Date Loaned

LiBra's 11-12-85			
JAN 28 2002			
DEMCO-292			

PUBLICITY AND DIPLOMACY

WITH SPECIAL REFERENCE
TO ENGLAND AND GERMANY

1890-1914

THE UNIVERSITY OF VIRGINIA
INSTITUTE FOR RESEARCH IN THE
SOCIAL SCIENCES

John Lloyd Newcomb, B.A., C.E., D.Sc., LL.D.
President of the University

Wilson Gee, M.A., Ph.D., D.Sc., LL.D.
Director of the Institute

Institute Monograph No. 27
(For list of other publications see page 483)

PUBLICITY AND DIPLOMACY

WITH SPECIAL REFERENCE TO ENGLAND AND GERMANY

1890–1914

BY

ORON JAMES HALE

ASSOCIATE PROFESSOR OF HISTORY
IN THE UNIVERSITY OF VIRGINIA

D. APPLETON–CENTURY COMPANY
INCORPORATED
FOR THE INSTITUTE FOR RESEARCH IN THE SOCIAL SCIENCES
UNIVERSITY OF VIRGINIA

NEW YORK   MCMXL   LONDON

To

EDWARD POTTS CHEYNEY

AND

WILLIAM E. LINGELBACH

THUS Government and Press have
lived and will live in wedlock with
one another, and in this wedlock
there is no divorce.

—*Chancellor Hans Luther at the German
Newspaper Congress, May 23, 1925.*

PREFACE

Lord Esher, referring in 1874 to the first results of the Education Act, noted in his diary: "It is pleasant to see the small and dirty boys reading the labels in the shop windows. It is one of the signs of the happier future." The first generation to benefit from the new standard of literacy cast its vote in a parliamentary election in 1892. The parallel generation in Germany, born during the period of the *Reichsgründung,* cast its first vote in the election of 1890. Early in the same decade, newspapers for the masses began to make their appearance in England and Germany. At first, the popular journals, while they had the format and periodicity of newspapers, were really entertainment fiction, designed to meet a growing demand from those who "just wanted something to read." With the political seasoning of this new electorate, the popular journals became more and more informational in their intent and function. It was popular literacy, manhood suffrage, and the mass circulation press that gave a distinct impress to the quarter of a century that elapsed between 1890 and the outbreak of the World War in 1914.

It was inevitable, under the circumstances, that in this era domestic, economic, and social issues should dominate the political scene in Western Europe—the élites of birth and skill, however, were scarcely challenged in their control of military and diplomatic relations. And yet, the new forces were not without effect upon the relations between the national states. An easy assumption, but one far from universally demonstrable, identified the new political power as Public Opinion, a term used to give a causal explanation of state actions in the international sphere. My reasons for rejecting this concept in favor of another—Publicity—can be briefly stated.

First, the term Public Opinion, because of its origin and generally loose usage, conveys the impression of rationality, public will, even sovereignty. Second, the singular noun "Opinion" connotes a unified opinion or a consensus. Such a condition is almost always an exception, for ideas and opinions usually develop as polarities. Third, too often the term Public Opinion is debased as a concept and becomes a mere stratagem. And finally, when transferred to a higher level of analysis and definition, it resolves itself into the metaphysical problem of universals, a discussion which, as John of Salisbury noted in the twelfth century, had already taken up more time than the Cæsars had occupied in conquering and governing the world.

When the concept of Publicity is substituted for that of Public Opinion, what springs into prominence is not the overtones of will, rationality, or sovereignty, but determinable actions—a speech is made and through the press is reported to an audience wider than that which actually heard the speaker's voice; an event occurs and is reported in the press; an editor or publicist has an idea and shares it with the readers of his journal. Publicity comprehends the news-reporting function of the press as well as the propagation of opinion. Moreover, in a historical study, this approach presents the press not as an impartial witness giving testimony but as a dynamic agency functioning in the drama of conflict and change. Finally, the concept includes the principal modes of enlistment and appeal —propaganda, agitation, and advertising.

This is a study, therefore, of the medium in which diplomats and statesmen worked rather than an exposition of the details of their policies. The foreign policy of the pre-War national state was usually determined and executed by a small circle of influential people and technical experts, customarily described in diplomatic reports as "influential circles" (*massgebenden Kreisen*). But this élite of skill and influence could not free itself entirely from the prejudices, the attitudes, and the opinions of the mass electorate, and these elements had to be reckoned with in the determination and execution of policies. The reality (but not the theory) of this relationship was best expressed by Lord Milner's categorical statement that "What is needed is a serious and resolute propaganda. The ordinary man has to be convinced of the burden before his answer is required."

I have endeavored to explore on a clinical level this triangular relationship between the public, the press, and the influential. For that purpose I have chosen for detailed examination the political and public relations of England and Germany. These two powers are selected because they best represent the two pre-War European systems of government—the parliamentary state and the continental bureaucratic state. Moreover, both were highly industrialized societies, both were economically expansionist, and the history of their relations presents a series of problems manifested in crises which lend themselves especially well to analysis.

In this field of politics and diplomacy, three studies have appeared only recently. Because of the advanced stage of my manuscript I could not benefit from their conclusions. I refer to R. J. Sontag, *Germany and England, 1848–1894* (New York, D. Appleton-Century Company, Inc., 1938);

E. Malcolm Carroll, *Germany and the Great Powers, 1866–1914* (New York, Prentice-Hall, Inc., 1939) ; and Pauline R. Anderson, *Background of Anti-English Feeling in Germany, 1890–1902* (Washington, D. C., American University Press, 1939). I should note in this connection that Chapter X of my study is a summary of my earlier volume, *Germany and the Diplomatic Revolution, 1904–1906* (Philadelphia, University of Pennsylvania Press, 1931).

In preparing and publishing this work I incurred many obligations. A fellowship from the Social Science Research Council in 1932–33 enabled me to spend a year in England and Germany, where most of the material for this study was gathered. Substantial assistance in the later phases of the work and in publication was generously afforded me by the Institute for Research in the Social Sciences, at the University of Virginia, and I wish to make special acknowledgment of the support and interest of the director, Dr. Wilson Gee, and for the assistance of his secretarial staff. I wish also to thank the Research Committee of the University of Virginia for a grant for photostatic work and traveling expenses. I am indebted to the directors and staffs of the following institutes and libraries: the Newspaper Division of the British Museum at Colindale, the Prussian State Library, the Reichstag Library, the Bavarian State Library, the Newspaper Division of the Library of Congress, the Hoover War Library at Stanford University, the Alderman Library at the University of Virginia, the Baker Library at Dartmouth College, the Institut für Zeitungswissenschaft in Berlin, and the Institut für Zeitungskunde in Munich.

I can not let pass the opportunity to express my appreciation for assistance and information from Mr. J. A. Spender, the late Dr. Friedrich Rosen, Mr. J. L. Garvin, Dr. Karl Bömer, Dr. Eugen Fischer, Dr. Friedrich Heilbron, Herr Hermann Lutz, Mr. Arthur E. Watson, managing editor of the *Daily Telegraph,* Mr. H. B. Carter, secretary to the managing director of Reuter's Limited, Mr. Tom Clarke, former editor of the *News-Chronicle,* and Professor Karl D'Ester. To my wife, Annette Van Winkle Hale, I owe special acknowledgment. It would be difficult to find words to convey the extent of my reliance upon her help and advice in every phase of the work from the copying and abstracting of material to the preparation of the index.

O. J. H.

University, Virginia.

CONTENTS

CHAPTER I

PUBLICITY AND DIPLOMACY

> There are only two ways of dealing with a democratic Press. The best way is to tell them everything; that bores them stiff. The second . . . is to tell them nothing, which at least provides them with the glory of a "secrecy" stunt. . . . The worst method is to tell them half-truths in the form of conciliatory leakages.
>
> Harold Nicolson, *Peacemaking*, p. 124.

When Woodrow Wilson proclaimed "open covenants of peace openly arrived at" to be one of the indispensable conditions of a new world order, he was censuring by implication the methods and machinery of pre-War international relations. This indictment, which was popularized under the slogan "Secret Diplomacy," was given an important place in the liberal democratic complaint against the old European order. Opposed to the view that unrestricted publicity would remedy a serious defect in the relations between nations is the opinion of Mr. J. A. Spender, one of England's most distinguished and responsible Liberal editors. "There has been much talk since the War of the evils of secret diplomacy," he writes, "but the dangers of a rash and inexpert handling of publicity are written just as large in the records." [1] On the surface the issue appears to be one of more publicity or less publicity. However, it is much more fundamental than that. It poses the problem of formulating and executing foreign policy under the conditions resulting from the transformation, during the nineteenth century, of the state composed of *subjects* into the state composed of *citizens*. The time span when this problem was most acute extended from the close of the era of absolute monarchy to the beginning of post-War totalitarianism. Manhood suffrage, universal literacy, and the mass circulation press were significant tokens of the new era. But from the dynastic subject-state was inherited the institutions, the procedures and terminology, and much of the spirit of foreign relations. Thus there arose a fatal dualism in the field of inter-state relationships. Any direct democratic action was excluded by the strict limitations imposed by the usual laws defining treason and by the state's constitutional monopoly of established agencies of diplomatic communication. Individual and group action was in the main limited to promotional activity and propaganda,

[1] *Fifty Years of Europe* (Lond., 1933), p. 239.

with the intention of enforcing or deterring action on the part of the constituted authorities. While electorates doubled and trebled with the trend toward universal suffrage, and while the agencies of communication and agitation were developing to gigantic proportions through technological advances, the balance of authority and control between parliament, ministry, and the professional foreign service remained practically unchanged.[2]

A new variable was injected into the situation with the unprecedented development of the popular press and the fierce blaze of publicity which accompanied the unrolling of international affairs. To the observer of the pre-War scene there appeared really to be two diplomacies: one, the official, involving ambassadors and foreign ministers, frock coats and high hats, secret treaties and confidential dispatches. The other, unofficial, whose agencies were the newspaper and periodical press, the public platform, the club, the *Stammtisch,* and the street corner. Outwardly the two systems appeared unrelated, each revolving in its own orbit. In reality they were cog-wheeled and helped each other 'round. The skilful operator knew how to throw them in and out of gear.

A two-fold classification of publicity in foreign affairs can be established on the basis of origin—publicity that emanated from official sources and publicity that sprang from private sources. In the latter category newspaper editors, party leaders, private persons, and pressure groups employed all the techniques of propaganda, agitation and advertising to bend the foreign policy of the government to their will. Until the nineteenth century, private publicity was of minor importance in the formulation of state policies toward other states. Prior to that time the chief agencies of publicity—the book, the periodical and the newspaper press—were subjected to the double yoke of princely monopoly and preventive censorship. Control of printing was as much a royal prerogative as the minting of coins. Official publicity, on the other hand, comes down in an unbroken stream from the days when Queen Elizabeth's ministers wrote and circulated pamphlets in the interest of the monarchy, when newspaper and periodical publication in France was a royal monopoly, and when the postmasters in the German states were the authorized editors of newsbooks and *Zeitungen.*[3]

[2] The problem in its larger aspects is considered by C. J. Friedrich, "Die Problematik der Willensbildung in der äusseren Politik," *Zeitschrift für Politik,* XXII (1933), pp. 645–63. Even in the post-War period hostility to direct democratic action is strong. Referring in the House of Commons to the peace referendum organized by the League of Nations Union, Sir John Simon declared that it "was mischievous to ask the opinion of 'uninformed persons' on such intricate questions as peace and war." (New York *Times,* June 28, 1935.)

[3] For official publicity practices in the age of absolutism see the important work by Erich Everth, *Die Öffentlichkeit in der Aussenpolitik von Karl V bis Napoleon* (Jena, 1931).

It is customary to think of Bismarck, Salisbury, and their contemporaries in the European chancelleries as confirmed partisans of diplomatic secrecy. And so they must seem to the post-War school of brass-band diplomats. Bismarck, none the less, was a skilled manipulator of the press and regularly employed publicity if it promised advantages, although he did not approve of the British practice of publishing diplomatic correspondence in parliamentary bluebooks. On one occasion he said that if diplomatic dispatches were published his work would be doubled, because he would be forced to write one dispatch to accomplish his purpose and another for publication.[4] The German ambassador, Paul Hatzfeldt, used to twit Lord Salisbury on his connection with the Standard, the leading ministerial organ in the London press. The little game that these two skilled practitioners used to play is described by Hatzfeldt in a report of May 12, 1897. "For years it has been my custom, which is well known to Lord Salisbury, to place before him the opinions of the Standard . . . as though they were inspired by him, while he always disclaims them, partly annoyed and partly joking, and will scarcely admit that he has ever read an article in this journal." [5]

As a matter of fact, practitioners of the "old diplomacy" regularly employed publicity in their diplomatic work. While there were no established canons to guide them in its use, they had certain practical rules which they observed. First of all may be noted their strong aversion to publicity while negotiations were in progress. This aversion did not arise necessarily from distrust of the public, but from the simple fact that anything revealed to their own countrymen was at the same time made known to the other parties in the negotiations. Secrecy, often maintained to avoid giving the opponent a material advantage, was usually branded by domestic political adversaries as a great conspiracy against the public welfare. This misinterpretation and misunderstanding has been, in part, the basis for condemnation of secret diplomacy.

Diplomatic history records many instances in which publicity was employed by one government to injure another, either in the estimation of its own citizens or in the opinion of other peoples. When Bismarck published Benedetti's draft treaty, proposing French annexation of Belgium, he practically assured English neutrality in the Franco-Prussian War. Another common publicity procedure involved deliberate trouble-making

---

[4] "Ich bin kein Anhänger der Blaubücher, obwohl sie bei anderen grösseren Staaten angenommen sind. Ich wiederhole meine Überzeugung, dass sie angenommen sind hauptsächlich aus Bedürfnissen der inneren Politik und Publizistik." Heinz Schulze, *Die Presse im Urteil Bismarcks* (Leipzig, 1931), p. 28.

[5] *Die Grosse Politik der Europäischen Kabinette, 1871–1914* (ed. by J. Lepsius, A. Mendelssohn-Bartholdy and F. Thimme. 40 vols., Berlin, 1922–27), XIII, 23. This official collection of German diplomatic documents is cited hereafter as *G. P.*

between allies by the publication of rumors that diminished or destroyed the mutual trust of their leading statesmen. A list of forged documents and apocryphal interviews appearing in the European press with that object in view would be a long one indeed. Publicity was also frequently invoked in the interest of security, as, for example, when an agreement between two governments was published so that the parties became publicly pledged. After the visit of the Czar to Potsdam in October 1910, Sazonov's first act upon returning to St. Petersburg was to give an interview to the Novoye Vremya reporting the substance of his conversations with the German authorities in Berlin. To the British chargé, Mr. O'Beirne, he frankly admitted that his object was to record publicly the concessions promised by the Germans with regard to the Russian sphere in Persia and the construction of railways in that region.[6] Breach of a publicly advertised obligation, as in this instance, would expose the delinquent to general reproach. An incalculable moral force was mobilized against Germany when she violated Belgian neutrality, which by treaty she was bound to respect. The frequent resort to publicity for obligations entered into by states was motivated quite as often by the desire to put the contracting powers on record as it was by the desire on the part of the authorities to take the public into confidence.

Publicity for military or alliance obligations was generally recognized as a valuable deterrent to potential aggressors or disturbers of the peace. The exact details of the Triple Alliance treaties, for example, remained secret until after the War, but the existence of the alliance and the nature of the military co-operation called for under the treaties were well known. This gave opposing powers certain valuable points of reference for shaping their own policy in the interest of European peace. Without public knowledge of its existence the Triple Alliance had no value in Bismarck's diplomatic system. It is well known that the permanent officials of the British foreign office favored transforming the Entente into a publicly acknowledged alliance. Here we observe practitioners of so-called secret diplomacy advocating publicity as a solution to a difficult problem, whereas Grey, the parliamentarian and public representative of his department, favored continuation of the Entente, implementing it by secret naval and military conversations.

So far, the points established relate to publicity for treaties, conventions, and military arrangements—all the result of arduous preparations and negotiations. Publicity in its various forms was never entirely excluded from the actual conduct of diplomatic business. At the beginning of nego-

---

[6] *British Documents on the Origins of the World War, 1898–1914* (ed. by G. P. Gooch and H. Temperley. 11 vols., Lond., 1926–38), X, pt. 1, 561–62.

tiations involving serious differences between governments, foreign ministers sometimes issued a public declaration of their final intentions. If delivered in forceful language it constituted a warning or a threat. Such publicity tactics, backed by armed determination, did on occasion force the opponent to abandon his claim or position. While impressing the opponent, it at the same time consolidated public attitudes at home behind the government. Such an uncompromising stand, accompanied by the mobilization of the press and a consequent blaze of publicity, was taken by the British government at the beginning of the Fashoda crisis in the autumn of 1898. "For the first time," says Kennedy Jones, "Fleet Street was invited to Downing Street." Faced with coercive demands, a united press, and overwhelming sea-power the French cabinet chose to retreat rather than fight. Such an inflexible stand at the beginning of negotiations limited the room for maneuvering; it was, moreover, a dangerous procedure because any settlement short of the complete fulfilment of original demands gave the appearance of a diplomatic defeat. At the beginning of Germany's Moroccan action in 1911, Kiderlen-Wächter countenanced, if he did not encourage, the public demand for territorial compensation in Morocco. When he emerged at the end of exhausting and critical negotiations with only a few thousand square miles of Congo swamp to show for all his trouble, the foreign office and government were bitterly criticized by aroused patriots and disillusioned colonialists.

In general, diplomats and foreign ministers preferred that knowledge of the actual details of negotiations be withheld from the public, especially if they anticipated a compromise outcome. When a point was reached beyond which they were determined not to retreat, their oath-helpers in the press were called in to make a display of what they called "our public opinion." The danger of this procedure lay in the possibility that publicists, politicians, and journalists might take the bit in their teeth and run away with public sentiment. Exclude the public, and the game was comparatively safe; turn on the publicity and a molehill might quickly become not simply a mountain, but a rocketing volcano.

When the assistance of publicity was invoked, two motives were generally discernible: first, the desire and the necessity to carry the public along with the government in a certain course of action which might eventuate in hostilities; and second, to undermine the opponent's position by appealing directly to the public upon which the opponent depended for support. For example, the wide publicity given in Germany to Woodrow Wilson's Fourteen Points was a potent force in breaking the war morale of the German people. Such a maneuver may, however, fail completely of its object and react with great damage to the user, as the history of the famous Daily Telegraph interview shows. Designed to convince the British that William II was England's devoted continental friend and champion, the interview was published in London with the approval of the German chancellor, after it had been corrected in detail by an official in the foreign office. Apparently no thought was given to its possible repercussions in Germany. In England the calculated indiscretions and typical exaggerations evoked polite snickers, but the interview came booming back to Germany on the telegraph wires, producing a grave constitutional crisis that shook the monarchy to its foundations.

Let us turn now from the consideration of motives and tactics, which inspired and conditioned official publicity, to the agencies and instruments commonly employed in giving currency to official views. Here a sharp distinction must be made between the parliamentary and the bureaucratic state. British practice may be taken as representative of the former, the German as typical of the latter. Official publicity channels in England included the public platform, from which cabinet members frequently reviewed foreign affairs, parliamentary bluebooks and debates in the House of Commons, and the daily press which, besides amplifying speeches and statements, received direct information and inspiration from cabinet members and the foreign office officials.

It was the boast of British statesmen and publicists that an official or semi-official press, subservient to the government and placing so much white paper at its disposal, was not a part of British public life. The party system as it operated in England, however, tended to produce all the features of a semi-official press. England has always been governed by political oligarchies, and party leader and party journalist were interchangeable rôles. Editors, statesmen, and officials were the products of the same public schools and universities, and they moved in the same social circles. All bore the trademark of the British ruling class. E. T. Cook, the first editor of the Westminster Gazette, described in his diary a dinner given at the House of Commons by Curzon. Present were Cook, Iwan-Müller of the Pall Mall Gazette, Balfour, Birrel, Arthur Hardinge and Asquith. Cook noted that they all "Arthured and Harryed and Georged." Mr. J. A. Spender, although he was not a member of the Liberal government, was entrusted with secrets of policy that were not known to the cabinet as a whole and he wielded more influence than many members of the ministry. Likewise, Mr. H. A. Gwynne, editor of the Morning Post, was a power in the Conservative party leadership. Party editors co-operated with party leaders, while the parliamentary whips kept the smaller journalistic fry in order. When we remember that the cabinet was in fact only a committee of party leaders, then it is plainly evident that when one cabinet retired and the opposition assumed power, the entire press of the incoming party became in a sense governmental. Although there was no central publicity bureau in the foreign office, direct contact with the press was maintained through departmental heads, the under-secretaries and, during Grey's régime, through his private secretary, Sir William Tyrrell.

Ministerial pronouncements on foreign affairs, which were common in England, were rare in Germany. Brief statements by the secretary of state and an occasional full dress debate in the Reichstag scarcely ever went beyond innocuous generalities. Having no constituencies, public appearances of imperial ministers were limited to the usual civic formalities. To get their views before the people German statesmen relied in the main upon a semi-official and inspired press operated from the foreign office by the secretary of state and the chief of the press bureau. The organs regularly employed were the Wolff Telegraphic Bureau, for official communications, the Norddeutsche Allgemeine Zeitung, for semi-official statements, and the Kölnische Zeitung, for inspired articles and trial balloons.

In the continental bureaucratic state where the chancellor and his secretaries stood above party, some instrumentality for publicizing policy was essential. Unlike a British cabinet, the German ministers had no party press upon which they could depend for support and through which they could air their views. They might be in favor with the press of one party today, and the same party press might be found in opposition tomorrow. The bureaucratic system, party instability, and the decentralization of the German press fixed the main outlines of the German official publicity system.

Strong condemnation on moral grounds marks almost every British reference to the German system of an official and inspired press. Shortly before the War Grey wrote: "The Press Bureau in Berlin has always been an obstacle to good relations between us. A Press Bureau is used to make mischief, and some German Diplomatists have done a good deal of mischief-making." [7] Sir Cecil Spring Rice, when he was attached to the embassy at Berlin, was even more condemnatory than Grey. Following a series of speeches on foreign affairs by Chamberlain, Hicks-Beach, and Balfour, in their respective constituencies, Spring Rice wrote to a friend:

It is certainly refreshing to read an English political speech after a German article. I like the thought of a man facing the vulgar people whose votes he has, and who will have to fight if there is a war, and telling them plainly as man to man what the Empire is for and what they are to fight for. The German writer, a dirty Jew generally, whom his employers are afraid to be seen talking to, gets his ideas from the Foreign Office in a back room; launches them

[7] B. D., X, pt. 2, 663.

in secret, is disavowed if necessary; generally, if successful, is rewarded with some piece of scandal or secret information—and that is the means they have here of making their political opinions known to the world.[8]

The deficiencies of the German system were glaring, but British methods were by no means as heroic and impeccable as Spring Rice portrays them. In Germany, as in most continental countries, public ministerial utterances carried the highest degree of official responsibility. It was sometimes necessary for the government to put its views before the public without limiting its future action by clothing those views with absolute authoritativeness. Hence the resort to semi-official and inspired publicity. The peculiar status of British cabinet members permitted them to achieve the same result from the speaker's platform with their words recorded and amplified by the daily press. Countless instances could be cited when a Chamberlain, a Winston Churchill, or a Lloyd George, either calculatingly or inadvertently, made provocative and incendiary statements touching Britain's relations with foreign countries. A polite inquiry at Downing Street by the government concerned usually received the stock answer: So and So was not speaking as a responsible member of His Majesty's Government, but as a private member of parliament addressing "the vulgar people whose votes he had." The foreign ambassador was certain to go away mumbling about Britain's peculiar institutions. Although the motive—avoidance of official responsibility—was the same on both sides, no other single feature of one another's diplomatic methods gave rise to so much misunderstanding.

Another misapprehension that produced much friction concerned the functioning of the party press in England and Germany. The British party system imposed certain restraints upon editors and journalists in their treatment of foreign affairs. The editor was an actor in the political drama; he played opposite the public man and shared party responsibility for success or failure of the play. In the bureaucratic state where party and parliamentary responsibility were non-existent, the political press was by and large unaccountable. The actors on the stage were all officials and bureaucrats; while editors and parliamentarians sat in the pit and galleries as an audience. Some functioned as a paid claque; others, friends of the actors, were sympathetic and helpful; a considerable number of critics caviled and jeered; while in the galleries the less well-behaved and politically unschooled howled and made obscene gestures at the players. Interpreting the German political scene in terms of their own experience, British observers attributed far more importance to the parties and their press than

[8] Stephen Gwynn, *The Letters and Friendships of Sir Cecil Spring Rice* (2 vols., N. Y., 1929), I, 246.

they actually possessed. Oftentimes from irresponsible press and party agitation they endeavored to deduce the policies and intentions of the government. And with what results? Well, it is no exaggeration to say that when one examines the English arsenal of anti-German propaganda in the decades before the War one finds that most of the weapons bore the trademark "Made in Germany." They were the excesses, the rudenesses, the beer-table fantasies and doctrinairisms of the Pan-Germans, the *Witzblätter,* the super-patriotic societies and the Social Democrats.

With the development of the cheap popular press, between 1890 and 1914, there was injected into the circle of defensive armament and diplomatic equilibration an uncontrolled publicity, direct and irresponsible. During this era, before the advent of motion pictures, the mass circulation press supplanted the old penny thrillers of blood and thunder and cheap romance. For millions of readers the yellow journals were not current or contemporary history but entertainment-fiction.[9] Harmsworth, Hearst, Ullstein, and Girardin discovered an entirely new reading public and habituated it to the daily newspaper. As Kennedy Jones, the technical creator of the Daily Mail, points out this new public was composed in the main of first generation products of universal suffrage and mass education—the sons and grandsons of men who had found excitement in public hangings and public whippings, rough sports and excessive drinking. The purveyors of yellow journals aimed to give these readers what they wanted; and the new reading public demanded, as one writer put it, "More chops, bloody ones with gristle." [10] Compensation for the monotony and drabness of modern industrial employment and urban life was provided by the vicarious thrill and excitement that came with the sensational exploitation of international conflicts and rivalries. Prior to the development of the mass circulation press foreign affairs were mainly the concern of a restricted circle of the politically initiated, the economically interested and the socially enfranchised. Publicity did not penetrate beyond the legislative halls and the select clientele of the mid-nineteenth century press with its three-decker editorials, verbatim parliamentary reports and long letters to the editor about "Compensation for Glanders," "Umbrella Stealing in St. Paul's," and "The Girls' Guild of Good Life." But now the blare of a brass band drowned the soft chamber music. For the first time manhood suffrage became aware of world politics; and it was like the discovery of a new

[9] The point is suggested by M. J. Adler, *Art and Prudence* (N. Y., 1937), p. 48. Along the same line see O. J. Hale, "Nationalism in Press, Films, and Radio," *The Annals,* vol. 175 (September 1934), 110–17.
[10] Quoted by W. L. Langer, *The Diplomacy of Imperialism* (2 vols., N. Y., 1935), I, 81. For Kennedy Jones' defense of sensationalism see *Fleet Street and Downing Street* (Lond., 1920), p. 310.

national sport in which all might join through the medium of the popular press.

In the new age of free expression and popular literacy the range and intensity of publicity increased a thousandfold, but far from always clarifying and enlightening it quite frequently served to articulate passion and excite prejudice. The new rough-rider school of journalists became the Jamesons of diplomacy! They were free with the spur but rarely used the bit. Sir Mount Stuart Grant-Duff, writing to T. H. S. Escott, expressed the opinion that "the diplomatists and foreign ministers of Europe would get on perfectly well together, and settle their own differences comfortably, but for the new journalists intermeddling and stirring up international jealousy and spite. It is a disgusting spectacle, which makes me feel thankful that I am seventy years of age." [11] Pre-War diplomatic records contain many strictures upon the irresponsibility of popular journalism and its baneful influence on international relations. In all this due allowance must be made for professional and class exclusiveness. But the course of events leading to the catastrophe of 1914 clearly showed that publicity was no substitute for intelligence and that mass democracy was as easily enslaved by shibboleths and stereotypes as were the subjects of dynastic despotisms in an earlier age.

[11] T. H. S. Escott, *Masters of English Journalism* (Lond., 1911), p. 338.

CHAPTER II

THE ENGLISH PRESS AND FOREIGN AFFAIRS

Unless we are read to-day we shall never be read. Hence our straining after effect, our exaggerated emphasis, our damnable iterations, our headlines and our booms. Let us strive and scream for to-morrow we die.

J. Saxon Mills, *Sir Edward Cook,* p. 213.

When W. T. Stead succeeded John Morley as editor of the Pall Mall Gazette, in 1883, a revolution of far-reaching consequence began in British journalism. What Matthew Arnold called the "New Journalism" made its way into the English press through the evening newspapers and Stead was its first successful practitioner. Brilliant, unconventional, and enthusiastic he shocked his respectable contemporaries in Fleet Street with his innovations. These innovations have long since sunk to the level of the commonplace, but in their day they were revolutionary. Stead improved the make-up of his paper by using headlines and cross-headings, developed the editorial paragraph or "Short Notes" and popularized the personal interview. Primarily a crusader, Stead defended sensationalism "up to the point that it is necessary to arrest the eye of the public and compel them to admit the necessity of action." Sensationalism to increase sales and profits, he condemned. His campaigns—"The Truth about the Navy," "Chinese Gordon for the Soudan," and "The Maiden Tribute of Modern Babylon," the latter a sensational exposé of the white slave traffic in London—established his reputation as a crusading journalist and led Lord Milner to characterize him as a "compound of Don Quixote and Phineas T. Barnum." His fiery opposition to the Boer War and his ardent public championship of spiritualism—the famous "Letters from Julia"—diminished his influence and authority with large sections of the public. His career ended in a double tragedy—he lost his life on the *Titanic* and he was unable to report the greatest news story of the decade before the War.[1]

In 1888 T. P. O'Connor founded the Star as a competitor to the Pall Mall Gazette in the afternoon field. The Star became a training school for

[1] F. Whyte, *Life of W. T. Stead* (2 vols., Lond., 1925) ; F. W. Hirst, *Early Life and Letters of John Morley* (2 vols., Lond., 1927), II, 92 ff. ; Harold Herd, *The Making of Modern Journalism* (Lond., 1927), chap. II ; J. Grande, *Constance Grande* (Lond., 1925), pp. 149–55. Constance Grande was Stead's secretary, interpreter and editorial assistant.

the oncoming generation of journalists who were to edit the papers for the masses. In all its features the Star represented a complete break with the journalistic traditions of the Victorian era. When Kennedy Jones and Alfred Harmsworth purchased the struggling Evening News and turned it into a valuable newspaper property the transformation of the evening dailies was complete. It was primarily entertainment that these papers offered. Selling at a half-penny, they brought sensational news reports, bright editorial paragraphs, theatrical, society, and sporting news, the gossip column, and the serial novel.

For some time the morning papers remained undisturbed by the revolution in evening journalism. They served quite a different public and the editors professed great disdain for the cheap evening papers, which seemed to have no aim beyond entertaining their readers. Since the middle of the century the Times had set the style for the morning press of London and the provinces. One journal might have a literary tone, another might emphasize commerce and finance, a third might cater to the aristocracy, but all deserved the appellation "serious." Politics was the staple of news, and each issue of the morning press seemed fitted to the Gilbert and Sullivan formula

> That every boy and every gal
>   That's born into the world alive
> Is either a little Liberal
>   Or else a little Conservative!

Parliamentary proceedings, speeches of political leaders, and special articles on the "issues of the day" took up most of the news space. The editorial page also ran heavily to politics. The leaders were dull and long-winded, cut to a standard literary pattern—exposition, discussion, and conclusion—and filling altogether three columns or more of the ordinary daily. In appearance, too, the morning papers were forbidding. Long columns of small black type unrelieved by headlines or cross-headings placed an unjust burden upon the reader. As for make-up and arrangement, these papers gave the impression of having been thrown together with a scoop; they were not even consistent in arranging the features on the same page in consecutive issues. Everything about the standard morning newspaper gave notice that it was edited for the upper classes of society and that no concessions would be made to the man in the street.[2]

A new era in English journalism began on May 4, 1896, when the first

[2] Indispensable for the make-up and typography of the English journals and the startling changes at the turn of the century is Stanley Morison, *The English Newspaper* (Cambridge, 1932), chaps. XV and XVI.

issue of the Daily Mail was offered to the public. Priced at a half-penny, it carried over into the field of morning journalism the standards and practices that had long prevailed in the popular afternoon press. Kennedy Jones and Alfred Harmsworth were not mere imitators, content to copy American methods. In creating the Daily Mail they applied the experience and knowledge acquired in building up the Evening News. In appearance and arrangement the Daily Mail did not differ radically from the established type of morning paper that sold for one, two, or three pence. Harmsworth and Jones believed that their creation, to be successful, must look like a morning journal rather than an afternoon paper, which meant that it must look something like the Times. Classified advertising occupied the front page; page two was given over to the City notes, law and police reports; page three contained domestic news; and page four the editorials and special articles. The featured news of the day appeared on page five—the "splash" page; sporting news filled page six; page seven, the magazine section, later became the woman's page; the last page, like the first, was devoted to advertisements. Editorial exhortation was reduced to a single column. A serial novel, human interest bits from "The World's Press," and spicy social gossip filled the space devoted to more serious purposes in the older journals.

Although in typography and lay-out the Daily Mail did not make a clean break with established practice, the spirit and purpose of the new journal were revolutionary. The right-hand "ear" on the front page bore the legend: "The Busy Man's Daily Journal"; however, it was not the patronage of the educated, critical newspaper public that was sought, but that of the new reading public that had snapped up George Newnes' weekly *Tit-Bits* and Harmsworth's *Answers*. Homeliness, variety, sensation were the conscious objectives of the editors. An entirely new scale of news values was created. What Kennedy Jones called "a good meaty crime" topped the list, followed by disasters on land and sea. Politics came far down the list, and only the human personal side had any pulling power—the rest was dead weight that had to be carried. As Philip Gibbs has written, "The Daily Mail, closely imitated by many others, regarded life as a variety show. No 'turn' must be long or dull. Whether it dealt with tragedy or comedy, high politics or other kinds of crime, it was admitted, not because of its importance to the nation or the world, but because it made a good 'story' for the breakfast table." [3] The Daily Mail was an immediate success. Within a few weeks it had a steady sale of 200,000 copies; by 1899 sales had risen to 700,000, and the Boer War brought circulation temporarily to the million mark.

[3] *Adventures in Journalism* (Lond., 1923), p. 99.

Thereafter, to 1914, the average daily publication hovered around 700,000. It was rumored that the profits exceeded a million pounds annually.[4]

In 1900, C. Arthur Pearson, a successful publisher of popular periodicals, launched the Daily Express as a competitor of the Daily Mail in the mass circulation field. The Express was the first important morning paper to display its main news offerings on the front page in the American manner. Both Harmsworth and Pearson, in the beginning, announced that their papers were independent of narrow party politics. For partisanship they substituted patriotism and imperialism. "Our policy," Pearson announced in the first issue of the Express, "is patriotic; our faith is the British Empire." Blustering chauvinism marked their treatment of foreign affairs.

Between 1900 and 1914 there was not a single English morning journal that did not undergo change as a result of the development of the popular press. Not that the established papers lost their subscribers to popular journals. The upper classes were satisfied with the papers they had always read and they scorned the cheapness and vulgarity of the Mail and the Express. The older papers might have continued in the old groove, ignoring the new arrivals, had it not been for one factor: advertising revenue. Advertising followed the largest circulations and commercial advertisers seeking the broadest markets transferred their patronage from the old to the new journals. For the sake of advertising revenue, which formed the economic foundation of their existence, the class papers were forced to compete with Harmsworth and Pearson for mass circulation. It was economic pressure that revolutionized the British morning press. By 1900 the pressure was felt in the business offices of the newspapers; by 1908 it was acute. Some journals ceased publication, others were consolidated with the more aggressive rivals, others, like the Daily News, were popularized and, with the price reduced to a half-penny, entered the competition for mass circulation. Some of the older newspapers held their position by improving news service and giving better value for a penny, without cheapening the spirit of the paper. The Manchester Guardian, which was in a serious position for a time, was saved in this way. But all, without exception, were forced to redefine news, to offer greater variety to the reader, to reduce the editorial space, to provide features for women, and to modernize make-up and typography. In 1908, Harmsworth's purchase

---

[4] *Daily News,* Jan. 2, 1914; Hamilton Fyfe, *Northcliffe: An Intimate Biography* (Lond., 1930), pp. 72–87, 113; F. A. MacKenzie, *The Mystery of the Daily Mail* (Lond., 1921); G. Weill, *Le Journal* (Paris, 1934), pp. 248–54; Morison, *op. cit.,* pp. 294–96; Herd, *op. cit.,* pp. 52–64; Kennedy Jones, *Fleet Street and Downing Street,* pp. 130–49. Northcliffe's originality in revolutionizing British daily journalism has been exaggerated. Although he kept in the background, Kennedy Jones, "whom all men feared and many hated," was the creative genius of the *Daily Mail.*

of the Times symbolized the complete conquest of the old journalism by the new.[5]

In the 1890's the penny evening papers in London were: the Pall Mall Gazette, Globe, Evening Standard, St. James's Gazette, and Westminster Gazette. Those selling for a half-penny were the Echo, the Star, the Sun, and the Evening News. The half-penny papers gave priority to crime, sports, and entertainment and scarcely touched foreign news and international affairs. The Evening News, purchased by Harmsworth and Kennedy Jones in 1894, was little more than a reflection of the Daily Mail. The Sun and the Echo disappeared and in 1905 the St. James's Gazette was merged by Arthur Pearson with the Evening Standard. Of the remaining evening papers the Pall Mall Gazette and the Westminster deserve special attention.

Under Morley, Stead, and E. T. Cook the Pall Mall Gazette was a Liberal party paper. When William Waldorf Astor purchased the paper in 1892 and turned it into a Conservative organ, Cook with the ablest members of the staff, including J. A. Spender and the cartoonist F. C. Gould, resigned and with the financial backing of George Newnes, a successful publisher of cheap periodicals, they founded the Westminster Gazette. Under the editorship of Harry Cust, sophisticated smartness was the chief characteristic of the Pall Mall Gazette. In 1896, during the Venezuelan crisis, Iwan-Müller wrote an article that offended Astor, who demanded his dismissal from the staff. Cust refused and both men resigned. Douglas Straight then became the editor, a position which he held from 1896 to 1909. During that period E. G. Barnard wrote the editorials on foreign affairs. In 1909, F. J. Higginbottom succeeded Straight and he in turn was followed in 1912 by Mr. J. L. Garvin, who restored the financial and spiritual life of the paper.[6] Although the Pall Mall Gazette was enlarged from eight pages to sixteen, it made no attempt to compete with the morning papers in the field of foreign intelligence, but depended largely upon the established news agencies. Its foreign policy was strongly imperialistic; it beat the drum for the navy and for national conscription, and it supported Grey's policy of ententes.

The finest tradition of English evening journalism was represented by

[5] The commercialization of the British press, that is its complete absorption into the capitalistic system and its standardization, rationalization and concentration, is the theme of the best work to date on modern British journalism by Max Grünbeck, *Die Presse Grossbritanniens* (2 vols., Leipzig, 1936), especially Volume I, pages 45–50. While dealing mainly with the contemporary press, Grünbeck brings together in the historical sections much scattered material. On the building of the trusts and the development of the financial structure of the press, since the beginning of the twentieth century, he has performed a task that excites the highest admiration.

[6] F. J. Higginbottom, *The Vivid Life* (Lond., 1934), pp. 134, 140, 183, 229.

the Westminster Gazette, which was founded in 1893 by George Newnes, with E. T. Cook as editor, J. A. Spender as assistant editor, and F. C. Gould as political cartoonist. The first issue (January 31, 1893) announced that the paper was a continuation of the Pall Mall Gazette under a new name and commented with some acerbity upon the Astor deal that had turned the old Pall Mall from a Liberal to a Conservative organ. "Legally a newspaper proprietor has as much right to part with his paper as another man to sell his stud. . . . But morally there is a wide and obvious difference." Unfortunately the practice became a common one in succeeding years as newspaper shares were sold and traded like mining stocks. Printed on green paper, tabloid size, with the leading article on the front page, the Westminster Gazette was a paper for the intellectual and political élite. The Saturday edition carried a prize and puzzle section which offered prizes for Greek and Latin verses. The chess column, literary notes and news, a London letter, and the pointed editorial paragraphs "Notes of the Day," written by Charles Geake, were among its notable features. For 'spot' foreign news the Westminster relied on the established agencies, but highly competent correspondents, who wrote interpretative and background articles, were maintained in the principal European capitals. Until his death, in 1909, the well known publicist J. L. Bashford represented the Westminster in Berlin. R. E. C. Long held the post until 1914. Lucien Wolf (Diplomaticus) was a frequent contributor of special articles on foreign affairs. From January, 1896, when J. A. Spender succeeded E. T. Cook as editor, to the merging of the Westminster with the News-Chronicle after the War, Mr. Spender's daily article on public affairs was one of the most authoritative features of English journalism. No one wrote on foreign relations with a greater sense of responsibility and moderation. The editor's close association with Grey and Asquith added to the paper's prestige abroad, where from 1906 to 1914 it was quoted with special attention as the semi-official organ of the Liberal government. Mr. Spender has always repudiated the suggestion that he wrote on assignment from his political associates. According to Mr. Spender, in his long association with Grey it was never suggested that he take one line rather than another. Views were exchanged, to be sure, and the information thus gained guided his pen, but of inspiration, common in France and Germany, there was none.

Financially the Westminster was never in a strong position. Its circulation probably never exceeded 50,000. It was reported that Sir George Newnes was losing ten thousand pounds yearly when he sold the paper in 1908. The sale was promoted by the Liberal party whips and the industrialist Mond became the chief shareholder in the new company. Lord

Riddell, who recorded this in his diary, admits the political importance of the paper because it was read by thinking people of all parties and trends of opinion. However, "The Westminster's trouble is that said thinking people don't appeal to the advertiser, so that the revenue from advertisements is inadequate." [7] Read by politicians and editors, the influence of the Westminster was out of all proportion to its circulation. The Daily Mail could scream and boom and boast of a million readers, but politically, up until the War, it was of much less consequence than the Westminster Gazette. [8]

Since the days of Thomas Barnes and John Walter II the Times had been regarded the world over as a national institution. In the last decade of the century its constituency was that solid section of English society called "the governing class"—the people to be found in the first class railway carriages, on the stock exchange, in the stalls of the London theaters, in the House of Commons and in the great country houses. A marked decline in fortune, if not in influence, set in with the publication of the Parnell forgeries, in 1887, and the heavy damages the proprietors were required to pay. W. T. Stead diagnosed the Times' difficulties as "mental paralysis gradually induced by uninterrupted prosperity." [9] But Moberly Bell, who became manager of the paper in 1890, found that it was far from prosperous. Its classified advertising was slipping away to the Daily Telegraph and the Morning Post. This was a serious loss because the small personal advertisements bring circulation as well as revenue. While other papers in the same class were offering their readers better service and at the same time reducing the sales price to two pence and one pence, the Times' price, until Northcliffe acquired control, remained pegged at three pence. As a matter of fact the "Thunderer" was suffering not so much from "mental paralysis" as from a weakening circulatory system. When Bell took charge the circulation had dropped to 40,000, and although he showed great ingenuity in devising schemes to increase sales the paper was barely able to hold its own. It had the best foreign news service of any English journal, the editorial department was second to none, and the financial, legal and political news was adequately reported; but the coverage of home news was inferior to that of its rivals. Moreover, the fundamentalist dogma of the nature of news prevailed at Printing House Square. Nothing was printed because it was interesting—it must be *important*. While this

[7] Lord Riddell, *More Pages from My Diary, 1908–1914* (Lond., 1934), p. 14.
[8] Information on the *Westminster Gazette* has been gleaned from the files of the paper, from Hulda Friedrichs, *Life of Sir George Newnes* (Lond., 1911); J. Saxon Mills, *Sir Edward Cook; A Biography* (Lond., 1921); J. A. Spender, *Life, Journalism and Politics* (2 vols., Lond., 1927), and *The Public Life* (2 vols., Lond., 1925); and from Mr. Spender personally.
[9] *A Journalist on Journalism* (Lond., 1892), p. 83.

satisfied and comforted its steady patrons, it repelled the younger people, who turned to journals that gave them what they wanted and not what the editors thought they ought to have. The Times' make-up was execrable. The paper was edited and printed in two sections. The "inside section" contained the editorials and the spot news; the "outside section" contained the accumulation of less important items from several days before. This quaint system provoked Northcliffe's comment that the Times people seemed to think that news like wine improved with age. In 1908 the paper was sold to Northcliffe, who broke down the conservative traditions of Printing House Square, reduced the price to two pence and sent the circulation figures up to 200,000. One of Northcliffe's associates reports that when he acquired the Times one third of its circulation was among colonial and foreign subscribers.[10]

During the greater part of the period covered by this study G. E. Buckle was editor-in-chief of the Times. He had succeeded Thomas Chenery in 1884 and did not resign until 1912, when Geoffrey Dawson (G. G. Robinson), who had been Lord Milner's secretary, and editor of the Johannesburger Star, was appointed to the post. However, it appears that the manager, Moberly Bell, and the foreign editor controlled the foreign news service and dominated the policy of the paper. Under Bell's management the position of foreign editor was held by Sir Donald Mackenzie Wallace until 1896, by Valentine Chirol until 1912, and thereafter, until he became editor in 1919, by Wickham Steed. The Times' foreign policy had undergone little change since 1788 when an announcement stated that it would be "like Janus, the Roman Deity, double-faced; with one countenance it will smile continually on the *friends* of *Old England,* and with the other will frown incessantly on her enemies." [11] While the Times' foreign department was independent of party and bureaucratic control, it was distinctly national and imperial; and Wallace, Chirol and Steed could usually be counted on to take a strong line in support of the foreign office.

Because of its completeness and authority the Times' foreign news service was held in higher regard than that of any other paper. The foreign office and everyone interested in high politics followed its reports closely; they were quoted and referred to on occasion by every paper in the country. The Times' correspondents in the European capitals were accorded recognition and favors usually reserved for diplomatic representatives. Close collaboration with the British embassies was everywhere an important feature of their activity. The reporting of 'spot news' of a relatively unimportant nature was left to Reuter's, but on momentous events

[10] Sir William Beach Thomas, *A Traveller in News* (Lond., 1925), p. 48.
[11] *The History of the Times* (Lond., 1935), I, 31.

their reports were supposed to make the agency accounts superfluous. Their chief duty under Moberly Bell's régime was "to comment on news rather than to give it." [12] This meant only one thing: policy, opinion and interpretation dominated news. This is apparent in almost every column of foreign correspondence.

From the Boer War to 1914 the news and editorial policy of the Times was consistently anti-German. Every means at the disposal of the editorial staff and the correspondents was employed in the campaign to "wake up England." When Northcliffe acquired the Times in 1908 he is reported to have said: "I shall leave the Editor unrestricted control, unless he should—which is incredible—fail to warn the British people of the coming German peril. I insist upon that duty being discharged." [13] Charles Lowe, who was the Berlin correspondent in the 'eighties, holds Bell responsible for the anti-German policy of the paper; and it may well be that Lowe's successors carried on under policy orders from the domineering manager. [14] After Lowe's violent quarrel with Bell, who forced his resignation, Brinsley Richards held the Berlin post for a brief time (d. 1892). Valentine Chirol occupied an exceptional position in the German capital until he quarreled with Marschall and Holstein. Boycotted by the chief officials of the Wilhelmstrasse, his usefulness was at an end and he was recalled to London in 1896, where he served first as assistant to Wallace and then as foreign editor. George Saunders went to Berlin in 1888 to represent the Morning Post, he married the daughter of Oscar Hainauer, Berlin banker and noted art collector, and became the resident correspondent of the Times in 1897. His service continued until 1908 when he was transferred to Paris and the Berlin post was entrusted to J. E. Mackenzie. Moberly Bell once remarked that "Our present Correspondent at Berlin [Mr. Saunders] enjoys the distinction of our having been twice requested to remove him." [15] There is no denying that in the Wilhelmstrasse the trend of Saunders' reporting caused much irritation. Saunders always regarded his warning activity in Berlin as a great national service. Temperamentally unsuited to the German atmosphere, he developed a deep antipathy to the country and its civilization. He was not a robust man and during his last years in Berlin he was frequently ill for long periods. His calls at the foreign office were irregular; for a time he would come every day, then stay away for weeks, sending an assistant in his place. Because of his position as the Times' correspondent, news and information came

---

[12] E. H. C. Moberly Bell, *Life and Letters of C. F. Moberly Bell* (Lond., 1927), p. 167.
[13] F. H. Kitchin, *The London 'Times' Under Moberly Bell* (Lond., 1925), p. 238.
[14] *The Tale of a "Times" Correspondent* (Lond., 1928), p. 301.
[15] *Life and Letters of Moberly Bell,* p. 172.

streaming in to him in spite of prolonged periods of inactivity. Saunders' feud with Richthofen may have had some influence upon the correspondent's reporting of German affairs. Von Richthofen, foreign secretary under Bülow, was a moderate man and reputedly Anglophile. At a social evening the two met and Saunders offered his hand, which the secretary refused to take, commenting bitterly: "No one has contributed more to the poisoning of public opinion in England against Germany than you." From that time the two never spoke.

Too much emphasis, however, should not be placed upon the personality of the Berlin correspondent. Probably more important was the policy laid down by the editors in London. Firmly convinced that the rising power of Germany is a menace to England and the Empire—political, economic and naval—the Berlin correspondent selects and reports those events that fit the pattern. The Vienna correspondent, Wickham Steed, observes and reports every reaction of German policy in the lands of the Dual Monarchy. In Paris William Lavino notes every sign of German intrigue against England and English policy. And so it goes on around the world. The result of the correspondence in the Times is a picture of Germany and German policy, which in its details may be true, but which taken as a whole is an artificial creation. The 'angling' or 'slanting' of the reports to fit the news policy is easily detected in the Berlin correspondent's reports on German press opinion, which was reported at greater length in pre-War dispatches than in post-War intelligence. By assembling editorial opinion from several journals and ignoring others almost any kind of an impression could be made. The Times' reports most frequently quoted the fantasies of the Pan-German press, the turgid squirts of the Krupp-controlled Berliner Neueste Nachrichten, and the nationalistic dogmas of the Post, the National-Zeitung, and the semi-official Kölnische Zeitung. Rarely were the moderate Vossische Zeitung, Berliner Tageblatt, or Frankfurter Zeitung quoted. Readers served daily with fare like this must have concluded that the German people were straining at the leash in their eagerness for war with England.[16]

In 1890 the Daily News was a prosy Victorian morning paper closely identified with the fortunes of the Liberal party. Edited by Sir John Rob-

---

[16] In addition to those cited above, the following works on the *Times* and its personnel are important: *The History of The Times*, vols. I and II, to be completed in three volumes; W. D. Bowman, *The Story of The Times* (N. Y., 1931); Fyfe, *Northcliffe*, pp. 122–36; Grünbeck, *op. cit.*, I, 193–209; Valentine Chirol, *Fifty Years in a Changing World* (N. Y., 1928); H. W. Steed, *Through Thirty Years* (2 vols., Lond., 1924); Max Pemberton, *Lord Northcliffe* (Lond., n.d.). Obituary notices in the *Times:* Moberly Bell, April 6, 1911; M. de Blowitz, Jan. 19, 1903; William Lavino, Aug. 6, 1908; George Saunders, Sept. 11, 1922. Personal reminiscences of Saunders by Mr. J. A. Spender and Geheimrat Friedrich Heilbron.

inson, the ownership was vested in a group of party leaders that included Arnold Morley, Henry Oppenheim, Lord Ashton, and Lord Brassey. Its circle of readers was drawn largely from the Non-Conformist middle class and its watchwords were free trade, religious freedom, and social reform. By some of its admirers it was dubbed "the conscience of the press," and the tone of its editorial page lent point to the remark of a writer that what England really needed was a book on *Moral Indignation: Its Cause and Cure.* Disturbed by the steady loss of subscribers and consequent decline in advertising revenue, the proprietors, in 1896, induced E. T. Cook to leave the Westminster Gazette and take charge of the paper. Between 1890 and 1900 the circulation declined from 93,000 to 61,000, the curve being identical with that of other morning dailies of the serious Victorian type. During the Boer War, Cook took a Liberal Imperialist line which left the Radical position unrepresented in the London morning press. In 1901 the paper was sold to a new company represented by Mr. Lloyd George. The major portion of the capital was supplied by Mr. George Cadbury, a wealthy Quaker manufacturer of Birmingham. A friend of E. T. Cook's said: "He [the friend] was surprised at their getting money from Cadbury. He had always failed. Cadbury used to say, 'Liberalism is too high and sacred a thing for money, but I will pray with you.' Probably Mr. Lloyd George had prayed." [17] Cook resigned the editorship rather than support the pro-Boer policy of the new owners, and his place was taken by A. G. Gardiner. H. N. Brailsford and H. W. Nevinson were for a time members of the editorial staff. G. H. Perris, a bitter critic of Sir Edward Grey's foreign policy, headed the foreign department until 1910. The leading articles on foreign affairs were written by Perris, Massingham or Gardiner.[18] Financially the Daily News under its new direction was not an immediate success. Racing tips and liquor advertisements were excluded and the paper assumed a higher moral tone than ever. A change came in 1907 when Mr. H. T. Cadbury became the business manager. In 1909 the company purchased the evening Star; in 1912 the popular Morning Leader was acquired and merged with the Daily News and the price reduced to a half-penny. The make-up and typography were radically altered; the first page became the main news page, headlines and features were employed to attract readers; the paper was popularized and became a serious competitor to the Daily Mail. A daily circulation of 500,000 was quickly achieved and sales continued to show an upward trend.

From 1906 to 1912 the editors of the Daily News concentrated on the

[17] Mills, *Life of Cook,* p. 196.
[18] Although Massingham became editor of the *Nation* in 1907, he still found time to write for the *Daily News.* One of the most forceful of political publicists, Massingham had previously been editor of the *Star* and the *Daily Chronicle.*

social reform program advocated by the Radical wing of the Liberal party. The second Moroccan crisis shocked the editors and owners and induced distrust and apprehension over the government's course in foreign affairs. A determined campaign against continental commitments was begun. The demand was for a Liberal and not a Conservative foreign policy. The "Grey Must Go" campaign, which threatened to split the party, found its strongest publicity support in the Daily News. Up to the last minute in 1914 Gardiner preached eloquently against declaring war on Germany.[19]

One of the oldest and most respected of English dailies, the Morning Post was associated for almost a century with the family of Borthwick. Peter Borthwick became editor of the paper in 1849; Algernon Borthwick purchased the paper in 1876 and stamped it with those Tory qualities which were rigidly guarded until its demise in 1937. In 1895, Borthwick was raised to the peerage, the customary reward of a political party. When Lord Glenesk died in 1908, the Post became the property of his daughter Lady Bathurst. "Fashionable" and "aristocratic" were the words most frequently used to describe the Post, for it devoted more attention to the political, social and literary preoccupations of the leisure class than any other daily paper. One of the first of the serious journals to reduce its price to a penny, this was the last concession to the new era, and in every other respect the editors and owners adhered strictly to the accepted canons of Victorian and Edwardian morning journalism.

In 1890 the Morning Post was an eight page paper (later 12, 16, 20) with its editorials filling five columns on page four, and its main news on page five. Domestic politics and foreign affairs held high rank in the apportionment of news space and its foreign correspondence, while not as complete as that of the Times, was equal to if not better than that of its other contemporaries. From 1897 to 1904 James Nicol Dunn was the managing editor although the Borthwicks never relaxed control of the paper's policy. Fabian Ware and Henry Spenser Wilkinson directed the fortunes of the paper until 1910 when H. A. Gwynne became editor. Gwynne was the Post and the Post was Gwynne during the last twenty-seven years of the paper's existence. He had been a correspondent for Reuter's Agency in many parts of the world before he became the foreign director; he left this position to become editor of the Standard and shortly thereafter he moved on to the Post. In 1904 the Tory imperialism of the Post, which opposed giving up anything or clearing out of any place, was

[19] Information about the *Daily News* drawn from the files of the paper; Mills, *op. cit.,* pp. 153–205; Morison, *op. cit.,* pp. 222–23, 305, 309; Grünbeck, *op. cit.,* I, 163–65; H. W. Nevinson, *More Changes More Chances* (Lond., 1925); H. Simonis, *The Street of Ink* (Lond., 1917), pp. 46–58.

expressed in its sharp criticism of the territorial sacrifices involved in the Entente with France. That mood passed, however, and the Post, particularly under Gwynne's direction, became one of the staunchest advocates of the Triple Entente and a bitter critic of German world policy.[20]

Although the proprietors of the Morning Post never relaxed control of the news and editorial policy, the influence of Henry Spenser Wilkinson as chief leader writer on foreign affairs from 1895 to 1909 was a factor of real consequence in the life of the paper. Born in 1853, Wilkinson attended Oxford, was called to the Bar, and then abandoned law for a position on the editorial staff of the Manchester Guardian. Like Eyre Crowe, whose sister he married, Wilkinson belonged to that stratum of the ruling class whose members kept off the stage and out of the limelight, but who through their knowledge as technical specialists were oftentimes more responsible for the course of affairs than those who took the bows and received the applause. Wilkinson was a close friend of Sir Charles Dilke, a disciple of Lord Roberts, a student follower of Mahan, an organizer of the Navy League, and an enthusiastic advocate of the Kipling-Rhodes-Roosevelt brand of imperialism. Between Crowe and Wilkinson there was at all times a lively exchange of ideas, and perhaps of information. That section of Crowe's famous foreign office memorandum of January 1907—"The Present State of British Relations with France and Germany"—which deals with the strategy and policy of the Empire is a *précis* of a book published by Wilkinson in 1897 entitled *The Nation's Awakening*.

Founded in 1855, the Daily Telegraph was the first four page morning daily to sell for a penny. J. M. Levy, the publisher, quickly located a public that valued a newspaper not simply for its politics but for its general news and information. In the Daily Telegraph, parliamentary reports and political speeches were accorded less space than in the older journals and a broader selection of news was offered the public. The tradition of a full page of editorials was strictly observed. However, instead of devoting the long and short leaders exclusively to domestic and foreign politics, the columns were filled to the prescribed length with a jumble of historical, antiquarian and scientific information written up with a pseudo-literary elegance. American women were "fair daughters of the Republic," milk became "lacteal accumulations," and grouse were "feathered denizens of

---

[20] Files of the *Morning Post*; R. Lucas, *Lord Glenesk and the Morning Post* (Lond., 1910); W. Hindle, *The Morning Post, 1772–1937* (Lond., 1937), chaps. XIII and XIV; H. Spenser Wilkinson, *Thirty-five Years, 1874–1909* (Lond., 1933); for the relations between H. A. Gwynne and Conservative party leaders see Austen Chamberlain, *Politics from Inside* (New Haven, 1937), pp. 138–40, 226, 364–65, 482–83.

the moor," who became "the premature victims of the predatory instincts of the prowling poacher." The Daily Telegraph was both the diet and the mirror of the rising middle class business circles of London. The tradition of progressive journalism was retained in the family of Levy-Lawson; and the son and grandson of the original proprietor surpassed other publishers in exploiting commercial advertising and in expanding circulation. In 1890 the Daily Telegraph had more than 200,000 subscribers.

Foreign news was important to the business and commercial class that favored the Daily Telegraph. One of the paper's notable features was a daily budget of gossip from the French capital, entitled "Paris Day by Day," which must have confirmed English readers in the opinion that the French were a frivolous and immoral people. E. J. Dillon, a journalist and publicist of European reputation, was the Telegraph's star traveling correspondent before the War. From 1885 to 1903–4 the paper was represented in Berlin by the most pro-German member of the British foreign correspondents corps, J. L. Bashford. Bashford also reported for the Westminster Gazette and contributed frequently to the English reviews. An ardent champion of German policy, Bashford was accorded many favors by the authorities and was decorated by the Kaiser. After Bashford's withdrawal, the Berlin post was occupied temporarily by Dillon and by Mr. Morrison, who also served the Daily News and the Daily Chronicle. In 1906 E. J. Wilcox became the resident correspondent, a post which he held until the outbreak of war in 1914.

During the period covered by this study, J. M. LeSage was managing editor of the Telegraph. There was no separate foreign department or foreign editor in the staff organization, the duties ordinarily connected with this position being performed by the managing editor. Among the distinguished journalists serving on the editorial staff were W. L. Courtney, J. L. Garvin, Iwan-Müller, Archibald Hurd, and Harold Spender. Of the Conservative morning dailies, the Telegraph was the least consistently Germanophobe in its treatment of news and in its editorial policy. Politically it was mildly Liberal until the party split over Home Rule; thereafter it was mildly Unionist, and during Balfour's leadership of the party was generally credited with being his personal organ and mouthpiece.[21]

More political in every respect than the Daily Telegraph was the London Standard, which during the Salisbury era was the recognized organ

[21] Files of the *Daily Telegraph* and information supplied by the present editor, Mr. A. E. Watson; H. W. Massingham, *The London Daily Press* (Lond., 1892), pp. 91–120; J. Courtney, *The Making of an Editor, W. L. Courtney* (Lond., 1930); Morison, *op. cit.,* pp. 266–70; Simonis, *op. cit.,* pp. 39–45; Grünbeck, *op. cit.,* I, 215–22.

of the Tory section of the Conservative-Unionist party. Massingham describes it in the 'nineties as "the most solid of British newspapers," a kind way of saying that it was very dull. Owned by the Johnston family it was edited in succession by W. H. Mudford, G. B. Curtis, H. A. Gwynne, and Herbert A. White. Particular importance attached to the Standard because of the close relations between Lord Salisbury and the chief leader writer on foreign affairs, Alfred Austin, who has been described as "a poet among leader writers and a leader writer among poets." This connection was known to the diplomats and foreign correspondents, and until Austin's retirement from editorial work in 1895 every pronouncement of the Standard on foreign affairs was attentively observed and carefully reported. With the competition of the popular press for circulation and advertising, around the turn of the century, the fortunes of the paper declined. In 1904 it was purchased by Arthur Pearson, H. A. Gwynne was made editor, and the policy was switched to support the Chamberlain tariff reform program. Circulation continued to decline as old readers died off. When the Pearson holdings were dispersed in 1910 it became the property of the Dalziel group. Under the editorship of Herbert A. White efforts were made to popularize the paper and to give it mass rather than class appeal. The experiment was unsuccessful, and during the War the Standard ceased publication as a morning journal and was merged with the Evening Standard.

In Berlin the Standard maintained a succession of able and distinguished correspondents. During the 'nineties the resident correspondent was William Maxwell, who later joined the staff of the Daily Mail. From 1904 to 1911 Herbert A. White represented both the Standard and the Daily Express. Maxwell and White avoided sensation, reported as objectively as they could and kept on good terms with the German foreign office. Unlike the Times' reports, those of the Standard were stamped with the old-fashioned idea that a responsible correspondent should work to improve official relations rather than to excite and exploit diplomatic difficulties.[22]

From its appearance in 1896 the Daily Mail, although it struck the level of the masses, gave due regard to the sensational aspects of foreign news. Large sums were expended on the perfection and expansion of its foreign correspondence. The tone in this section of the paper was always patriotic and imperial. The Daily Mail outstripped all rivals in its screeching jingoism. "If Kipling be called the Voice of Empire in English literature,"

[22] Files of the *Standard*; J. D. Symon, *The Press and Its Story* (Lond., 1914), pp. 199–203; Sidney Dark, *Life of Sir Arthur Pearson* (Lond., 1922), chap. VI; *The Autobiography of Alfred Austin* (2 vols., Lond., 1911), II, 209, 215; Riddell, *More Pages from My Diary*, p. 147; Massingham, *op. cit.*, pp. 73–89; Grünbeck, *op. cit.*, I, 228–29.

writes Kennedy Jones, "we may fairly claim to have been the Voice of Empire in London journalism." [23] Contrary to statements frequently encountered, the Daily Mail was not anti-German from the day of its foundation. To be sure, in its pattern of news presentation all countries were envious rivals of the British Empire, but from time to time particular governments were singled out for special abusive treatment. On November 9, 1899, it was the French who had "succeeded in thoroughly convincing John Bull that they are his inveterate enemies." And shortly thereafter, they were to be "rolled in mud and blood." At the height of England's world-wide unpopularity, during the Boer War, the Kaiser was welcomed on a visit to England with a boot-licking editorial that went beyond the bounds of good taste, and a political cartoon that bore the significant title, "A friend in need is a friend indeed." When popular opinion shifted, Northcliffe swam in the new current. By 1905 the owners and editors of the Daily Mail were obsessed with the German peril; and until 1912, when a general lull in press polemics set in, the Northcliffe organ was one of the most disturbing publicity factors in the relations between the two governments and their peoples. After the crash in 1914, Northcliffe posed as the prophet who had foretold the war with Germany, and attacked the pacifists and moderates who had worked for peace and opposed intervention. When these attacks became personal, A. G. Gardiner, the editor of the Daily News, replied with an indictment of Northcliffe that deserves to be recorded.

Your claim to be the true prophet of the war does not call for dispute [wrote Gardiner]. You say that we prophesied peace. Yes, we not only prophesied peace, but we worked for peace, just as you prophesied war and worked for war. We lost and you won. It has always been your part to prophesy war and to cultivate hate. You have been the incendiary of journalism for twenty years. You have spent your life in an infamous servitude to the changing passions of the hour.[24]

On all matters affecting news and editorial policy the Daily Mail staff took orders directly from Northcliffe. Until 1899, when Thomas Marlowe was made chief editor, the direction of the paper was really in commission. Marlowe was an efficient chief of staff rather than an independent editor. H. W. Wilson, an authority on national defense and editor of the *Navy League Journal,* was the chief leader writer. Fenton Macpherson directed the foreign department. Among the star reporters who at various times served the Mail were Charles Hands, George Steevens, Philip Gibbs, Hamilton Fyfe, and Valentine Williams. In the Daily Mail, regular cover-

[23] *Fleet Street and Downing Street,* p. 149.
[24] *Daily News & Leader,* Dec. 5, 1914.

age of news in a foreign capital by a resident correspondent was subordinated to the sending of "specials" to write up in sensational form the topic or topics that could be pushed into the circle of reader interest. The one exception to this was Berlin, where the Daily Mail was represented from 1906 to 1914 by the American, F. W. Wile. Sidney Whitman described Wile as "quite harmless before he had taken Harmsworth's 'shilling.' " Although he was also correspondent of the New York Times and the Chicago Tribune, he was always rated in the black books of German officialdom as "the Daily Mail man." The disfavor which he incurred in Berlin is understandable in light of his own statement in *Who's Who* (1918) that he "Specialized . . . in reporting Germany's palpable preparations for war ashore, afloat and aloft." On the outbreak of hostilities in 1914 Wile expected to drop his Daily Mail connection and remain in Germany to report the war for the New York Times and the Chicago Tribune, but the German authorities refused him the necessary credentials and he left the country with the British embassy staff and the other English newspaper correspondents.[25]

Founded by Sir Arthur Pearson in 1900, the Daily Express was the Mail's chief rival in circulation and sensationalism. Pearson directed the paper personally until 1904 when R. D. Blumenfeld, an American journalist, was appointed editor. In addition to founding the Express, Pearson built up the first great newspaper chain in England, bringing under his control five provincial papers and three London journals—the Standard, Evening Standard, and St. James's Gazette. Incapacitated by blindness, he disposed of his newspaper interests in 1912. The Daily Express became the property of a syndicate organized by Blumenfeld. At that time the Express had a circulation of about 400,000. With its feature news on the front page, with its stunt displays, and its dramatization of the news, it sought to excite and stampede rather than to inform its readers. During the Pearson régime, the Express was a particularly raucous advocate of tariff reform. Foreign affairs were sensationalized and the tone of the paper was strongly imperial. When the German peril was exploited it was for business reasons, or in the interests of tariff reform. In Herbert A. White, the resident correspondent in Berlin from 1903 to 1911, the Ex-

[25] F. W. Wile, *The Assault* (Indianapolis, 1916), *passim; Memoirs of Count Bernstorff* (N. Y., 1936), p. 79. On Northcliffe and the policies of the *Daily Mail:* Kennedy Jones, *op. cit.;* H. Morgan-Browne, *Concerning the Daily Mail* (Lond., 1907), a severe but just indictment; Max Pemberton, *Lord Northcliffe,* and McNair Wilson, *Lord Northcliffe* (Lond., 1927), are uncritical and of no great importance; J. A. Hammerton, *With Northcliffe in Fleet Street* (Lond., 1932), deals frankly with Northcliffe's character; Tom Clarke, *My Northcliffe Diary* (Lond., 1931), is important for the publisher's last years; H. Fyfe, *Northcliffe: An Intimate Biography,* is the most authentic portrait and the best appraisal of his influence on British journalism.

press had an able and responsible representative whose careful reporting stood in marked contrast to that of the Daily Mail's agent.[26]

In reporting and interpreting foreign news London journalism was pre-dominant in the provinces. The mass production papers became national in distribution with the establishment of provincial editions in Birming-ham, Manchester, Liverpool and Glasgow. By purchase and merger, chains were formed and controlled from London. Many well established provin-cial papers failed under heavy competitive conditions or were purchased and merged with other newspaper properties. London, moreover, was the bottleneck of all foreign news appearing in the regional press. All the reports of the news agencies were distributed from the capital and many local journals depended for foreign news on the leading London dailies with their unrivaled independent correspondence services. Every impor-tant provincial paper had a private London wire and a well staffed bureau in the capital which tapped all the vast news resources of the government bureaus, the parliamentary lobby, and the foreign embassies. Very few of the regional journals, however important they were in national affairs, gave anything like the space to foreign news that London papers gave, and throughout the period here under review they generally followed the lead of the metropolitan press in interpreting and judging foreign develop-ments.

A notable exception, however, was the Manchester Guardian, which, among provincial papers, was pre-eminent both in respect to its political influence and the ability with which it was edited. Liberal to the core, its position in the front rank of British journalism was largely attributable to the character and personality of one man, Mr. C. P. Scott, the editor and principal owner. Equally distinguished were Scott's collaborators on the editorial staff. W. T. Arnold was the chief leader writer until his retire-ment in 1898. He was succeeded by C. E. Montague, Scott's son-in-law. Herbert Sidebotham, who joined the staff in 1895, made foreign affairs his special province, but both Scott and Montague shared with him the edi-torial writing in this field. Until shortly before the War, the Guardian did not have an extensive foreign news service, but relied upon the agencies and the London journals for its foreign reports. The maintenance of an independent news service was a luxury which the Guardian could ill afford at the turn of the century. Competition from the popular mass circulation papers brought the sales down; the unpopular stand which the editors took during the South African War made "giving up the Guardian" a highly

---

[26] Files of the *Daily Express;* Simonis, *Street of Ink,* pp. 76–78; Dark, *Life of Sir Arthur Pearson;* R. D. Blumenfeld, *R. D. B.'s Diary,* (Lond., 1930), and *The Press in My Time* (Lond., 1933); Morison, *op. cit.,* pp. 304–5; Grünbeck, *op. cit.,* I, 155.

patriotic act on the part of many of its old patrons. The profits, which between 1870 and 1898 ran from twelve to twenty-four thousand pounds per year, dropped to twelve hundred in 1905. With the death of the chief stockholder, J. E. Taylor, in 1905, all the shares were acquired by the Scott family and the editor had a free hand in restoring the fortunes of the Guardian. Modernization of the plant, improvements in the distribution system, more attention to the advertising department, and adoption of new features to broaden the paper's appeal resulted after 1910 in a rapid improvement in its financial condition. Thus the Guardian escaped the fate that befell so many of its contemporaries—popularization and cheapening for the masses, on the one hand, loss of independence and individuality by absorption in a newspaper chain, on the other.

Until about 1910, when its world wide news service was developed, the Guardian was more important for its views than for its news. C. P. Scott's position in the Liberal party, his relations to Campbell-Bannerman, Asquith, Morley, Lloyd George and Loreburne, together with his conception of journalism as a public trust and a profession, made this inevitable. As editor, Scott's chief concern was the first leading article, which was always devoted to some public issue. "This was the Long Leader, prime instrument of policy, the voice, persuasive or protestant, for whose utterance, more than for any other single purpose, he believed the paper to exist." [27] Keeper of the tradition of Cobden, Bright and Gladstone, the Guardian upheld the cause of international peace and understanding. Its interpretations and judgments of foreign affairs were invariably sane, just and independent. It was always in opposition to nationalist and jingo opinion and from the time of the Agadir crisis it carried on a campaign for reconciliation with Germany and withdrawal from the continental commitments incurred by Britain under the Triple Entente.

Politically the most important newspaper in the industrial Midland region was the Birmingham Daily Post. It was a standard eight page, eight column morning daily, concentrating upon local affairs and national politics; it did not attempt to compete with the metropolitan dailies in covering the foreign field. Originally Liberal in politics, it followed Joseph Chamberlain out of the party in 1886 and thereafter, through its local associations, it was closely linked to the fortunes of the Unionist leader. The ownership and publication of the Daily Post was a family enterprise. In 1894 when the editor and part owner, Sir John Jaffray, retired, the

[27] J. L. Hammond, *C. P. Scott of the Manchester Guardian* (Lond., 1934), p. 305. Chapter XVII, "C. P. S. in the Office," is an intimate picture of a great editor and the daily routine in a newspaper office. Further information on the *Guardian* from the files and from Oliver Elton, *C. E. Montague: A Memoir* (Lond., 1929); Grünbeck, *op. cit.*, I, 261–68.

paper became the property of John Feeny, son of the original founder. On his death in 1905 control of the paper passed into the hands of his nephew, Mr. Charles Hyde. During Mr. Feeny's illness, the managing editor refused to follow Chamberlain in his campaign for imperial preference. A family conference was held and on the advice of Mr. Law, one of the proprietors of the Edinburgh Scotsman and a close family friend, the editor was told that he must support Chamberlain or resign. When Austen Chamberlain succeeded to his father's place in the Unionist party, the alliance with the Birmingham Post was continued through the paper's chief London correspondent, Sir Alfred Robbins.[28]

Until their amalgamation in 1904, two papers divided the morning field in Liverpool: the Liverpool Post and the Liverpool Mercury. The managing editor of the combined papers was Sir Edward Russell and the business director was A. G. Jeans. Liberal in politics, the Daily Post and Mercury was gradually popularized and its appeal broadened until it acquired the largest circulation of any newspaper in the Liverpool area. The emphasis upon commercial, financial and shipping news reflected the economic life of the region and strongly influenced the treatment of foreign affairs. Unlike the London political press, which drew a picture of a world composed of clashing rivalrous entities, the Liverpool Post and Mercury wove a world pattern of swiftly and smoothly moving commodities. The greater part of its supply of foreign news was drawn from the London agencies, but in Paris, Berlin and St. Petersburg it shared the services of special correspondents with the London Daily Chronicle.[29]

The Glasgow Herald, established in 1783 as the Advertiser, was one of the largest and most influential morning dailies circulating in Scotland, North England and North Ireland. In physical make-up and in news criteria it adhered closely to the Victorian tradition, although it underwent some modification in the matter of style and in the addition of features to broaden appeal. Dependent in the 'nineties upon the agencies and the London dailies for its foreign news, it had built up by 1913 a fairly complete special service covering Paris, Berlin and New York. In London it maintained a large staff for reporting national affairs and general news. In politics it was mildly Unionist, but in this field as well as in foreign affairs its judgments were notably independent. Dr. C. G. Russell was editor from 1888 to 1907, when he was succeeded by Dr. William Wallace.

[28] A. Chamberlain, *Politics from Inside*, pp. 48–49, 201, 446–47; Riddell, *More Pages from My Diary*, pp. 71–72; Simonis, *op. cit.*, pp. 188–89; Symon, *op. cit.*, p. 160; Grünbeck, *op. cit.*, I, 259.
[29] Files of the *Daily Post and Mercury;* Simonis, *op. cit.*, pp. 208–11; Grünbeck, *op. cit.*, I, 269–73.

F. Harcourt Hitchin, formerly assistant manager of the Times under Moberly Bell, became the editor in 1909.[30]

Sometimes called the Times of the North, the Edinburgh Scotsman was generally regarded as the leading political paper in Scotland. Founded in 1816, as a radical Whig organ, it followed the conservative course of the upper middle class until at the beginning of the present century it was recognized as the chief representative of Scottish Conservatism. An eight page, eight column morning daily, carrying four and five columns of dull editorial matter, the Scotsman made fewer concessions to the new journalism than did the London Times. When the Times, in 1907, departed from its ancient tradition and began to give titles to its editorials, the Scotsman clung to the old practice of printing its long political disquisitions without captions. Unrelieved solidity, and information rather than entertainment, is the impression that this journal gives. Dr. Charles A. Cooper, a prominent publicist, was editor from 1876 to 1906 when he was succeeded by J. P. Croal, for twenty-five years the chief of the Scotsman's London bureau. Like the majority of provincial papers it depended on the agencies for its foreign news except in crisis periods when it drew freely upon the special correspondence of the Times and Daily Telegraph.[31]

Only a few of the provincial newspapers before the War were in a position to maintain their own correspondence service on the continent. At least ninety-five per cent of the foreign news reports appearing in the newspapers of Birmingham, Glasgow, Liverpool, and Edinburgh, were taken from the London journals or supplied by the commercial news gathering agencies. Organized in 1868, the Press Association, like the Associated Press in the United States, was a co-operative news agency designed to meet the needs of the regional press. Besides its service of domestic news it had a monopoly upon the provincial distribution of the Reuter reports and the special correspondence of the Times. These dispatches appeared in the local papers under the heading "Press Association Foreign Special." The Central News Agency, which was founded in 1870, was a commercial news distributing concern which offered a national news gathering service to its subscribers. Around 1900 the Central News Agency broadened its field of operation and in competition with Reuter's began the gathering and distribution of continental news. Another commercial agency, the Exchange Telegraph Company, specialized

[30] Files of the *Herald;* Simonis, *op. cit.,* pp. 201–3; Symon, *op. cit.,* p. 163; Grünbeck, *op. cit.,* I, 278–82.

[31] Files of the *Scotsman;* C. A. Cooper, *An Editor's Retrospect* (Lond., 1896); Symon, *op. cit.,* pp. 162–63; Simonis, *op. cit.,* pp. 196–98; Grünbeck, *op. cit.,* I, 284–90.

in financial and sporting news, but in the decade before 1914 it extended
its correspondence service to the main news centers of the world and
began to supply its subscribers with general news reports. In the gathering, preparation and distribution of material, the Exchange Telegraph
sought to meet the special needs of the popular afternoon and evening
papers, which constituted its chief clientele.

While the above mentioned agencies were important in providing the
regional press with both domestic and foreign reports, the metropolitan
dailies were likewise dependent upon Reuter's Agency for much of their
European news. Oldest of the news agencies, it easily surpassed its competitors in the completeness and reliability of its service. Reuter's service
was world-wide and through its cartel arrangements with the national
news agencies of France, Germany, Russia, Austria and the United States
its position was quasi-monopolistic. In Germany its agents had exclusive
right to the reports of the Wolff Telegraphic Bureau and every important
news center was served by a full or part-time correspondent. All political
news reported by Reuter's in Germany was cleared from Berlin where
the Agency's office was maintained. The directors of the Berlin bureau
during the period covered by this study were E. A. Brayley Hodgetts
(1890–91), Gordon Smith (1891–99), A. Harrison (1899–1904), G. Valentine Williams (1904–09), and Lester Lawrence (1909–14). Straight
factual reporting with great emphasis upon completeness and accuracy
was the chief aim of Reuter's service. Their correspondents were supposed to report the facts without interpreting or editorializing. On
the occasion of an important speech by the German chancellor, Reuter's
would supply a long abstract, or quote such parts as pertained directly to
English interests. Interpretation or comment was left to the special correspondents or the editorial writer. 'Spot' news reports were furnished
by the agency; the special correspondent developed the background, covered the field of editorial and party opinion, and tried to give significant
meaning to the event reported.[32]

Special importance attaches to the reportorial function performed by the
newspaper correspondents. Before the advent of radio broadcasting, the

[32] On the history and organization of Reuter's Agency see Friedrich Fuchs,
Telegraphische Nachrichtenbüros (Berlin, 1919), pp. 34–72; W. Schwedler, *Die
Nachricht im Weltverkehr* (Berlin, 1922), pp. 9–14; F. Leiter, "Reuter, Havas,
Wolff, k.k. Telegraphen-Korrespondenzbüro," *Oesterreichische Rundschau*, Bd. 44
(1915), pp. 58–73; Otto Groth, *Die Zeitung* (4 vols., Mannheim, 1928–30), I, 502–8;
H. M. Collins, *From Pigeon Post to Wireless* (Lond., 1925), *passim*. For the other
English news agencies see Simonis, *Street of Ink*, pp. 165–81; *The Newspaper Press
Directory* (Lond., 1913), p. 257. For the personnel of Reuter's Berlin bureau and the
dates of service, I am indebted to the Managing Director of Reuter's Limited.

daily press was the principal means of reporting events and occurrences in foreign lands. All possibility of individual reader control over this aspect of news presentation was remote, whereas in the domestic field the reader might be and frequently was in a position to test the accuracy of reports. The great news agencies, the special correspondents, governmental press bureaus, telegraph and news editors were all interposed like a succession of filters between the world of events and the ultimate consumers of news. Every act of these middlemen in selecting, forwarding and processing the news reports was highly subjective. The criteria governing the selection were established in the main by institutional practice, but they were not so rigidly defined as to exclude the subjective judgments of the correspondents. The old peasant who racked his brain over the problem as to how it was that always just enough occurred in the world to fill the four pages of his weekly paper had fastened upon the most significant problem of modern journalism. But not only was selection made with regard to space limitations, but bias too might determine the printing of one report and the suppression of another. Any journalist or any student of the press knows how easy it is to select authentic facts to tell fabulous untruths. The foreign correspondent was under an obligation not only to secure the news but also to select and report it fairly and objectively.

German news in the British newspapers was selected and forwarded by a small corps of about twelve resident correspondents, most of whom had their headquarters in Berlin. The mere fact that Berlin was the focus of their activities produced a false perspective because, unlike Britain and France, where London and Paris were the unquestioned centers of national life, Germany in every major aspect of life, except the governmental, was decentralized. Most of the correspondents served more than one paper. H. A. White represented the Standard, the Daily Express, and the American United Press; F. W. Wile reported not only for the Daily Mail but also for the New York Times and the Chicago Daily News; J. L. Bashford wrote for the Daily Telegraph and the Westminster Gazette; and for a time Mr. Morrison represented the Telegraph, Chronicle, and Daily News. Each correspondent knew the special requirements of the paper or agency that he represented and these he tried to meet. Policy orders or directives from his editor provided him with definite criteria for selection and treatment of news. Correspondents for the serious dailies were under less compulsion to select sensational and startling incidents for reporting than were the representatives of the mass circulation papers. The former could be certain that their material would be used if it was important and informative, the latter must meet the selective standards of popular journalism, which required novelty, sensation and entertainment.[33]

Considerations of high national policy frequently influenced the work of the correspondents. A good example of this is afforded by the contrasting tone of British reporting from Paris and Berlin between 1904 and 1914. There was a marked delicacy, indulgence and reserve in reporting events in France. The Paris correspondent rarely indulged in criticism because that "would be bad for the Entente." The correspondent in Germany was under no such restraint. He had free rein to report German ambitions, the brutal conduct of the police, mistreatment of army recruits, and the choicest examples of the stupidity of German officials and professors.[34] In general, the power which the foreign correspondents wielded cannot be overestimated, for they controlled the news valves regulating the flow of reports and intelligence out of which were fashioned the pictures and stereotypes of Germany and German policy which Englishmen carried in their minds.

Foreign capitals were not the only centers of news affecting diplomatic relations. In all transactions in which the British government was involved, the foreign office itself was a potential source of information of the greatest interest and value to the daily press. We have very little detailed knowledge of the relations between this department of government and the newspapers. The most recent historians of the foreign office, writing of the pre-War years, simply note that

There was little contact with the Press in the old Foreign Office; certain newspaper writers, especially those representing The Times newspaper and other great British journals, were of course in touch with it, but there were not the regular inquiries at the Office, and the regular supply of information to them, which is to be found today. The business of informing the Press, or rather of answering inquiries where any answer could be given, was before 1914 in the hands of one of the Private Secretaries. . . .[35]

As a matter of fact, to all but a few favored journalists and publicists the atmosphere of the foreign office was cold if not actually hostile. Kennedy Jones has described the reception that the journalist might expect in the old days at the foreign office:

Here he was ushered into a chilly waiting room by a still more chilly attendant, and after having declared his business was left to his own reflections for an indefinite time. Then the attendant would return, probably munching

---

[33] As Harold Nicolson says in his novel, *Public Faces* (Lond., 1932), "Information is never news provided it be full, accurate and not exclusive."
[34] "Germany and the British Press," *New Statesman*, May 30, 1914.
[35] Sir John Tilley and Stephen Gaselee, *The Foreign Office* (Lond., 1933), p. 278.

toast if it was tea-time . . . and with a lofty air would announce: "The Foreign Office has no communication to make, but it may issue a statement later." [36]

One of the first significant departures from this state of mysterious aloofness toward the press occurred at the time of the Fashoda crisis, when the journalists were taken directly into the confidence of the foreign minister. "For the first time," writes Kennedy Jones, "Fleet Street was invited to the Foreign Office." The results of this mobilization of publicity forces are evident in the unanimity and the vehemence with which the government's position was supported by the British editors.[37]

In ordinary times contact with the press was maintained through a limited number of journalists who were persona grata with the department heads, and who, in most cases, represented the serious political or class papers rather than the popular mass circulation journals. Among those who stood in close and regular relation to the foreign office may be mentioned Donald Mackenzie Wallace, Valentine Chirol, and Wickham Steed, as foreign editors of the Times; H. A. Gwynne, as foreign editor of Reuter's Agency and later editor of the Standard and Morning Post; E. J. Dillon of the Daily Telegraph; Lucien Wolf, foreign editor of the Daily Graphic; Spenser Wilkinson of the Morning Post; J. A. Spender, editor of the Westminster Gazette; and Fenton Macpherson, foreign editor of the Daily Mail. The directors of foreign policy, even in their position of relative isolation, were not indifferent to the attitude of the press toward their work. And as Harold Spender has recorded, the foreign office "did not scruple to use its distribution of news as a means for controlling newspapers. If a newspaper criticized a Foreign Secretary too severely he had a very simple means of punishment—he closed the door of the Foreign Office to that paper. . . ." [38]

Foreign secretaries were always extremely guarded in any statements bearing on the relation of their department to the press. The only formal statement on the subject that we have was made by Grey in the Commons on November 31, 1911:

Certain representative newspapers and Press agencies receive any communications with regard to foreign affairs which are suitable for publication. Such information is, for the most part, confined to appointments and changes in His Majesty's Diplomatic Service. If inquiries are made at the Foreign Office with regard to specific facts they are answered when it is possible to do so without prejudice to public or private interests. . . . There is no regular organization in connection with the Foreign Office for inspiring any Press

---

[36] *Fleet Street and Downing Street,* p. 95.
[37] *Ibid.,* pp. 96–97; T. W. Riker, "A Survey of British Policy in the Fashoda Crisis," *Pol. Sci. Quar.,* XLIV (1929), 54–78.
[38] Harold Spender, *The Fire of Life* (Lond., 1926), p. 154.

agency or newspaper in order to put forward, either officially or semi-officially, the views of His Majesty's Government with regard to foreign affairs.[39]

This was a factual understatement. While it was true that there was no press bureau in the foreign office, Grey's remarks leave entirely out of account the informal and unorganized relationships that were maintained with the editors and writers on the principal political dailies. As Grey's private secretary, one of Sir William Tyrrell's duties was to keep in touch with the leading figures in the world of journalism, to convey information to the press, and to interpret and explain the foreign secretary's policies.[40]

Tradition as well as service rules forbade members of the diplomatic staff to write for publication, but the prohibition did not extend to the furnishing of information for articles in the press. Here again the relations with journalists were entirely personal and informal. Sir Cecil Spring Rice, for example, corresponded regularly with his friends Leo Maxse of the *National Review* and St. Loe Strachey of the *Spectator;* he supplied J. L. Garvin with material for an article on "The German Peril" for the *Quarterly Review;* and throughout his long career in the foreign service he carried on a lively political correspondence with his friend Valentine Chirol.[41] In the foreign office as well as in the embassies the furnishing of information was held out as a favor, and usually a personal one, and never acknowledged as a right. Equality of treatment for all accredited journalists could not be countenanced, and such was the tradition of the service that too close contact with the press as a whole was held to be perilous, vulgar and improper.

Besides direct contact, as described above, the press mediated in still another way between diplomatists and the public. Information supplied by the foreign minister in parliamentary debates on foreign policy, in response to questions in the House, and in parliamentary bluebooks, reached the public through the newspapers. However, the importance of this service of information depended entirely upon the will of the foreign minister and the extent to which he thought it necessary or advisable to take parliament into his confidence. It would be natural to assume that with the democratization of the franchise and the tremendous development of modern publicity this channel of information would assume greater importance. As a matter of fact, just the reverse tendency developed and this source of news, illuminating foreign affairs, tended to dry up. As politics became more and more concerned with domestic social issues, less

---

[39] *Parl. Deb.*, 5th Ser., vol. 32, 564.
[40] *Lord Riddell's Intimate Diary of the Peace Conference* (N. Y., 1934), pp. 219–20, 278.
[41] Stephen Gwynn, *Letters and Friendships of Sir Cecil Spring Rice*, I, 436–37, II, 144.

time was given on the calendar to foreign policy debates. As parliament became less of a gentleman's club, the curtain of class exclusiveness and bureaucratic secrecy was drawn more closely around the conduct of the nation's foreign relations. This trend is clearly revealed in the policy of bluebook publication. More information was made available to parliament and the nation by the publication of papers during Lord Salisbury's conduct of the foreign office than during Grey's administration of that department.[42]

Although the foreign service professionals were in a position to control information about the work of their department, this did not mean that they were delivered from the influence of daily journalism. The pressure of publicity became greater as they became more secretive about the preparation of policies. At this point the distinction between official publicity emanating from a government department and private publicity originating with a correspondent, an editor or a newspaper proprietor, is of signal importance. Private publicity, whether news, interpretative comment, or straight exhortation could not be entirely ignored by those who shaped policies. For the foreign secretary and his staff the domestic and foreign press was a primary source of information. One of the routine functions of ambassadors and ministers was to follow and report on the press of the country to which they were accredited. The important British papers were carefully read by the foreign office officials both for their news reports and their editorial reactions. Although Grey was occupied for eight hours a day—excluding week ends—with dispatches and conferences, and although attendance at the House of Commons took much of his remaining time, he regularly read the Times in the morning and the Westminster Gazette in the evening. Press articles appearing in other organs were clipped by the clerks and, if judged to be of sufficient importance, came to his desk in the regular course of business. The papers that were carefully read in the foreign office were not those boasting the largest circulations, necessarily, but those that were most highly regarded and regularly read by the politically effective sections of the population. The list included the Times, Morning Post, Daily Telegraph, Daily News, and Manchester Guardian among the morning journals, and the Westminster Gazette and the Pall Mall Gazette among the evening papers. As potential trouble makers, the mass circulation journals, such as the Daily Mail and the Express, were carefully watched by the officials. Their puffs and screams, and a tendency to turn international relations into a series of stunts and

---

[42] For the publication policies of British foreign ministers see the historical introduction in H. Temperley and L. M. Penson, *A Century of Diplomatic Blue Books, 1814–1914* (Lond., 1938).

sideshows, frequently resulted in serious embarrassment for the diplomats. These papers and their representatives could not be ignored, but in general the attitude of officialdom toward them was marked by reserve and suspicion.[43]

In still another way the press directly affected the foreign office and its work. A very large proportion of the questions, oral as well as written, that was put to the foreign secretary during the question hour in the House of Commons was inspired by some item of news, or suggested by an editorial statement in the daily press. A brief dispatch from an obscure correspondent in a still more obscure post could, and frequently did, lead to an embarrassing question in the House of Commons. A calculated indiscretion by a foreign statesman might result in pertinent questions that endangered a whole line of policy. Resulting political repercussions might even threaten the position of the cabinet. This was the peculiar and incalculable power of the press which foreign office officials feared and dreaded.

Between 1890 and 1914 the British newspaper press underwent many changes in spirit, content and physical appearance. Millions of people who had not before been subscribers to the older journals, now became regular newspaper readers. The publicity given to politics and foreign affairs was increased a thousand times. More people were informed, or misinformed, about the Empire and England's relations to her neighbors than ever before. We cannot infer from this any extension of popular control over those relations, because the balance between parliament, cabinet and foreign office remained unchanged. A higher regard for the increasing power of publicity marked, however, the attitude of the foreign office officials. The metropolitan papers, because of their superior resources, dominated the publication of news and opinion on foreign affairs. The extension of the area in which London papers circulated, through the exploitation of rapid communications, the concentration of newspaper properties in the hands of a single individual or trust, the development of the news agencies in London, through which were filtered the foreign reports reaching the provinces—all assured to London journalism a disproportionate influence in publicizing foreign affairs. Moreover, the leadership of London was reinforced by the natural tendency of provincial editors to follow the metropolitan editor because of his great prestige. The mass of news and opinion poured out daily by the press was the work of many hands and brains. Gathered by the correspondents from many sources, prepared for the wires and telegraphed to London, where it was submitted to the rigid selective

[43] For information on the foreign office and the newspapers I am indebted to Mr. J. A. Spender.

standards of the news editor, it was then processed for reproduction in the newspapers. From this mass of stuff readers received their impressions of foreign countries and foreign peoples. Foreign news dispatches might clarify a situation, modify opinions, or confirm existing preconceptions and stereotypes. Popular leaders and technical specialists could not ignore the increasing power of the great engines of publicity and propaganda.

CHAPTER III

THE GERMAN PRESS AND FOREIGN AFFAIRS

The Imperial Chancellor does not need to beg favors of the press. The newspapers flock to him because of the valuable information that flows from the foreign office.

Otto von Bismarck.

Foreign policy cannot be conducted without the press.

Marschall von Bieberstein.

It is often said by apologists for the press that every country has the kind of newspapers that it deserves. This is a truism and requires no elaborate demonstration. The history, national economy, political institutions, educational level, and the general *Weltanschauung* of any nation condition and determine the physical and intellectual characteristics of its press. A London daily transplanted to Berlin, printed in German, and endowed with a million subscribers, would go under in a very short time. Likewise, a German journal of the first rank published in London in the English language could not survive without unlimited subsidy. No institution in the modern world expresses and represents more distinctly the differences between national cultures than the newpaper press. While the history of the institutional growth of the English and German press shows a pronounced parallelism in mechanical techniques, organization, and relation to the cultural environment, nevertheless, the relationship of the two is no closer than that of species within the same genus.

Among the most evident differences should be noted, first, the decentralization of the German press as distinguished from the English. Nothing comparable to London's domination of British journalism existed in Germany. Berlin, to be sure, was an important news center and every important paper in the Reich maintained a bureau there, but of the five German papers with European reputations only two were published in the capital. Second, there is no need to dwell upon the particularism that prevailed in certain sections of the country, especially in the South, and the religious cleavage that intensified sectionalism. These divergencies were sharply reflected in the newspapers and their subscription lists. In external appearance, too, there were marked differences between English and German newspapers. Nothing like the great blanket folios of the Times and Telegraph were known in Germany, where the standard size was slightly larger than the modern American tabloid. The first page of the standard London morning paper carried classified advertising, while the front page of its German counterpart was given over usually to a long scholarly feature article, which was derived from, or suggested by, some significant news event of the day. In the amount of printed material offered the leading German journals outdid the English. Resembling the American press, the German newspapers, besides general news, published a great deal of matter on literature, art, music, and the theater, sports, business, religion, travel, science, and fashions, an entertainment section for women, together with a large acreage of advertising. This material was generally arranged and presented in special supplements to the first or main news section. The variety and technical excellence of the special articles on economics, art, music, literature, and science, gave to German journalism one of its most praiseworthy qualities. Weak on news coverage, as compared to the British journals, the German press surpassed that of any other country as an educational and cultural medium.

The great circulations acquired by the popular English dailies were never equaled in Germany. In 1896–97 the average daily circulation for the established Berlin newspapers was 38,500.[1] In the same year, over the entire Reich, the average circulation, including dailies and weeklies, was 3600. In 1912 only sixteen German papers had circulations of over 100,000, but there were 292 papers with circulations of 10,000 or more. The sales of the Berlin Morgenpost reached 400,000, which was about half the circulation of the Daily Mail. In the same year (1912), the Lokal-Anzeiger of Berlin achieved sales of 250,000 and the Berliner Tageblatt claimed 215,000. While circulations were quite modest, Germany supported a large number of newspapers. Disregarding minor statistical discrepancies, it appears that there were about 3000 daily and weekly newspapers in Germany in 1890, about 3500 in 1901 and about 4000 in 1914. The total edition of all newspapers rose from eight million in 1885 to sixteen million in 1913.[2] It is evident from the figures given that the Germans

[1] Hjalmar Schacht, "Statistische Untersuchung über die Presse Deutschlands," *Conrads Jahrbücher,* 1898, pp. 503 f. The statistical studies on the German press are numerous; and the literature of investigation and research on German journalism is more extensive than for any other country. It is best approached through the bibliographical aids afforded by Karl Bömer, *Bibliographisches Handbuch der Zeitungswissenschaft* (Leipzig, 1929) and *Internationale Bibliographie des Zeitungswesens* (Leipzig, 1932); also the voluminous bibliography in Otto Groth's *Die Zeitung* (4 vols., Mannheim, 1928–30), IV, 349–582. Groth's volumes on the German press constitute the most scholarly systematic study of modern journalism in all its manifold aspects. Anyone concerned with the German press—political, cultural, technical, social, or historical—must consult this truly monumental work.

[2] Paul Roth, *Die Programme der politischen Parteien und die politische Tagespresse* (Halle, 1913), pp. 10–11, 72; P. Stocklossa, "Die periodischen Druck-

were a newspaper reading people, but their press was more diverse and the general product less standardized than the British; this points to the obvious conclusion that the subscribers or purchasers of a German newspaper formed a more homogeneous group with more definitely articulated tastes, preferences and interests than the reading public of a mass circulation English newspaper.

Particularism, confessional differences, and the multiple party system in the political life of the country contributed to the maintenance of a large number of papers with modest circulations. Another characteristic of the German press was the predominance of the editorial program over all other aspects and functions of the newspaper. It was a principle of British journalism that the editorial and news departments be clearly separated, that one should not intrude upon the other. This was an ideal, of course, and was not always achieved in practice. But in the German press the news report had to be stamped with the editorial viewpoint either by comment on the report itself or by rewriting the report so that it harmonized with the personality and convictions of the paper. English news reports frequently ran counter to the political, cultural and social viewpoints represented on the editorial page. In the German paper everything had to be harmonized and stamped with the editorial values for which the journal stood. The German newspaper, therefore, possessed an organic and spiritual unity that was frequently lacking in British organs.

Nowhere was this more clearly the rule than in the political press. It was axiomatic that a newspaper could not live indefinitely on German soil and maintain neutrality toward the current social and political conflicts, a neutrality that was a condition for the success of the popular press in England and America.[3] While a politically neutral "business press"— the *Generalanzeigers*—did develop in Germany, still to a far greater extent than in the Anglo-Saxon countries a determined viewpoint in both news and editorial features was demanded by the German reader. "A newspaper without opinions is like a man without opinions," is a statement frequently heard in Germany. Throughout the nineteenth century the German press had developed as a medium for expressing positive views, not only in politics but also in literature and art. "Die Feder als Waffe zu benutzen" is expressive of well-known aspects of German political, academic, and literary life, and reflects accurately the average German's attitude toward the press. Objectivity was not expected of the press.

schriften Deutschlands," *Schmollers Jahrbuch*, 1913, Heft 2; published statistical studies are summarized in W. Schöne, *Die Zeitung und ihre Wissenschaft* (Leipzig, 1928), pp. 93–124; and in Groth, *op. cit.*, I, 205, 251–59.

[3] W. Bauer, *Die öffentliche Meinung in der Weltgeschichte* (Potsdam, 1929), p. 356.

A Conservative paper must suppress or pass over with a sneer the speech of a Socialist leader. Had the editors done otherwise, the readers would have complained and canceled subscriptions. One did not subscribe to a Conservative paper to read Socialist speeches. The German demanded partisanship and he got it. Violence in political writing and reporting was one of the characteristic features of German journalism. The Kreuzzeitung referred to the "monkey-like quickness" of the Progressive editors, "who lie like the devil and deceive on principle." The Börsen-Courier referred to its Conservative contemporary as a "filthy sheet." To find in English political journalism anything approaching the scurrility and vituperation common in the German political press, one would have to return to the early decades of the nineteenth century when the Times alluded to the Chronicle as a "squirt of dirty water" and to the Standard as a "stupid and priggish print, which never by any chance deviates into candour." The German tradition of vilifying political opponents was carried over into the field of international affairs and caused much trouble and created much bad blood abroad.

Not only was the tradition of political journalism different in the two countries, but the press also bore a different relation to the organized parties. Much earlier than in Germany, the press in England exploited the rich mine of commercial advertising. It found a new economic life stream in the purchasing public and was freed from dependence upon the party pantry. This made it possible for political writers and editors to assume the rôle of independent advisers and critics. This aloofness toward narrow party politics was most pronounced in the new mass circulation press, for its creators and promoters realized that a sharply defined party policy narrowed the circle of readers and impaired the value of the paper's advertising space. In the election campaign of 1906, for example, Northcliffe beat the drum for Chamberlain and Imperial Preference. When the returns were in he found himself on the unpopular side by a thumping majority. From this experience Northcliffe concluded that a newspaper for the masses could not afford to be identified with a positive political program, so thereafter, while showing preference for Conservatism, he avoided unconditional support of party issues and party leaders. In the political field, broader questions such as the Empire, the navy and the German peril were boomed and puffed, because these were questions which did not have to be voted on.[4] In England, political campaigning for men or issues was divorced from popular journalism.

After 1848, as the German political authorities relinquished control of the press, the political parties began to develop newspapers as instruments

[4] H. Fyfe, *Northcliffe*, p. 114.

of agitation and enlistment. The political press became as closely controlled by the parties as it had been previously by the government. Censorship by the party committee took the place of censorship by state officials. Exclusive of a few outstanding newspapers, a "free press," in a political sense, never existed in Germany. Conservatives, Centrists, and Social Democrats did lip service to freedom of the press, but if one of these parties had completely dominated the government, it is doubtful if the principle would have been observed. Bismarck's tirade against the German political parties was not entirely senseless: "They understand by 'Freedom' really 'Domination'; by 'Freedom of Speech' they mean 'domination of the speaker'; by 'Freedom of the Press' they mean predominance and prevailing influence of the editors and the newspapers." [5] Neither the government nor the party leaders ever admitted that political journalism was a co-ordinate power in the political process. Their view of the press was essentially dictatorial and authoritarian. They would have agreed with Napoleon that "A publishing establishment is an arsenal to which everyone should not have access." [6]

Five newspapers in Germany were outstanding in the field of foreign affairs. Their importance was derived either from the completeness of their news service, the authority of their comment and interpretation, or the special sources of information which they commanded. These journals, which were those most likely to be seen on the newsstands in London, Paris, Rome, and Viènna, were: the Berliner Tageblatt, Kölnische Zeitung, Frankfurter Zeitung, Münchner Neueste Nachrichten and the Vossische Zeitung. Two were published in Berlin, and one each in Cologne, Munich, and Frankfort. The Tageblatt, Vossische Zeitung, and Frankfurter Zeitung were liberal-democratic in their policies; the Kölnische Zeitung and the Münchner Neueste Nachrichten, although not controlled by the party, were aligned with the National Liberals. None was a party paper in the German sense: that is, supported out of party funds and under the thumb of the party functionaries. As successful publishing ventures, they were secure from party domination.

Rudolf Mosse, founder of the Berliner Tageblatt, was not a journalist but a business man. The advertising agency, which he established in 1867, was caught up on the crest of German commercial expansion and formed the economic basis of his later publishing ventures. Founded in 1872, as a

[5] Quoted in H. Schulze, *Die Presse im Urteil Bismarcks*, p. 193. On the history and characteristics of party journalism see Groth, *op. cit.*, II, 370–541.

[6] Quoted in Bauer, *op. cit.*, p. 264. For an example of party control and censorship see the directives of the Augustinus-Verein, the central organ of the Catholic party press, published by Groth, *op. cit.*, III, 318–19. Party censorship extended even to the advertising matter.

local Berlin paper, the Tageblatt became a journal of national and international importance. Its rise to first rank among German papers is attributable in the main to the energy and ability of Arthur Levysohn, who became chief editor in 1881. Trained in the lighter Viennese tradition of journalism, he imparted to the Tageblatt originality and lightness, which were lacking in the serious political press of North Germany. He also organized an excellent foreign news staff and moulded the liberal-democratic editorial policy. Levysohn contributed each week a front page review of foreign and domestic politics. This weekly review was one of the notable features of German political journalism. Theodor Wolff, who succeeded Levysohn in 1907, had been for years the Tageblatt's correspondent in Paris where he occupied an important position in the journalistic and diplomatic life of the French capital. Under Wolff's editorship the Tageblatt's reputation for complete and accurate reporting, for political independence and progressive policies was ably maintained. Among the serious political papers in Germany, the Tageblatt had the largest circulation. In 1897 it had 60,000 subscribers; by 1902 the number had increased to 76,000; by 1912 it had tripled its circulation, which stood at 215,000.[7]

One of the oldest of the German dailies, the Vossische Zeitung, with its emphasis on literature, art, science, and education, appealed especially to the liberal intelligentsia of Berlin. Through several generations this paper was owned and directed by the families Müller and Lessing. Its doctrinaire liberalism, the intellectual tone, and the professional rather than the business spirit which predominated in the editorial and business offices placed the Vossische Zeitung at a disadvantage in the sharp competition with the popular business press in the years immediately preceding the War. Upon the death of Robert Lessing in 1913 the paper was sold by its banker creditors to the Ullstein concern, publishers of the popular, sensational Morgenpost. This change of owners was in every way comparable to Northcliffe's purchase of the Times. The Vossische Zeitung was edited, during the period covered by this work, by Friedrich Stephany, Dr. M. Grunwald and Georg Bernhard.[8]

A special chapter in the history of German journalism belongs to the Kölnische Zeitung. Founded in the eighteenth century, its national and international reputation was established by the owner and publisher, Joseph du Mont, who assumed control of the paper in 1831. The Kölnische Zeitung was the first German newspaper to use the steam driven

[7] Files of the *Berliner Tageblatt;* Emil Dovifat, *Die Zeitung* (Gotha, 1925), pp. 67–71; Roth, *op. cit.,* p. 43; Groth, *op. cit.,* III, 276 ff.

[8] Files of the *Vossische Zeitung;* Dovifat, *op. cit.,* pp. 44–49; Roth, *op. cit.,* p. 43; "Vossische Zeitung" in *Fünfzig Jahre Ullstein* (Berlin, 1927). Circulation figures are not available, but it is unlikely that average sales exceeded 100,000.

mechanical printing press; it was the first to employ the telegraph for transmitting news; it was the first German paper to publish a serial novel. The special correspondence of the Kölnische Zeitung in the quarter century before the War was excelled only by the London Times. Independent of party control, it generally supported the National Liberal program. Much of its political prestige was derived from its position as an inspired, almost semi-official, organ of the Berlin foreign office. It was not unusual to find the editors opposing the government on domestic issues, but in the domain of foreign policy they supported the Wilhelmstrasse through thick and thin. For public men and journalists, at home and abroad, the Kölnische Zeitung was an invaluable barometer of official opinion. For this reason it was quoted by the foreign press more often than any other German newspaper. During the period covered by this study the Kölnische Zeitung was edited first by Dr. August Schmits (1872–1901) and then by Ernst Moritz Posse (1901–22), one of the outstanding figures in modern German journalism. The director of the Berlin bureau was the link between the editorial staff in Cologne and the officials in the Wilhelmstrasse. From 1884 to 1904 this important and highly responsible position was filled by Dr. Franz Fischer. His was a gifted political intelligence and at the height of his career his advice and opinion on all major governmental moves was sought by Berlin officialdom. Fischer's successor was Arthur von Huhn, who had represented the paper, first, in the Balkans, then in Paris. From 1892 to 1904 he served with Fischer in Berlin; after the latter's death he became the principal political correspondent, a position he held until his own death in November 1913. In the diplomatic and political world the Berlin dispatches of the Kölnische Zeitung were carefully observed; for this was a channel frequently employed by the Wilhelmstrasse for important announcements, for trial balloons, and for launching diplomatic campaigns. An asterisk (*) placed before a Berlin dispatch dealing with foreign policy indicated that it rested upon information from official sources.

One of the ablest members of the Kölnische Zeitung's large staff of foreign correspondents was Dr. Hans Paul Esser, who represented the paper in London from 1895 to the outbreak of the War. Every day after a careful perusal of the London morning papers he dispatched a telegraphic summary of important news and opinions; this was followed by a written report in which he interpreted and commented on the news of the day. A collection of his correspondence at the end of a year would have presented an intelligent chronicle and interpretation of the domestic and foreign politics of Great Britain. Although seventy-five years of age in 1914, he was put in an alien enemy concentration camp. When he fell sick he was released and taken into the home of an English friend, but he died, a victim of the war psychosis, on June 16, 1915. Among the correspondents of ability and reputation who represented the Kölnische Zeitung in Europe were Dr. Schneider and Dr. Kröger (Paris), Dr. Noack (Rome), Dr. Ullrich (St. Petersburg), Dr. Meissner and Dr. Bungers (Vienna).[9]

Of the politically important papers in South Germany the Münchner Neueste Nachrichten had by far the largest circulation (90,000 in 1899; 120,000 in 1912). A non-party journal, it proclaimed itself "national and liberal." Founded in 1848 it was brought to the front rank of German newspapers by the publishers Julius Knorr and Dr. Georg Hirth. Dr. Friedrich Trefz was chief editor for thirty-six years (1890–1926). Professor Ernst Francke of Berlin, who was on intimate terms with the officials of the foreign office, contributed special political correspondence to the Munich paper and used the same information for bi-weekly articles in the Hamburgischer Correspondent. From its London correspondent, Dr. Otto Gaupp, the Münchner Neueste Nachrichten received both mail and telegraphic reports. Many of the important articles on national politics and foreign affairs originated in the Berlin bureau, which accounts in part for the strong national note which the Neueste Nachrichten sounded in particularist Bavaria.[10]

Distinguished for its moderation, the extent and authority of its news reports, the variety and quality of its cultural material, and the ability with which it was edited, the Frankfurter Zeitung stood in the forefront of German journalism. Founded in 1856 by Leopold Sonnemann as a business and stock exchange paper, the development of a general news service and the addition of literary and entertainment features gave it an established position in the German press. Politically the Frankfurter Zeitung advocated a liberal-democratic policy, which was to be realized by constitutional reform and the establishment of parliamentary responsibility in the government. Sonnemann devised for his paper a constitution unlike that of any other German journal. The anonymity of editors and contributors was an iron rule; and after the resignation of the first editor-

[9] Johannes Lehmann, *Die Aussenpolitik und die Kölnische Zeitung während die Bülow-Zeit, 1897–1909* (Bleichrode am Harz, 1937), pp. 7–49, presents much interesting material on the political character, personnel, and inside workings of this influential paper. Also Dovifat, *op. cit.,* pp. 54–59; Roth, *op. cit.,* p. 37; Groth, *op. cit.,* II, 221–29. The publishers of the *Kölnische Zeitung* also owned and published the influential *Strassburger Post,* using the same correspondence service for the two papers.

[10] Files of the *Münchner Neueste Nachrichten;* Dovifat, *op. cit.,* pp. 53–54; Roth, *op. cit.,* pp. 37–38; E. Löbl, *Kultur und Presse* (Leipzig, 1903), pp. 160, 164; F. Trefz, *Fünfundsiebzig Jahre Münchner Neueste Nachrichten* (Munich, 1922); information supplied by Geheimrat Friedrich Heilbron.

in-chief, the administration and policy of the paper was entrusted to an editorial board; all matters of business affecting the newspaper staff and the publishers were settled in regular conferences between representatives of the two sides of the enterprise. The independence of the editorial staff, as against the directors of the publishing business, was surrounded with as many guarantees as Sonnemann could devise. August Stein, chief of the Berlin bureau, occupied a position in the political and professional life of the capital that was accorded to but few journalists in pre-War Germany. His genial personality, political sagacity and journalistic ability won for him universal respect and a large circle of friends. Highly regarded by German officials, personal friend of ministers and chancellors, he was justly regarded as one of the best informed journalists in Germany. A close friend and intimate of Hammann, the director of the press bureau, Stein's dispatches, from 1891 to 1914, constitute one of the best indexes to official attitudes and views on major questions of foreign policy.[11]

The five important journals described above are clearly distinguished from their contemporaries by the size of their circulations, the extent and reliability of their foreign news reports, and their relations to the foreign office, which enabled those papers to appear before the public as "well informed." All were political organs in that they supported in a broad way the program of one of the major parties, but they were not strictly speaking party organs. The profession of journalism and the business of publishing news came first and the solid financial foundation of these successful enterprises made them independent of party support and its inevitable concomitant—party dictation.

In pre-War Germany the press of the political parties possessed four general characteristics. First, most of the strictly party journals were founded by a party committee and supported by party funds or by contributions from wealthy individual party members; second, strict adherence was enforced, both in news and editorial policy, to the party line and the definition of news was limited to political subjects; third, the papers drew their subscribers almost entirely from the party membership; and fourth, the party interest was absolutely predominant in the editorial room, which was supervised and controlled by a party leader in the Reichstag or by a party committee. If we exclude the Social Democratic Vorwärts, which had a circulation of 150,000 in 1913, we may also

---

[11] Dovifat, *op. cit.*, pp. 60–67; *Geschichte der Frankfurter Zeitung, 1856–1906* (Frankfort, 1906); *Es war alles ganz anders. Aus der Werkstätte eines politischen Journalisten, 1891–1914* (Frankfort, 1923), presents essays and memoranda by August Stein from the archives of the *Frankfurter Zeitung*. Otto Hammann, *Bilder aus der letzten Kaiserzeit* (Berlin, 1922), pp. 55–56.

say that the party journal was distinguished by its modest circulation.[12] The German party paper normally circulated between ten and thirty thousand copies. They were, in general, further distinguished in their content by the amazing disproportion between news and views. Speeches of party leaders, political announcements, news of party activity and polemical attacks upon opposing political groups made up the bulk of the material offered readers of these papers; a minimum of space was accorded to general news and features. Most of them were content to reproduce the brief, colorless Wolff dispatches and what they could reasonably take from the larger papers. True, not all party organs were so narrow and unimportant. The Kölnische Volkszeitung, the leading Catholic paper, had a creditable news service, was ably edited, and had a large circulation; but for one such party paper there were ten that deserved the appellation of *Käseblätter*—that is, mainly useful for wrapping cheese.

The multiplicity of parties and organized factions made of political journalism a confused and intricate pattern. Four large groups corresponding to major party alignments are, however, distinguishable. First, the parties of the right embracing the Conservatives, Free Conservatives and certain smaller fractions under the title of "Economic Union" (*Wirtschaftliche Vereinigung*); second, the liberal parties, including the National Liberal, South German Democratic party and the Progressive Peoples party; third the Catholic Center with the national minorities, Poles, Guelfs, and Alsatians under its wing; and fourth, the Social Democratic party.[13]

From its foundation by a group of Prussian reactionaries in 1848, the Neue Preussische Zeitung, better known as the Kreuzzeitung, was the leading Conservative party organ. Bismarck was an early contributor and Von Roon was a member of the original directing committee; the shareholders were all of the Prussian nobility. Junker class obstinacy and jack-boot roughness characterized the editorial expression of opinion toward all progressive governmental policies. The policy of the Kreuzzeitung was under the absolute control of the parliamentary oligarchy and most of the political articles were written by party officials

[12] The German party paper was rarely self-supporting. Eugen Richter's *Freisinnige Zeitung* frequently incurred a deficit of 120,000 marks per year. Deficits were covered by contributions from party members, from appropriations out of party funds and from publication of party handbooks and election material. L. Ullstein, *Eugen Richter als Publizist und Herausgeber* (Leipzig, 1930), pp. 113–29.
[13] On the political parties see Ludwig Bergsträsser, *Geschichte der politischen Parteien in Deutschland* (Berlin, 1932); C. Grotewold, *Die Parteien des deutschen Reichstags* (Leipzig, 1908); Paul Roth, *Die Programme die politischen Parteien und die politische Tagespresse in Deutschland;* and the detailed scholarly treatment of the party press in Groth, *op. cit.*, II, 370–541.

and deputies. Among Conservative leaders who played the dual rôle of
politician and journalist, Wilhelm von Hammerstein, chief editor from
1881 to 1895, is best known. Devoted to the defense of narrow class interests and values, the Kreuzzeitung had no great appeal outside the
restricted political circle for which it was written, and the preference
of many Conservatives for the popular Progressive papers was more than
once a matter of editorial complaint. "We make war to the knife against
the Progressives," the editor wrote on one occasion, "and we become
angry at the senseless attacks of their papers—but we subscribe to them
nevertheless and use them for our advertisements." (December 21,
1897.) By far the most renowned feature of the Kreuzzeitung was the
Wednesday review of foreign policy and international affairs by Professor Theodor Schiemann, a German Balt, and an authority on Russian
history. Schiemann's first journalistic connection was with the Allgemeine Zeitung of Munich (1887–93); in 1893 he began to write for
the Kreuzzeitung. He cultivated assiduously connections with high military and civil officials and through his friendships with Waldersee, Bernhardi, Miquel, Holstein, Hammann, Bülow, and eventually, William II,
he came to deserve quite properly the designation "well informed."
From 1902 to 1905 Schiemann was on intimate terms with Holstein;
he called at the foreign office once or twice a week for a discussion of
current affairs and Holstein allowed him to read selected dispatches for
his information and guidance. In all that he wrote Schiemann was, of
course, an ardent champion of national policy and since the patriotic front
against the outside world was a Conservative tradition, Schiemann was
free from interference by the party committee that supervised domestic
policy in the Kreuzzeitung.[14] While the Kreuzzeitung remained the
principal party organ, the Conservatives strengthened their position in
the press by organizing, with capital furnished by party friends, the
Deutsche Zeitungsgesellschaft which by purchase and consolidation ac-

[14] Files of the *Kreuzzeitung;* Dovifat, *op. cit.,* pp. 48–53; Roth, *op. cit.,* pp. 17–18;
Groth, *op. cit.,* II, 460–62; Schulze, *Presse im Urteil Bismarcks,* pp. 7–14; H. Leuss,
Wilhelm Freiherr von Hammerstein, 1881–1895 (Berlin, 1905). On Schiemann and
his connections see the obituary in the *Deutsches biographisches Jahrbuch,* 1921,
pp. 216–22; H. Rogge, *Friedrich von Holstein: Lebensbekenntnis in Briefen an eine
Frau* (Berlin, 1932), pp. 224, 240; F. Rosen, *Aus einem diplomatischen Wanderleben
—Auswärtiges Amt, Marokko* (Berlin, 1931) pp. 23 f.; Graf Anton Monts, *Erin-
nerungen und Gedanken* (Berlin, 1932), p. 364; *Memoirs of Prince von Bülow*
(4 vols., Boston, 1931–32), II, 16, 91–92, 149, 226, 268; Friedrich von Bernhardi,
Denkwürdigkeiten aus meinem Leben (Berlin, 1927), pp. 213, 281, 290–92, 311–19.
Much interesting detail on the political direction of the *Kreuzzeitung* is given by
Count Westarp, *Konservative Politik im letzten Jahrzehnt des Kaiserreiches* (2 vols.,
Berlin, 1935), I, 43, 400–2. For the financial scandal of the *Kreuzzeitung* in 1895
see H. O. Meisner, *Denkwürdigkeiten des Grafen Waldersee* (3 vols., Stuttgart,
1922), II, 357–60.

quired the Reichsbote (1911), Berliner Neueste Nachrichten, Deutsche Zeitung, Deutsche Warte, and Deutsche Nachrichten. No one of these had any considerable circulation.[15]

Founded in 1866 as an organ for the propagation of highly speculative railway operations, the Berlin Post was sold in 1874 by a Berlin bank, into whose hands it had fallen, to a group of leaders of the Free Conservative party. One of the principal stockholders was the steel magnate, Freiherr von Stumm (1836–1901), and associated with him were eleven great industrialists and financial supporters of the party.[16] Because of its frequent use as a semi-official mouthpiece from 1870 to 1890, it was sometimes referred to as the "ambassadors' paper." After 1890 it was still used by government officials as a place to plant semi-official articles, but not with the same regularity as in the earlier period. The biography of Wilhelm von Kardorff, leader of the Free Conservative party, affords some revealing information on the relations of a party leader to the party's principal journalistic organ. As leader of the parliamentary group in the Reichstag, Kardorff was a member of the committee that supervised the party paper. Like other party leaders, he divided his time between committee work, the Reichstag, and writing articles for Die Post. In January 1891, when the editor of Die Post, Dr. Kayssler, published an article originating in official circles supporting Caprivi's low tariff treaty with Austria, Kardorff wrote and published the next day an article opposing the treaty and giving the party line. This was the beginning of a break between Kardorff and Die Post. Stumm, the principal owner, approved the Caprivi treaties with Russia and Austria because they opened markets to German industry; Kardorff opposed them because of the sacrifices required of German agriculture. In the end Kardorff resigned from the Post's committee of control and established relations with the Berliner Neueste Nachrichten, which henceforth received and published his political articles.[17]

Like Die Post, the Berliner Neueste Nachrichten was unimportant as an organ of news; its standing was derived from its position as the mouthpiece of the heavy industries of the Ruhr and Rhineland. Founded in 1880, the Krupp and Donnersmarck interests acquired control of the journal during the 'nineties. Reorganized as a joint stock company in 1901, the controlling stock was divided among several representatives

[15] Westarp, op. cit., I, 400–1.
[16] For the list of stockholders see Groth, op. cit., II, 460. For the attitude of the owners toward the paper and its editor see F. Hellwig, Carl Ferdinand Freiherr von Stumm-Halberg (Heidelberg, 1936), pp. 262–70, 442–45, 480–81.
[17] Siegfried von Kardorff, Wilhelm von Kardorff, 1828–1907 (Berlin, 1936), pp. 234–38, 293–97; Schulze, op. cit., pp. 62–63; Groth, op. cit., II, 193, 203, 460, 574.

of Westphalian industry.[18] Published in a morning and afternoon edition
of eight and four pages, it was devoted almost exclusively to political
topics, which were treated always from the standpoint of the interests of
the heavy industries. Protective tariffs for German industry and support
of government armaments programs were fixed news and editorial policies. The fury with which the editors always intervened when the subject
of private manufacture and sale of arms and munitions to foreign countries arose left no room for doubt as to whose interests were being
served.[19] During the last decade of the century the Berliner Neueste
Nachrichten enjoyed a certain prestige in political circles because it was
edited by Hugo Jacobi, a political publicist of considerable standing,
who was often called on by Hohenlohe for advice, and who frequently
served as a mouthpiece for Miquel, the minister of finance. Of an entirely different character was Viktor Schweinburg, the business manager,
who represented the proprietors. He also operated a political correspondence service, the Berliner Politische Nachrichten, occasionally employed
for semi-official and inspired statements and articles. Schweinburg also
played an important part in organizing the Navy League and served as
its first secretary. He was forced to resign the secretaryship when
charged with using his position for his own financial gain. In the *Haus-
blatt* of the armaments ring, foreign affairs could be handled in only one
way—that is, totally perverted to serve the financial interests of those
who profited from hostility, fear and ill will among nations. With regard
to Tirpitz' naval program the Berliner Neueste Nachrichten was the
ardent champion of the thesis that Britain was "the enemy" against
whom more, and still more, ships must be built.[20]

In the ranks of conservative papers the Deutsche Tageszeitung occupied a singular position. It was the official organ of the Agrarian League,
one of the most powerful politico-economic groups in pre-War Germany.
The League was organized by the large estate owners to represent agricultural interests and to fight the Caprivi tariff treaties, which, on the
whole, favored industry at the expense of agriculture. Financed by stock

[18] The list of stockholders is given by R. Brunhuber, *Das deutsche Zeitungswesen*
(Leipzig, 1908), p. 17; all were mining, steel and engineering concerns.
[19] "Die deutsche Waffen-Industrie und das Ausland," No. 547, Nov. 22, 1900.
[20] Files of the *Berliner Neueste Nachrichten;* Eckart Kehr, *Schlachtflottenbau
und Parteipolitik, 1894–1901* (Berlin, 1930), pp. 169–70, 184–88; Groth, *op. cit.,* II,
461, 576, 580. On Schweinburg: letters in the *Berliner N. N.,* No. 1, Jan. 2, 1900,
and *Die Post,* No. 2, Jan. 3, 1900; *Wer Ists?,* vol. VI, 1559. On Jacobi: Kardorff,
op. cit., pp. 303, 308–9, 316–17, 338–39. The newspaper properties of the Conservative
Westphalian industrialists were concentrated after 1902 in the Deutsche Verlag
which acquired and published the *Berliner Neueste Nachrichten,* and the *National-
Zeitung.* The biggest coup of the Rhenish industrialists was the acquisition in 1913
of the Scherl Verlag with its numerous newspapers and periodicals.

sales to members of the League, the Deutsche Tageszeitung was launched in 1894. To Dr. Georg Oertel, a shrewd politician and able editor, must go most of the credit for forcing the program of the Agrarian League upon the Conservative party. The Deutsche Tageszeitung was his sword in this campaign. Oertel made out of the paper a lively journal with a wider appeal than the party or pressure-group organ usually possessed. Count Reventlow, a prolific writer on foreign affairs and national defense, and a leading Pan-German, was for a long time a regular contributor and later became a permanent member of the editorial staff.[21]

Generally described as Conservative or Nationalist was the Deutsche Zeitung (Berlin), an insignificant scissors-and-paste daily edited, and largely written, by Friedrich Lange. It was a vehicle for personal policies and opinions of the fanatical editor and a small group of followers. Friedrich Lange (1852–1917) was editor of the Tägliche Rundschau from 1882 to 1895; he was closely associated with Karl Peters in his plans for East African colonization. Later he founded the *Deutschbund für reines Deutschtum,* a satellite of the Pan-German League, with a program that anticipated the political and racial policies of Adolf Hitler. Lange was a fanatical doctrinaire whom the Liberal Anglo-Saxon always meets with a mixture of dislike and misunderstanding. Impractical, fanatical, lacking a sense of humor, operating always on principle and never on a basis of compromise, despising opportunists and hypocrites above all things—Lange was the typical doctrinaire. The journal which he edited from 1895 to 1912 was unimportant so far as the German newspaper public was concerned, but so unbalanced were its outpourings, so blatantly chauvinistic, that in dull times foreign correspondents turned to its columns for their daily insult, which they would transmit as a sample of German press opinion. The Deutsche Zeitung was better known to the readers of the London Times than to the people of Berlin.[22]

National Liberalism was more strongly represented in the provincial press than in the press of the capital. This had not always been so. Organized in 1848 as a joint stock undertaking by a party committee, the National-Zeitung was a rival of the Vossische Zeitung at one time for the position of Berlin's leading paper. As long as Bernhard Wolff, the founder of Wolff's Telegraphic Bureau, directed its publishing and financial affairs, the paper flourished. But with his withdrawal and the split in the National Liberal party in 1880, the fortunes of the National-Zeitung began to decline. Between 1900 and 1907 it was completely out-

[21] Dovifat, *op. cit.,* pp. 74–76; Roth, *op. cit.,* pp. 26–27; Bergsträsser, *op. cit.,* pp. 123–24; Westarp, *op. cit.,* I, 196–97.

[22] Files of the *Deutsche Zeitung; Deutsches biographisches Jahrbuch,* 1917–1920, pp. 94–99; Groth, *op. cit.,* II, 587, IV, 341.

distanced by new competitors and threatened with extinction. Financial
support was found for the paper when the majority stock was acquired
by the steel interests. Presumably the chief owner was Freiherr von
Stumm, who also controlled Die Post, since both papers in 1908 were
published by a single dummy corporation that cloaked the real ownership.[23] When the National-Zeitung became a megaphone for selfish private economic interests, the subscribers dropped off rapidly. Finally,
in 1911, it was transformed into a sensational evening boulevard paper
in the Viennese style. The history of the National-Zeitung parallels
closely the history of other papers that came under the domination of the
great industrialists.[24] A cursory examination of the files of this paper
while it was still a party journal reveals the weaknesses of its class. The
news service was negligible, politics dominated everything, and it lacked
freshness and spirit. There was no separation between news and editorial
comment; even written reports from occasional correspondents abroad
were smothered with editorial effusions. The following is an example:
On January 6, 1896, a quarter of a column dispatch was published from
a London correspondent. Without a break in the column the editor continues: "So much for our correspondent. To his communication we add
the following." Then came two columns of editorial interpretation, sup-
position, and insipid historical background. A newspaper edited on these
lines could not hope to compete with the rapidly developing popular
press.[25]

Representative of the National Liberal press in the provinces was the
Schwäbischer Merkur, published at Stuttgart in two daily editions. It
had between ten and twelve thousand subscribers and almost no street or
railroad station sale. It was published in tabloid size in twelve or fourteen pages. The first page carried three columns allotted as follows:
columns one and two, telegraphic dispatches, special Berlin correspondence, and abbreviated Wolff telegrams; the third column was given over
to the special article, usually political. The second page contained general
news of the Reich and reports, written and telegraphic, from European

[23] *Schwäbischer Merkur,* No. 570, Dec. 5, 1908. About this time, Dr. Reismann-
Grone, Pan-German publisher of the *Rheinisch-Westfälische Zeitung,* acquired control of the Berlin *Post.* To what extent he was backed by Westphalian industrial
capitalists cannot be determined.

[24] Ludwig Bernhard quotes the director of the *Reichsverband deutscher Industriellen,* Bueckh, as follows: "Wie es uns mit der 'Nationalzeitung' und anderen
Blättern ergangen ist, so wird es uns immer wieder ergehen. Die Industriellen haben
kein Talent für die Presse. Sobald in einer Zeitung industrielle Einflüsse massgebend
werden, geht das Blatt zugrunde." Ludwig Bernhard, *Der Hugenberg-Konzern*
(Berlin, 1928), pp. 57–58.

[25] Files of the *National-Zeitung;* Dovifat, *op. cit.,* pp. 41–43; Bernhard, *op. cit.,*
pp. 40–41. From 1884 to 1897 Dr. Heinrich Bauer was assistant editor in charge of
foreign correspondence. (*Deutsches biographisches Jahrbuch,* 1902, pp. 73–74.)

capitals. When the Reichstag was in session, the parliamentary report required one or two pages. The remaining pages were taken up with market reports, advertising, and various supplements presenting articles on art, literature and science. Although independent of party control, the editors supported the National Liberal program. The policy on foreign affairs was strongly nationalistic, sometimes aggressively so, and the paper championed commercial, naval and colonial expansion. The Pan-Germans, the Navy League, and the Colonial Society were accorded considerable space.[26]

The Magdeburgische Zeitung and the Hannoverscher Kurier, also provincial National Liberal papers, were, like the Schwäbischer Merkur, family owned and operated enterprises, enjoying about the same circulation and appealing to the same well-educated middle class whose interests were commercial and industrial rather than agricultural.[27]

Close co-operation between the Center party and the daily press was a marked feature of Catholic journalism. The great majority of the papers were originally founded by committees or Catholic lay clubs, while the priesthood always displayed a lively interest in their parishioners' newspapers. In 1850 there were only fifty-five Catholic newspapers in all Germany, and they were of slight importance; by 1870 there were 150. The *Kulturkampf* increased not only the number of papers, but doubled the circulation of the Catholic press. By 1890 the Catholic press had nearly a million subscribers, and by 1912 it had passed two and a half million. One result of the *Kulturkampf* was the foundation of the *Augustinusverein* (1879). This association had as its objectives the co-ordination of policy in the Catholic press, the regulation of competition between Catholic publications, and the forging and maintenance of bonds between the press and the Center party. The membership of the *Augustinusverein* was composed of representatives from the priesthood, party leaders, publishers and editors. Unity and direction in political and confessional publicity was achieved through this institution to a degree unmatched in the press of any other party except the Social Democratic. Because of its strong confessional and political character the Catholic press never developed journals for the masses. The largest Catholic paper in 1912 was the Essener Volkszeitung with 56,000 subscribers. With a circulation in 1912 of 30,000, the Kölnische Volkszeitung was

[26] Files of the *Schwäbischer Merkur*. Dr. Hermann Elben (1823–1899), owner and publisher, was a leader of the National Liberal party. (*Deutsches biographisches Jahrbuch*, 1899, pp. 41–45.) He was followed by his son, Karl Elben, who directed the paper until his death in 1914.

[27] On the relations of the National Liberal party to its press see Groth, *op. cit.*, II, 454–57.

the leading Catholic daily in Germany and gave the lead to the entire Center press of the Rhineland. Owned by the Bachem family and edited by a leading Catholic publicist, Hermann Cardauns (succeeded in 1907 by Dr. Wiesemann), the Kölnische Volkszeitung issued three daily editions. It was inferior to its rival, the Kölnische Zeitung, in its foreign news service, relying in the main on the agencies and occasional specials. From a London correspondent it received regularly a news letter, which it ran under the heading "Allerlei von der Themse." A moderate and tolerant tone marked the treatment of foreign affairs. The "hurrah patriotism" of Conservatives, National Liberals, and Pan-Germans was consistently and sharply denounced. However, in the Kölnische Volkszeitung, as in the other Catholic papers, an unsympathetic attitude toward England prevailed because of British policy toward Catholic Ireland.[28]

To a greater extent than any other party, the Social Democratic organization created, owned and controlled its own press. The editorial personnel and the administrative committees were recruited from the party leadership; the political policies, the selection and treatment of news, and the general principles of publication were determined solely by the political objectives of the party organization. The Social Democratic press lived by and for the party. All of the features common to the Socialist papers were strongly represented by the central organ of the national party, the Vorwärts (formerly Berliner Volksblatt). With a circulation of 150,000 in 1912, it was the most widely read of the party journals. Besides serving as the principal organ of the party leadership, it was also the local organ of Berlin's Social Democracy. Administrative and editorial control was divided between the executive committee of the national party and a press committee chosen from the party membership. The latter was supposed to represent the interest of the rank and file against the monopolizing tendencies of the official oligarchy. The foreign news service of the Vorwärts was insignificant. Occasional correspondents surveyed and reported current developments abroad in labor politics and socialism. International politics were treated solely from the standpoint of Socialist theory and party ideology. The result was a sterile negativism monotonously expressed in the stereotypes of antimilitarism, anti-imperialism, and proletarian solidarity. So far as the party leaders and editors studied foreign affairs it was mainly for the

[28] Files of the Kölnische Volkszeitung; W. Kaupert, Die deutsche Tageszeitung als Politicum (Freudenstadt, 1932), pp. 91–101; Hermann Cardauns, Fünfzig Jahre Kölnische Volkszeitung (Cologne, 1910); Dovifat, op. cit., pp. 76–79; Roth, op. cit., pp. 45–53; Groth, op. cit., II, 430–53. The best survey of the history of the German Catholic press is K. Löffler, Geschichte der katolischen Presse Deutschlands (Munich, 1924).

purpose of gathering material for use against the German government or to illustrate the class struggle.[29]

Outside the circle of party journalism in Germany were a number of papers which were unmistakably organs of political opinion. Disclaiming allegiance to any party, they appealed to the public as independent, non-partisan, or non-political. Outstanding in this group was the Tägliche Rundschau, founded in Berlin in 1881 by the publisher Bernhard Brigl as a "paper for the non-political." It soon found a small but loyal group of readers among government officials, army officers, and in literary and academic circles. Under the editorship of Friedrich Lange it lost its non-political character and became an exponent of aggressive German nationalism, a champion of the Evangelical League, and a bitter foe of international Catholicism. In 1896 Lange was displaced by Heinrich Rippler, who edited the paper with great ability and rare independence until it was purchased and slaughtered by Stinnes in the inflation period following the War. The super-nationalism of Lange's day continued. Standing aside from the daily battle of parties, the editors advocated a strong national policy—naval, colonial, and commercial. In this they were very close to the Pan-German League. As a matter of fact one of the staff, Dr. H. Wagner, was editor of the *Koloniale Zeitschrift,* and Rippler was a member of the executive committee of the Pan-German society.[30]

A unique position was occupied by the Norddeutsche Allgemeine Zeitung. It appealed to subscribers on the ground that it "stands above party, maintains itself uninfluenced by factional spirit and pursues none other than national interests." From 1863, when it first came under the influence of Bismarck and received a considerable subvention from the government, until 1918 it was the semi-official organ of the German government. The economic dependence of the journal upon the government varied with the years and ranged all the way from outright subsidy, to exclusive news rights, official advertising contracts, and a standing government order for five thousand copies daily. In return the Norddeutsche was obligated to receive and publish semi-official pronouncements, corrections and explanations, and to support without reservations the official policies, domestic and foreign. The closest co-operation between high officials of the government and the editors of the paper was required by this arrangement and to assure harmony the authorities exercised the

---

[29] The best study of the Socialist press in Germany is L. Kantorowicz, *Die sozialdemokratische Presse Deutschlands* (Tübingen, 1922); Curt Schoen, *Der Vorwärts und die Kriegserklärung* (Berlin, 1929), pp. 1–13; Dovifat, *op. cit.,* pp. 83–88; Groth, *op. cit.,* II, 406–30; Kaupert, *op. cit.,* pp. 102–11; Roth, *op. cit.,* pp. 60–69.

[30] Files of the *Tägliche Rundschau;* Dovifat, *op. cit.,* pp. 71–74; Kaupert, *op. cit.,* pp. 87–88; Groth, *op. cit.,* II, 268, 536, 555.

right of approving changes in the editorial personnel of the paper. Very early in its history the Norddeutsche became the property of the brothers Ohlendorff; later, around 1914, it passed into the possession of the Reimar Hobbing publishing concern and eventually became a part of the Stinnes industrial empire. The first editor-in-chief was August Brass, who was succeeded in 1865 by Emil Pindter. When Pindter retired in 1894 the political editorship was entrusted to Dr. M. Griesemann and the post of general director was filled by Herr von Ehrenberg. Another editor-in-chief, Dr. Wilhelm Lauser, after a brief period of service, resigned in 1902 and was succeeded by Otto Runge who directed the paper until its disposition during the period of the War.

The Norddeutsche was primarily an editor's paper, preponderantly political, and therefore had slight appeal for the general newspaper reader. Published in the afternoon, it was available to the editors of the great morning dailies for the next day's issue. Any inspired statement or semi-official pronouncement was certain of quotation and comment in the entire German daily press. The first left-hand column on the front page carried the daily political survey, made up of short paragraphs, half news and half editorial interpretation. It was in this section that the famous *entrefilets* on foreign policy usually appeared. Frequently these semi-official announcements, corrections, or expressions of official views were set in different type to emphasize their special character; sometimes the source was indicated by the well-known introduction—"We are able to state on the highest authority. . . ." The reporting of foreign news and editorial comment thereon was always restrained, almost colorless, so that any deviation from the straight factual line was certain to attract wide attention as a move inspired by official circles. As an important cog in the press apparatus of the German government the Norddeutsche deserves special study and attention. Only enough has been set down here to indicate its place and function in the political process. In succeeding chapters its actual operation in crisis periods will receive special emphasis.[31]

All of the journals described above were distinctly political in character. They represented viewpoints, programs and values in the public life of Germany. In so doing they fulfilled the tradition of the newspaper press in the nineteenth century. Beginning in the 'eighties this tradition was challenged by the development of a new type of newspaper, gener-

---

[31] The best treatment of the *Norddeutsche* is J. Boehmer, "Die Norddeutsche Allgemeine Zeitung," *Zeitungswissenschaft, Monatsschrift für internationale Zeitungsforschung,* vol. I (1926), No. 7; Groth, *op. cit.,* II, 183, 201, 232, 267, 575; *Norddeutsche,* No. 232, Oct. 3, 1911 (celebrating the fiftieth anniversary of its foundation); *Die Post,* No. 155, June 9, 1894.

ally referred to as the *Lokal-* or *Generalanzeiger* press. Designed to meet mass demand at a low price, the *Generalanzeiger* press was founded on the local market for news, advertising, and entertainment. Provincial and narrow in outlook, it brought little or no foreign news and recorded only the most sensational incidents in domestic politics. Politically colorless, this press aimed to please everyone and offend no one. Crime, catastrophe, divorce, and human interest stories, together with special features, such as the household and kitchen columns, legal advice, and the serialized novel, constituted the staple fare offered the new reading public.

Like the popular press in England, the success of the *Generalanzeiger* press threatened the economic foundations of the older journalism. The danger was met in several ways. Many publishers set up alongside their old established journals a *Generalanzeiger* for their locality. The Kölnische Zeitung published the Stadtanzeiger with a circulation of 100,000; the Münchner Neueste Nachrichten issued the *Generalanzeiger* for Munich, which had a circulation of 80,000; and the Schwäbischer Merkur was paired in Stuttgart with the Schwäbische Kronik. Other publishers broadened the appeal of their papers to meet the new competition and sought new capital for the modernization of their technical equipment. Some of the old established journals were unable to survive as independent organizations and were bought up by younger competitors in the process of capitalistic concentration and trust building. The Vossische Zeitung, for example, after a vain effort to compete with the mass circulation papers in Berlin was taken over by the firm's creditors in 1911 and subsequently sold, together with the printing plant and publishing business, to the Ullstein concern.[32]

August Scherl, a man of great ingenuity, energy and business ability, was the pioneer in developing the *Generalanzeiger* press. The founding of the Berliner Lokal-Anzeiger, in 1883, was a significant event in the history of German journalism. Scherl is credited with three innovations: first, a cheap and reliable distributing system for his paper, covering every section of Berlin; second, the popularizing of the classified advertisement by a low charge based on the number of words; and third, the establishment of an extensive local news gathering system for reporting everyday occurrences of particular interest to Berlin readers. The paper was a great success; the circulation rose rapidly to a quarter of a million. In the beginning the Lokal-Anzeiger was politically colorless. By

---

[32] Bernhard, *Der Hugenberg-Konzern*, pp. 41–42. The details of the *Vossische's* financial history are given by Dr. Max Osborn, "Die Vossische Zeitung seit 1904," in *Fünfzig Jahre Ullstein*.

1890, however, it was given a definite conservative direction. In return for occasional exclusive news scoops, provided by the chancellery or foreign office, the editors glorified the monarchy and supported the state and its policies.

While the Lokal-Anzeiger was the paper of Berlin's *Kleinburgertum,* the Morgenpost, founded in 1898 by the Ullstein firm was the daily paper of the working class. It was even less discriminating and more sensational than the Scherl organ. The Morgenpost, which had average sales of 350,000 in 1912, was not identified with any political party; it was a strictly business enterprise, but in accord with the general *Weltanschauung* of its readers and publishers it had a democratic, radical tone.

Three publishing concerns and three newspapers dominated the popular field in Berlin: Mosse with the Berliner Tageblatt, Scherl with the Lokal-Anzeiger, and Ullstein with the Morgenpost. Consternation was produced in official circles when, after considerable tinkering with the financial structure of his numerous enterprises, Scherl let it be known that he was contemplating the sale of the Lokal-Anzeiger and the parent publishing business. The likely purchasers were Rudolf Mosse, who already owned a considerable number of shares, and the Ullstein brothers —both concerns democratic and both Jewish, and therefore a double danger in the eyes of the government officials and the supporters of the existing social and political order. As early as 1907 the German government, through Otto Hammann, showed deep concern for the financial future of the Scherl enterprise. In 1913, upon the initiative of the imperial chancellor, Bethmann-Hollweg, a group of bankers and industrialists from the Ruhr and Rhineland purchased the majority stock of the Scherl publishing company. These men, in their opinion and in the opinion of the authorities, had performed a patriotic duty—they had saved Berlin from the domination of Mosse and Ullstein.[33]

Scherl's practical demonstration that large profits were to be made from producing cheap newspapers for the masses, attracted capital to this field and in a remarkably short time the *Generalanzeiger* press was established in every city in Germany. Scherl and Ullstein undertook the establishment of newspaper chains, but their efforts to extend their power beyond Berlin met with only moderate success. W. Girardet and August Huck were the outstanding promoters of the *Generalanzeiger*

---

[33] Out of the union between the Scherl publishing company and the Rhenish industrialists emerged the post-War Hugenberg organization, representing in the newspaper business the principle of industrial concentration. For the history of this deal see Carl Fürstenberg, *Die Lebensgeschichte eines deutschen Bankiers* (Berlin, 1931), pp. 484–85; and Bernhard, *Der Hugenberg-Konzern,* pp. 42–49. Bernhard was one of Hugenberg's associates and had access to important private documents.

press in numerous German cities. Huck was the founder and part owner of a dozen or more papers of this type in South and East Germany, while the firm of Girardet established papers in the principal industrial centers of Westphalia. In sales the *Generalanzeiger* press completely outstripped the old established newspapers. In 1912 ten of the sixteen papers with circulations of 100,000 or more were of the *Generalanzeiger* class.[34]

In England the gulf between the new journals and the old was bridged by compromise, imitation and bankruptcy. In Germany, down to 1914, the rise of the cheap popular press, while not without influence on the old established journals, resulted in the old and the new existing side by side as two distinct types. Fusion and the emergence of a new form did not occur until after the War under the impact of political and economic upheaval. With a few exceptions, such as the Lokal-Anzeiger and the Morgenpost, the *Generalanzeiger* press was politically undeveloped and colorless. In the dispatches of the British correspondents in Germany it would be difficult to find a score of references to this non-political local press.[35]

In the history of the German press no single topic has inspired more curiosity and speculation than the relations of the newspapers to the government. Because official press policy was from time to time an issue in political debate much that has been said and written is gross exaggeration. The Bismarckian system of press control and inspiration during the period of the *Reichsgründung* is familiar in its main outlines through the revelations of Bismarck's subordinates and the researches of later scholars. A generation of English statesmen and publicists derived their main impressions of Bismarckian statesmanship from the published diaries of Moritz Busch. The stereotype of Machiavellism which they ever after applied to German political methods was derived almost exclusively from this source.

For Bismarck the press was never more than an agency to be bribed, bludgeoned, or cajoled to do his bidding and to assist in the realization of his political objectives. His more incautious critics felt the weight of the press law; with some publishers and editors his agents struck a bargain—exclusive bits of news and information in return for editorial

---

[34] Some of the most successful *Generalanzeigers* were those in Breslau and Frankfort (150,000), Hamburg, Dortmund and Hanover (100,000), and the *Bayerischer Zeitung* (100,000). Roth, *op. cit.*, p. 72.

[35] On the history and characteristics of the *Generalanzeiger* press see Groth, *op. cit.*, I, 222 ff., 926, II, 536–41; Dovifat, *op. cit.*, pp. 89–103; Kaupert, *op. cit.*, pp. 87–90; Bernhard, *op. cit.*, pp. 25–49; A. Bernstein, "Wie die Berliner Morgenpost wurde," in *Fünfzig Jahre Ullstein*. Carl Fürstenberg (*Lebensgeschichte*, pp. 320–26) gives some interesting personal reminiscences of the eccentric August Scherl.

support; and in a good many identifiable instances support was purchased by subventions to editors and free lance journalists out of the
secret funds at the disposition of the officials.[36] During the last decade
of Bismarck's rule the range and intensity of his efforts to influence and
control the press in the interest of his policies notably declined, and
in 1890 new men brought with them new methods.

As a matter of fact the conditions of journalism and newspaper publishing in 1890 were no longer what they had been in 1870. The press
had shared in the economic advance of the preceding decades and in many
instances a firm economic foundation had freed the publishers from dependence upon individual or official patronage. With a vast public becoming rapidly habituated to the reading of a daily newspaper, with a
steady flow of capital into the business of newspaper production, the
representatives of the press no longer had to goosestep on orders from
above. Better treatment, with more regard to the professional integrity
that editors owed to the public, was now required of the government. The
publicity which ministers needed in pursuit of their policies was to be had
in as great or even greater measure than ever before, but not on the old
terms of fear and subsidy. A new conception of the press as an independent
co-operating agency, mediating between the public and the government,
arose and began to gain currency. Those who saw in the government's
press policy after 1890 only a continuation of Bismarckian methods were
blind to the new forces operating in the economic and political life of the
country. That is not to say that all abuses were removed and that an ideal
system was developed. But new men and new procedures, which made
their appearance on Bismarck's departure, justify Otto Hammann's application of the term "New Course" to the government's press relations
as well as to the new direction given to public policies.

Five years after Bismarck's resignation we find Count Waldersee, at
the ceremonial opening of the Kiel Canal, complaining of official recognition and favor shown to the press on that occasion. "What pleased me
least about the Canal festivities was the treatment of the press," he wrote
in his diary. "Never have these gentlemen been courted as they have
here. They were assigned to a special ship with an officer as guide. They
were given special places everywhere and on all sides they were paid
special compliments. A complete capitulation before this new power." [37]

[36] For a complete summary of the material on the Bismarckian system and a fair
judgment on it see Groth, *Die Zeitung,* II, 192–217; also Schulze, *Die Presse im
Urteil Bismarcks, passim;* for the last word on the use of secret funds see the testimony of Prof. Wilhelm Mommsen, summarized by Groth, *op. cit.,* II, 205.

[37] Waldersee, *Denkwürdigkeiten,* II, 351. The Hamburg-Amerika Company provided the vessel and Otto Hammann was official host to the foreign and German
correspondents. (*Deutsches biographisches Jahrbuch,* 1928, p. 98.)

The change that had taken place merited Waldersee's notice but not necessarily his displeasure. The "Hammann System" had displaced the Bismarckian system. The institutions, techniques and personalities of the new order, which was to prevail until the War, deserve adequate description.

Bismarck had operated with a remarkably simple press apparatus. The Literary Bureau in the Prussian ministry of the interior had been established in 1848 to influence and direct the press in the interest of official policy. According to Julius von Eckardt, who served in the bureau in the 'eighties, it was poorly organized and its work not very effective. The four or five officials in the bureau were occupied mainly with the preparation of an official and a semi-official correspondence service for the official district papers (*Kreisblätter*) and the smaller provincial journals.[38] One of the most important tasks was the preparation of press clippings for submission to the Kaiser. One of the officials of the bureau, testifying in the famous Tausch case, asserted that they selected extracts from the press of all shades of opinion from Conservative to Social Democratic. The imperial *dossier* was prepared in three exemplars—one for the Emperor, one for the imperial chancellor and one for the minister of interior. The reports for the Kaiser went through many hands and were subject to control by the responsible ministers. Count Westarp, who was employed in this work several years later, gives the same impression of bureaucratic routine and dullness.[39]

The Literary Bureau confined itself to domestic affairs; foreign policy press relations were conducted through the press department established in the imperial foreign office in the spring of 1871. The first director was Professor Ludwig Aegidi, who occupied the post until 1877; in 1890 the director was Rudolf Lindau, who, with the assistance of one clerk, attended to the current business of the department, while Kiderlen-Wächter (1888–94) handled all matters relating to high policies and cultivated relations with the correspondents of the important foreign newspapers. In the interim between Lindau's resignation in 1892 and Hammann's appointment in 1894, the routine work was done by Constantin Rössler, who was transferred temporarily from the Literary Bureau.[40]

For four years Caprivi struggled with the problems of policy and

---

[38] J. von Eckardt, *Lebenserinnerungen*, II, 66, quoted in Groth, *op. cit.*, II, 214–15.

[39] *Konservative Politik*, I, 10; Waldersee, *Denkwürdigkeiten*, II, 93 n.; *Daily Mail*, Berlin correspondent, quoted *Deutsche Ztg.*, No. 239, Oct. 2, 1900.

[40] Otto Hammann, *Der neue Kurs* (Berlin, 1918), p. 10; J. von Eckardt, *Aus den Tagen von Bismarcks Kampf gegen Caprivi* (Leipzig, 1920), p. 5; Groth; *op. cit.*, II, 218–19; Waldersee, *op. cit.*, II, 93.

administration arising out of the government's relations with the press. At the beginning of his chancellorship he announced in the Prussian Landtag that he would abandon the practice of inspiring the press in matters of domestic politics. His government, he announced, would be more moderate in the semi-official use of the press in the conduct of foreign affairs, although it was sometimes imperative that communications on foreign policy appear in papers other than the strictly official organs such as the Reichsanzeiger.[41] He next dealt with the famous Guelf fund, the source of many a bitter attack on Bismarck. In 1866 the private fortune of the house of Hanover had been confiscated by the Prussian government. The property was valued at about $10,000,000 but yielded only about $125,000 annually. The government was not required to account for the use of this income and in the public mind it became associated with political bribery, domestic espionage and press corruption. The climax was reached in 1891 when it was revealed that $85,000 had been paid out of the fund at one time by Bismarck to save a cabinet member from a scandalous bankruptcy. In March 1892, with the consent of William II, Caprivi restored the fortune to the Duke of Cumberland, heir of the house of Hanover. In the budget that year the secret fund for the foreign office was raised from 50,000 marks to 500,000 marks.[42]

Caprivi's abandonment of the policy of influencing the press in domestic matters left the field free for his opponents and in a short time twenty-five volumes of newspaper clippings recording Bismarck's campaign in the press against the "New Course" accumulated in the foreign office. In the spring of 1892, when Bismarck's campaign against the new régime was intensified, Caprivi decided on a counter-offensive. Julius von Eckardt, who had already published a defense of Caprivi's foreign policy,[43] was recalled from his consular post at Marseilles and entrusted with the preparation of a general defense of Caprivi's policies against the attacks of the Bismarck *fronde*, the colonialists, and the agrarians. On instructions from the chancellor the secret files and press clippings

[41] London *Times*, Berlin dispatch, April 17, 1890. The correspondent noted that after Caprivi took office "some of the journals (like the *North German Gazette* and others that could be named), which used to fatten on the scraps of information and inspiration flung them by the official servants of Prince Bismarck, have been afflicted with a famine-stricken and paralyzed look."

[42] *Times*, Berlin dispatch, March 14, 1892; *Vorwärts*, No. 255, Nov. 1, 1900; Hammann, *Der neue Kurs*, pp. 16–17. In 1895–96 the secret fund of the Prussian ministry of the interior for "general police purposes" was increased to 200,000 marks. The Prussian state ministry received annually 93,000 marks "for general political purposes." What was allotted for intelligence services for the war and navy departments cannot be ascertained. Altogether the imperial and Prussian governments probably did not have more than a million marks for secret purposes.

[43] *Berlin-Wien-Rom* (Leipzig, April 1892). For the circumstances see Eckardt's *Bismarcks Kampf gegen Caprivi*, pp. 18–26.

were placed at Eckardt's disposal. In the foreign office, Holstein and Kiderlen took it ill that an outsider, a consul general, was brought in on the chancellor's initiative to undertake this most important and delicate task. Before the work of composition had actually begun, however, the Friedrichsruhe campaign slackened and Caprivi, not wishing to start the agitation anew by the publication of a semi-official volume, abandoned the project.[44]

Caprivi's principal success in the field of public relations was achieved in connection with army reform. The propaganda for this measure, which involved dissolution and re-election of the Reichstag, was conducted by Major Keim with the assistance of Otto Hammann. The latter came in contact with Caprivi during this campaign, and shortly after the military measures were safely under cover Hammann was appointed chief of the press division in the foreign office and adviser to the chancellor in all matters touching the press. On January 1, 1894, Caprivi issued an administrative order to all the ministries requiring them to clear political communications to the press through Hammann's bureau; information on departmental work, without political implications, could be communicated directly to representatives of the newspapers. Caprivi was aiming at unity and responsibility in the government's relations with the political press. Publicity on domestic as well as foreign affairs was to be concentrated in Hammann's bureau and the director was to be jointly responsible to the foreign secretary and the chancellor. Within this administrative framework Hammann developed, under Caprivi's successors, the institutional practices and procedures generally referred to as the "Hammann System."

Born in 1852 of a Thuringian family, Hammann studied law and then drifted into political journalism. He came to Berlin in the 'eighties where he corresponded for the Schlesische Zeitung, Hamburgischer Correspondent, the Allgemeine Zeitung of Munich and the Pester Lloyd of Budapest. From 1890 to 1893 he edited the Neueste Nachrichten, the official press correspondence service issued by the Literary Bureau. During his first years as press director under Hohenlohe and Marschall, Hammann was heavily burdened with work arising out of the Leckert-Lützow and Tausch cases. As a matter of fact the press bureau was directly involved, and Marschall, giving testimony on the relations of the foreign office with the press, described the work of the bureau as follows:

These relations are carried on for the most part by Secretary of Legation Dr. Hammann, who is my representative in press matters. He has considerable freedom of action in this field. He comes in the morning to me and asks:

[44] Eckardt, *op. cit.*, pp. 44–66.

What can one say on this question, or can one say anything? He then receives the representatives of the press—also with respect to persons he has full responsibility, understanding naturally that only trustworthy persons are received—and they receive the information from him. It happens that from time to time articles are directly inspired; as a rule I attend to that. I personally have few contacts with the press, I receive only the representative of the Kölnische Zeitung and occasionally correspondents of the English papers. My press official has the strictest instructions to limit his information to the affairs of the Foreign Office and not to go outside that field unless he has specific orders from the Imperial Chancellor respecting internal affairs.[45]

When Bülow succeeded Marschall as foreign secretary in 1897, Hammann's influence was greatly extended by virtue of the new minister's regard for the power of the press. When Bülow became chancellor, three years later, he announced that he would keep matters concerning "press, police and personnel" in his own hands. He kept his word as regards the press and Hammann reported direct to the imperial chancellor as though he were a secretary of state. Hammann had previously worked with one assistant. Bülow gave him two more. The tendency for high officials to pursue a personal or departmental press policy was checked—they felt the sharp bit that Bülow put in their mouths. Gradually under Hammann and Bülow almost the entire work of cultivating and informing the press was carried on by Hammann's bureau. While they were never able to break the power of the Literary Bureau over the provincial Prussian press, they achieved a degree of co-ordination by shuffling one of Hammann's confidants into the directorship of the rival department.

An amazing amount of work was performed by Hammann and his three assistants (Heilbron, Esternaux, and later Riezler). The day began with the reading and clipping of the newspapers by Esternaux, who came at an early hour so that the clippings could be sorted and placed on the desks of the chancellor, foreign secretary, and under-secretary. When Hammann arrived much of the routine detail had been attended to. On his desk usually lay directions from the chancellor on matters requiring immediate attention. Daily, between eleven and twelve, Hammann was summoned to conference with the chancellor, and all current problems involving press relations were discussed. Loebell, chief of the chancellery under Bülow, and Wahnschaffe, who filled that position under Bethmann-Hollweg, were usually present, and department heads also participated when affairs touching their work were under discussion. The results of the conference guided Hammann in his interviews with the journalists,

---

[45] Brunhuber, *Das deutsche Zeitungswesen*, pp. 63–64. Brunhuber (pp. 44–74) gives a detailed description of the official and semi-official press system.

which began immediately after returning to his office. The officials also assembled daily a collection of clippings from the German and foreign press to be sent to the Emperor. These often came back with extensive marginal notes and comments, which served as a barometer of the Kaiser's disposition and sentiments. It was also in the press bureau that Bülow's brilliant 'extemporaneous' speeches were prepared. The smallest detail of wording and phrasing was carefully discussed by Bülow, Loebell and Hammann. Bülow's powerful memory enabled him to learn by rote speeches that required one or two hours to deliver. Bethmann used the concepts prepared for him by Hammann and his assistants, but did the composing himself. His speeches lacked the trenchant and pithy qualities of Hammann's product. On one other aspect of Hammann's duties there is almost no information. Reasonable inference from chance remarks indicates that he had some responsibility or voice in the disposition of the secret funds of the foreign ministry. Altogether the chief of the press bureau played an important part in the day to day affairs of government.

Bülow's efforts to centralize the official service of information in one bureau were only moderately effective. Under his successor serious administrative difficulties developed. The press chief was responsible to both the foreign secretary and the chancellor. When these two officials did not see eye to eye Hammann's position was anything but a bed of roses. A bitter feud developed between Hammann and the foreign secretary, Schoen. The latter was supported by the foreign office personnel, while Hammann relied upon the support of the chancellor. A plan for administrative reorganization was brought forward at this time but failed of adoption. Kiderlen-Wächter inherited the departmental feud as well as the plan of reform. The substance of the plan called for the transfer of Hammann's bureau to the chancellery, and the establishment of a separate division for press affairs in the foreign office under the immediate and complete control of the foreign secretary, with a liaison officer to co-ordinate the work of the two bureaus. The plan failed again of adoption in 1912. Meanwhile, Hammann found himself further and further removed from the indispensable sources of information on foreign policy. His right to receive the foreign dispatches and telegrams in the usual routine was sharply curtailed by Kiderlen, and he was without information on some of the most important moves in foreign policy. Von Jagow avoided relations with Hammann and placed his confidential press contacts in the hands of a departmental official, Wilhelm von Radowitz. Thus by 1914 the old condition of decentralization and irresponsibility, which Hammann had found on assuming office, again prevailed in the relations of the government to the press.[46]

Among the greatest hindrances to a unified service of information was the existence in certain government departments of special press bureaus, and in others of officials who regularly maintained personal contacts with favored representatives of the press. In 1897 Tirpitz set up a news and propaganda department in the ministry of marine to publicize and support the new naval program. When the naval policy reacted upon Germany's relations with England and raised the most serious political issues, the two publicity bureaus became engaged in an interdepartmental press feud. Contrary to his policy of centralization, Bülow authorized the establishment of a special publicity bureau in the treasury department to explain and popularize the proposed reform of imperial finances in 1908–9. However, it was not as easy to arouse the enthusiasm of the German people for the assumption of new tax burdens as it had been to awaken popular ardor for a powerful navy that would bear the German flag proudly into every ocean.[47] Many officials in important posts maintained secret press connections and pursued personal and departmental policies with little regard to the unity and general direction of policy. Dr. Johannes Miquel, minister of finance, and an important figure in domestic politics, used two journalists, Hugo Jacobi and Viktor Schweinburg, as his special agents in political publicity. Baron Holstein maintained steady personal relations with a few favored journalists and eventually broke with Hammann over the direction of press affairs in the foreign office. He was on intimate terms with Valentine Chirol during the latter's years in Berlin; he regularly received Schiemann and gave him information and counsel for his articles in the Kreuzzeitung; but his closest journalistic connection was with Justizrat Fischer of the Kölnische Zeitung. Almost daily Fischer called on Holstein in his office in the Wilhelmstrasse. There he retailed to the recluse all the gossip and information that he had picked up in political, diplomatic and financial circles. He then read telegrams and dispatches which Holstein had put aside for him and received the advice and counsel of his friend on the

[46] The indispensable sources for the history of the press administration are: *Deutsches biographisches Jahrbuch,* 1928, pp. 96–105, the best biographical sketch of Hammann, by his co-worker, Dr. Friedrich Heilbron; Hammann, *Der neue Kurs,* chap. VI, "Offiziöse Presswirtschaft"; Freiherr von Schoen, *Memoirs of an Ambassador* (Lond., 1922), pp. 126–27; E. Jäckh, *Kiderlen-Wächter: der Staatsmann und Mensch* (2 vols., Stuttgart, 1924), II, 101–4; O. Grosse, *Die Beamte und die Zeitung* (Jena, 1927), *passim;* W. Heide, *Diplomatie und Presse* (Cologne, 1930); Groth, *op. cit.,* II, 218–36. The writer is also indebted to Geheimrat Heilbron for information regarding the organization and work of the information division.

[47] Reinhold von Sydov, "Fürst Bülow und die Reichsfinanzreform, 1908–9," in *Front Wider Bülow* (ed. by Friedrich Thimme, Munich, 1931).

treatment of the current questions in reports to his paper. Even after his resignation Holstein continued to cultivate relations with the press, carrying on a lively political correspondence with the editor of the Neue Tageblatt in Stuttgart and writing and publishing articles in the Schlesische Zeitung,[48] Kiderlen-Wächter, Tschirschky, Marschall and other members of the foreign service had their personally preferred channels of publicity. It is impossible to verify or disprove the many references to personal press intrigues and attacks that one encounters in the diaries and memoirs of this period. That personal attacks to injure or discredit a rival were frequently inspired in the press is beyond doubt. But many high officials were too inclined to attribute normal press criticism of their official acts to the back stairs work of a jealous rival.

The central bureau for press affairs presided over by Hammann was the principal source from which the public derived its information on the government's foreign relations. The media for communicating this information were the newspapers and the news agencies. The nature and character of the relationships of these media to the central government constitute the central feature of the Hammann system. In 1901 an administrative order was issued requiring Prussian and imperial officials to publish all official announcements, such as appointments, resignations, departmental orders, etc., in the Reichs- und Staatsanzeiger. All semi-official announcements, explanations, projected legislation, and articles in defense of official measures, were to be published in the Norddeutsche Allgemeine Zeitung and in the Berliner Korrespondenz, which had been established in the Literary Bureau in the ministry of interior in 1894 to take the place of the defunct Neueste Nachrichten (Korrespondez).[49] During the Bülow era, the Süddeutsche Reichskorrespondenz, a political news service edited by Herr Katz in Karlsruhe, was recognized as "highly official." It was frequently used by the chancellor for unofficial statements and explanations of policy. Through these agencies the daily press received a vast amount of routine political and governmental news. More important than these, however, for the foreign affairs of the Reich, was the direct contact maintained with the journals of national importance through the press bureau and through the semi-official relations with the national news agency, the Wolff Telegraphic Bureau.

Hammann placed the relations of the foreign office to the newspaper

---

[48] Hammann, *Der neue Kurs,* pp. 91–92; Holstein, *Lebensbekenntnis,* pp. xliv–xlv, 140–41, 208–10, 224; Rosen, *Aus einem diplomatischen Wanderleben,* I, 23 ff.; H. O. Meisner, "Gespräche und Briefe Holsteins, 1907–9," *Preussische Jahrbücher,* April–September 1932.

[49] For a summary of the administrative decrees relating to the press relations of the government see Groth, *op. cit.,* II, 231–32.

representatives on an entirely new basis. The attitude of disdain and suspicion which the high bureaucracy was wont to assume toward the journalist disappeared, and was replaced by a spirit of confidence and regard based upon the recognition of the legitimate functioning of the correspondents' corps in the business of securing and disseminating news of the government's activity in foreign affairs. The emphasis in the work of the bureau was shifted from the writing and planting of articles in the press, as it was carried on in the days of Moritz Busch and Professor Aegidi, to the development of the bureau as a source of news and information for the agencies and the daily papers. Articles originating in the information bureau continued to appear in the press from time to time, but their number and importance steadily declined. The doors of 76 Wilhelmstrasse were open to all accredited journalists, German and foreign, without respect to party affiliations. A steady stream of routine information passed in this way into the news channels. Special questions could be put to Hammann, Heilbron or Esternaux. There was no assurance, however, that an answer would be given or that any exclusive information would be forthcoming. As a matter of fact, the plums of exclusive and significant information—and this is the most common journalistic complaint against the Hammann system—were reserved for a small inner ring of journalists who stood in close personal relations to Hammann and who enjoyed his special confidence and trust. Most of the delicate publicity work in connection with high policy was handled through this group. The basis of this relationship was as old as political journalism—from the government a steady flow of exclusive information in return for support and assistance in executing its policies. Among the journalists who enjoyed the confidence of the press chief and who received special favors at his hands may be mentioned: Huhn and Fischer (Kölnische Zeitung), Stein (Frankfurter Zeitung), Engel (Reichsbote), Schiemann (Kreuzzeitung), Fitger (Weser-Zeitung), Francke (Münchner Neueste Nachrichten), and Mantler (Wolff's Bureau). It was in the correspondence and dispatches of these men that the initiated looked for an accurate reflection of the views and opinions of the foreign office on current diplomatic questions. They were generally referred to as "well informed." In the decade before the War, two of the journals, the Kölnische Zeitung and the Frankfurter Zeitung, occupied a special position. It was in these journals, as Bethmann-Hollweg informed the Austrian ambassador, that semi-official communiqués with easily recognizable symbols, were ordinarily published.[50] The special preference enjoyed by some

---

[50] *Oesterreich-Ungarns Aussenpolitik von der Bosnischen Krise 1908 bis zum Kriegsausbruch 1914* (8 vols., Vienna, 1930), III, 742. A threat to deprive a journal

of the leading journals and journalists was in the main the basis of official influence upon the political press. It is on this ground that legitimate criticisms were made by working journalists. A second justifiable criticism was that of official *"Schönfarberei,"* that is of representing everything connected with the government's diplomatic moves in a falsely optimistic light. Political news is inevitably colored at the source. The editor of the Kölnische Volkszeitung, criticizing the "Hammann System" on the occasion of the press director's retirement (1916), wrote: "I know of no event during the past ten years to which the stereotyped advice in the foreign office was not given: 'Maintain complete reserve, better say nothing.' " [51] Special preference, suppression of unpleasant facts, and false optimism—these are the legitimate grounds for indicting the "Hammann System."

More important than all of the other instrumentalities and means employed in publicizing official policy was the principal German news agency, Wolff's Telegraphic Bureau (WTB). With the exception of the few great dailies which maintained an organization of foreign correspondents, the Wolff Bureau had almost a monopoly in the supply of foreign news to German newspapers of all ranks. The news report, appearing simultaneously in thousands of papers and read by millions of people, produced an effect of far greater magnitude than the editorial, the feature article, or the commentary. Official influence, even though it was slight, upon this central organ of news distribution afforded the government more power over the public mind than any other form of press influence.

Founded in 1849 by Dr. Bernhard Wolff, the Wolff Telegraphic Bureau advanced in the wake of Prussia, and the political predominance of the one opened the way to the news reporting predominance of the other. Very early the Prussian authorities realized the political importance of the service supplied by Wolff. In the 'sixties the government intervened to prevent the invasion of Wolff's territory by the Reuter Agency and in 1870 the authorities assisted in the negotiation of the first cartel agreements between Wolff, Reuter, and Havas. On the initiative of the Italian statesman Crispi, in 1887, the news agencies of the Triple Alliance powers united with Reuter to combat Havas. Meeting with little success, and forced to pay a high price for Reuter co-operation, the original cartel arrangements were revised and restored in 1900. Shortly thereafter the Associated Press became a member of the group.[52]

---

of these favors was usually sufficient to secure compliance with the government's wishes. In 1912 Bethmann threatened to break official relations with the *Kölnische Zeitung. (Ibid.,* III, 781.)

[51] Quoted F. Fuchs, *Telegraphische Nachrichtenbüros,* p. 249.

[52] The Prussian authorities assisted in the financial reorganization of Wolff's

These cartel agreements, although they were negotiated under the supervision of the government and although they affected the public interest in a vital manner, were never published. In general, the agreements were known to provide for an exchange of news reports between the members and to assign to each member its area in the world news market. To Reuter went the British Empire and the Orient, to Havas, Southern Europe and South America; and Wolff was restricted to Central and Eastern Europe. To round out its service in this area Wolff concluded exchange agreements with the semi-official Austrian agency and the Russian Telegraph Agency.

Before the War, Wolff was often criticized for the inadequacy of its foreign news gathering service and its dependence upon Reuter and Havas for its reports from the British Empire, the Orient and South America. A striking example of its dependence is afforded by the Algeciras Conference. During the first part of the conference Wolff had no representative at Algeciras, but was satisfied to feed to its German subscribers the plainly biased dispatches of Reuter and Havas, which it received through the exchange agreement. Only after loud protests from German editors did the agency make provision for independent reports. In the principal centers where Wolff connected with the cartel agencies— London, Paris, St. Petersburg, Vienna, Rome, and New York—it maintained a representative whose task it was to select from the reports filed by the affiliate those which were judged to be of interest to Wolff's German subscribers. These agents did not, however, function as independent correspondents. While the patriotism of many German critics may have led to the exaggeration of this deficiency in the Wolff organization, it cannot be denied that through its dependence on Reuter and Havas a great deal of political contraband was smuggled into the German press.[53]

In Germany Wolff's position was unchallenged until just before the War. In 1905 it had 2300 subscribers among the newspapers, banks, and exchanges, and its telegraph, cable and telephone tolls for the year exceeded a million marks.[54] Its quasi-monopolistic position was supported

---

Bureau in 1871. Reuter did not withdraw from Hamburg until 1900. Hammann, *Der neue Kurs*, pp. 133–34; Fuchs, *Telegraphische Nachrichtenbüros*, pp. 72–96, 197–208, is the best historical account, and affords the best treatment of the cartel arrangements; W. Schwedler, *Das Nachrichtenwesen* (Gotha, 1925), pp. 126–32, gives a brief account of the development of the Wolff enterprise; also Groth, *op. cit.*, I, 490 ff.

[53] For criticisms of Wolff's shortcomings see Fritz Waltz, *Die Presse und die deutsche Weltpolitik* (Zürich, 1906), *passim;* N. Hansen, "Depeschenbureaus und internationales Nachrichtenwesen," *Weltwirtschaftliches Archiv*, vol. III (1913), pp. 78–96; Fuchs, *op. cit.*, p. 251; Groth, *op. cit.*, I, 527–28, 534–36, 541–47, reviews the literature of attack and defense and delivers a measured judgment.

[54] Groth, *op. cit.*, I, 497.

by the government and in return it submitted to a certain degree of control and direction by the government authorities, particularly where its activities touched the foreign affairs of the Reich. The degree of dependency in which Wolff stood to the foreign office has been hotly debated. The government certainly did not exercise a preventive censorship over the agency's political news service, nor was the government interested financially in the agency.[55] At the time when Wolff was threatened by the competition of Reuter, the government agreed to give it priority over all other private organizations in the transmission of its dispatches by the state telegraph system. This privilege was withdrawn in 1904. More important than this, however, was the monopoly that Wolff possessed, against all other news agencies, of reporting and circulating all official and semi-official publications and announcements not published first in the Reichsanzeiger or Norddeutsche. The business value of this monopoly is readily apparent; every newspaper of consequence in Germany was of necessity a subscriber to Wolff's service. Through the Wolff agency, with its thirty-six branches, the government was assured that its policies and acts would receive the widest publicity. It was the advantage that each party derived from the connection that inevitably gave the alliance a political character.[56]

Given the highly preferential position enjoyed by the Wolff Bureau, there was bound to be more consideration for the government and the requirements of its policies than there would be in the case of an independent agency whose sole purpose was to gather news and sell it at a profit to subscribers. A good example of the co-operation between the government and the news agency is afforded by the reporting of the Kaiser's speeches. On all William II's journeys, a representative of Wolff's Bureau traveled with the entourage. (Hofrat de Grahl, a former Austrian officer, until 1896; thereafter, Hofrat Georg Schneider.) When the Kaiser spoke extemporaneously or departed from his manuscript, which he did too frequently, in his public addresses, his words were taken down in shorthand by the *Hofberichterstatter* and the final draft was corrected and edited with the co-operation of the chief of the Emperor's civil cabinet and the representative of the chancellor. The consequences that would have ensued from publication of many indiscreet statements and remarks were thus oftentimes avoided. After official approval the final text

[55] According to E. Heerdegen, *Der Nachrichtendienst der Presse* (Leipzig, 1920), p. 39, the majority stock was owned by the Bleichröder Bank. Paul von Schwabach, the director of Bleichröder's, was chairman of the board.

[56] The contractual relations are specified in Groth, *op. cit.*, I, 537–39; also by the general director of Wolff's Bureau, Dr. Hermann Diez, *Das Zeitungswesen* (Leipzig, 1910), pp. 89 ff.; Fuchs, *op. cit.*, pp. 238–53, *passim*.

was telegraphed to Berlin and distributed to the sub-agencies throughout Germany and through them to the subscribing newspapers. Consideration for the government's foreign policy was also shown in reporting and circulating news reports, particularly those of foreign origin. Dr. Mantler, political director of the Wolff Bureau, kept in close touch with Hammann, coming daily to the foreign office to receive information and reports and to discuss current publicity problems arising out of government policies. When a foreign report of doubtful authority, or a report which might be detrimental to the Reich's policy, was received in the central Wolff Bureau, it was customary to refer it to Hammann's department for approval, verification or denial. As a result of this voluntary control the Wolff dispatches assumed a degree of semi-official authority. However, the great masses of political news reports and announcements that passed daily through the Wolff Bureau were never seen by the officials in the foreign office until they appeared in the newspapers.[57]

One charge leveled at Wolff's, for which there was considerable justification, concerned its reporting of reactions abroad to German foreign policy. It was standard practice to quote the editorial comment of a number of journals. By selecting and transmitting extracts, of which a majority were favorable, Wolff's political service could create the impression that German policy was meeting with universal approval abroad. Oftentimes, as a matter of fact, a wider selection of press extracts would have produced a much less optimistic impression. The only check on this practice was afforded by the few financially strong newspapers that maintained their own correspondents in the principal European centers of news.[58]

Louder and louder grew the protests over the German dependence on foreign owned and foreign controlled news agencies. They came not only from patriots and publicists but from representatives of industry, finance, commerce, and shipping. Finally in the winter of 1913 sixteen representatives of the most important business interests in Germany, with the co-operation of the foreign office, organized the *Syndikat Deutscher Ueberseedienst* for the purpose of founding a world-wide German news service. In 1914 national groups backed by their governments and their capitalists were preparing to do battle for world communications.[59]

[57] For the factual description of the relations between Wolff's Bureau and the authorities I am indebted to Geheimrat Heilbron.
[58] *Frankfurter Ztg.*, No. 327, Nov. 26, 1900.
[59] Bernhard, *Hugenberg-Konzern*, pp. 60–65; F. Leiter, "Reuter, Havas, Wolff, k.k. Telegraphen-Korrespondenzbüro," *Oesterreichische Rundschau*, vol. 44 (1915), p. 70, gives the names of the sixteen committeemen.

It cannot be gainsaid that the German public was dependent to a very large extent on English sources for its news of the world. Because of its far-flung cable monopolies and its great dailies with extensive private correspondence services, London was the focal point of news gathering. A casual examination of the foreign dispatches in the five leading German papers gives the impression that fully half bore the following introduction: "Der 'Daily Chronicle' lässt sich aus Rom melden. . . ." or "Wie uns ein eigener Drahtbericht aus London mittheilt. . . ." While Reuter's Agency covered Germany, as it did the rest of the world, with its own newsgathering staff, Wolff's maintained one representative in London, who simply turned the valves and watched the Reuter reports flow into the Wolff pipes.

In bringing to the German public adequate and accurate news of British affairs, the correspondents of the principal German newspapers made up for some of the deficiencies of Wolff's service. Only the five or six leading journals, however, maintained full time independent representatives in the capital of the world's greatest empire, and their cable and telegraph allowances must have been modest indeed compared to those of their British colleagues in Berlin. Moreover, the professional and political position of the German correspondents in London was inferior to that enjoyed by the representatives of the London press in Germany. As a matter of fact, English correspondents were accorded favors by German statesmen that were denied their own countrymen in the journalistic profession. Every resident correspondent in Berlin had access to the press gallery in the Reichstag; foreign correspondents were excluded from the reporter's gallery in the House of Commons. Nor were the British officials who controlled the sources of political news particularly well-disposed toward foreign journalists. On the occasion of Queen Victoria's funeral the correspondent of the Kreuzzeitung commented at some length on the difficulties encountered by the foreign press in London. At the funeral ceremonies no facilities or arrangements were provided for the visiting correspondents. With the exception of the admiralty, war office, and police departments, the British divisions of government and administration did not accord recognition to foreign journalists. According to this correspondent, a foreign journalist who sent his professional card, with the name of his newspaper, in to a minister or high official would be turned away; if he sent in his private card he would be received.[60] While the editors of the leading British journals expected foreign governments to extend privileges and courtesies to their rep-

[60] *Kreuzzeitung,* No. 77, Feb. 15, 1901.

resentatives, it was a common complaint among foreign correspondents in London that they were ignored by the public and the government.[61]

Officials of the German embassy in London maintained closer relations with their own correspondents than did most of the German missions. Successive counselors of embassy—Pückler, Eckardstein, Bernstorff, Stumm, and Kühlmann—co-operated with their own countrymen and cultivated relations with the British press. In the business of transmitting news and reporting the English scene, the Wolff correspondent occupied, of course, a key position. This post was held for many years by Major Piper. Shortly after 1904 he was succeeded by Dr. Hans Plehn (1868–1918). The latter was a scholar, a student of world affairs and an able political journalist. In collaboration with Kühlmann he wrote and published the well known brochure on German foreign policy, *Deutsche Weltpolitik und kein Krieg* (1913). He was also the author of several works on history and politics. Dr. Hans Paul Esser (1839–1915) succeeded Dr. Karl Schneider as correspondent of the Kölnische Zeitung in 1895 and was active until the War. He was well connected with the Anglo-German circle in London, he was on confidential terms with Eckardstein and was regarded as trustworthy and reliable by the embassy officials.[62] During this period the Frankfurter Zeitung was represented first by Dr. Bernhard Guttmann, who had previously served in Egypt, and then by Dr. Otto. Both seem to have been prudent and impartial reporters. From 1898 to 1912 Dr. Otto Brandes corresponded for the Berliner Tageblatt. Between 1912–14 only temporary appointments were made. Emil Ludwig occupied the post early in 1914. Dr. Gaupp, an able Swabian journalist, corresponded for the Münchner Neueste Nachrichten and the Hamburger Fremdenblatt from 1892 to 1914. The Vossische Zeitung was represented by Moritz Sasse until his death in 1905; until 1910 the paper was represented by C. C. Schardt and thereafter until the War by Dr. Johannes Tschiedel.[63] Judging by the reports which these men composed for their papers they were moderate minded, reasonable and generally sympathetic reporters of the British scene. None of the group ever got into the black books of British officialdom as did Saunders in Berlin.

In its treatment of foreign affairs the German press displayed many

[61] See Valentine Chirol's arrogant letter to Count Bernstorff, June 17, 1904. *Memoirs of Count Bernstorff,* p. 86.

[62] J. Lehmann, *Die Aussenpolitik und die Kölnische Zeitung,* pp. 26–27; Freiherr von Eckardstein, *Lebenserinnerungen und politische Denkwürdigkeiten* (3 vols., Leipzig, 1919–21), III, 116–18, 126, 165; information supplied by Reuter's Limited, Aug. 10, 1935.

[63] *Fünfzig Jahre Ullstein,* pp. 233, 249; *Deutsches biographisches Jahrbuch,* 1905, p. 240; information supplied by Geheimrat Heilbron.

shortcomings and deficiencies. On the editorial side the tradition of political responsibility that had developed with liberal institutions in England, was lacking in Germany. All too often freedom of opinion meant freedom for recrimination and abuse of other peoples and governments. Responsibility and political self-discipline were relatively undeveloped. There was some justification for Bülow's constant complaint of the tactlessness of certain sections of the German press in dealing with current issues of diplomacy. The multiplicity of parties, the bitterness of the domestic political strife, and the rigid control of party committees over the political press, frequently resulted in the subordination of the nation's foreign policy to narrow partisan interest. As regards this, Pan-Germans, Socialists and Conservatives could all be brought under one hat. In art, literature, social policy and administration, in commerce, finance and industry the editorial and informational functions of the German press were more satisfactorily developed than in international affairs. Otto Groth states that journalistic recruits were usually assigned to the latter field because it was thought that in this department beginner's mistakes would do the least harm.[64]

The insufficiencies of the German press in its service of information about world events have already been stressed. Decentralization of the press, modest circulations, and limited capital account for the failure of the German newspapers to measure up to the English metropolitan press. Reuter's Agency charged the London newspapers double the amount for its service that Wolff could charge in Germany. And it followed that inadequacy of reporting made for inadequacy of judgment and interpretation. The government, too, was in part responsible for the mistakes and failures of the press in this scene of action. For Bismarck the press was never more than an instrument to be used in his diplomatic operations. While conditions changed considerably after 1890, his successors never encouraged or educated the press to take its place as an independent but co-operating agency in the determination and conduct of foreign relations. The institutions and practices developed by the administrative authorities were devised primarily to influence the press and through it the public. Rarely, however, was the government able to secure a united press front. With respect to this much discussed feature of German political life, the peculiarities of the constitutional system have rarely been taken into account. In the parliamentary state, with its theory of strict and direct accountability and the highly developed system of interpellation, the chief of state made his announcements, explanations, and corrections in parliament and the representatives

[64] *Die Zeitung*, I, 834.

jealously guarded this right of priority to information as against the claims of the press. Instead of holding a press conference, a British prime minister or foreign secretary made his announcements in the House of Commons and the newspapers communicated them to the public. Under the German constitution the ministers were not responsible to the Reichstag and the system of interpellation was atrophied. Once or twice a year the chancellor or foreign minister delivered a monologue on the Reich's foreign policy, usually in response to an interpellation arranged in advance with a National Liberal deputy. There grew up a more or less organized system of official, semi-official and inspired press communications through which the government disclosed to the public what, under the circumstances, they wished to let it know about official attitudes, intentions and aspirations. Similarly in the United States there has developed an extra-constitutional system of presidential and departmental press conferences for direct communication with the public. In general it was not the subjective quality and form of the press, in any land, that determined its relations to the state, but rather it was the constitutional relations and practices that gave to the press its position in the power configuration.

CHAPTER IV

COLONIALISM AND THE CONTINENTAL BALANCE

It must be acknowledged that there never was a country which, having won so much military glory as Germany, has shown less disposition to use its power for offence instead of defence.

The Times, September 29, 1891.

On the afternoon of March 18, 1890, Reuter's agent in Berlin flashed to London the news of Prince Bismarck's resignation. He "broke" for Fleet Street the most important story that had come from abroad since the news, five years before, of the murder of Chinese Gordon at Khartoum. The ponderous editorials that appeared the next morning in the Times, the Post, the Standard, the Telegraph, and the Daily News all paid tribute to the man who had so markedly influenced the course of history, and who by the force of his personality and his key position in the political world had controlled the destinies of Europe for twenty years. "A bulwark of security," "a steadying force in European politics," "a dominating influence," were some of the tributes to Bismarck's statesmanship. All sounded a note of concern for the future. "Has the young Emperor the necessary patience and tact to keep the peace, as Prince Bismarck has kept it in the face of many temptations and opportunities for war?" asked the leader writer on the Pall Mall Gazette.

Doubtless the general feelings expressed by the editors were shared by Lord Salisbury and his assistants at the foreign office. Their interest in the change at Berlin was, however, more direct and intense because of important negotiations then in progress concerning disputed territorial claims in East Africa and Zanzibar. The origin and nature of these conflicting claims belong to the history of European exploitation of Africa.

Lord Salisbury's first proposal of arbitration, made in 1889, gradually faded into the background as the details of a general clearing agreement were hammered out in discussions between the English foreign secretary and the German ambassador, Count Hatzfeldt. The technical problems of frontier delimitation were made the subject of direct conversations between Sir Percy Anderson of the colonial department of the British foreign office and the German foreign office representative, Dr. Krauel. These conversations were momentarily interrupted by the chancellor crisis in Berlin, but by the middle of June a practical agreement was reached on the major points, the terms of which were made public on June 17. Formal ratification took place on July 1.[1]

Although the details of procedure, involving disagreements, concessions, and compromises were withheld from the press, publicity factors of great importance entered into the conversations between the German and English representatives. In Germany the main pressure groups were the German East Africa Company, whose immediate economic interests were involved, and the *Kolonialverein* representing commercial, industrial, scientific, cultural and political circles interested in colonial expansion.[2] The chief pressure groups in England were the British East Africa Company, organized by Sir William Mackinnon, and certain trading concerns interested in commerce with Zanzibar, Witu, and Uganda. From Hatzfeldt's conversations with Salisbury it is evident that had it been possible to handle the entire affair as a simple deal in African real estate, in which only the foreign offices were concerned, it could have been settled in short order by a series of mutual compromises. However, representatives on both sides had to proceed cautiously in the matter of concessions because of what they referred to as "their public opinion." It was thus that they dignified the opinion of promotional and economic groups. Sir Percy Anderson revealed the real source of pressure when he remarked to Hatzfeldt that "The British colonial companies possess great power and influence here." [3] Salisbury, moreover, consulted the directors of the British companies at each critical juncture, and likewise Marschall, the new German foreign secretary, came to terms with the German East Africa Company over the cession of Witu.[4] The foreign ministers, then, carried on simultaneously negotiations with one another and with the interest groups of their own countrymen. Failure to satisfy the latter might lead to public agitation by the interest groups, with attendant unwelcome publicity in the press that would produce serious repercussions in their respective parliaments. Because of the party cabinet system of government in England and the strength of the English pressure groups involved, Salisbury was in more immediate danger of serious embarrassment than the German foreign minister. Hatzfeldt refers in his dispatches on several occasions to the "inflammatory attacks" and the "rousing speeches" of H. M. Stanley as the cause of Lord Salisbury's caution in pursuing the negotiations. At one point Salisbury hinted that

[1] Details of the negotiations are given in *Die Grosse Politik*, VIII, 1–36.
[2] M. E. Townsend, *The Rise and Fall of Germany's Colonial Empire, 1884–1918* (N. Y., 1930), pp. 81–84, 131 ff.
[3] Hatzfeldt to Caprivi, April 30, 1890; *G. P.*, VIII, 9.
[4] *G. P.*, VIII, 14, 16.

it might be advisable to postpone the negotiations until the excitement aroused by Stanley had subsided.[5]

What was the nature of this activity that made Salisbury so cautious? How was it engendered and how did it involve the public and its relations to parliament and the cabinet? In the spring of 1890 H. M. Stanley returned to civilization from the last of his great African expeditions. Stanley and his exploits had symbolized for contemporaries the romance and riches of the Dark Continent, and had centered public attention on the general European scramble for markets and colonies. The Emin Pasha Relief Expedition, headed by Stanley, was organized and financed through the efforts of Sir William Mackinnon, dominant figure in British trading relations with East Africa and chairman of the British East Africa Company. The ostensible object of the expedition was the rescue of Emin Pasha, a German adventurer in the Egyptian service, from his revolting subjects in the Equatorial Province on the upper Nile. As a publicity coup, the 'rescue' aspect of the expedition was a fiasco. Emin Pasha did not want to be 'rescued' and only reluctantly accompanied Stanley back to civilization. On making contact with Germans on the coast he took service with them and began concession hunting in British spheres. Stanley, however, had concluded numerous treaties with native chieftains on behalf of Mackinnon's East Africa Company, which later became the basis of the British East Africa Protectorate.[6]

Stanley arrived in England while the foreign office was negotiating with Berlin a settlement of their conflicting claims in East Africa. In the interests of the British East Africa Company, Stanley began a public campaign to awaken the English to a realization of the value of the African stakes involved. Ten thousand people attended the reception given in his honor by the Royal Geographical Society. The press was at his service and he was invited to address countless societies, chambers of commerce, geographical and exploration societies. He initiated a campaign to prevent Salisbury from sacrificing through concessions to Germany the interests of the British trading and colonizing companies. In a speech before the London Chamber of Commerce, he referred lugubriously to the future of the British East Africa Company, scored the apathy of the British public toward the

[5] *G. P.*, VIII, 14–15.

[6] *Dictionary of National Biography*, Supp. vol. III. Sketches of William Mackinnon and H. M. Stanley. An unflattering portrait of Mackinnon is drawn by Sir Harry Johnston, *The Story of My Life* (Indianapolis, 1923), pp. 137–38. A German committee was likewise organized to send an expedition under Karl Peters to 'rescue' their German countryman. When Peters found that he had been forestalled by Stanley, he turned aside to Uganda, 'rescued' the native ruler there and placed him by treaty under German protection. (Sketch of Karl Peters by Heinrich Schnee in *Deutsches biographisches Jahrbücher*, 1917–1920, pp. 285–98; Townsend, *op. cit.*, pp. 136–37.)

value of the territories involved, and hinted darkly at the extent of the contemplated concessions in East Africa. The Times' editor was moved by Stanley's remarks to declare that "it would be very undesirable for the Government to come to any agreement as to the delimitation of African territory which should not be acceptable to the great trading companies." (May 23, 1890.) The leader writer on the Morning Post wrote: "It would be a thousand pities if the Government carried through their arrangements with Germany under the impression that Mr. Stanley's remark about the carelessness of English public opinion is to be taken as literally true. Six months ago it is quite likely that the country would have received the tidings of any number of compromises with indifference. . . . But the intense and magnetic influence of Mr. Stanley's recital has done much to falsify his sorrowful accusation as to national indifference." (May 27, 1890.)

At Edinburgh, where he opened the new rooms of the Royal Scottish Geographical Society, Stanley made a speech lauding the British East Africa Company "because it represented more than all the other companies combined the future of British influence in East Africa." The chairman in moving a vote of thanks said that "he hoped that until the noble cause to which the lecturer had devoted himself was thoroughly taken up by this country he would not be allowed to cease from his labours. (Cheers). In reference to the present question of English and German influence in Africa Lord Lorne said he hoped our Government would hold firm (cheers), and that we would be enabled to have those portions of the country which were justly our due, from the efforts of our missionaries and our pioneers and the money which we had already expended on them. (Cheers). He hoped, for instance, that the land which they saw on the map to the west of Victoria Nyanza would in the future be seen with a portion colored red (cheers); and that the way to it would be freely opened." [7]

On June 12, Stanley was presented with the freedom of the city of Glasgow. On that occasion he made a virulent attack on German claims in East Africa, again deplored the apathy of the English people toward the African question, and urged the necessity for England to secure the uttermost limits of her claims. In bright colors he painted the future of the territory around Victoria Nyanza: "On its shores were about twelve millions of docile, workable, teachable Africans. All the labour that any British company would need could be brought from Uganda for the construction of the railway, for manning the steamers . . . and for carrying to further regions the blessings of commerce. (Cheers)." In conclusion,

[7] *Times,* June 10, 11, 1890.

Stanley, who at that time was an American citizen, put this question to his audience: "Why should the gentlemen of the Foreign Office feel that it was a distasteful task to bring more regions within the influence of civilization and subjects of Queen Victoria? (Cheers)." [8]

The "gentlemen of the Foreign Office" were by no means unaware of the task they were expected to perform. Stanley on the stump, supported by a swelling editorial chorus and with acres of space in the news columns at his disposal, made it impossible to forget that any agreement disadvantageous to the great trading companies would produce unpleasant repercussions in parliament and in the cabinet. Thus was "public opinion" manufactured. It did not come welling up spontaneously from the masses who ogled and gaped at Stanley wherever he appeared, but its appearance was evoked by a combination of circumstances, an arresting personality, and the activity of an interested pressure group. It was a clear-cut case of the complete identification of the interests of an economic pressure group with the interest of the nation. [9]

In Germany nothing comparable to Stanley's agitation developed during the course of the negotiations. However, when Salisbury at one point suggested postponement he was warned that Dr. Peters was expected to arrive on the coast from his Uganda expedition at the end of June and that in view of his well known character they might expect him to start agitating on behalf of his native treaties in a manner that would be as embarrassing for England as Stanley's activity had been for Germany. [10] Since details of the negotiations were withheld from the press, only rumors and uncontrolled reports reached the German public. Colonial enthusiasts voiced their demands through the press, but there was no outstanding public figure to crystallize and direct the agitation. Marschall consulted the German East Africa Company where its interests were concerned, but the broad lines and details of the accord were worked out in the comparative isolation of the German foreign office.

The provisions of the Helgoland-Zanzibar treaty may be briefly summarized: The German government renounced all claims to Witu, Zanzibar and Uganda in return for English recognition of German claims to the coast of the mainland opposite the island of Zanzibar and the hinterland as far as the lakes Tanganyika and Nyassa, thus giving German South East Africa and the Congo Free State a common boundary and ending the imperialist dream of a British empire in Africa stretch-

[8] *Times*, June 13, 1890.
[9] The strongest editorial support of the Stanley agitation on behalf of Mackinnon's British East Africa Company was given by the *Pall Mall Gazette*, the *Times*, the *Standard*, and *Morning Post*.
[10] *G. P.*, VIII, 21.

ing from the Cape to Cairo. In return for the abandonment of German claims in Africa, England ceded to Germany the island of Helgoland in the North Sea. Helgoland was the sugar coating that should sweeten the bitter pill of German abandonment of a great empire in Africa. Its acquisition was regarded by the Emperor and his advisers, Caprivi and Marschall, as of supreme importance, outweighing all considerations of African territory. Why? Because it was the key to Germany's North Sea gateway. The military value of the Kiel canal, then under construction, hinged largely upon the acquisition and fortification of Helgoland.[11]

The publicity tactics of the Wilhelmstrasse in dealing with the completed treaty revolved around the Helgoland acquisition. An inspired article in the Norddeutsche, on June 16, was obviously designed to prepare the press for the unfavorable colonial provisions. All mention of Helgoland was withheld until June 17, when a summary of the agreement was published in a special afternoon edition of the Reichsanzeiger. Publicists, editors, and politicians were taken completely by surprise. Prepared for serious colonial losses they now learned of the acquisition of German land peopled by Germans, and formerly held by a foreign power. The immediate reaction was altogether favorable to the government.[12] After the first round of patriotic huzzas over the sand and rock of Helgoland, the full extent of the government's colonial renunciations in favor of England began to be appreciated. A sharp change in press opinion set in. The question which commentators weighed was: Is the acquisition of Helgoland sufficient compensation for the sacrifices we make in Africa? Bitter, hostile criticism was poured upon the accord by those interested in colonial expansion, and many writers who approved the agreement as a whole found the abandonment of Zanzibar, Witu and Uganda a bitter pill to swallow. "We have traded three kingdoms for a bathtub," was Karl Peters' bitter comment. His judgment seemed to be confirmed by Stanley's oft quoted remark that England had acquired a new suit of clothes in exchange for an old pants' button.[13]

The government was hampered in its defense of the agreement because

---

[11] G. P., VIII, 16–25, passim. See also William II, My Memoirs (N. Y., 1922), pp. 55–56.

[12] Berlin dispatches to the Times and Daily Telegraph, June 19, 1890; comments on June 18 of the leading Berlin papers including Die Post, National-Zeitung, Vossische Ztg., Berliner Tageblatt, Tägliche Rundschau, and Kreuzztg.

[13] Manfred Sell, Das Deutsch-Englische Abkommen von 1890 im Lichte der deutschen Presse (Berlin, 1926), p. 39. Sell's study of the reception of this agreement by the German press is so complete that further combing of the newspaper files yields very small returns. The reports of the English correspondents in Berlin bear out his conclusions with regard to the change in German press opinion. Daily Telegraph, Morning Post, Times, June 23, 1890.

final signature was delayed until July 1, and the necessary parliamentary action for transfer of the island was not completed until the end of the month. Meanwhile, opponents of the accord propagated the view that Helgoland was valueless except as a pleasant place for Sunday excursionists. Until all details of the transfer were completed, the German government could not publicly declare that the island's value was chiefly military and strategic. Finally, on July 29, the German government published in a special supplement to the Reichsanzeiger a memorandum that was a complete statement of the motives behind the agreement with England and a blanket defense of the colonial clauses of the treaty. In the press and later in the Reichstag, the official case emphasized the fairness of the boundary adjustments, claimed that the abandonment of the island of Zanzibar did not impair the value of the coastal mainland remaining in German possession, and maintained that Helgoland, because of its strategic position, was indispensable to Germany and of more value than ill-defined claims in Africa. Finally, the public was asked to judge the agreement as a whole, particularly in reference to its bearing on the maintenance of close and cordial relations between England and Germany. In the memorandum published in the Reichsanzeiger it was specifically stated: "We sincerely desire to secure for the future the former good relations with England," and in the Reichstag, Caprivi quoted a marginal comment by Bismarck apropos of Anglo-German difficulties in Africa: "England is worth more to us than Zanzibar and all East Africa." [14]

No amount of emphasis in official publicity on the larger aspects of the accord could still the outcry in colonial circles over England's walking off with the lion's share of African territory. This disappointment and dissatisfaction led to the foundation, in the spring of 1891, of the *Allgemeiner deutscher Verband* under the presidency of Karl Peters; in 1894 it became the *Alldeutscher Verband*—the Pan-German League, which embraced all the forces in Germany hostile to England and to English policy.[15] Henceforth the raucous voice of the Pan-Germans, proclaiming their vague and ill-defined ambitions, was a constant factor in the public relations of England and Germany.

Outside the circle of colonial enthusiasts, editorial evaluation of the treaty corresponded closely to the opinions expressed later in the Reichstag by party leaders. The Conservative press, reflecting the lack of party

[14] Sell, *op. cit.*, p. 54.
[15] Mildred S. Wertheimer, *The Pan-German League* (N. Y., 1924), pp. 22–38; Townsend, *op. cit.*, pp. 162–65; Johannes Ziekursch, *Politische Geschichte des Neuen Deutschen Kaiserreiches* (3 vols., Frankfort, 1925–30), III, 28–31.

unity toward colonial expansion, expressed divergent opinions on the value of the accord. The Kreuzzeitung, in general, approved it ; the Post joined in the first chorus of praise, then swung sharply into opposition ; the Reichsbote blew hot and cold.[16] The National Liberal party press was the ardent champion of expansionist ideals. The first impression of the agreement registered in this quarter was favorable, but the colonial disadvantages were soon uppermost and as the debate continued the criticism from this direction became more determined and aggressive. The National-Zeitung alone among the important party papers consistently defended the agreement.[17] The Center press, in general opposed to colonial adventures, raised no objection to the abandonment of claims to African territory. The Catholic press alone shared fully the government's optimistic evaluation of the accord.[18] The *Freisinnige,* or liberal-democratic press, cheered the agreement because it contained "squirts of cold water against the colonial fanatics." This partisan acclamation only damned it further in the eyes of Conservatives and National Liberals. High praise from the Berliner Tageblatt, Frankfurter Zeitung, and Vossische Zeitung was of questionable value in the scheme of official publicity, for such jubilation from this quarter bore too much the appearance of a celebration of an English diplomatic victory over Germany.[19] The Social Democratic papers expressed no opinion on the value of the agreement, but in accord with party principles and tactics used it as a point of departure for general attacks on "the system." [20] Such in brief is the picture revealed by the party press : On the side of the government, was the press of the Center and the Democratic parties ; in opposition was the greater part of the Conservative press and the most important National Liberal organs. In time, however, the outlines of the picture were blurred. As Germany moved into the era of *Weltpolitik,* and overseas expansion became the watchword of ever widening circles, the Helgoland-Zanzibar accord became a symbol of a lost empire in Africa. By 1896 even the editor of the Vossische Zeitung spoke bitterly of how Germany had been done out of Zanzibar.[21]

In England a battery of big guns was marshaled in defense of Salisbury's treaty and isolated attempts at opposition were soon squelched. The Times, Daily Telegraph, Standard, and Morning Post led the chorus of approval ; the Liberal Daily News was not openly hostile ; and

---

[16] Sell, *op. cit.,* pp. 72–79.
[17] *Ibid.,* pp. 79–87.
[18] *Ibid.,* pp. 87–90.
[19] *Ibid.,* pp. 90–95.
[20] *Ibid.,* pp. 95–98.
[21] *Vossische Ztg.,* No. 466, Oct. 3, 1896.

only the Pall Mall Gazette and the Star denounced the agreement as a shameful betrayal of British interests.[22]

In concluding the Helgoland-Zanzibar agreement Bismarck's successor, Caprivi, clearly revealed his disinclination to allow colonial questions to endanger Germany's position in Europe. His was a continental viewpoint first and foremost. The close understanding that had existed between London and Berlin since 1887 was more necessary than ever after the non-renewal of the Russian reinsurance treaty and the indications that soon appeared of a morganatic marriage between St. Petersburg and Paris. Caprivi, strongly inclined toward England, found the basis of co-operation with that power already laid by the Mediterranean accords of 1887. Through these agreements England had become one of the weightiest of the flying buttresses supporting Bismarck's intricate Gothic edifice of European treaties and agreements. The first and second Mediterranean accords, inspired and promoted by Bismarck, linked Austria, Italy and England together in defense of the status quo against any forward movement in that area by France or Russia.[23] So far as disturbance of the peace in the Mediterranean was concerned, the Triple Alliance through these two vital connections became a Quadruple Alliance.

The Mediterranean, one of the most important arteries of Empire communication, was Lord Salisbury's constant concern. The protection of British interests in this region through a close connection with two members of the Triple Alliance, was a feature of his policy. Salisbury leaned on the Triple Alliance and was definitely concerned with its preservation. Hatzfeldt, the German ambassador at London, reviewing the Conservative government's policy, wrote on November 24, 1892:

On the whole . . . Lord Salisbury was perfectly clear on the European situation and on the aims he must follow in foreign politics in the interests of his country, even if he endeavored . . . to involve in obscurity his leanings toward the Triple Alliance and his actions in support of it, in order not to give to his opponents weapons which they might use against him. Above all we can consider that he held it to be of supreme interest to England to join Austria, Italy, and perhaps also ourselves, in stemming the Russian advance towards Constantinople and the Dardanelles and to prevent the excessive development of the power of France and of French influence in the Mediterranean.[24]

---

[22] Daily Telegraph, Times, Post, and Standard, June 18, 19, 1890; Pall Mall Gazette, June 18, 19, 20; Star, June 18, 19.

[23] W. L. Langer, European Alliances and Alignments, 1871–1890 (N. Y., 1931), pp. 398–401, 439–41; Lady Gwendolen Cecil, Life of Robert Marquis of Salisbury (4 vols., Lond., 1921–28), IV, 20–24.

[24] G. P., IX, 90, Nov. 24, 1892. Also W. Herrmann, Dreibund, Zweibund, England 1890–1895 (Stuttgart, 1929).

Definite limits, however, were set to Salisbury's co-operation with the Triple Alliance and its members. This was clearly shown in May 1891, when the Italians, negotiating with London through Berlin, sought to expand the agreement of 1887 to a definite alliance. The nervousness of his colleagues, embarrassing questions in parliament from the Francophile Labouchère, and the cabinet's unwillingness to conclude military alliances caused Salisbury first to interrupt the conversations and then to avoid their renewal.[25] Nevertheless, until he left office, the prime minister was frank in stating to Hatzfeldt that, in his opinion, close and friendly relations to the Triple Alliance was the best means of securing the peace of Europe and the interests of Great Britain.

An examination at this time of the files of the leading Conservative and Unionist newspapers reveals a community of agreement and understanding between the foreign office and the press that gives meaning to the somewhat cryptic remark of Lady Gwendolen Cecil that "Even Lord Salisbury made occasional use of his under and private secretaries." [26] In the press the Triple Alliance was praised as a "Triple League of Peace," while France and Russia were branded as potential disturbers of the status quo. In the spring of 1891, the Triple Alliance was due for renewal. Italy was reminded of the benefits of alliance with the Central powers and assured that England was keenly conscious of their community of interests in the Mediterranean.[27] Special importance attaches to a long article in the Standard (June 4, 1891) on England's relations to Italy and the Triple Alliance. Salisbury directed Hatzfeldt's attention to the article; it was transmitted to Berlin and laid before the Emperor who commented approvingly in his usual racy style.[28] This bit of by-play is given meaning by a knowledge of the relations between Salisbury and Alfred Austin, chief writer on foreign affairs for the Standard and probable author of the article. Austin, who was later appointed poet laureate by Salisbury, combined editorial writing for the Standard with the writing of indifferent poetry. He was a frequent visitor at Hatfield and maintained a regular political correspondence with the prime minister. From the guarded remarks of Salisbury's biographer, Lady Cecil, we infer that this connection was mutually advantageous in that Austin's pen was guided by his knowledge of the statesman's mind while Salisbury was able to give a lead to press opinion without assuming responsibility

25 G. P., VIII, 43–50; Cecil, op. cit., IV, 381–82; W. L. Langer, The Diplomacy of Imperialism, I, 18–20.
26 Cecil, op. cit., IV, 294.
27 Standard, May 6, 7; Times, April 14, June 11; Morning Post, June 3, 1891.
28 G. P., VIII, 59.

for an official statement. Such a connection, quite different from the German practice of inspiration or direct composition of articles, led to a marked synchronization of the Standard's editorial viewpoint on foreign affairs with the opinions of the prime minister.[29] The politically initiated, who saw in Austin's editorials a clear reflection of Salisbury's views on domestic and foreign policy were frequently justified in so doing. The Standard's leader of June 4—the florid prose is unmistakably Austin's—stated that while England was not bound by definite engagements to render armed assistance to Italy in the Mediterranean, nevertheless, their common interests would force England to range herself on Italy's side in any dispute with France over predominance in that region. The Triple Alliance was praised as a "League of Peace" which prevented France and Russia from upsetting the status quo. England's sympathies, no less than her interests, inclined her to support and favor this group. "The Triple Alliance, it cannot be too often repeated, is a defensive compact and a defensive compact only." Which remark brought a "Bravo" from the Kaiser.[30]

During the summer of 1891 the visit of the French naval squadron to the Russian port of Kronstadt overshadowed all other events in the field of diplomacy. Signifying as it did a future of political co-operation between France and Russia, it excited comment in every European capital. Counter demonstrations were staged by the Triple Alliance powers in conjunction with England. William II triumphantly announced the renewal of the Triplice; he followed this with a state visit to England; the British Mediterranean squadron was host to Emperor Franz Joseph of Austria and King Humbert of Italy. Of these events the Conservative and Unionist journals were the inspired reporters and interpreters. The Standard, Daily Telegraph, and Times acclaimed the renewal of the Triple Alliance with the semi-official formula, and all three praised it in identical words as the "League of Peace." But the Times in advance of its contemporaries proclaimed the solidarity of England and Germany: "The union of England and Germany in the cause of peace and civilization may be as solid and valuable as if it were embodied in a formal treaty and supported, as it would be, were the necessity to arise in the future as it has arisen in the past, by a conjunction

[29] Cecil, *op. cit.*, IV, 24–25, 56–57, 83, 205. An example of the communications that passed between the two is a note from Salisbury to Austin on August 12, 1888: ". . . as to my Mansion House speech—take it as it was spoken—don't read anything into it that was not there—and you will find it a string of truths, which verge on truisms." Another instance of Salisbury's use of publicity is recounted by Sir Harry Johnston, *The Story of My Life*, p. 205.

[30] *G. P.*, VIII, 59.

of the forces of the greatest naval Power with those of the greatest military Power in the World." [31]

On the occasion of William II's visit the high political tone assumed by the leader writers, and the purple panegyrics with which they greeted the royal guest, took on the appearance of a demonstration of British solidarity with the Triple Alliance against France and Russia.[32] The foreign correspondents harmonized their reports with editorial policy. Everything that detracted from the Kronstadt demonstration was reported and every sign of difference or disagreement between France and Russia was magnified. An extreme manifestation of this policy is found in a report from the Paris correspondent of the Times who gave currency to what must have been an unsubstantiated rumor. "It is said," he wrote, "that proofs have been given to the French Government—one amongst a hundred horrible episodes—that young Jewish women, students of medicine at Moscow, have been allowed by the police to complete their studies only on condition of becoming enrolled on the list of prostitutes (the only class tolerated without religious distinction), and that they have been compelled to enter houses of ill-fame at least once in order that their names might be put on the recognized lists." (June 9, 1891.) The correspondent of the same journal in Russia dwelt with considerable satisfaction on the anomalies of the situation in Kronstadt, pointing out that the air of the Marseillaise was permitted, but not the revolutionary words; Russian toasts were addressed to President Carnot and not to the French Republic; the people were allowed to shout *vive la France* but not *vive la république*.[33] The Daily Telegraph (July 27) remarked that "The friends of peace are allied; its enemies find it difficult to coalesce." While the Morning Post (July 27) comforted its readers with the reflection that "The interest of the scene at Cronstadt . . . seems to derive its importance chiefly from the internal contrasts presented by the two states concerned." Austin, in the Standard, enlarged upon the aggressive potentialities of the Franco-Russian combination in questions affecting Egypt and the Straits. The power of such a combination to injure its neighbors was unquestionable, hence "Their neighbors . . . can only stand ready-armed to ward off the danger." (July 26.)

The angling of news, the reporting of rumor as fact, the suppression of reports out of harmony with policy trends are clearly discernible in the English Conservative-Unionist press. Directed at this time against

---

[31] *Times*, July 1, 1891. Also *Standard,* and *Daily Telegraph,* June 30.
[32] *Daily Telegraph,* July 6; *Morning Post,* July 14; *Times,* July 4; *Standard,* July 4, 6, 10, 11, 13, 1891.
[33] *Times,* July 27, 1891.

France and Russia, the same tactics were later employed effectively against Germany. Then the Berlin news reports blossomed with stories of "military murders," subaltern brutality in the army, student dueling, and stupid bureaucrats. But in 1891 the combination of France and Russia, and not Germany and her allies, seemed to menace British interests.

It must not be supposed that the golden opinions which the Conservative editors expressed about the Triple Alliance, Germany and the German people constituted in any strict sense the public opinion. It was rather an expression of co-ordinated understanding between Conservative editors and journalists on the one hand and the government and the foreign office on the other.

Salisbury's policy of leaning on the Triple Alliance and giving the appearance of hostility to France had numerous critics in Liberal ranks. Opposition, moreover, was frequently voiced in the Liberal press to Salisbury's tendency to timber up his Mediterranean policy with continental supports. It is not surprising, under the circumstances, that a feeling of uneasiness and uncertainty should have appeared in German diplomatic circles when, in August 1892, the Conservative government resigned and a Liberal cabinet led by Gladstone took its place. For the Wilhelmstrasse the one bright spot in an otherwise cloudy situation was the exclusion from the cabinet of Francophile radicals of the stamp of Dilke and Labouchère and the appointment of Lord Rosebery to the foreign office. "Our only dependable friend in the English cabinet," was Hatzfeldt's compliment to Rosebery.[34] A measure of reassurance was forthcoming, as the new foreign secretary informed Hatzfeldt that he had no intention of breaking the continuity of British foreign policy.

However, with the Liberals in office the coefficient of unpredictability attaching to British policy became considerably higher. Gladstone's publicly stated dislike of the continental system of alliances was a factor as was also the Liberal tendency to concentrate on the domestic political program. The Liberal party appealed to those whose major interests were social and economic rather than imperialistic. The Conservatives claimed special competence in Empire affairs, whereas the Little England er tradition made the Liberals suspect in nationalist circles. The preceding Gladstone government had an unhappy record in foreign affairs, and many individuals, who were not strongly partisan, felt that Imperial interests were safer with the Conservatives than with the Liberals. Then, too, the heavy press battalions were on the Conservative

[34] *G. P.*, VIII, 402. The Germans undoubtedly overestimated Rosebery's inclination toward the Triple Alliance. In a letter to Gladstone, July 16, 1891, he expressed out and out isolationist views. Marquess of Crewe, *Lord Rosebery* (2 vols., Lond., 1931), II, 374–75.

side. This weighed more heavily in the conduct of foreign policy than in the field of domestic affairs where party organization and direct contact between constituents and their parliamentary representatives diminished the importance of the press.

When Hatzfeldt tried to draw the new minister on the Mediterranean issue and the need for clarifying the relations of England to Austria and Italy, he met with evasion as "masterful" as Salisbury's "inactivity." [35] In the summer of 1893, when the Siamese crisis over the French blockade of Bangkok arose, Rosebery made gestures toward Berlin that gave rise to the opinion that he contemplated having it out with the French if he were assured of support by the Triple Alliance. The crisis passed as rapidly as it had developed. Rosebery's gesture was probably a diplomatic feint. Whether it was or not, it awakened the suspicion in Berlin that he had been seeking "not an ally but a lightning conductor." [36] This impression was considerably strengthened by direct and inferential references to the close understanding between England and the Triplice that appeared in the Daily Telegraph, Morning Post, Standard and the Daily News. The Morning Post's leader writer went so far as to declare that "Even in Siam there is a complete identity of interest between the Teutonic states." [37]

In the autumn of 1893 these newspaper warnings were repeated on the occasion of the visit of the Russian fleet to Toulon and the fortnight of nationalist delirium in which the French indulged. All sorts of alarmist rumors appeared as to intended Franco-Russian co-operation in the Mediterranean, particularly with regard to the Straits and British occupation of Egypt. The emotional orgy that accompanied the appearance of the Russian sailors and officers in France, furnished English press correspondents with the liveliest copy of the year. There was a good deal of malicious banter in the many columns of descriptive comment, but underneath the mild-mannered fun ran a note of sincere concern for the future of Britain's position in the Mediterranean.[38] Fear of aggressive action by the new combination in that area led to conversations between London and Vienna, which had as their object the establishment of a common front on the Near Eastern question. These negotiations were

---

[35] G. P., VIII, 84, 89; Langer, op. cit., I, 40; Herrmann, op. cit., pp. 42–57.

[36] Ibid., VIII, 125. On the Siamese crisis see also Crewe, Lord Rosebery, II, 424–27; Langer, op. cit., I, 43–44.

[37] Morning Post, July 31; Daily Telegraph, July 26; Standard, July 29; Daily News, August 1.

[38] Daily Telegraph, Oct. 14, 19; Standard, Oct. 13, 18, 26; Morning Post, Oct. 13, 17, 23, 25; Times, Oct. 14, 17, 25; Daily News, Oct. 14, 17, 20. See also E. Malcolm Carroll, French Public Opinion and Foreign Affairs, 1870–1914 (N. Y., 1931), pp. 158–59.

no more fruitful than previous attempts at agreement. Any obligation assumed by Austria was bound to affect her allies, and the British were unwilling to engage themselves definitely to the Triple Alliance.[39]

Another consequence of the Franco-Russian demonstration was the raising of a naval scare over the inadequacy of British forces in the Mediterranean. It ran a course similar to later naval scares in which Germany figured as the bogey. Unless a large increase in construction were undertaken immediately, it was asserted, the combined French and Russian fleets would be superior to Britain's in 1898. The Conservative journals broke out in a rash of naval arithmetic; and in parliament Lord George Hamilton, Arthur Balfour and Sir Ellis Ashmead-Bartlett taxed the government with neglect of British naval security, and predicted that unless steps were taken immediately to restore their superiority England would have to cut and run from the Mediterranean.[40] It was a dark picture, indeed, that the Conservatives conjured up in the press and in parliament. The Times in concluding its survey of events for the twelve months of 1893 could find only one cheering feature: "It has been a year of menace and danger, but not a year of catastrophe. The Great European War has not broken out." (Dec. 30.)

The next turn of the wheel brought Berlin and London into an embarrassing collision. A certain soreness had been developing for some time in official German circles at British lack of consideration for German colonial aspirations. While there was no desire in Berlin to abandon co-operation in the field of general policy, London must be made to realize that a legitimate claim could be made for English support in the colonial field in return for German support of England's general policy. The attempt to reopen the Samoan question with this argument failed utterly. Rosebery, who had succeeded Gladstone at the head of a cabinet that was all at sixes and sevens, dared not add to the number of the government's opponents by a weighty concession to the German colonial appetite.[41]

Faced with Rosebery's resentment at importunities and attempts to wheedle colonial advantages, German authorities set about bringing pres-

---

[39] *G. P.,* IX, 134–39. For a full discussion of the diplomatic situation see Langer, *Diplomacy of Imperialism,* I, 51–58; Herrmann, *op. cit.,* pp. 86–121.

[40] Article by Lord George Hamilton in the *Nineteenth Century,* December 1893; criticism in the *Daily News,* Dec. 7; general debate in the House of Commons on Dec. 19, *Parl. Deb.,* 4th Ser., vol. 19, 1771 ff.; Lord Charles Beresford, "A Programme for Proposed Increase of the British Fleet," *Daily Telegraph,* Nov. 21; meeting of the London Chamber of Commerce urging naval increases reported in *Daily Telegraph,* Dec. 13; agitation throughout December in the entire Conservative press. The cabinet situation produced by the naval question is described in Crewe, *Lord Rosebery,* II, 435–37; and Langer, *op. cit.,* I, 49–51.

[41] *G. P.,* VIII, 402–39, *passim.*

sure to bear wherever opportunity afforded, in order to bring home to
the directors of British policy a realization of the value of German friendship. Egypt was of course the most powerful lever in German hands and
it was employed during the summer of 1894 to move the British in the
direction desired by the Wilhelmstrasse.[42] At the same time Rosebery
and the foreign secretary, Kimberley, by a maladroit move placed themselves in a position vis-à-vis Germany from which they were able to
escape only by a humiliating withdrawal.

At Brussels on May 12, 1894, was concluded a treaty between Great
Britain and the Congo Free State in which the former agreed to cede her
rights over the Bahr-el-Ghazal to the Congo government, a cession calculated to block a French advance from Equatorial Africa toward the head-
waters of the Nile. In return for her rights, Britain received an indefinite
lease upon a strip of territory twenty-five kilometers wide between Lake
Tanganyika and Lake Albert Edward. The Zanzibar-Helgoland agreement had extended German Southeast Africa to the boundary of the
Congo Free State. By leasing this strip the British hoped to re-establish
direct connection between their possessions in South Africa and Uganda.
The establishment of such an "English girdle" around German Southeast
Africa had been proposed during the negotiations in 1890 but was abandoned as a result of sharp German protest. Since Berlin had not been
informed of the preliminaries of the Anglo-Congolese treaty, it now appeared that the Rosebery government had resorted to a sharp trick in
order to realize, against German opposition, the Cape to Cairo dream of
English colonial enthusiasts. Parallel protests, based upon the claim that
the agreement violated pre-existing conventions, were immediately forthcoming from Berlin and Paris. The French objected to the cession of the
Bahr-el-Ghazal and the Germans objected to the leasehold conveyed in
Article III. They did not act jointly and on the same grounds, but their
parallel action intensified the pressure upon Brussels and London.

In lodging an official protest with the government of the Congo Free
State on May 27, Marschall referred to the unfavorable reception accorded the treaty by "our public opinion." [43] While it is true, as the
Times Berlin correspondent reported, that such moderate organs as the
Vossische Zeitung were critical of this latest development, the really
sharp protests came from those journals that regularly voiced the sentiment in colonial circles. The National-Zeitung and Tägliche Rundschau
took the lead for this group. The Hamburger Nachrichten, on purely
partisan grounds as the megaphone of Bismarckian opinion, twitted the

---

[42] G. P., VIII, 215–30.
[43] Ibid., VIII, 430.

government on this latest return which it had realized from its friendly policy toward England. The Hammerstein group in the Conservative party through its organ, the Kreuzzeitung, was ready to attack Caprivi on any pretext. It was not so much German "public opinion" that Marschall had in mind, probably, as the exigencies of the domestic political situation and the desirability of placating malcontent groups or cutting the ground of opposition from under their feet.

Over the bullyragging papers the press bureau in this case had no influence. Their ill-considered attacks on the latest manifestation of English "underhandedness" could not be curbed. Papers such as the Vossische Zeitung, Berliner Tageblatt, Frankfurter Zeitung, and Kölnische Zeitung kept well within the bounds of diplomatic etiquette, although they firmly supported the foreign office protest. Marschall's task was facilitated by the attitude of the British correspondents in Berlin. While they completely disregarded or referred only obliquely to the tirades of the jingo and opposition papers, they stated clearly and even sympathetically in some instances, the Wilhelmstrasse's objections to the agreement. The correspondent of the Morning Post wrote: "To spring upon Europe a mere paper agreement, which was sure to be met with a universal protest, seems on the face of it both bad diplomacy and weak policy. . . . Fortunately there never was a German Government animated by more friendly and conciliatory feelings toward England than the present one; and if adequate, and above all, prompt, English assurances and guarantees are afforded they will undoubtedly meet with a favorable reception. It is most desirable that public feeling in Germany should not be left under the impression that Germany is the victim of a conscious or unconscious act of bad faith." (June 2.) This tips the balance rather far in favor of the Wilhelmstrasse against Downing Street, but the Times and Standard correspondents reported in the same vein.[44]

The first formal German protest was sent to the Congo State government in Brussels, but practically the same communication was made in London. On June 5 Lord Kimberley acknowledged the German statement but he did not meet the issue. On June 8 Sir Edward Grey answered a question for the government in the Commons in words chosen to give the impression that German objections had been met with satisfactory explanations.[45] As a matter of fact, at the time Grey spoke, a sharply worded note was being prepared in Berlin for delivery to the British foreign office. Presented on June 11, it stated the German objections to Article III as follows: Since the lease of the corridor had no

[44] *Times*, May 26, June 13, 16; *Standard*, June 8; *Morning Post*, June 7.
[45] *Parl. Deb.*, 4th Ser., vol. 25, 693–94.

time limit, it amounted in effect to a cession of territory and altered the boundary between German Southeast Africa and the Congo State; second, the proposed cession would injure Germany's political position in that region and impair her trade connections with the Congo Free State; these reasons, which had been presented in opposition to the British request for a leased strip during the negotiations in 1890, were still valid.[46] The official position was further explained in a dispatch from the Berlin correspondent of the Times, who, after making the points contained in the note, added: "Perhaps what has caused even greater soreness here than the Agreement itself is the way in which it was concluded and sprung upon Germany as an accomplished fact. . . . Whether Germany's sensitiveness be or be not exaggerated, the spirit of moderation in which her Government has hitherto sought to approach this question must not be mistaken for weakness or irresolution. The Emperor and the Chancellor, notwithstanding their earnest desire to persevere in the friendly policy towards England which has distinguished the new régime without, it must be confessed, in any way contributing to its popularity, are, I understand, thoroughly determined that Germany's voice shall be heard and her interests respected in this matter. . . ." (June 12.) The nature and content of the German note were revealed in a semi-official communication appearing in the Kölnische Zeitung.[47] The statement of the official position was prefaced with this remark aimed at Grey's announcement in the Commons: "In view of repeated English attempts to represent German opposition to the Anglo-Congolese treaty before public opinion as inconsequential, or through evasive statement of the London cabinet as already settled, we feel it necessary once more briefly to state the objections." A Berlin dispatch the next day referred again to Grey's statement in the Commons and gave the dates of the delivery of the German protest notes in London.[48] In this way the false impression produced by Grey's statement was removed.

While the Berlin correspondents reported the polite but firm official viewpoint and disregarded the Anglophobe effusions of the chauvinistic papers, the Conservative editors in London trained their heavy guns upon France, where agitation in press and parliament reached its height with Hanotaux' declaration in the Chamber that so far as France was concerned the Anglo-Congolese agreement was "null and void."[49] Con-

---

[46] G. P., VIII, 442–43.
[47] No. 497, June 15. Quoted also in the Times, June 16.
[48] Quoted in Die Post, No. 163, June 17. That this incident gave Grey a bad impression of German policy—he referred to it frequently in later years—may be due to the sharp manner in which he was caught up in the inspired press.
[49] Standard, Paris correspondent, June 8.

demning the French trouble makers and excusing the British foreign office, they spoke no ill of German action. The Standard leader writer, presumably Austin, contrasted French action with Germany's. The latter was "unexceptionable in every respect." "In a word [Germany] has behaved as one self-respecting and well-mannered state behaves to another." (June 14.) A Times editorial said that "The German Government . . . has never assumed an unfriendly or vindictive attitude." Admitting that the Germans had some cause to complain of the manner in which the lease of the twenty-five mile strip had been secured, the writer states that "there is no doubt whatever that our Foreign Office was innocent of any intention to trample on German rights, and was greatly surprised at finding its action attacked on the ground of want of straightforwardness and regard for treaty obligations." (June 19.) The leading Liberal papers ignored the German action.[50]

Rosebery, faced with the determined opposition of France and Germany, was eventually forced to retreat. He first, however, toyed with the idea of a general conference which should confirm England's position in Egypt and the upper reaches of the Nile. Abandoning this line he sought to frighten the Germans into dropping their objections to the agreement. Writing to the Queen, he reported that he had used language to the Austro-Hungarian ambassador that would "ricochet through Vienna to Berlin." The import of his statement was that he would reverse his entire European policy and come to terms with France and Russia if the Germans were not more reasonable. He further protested that instead of "friendly remonstrances" Germany assumed "a tone which she might properly use in addressing Monaco." [51] The Berlin foreign office stuck to its guns, however, and in the end Rosebery agreed to drop Article III from the treaty, explaining to the Austrian ambassador that "After due reflection I am convinced that the corridor ceded by the Congo has not enough value to justify changing my whole policy." [52]

On cancellation of Article III, German objections to the treaty were immediately withdrawn. All the elements of a bitter press war had been present. For avoiding it credit is due the British editors and correspondents, who, conscious of the difference between a major policy of govern-

---

[50] An exception was a statement in the *Westminster Gazette,* June 15, charging Germany with a dog-in-the-manger policy and concluding that in view of what England had surrendered to Germany in the agreement of 1890 "we may fairly refuse to have our negotiation of a modest lease from the Congo State upset by Germany."

[51] Crewe, *Lord Rosebery,* II, 448–49.

[52] *G. P.,* VIII, 472. For the wider diplomatic implications of the entire incident see Langer, *op. cit.,* I, 135–41; Herrmann, *op. cit.,* pp. 125–40.

ment and a minor colonial dispute, and well aware that the foreign office had blundered badly, kept the torches away from the powder kegs.[53]

In view of the severe criticism to which Caprivi's foreign and colonial policy had been subjected by the malcontent German press, it would not have been surprising if political credit had been manufactured by the government from the success with which German interests had been defended in the brush with England. This, however, was not the case. In the papers close to the Wilhelmstrasse or friendly to Caprivi, the English retreat was not celebrated as a diplomatic victory. This section of the press closed the incident with an expression of approval for the general policy of friendliness and co-operation between Berlin and London.[54] On the other hand, three papers, motivated by hatred for Caprivi's policy, endeavored to turn the government's victory into a defeat. The National-Zeitung, closely related to colonial circles, ignored the favorable outcome of the dispute. The Tägliche Rundschau, whose editor was the colonial enthusiast, Dr. Lange, reproached the government for having failed to make a demand for compensation that would remove the mistakes of 1890. This deal he declared was like all others which Caprivi had concluded with England: Germany agreed to limit her colonial development in a certain direction for all time, while England won an indisputable legal title for an extension of her power; since that corresponded to their mutual desires, the bargain was sealed with a friendly handshake. The editor could see no positive advantage to Germany in having maintained simply the status quo.[55] The Hammerstein faction of the Conservative party, which was shortly to bring about Caprivi's fall, launched a bitter attack in the Kreuzzeitung. The semi-official press apparatus was immediately set in motion. A sharp article appeared on June 27 in the Norddeutsche setting forth the official view and reprimanding the Kreutzzeitung.[56] The Kölnische Zeitung published a dispatch from its Berlin correspondent, Justizrat Fischer, attacking Hammerstein and the Kreuzzeitung. Taking up the complaint that the government should have worked for compensation rather than the return of the status quo, the correspondent asked: "Would they foul their own

[53] Six years later Rosebery told Count Metternich that Sir Percy Anderson, the expert in African affairs, had been asked at the time of the corridor negotiations if German rights were involved. He had answered in the negative, and Rosebery had never spoken to him since. (G. P., VIII, 473–74 n.)

[54] Times Berlin correspondent, June 22, 23; Kölnische Ztg., No. 520, June 23; Hamburgischer Correspondent, Berlin dispatch quoted Die Post, No. 167, June 21; Frankfurter Ztg., No. 177, June 28; Die Post, No. 169, June 22, article entitled "Deutschland und der Congostaat," obviously inspired.

[55] Tägliche Rundschau, No. 143, June 22.

[56] The article was reproduced in all the papers friendly to Caprivi. Frankfurter Ztg., Berlin dispatch, No. 177, June 28.

nest?" [57] A similar rebuke was delivered in Die Post, where those who held that the government should have repudiated its own stand on international law, for a *price,* were branded as lacking in elementary appreciation of right and wrong.[58]

The domestic repercussions of the dispute threw into sharp relief one of the chief differences between the English and German party press in the handling of foreign affairs. The English Conservative editors studiously refrained from partisan exploitation of the government's retreat. A Conservative press campaign would have been a serious blow to the already tottering Rosebery cabinet. There was always in England, however, a certain limit beyond which responsible editors hesitated to go in turning developments in foreign policy to party purpose and advantage. No such reserve was ever manifested by the party papers in Germany. Here responsibility was completely divorced from publicity and criticism.

[57] No. 535, June 28, 1894.
[58] No. 171, June 25, 1894.

CHAPTER V

THE PRESS AND THE KRUGER TELEGRAM

To go to war for newspaper articles! It sounds absurd; and yet that is what almost every English resident in Germany must be inclined to wish.

Sir Cecil Spring Rice to Valentine Chirol, October 9, 1898.

"The relations with Germany continue the same, viz., a coolness, if not more between the Courts, a little bickering between the people, and the most absolute cordiality and confidence between the Governments." In this sentence Maurice de Bunsen, a fairly shrewd observer, summed up the relations between England and Germany during the early 'nineties.[1] A radical change occurred toward the middle of the decade. The coolness between the courts was intensified, an atmosphere of the clenched fist and cocked pistol replaced "a little bickering between the people," while injured sensibilities and suspicious concern were nursed alike by German and English officials. The Kruger Telegram, accompanied as it was by a blaze of publicity, marked a turning point in the public relations of the two countries.

For some time, grievances, real and fancied, had been nursed by German officials. These were not infrequently voiced in the press. Marschall taxed the British with senseless opposition to German economic and colonial expansion in Africa.[2] In the press, complaints increased at the way the dice had fallen for Germany in the African gamble. The Anglo-Congolese brush of the preceding year was symptomatic of the increasing friction. Editorial bickering over German co-operation with France and Russia in the Far East further disturbed the press relations between the two countries. The increasing tendency shown in German policy to take an independent line in extra-European affairs was regarded in London with astonishment not unmixed with distrust.

On Count Caprivi's resignation from the chancellorship, in October 1894, his post was taken by Prince Hohenlohe whose sympathies and connections inclined him toward St. Petersburg rather than London. In

---

[1] E. T. S. Dugdale, *Maurice de Bunsen* (Lond., 1934), p. 80.
[2] Marschall to Bülow, Feb. 4, 1895; *G. P.*, VIII, 474–75. W. J. Stillmann, the *Times* correspondent in Rome, had asked Bülow for material for an article on Anglo-German relations. The request, passed on to Marschall, brought forth this indictment of British obstruction.

Russia Nicholas II succeeded his father, the Slavophile Alexander III; the same year witnessed the end of the bitter Russo-German tariff war. As a result of these changes, a considerably better atmosphere prevailed in the relations between the two countries. Caprivi had cut the wire to St. Petersburg, he had favored a closer English connection and had opposed unlimited colonial expansion. His influence on German policy was now removed. The significance of the change in personnel was fully appreciated by the British press correspondents in Berlin, who had consistently championed his policies during the previous four years. Their news dispatches clearly reveal their hostility to the political forces that had brought about Caprivi's resignation, namely, the agrarians, the Bismarckians, the colonial chauvinists and the Social Democrats.[3]

Outside the field of foreign policy incidents occurred that occasioned sharp exchanges between English and German editors. The ramming of a North German Lloyd liner by an English tramp steamer, with a heavy loss of life, complaints of English travelers who had run afoul of German police regulations, the marked increase in the number of prosecutions for *lèse majesté* and other indications of a return to more reactionary policies in Germany provided fuel for editorial controversy. Leading German papers brought accusations of industrial espionage against delegates from the British Iron Trade Association who visited Germany in the summer of 1895.[4] Ill will and hostility seemed to motivate the selection and presentation of news.

More serious than these incidents, and entirely within the circle of diplomatic relations, was Germany's co-operation with the Dual Alliance in the Far East, in direct opposition to British interests and British policy. With the outbreak of the Sino-Japanese War the British foreign office, anticipating serious trade disturbances in China, took the initiative in proposing joint intervention by the great powers. German officials refused to co-operate and nothing came of the British proposal. At the close of the war, however, the directors of German policy responded with alacrity when Russia proposed intervention to thwart the Japanese claim to a territorial foothold on the mainland. English correspondents and editors were unsparing in their criticism of German participation in the coercive coalition. "Germany, standing shoulder to shoulder with the allies of Cronstadt, is about to snatch the chestnuts out of the fire for Russia," wrote George Saunders, the Berlin correspondent of the Morning Post, on April 23. German policy, in Russian

[3] *Times, Standard, Daily News, Daily Telegraph,* Oct. 26, 27, 28, 29, 1894. These journals were represented in Berlin, respectively, by Valentine Chirol, William Maxwell, Mr. Morrison, and J. L. Bashford.

[4] *Times,* Berlin dispatch, Aug. 17.

leading strings, aimed at a general redistribution of colonial possessions. Therefore, continued Saunders, "it behooves England to take these wayward ambitions into account, and to lose no opportunity of relegating them to their proper place with a friendly but strong hand." (April 29.) German action was denounced as "inexplicable and grossly inconsistent" by the Daily Telegraph, and as "at once useless, mischievous, and irritating" by the Daily News.[5] The Standard's leader writer could not decide whether German conduct was attributable to "the sudden impulses of Germany's Ruler," or to "a perverse desire to do the opposite of whatever is done or favoured by Great Britain." (April 26.) English press criticisms were answered and German policy defended in obviously inspired articles in the Norddeutsche and the Kölnische Zeitung.[6] Official publicity, however, did not silence the critics in the English press or in the liberal-democratic organs in Germany where it was insisted that the Wilhelmstrasse had engaged German policy in the service of Russian interests.

In semi-official publicity the underlying motives of German action were not revealed. The safeguarding of commercial and economic interests was the main reason advanced, but in the eyes of Holstein, Marschall, and the Kaiser far greater issues were involved. To be "in at the kill" in case of a general handing around of compensations, to pave the way for future acquisition of a commercial and naval base in the Orient, and to win the good will of the Czar and his advisers were important considerations. The Triple Alliance could not but benefit by the direction of Russian expansive forces toward the Far East with a consequent relief of pressure upon the eastern frontiers of Austria and Germany and an abatement of Russian activity in the Balkans and at Constantinople. Nor did they anticipate a permanent estrangement from England as a result of this "extra waltz." On the contrary, the British would see that without German support they were powerless against France and Russia in the Far East. As a consequence of this little lesson English statesmen would be inclined in the future to place a higher value on German good will. German action foreshadowed the policy of the "free hand." As the Franco-Russian bloc became more aggressive in its attitude toward the British Empire, Germany could tip the balance for one or the other.[7]

---

[5] April 26, Aug. 14, 1895.

[6] *Norddeutsche*, No. 199, April 29; *Kölnische Ztg.*, quoted in *Die Post*, No. 126, May 9.

[7] On German participation in the Far Eastern coalition and its significance for the alignment of the powers, see Eric Brandenburg, *Von Bismarck zum Weltkriege* (Berlin, 1927, rev. ed.), pp. 46–63; Friedrich Meinecke, *Geschichte des deutsch-*

It is the nature of the press that it never permits a particular question to be followed to a final mathematical conclusion. In striving for actuality the startling event of today crowds out the equally startling event of yesterday. Political occurrences arise, have their short day in the public prints and disappear behind a new screen of printer's type and printer's ink. Questions are frequently revived in association with subsequent occurrences which possess publicity values. When William II visited Cowes in August 1895, the usual hearty welcome was not forthcoming from the English press. On the contrary, the Standard, which was a recognized ministerial organ, took the Emperor to task for associating his government with the action of the Dual Alliance in the Far East. The press attacks appear to have rankled in the Kaiser's mind even more than the personal disagreement with Lord Salisbury which terminated the momentous interview at Cowes on August 5.[8] Six months later he referred to them in a letter to his grandmother, Queen Victoria, and although he cited the anger of "our press" and "Germany's *amour propre*" we may safely assume that he was expressing his own feelings. "Our press," he wrote, "is still angered by the Standard Articles which appeared when I was in Cowes and which were very unkind to me personally, and which wounded Germany's *amour propre* more deeply than the authors might have thought." [9]

The first Standard article, an editorial welcoming William II to England, was published on August 5. The florid style, the personal flattery of the Emperor, and the political ideas expressed point unmistakably to the chief leader writer, Alfred Austin, as the author. Because it was well known in journalistic circles that the Standard maintained connections with Lord Salisbury, the editorial was seized upon by German press representatives as a semi-official utterance. Austin, in the interests of the Conservative government that had recently returned to power, apparently intended to close the breach that had opened between England and the Triple Alliance during Rosebery's administration.

Beginning with a eulogy of the "young Emperor" (who was almost forty), the author went on to welcome William II to England and suggested that he would have an opportunity to inform himself on English

englischen Bündnisproblems, 1890–1901 (Munich, 1927), pp. 24–31; W. L. Langer, *The Diplomacy of Imperialism*, I, chap. VI.

[8] On the conversations pertaining to Salisbury's plan for partitioning the Turkish Empire see R. J. Sontag, "The Cowes Interview and the Kruger Telegram," *Pol. Sci. Quar.*, XL (1925), 217–47; Brandenburg, *op. cit.*, pp. 64–69; Meinecke, *op. cit.*, pp. 32–53; Langer, *op. cit.*, I, chap. VII.

[9] Sir Sidney Lee, *King Edward VII* (2 vols., N. Y., 1925–27), I, 671. To the same articles the German chargé d'affaires in Vienna attributed the bitter press polemics of the autumn of 1895. *G. P.*, X, 147.

public opinion and to benefit from the political wisdom of his grandmother and her experienced ministers. It was regrettable that between
two countries which were naturally "friends and allies" there had developed misunderstandings and differences during the Liberal tenure of
office. He noted and deplored the tendency in German policy to try
diplomatic experiments which "seemed more than once to borrow the
dexterous, not to say ambidexterous, policy of his first Chancellor." "To
this country," the writer continued, "it is a matter of indifference who
did, and who did not, interfere between Japan and China. But as two of
the Powers that decided to take that course were represented . . . as
having thereby effected a valuable diplomatic and commercial triumph
over England, we perhaps had some right to be surprised at finding
Germany in their company. . . . The good will of this country, which
Germany has long enjoyed, is of much more value to it . . . than any
momentary result that may accrue from coquetting with France or Russia. . . . In little matters as in big, in great European and Asiatic questions as in subordinate Colonial ones, Germany and England should treat
each other in a frank and friendly spirit." The second Standard editorial,
of August 10, provided fresh fuel for controversy by speaking of English
"complaisance" toward German colonial enterprise, emphasizing the
value of "our good will" for Germany, and regretting that "the eccentric
course occasionally pursued by the Berlin Foreign Office has shown so
little regard for our convenience and susceptibilities, and has been attended with so little profit for the Fatherland." [10]

An examination of the German newspapers substantiates the statement
of William Maxwell, Berlin correspondent of the Standard, that "For
many years past no newspaper article has created so much excitement as
the recent leader welcoming the Emperor William on his present visit to
England." (Aug. 9.) Comment ranged all the way from the venomous
outpourings of the Hamburger Nachrichten to the regretful excuses of
the Kölnische Volkszeitung and the dignified reproaches of the semi-
official Norddeutsche. "Pedantic," "tactless," "clumsy," "politically
naïve," and "outside the bounds of good taste" were some of the milder
descriptive terms used. "Insolent," "rude," "injurious," "repulsive,"
"patronizing," "impertinent," and a "tactless provocation" were employed by more outspoken commentators. Others referred to the Stand-

---

[10] Deep resentment was also created by an editorial in the Liberal *Daily News*
(Aug. 7) attacking William II for a breach of English hospitality. The occasion for
this was the Kaiser's harangue of the personnel of the cruiser *Wörth*, lying then in
the Solent, on the anniversary of the famous battle of the Franco-Prussian War. It
was not the Conservative but the Liberal press that reprimanded the Emperor and
ostentatiously apologized to the French. Cf. Lee, *King Edward VII*, I, 671.

ard's articles as an expression of "arrogance and jealousy," and of "haughtiness and pedantry," that sprang from an "exaggerated consciousness of England's position in the world." One editor, disregarding the limits usually observed in international debate, labeled the articles "political-colonial expectorations." The saner critics objected to the Standard's articles because the personal rule of the Kaiser was emphasized to the exclusion of his responsible ministers and the German people; it was German and not English public opinion that William II had to take into account. Not a few made the point that the Emperor governed Germany as the grandson of William I, and not as the grandson of Queen Victoria. German colonies, moreover, were acquired not by English "permission" but in the face of active English ill will and no one could forget "the cheatings which Germany suffered at the hands of England during Count Caprivi's chancellorship." Furthermore, the Standard wanted Germany to go hand in hand with England, while England, without assuming any risks or obligations, continues to regard as entirely "subordinate" the colonial questions in which Germany is interested.[11]

Indicative of the attitude of the Wilhelmstrasse toward the witches' Sabbath of the political publicists was the reserve maintained by the Kölnische Zeitung and the Norddeutsche. On August 13, the former published a statement flatly denying that the Standard spoke for the British cabinet. While German editors, it continued, were quite within their rights in protesting at the "supercilious pedantries" (*hochnasigen Schulmeistereien*) of the Standard writer, the articles revealed nothing of the plans and the views of Lord Salisbury.[12] On the same day, the Norddeutsche broke its silence with regard to the heated press campaign. The cause of Anglo-German friendship, it said, had been badly served in attributing Germany's acquisition of colonies solely to British charitableness. The Norddeutsche also noted with approval the general press resentment of the Standard's "arrogant remarks about the highest representative of the German nation when he was a guest at the English court."[13]

These two articles were doubtless calculated to take the edge off the more violent criticisms by denying the official origin of the Standard articles. But they also recognized the justness of the widespread resentment at the tactless criticism of the Emperor and his policies. A violent

[11] The above summary is based on articles appearing in all sections of the German press from August 6 to September 6: *Hamburger Nachrichten, Hamburgischer Correspondent, Magdeburgische Ztg., Hannoverscher Kurier, National-Zeitung, Tägliche Rundschau, Berliner Tageblatt, Leipziger Tageblatt, Dresdner Journal, Deutsche Tagesztg., Reichsbote, Berliner Neueste Nachrichten, Freisinnige Ztg., Germania, Die Post, Münchner Allg. Ztg., Kreuzzeitung, Kölnische Volksztg.*
[12] *Kölnische Ztg.*, quoted in *Die Post*, No. 221, Aug. 14.
[13] *Norddeutsche* quoted in *Die Post*, No. 221, Aug. 14.

counterdemonstration might have resulted had the provocative utterances of the German editors been reported in detail in the English press. Correspondents and editors apparently regarded the dispute as peculiarly the Standard's affair and refrained from extensive direct quotation of the wilder manifestations of German editorial anger. The correspondent of the Morning Post, however, complained that the German press was unduly sensitive to unintentional slights and that this attitude hindered the calm and unbiased conduct of relations between the two countries. "In this respect," he continued, "the German press sins far more flagrantly than the English, and if anyone were malignant enough to wish to cast an apple of discord between the two countries, he would only need to send over a weekly budget of the vicious attacks on England and all things English which are constantly appearing in journals so prominent as the Post, Kreuzzeitung, Berliner Tageblatt, and even the more enlightened Cologne Gazette." (Aug. 13.) The Standard articles and the resultant polemics that continued unbroken throughout the autumn of 1895 contributed to the exaggerated suspicions which Marschall, Hohenlohe and the Kaiser entertained with regard to English policy. The baneful and paralyzing effect of these suspicions was clearly revealed in connection with the Turco-Armenian crisis that agitated the European chancelleries during the closing months of 1895.[14]

German co-operation with France and Russia in the Orient, the suspicious rejection of Salisbury's solution of the Near Eastern question, and the nagging, unfriendly criticism of British policy by the German press led up to the bitter clash over South Africa. Viewed with these related events in the immediate background the terrific explosion in the British press over the Kruger Telegram appears, not as an isolated event, but as a regular link in the chain of cause and effect.

Public attention was focused on the South African Republic by the discovery of the fabulous gold mines of the Witwatersrand where fortunes were made and lost overnight. Through the democratization of finance capitalism by the issue of stocks and debentures countless thousands of Europeans shared the excitement, the losses and gains, occasioned by the exploitation of the mines. The corner of the London exchange where the wild trading in South African gold mining shares took place was popularly known as the Kaffir Circus. The political destiny of the Transvaal was a matter of supreme public interest, and every move in the political game of Boer versus Briton was accorded a generous allotment of space in the daily press of two continents. As the Transvaal

[14] *G. P.,* X, 71, 81, 107, 121, 147, 153, 189, 209.

authorities became more and more suspicious of the motives of Cecil Rhodes and the Rand capitalists, the encouragement of German enterprise and capital as a make-weight against the British became a marked feature of President Kruger's policy. German money and engineering skill had contributed to the construction of the railroad from the Transvaal to Delagoa Bay, thus making the country independent of outlets through British territory. In the dynamite monopoly, the banks, and other public enterprises the Germans were accorded special consideration.[15]

Political relations between Berlin and Pretoria were sedulously cultivated by Boer and German authorities. British dissatisfaction at German meddling and intrigue grew apace. In January 1895, Cecil Rhodes, then in London, gave an interview to the correspondent of the Kreuzzeitung in which he made some uncomplimentary remarks about German colonial enterprise in South West Africa. Malet, the British ambassador in Berlin, characterized these aspersions as "intolerably galling." In referring to the Transvaal, Rhodes said that since the English were going there in great numbers the problem would soon be solved by absorption.[16] Within a week after Rhodes' flight into publicity Malet was taxing Marschall with encouraging Kruger's intransigence toward British authorities. The Transvaal was a "point noir" for England, he said. Marschall, with considerable asperity, challenged Malet to reconcile his government's alleged concern for the status quo with Rhodes' public proclamation of a policy of federation and absorption.[17] Later, in October, Malet referred again to Germany's encouragement of Kruger and warned Marschall that a continuation of the present policy might have serious consequences. The Emperor interpreted Malet's remark as a threat of war, "all on account of a few square miles full of negroes and palm trees. . . ." [18] Salisbury disavowed Malet and the incident was smoothed over; but the clash of opinion and policy over South Africa remained. It became, to use Garvin's apt phrase, "the nail working up in the shoe." [19]

Scarcely had ruffled tempers been stroked down when the searchlight of publicity was turned full upon South African affairs by the Jameson Raid. The history of that inglorious *Putsch* need not be retold here. Garvin in his biography of Joseph Chamberlain, and Lovell in his study

---

[15] R. I. Lovell, *The Struggle for South Africa, 1875–1899* (N. Y., 1934), pp. 342–47; R. W. Bixler, *Anglo-German Imperialism in South Africa, 1880–1900* (Ohio State University, 1932), pp. 57–71; Langer, *op. cit.,* I, 213–32.
[16] *Times,* Berlin dispatch, Jan. 28, 1895; *British Documents on the Origins of the War,* I, 326; Lovell, *op. cit.,* pp. 349–55.
[17] *G. P.,* XI, 3–5.
[18] *Ibid.,* XI, 5–10. Mem. by Marschall, Oct. 15; William II to Marschall, Oct. 25.
[19] J. L. Garvin, *The Life of Joseph Chamberlain* (3 vols., Lond., 1932–34), III, 64.

of clashing imperialisms in South Africa—both fresh and spirited accounts
—reveal how the conspiracy was matured by Rhodes, the premier of the
Cape Colony, and his associates; how the colonial office was prepared to
take advantage of the expected revolution promoted by the Reform Committee and Rhodes' agents in Johannesburg, and in pursuance of that
policy authorized the stationing of Jameson's forces on the Transvaal
frontier; how the revolution in Johannesburg fizzled out because of dissension among its promoters as to the flag they were to act under—the
Vierkleur or the Union Jack; how Jameson, unrestrained by Rhodes and
flagrantly disobeying official orders to withdraw, led his men toward
Johannesburg to "float the revolution" and fell an easy prey to Oom
Paul's commandos. The proposed action pattern was one frequently employed with great success by Anglo-Saxons in extending the boundaries
of empire. The defeat at Krugersdorp and the surrender at Doornkop
humiliated the British and freshened the painful memories of Majuba
Hill.

Of more immediate concern in this study than the ramifications of the
Rhodes conspiracy are the publicity manifestations in the press and their
influence on the relations between Berlin and London. Apprehension,
wounded pride, and resentment marred the holiday season for nationally
minded Englishmen; blow followed blow with the force and regularity of
a triphammer until finally William II's telegram of congratulation to
President Kruger produced an explosion of wrath and fury which, while
it worked itself out in the press largely through insults, abuse and strong
language, might easily have been turned in the direction of war. The
newspaper press, by articulating the resentment and the ill-feeling of its
constituency toward Germany, acted as a national safety valve and reduced the dangerous pressure for war-like action. Even a fight to the last
column of type has advantages over the grimmer reality of iron and steel.

Taut nerves and ruffled feelings already existed in Fleet Street and
Downing Street as a consequence of President Cleveland's Venezuelan
message, which had burst upon the ministry and the public with the force
of a bombshell just a week before Christmas. On Boxing Day reports of
the grave tension and impending revolution in Johannesburg monopolized
the news and editorial space in the London morning papers. From that
point events moved in double-quick time to a climax. On Tuesday, December 31, the papers carried the news both of Jameson's invasion of the
Transvaal and Chamberlain's repudiation of this "flagrant piece of filibustering." [20] On New Year's Day the Times published the "women and

[20] Garvin, *op. cit.*, III, 90.

children letter" supplied by Rhodes' agent Harris, who had thoughtfully furnished it with a falsified date (December 28). This letter, which Garvin calls a "moral forgery," turned Jameson from a freebooter into a mediaeval knight, who, in the best chivalric tradition was riding to rescue the helpless women and children of Johannesburg. The floodgates of Victorian sentimentalism were opened. The Times accompanied the letter with a florid editorial to the effect that even though Jameson had been repudiated by the colonial office and the high commissioner in South Africa, if it later appeared that British property and lives were threatened his act would meet with the approbation of the British people even though it may have been *"technically incorrect."* [21] On Friday morning, January 3, came the bitter dénouement—news of Jameson's surrender at Doornkop. The cup of bitterness and humiliation was near to overflowing. From this pit of black despair the nation was lifted the next day on a tidal wave of jingo patriotism engendered by the publication of the Kaiser's telegram to President Kruger. Venezuela, the Raid, and the Telegram— two insults and one national humiliation in a fortnight. Under these circumstances it is not surprising that British reserve was shattered. For a time it looked as though England might slip her cables and roll away on the deep ground swells of national feeling.

In Germany the news of Jameson's invasion of the Transvaal created quite as much excitement as it did in England. The government was urged by the leading journals to act quickly and forcefully on behalf of Boer independence. The security of their Boer kinsmen, the balance of power in South Africa, and German economic interests in the Transvaal were at stake. [22] Jameson's defeat and capture was hailed by German editors as though it were a victory for German arms. The London dispatches stating that Jameson had been disavowed by the British authorities were received with artless incredulity by a considerable section of the press. Editorial comment as well as the London telegrams hinted at a general conspiracy which the colonial office had been forced by circum-

---

[21] *Times,* Jan. 1, 1896.

[22] *Vossische Ztg.,* No. 1, Jan. 1; *National-Zeitung,* No. 1, Jan. 1; *Berliner N. N.,* No. 1, Jan. 1; *Kölnische Ztg.,* No. 4, Jan. 2; *Kreuzzeitung,* No. 2, Jan. 2; *Frankfurter Ztg.,* No. 2, Jan. 2. Dr. M. Grunwald, foreign editor of the moderate *Vossische Zeitung,* wrote: "It is the duty of the Imperial Government to take immediate and energetic measures for the protection, not only of German interests in the Transvaal but also of our Boer kinsmen. No protest against British aggression can be too sharp; and we hope that the secretary of state of the South African Republic, Dr. Leyds, who is at present in Berlin and who has made several visits to the foreign office, is in a position to wire his government in Pretoria the assurance that the independence of the Transvaal must remain unimpaired and that the German Empire is strong enough to extend its protection to the Boer states and not solely in a diplomatic way." (No. 1, Jan. 1.)

stances to disown. Suspicion could not be removed simply by telegraphing Jameson: "Turn back, my good fellow, we have been discovered." [23]

Lyrical acclaim greeted the Kaiser's telegram to President Kruger. Although it was a diplomatic impromptu imposed upon the Emperor as a substitute for measures of a more serious and provocative nature, the telegram was an official publicity act of the highest importance.[24] Dispatched to Pretoria at twenty minutes past eleven in the morning, following the conference at the chancellor's palace, the telegram was communicated immediately to Wolff and Reuter's for publication. Unaccompanied by comment, it was reproduced on the front page of the Norddeutsche the same afternoon. There is no point in quoting here the ecstatic comments of the German papers on January 4. An examination of the newspaper files for that date shows a rare unanimity of opinion among all parties and groups. Even the Social Democratic Vorwärts grudgingly admitted that "up to a certain point we agree with the Emperor in this question." No wonder Marschall noted in his diary: "Our press is first-rate, all parties united, and even Aunt Voss will fight." [25]

Throughout the crisis produced by the Raid and the Telegram the levers of diplomacy and publicity were in Marschall's hands. When he learned of the Raid shortly after noon, on December 31, he instructed Hatzfeldt to inquire in London if Jameson's action were approved by the British government. If it was, he should request his passports. At the same time Marschall warned Lascelles, Malet's successor at the British embassy, that annexation of the Transvaal would not be tolerated. The German consul at Pretoria was authorized to requisition fifty men from the *Seeadler,* then in Delagoa Bay, for the defense of the consulate and German property. A request for permission to send the detachment through Portuguese territory was made in Lisbon. Salisbury's complete disavowal of Jameson, with assurances that he desired the maintenance of the status quo, reached Marschall through both Hatzfeldt and Lascelles on January 1.[26] Shortly after receiving this assurance, Marschall, in

[23] *Kreuzzeitung,* No. 4, Jan. 3. Also *Kölnische Volksztg.,* Nos. 5, 7, Jan. 3, 4; *Berliner Tageblatt,* No. 3, Jan. 3; *Vossische Ztg.,* No. 4, Jan. 3; *Berliner N. N.,* No. 3, Jan. 3.

[24] On the genesis of the telegram and the question of intellectual and literary authorship see Friedrich Thimme, "Die Krugerdepesche," *Europäische Gespräche,* May–June, 1924, pp. 201–44. Langer evaluates the considerable literature pertaining to this question in *The Diplomacy of Imperialism,* I, 234–38. In literal translation the telegram read: "Berlin, January 3, 1896. I express to you my sincere congratulations that, without appealing for the help of friendly Powers, you with your people and with your own energy succeeded, against the armed bands which invaded your country as disturbers of the peace, in re-establishing the peace and protecting the independence of the country against attacks from without."

[25] From Marschall's unpublished diary, quoted by Thimme, *op. cit.,* p. 213.

[26] *G. P.,* XI, 16–25; Marschall's diary quoted by Thimme. The German public was

an interview with Herbette, the French ambassador, broached the subject of an understanding between the continental powers—i. e., to set limits to British expansion.[27] Lascalles had already been warned by the foreign secretary that England should not count too strongly on the antagonisms of the continental powers—under severe provocation they might come to an agreement at her cost and "cut straps from English leather." [28] On January 2 the outcome of Jameson's invasion was still uncertain. On the basis of reports from Pretoria, Marschall suspected that the English authorities, in the event of Jameson's success, were preparing to reap the fruits of his illegal action. He therefore instructed Hatzfeldt to deliver a formal note in London stating that Germany would not recognize any change in the legal status of the Transvaal that might result from Jameson's invasion or its consequences.[29]

While bombarding London with protests, Marschall employed every available agency of publicity to give emphasis and point to his diplomatic warnings. In a long conversation with Valentine Chirol, on January 2, he explained the German position and pointed out how British policy might force the continental powers into an alliance to defend their interests. His views were placed before the political public through Chirol's dispatch of January 2.[30] This dispatch began with a statement calling attention to German interests in the Transvaal. More important, however, was the sharp warning addressed to London:

But I am not speaking without authority when I state that as far as Germany is concerned the issue of this Question may determine her whole policy toward England, whether it shall continue to be, as during the last six years at least, one of friendship and good will, or whether it shall be one of calculated hostility. . . . British statesmanship has been for some time past suspected here of speculating for its own purposes upon the apparent division of Continental Europe into two irreconcilable camps, and of even encouraging that division in order to secure for itself greater liberty of action in other parts of the world. . . . But it is contended that the antagonism which undeniably exists between certain Continental Powers is, perhaps, not so profound or insurmountable as England believes, and she may some day be herself surprised to see how easily it might make room for a combination directed against herself.

informed of the official *démarche* in London by a Berlin telegram published in the *Kölnische Zeitung* (No. 2, Jan. 1). This was immediately communicated by Reuter's agent in Cologne to the London press.

[27] *G. P.,* XI, 69–71.

[28] Marschall's diary, quoted by Thimme, *op. cit.,* p. 210.

[29] *G. P.,* XI, 26–27. On the news of Jameson's surrender, Hatzfeldt recovered the note unopened from the British foreign office. Some writers have referred to this note as an "ultimatum." It was of course in no sense an ultimatum; it was a solemn protest and declaration of policy delivered in the most formal manner known in diplomatic practice.

[30] Marschall's diary, quoted by Thimme, *op. cit.,* p. 211; *Times,* Jan. 3.

England might be in a position to play a reckless game in South Africa, the dispatch concluded, but in North Africa her position was not so invulnerable; and the Egyptian question was not the only one which might be used to compose continental differences at England's expense. Indicating clearly the official source of his information, Chirol said: "I have felt it my duty to place these views on record."

According to Chirol, when the Telegram was communicated to the press, Marschall summoned him to the foreign office to inform him that the congratulatory message was not an isolated, impulsive act of the sovereign, but a state measure designed to teach the English a lesson.[31] Chirol's dispatch to the Times (Jan. 4) emphasized this point, and the information, which fixed the official character of the Telegram, materially heightened English resentment. At the ministerial council, on the afternoon of January 4, reports were brought to Marschall of the hostile reaction of the British press to the Telegram. He immediately summoned Justizrat Fischer, chief of the Berlin bureau of the Kölnische Zeitung, and dictated a statement for his paper. It appeared without a heading or a date line in the first morning edition of January 5 (No. 11). "The language employed by the English press with reference to the German Emperor's telegram to President Kruger does not frighten us," the article began. It declared the German press to be united behind the Emperor and his government, and that the Liberal press in England took a different line from the Times and the Standard. The union of all South Africa, the object of English policy, would entail grave disadvantages for Germany and other states whose subjects had financial interests in the Transvaal; these powers had a direct interest in seeing that the Boers had made their last trek. "It is not Germany's custom to interfere with the rights of others, but there is a unanimity of opinion in Germany that all arrogant claims injurious to her interests must be energetically withstood. It is to be hoped that the English press will not imagine that threats will exercise the slightest influence upon the attitude of the German Government."

The implication that the Transvaal was an independent state incurred the sharpest criticism in the English press. Marschall, therefore, concentrated on the legal angle of the case; he reverted to his earlier official rôle and became again the fiery public prosecutor intent on establishing a point of law. On January 5, according to his diary, he conferred with Fischer

---

[31] Valentine Chirol, *Fifty Years in a Changing World*, pp. 279–80. Marschall's diary records an interview with Chirol on Jan. 4, but not on Jan. 3. Chirol's memory may be at fault here. Certain it is that he talked to someone in authority on Jan. 3 for he reported the names of the officials present at the conference in the chancellor's palace where the telegram was drafted.

on the legal aspects of the Transvaal dispute.[32] The result was the article entitled "The Independence and Sovereignty of the Transvaal State," appearing in the Kölnische Zeitung on January 6 (No. 15). It was a closely reasoned brief showing that English suzerainty had been abrogated by the Convention of 1884. British rights, which it was alleged Germany had invaded, no longer existed. In support of his position Marschall quoted Lord Derby's letter of February 15, 1884, which interpreted the Convention in a manner indicating that the "suzerainty" reservation in the earlier convention (1881) had now been abandoned.[33] After this display of legal logic and documents Marschall called on the British press to cease its unfounded attacks on Germany. Protection of German interests through the maintenance of the status quo was the only motive behind German action; this did not require permission of the English press.[34]

Slight notice of Marschall's legal brief was taken in the English press; there was no abatement of the attacks. An entry in his diary on January 7 notes: "Hammered out an article this morning for the Kölnische Zeitung contra Times and Standard." The late evening edition carried the article in the form of a Berlin telegram. "The correctness of the German proverb, 'Blind zeal is only harmful,' is again confirmed by the attitude of the greater part of the British press," wrote Marschall. Then follows a brief restatement of the Wilhelmstrasse's position. "Germany," the telegram concluded, "will refrain from exceeding the limits of her rights and treaties. The insulting remarks of the English press engender in us no heat whatsoever. We are mindful of the saying, 'Abuse shows a bad cause.'"[35]

On January 8 Marschall's diary records the appearance of another insolent article in the Times. Still intent on pumping his views into the London press, he granted an interview to J. L. Bashford of the Daily Telegraph. In his dispatch, published in London on January 9, Bashford denied a score of rumors concerning the German government's contemplated dispatch of armed forces to Pretoria at the first news of Jameson's invasion. The source of these explanations was, of course, not mentioned, but their tenor clearly indicated that they originated in an authoritative quarter.[36]

---

[32] Thimme, *op. cit.,* p. 214.

[33] On this question see Lovell, *Struggle for South Africa,* pp. 43, 58–62.

[34] This article was reproduced in full on the front page of the *Norddeutsche* on the following day. (No. 10, Jan. 7.) According to the press methods of the Wilhelmstrasse, this stamped it with semi-official authority. In an interview with Lascelles and in a dispatch to Hatzfeldt (Jan. 6) the same arguments and the identical supporting documents were employed by Marschall. *G. P.,* XI, 39–41.

[35] *Kölnische Ztg.,* No. 19, Jan. 7.

[36] Bashford was indefatigable in presenting through his dispatches the official explanations of the Wilhelmstrasse. They had little effect on the editorial policy of

Another *"sehr törichten Artikel"* in the Times is noted by Marschall on January 9. After consulting Fischer about a reply, he authorized another disquisition on the suzerainty question for the Norddeutsche. Like the preceding article in the Kölnische Zeitung this was concerned with establishing legal justification for German intervention. To bolster the claim that suzerainty rights had been abolished in 1884, Marschall cited the international postal conference held at Vienna in 1891 at which the Transvaal had been represented on equal terms with Great Britain without protest from London.[37] This semi-official legal statement of the German position was reproduced next day in all the important German newspapers.

Marschall's publicity tactics had three objectives: First, to establish in the eyes of the German political public the legality of the government's action in the face of bitter English criticism, and to consolidate the credit which had accrued to the government for its vigorous defense of the national interest; second, to convince the English that in dispatching the Telegram and in preparing to land troops in case of revolutionary disturbances in the Transvaal the Emperor and his ministers were acting on well-defined treaty rights; third, to warn British authorities and political circles that a policy of force or coercion against the Transvaal would alienate Germany and encourage the formation of a continental league. Only in the first instance can it be said that Marschall's publicity policy was a success; in the press, and subsequently in the Reichstag, the Wilhelmstrasse reaped a rich harvest of praise and approval. In England, however, Marschall's attempts to influence press opinion by legal arguments, or by conjuring up the specter of a continental bloc, were fruitless.

Marschall's preoccupation with press matters is readily understandable when one contemplates the violent repercussions produced in England by the Kaiser's telegram. By this one stroke Jameson was established as a popular hero, William II as a popular villain. The Telegram was regarded as certain proof of a German conspiracy with the Boers to subvert England's position as "paramount Power" in South Africa. It was imperative, therefore, that German interference be rejected regardless of consequences. Opinions and attitudes were expressed in the news and editorial columns of the daily press, in letters from readers, in public speeches, in patriotic demonstrations at the theaters and music halls, in street demonstrations against Germans, and in appeals for a boycott of German goods.

---

the Daily Telegraph, being generally passed off with a remark such as "It is an ingenious explanation that our Berlin correspondent offers, but the facts seem to indicate the contrary. . . ."

[37] Marschall's diary, quoted by Thimme, *op. cit.*, p. 214; *Norddeutsche*, No. 14, Jan. 9.

The Times took special umbrage at the reference to Kruger's repelling the invasion "without the help of friendly Powers" and the "unqualified reference to the 'independence' of the Transvaal." Never, declared the Times, shall we "relinquish our historical claims at the bidding of the German Emperor; nor shall we fail to maintain them, if the necessity be forced upon us, by sacrifices similar to those upon which they are founded." Editorial tribute was paid to Dr. Jameson and "his gallant little band of adventurers" whose filibustering was hailed as a "revival of the daring Elizabethan spirit." The public was informed that "as surely as South Africa is destined to be settled and developed by white men, so surely will that enterprise be controlled by the British race and no other." [38] The leader writer on the Morning Post recommended the recall of the Mediterranean fleet and its junction with the Channel fleet as the proper answer to the Emperor's telegram, which he characterized as a "piece of gratuitous mischief." [39] The Daily Telegraph printed its South African dispatches under the heading, "German Intrigues Against England." In the editorial columns ecstatic references to the "Star of Patriotism" alternated with abuse of William II, who was denounced, particularly, for taking advantage of England's embarrassment to force colonial concessions. "He will not win by these unfriendly tactics one inch of the lands, one wave of the waters for the possession of which he has descended to methods incompatible with his station and his British breeding." [40] The Standard, which showed fight from the beginning, denounced the Telegram as "a strikingly unfriendly act"; the Transvaal was under the protection of the Queen and no country had the shadow of a right to intervene. "Honour still comes first in the calculations of Englishmen, and those critics are greatly deceiving themselves who imagine that the 'nation of shopkeepers' is not also in the hour of need a nation of combatants. . . . They are simply insane who fancy that it is a light thing to rouse the fighting instincts and to challenge the immense resources of the British Empire." [41] In the flippant tone that pleased its sophisticated clientele the Pall Mall Gazette referred to the Telegram as "very sad and very dreadful." It contained, however, the editor noted, "three contributions to the better ordering of the world, to wit: (a) the Transvaal is an independent Power; (b) Germany is its ally; (c) if President Kruger had asked for help against Dr. Jameson, he,

---

[38] Jan. 4, 5, 6, 9. The *Times* was in a special sense the spokesman of Rhodes and the Chartered Company. The connecting link was Miss Flora Shaw—later Lady Lugard —a member of the *Times* staff in London, who possessed the Chartered Company's secret cipher for direct communication with Rhodes in Capetown. Lovell, *op. cit.*, p. 15; Bixler, *op. cit.*, p. 79; Garvin, *op. cit.*, III, 70, 82.
[39] *Morning Post,* Jan. 4, 8.
[40] Jan. 4, 6, 7.
[41] Jan. 4, 6.

William, would have saddled up and proceeded southward." In conclusion the editor stated: "It does not hurt us, and the Kaiser has to be amused. If it should ever pass out of the sphere of Imperial frivolity we hope Count Hatzfeldt will let us know." [42]

Leading Liberal journalists in London, while less exalted in expressing their patriotic indignation, were in hearty accord with their Conservative colleagues on the question of England's suzerainty rights and the necessity for maintaining them. While stating this unequivocally in the Westminster Gazette, E. T. Cook at the same time denounced as "enemies of their country and of their kind" those jingoes "who lightly talk of war and needlessly inflame popular passion." [43] W. T. Stead, friend and admirer of Rhodes and Jameson, contributed to the Westminster Gazette (Jan. 6) a puckish article entitled "Dr. Jim of Berlin," in which he drew a striking parallel between the Emperor and Dr. Jameson. Both erred through the same besetting sin—reckless haste. "The excellent Kaiser has been displaying in a more exalted station the very same qualities which have landed our Doctor Jim in Pretoria Gaol," he wrote. "Hence amid the confused and clashing factions who shout this morning for the Kaiser and against Dr. Jameson, or for Dr. Jameson against the Kaiser, I find myself able to shout as lustily as any for both the distinguished representatives of lawless enterprise and magnificent indiscretion." [44] The Daily News carried water on both shoulders. It denounced Jameson, Rhodes, and the Chartered Company, but styled the Emperor's telegram "ill-timed and imprudent." British rights under the Convention of 1884 must be maintained, the editor declared, although he did not define those rights or state how they had been violated. ". . . we cannot set aside a treaty at the bidding of any personage, however exalted." And finally: "The conduct of the Government in this matter is not open to the censure of any foreign Power." [45]

Provincial editors did not enter wholeheartedly into this rivalry of railing. The Liberal Manchester Guardian refrained from disparaging remarks about the Emperor and German policy, but it too insisted that

[42] Jan. 4. Four days later (Jan. 8) the editor had come to the conclusion that the act was not one of those "spontaneous exhibitions of eccentricity" but the climax of "a deliberate and carefully considered policy . . . to strike a blow at British influence. . . ."

[43] Jan. 4, 6, 8. J. A. Spender had already been appointed editor of the Westminster, but Cook remained in charge until January 30, when he took over the editorship of the Daily News. Spender did not share Cook's tender regard for the "South African heroes," Rhodes and Jameson. Spender, Life, Journalism and Politics, I, 79–80.

[44] Stead, whose life was a series of crusades utterly lacking in consistency, rivaled the wildest jingoes during the Telegram crisis. Later, during the Boer War, he was the mainspring of the pro-Boer agitation. See Frederic Whyte, Life of W. T. Stead, II, 88–100.

[45] Jan. 6, 7.

British rights be upheld.[46] While Chamberlain was commended for his prompt and vigorous action, the Times and other imperialist organs were blamed for German and continental hostility—they had counseled in the beginning a policy of "wait to see whether the offence brought us a hand-some addition to our African estates." [47] To the Unionist Glasgow Herald William II was the "Jameson of diplomacy"; after the first outburst of resentment it took a cooler view of the matter and called upon the balanced judgment of the provinces to counteract London jingoism. There was no excuse, it said, for the feeling expressed that: "England must thrash somebody!" [48] Likewise the Scotsman contented itself with a very mild reproof, but each day the London wire brought from the capital a budget of editorial opinion of the most inflammatory kind.[49] The Unionist Birmingham Post, owned by the Feeny family, and associated with the political fortunes of Joseph Chamberlain, saw in the Telegram an indication of a desire to profit from the difficulties created by Cleveland's Venezuelan note and the crisis in South Africa. The editor pontificated: "We are not to be bullied, and those who are reckoning on playing that game had better lay their account with an assurance that, for the sake of keeping a nominal friendship, or maintaining a hollow peace, we shall not be driven to degrade our position, or to abandon our rights." (Jan. 6.) While editorial opinion in the provincial papers was, in the main, less censorious than that of the London press, the belligerent sentiment of the capital found expression in the daily reports of "Our London Correspondent." London editors, cheered on by the armchair and pavement patriots, took the bit in their teeth and ran away with national sentiment.

In the choice of words, certain restraints were imposed upon editorial writers which did not apply to letters from subscribers. Here feelings and convictions were expressed in language direct and sometimes picturesque. The Times and the Morning Post were favored by the choleric old gentlemen of the Carlton, Athenaeum, and St. James's clubs, who signed their letters "Ignotus," "Briton," "Japhet," "Staunch Conservative," "Octogenarian," and "Ubique," etc. "True Briton" demanded that the Emperor's name be removed from the Army and Navy lists; another demanded that parliament be summoned immediately to vote fifty million pounds for the perfection of English defenses; while another declared that "we do not want him [William II] to come over here next summer masquerading in a British uniform." "A Peace-Loving Physician" wrote to the Times begging the editor to stand to his guns and calling upon the

---

[46] Jan. 6. British editors did not bother to define or state those rights.
[47] Manchester Guardian, Jan. 7.
[48] Jan. 4, 9, 13.
[49] Jan. 4, 7, 8, 9.

country to "fight to her last shilling and her last man." A correspondent wrote to the Standard that the Germans would endeavor to form a continental coalition against England. "We can at pleasure trump their trick (a dirty one at best) by making friendly concessions to France in Egypt, and leaving Russia a free hand in Turkey, in return for their co-operation against Germany." "Better an open enemy than a treacherous friend," wrote "W. P. H.," while "Commander, R. N." wrote that the behavior of the German nation at the present crisis is a disgrace to any educated, civilised, and reflecting people. . . ." "Vindex" called on the government to exact an apology, "failing this, we should withdraw our Minister and, if necessary, declare war." Incendiary communications continued to appear in the letter columns of the Conservative press long after the actual diplomatic crisis was past.[50] All were expressive of the spirit "We don't care a damn how many of you there are. . . ."

Reports from public meetings held during these days reveal sentiments no less bellicose than those expressed in the flood of letters from patriotic readers to patriotic editors. At a public dinner held at Chard, Somersetshire, the mayor asked the assembly to drink to the health of the royal family "except one grandson of the Queen." "This was received with the utmost enthusiasm, the name of the German Emperor being met with groans and hisses, and the National Anthem sung with much fervour." [51] Brigadier-General Bulwer promised an audience at Dereham that if the Emperor landed some marines "from a few trumpery ships in Delagoa Bay," they would soon be made prisoners. "It was not the first time England had fought the whole world and blockaded every harbour on the Continent, and England was prepared, if necessary, to do it again." [52] Sir William Grantham, distributing medals to a company of Volunteers, said that the German Emperor "had taught English people to know how strong they were at home. . . . He had shown England his true colors and it had put England on her guard." [53] Prolonged cheering greeted Mr. Balfour's unequivocal declaration at Manchester: "We control the external relations of the Transvaal, and we will admit no foreign interference." [54] Vehement hissing greeted every mention of William II's name at public meetings.

In the press and on the stump those to whom the editors always referred as "thinking people" gave oral expression to their emotional atti-

[50] The examples above are selected from the *Times*, Jan. 6, 7, 8, 9, 11, 14; *Standard*, Jan. 7, 8; *Morning Post*, Jan. 7, 8, 15; *Glasgow Herald*, Jan. 5, 13.
[51] *Glasgow Herald*, Jan. 8.
[52] *Daily News*, Jan. 9.
[53] *Daily News*, Jan. 11.
[54] *Standard*, Jan. 16.

tudes. In the absence of a cheap popular press—it was still in the womb—
the lower classes demonstrated in the music halls and theaters. Topical
verses containing offensive references to the German Emperor and his
people evoked roars of approval from the pit and the gallery: Cecil Rhodes
and Dr. Jim were cheered by a million cab drivers.[55]

These last demonstrations, before the popular press displaced the music
hall and the ballad as important agencies stimulating and expressing the
robust sentiments of the lower classes, deserve to be recorded. At the
Prince of Wales Theater Miss Addie Conyers sang "a political and topical
song" entitled "Something to Play With." "In this had been interpolated
some stirring verses upon current events, the latest being some trenchant
lines upon the recent action of the German Emperor in connection with
Transvaal affairs. Upon Miss Conyers singing this with stimulating verve
and patriotic spirit, the audience was moved to an extraordinary demonstration of national enthusiasm, and applauded song, sentiment, and singer
with tremendous vigour." [56] At Daly's Theater Mr. Hayden Coffin sang
a song before enthusiastic audiences entitled "Hands Off!" Included
were several direct references to William II, one verse starting, "Let
Pinchbeck Caesar strut and crow." Before the Lord Chamberlain intervened to secure a revision of certain lines the chorus ran as follows:

> Hands off, Germany! Hands off, all!
>   Kruger boasts and Kaiser brags; Britons hear the call!
> Back to back the world around, answer with a will—
>   England for her own, boys! It's Rule Britannia still! [57]

A writer on the Westminster Gazette (Jan. 13) was unkind enough to
remark that "The poem itself is not very much worse than the contribution of the new Poet Laureate to the Times."

This shot was aimed at Alfred Austin and his poem entitled "Jameson's
Ride," which was published in the Times on January 11 and recited by
Mr. E. H. Vanderfeldt—note the name—at the Alhambra on January 13.
A reporter for the Standard, on January 14, describes the performance:

When the curtain rose it disclosed a rugged African bush scene, with a large
piece of rock as a centre piece. Standing beside this was Mr. Vanderfeldt,
dressed in the costume of Jameson's men—a brown shooting jacket, buff jack
boots, and a sombrero hat, while in his hand was a rifle. The cartridge belt
was empty. Tremendous cheering greeted the rising of the curtain, and it was

[55] When Jameson, under arrest, landed in England, February 22, 1896, the *Evening
News* published a three column picture of Dr. Jim with the caption: "God bless you,
Doctor Jameson, here's your country's love to you." (Kennedy Jones, *Fleet Street
and Downing Street*, p. 144.) At this time, Jones and Harmsworth were experimenting in the *Evening News* preparatory to launching the *Daily Mail*.
[56] London correspondent of the *Liverpool Post*, Jan. 9.
[57] *Standard*, Jan. 14.

not for several minutes that it subsided. Standing with his shoulders well back, his right hand grasping the muzzle of his gun, Mr. Vanderfeldt commenced. In the first line, which begins with the words—"Wrong! Is it wrong?", a man in the gallery shouted "No!" several times. As the concluding words [of the poem] were said, a remarkable scene ensued. Cheer after cheer rose from all parts of the house, and an occupant of one of the front boxes shouted out "Three cheers for Dr. Jameson and his men." A great burst of cheering followed. . . . At length the band played the National Anthem, and the whole audience rose and again cheered.

The first three and concluding stanzas of this poem which so moved music hall patrons ran as follows:

> Wrong! Is it wrong? Well, may be:
>   But I'm going boys, all the same.
> Do they think me a Burgher's baby,
>   To be scared by a scolding name?
> They may argue, and prate, and order;
>   Go, tell them to save their breath:
> Then, over the Transvaal border,
>   And gallop for life or death.
>
> Let lawyers and statesmen addle
>   Their pates over points of law:
> If sound be our sword, and saddle,
>   And gun-gear, who cares one straw?
> When men of our own blood pray us
>   To ride to their kinsfolk's aid,
> Not heaven itself shall stay us
>   From the rescue they call a raid.
>
> There are girls in the gold-reef city,
>   There are mothers and children too!
> And they cry, "Hurry up! for pity!"
>   So what can a brave man do?
> If even we win, they'll blame us:
>   If we fail they will howl and hiss.
> But there's many a man lives famous
>   For daring a wrong like this!
>
> I suppose we were wrong, were madmen,
>   Still I think at the Judgment Day,
> When God sifts the good from the bad men,
>   There'll be something more to say.
> We were wrong, but we aren't half sorry,
>   And, as one of the baffled band,
> I would rather have had that foray
>   Than the crushings of all the Rand.

Austin's "vigorous tribal lay" and the Alhambra demonstrations, which it evoked, were regarded by many as incompatible with the dignity of a poet laureate. The Daily News, in a blistering editorial on "The Laureate of the Music Halls," ridiculed Austin's poem and recommended withdrawal of "his annual allowance of victuals, which may be described as the board wages of his Muse." [58] Uncomplimentary references came from the highest quarters. The Queen and the Prince of Wales regarded it as a regrettable blunder, while Lord Salisbury, who had secured Austin's appointment to the laureateship only a week before, was unquestionably greatly embarrassed. He wrote to Victoria: "It is a pity that this effusion was his first performance. Unluckily, it is to the taste of the galleries in the lower class of theatres, and they sing it with vehemence." [59] Salisbury was sincere in his disapproval; as a statesman of the old school the irruption of the chauvinistic masses into the field of foreign policy was certain to disturb him.

British ill-feeling was not exhausted by press polemics and music hall sentiments. In East London there were street demonstrations against German residents. Brawls between German and English sailors were reported from the London docks. German shops and clubs were closed for a time. German members of the Baltic Exchange were hissed by their English associates. According to reports there were numerous dismissals of German assistants by London firms; appeals to boycott goods from the "Fatherland" appeared in the English press. The genuine concern of the Norddeutsche's London correspondent was voiced in a letter, dated January 9: "People in Germany should not deceive themselves. There prevails at present in England an irritation toward everything German such as never before existed. It has seized all parties and all classes of the population." Queen Victoria commanded Lord Salisbury to "urge the police to watch and prevent ill-usage of innocent and good German residents." [60]

Another significant aspect of the public alarm and clamor was the accusation in the English press that German policy aimed at the eventual destruction of Great Britain as a world power. This bald assertion, which later became an article of faith with the Germanophobe school of publicists

---

[58] Jan. 13. Less topical but more exalted was Austin's second performance, published in the *Times*, February 6, entitled, "Who Would Not Die for England?"

[59] Salisbury to Queen Victoria, Jan. 16, 1896; *Letters of Queen Victoria, 1886–1901* (3rd ser., 3 vols., Lond., 1930–32), III, 24. Also Lee, *King Edward VII*, I, 718.

[60] *Ibid.*, III, 13. The demonstrations, brawls and boycott appeals were reported in Press Association dispatches in the *Scotsman*, Jan. 8, 14, and other papers; *Daily News*, Jan. 11; *Berliner Tageblatt*, No. 11, Jan. 7; *Kölnische Ztg.*, No. 20, Jan. 9; *Vossische Ztg.*, No. 16, Jan. 10; *Norddeutsche*, No. 17, Jan. 11.

and diplomats, was based upon the following unfounded assumptions:
Germany intended to annex Holland; using Holland as a base the general
staff planned to invade and conquer England; German historians and
history books preached hatred of Great Britain and the destruction of her
Empire as a patriotic duty.[61] In time this became a fixed publicity stereotype in political journalism.

Both Queen Victoria and the German ambassador, Count Hatzfeldt,
urged Salisbury to use his influence with the journalists to mitigate the
violence of the press campaign. There is no evidence of the prime minister's exertions, although he had readily agreed to do what he could.[62]
In fact, it was Chamberlain and not Salisbury who influenced the press
during the crisis. To journalists, the colonial secretary was the most
accessible of all public men of his day. He broke all precedents in official
dealings with the press when he opened wide the doors of the colonial
office, provided the reporters with rooms in which they might wait and
work, and supplied them with information through his departmental
heads and his private secretaries.[63] It was also Chamberlain who suggested that a public gesture of defiance be made in reply to the German
publicity measures. On January 4 he wrote to Salisbury that the injured
vanity of the nation required an "Act of Vigour" which should take the
form of a defiance of some one of England's several foes. He suggested
four possibilities: (1) A threatening dispatch to Germany, to be given
to the press immediately; (2) a pretentious commissioning of ships of
war and preparation of troops for dispatch to South Africa; (3) an ostentatious offer of funds to the colonies for the extension of their naval
and military defenses; (4) an immediate agreement with the United
States in the matter of the Venezuelan boundary.[64] The second suggestion—commissioning of a special squadron—had been contemplated at
the admiralty as a result of Cleveland's Venezuelan manifesto. Suggested
by Goschen, first lord of the admiralty, to Lord Salisbury as a general
precautionary measure on December 31, the government acted quickly
in the new situation created by the Kaiser's telegram. Communications

[61] "Occasional Correspondent," *Times,* Jan. 7, 9; letter from Major General Alexander Elliott, *Times,* Jan. 9; "An Indian Magistrate," *Daily News,* Jan. 10; "Well-
wisher to Old England," *Daily News,* Jan. 16; interview with F. S. Stevenson, M. P.,
Standard, Jan. 9.

[62] *Letters of Queen Victoria,* III, 13; *G. P.,* XI, 53–56.

[63] Jones, *Fleet Street and Downing Street,* pp. 94–95. The colonial office's South
African dispatches, with the official replies, were given immediately to the press for
publication. The colonial secretary's courtesies to the press were acknowledged publicly by the president of the Institute of Journalists. *Daily News,* Jan. 13, 1896. Cable
communications were interrupted for a time, immediately following the Raid. When
resumed, official dispatches were of course given preference over press cables. Some
of the *Times'* cables from South Africa were delayed four or five days.

[64] Garvin, *op. cit.,* III, 95-96.

between Goschen, Chamberlain, and Lord Salisbury resulted in an administrative order for the formation of the celebrated "flying Squadron." [65] For Chamberlain the chief value of this action lay in its publicity effect. It therefore seems altogether likely that the government's intentions were communicated to the press on the initiative of the colonial secretary.

While Chamberlain was pressing for an "Act of Vigour," which was bound to excite passions still further, the Queen was distressed at the tone of the press and the danger of war. By a curious slip of the pen she urged Salisbury "to pour oil on the flames." But her intent was clarified in the next sentence. "Could you not hint to our respectable papers not to write violent articles to excite the people?" she wrote to Lord Salisbury. "These newspaper wars often tend to provoke war, which would be too awful." The prime minister could give her little comfort beyond assuring her that he had "strongly discouraged" violent language and precipitant action. He confirmed the Queen's anxiety over the press war when he wrote: "The more irresponsible newspapers in both countries do infinite harm." [66]

The dramatic qualities of the government's action deeply impressed the journalists: a simple administrative order creates a special fighting squadron while Lord Salisbury attends a country ball! For a week (January 8–15) English editors indulged in an orgy of speculation, publishing interviews with retired admirals, reports from the dockyards, cheers for the government, and manifestoes directed at Germany. News editors dipped into their heavier type to announce the military preparations: "The Anglo-German Crisis—Government's Precautionary Measures—British Flying Squadron Commissioned—Activity at the Dockyards—War-like Preparations—Britain Answers the Kaiser." The ultimate destination of the special squadron was a subject of the wildest speculation. In the press it was sent successively to Delagoa Bay, the North Sea, the Baltic, the Mediterranean, the Dardanelles, and Bermuda. Some journals required as many as eight solid Victorian columns to chronicle these war-like preparations for the preservation of peace.[67]

[65] A. D. Elliott, *Life of George J. Goschen* (2 vols., Lond., 1911), II, 204–5; *Letters of Queen Victoria*, III, 16–17. Goschen's account does not agree with Salisbury's explanation to the Queen, who learned of this important step from the newspapers. On January 8, Salisbury wrote to Victoria: "I was as much surprised as Your Majesty to see in *The Times* the account of the intention to send a flying squadron and troops to the Cape. I first heard the project yesterday, but I did not understand it to be mature. Your Majesty certainly ought to have been consulted before the newspapers were allowed to know what was proposed. But their emissaries swarm all over the public offices, and it is very difficult to keep things from them." *Ibid.*, III, 12–13. The *Times* announced this measure on its own responsibility (Jan. 8) and a few hours later it was officially confirmed and details as to ships, etc., given.
[66] *Letters of Queen Victoria*, III, 13–14.
[67] These statements are based on an examination of the following papers from

Editorial comment was pitched in the same shrill key. The chief leader writer on the Morning Post, presumably Spenser Wilkinson, wrote: "The Government has acted in the sense of the nation, and by putting into commission an additional squadron has shown the world that for England's honour England, the peace-loving commercial England of today, will fight. . . . Since the announcement that the Government has taken the sole course that could satisfy the national feeling and has begun to arm, every Englishman and every English woman breathes freely. We are ourselves again." [68] From Edinburgh came the voice of the Scotsman: "Let our Presbyteries pray for peace with all their might, and let all the people say amen; but the Queen's Ministers must see that the army and navy are ready for war." (Jan. 10.) The leader writer on the Daily Telegraph thanked William II for having evoked in England "such a manifestation of united and unshrinking patriotism as has perhaps never before been witnessed." (Jan. 9.) On January 14, the Standard, noting that the crisis was less acute, pointed the moral for all who might read: "The strong man armed will now, it may be hoped, keep his goods in peace. . . . We cannot help ascribing the disappearance of danger in large part to the prompt demonstration that we were capable of defending ourselves."

Only the Westminster Gazette and the Manchester Guardian disturbed the harmony of the patriotic chorus. However, neither Cook nor Scott disapproved of the government's military measures. In fact on January 7, before the government's intentions were communicated to the press, the following significant statement appeared in the Westminster's "Notes of the Day": "But if . . . the Government should tell us that, in view of the present foreign situation, it is desirable to strengthen the Navy that we may be in a position to meet any fortuitous concourse or possible combination of hostile forces against us, no one on the Liberal side, we feel sure, will desire to limit their discretion." The attitude of the leading Liberal organs was summed up in the moderate counsel delivered by the Westminster Gazette: "Let us do all that is necessary quietly and unostentatiously to prepare for all emergencies; but do not let us rave or bluster, lest we increase the tension which we desire to relax." (Jan. 8.) [69]

Occupying a central place in English estimations of the seriousness of the crisis was the widespread conviction that an official German plot for military intervention in the Transvaal had been uncovered. The 'plot' theory was based in the main upon reports appearing in the Times from Berlin and Capetown. As early as January 4 it was stated in the English

Jan. 8 to 14: *Times, Standard, Daily Telegraph, Morning Post, Pall Mall Gazette, Birmingham Daily Post, Scotsman, Liverpool Daily Post, Glasgow Herald.*
[68] *Morning Post,* Jan. 9.
[69] Similarly the *Manchester Guardian,* Jan. 9, 10.

press that marines had been landed from a German war vessel in Delagoa Bay. A telegram from Berlin to the Kölnische Zeitung, reproduced in special type used for semi-official communications, flatly contradicted the report; such a step had been contemplated for the defense of the consulate, but was abandoned because Jameson's defeat and the collapse of the revolution in Johannesburg had made it unnecessary.[70] In one of his inspired articles in the Kölnische Zeitung, Marschall cited this contemplated measure as proof of the government's determination to protect German interests. The government's intention, he continued, "will not fail to call forth throughout the Empire and among all patriotic Germans on the face of the earth feelings of legitimate pride such as those which responded in former days to the lightning flashes from beneath the bushy eyebrows of the first German Chancellor." [71] Naturally, this effusion was quoted by Chirol in his report to the Times (Jan. 6). Further, the Capetown correspondent reported, on January 7, that the Transvaal's European diplomatic representative, Dr. Leyds, was in Berlin to arrange for the settlement of five thousand German military colonists in the Transvaal. E. Ashmead-Bartlett, a leading Conservative jingo, declared in a letter to the Times (January 9) that "Dr. Leyds . . . has been a month at Berlin with his pocket full of secret service money, working the German Press and seeking for a German protectorate." An official denial that Leyds was enlisting military colonists was published in the Kölnische Zeitung.[72] But the editors of the Times continued to prattle about "long matured plans" and "antecedent and elaborate preparations to interfere in the Transvaal." [73] Cecil Spring Rice, secretary of the embassy in Berlin, writing to Villiers, assistant under-secretary in the foreign office, said: "I don't think it is possible to deny that a plot of some sort existed." [74] Every wild rumor indicating that the German government had planned a military coup in South Africa was seized upon and exaggerated in the English press, until finally it became an accepted proposition that the Germans had engineered a vast conspiracy against Britain's position in South Africa.[75]

[70] No. 9, Jan. 4. To the German request for permission to land and transport a detachment of fifty men for guard duty at the Pretoria consulate, the Portuguese government at first gave an evasive answer. The desired permission was subsequently promised should further disturbances occur. G. P., XI, 19–20.
[71] No. 11, Jan. 5.
[72] No. 19, Jan. 7 (Berlin telegram).
[73] Times, Jan. 13.
[74] Gwynn, Letters and Friendships of Cecil Spring Rice, I, 189–90.
[75] This was the theme of numerous periodical articles. Typical is one by W. T. Stead in the Review of Reviews, February 1896: There were two plots against the Transvaal—one German and one organized by Rhodes. ". . . by his British plot against the German plot he [Rhodes] was able to checkmate the German conspiracy. He fought fire with fire."

Official and semi-official German denials, while reported by the Berlin correspondents, were lost in a flood of recrimination and abuse. When noticed they were made the butt of malicious editorial comment. "Those famous marines from the *Seeadler*," wrote the Times' editor, "were at first the symbol of Germany's unalterable resolution to assert at least equal rights in the Transvaal, then they were reduced to the humble rôle of simple policemen, while now, as our Berlin correspondent remarks, they are represented merely as a few honest fellows seeking to relieve the monotony of shipboard by a harmless picnic." (Jan. 10.) In the eyes of British imperialists, the discovery of this German conspiracy completely overshadowed Jameson's "boyish exploit" and justified the government's menacing tabulation of guns and ships.

War was so strenuously written up on both sides of the Channel that an armed clash seemed inevitable. "What beasts newspapers are," was Spring Rice's comment. He wished that "a few newspaper editors could be hanged." [76] Such a crisis, however, could not be prolonged indefinitely. The first break came with the reception in Berlin of reports of British military preparations. The London telegrams announcing the formation of the special service squadron worked on the German editors like "a jet of cold water," according to the correspondent of the Morning Post. (Jan. 10.) Whether it was the news of English military measures that worked the change in the German press, or whether it was, as the Daily News correspondent asserted, the injunction delivered by the foreign office to the press not to aggravate the situation further, cannot be determined. There was, however, a notable abatement in the acrimonious language employed toward England. British military preparations were greeted with comparative calm and German editors seemed singularly indifferent to the purpose and possible destination of the flying squadron.[77] In the offices of the Kreuzzeitung, the National-Zeitung, and Berliner Neueste Nachrichten the Hotspurs abruptly lowered their voices, and from the press disappeared all references to intervention in South Africa either singly, by concert or by conference. The editor of the Standard claimed a victory for the English press. "If the Germans have a foible," he explained, "it is to raise their voices in argument beyond the pitch of good manners, and not to lower their tone until over-shouted." (Jan. 9.) Thus by over-shouting in a time of serious international tension did the

[76] Gwynn, *op. cit.*, I, 187–88.

[77] Berlin dispatches, *Daily News,* Jan. 9; *Standard,* Jan. 9; *Morning Post,* Jan. 9, 10; *Times,* Jan. 10. The *Daily News* correspondent reported further : "On good authority [Marschall or Hammann?] I am able to state that the Government here is determined not to let itself be carried away in taking over-hasty steps, either by the vehement and even threatening language of some of your contemporaries, or by the militant measures announced."

press perform what Victorian after-dinner speakers called its "beneficent mission."

A return to moderation on the part of the German journalists was followed within a few days by a relaxation of the tension in England. This was doubtless the result of a calculated indiscretion on the part of some high German official. Queen Victoria, in a letter to her impulsive grandson, had mildly protested at his telegram to President Kruger and the implication of unfriendliness which it bore. On January 8, William II answered his "Most beloved Grandmama" in a long letter in which he vehemently disclaimed the unfriendly motives attributed to him in England. It was as a champion of law and order and as a defender of the Queen's authority—so sorely flouted by Jameson and his men—that he had given public expression to his feelings. As usual he had been misunderstood and misrepresented. All the blame was laid on the English press.[78]

J. L. Bashford, Berlin correspondent of the Daily Telegraph, learned of the exchange of letters and reported it to his paper. Confirmed by William Maxwell, the correspondent of the Standard, and an unnamed person close to the Queen's court, the report was dressed up to make it appear that the Emperor had tendered an official apology and explanation. A picture of William II eating humble pie at the bidding of his grandmother was presented by some of the jingo papers and, though largely an invention, it was a soothing plaster for lacerated feelings.[79] These exaggerations provoked heated rejoinders in Germany, the Kölnische Zeitung declaring that the German Emperor had not the slightest reason to explain or justify his actions, least of all to the English. An official note in the Norddeutsche emphatically denied that excuses or explanations had reached London from any authoritative quarter in Berlin.[80] From this point on the press war tailed off into individual feuds. The editors of the Hamburger Nachrichten, for example, engaged the editors of the Standard; while the Times and the Kölnische Zeitung indulged in an endless exchange of sour jibes. One article in particular, entitled "Peace Without Honor" (*Friede mit Schande*), appearing in the Kölnische Zeitung, enraged Chirol who asked the foreign office press bureau to reconcile this article in a paper used for semi-official communications

---

[78] The complete text of the letter is given by Thimme in *Europäische Gespräche*, January–June, 1924, pp. 243–44; excerpts in Lee, *King Edward VII*, I, 726–27. For the Kaiser's explanation to a private friend in England see Charles à Court Repington, *Vestigia* (Boston, 1919), pp. 191–92.

[79] *Daily Telegraph*, Jan. 11; *Morning Post*, Jan. 14; *Scotsman*, Jan. 13; *Birmingham Daily Post*, Jan. 14, 15; *Standard*, Jan. 11, 14, 15.

[80] *Kölnische Ztg.*, No. 36, Jan. 13; *Norddeutsche*, No. 23, Jan. 14. Accompanied by sharp condemnation of this latest example of English perfidy, the *Norddeutsche's* statement was reproduced next day in all important German journals.

with the assurance that the German government wanted an amicable settlement of the affair.[81]

With the publication of the White Book on South African affairs and the full dress Reichstag debate on German policy on February 13, all the cobs and tailings of the controversy were again augered through the press machine; but the second threshing yielded only a few shriveled kernels, while an adverse wind enveloped machine and operators in a blinding, irritating cloud of chaff and dust. Marschall's spirited defense and explanation in the Reichstag met with unreserved approval in all sections of the German press.[82] His general thesis was that on the basis of existing laws and treaties Germany had acted to defend her economic interests; her policy from beginning to end had aimed at the preservation of the status quo in South Africa. The documents published in the White Book, on February 12, were carefully selected and edited to conform to this general thesis. At Hatzfeldt's insistence all references to the suzerainty question were excluded as was all other matter that might provide fresh fuel for press polemics.[83] The speech and the supporting documents were thus harmonized to produce the desired publicity effect both at home and abroad. English editors were openly skeptical, and justly so, of the truth of Marschall's assertions. His legal position they interpreted as a claim to a right of veto upon any change in the political position of the Transvaal or any move toward an economic union of the South African states. Without mincing words they affirmed England's intention to deal with the situation according to her own will, at her own time, and without reference to foreign opinion.

Throughout the spring and summer the unrestrained exchange of ignoble taunts and poisonous calumnies continued in the press. Here and there the voice of reason and caution was raised, but without any lasting

---

[81] *Kölnische Ztg.*, No. 35, Jan. 13; *Times,* Jan. 14. The following was the most offensive passage: "Let the European Powers recall that the English, to use Macauley's words, have now imported into Africa, as formerly into Asia, their power but not their morality. . . . Fighting continually against savages, the English have become savages themselves; they have adopted the warfare of savages and now attempt to treat Christian whites as if they were pagan negroes."

[82] Describing the Reichstag session of February 13, the parliamentary correspondent of the *Berliner Tageblatt* commented on the unusual agreement among all parties. The Center, Conservative, Progressive and National Liberal parties, and even the Socialists, praised the government for its defense of German interests (*Berliner Tageblatt,* No. 81, Feb. 14). The political press echoed the party spokesmen in the Reichstag: *Frankfurter Ztg.,* No. 45, Feb. 14; *Vossische Ztg.,* No. 76, Feb. 14; *Kölnische Volksztg.,* No. 104, Feb. 14; *National-Zeitung,* No. 104, Feb. 14; *Kölnische Ztg.,* No. 142, Feb. 14; *Schwäbischer Merkur,* No. 37, Feb. 14; *Berliner N. N.,* Nos. 75, 79, Feb. 14, 16, quoting *Kreuzzeitung, Die Post, Rheinisch-Westfälische Ztg., Dresdner Nachrichten, Leipziger N. N., Hannoverscher Kurier; Norddeutsche,* Nos. 76, 77, Feb. 14, 15, quoting numerous other papers.

[83] On the preparation of the White Book, *Aktenstücke betreffend die Südafrikanische Republik,* see G. P., XI, 48–49.

effect. In October the campaign was renewed on both sides with redoubled vigor. British foreign policy was subjected in Germany to bitter and hostile criticism and English editors answered their detractors in language seldom employed in the dignified British press.[84]

Special importance attaches to the work of the foreign correspondents as collectors and transmitters of news and opinion during the January crisis. The work of the German representatives in London is relatively less important than that of the English group in Berlin. The former were mainly concerned with forwarding to the German papers and news agencies the dispatches received in London from South Africa. This work was done for the Vossische Zeitung by Moritz Sasse, for the Kölnische Zeitung by Dr. Hans Esser, for the Münchner Neueste Nachrichten and Hamburger Fremdenblatt by Dr. Gaupp, and for Wolff's Telegraphic Bureau by Major Piper. Practically all the news from the Transvaal was pumped into Germany from London, being for the most part condensations of the dispatches of Reuter's Agency, the Times, Telegraph, and Standard. It was not until January 13 that the Berliner Tageblatt began to publish dispatches direct from South Africa. Piper, through Wolff's Bureau, sought to follow the main currents of London editorial opinion in addition to reporting 'spot news.' In the main his reports seemed accurate and fair, although George Saunders, Berlin correspondent of the Morning Post, accused Wolff's Bureau of garbling and twisting one of the Post's editorials.[85]

Saunders, who became the Times' representative in January 1897, sent the most inflammatory dispatches and displayed the greatest hostility toward German policy. Repeatedly he warned the Post's readers to be prepared "not only for violent or subtle acts of aggression, but for hostile manoeuvres and the tortuous methods of the new German diplomacy which may have many surprises in store for us." [86] Between Chirol and Saunders there was a genuine community of feeling and opinion in the matter of Anglo-German relations. Chirol favored a close understanding between the two governments, but sincerely mistrusted the aspirations and desires that were frequently voiced in the German press. His experience in Berlin at this time did not swing him entirely over to an anti-German posi-

[84] The *Pall Mall Gazette* was quoted by *Vossische Zeitung* (No. 491, Oct. 18) as saying : "Insolence is the only article produced in Germany that is not manufactured better elsewhere." *Daily Telegraph,* Oct. 16 : "Criticism 'Made in Germany' of British policy, British character, and British motives, is as cheap, and we may safely add as nasty, as the commodities which have turned that phrase into a byword." *Times,* Oct. 20 : "We do not attach much importance to the cheap little sneers which give German newspapers, even when inspired by the Foreign Office, so much delight."

[85] *Morning Post,* Jan. 6.

[86] *Morning Post,* Jan. 11, 1896. In a similar vein, Jan. 4, 6, 7, 14.

tion, but it put him in a very bad temper and his dispatches clearly showed it.[87] Later, under the impression created by German press hostility during the Boer War, his suspicions of aggressive intentions hardened into convictions. That Chirol should have gone immediately to the foreign editorship of the Times with the bitter memories of January 1896 fresh in his mind had serious consequences for the public relations of the two countries. William Maxwell of the Standard and J. L. Bashford of the Daily Telegraph reported fairly and without bias the events and opinions which they noted in the German capital. They avoided quoting the more provocative utterances of the chauvinistic press and placed before their readers the views of the Berlin government. Their influence was ameliorative rather than aggravating, although they were unable to guide editorial opinion along the same line.

From January 1896 to the outbreak of the Boer War in October 1899, the South African question moved across the pages of the daily press. The trial of Jameson and the British officers, in July of 1896, the thorough whitewashing of the entire affair by the parliamentary investigating committee in 1897, and Chamberlain's prolonged diplomatic duel with Kruger were reported at length in the German journals.[88] Except in a few isolated instances German press comment was consistently hostile. Spring Rice described it as "a systematic campaign of slander, which sometimes goes into winter quarters, but never makes peace." [89] The outbreak of the Boer War gave rise to a malignant and persistent campaign of abuse and reprobation that eventually raised a Chinese wall of misunderstanding between the British and German peoples.

When the text of the Kaiser's telegram to Kruger was drafted, Baron Marschall boasted that it would be a "knock-out" (*ein Schlager*). But German officials were taken aback and surprised at the intensity of the reaction in England. German scholars, too, have been at a loss to explain it.[90] Otto Hammann takes the position that the Telegram was only the

[87] Gwynn, *op. cit.,* I, 191; Chirol, *Fifty Years,* pp. 281–82. Chirol left Berlin in April 1896. The post was occupied temporarily by Wickham Steed until Saunders was free from his engagement with the Morning Post in January 1897. Steed, *Through Thirty Years,* I, 74.

[88] The ineffectiveness of the investigating committee was the subject of a striking cartoon by F. C. Gould in the *Westminster Gazette.* The members of the commission, dressed as mourners, are grouped around a large tombstone bearing the following inscription : "In MEMORIAM—The South African Committee— It respected Confidences— It discovered the Obvious— It avoided the Obscure— It compromised no man—Fortified by unctuous rectitude, and an unsuspicious disposition it was unsparing of WHITEWASH. Died in the Odour of Inanity, June 4, 1897. 'Let Resignations Wait.' "

[89] Gwynn, *op. cit.,* I, 261.

[90] Thimme, "Die Krugerdepesche," *Europäische Gespräche,* January–June, 1924, p. 234 n.

fuse that fired a magazine already fully charged by English jealousy of German economic success in competition with England in world markets.[91] Moreover, in a study by an American scholar it is maintained that political rivalry and political crises in Anglo-German relations sprang from the alkaline soil of commercial competition.[92] Simply demonstrating that there were economic issues involved in the South African clash and that in the six months following that crisis there was a lively campaign in the English press against goods "Made in Germany" does not, in the writer's opinion, prove the case for economic determinism. Was it not altogether natural that during and immediately following this political crisis, when threats of war were bandied about, that Germany should be dressed up and exhibited in the English public prints as the unscrupulous salesman rather than the valued customer? In the very first days of the crisis economic boycott of German goods and services was advocated as a proper reprisal for German political impoliteness.[93] Certainly, the demonstration on London's Baltic Exchange against the German members was an expression of patriotic resentment rather than economic jealousy. Out of these demands for economic reprisal developed the campaign in the English press during the summer and the autumn against German industrial and commercial competition.[94] It was exploited and sensationalized by the press because it made good copy during the dog days, and because the full force of British prejudice against Germany had been aroused by the political crisis produced by the Kruger Telegram. The famous *Germania est delenda* article, published in the *Saturday Review* the following year (September 11, 1897), represented an unsuccessful attempt to revive the alarms of the previous summer. Although it did yeoman service later in the hands of Tirpitz' press bureau, it attracted practically no attention at the time of publication. Political passions had cooled in the meantime.

A second fact that contravenes the thesis that the outburst in England

[91] Hammann cites the supporting opinions of Hermann Oncken and Count Reventlow. *Der neue Kurs*, pp. 186–88.

[92] R. J. S. Hoffman, *Great Britain and the German Trade Rivalry, 1875–1914* (Philadelphia, 1934).

[93] The Gillingham school board calling for tenders for clocks ordered that German goods be ruled out. (*Daily News*, Jan. 11.) A special article in the *Times* (Jan. 14) on "Germans in England" raised the bogey of German clerks, teachers, and waiters. A Press Association dispatch (*Scotsman*, Jan. 14) reported a serious falling off of English orders from German firms. This was confirmed by a letter from a German firm in London published in the *Berliner Tageblatt*. (No. 28, Jan. 16.) Considerable prominence was given in the German press to London reports of economic reprisals: *Berliner N. N.*, Nos. 10, 17, Jan. 7, 11; *Norddeutsche*, No. 17, Jan. 11; *National-Zeitung*, No. 26, Jan. 14 (letter to the editor from Robert Koch, director of the Deutsche Bank); *Hannoverscher Kurier*, quoted *Berliner N. N.*, No. 23, Jan. 15; *Schwäbischer Merkur*, No. 12, Jan. 16.

[94] The campaign is described in detail by Hoffman, *op. cit.*, pp. 244 ff.

was an expression of accumulated ill will because of German commercial
success is revealed by an examination of the leading papers of London and
the provinces. Such an examination shows that the least bellicose at the
height of the crisis and the first to recover their balance and speak of the
tradition of Anglo-German co-operation were those journals located in
the industrial and commercial centers of the country. Particularly noteworthy in this respect were the Daily Post of Liverpool, the Glasgow
Herald, the Scotsman of Edinburgh, the Manchester Guardian, and the
Birmingham Post. In London it was the editors of those papers whose
patrons were the commercial and industrial classes who began first to
temper their language with regard to German policy, namely, the Daily
Telegraph, Daily News, and eventually the Standard. During this and
later crises down to the War, the foci of Germanophobe fermentation were
those daily and weekly publications whose interests were furthest removed
from the industrial and commercial life of the country, whose general emphasis was literary or political, or whose appeal was to the world of high
society and the personnel of the national services. Recitation of the names
—Times, Morning Post, National Review, Spectator, and Saturday Review—tells the story. The economic motive certainly dominated the policies of the popular papers, such as the Daily Mail, but it was primarily
their own economic interest—increased circulation and advertising revenue—that led them to pound the drum and paint the devil on the wall.[95]

There is no inexplicable mystery about the outburst of popular hostility toward Germany. Neither the aristocratic clubman who wrote a
scorching letter to the Times, nor the middle class jingo who wrote threatening letters to the German ambassador, nor the Whitechapel guttersnipe
who hurled insults at German Jews, was motivated primarily by economic considerations. Such reactions were provoked by the experience of
a vicarious insult suffered from a foreign monarch. Beyond a doubt economic motives prevailed in relatively small pressure and action groups;
but the public, the vast mass of the people, came fully into the picture during this crisis because the common emotion of national patriotism was
deeply stirred. "The nation is in a fighting mood," was the way contemporary observers described this complex psychological phenomenon. All
the stereotypes, symbols, values, and ideologies associated with the wor-
ship of the national state, which the unthinking regarded as something

[95] The *Daily Mail* was born four months too late to participate in the Transvaal
crisis, but its aftermath was exploited to the utmost. From May to November its
columns were opened to letters on German competition, while editorials and special
articles preached the menace of German trade and the disloyalty of German clerks
employed by English firms. Outstanding in their cheap sensationalism was a series of
articles by Gilbert Burgess, entitled "Germany as She Is." (Aug. 17–Sept. 7.)

created in their own image, seemed endangered. Threats, retaliatory gestures, and verbalizations of aroused and hostile attitudes were provoked all along the line. There was, indeed, little of the "public opinion" of the nineteenth century democratic theorists in this English outburst. The rational process, the considered judgment based upon facts, was entirely absent.

Paul Hatzfeldt, the German ambassador, drew a sharp distinction between the government and the emotionally aroused masses. "It is not so much a question of ill-humor on the part of the English Government," he wrote in retrospect, "but of deep-seated bitterness among the public, which has manifested itself in every way. . . . The general feeling was such—of this I have no doubt—that if the Government had lost its head, or on any ground had wished for war, it would have had the whole of the public behind it. The consideration that we could contribute essentially to England's difficulties in other parts of the world remained absolutely without effect upon the ignorant masses of the population. England's ostensible isolation likewise made no impression. They gloried in the proud feeling that England was strong enough to defy all her enemies." [96] The threats contained in the Venezuelan message, the humiliating dénouement of the Jameson Raid, and the unmitigated condemnation of English freebooting in the entire continental press, capped by William II's congratulatory telegram to President Kruger convinced the Englishman that all the world was arrayed against him. The brunt of English resentment, however, fell upon Germany. Of all Britain's enemies she was singled out for castigation. The unfortunate Telegram was largely responsible, but differences outside of South Africa were undoubtedly contributory causes. Anger over the Wilhelmstrasse's co-operation with France and Russia in the Far East, resentment at Germany's "thumbscrew policy" in colonial competition with Great Britain, the divergence of views and policies in the Armenian question, the apparent desertion at a critical moment of a hitherto politically reliable continental friend—all these matters were productive of much ill will and hostility. The Telegram itself was interpreted as a challenge to Britain's supremacy in South Africa; as a denial of the imperialists' claim to control the foreign relations of the Boer republic; as a statement of Germany's willingness to extend aid other than diplomatic to the Transvaal; and the fact that it was wrapped up in a friendly message to Kruger made it not a whit less offensive and provocative in the eyes of patriotic Englishmen.

What took experienced German and English observers—Salisbury, Moberly Bell, Hatzfeldt—by surprise was that *"all* classes" joined in the

[96] Hatzfeldt to Holstein, Jan. 21, 1896; *G. P.,* XI, 53.

hisses for "Bumptious Billy of Berlin." [97] The public's enthusiasm for Jameson testified to the popularity of the New Imperialism with the masses.[98] It was, in fact, the working of this imponderable that threw the Wilhelmstrasse's elaborate diplomatic equation out of balance. A nicely calculated cabinet policy assisted by winks and tips toward the newspapers went completely awry as a result of the intervention of the British public, which, in the main, interpreted German action as a threat and a challenge to the Empire. The directors of German policy had no idea of engaging the military and naval power of Britain. They contemplated rather a diplomatic campaign in the chancelleries of Paris, London, and St. Petersburg. That campaign had two objectives: First, to halt British absorption of the Transvaal; second, by conjuring up the specter of a continental league to frighten Britain into greater dependence upon the Triple Alliance. The feelers that were put out toward France and Russia on this occasion envisaged possible co-operation in questions affecting their mutual interests outside Europe, after the manner of their action against Japan in 1895. That England was courting the danger of a continental league by her covetousness was the refrain of Marschall's communications to the English correspondents and the British ambassador. To this extent the motives of German policy were revealed in the English press.[99] The German plan was logical and based upon nicely calculated compensatory diplomatic strains and stresses, but the structure was brought tumbling to the ground before half erected by total miscalculation of the publicity factors involved. Baron Holstein, witnessing the explosion produced by the Telegram, realized immediately that the plan had miscarried. "Let us be happy," he wrote to Hatzfeldt, "if the affair now ends as it seems to be doing—with a small diplomatic success for Germany and a little political lesson for England." [100] Even this was a too sanguinary view as later events were to show. German action did not prevent the eventual con-

---

[97] Moberly Bell, *Life and Letters,* p. 212.

[98] In this connection see the brilliant analysis of the social forces behind late Victorian imperialism in Langer, *Diplomacy of Imperialism,* I, chap. III.

[99] Chirol analyzed them correctly enough in his dispatch to the *Times* on January 7: "The purpose of that telegram was clearly twofold. It was a bid for popularity at home, which, in the present internal situation, was eminently desirable, and it was a warning to England that she could only find salvation in closer contact with Germany and her allies." Holstein expounded the same thesis to Chirol in an interview on January 8. (*G. P.,* XI, 41–42.) The editor of the *Daily News,* interpreting the Berlin dispatches, said that "She [Germany] wants to drive England into the Triple Alliance by an ostentatious display of her hate." (Jan. 8.) *Westminster Gazette* on Jan. 11: "The attempt to crowd us into the Triple Alliance has failed."

[100] Jan. 10; *G. P.* XI, 49. No little concern was created in the Wilhelmstrasse by the subsequent campaign in the English press for a rapprochement with France and Russia—the very opposite of what they had hoped to accomplish. The lead in this movement was taken by J. A. Spender in the *Westminster Gazette* and by E. T. Cook in the *Daily News.*

quest of the Transvaal, and the English seemed not at all impressed by the "political lesson" which Marschall and Holstein sought to impart. Marschall, too, received a little lesson, the text of which he expounded to the German ambassador in St. Petersburg: "For Germany there lies in the experience of the Transvaal question a cautionary reminder for the handling of existing and future points of difference between us and England. The idea that provisional co-operation between the Continental Powers is the best means to settle pending disputes between England and the Continent—simply through diplomatic pressure and without war—appears impracticable in view of the attitude of France." [101] Neither Salisbury nor his counselors in the daily press were convinced that the security of the Empire lay in a close relationship with the dominant partner of the Triple Alliance, while the public at large was filled with mistrust and suspicion of those vague and ill-defined ambitions which seemed to inspire German policy.

[101] Jan. 19; *G. P.,* XI, 83.

CHAPTER VI

PUBLICITY AND THE BIRTH OF *WELTPOLITIK*

In unserem Volke stact noch immer der Peter in der Fremde, der sich nach dem warmen Ofen zurücksehnt und ein unüberwindliches Gruseln vor der Fahrt über das Meer empfindet. Aber ein Volk, das in dem universalen Zeitalter nicht seefest und seetüchtig ist, spielt keine Rolle in der Weltgeschichte mehr, ein Volk ohne Flotte hat im 20. Jahrhundert für die Entwicklung der Kultur werth und Bedeutung verloren, weil es von dem Welttheater verschwindet und zum Statisten herabsinkt.

National-Zeitung, December 19, 1897.

In the four years from 1895 to 1899, Great Britain faced the possibility of war with four of the great powers: with the United States over Venezuela, with Germany over South Africa, with Russia in the Far East, and with France at Fashoda. In each case it was an outlying post of her commercial and territorial empire that was threatened; her security and influence in Europe were unaffected. In reality since the conclusion of the Franco-Russian Alliance, a continental equilibrium was restored that discouraged assaults on the status quo except under the greatest compulsion or provocation. Such a situation was to England's advantage. Proponents of splendid isolation argued that Britain, possessed of supreme naval power and holding the balance between the continental groups, could maintain and even extend her territorial and commercial empire. In the crises between 1895 and 1899 this formula, however, failed to lead in all instances to a correct British solution. The Venezuelan imbroglio was compromised; Germany backed down in South Africa only when threatened with force; and the back door to Egypt was held against French entrance by the same method. But in the Far East the British failed utterly to stop the Russian steam roller. Freezing of the continental status quo was not an unmixed blessing for British policy. It intensified competitive activity outside Europe in the drive for colonies, markets, and investment opportunities. Diplomacy backed by a superior navy enabled Britain to meet any one power in the game of imperialism, but could she withstand a coalition of three aggressive continental states? What if Russia, France, and Germany should unite "to cut straps from British leather"? Could Britain withstand the Dual Alliance if the weight of that continental com-

138

bination were thrown against the British Empire? Under the pressure of circumstances the British cabinet began a search for insurance to cover the risks of empire. That is the real significance of Salisbury's approach to Russia in 1898, of the Portuguese colonies agreement with Germany, of Chamberlain's alliance proposals to Berlin, of the Yangtze agreement with Germany in 1900. It was the policy of insurance that led eventually to the Anglo-Japanese Alliance, the entente with France and the understanding with Russia.

For better than two years Salisbury cast his fly in Russia's direction— he never got a solid strike. Meanwhile, German statesmen were enjoying their renewed cordiality with Russia; they drew concrete profit from it in the Far East and cultivated this friendship as a means of neutralizing the anti-German import of the Franco-Russian Alliance. With the Austro-Russian agreement of May 1897, defining and acknowledging their claims on the Turkish Empire in Europe, a heavy mortgage was lifted from the Triple Alliance. Thus relieved, Germany was in a position to take an "extra waltz" with any partner who offered a hand.

The time and circumstances were favorable for launching fully into the stream of world politics. The first fanfaronade proclaiming the "Greater German Empire" outside the limits of the Fatherland came from the Emperor on the occasion of the twenty-fifth anniversary of the foundation of the Reich. (Jan. 18, 1896.) In the following year Bernhard von Bülow succeeded Marschall as foreign secretary, and Admiral von Tirpitz became minister of marine. Bülow and Tirpitz sought to realize the Emperor's dream of a colonial and commercial empire floating on a powerful navy. Intensive pursuit of *Weltpolitik* was inaugurated with the acquisition of Kiao-chow and the simultaneous publication of the first naval bill.

In England, as the press cooled down after the Kruger Telegram, the greatest confusion of counsel prevailed. There were those who spoke out boldly for a settlement all along the line with France and Russia. Others took great care to bring this possibility to the attention of German editors without, however, urging it upon the Queen's ministers. Some thought that time and common sense would restore the defense of Britain's flank previously afforded by the Triple Alliance. Still others, apprehensive of the future in the Near and Far East, frankly admitted that splendid isolation involved too many risks; they could be covered more cheaply by concessions to Germany and her partners than by sacrifices to the Franco-Russian combination. England should come to terms with the Triple Alliance, draw France to her side by worthwhile concessions, and thus arrayed with friends withstand Russia all along the line. Such was the import of a series of articles by Spenser Wilkinson, published in the Morn-

ing Post during February and March 1896.[1] Long-range views and future
programs constituted in the main, however, a field reserved for the
monthly reviews. Journalism and journalistic comment was concerned
with the events of the day. They could not be detached from the current
of affairs. Publicity by the clock, measuring the time between one edition
and the next, gave little opportunity for a long and considered look into
the future. Moreover, in so far as England and Germany were concerned,
time and circumstances afforded little relaxation of the tension and no
opportunity for the speaking of a friendly word. In fact every reported
incident evoked bitter comment and such comment became in turn the
occasion for further polemics.

An acrimonious dispute raged during October 1896 over German protection of the Mohammedan pretender to the throne in Zanzibar. This led
to a general exchange of taunts and calumnies.[2] When Rosebery referred
in a speech at Edinburgh to "the frantic eagerness" with which England
had acquired territory during the preceding twelve years (2,600,000
square miles since 1884), the Berlin papers provided appropriate comment on "British landgrabbing" and "English covetousness." In turn,
when Bismarck revealed the secret of the Russian reinsurance treaty in an
article in the Hamburger Nachrichten, and set the German political world
by the ears, he afforded the English editors a good opportunity to express
their *Schadenfreude* and to editorialize on the innate duplicity of German
foreign policy.[3] A warning to the German press for its "unprovoked
and needless attacks upon England," delivered by Lord George Hamilton,
secretary of state for India, drew the following reply from the Vossische
Zeitung:

[1] The most important of the series were those of February 17, 20, 24, 26, March 2,
5, 9. Because of their frank statement of Britain's need, Spring Rice wrote from his
observation point in Berlin that "Articles like those in the *Morning Post* are instruments in the hands of our enemies here." (Gwynn, *Letters and Friendships of Cecil
Spring Rice*, I, 204.) Subsequently expanded, the articles were published in book
form in 1897 with the title, *The Nation's Awakening.*

[2] The unsavory debate is fully reported in the *Vossische Ztg.*, Nos. 466, 467, 468,
480, 490, Oct 3, 4, 5, 12, 17; *Times,* Oct. 16, 19, 21; *Daily Telegraph,* Oct. 16, 19;
Standard, Oct. 24, quoting *Kreuzzeitung, National-Zeitung, Berliner Tageblatt,
Hamburger Nachrichten,* and *Die Post; Morning Post,* Oct. 19; *B. D.,* I, 327;
Letters of Queen Victoria, III, 71, 87.

[3] All the London morning journals commented on the revelations. Particularly
outspoken were the editorials in the *Daily Telegraph,* Oct. 29, Nov. 6; and the *Standard,* Oct. 26. The agitation in Germany continued for a month. The original article
and subsequent explanations and rejoinders from the *Hamburger Nachrichten* are
reproduced in Hermann Hofmann, *Fürst Bismarck, 1890–1898* (3 vols., Stuttgart,
9–11 ed., 1922), II, 370–389. Also Fürst Hohenlohe-Schillingsfürst, *Denkwürdigkeiten der Reichskanzlerzeit* (Berlin, 1931), pp. 270–78; Waldersee, *Denkwürdigkeiten,* II, 375–77. Schulthess, *Europäischer Geschichtskalendar* (1896), pp. 112 ff.,
gives a good account of the domestic press dispute in which Clerical, Socialist, and
Liberal papers were aligned with the semi-official journals against the Bismarckian
organs.

The German press does not want Lord George Hamilton's advice. . . . The Secretary of State for India would do better to trouble himself less about the German press and more about the duties of his office, and, for example, to think how he can avoid the menacing famine in India. That would anyhow be a better and more suitable return for the five thousand pounds a year salary he receives as Secretary of State for India.[4]

But mendacity reached its highest point with the circulation in the German press of the charge that the great dock workers' strike at Hamburg was provoked and financed by English shippers in agreement with their workmen.[5] Thus the steady flow of accusation and retort went on week after week.

How did the constant editorial bickering and unfriendly interpretation of every news report react upon the diplomatic relations of the two governments? We do not find Salisbury and Hatzfeldt imitating the editors. Personal relations remained cordial and unstrained. However, a notable reserve was imposed upon the British minister in entertaining any proposals or projects emanating from Berlin, and Hatzfeldt advised his foreign office against the extension of their diplomatic activity beyond ordinary current business. In the main, the effect of the press was negative and restraining rather than positive and directing.

William II, who placed great value upon his personal popularity in England, felt the press feud most keenly. He could not have relished the appellation "William the Witless," which was at that time current in the jingo press of London.[6] In response to a protest made informally through the British military attaché, Salisbury replied that he was without the means or power to control the British press. The Emperor bombarded Hohenlohe with messages expressing his fear that the English press campaign might be a prelude to a raid on their colonies. It was madness to have initiated a colonial policy without a strong navy. Their colonies had become an "Achilles heel" and their great merchant marine was defenseless before Britain's strong fleet of cruisers.[7] In November, the Kaiser, in a conversation with Lascelles, expressed his deep concern over the newspaper bickering. He, personally, would oppose the press agitation and continue to work for good relations; he hoped that "a fair amount of reciprocity" would be shown by England, especially in the press.[8] What he meant by "a fair amount of reciprocity" was revealed shortly thereafter when the Hamburger Nachrichten reported that the dock workers' strike

[4] No. 534, Nov. 12, 1896.
[5] The occasion was the visit of Tom Mann, the English labor leader, to Hamburg. *National-Zeitung*, No. 694, Nov. 28.
[6] *Daily Mail*, Nov. 3, 1896.
[7] *G. P.*, XI, 185; XIII, 3–4.
[8] *Ibid.*, XIII, 7.

was instigated and supported by English commercial interests. Fearing that the report would arouse the press still further against England he appealed to Lascelles to secure publication of an official denial by the English government. Salisbury replied that "The imputation is so devoid of foundation that an official denial would be received with ridicule." The Emperor made a second and more pressing appeal, and this time Salisbury, somewhat grudgingly, communicated with Sir Donald Mackenzie Wallace, the foreign editor of the Times. The desired statement, ridiculing the rumor as a Friedrichsruhe invention, appeared in the Times on December 5, and was given general circulation through Reuter's Agency. In acceding to the Emperor's request, Salisbury was careful to protect himself by the customary foreign office formula in such matters. "But please impress on His Majesty," he cautioned Lascelles, "that we are absolutely without the means of influencing or controlling the press, and I cannot be sure as to the effect which may be produced by my appeal to Wallace." [9] This single instance of official intervention in press matters did not become the entering wedge, as the Emperor doubtless hoped it would, for a general movement on the part of the government to influence the press to assume a more temperate attitude. When Curzon, Salisbury's parliamentary under-secretary, visited Berlin in April 1897, the problem of press relations occupied a prominent place in his discussions with Baron Marschall. Curzon said that the impression seemed to prevail in Berlin that the British government could control the press; this, in fact, they could not do. Marschall replied that the English belief that the greater part of the German press was under the influence of the government, and that unfriendly attacks were inspired by the foreign office, was equally without foundation. Curzon did not altogether agree that this was a correct statement of English belief. They could not fail to be impressed, he said, when an obviously inspired article appeared one day, to be followed the next day in the same journal by unmerited criticism. Marschall countered this by pointing out that the Standard, which was the recognized official organ of the Conservative party, was of all English papers the most unrestrained in its attacks on Germany.[10] Marschall closed this subject with the admission that the sympathy for England which had formerly prevailed in Germany had, in the main, disappeared because of England's

---

[9] G. P., XIII, 8–11; Hohenlohe, Denkwürdigkeiten, p. 284.

[10] This was in a measure true. But the Germans were apparently unaware that a change had occurred with Alfred Austin's resignation from the editorial staff, toward the close of 1896. The paper, of course, through its editor, William Mudford, maintained its party contacts, but the intimate relationship with Lord Salisbury no longer existed. Autobiography of Alfred Austin, II, 215 ff. On Mudford as an editor see F. J. Higginbottom, The Vivid Life, pp. 69–70.

unfriendly attitude toward German colonial expansion, particularly in Africa.[11]

This mutual misunderstanding of the relations of the two governments toward their own press and the responsibility for its utterances was never cleared up; it remained a fertile source of suspicion and dissatisfaction in the most influential quarters. English officials, influenced by British correspondents in Berlin, never believed that the German foreign office had clean hands in the matter of anti-British press campaigns; German officials, on the other hand, were loath to accept repeated assurances that Downing Street was without any power to modify the hostile publicity that accompanied every move of German diplomacy. Press campaigns in general, then, had an adverse direct effect upon the official relations of the two governments. Their effect on the general public, though indirect, was no less detrimental. The more violent and unrestrained tone in which politics were handled in the German press did inestimable damage in England. This was clearly expressed by the London correspondent of the Allgemeine Zeitung of Munich in a general warning to the German press:

The Berlin papers ought not always to answer the leaders of *The Standard* and other papers on Germany with ball cartridge. . . . The English are accustomed to politeness, even when they know that they are in the wrong. The angry replies of the German papers are followed by retorts from the English Press which, on account of its enormous influence on British public opinion, create deep and lasting ill-feelings in England against Germans.[12]

Irresponsible publicity hampered the formal conduct of relations and led old-school statesmen to despair of the popular press and universal manhood suffrage.

From the documentary record for 1897 one might conclude that there was little to attract public interest in the relations between England and Germany during that year. An examination of the files of the press, however, reveals more interest, expressed in terms of space allotment, than in other years when the diplomats were preoccupied with matters of vital concern to both governments. The long drawn-out duel between Kruger and Chamberlain was followed in great detail by the German press. The parliamentary inquiry into the Jameson Raid began in February 1897, and dragged on for five months. The proceedings of the committee and the manifest reluctance to probe deeply around the foundations of Rhodes'

[11] *G. P.*, XIII, 12–13; Earl of Ronaldshay, *The Life of Lord Curzon* (3 vols., N. Y., 1928), I, 247–49.

[12] Quoted in the *Standard*, Oct. 23, 1896.

policy in South Africa offered many opportunities for caustic criticism.

In April a sharp clash occurred between Chamberlain and Kruger. The Transvaal was arming and Kruger stood his ground. Military reinforcements were sent to Natal and eight British warships were dispatched to Delagoa Bay. The naval demonstration, described by J. L. Garvin as "a warning shot" fired "across Mr. Kruger's bows," was interpreted in Germany as a move preliminary to the seizure of Delagoa Bay and the military suppression of the Boer republic. England, it was charged, was creating a pretext for armed intervention. A declaration of pacific intention issued through Reuter's Agency failed to quiet the clamor. "In spite of all peaceful assurances from England a real feeling of distrust as to her intentions is quite justified," declared the Vossische Zeitung.[13] The hue and cry continued. England was threatened with the Concert of Europe; the familiar themes of "British egoism," "British landgrabbing," and "British perfidy" were paraded through the press by excited editors. The shouting reached its climax in a statement from a writer in the Kreuzzeitung: "England foments hatred between the nations, sets on foot revolutions and wars in order . . . to play at catchball in other parts of the world. England is proclaiming today in all sorts of phrases that she must have the Transvaal, which is treading upon freedom, and that none but the English can be allowed to possess the richest gold and diamond fields."[14] This puerile calumny was met in the British press by the explanation that the dispatch of warships to Delagoa Bay was a measure to forestall a concerted Boer-German seizure of Portuguese territory. The Times correspondent in Lisbon obligingly reported that the Portuguese press accepted British action as a demonstration against a possible Boer-German raid.[15] When one compares the relatively simple diplomatic record of this incident with the reckless exaggerations of the press, the issue of responsibility is presented in a striking manner.

The violent partisanship displayed by the German press for the Boer cause raised the question in Hatzfeldt's mind as to the wisdom of continued

[13] No. 257, April 23, 1897.

[14] Quoted in Bashford's dispatch to the Daily Telegraph, May 4. The more exaggerated rumors and charges are found in the National-Zeitung, Nos. 191, 195, 208, 210, 225, March 20, 23, 29, 30, April 4; Vossische Ztg., Nos. 153, 154, 160, 163, 172, April 1, 3, 7, 12; Times, Daily Telegraph, and Daily Mail gave full reports, April 29, 30, and May 4. Delagoa Bay, through which Kruger was arming his country, was the key to the South African question. Although a forcible seizure was apparently not contemplated by the British, their diplomacy at this moment was leaving no stone unturned in an effort to acquire by lease or purchase the harbor at Lourenço Marques and the railroad to the Transvaal. (B. D., I, 44–48; Garvin, Life of Chamberlain, III, 307–10; G. P., XIII, 13; Langer, Diplomacy of Imperialism, II, 521–22.)

[15] Times, April 23, 29; Vossische Ztg., No. 257, April 23; National-Zeitung, No. 268, April 29; Morning Post, April 24; Westminster Gazette and the Globe, cited by Vossische Ztg., No. 195, April 27; Kölnische Ztg., No. 370, April 23.

opposition to Great Britain in South Africa. Close analysis of objectives and instrumentation showed that Germany could not prevent British absorption of the Transvaal. The Delagoa Bay episode revealed the connection between the Transvaal and the Portuguese colonies. Would it not be more realistic, as well as profitable, to abandon opposition to Great Britain's policy toward the Boer republics and seek compensation in Portugal's African colonies? This policy was advocated by Hatzfeldt and approved by the Emperor. The moment was not opportune for striking a bargain, but the formula was applied in the following year by Bülow in the Portuguese colonies agreement.[16]

Less acrimonious than the dispute over Delagoa Bay, but fraught with greater consequences for the future, was the German acquisition of an independent foothold in the Far East through the seizure of the Chinese port of Kiao-chow. For three years the German foreign office and admiralty, urged on by the Emperor, had been casting about for a suitable naval base in the Far East which could be acquired and developed as a commercial and cultural center. It was a difficult task to find a port that met the naval requirements, that promised a rich field for economic development, and that, at the same time, could be secured without provoking the opposition of England or Russia.[17] Kiao-chow, on the south side of the Shantung peninsula, was finally fixed upon as the most desirable place they might hope to acquire. It cannot be said that pressure of public opinion forced the government to act. To be sure, in March 1896, Councillor Klehmet drew up a memorandum on the need for a naval station on the Chinese coast in which he stated that "public opinion," as expressed in the press and in the resolutions of colonial and commercial societies, called for government action.[18] The impulse came not from the public but from the Emperor and his advisers. The murder of two German Catholic missionaries by Chinese bandits in Shantung province, on November 1, was the "incident" for which the Germans had long been waiting. After notifying the Czar of his intention, the Emperor ordered the Far Eastern squadron to occupy Kiao-chow Bay until satisfaction for the outrage could be secured from the Chinese government. The leasehold and extensive economic concessions which were subsequently extorted from the

[16] *G. P.*, XIII, 16–27.

[17] On the preliminary surveys and discussions see *G. P.*, XIV, 5–64; Admiral von Tirpitz, *My Memoirs* (2 vols., N. Y., 1919), I, 91 ff. Langer's excellent account of the diplomacy of the Far Eastern crisis that began with the German landing at Kiao-chow makes it unnecessary to touch on that part of the story except to make clear its accompaniment of publicity. (Langer, *Diplomacy of Imperialism*, I, 445–80.)

[18] *G. P.*, XIV, 25–26. As evidences of public demand for this step were cited articles from *Kreuzzeitung, Deutsche Tagesztg., Hamburger Nachrichten, Hannoverscher Kurier, Münchner N. N., Münchner Allg. Ztg., Magdeburger Ztg.,* and *Frankfurter Ztg.*

Chinese as the price of German satisfaction were only secured after protracted negotiations. In consequence of the vigorous opposition offered
by the Russian foreign office, the directors of German policy were, for
about a month, by no means certain of the outcome of the enterprise.

Considerable restraint in the use of accompanying publicity was imposed upon German officials because the ultimate objective—permanent
occupation of Kiao-chow as compared to the immediate aim, punitive
action—could not under the circumstances be openly avowed. Official publicity policy may be clearly traced in the comments and the silences of the
Norddeutsche and the Kölnische Zeitung. The news of German troop
landings at Kiao-chow appeared simultaneously, on November 16, in the
English and German press. The Norddeutsche simply reproduced the telegram appearing in the Kölnische Zeitung; confirmation by official announcement did not follow until the 20th.[19] From that time until December 7 any newspaper reader entirely dependent on the Norddeutsche for
information would have been unaware of the important events transpiring
in the Far East. There was no mention of Kiao-chow or of the diplomatic
situation created by German action, and no foreign or domestic press
comment was quoted. When the substance of German demands at Peking
became known through Reuter's correspondent at Shanghai, the reserve
of the semi-official organ was in part abandoned.[20] When the Russian fleet
went into winter quarters at Port Arthur, the Norddeutsche published a
foreign office statement: "This Russian announcement of the temporary
occupation of Port Arthur as a winter harbor does not come as a surprise
to German statesmen." [21] The import of this statement was that Russian
action had no aggressive implication as far as Germany was concerned,
but on the contrary the two powers were in complete accord. On the next
day appeared a sharp rebuke to those journalists who were saying that
these events marked the beginning of the partition of China. Henceforth,
the Far Eastern question was handled in a normal fashion. A column and
a half on the front page was accorded to Reuter's dispatches and the Kölnische Zeitung's telegrams, Archibald Colquhoun's letter to the Times
on British Far Eastern policy, and the reported movements of the Japanese fleet. It was as though the editor had been adventuring with Marco
Polo and had suddenly discovered China.[22]

Just as significant as the reserve of the Norddeutsche was the news and
editorial policy of the Kölnische Zeitung. If the Emperor had had his way

[19] Norddeutsche, Nos. 377, 380, Nov. 16, 20.
[20] Nos. 397, 398, Dec. 7, 8. Reuter's dispatch in the Times, Nov. 30, 1897.
[21] No. 410, Dec. 20. Almost word for word the same statement was published in a
Berlin telegram to the Kölnische Zeitung.
[22] Norddeutsche, No. 412, Dec. 22.

the foreign office would have been deprived of its valuable connection with this journal. Because of an editorial slur on a member of his military entourage William II, in January 1897, ordered a boycott of its representatives. Under pain of immediate dismissal German officials were forbidden to give subsidies and tips of exclusive news, or to receive its correspondents. Hohenlohe refused point blank to obey the order, declaring that as long as he remained in his post he must be free to choose those journals that were to receive special information. In the conduct of foreign affairs, he said, only those papers were useful whose articles were read and given consideration abroad.[23] There was no break in the customary relations between the Wilhelmstrasse and Dr. Fischer. Playing its usual rôle of inspired spokesman, the Kölnische Zeitung published all news reports on the Far Eastern situation. But at first not a single hint was given that the landing at Kiao-chow had other aims than to implement diplomatic demands for reparation. Then, very lightly, the subject of more far-reaching concessions was touched upon. On December 4, it published for the first time a long article in which was mentioned as possible demands the concessions that were eventually extorted from Peking—lease of Kiao-chow, railroad concessions and mining rights in Shantung province.[24] In the bitter polemics that broke out between English and Russian journalists, following the announcement that the Russian fleet would winter at Port Arthur, the Kölnische Zeitung warily guarded its neutrality. When the British countered the Russian move by occupying Weihaiwei, in April 1898, a Berlin telegram signaled to the German press that the government's policy was not affected. "For Germany it is a matter of indifference which flag waves over Weihaiwei." [25] This was correctly interpreted in the press to mean that Germany stood aloof from Anglo-Russian rivalry in the Gulf of Pechili.

No reserve was imposed upon the papers outside the circle of official and inspired organs. The Conservative and National Liberal journals demanded at the outset that a permanent foothold be established at Kiao-chow. "It is an opportunity to do what should have been done long ago," declared the Kreuzzeitung on receipt of the news of the landing of German troops. "It is unthinkable that Kiao-chow should ever fall again into the hands of the Chinese." [26] The leading democratic journals, while less rhetorical, approved the government's vigorous action.[27] The prompt pro-

[23] Hohenlohe, *Denkwürdigkeiten*, pp. 291–92.
[24] No. 1075, Dec. 4, 1897.
[25] The telegram was reprinted in special type in the *Politische Übersicht* of the *Norddeutsche*. (No. 81, April 6, 1898.)
[26] Nos. 539, 549, Nov. 17, 24.
[27] *Berliner Tageblatt*, Nos. 624, 627, 630, 645, Dec. 9, 10, 12, 20; *Vossische Ztg.*, Nos. 567, 569, 573, Dec. 3, 4, 7; *Frankfurter Ztg.*, No. 335, Dec. 3.

tection afforded the Christian missions also won the support of leading Catholic and Protestant journals, the Protestant Reichsbote making the point that it was more important to protect missionaries than traders because the former stood in close touch with the masses of the people and were the agents of culture.[28] When it became apparent, however, that the affair was becoming an imperialistic adventure and an advertisement for the new navy law, the Catholic press began to cry halt and demand information.[29] It was too late. The Center party had incurred a moral obligation to support the new program of naval imperialism.

As events in the Far East unfolded the German editors kept an anxious eye cocked on London. British press comment was reported in detail in those journals remote from the influence of the Wilhelmstrasse. To their readers they conveyed the impression that English editors were sick with envy, that they were encouraging the Russians and the Japanese to make trouble for Germany, that every effort was being made to sow suspicion and distrust of German policy in the Far East.[30] While unfriendly comment was by no means absent from the British press, the Germans were mistaken in attributing it to envy and jealousy. The general attitude of the English press coincided with the personal attitude of Lord Salisbury, who confided to Lascelles that "the mode in which the purpose of Germany had been attained impressed me more unfavourably than the purpose itself." [31] German action at Kiao-chow Bay was at first viewed as a particularly strong measure to secure prompt redress in Peking. The Times, for example, thought that it showed "a just appreciation of the Chinese character," and wondered "why we do not always follow the more effectual method." (Nov. 16.) Admiration turned to chagrin when it became known that the Germans were seeking cession of Kiao-chow under lease from the Chinese government. "Altogether out of proportion to the offence committed," "manifestly unjust," "a high-handed action," "a land-grabbing expedition," were some of the editorial comments which were coupled with minute analysis of Russian and Japanese interests that would be injured by German command of Kiao-chow.[32] Some editors hinted vaguely at forceful expulsion of the Germans from Kiao-chow. But who was to bell the cat?

---

[28] *Reichsbote* quoted by *Die Post*, No. 332, Dec. 4.
[29] *Kölnische Volksztg.*, No. 861, Nov. 27; *Frankfurter Ztg.*, No. 353, Dec. 21, quoting the *Centrums-Korrespondenz* and the *Kölnische Volksztg.*
[30] *Die Post*, Nos. 317, 319, 347, Nov. 19, 21, Dec. 19; *Berliner Tageblatt*, Nos. 627, 630, 645, Dec. 10, 12, 20; *Vossische Ztg.*, Nos. 573, 583, 589, Dec. 7, 13, 16; *Kreuzzeitung*, Nos. 573, 605, Dec. 8, 28, 1897.
[31] Salisbury to Lascelles, Jan. 12, 1898; *B. D.*, I, 4.
[32] *Times*, Nov. 24, 30; *Pall Mall Gazette*, Nov. 30; *Morning Post*, Nov. 30, Dec. 4; *Westminster Gazette*, Nov. 30, Dec. 1; *Standard*, Dec. 8; *Daily Mail*, Dec. 1, 2, 10.

What drew the fire of English editors was the theatrical manner in which the affair was treated by the Emperor and the German press. Colonial expansion and sea-power were the Siamese twins of *fin de siècle* policy. William II was determined to make all the capital he could for the new navy bill from the Kiao-chow incident. The navy bill was presented to the public and the Reichstag at the very time German troops were landing at Kiao-chow Bay. The Kaiser, in opening the new legislative session read the speech prepared for him by his ministers, then launched into an extemporaneous harangue on behalf of the German navy, and linked the question of sea-power with the events then transpiring in the Far East.[33] This was nothing compared to the "Dear Henry," or: "Mailed Fist" speech, which he delivered at Kiel on December 15. Two cruisers and a small contingent of troops had been quickly prepared for dispatch to the Far East under command of the Emperor's brother, Prince Henry. On the eve of their departure, word was received at the foreign office that Russian opposition to German occupation of Kiao-chow had been abandoned. The Emperor was jubilant. In the afterdinner speech in the castle at Kiel, he let himself go. His theme was German imperial destiny and he provided his own text: *Reichsgewalt bedeutet Seegewalt*. After a short lecture on this subject he addressed himself directly to his brother Prince Henry. "My dear Henry" was adjured to make it clear to everyone in the Far East that "the German Michael has set his shield, adorned with the Imperial eagle, firmly upon the ground," and that "whoever asks him for protection will receive it." "But should anyone essay to detract from our just rights or to injure us, then up and at him with your mailed fist, and if it is God's will, weave for your youthful brow a wreath of laurel which no one in all the German Empire will begrudge you." Prince Henry's reply was even more bombastic and politically inept. He modestly disclaimed any desire for laurel wreaths. His one object would be to "proclaim the gospel of your Majesty's hallowed person to all who will hear it, and also to those who do not want to hear it." After referring to the Kaiser's "crown of thorns" he closed with words appropriate to the court of Louis XIV: "most august, most mighty, beloved Emperor, King and Lord, for ever and ever." Bülow, who witnessed this forensic bout over the champagne and cigars, wished to tone down the report to be given to Hofrat Schneider for release through Wolff's Bureau, but he was dissuaded by Lucanus, the chief of the Kaiser's civil cabinet.[34] Un-

---

[33] Schulthess, *Europäischer Geschichtskalendar*, 1897, pp. 147 ff. Bülow, *Memoirs*, I, 221–22.

[34] Bülow, *Memoirs*, I, 236–39. The unedited version was distributed by Wolff's Bureau and published on December 16. The criticism in the German press was by no means as universal as Bülow would have us believe.

qualified approval of the royal rhetoric was expressed in the Leipziger Neueste Nachrichten, the Westdeutsche Zeitung, the Dresdner Journal, the Karlsruher Zeitung, and the Rheinisch-Westfälische Zeitung, all noted for their "hurrah patriotism." The editor of the last named journal, the Pan-German Dr. Reismann-Grone, was more juvenile even than the royal brothers: "Since Prince Henry the Navigator began his great work in 1420, with which Portugal's greatest age began, no Henry and no royal prince has ever put to sea accompanied with such universal hopes. . . . Hail to the German Prince Henry the Navigator!" [35] The Conservative Kreuzzeitung took exception to Prince Henry's choice of words. Only one King had worn "a crown of thorns," it pointed out, and there was only one "gospel" to preach to Christians. The "mailed fist" phrase met with full approval.[36] The Catholic organs, Germania and Kölnische Volkszeitung, ventured similar criticisms, although their words were carefully chosen to avoid prosecution for lèse majesté.[37] The liberal democratic organs, Berliner Tageblatt and Vossische Zeitung, offered no criticism. The Berlin correspondent of the Frankfurter Zeitung, August Stein, suggested "a little less heroic pathos" in royal speeches obviously designed to help along the navy law.[38]

The German people never knew how the Emperor in some of his higher moments impressed the rest of Europe. To have printed on this occasion direct quotations from the English press would have brought the editors into collision with the authorities. Smiles, snickers and malicious laughter greeted the inflated oratory of William II and his brother. Quoting all the best lines with the greatest glee, the Times concluded that "the Kiel speeches must rank amongst the most unhappy that have yet fallen from the lips of their exalted authors." "It is understood," wrote the editor of the Pall Mall Gazette, "that Lord Salisbury has received an assurance that Malta and Ceylon shall not be knocked out of the water, and that there is no reason at present to widen the Suez Canal." "My Dear Henry," "The Emperor's Rhapsody," and "My Only Brother," captioned the reports in the London press. The Daily Telegraph labeled the speeches "inflated pother about a commonplace cruise in Chinese waters." The Berlin correspondent of the Morning Post scoffed at the Emperor's "investing a punitive and land-grabbing expedition with the nomenclature and phraseology of a new Crusade." The Daily News thought that what Prince

---

[35] The super-patriotic journals are quoted in Die Post and the Kölnische Volksztg., Dec. 17–19.
[36] No. 590, Dec. 17.
[37] Germania, Dec. 16; Kölnische Volksztg., No. 915, Dec. 17.
[38] Vossische Ztg., No. 589, Dec. 16; Berliner Tageblatt, No. 638, Dec. 16; Frankfurter Ztg., No. 349, Dec. 16.

Henry had to endure in leave-taking would be "his most 'significant sacrifice on the altar of patriotism.' " "Let him weave as many laurels as he may 'around his youthful brow' so long as we retain [in the Far East] our business lead," the editor concluded. William II and his brother came in for some tart chaffing from Mr. Spender in the Westminster Gazette. "This method of working off the martial steam is not exactly our method," he wrote. "The sacrifice which the Emperor is making in sending his brother on a cruise leaves us with dry eyes. . . . Of course, we know why he shouts in public this way—it is all part and parcel of a plan to get the Reichstag to pass his Navy Bill." Altogether the English press comment was singularly lacking in appreciation. This was attributed by German editors to malice and envy.[39]

What the British editors failed to acknowledge was that in seizing Kiaochow the Germans were paying them the sincere compliment of imitation. The murder of missionaries, the dispatch of warships and landing of troops to prevent a repetition of the outrage, the forgetting to withdraw, the sending of military expeditions into the hinterland, and eventual lease of a port with an entire province attached to it was as genuinely British as roast beef and Yorkshire pudding.

The amused tolerance displayed by British editors gave way to alarm with the announcement on December 20 that the Russian Far Eastern squadron was taking up winter quarters in Port Arthur. Confiscation was becoming contagious and the more outspoken imperialistic journals began to assume a harsher tone toward the German adventure. "The German Emperor, by a characteristically theatrical effect, has forced the hands of Europe," was the peevish complaint of the Pall Mall Gazette. Why should Prince Henry's ships be allowed to coal in British stations all the way to the Far East? Spenser Wilkinson, in the Morning Post, suggested that the British and Japanese fleets join forces in China to give Prince Henry a proper reception.[40] When the Kölnische Zeitung and the Norddeutsche hinted that Russian action was no surprise to Berlin statesmen, the British press raised the specter of a Far Eastern Triplice and the immediate partition of China.

In unreasoning panic English publicists turned upon Lord Salisbury's government and the foreign office. Special and agency correspondents cabled the most sensational dispatches from Peking and Shanghai. Editors drew extreme conclusions. The government had been outwitted, the partition of China had begun, Britain's mercantile supremacy in the Ori-

[39] *Times*, Dec. 20; *Pall Mall Gazette*, Dec. 16; *Daily Mail*, Dec. 17; *Daily Telegraph*, Dec. 17; *Morning Post*, Dec. 16, 17; *Daily News*, Dec. 17, 23; *Westminster Gazette*, Dec. 17, 21; *Standard*, Dec. 17.

[40] *Pall Mall Gazette*, Dec. 22; *Daily Mail*, Dec. 29; *Morning Post*, Dec. 21, 30.

ent was being undermined while the foreign office pursued a policy of "masterly inactivity." "Our Foreign Office, our War Office, and our Admiralty do not exist for the purpose of gazing with empty looks of scientific curiosity at the partition of China," declared the Standard, a paper hitherto staunch in its support of Salisbury's foreign policy. Until well into the spring of 1898 the government's policy, or lack of policy, in the Far East was the target for Conservative-Unionist and Liberal journalists alike.[41] Behind the press agitation was the additional force of widespread criticism from the political platform, attacks in the House of Commons, deputations to the foreign office, and numerous communications in the letter columns of the daily papers. No British government could be indifferent to such pressure.

Chamberlain sensed that political necessity required vigorous action, and Lord Salisbury cynically agreed "that 'the public' will require some territorial or cartographic consolation in China," although he doubted its utility and deprecated the expense. Before moving to occupy Weihaiwei overtures were made to Russia with a view to eliminating rivalry and promoting co-operation in the Near and Far East.[42] This turned out to be a blind alley when the Russians, heedless of Salisbury's approach with an olive branch in one hand and rich gifts in the other, wrung from the weak Chinese government the lease of Port Arthur and Talienwan, railway building rights in Manchuria and predominant diplomatic influence at Peking. British lease and occupation of Weihaiwei, across the Gulf of Pechili from Port Arthur, was a gesture of retaliation. Amidst unprecedented clamor in the press and serious alarm and bewilderment in political circles Chamberlain took the frying-pan in his own hand in an effort to save the British pancake. It was the complete debacle of British policy in the Far East and the consequent embarrassment of the government at home that inspired Chamberlain's alliance overtures to Germany in March 1898.[43]

Meanwhile, in Germany the Anglo-Russian dispute was regarded as a piece of good luck. The annoyance manifested in the English press at German action had been superseded by near-panic over the Russian advance in Manchuria. British critics of German policy were further disarmed by the announcement in the press that Kiao-chow would be developed as a

[41] It would be tiresome to review all the adverse publicity. Notably strong protests were: Standard, Dec. 20, 28, Jan. 7, March 26; Daily Mail, Dec. 22, April 2, 7; Morning Post, Dec. 21, 23, March 23; Times, Dec. 20, 22, 28 and throughout the first four months of 1898; Daily News, Dec. 20, 21, 22; Westminster Gazette, Dec. 23, March 28, April 25, 26, 27.

[42] Garvin, Life of Chamberlain, III, 248–49; B. D., I, 5–30, for the details; also the complete account in Langer, Diplomacy of Imperialism, II, pp. 467 ff.

[43] Garvin, Life of Chamberlain, III, 254 ff.; Langer, op. cit., II, 485 ff.

free port.[44] English editors and politicians were led by this gesture to assume an identity of interest in preserving the open door for commerce in opposition to the monopolistic tendencies of Russian policy. They were inclined to forgive Germany, although by her Kiao-chow adventure she had been to a considerable degree the author of British embarrassment.

The Germans had every reason for self-congratulation on the outcome of the bold move in the Far East. They had acquired a valuable foothold in China and demonstrated the need of sea-power. Public attention was diverted from furious party strife to larger national aims—overseas expansion and its corollary, naval power. The year closed with a chorus of patriotic exultation. "The glad tidings from the Far East comes like a gust of fresh sea air into the stifling and stagnant atmosphere of German party life." [45] The Norddeutsche in the spirit of the Kiel toasts, said good-by to the year 1897. "When the muse of history turns the page headed '1897' she will linger pensively over the place where in shining characters it is written: 'Landing of the Germans on the strand of the Yellow Sea.' . . . The Imperial standard is hoisted on the mainmast, and as the epic hero of the French story shouted to his men to follow his plumes into the thickest of the fight, so the legend of 'God with us' on the Iron Cross finds its way to the heart of all Germans and kindles there a fire of enthusiasm. Begone all the pettiness and faint-heartedness that burdened and imprisoned the German soul!" [46]

Critics of German policy sensed the connection between the exaggerated publicity of the Far Eastern venture and the new navy law. Tirpitz, who was just introducing his naval program to the public and the Reichstag, was apprehensive of the effect of the Kiao-chow move. He doubtless feared that his opponents would find in it proof of their assertion that a greater navy was wanted not for defense but for purposes of aggression.[47] His apprehension was unfounded. The success of the Far Eastern enterprise raised patriotic feelings and reacted favorably on the navy bill in the Reichstag. At the same time the acquisition of a Chinese port gave naval enthusiasts an opportunity to impress upon the public the great need for a fleet to protect their expanding overseas interests.

A detailed study of the origins of German naval policy lies outside the scope of this study. Nor can space be claimed for an extensive analysis of the propaganda campaign that accompanied the launching of the first naval

---

[44] *G. P.*, XIV, 140–48; *Times,* Jan. 24, 1898. But the German government avoided anything like a pledge, refusing even to make it a matter of official record by publication in the *Reichsanzeiger*.

[45] *Die Post,* No. 357, Dec. 31.

[46] *Norddeutsche,* No. 419, Dec. 31.

[47] Hohenlohe, *Denkwürdigkeiten,* p. 412.

law. Eckhart Kehr in his notable work, *Schlachtflottenbau und Partei-politik, 1894–1901,* leaves but little to add to that theme, while Hans Hall-mann in two volumes, *Krügerdepesche und Flottenfrage* and *Der Weg zum deutschen Schlachtflottenbau,* has explored the origin and evolution of Tirpitz' program, basing his study upon archival material and private papers not available to other scholars. What concerns us here is the publicity and propaganda features of the campaign which affected di-rectly or indirectly the relations between England and Germany.

Tirpitz gives in his memoirs a brief description of the programmatic publicity effort made in the summer of 1897 to prepare the nation for the new navy law.[48] However, to Tirpitz alone, and to the efforts of those whom he enlisted in this work, should not be ascribed the success that the bill scored with the nation and the Reichstag. Bülow, for example, was tremendously impressed with Tirpitz' performance and was led into the false belief that a publicity bureau was all one needed to overcome public inertia and hostility in matters of important national legislation. Behind Tirpitz' success in popularizing the German navy was a com-plex web of social, psychological, and economic forces. The "climate of opinion" resulting from these forces was favorable to the development of German sea-power; Tirpitz supplied the program and organized and concentrated around it the public attitudes and opinions requisite for favorable action in the Reichstag.

British Imperialism and German *Weltpolitik* were products of similar social, economic and ideological compulsions. Basic in both imperialisms was the technological transformation of industry leading to mass produc-tion, the expansion of overseas trade and the search for markets, raw materials and investment opportunities. The great stampede to annex territory, establish spheres of influence, or to exploit economically the undeveloped portions of the globe was the central feature of world history at the turn of the century. Ruthlessness toward native populations and a fang-and-claw attitude toward rivals were rationalized in a manner satisfactory to the élites of industry, finance and politics. Science and exploration, religion and the civilizing mission, the adventure and romance connected with colonial activity cloaked the less idealistic aspects of imperialism.[49]

Most compelling of all the rationalizations of individual and corporate

[48] Tirpitz, *My Memoirs,* I, 142 ff.; far more detailed and revealing is Kehr's *Schlachtflottenbau und Parteipolitik, 1894–1901* (Berlin, 1930), pp. 93–120.
[49] The travel literature of the period associated with the names of Stanley, Peters, Johnston and others, represents a fusion of these interests. Johnston's first African journeys were ostensibly scientific—zoological, botanical, and philological—but he carried in his baggage form treaties supplied by the foreign office for negotiation with tribal chieftains. (Sir Harry Johnston, *The Story of My Life,* pp. 110–39.)

conduct in this field, however, was the strong cast of contemporary thought, generally termed "Social Darwinism." A biological theory, applied by analogy to human society, it justified economic individualism, proved the biological necessity of war for the progress of the human race, afforded a whole armory of arguments for international competition on political and economic levels, gave a scientific complexion to contemporary racial theories, and made of overseas expansion a test of a nation's fitness and ability to survive. Nations were organisms and as such were subject to the compulsions of Darwinian laws. Nationalism, economic endeavor, and international conduct were synthesized anew, and the progress theory was restated in terms of struggle and survival. In consequence there was stamped upon the Imperialism and *Weltpolitik* of the 'nineties a ruthless and brutish character unrestrained by moral or religious sanctions.[50] There is scarcely a single contemporary source that is not shot through with the preconceptions of evolutionary thought. One meets them on every hand in the periodicals, the daily press, private letters and journals, popular literature and poetry, and above all in the speeches and addresses of statesmen and national leaders.[51]

Imperialism, or *Weltpolitik,* justified by theories of biological determinism, had sea-power as its chief instrumentality. Only through sea-power could an overseas empire be won and held. That was the burden of Admiral Mahan's epoch-making treatise, *The Influence of Sea Power Upon History,* published in 1890. Immediately it became the Bible of imperialists and navalists throughout the Western World. Following the first work with a series of volumes sustaining the thesis that command of the sea had been decisive in all past duels for empire, Mahan fathered a cult whose members on the platform, in periodicals and in the

[50] For the historical genesis of Social Darwinism and an analysis of the contributions of its leading exponents—Bagehot, Gumplowicz, Ratzenhofer, Novicow, Vacher de Lapouge—see the admirable treatment in F. N. House, *The Development of Sociology* (N. Y., 1936), chap. XIV, "Social Darwinism." Also R. C. Binkley, *Realism and Nationalism* (N. Y., 1935), pp. 25–31; and for contemporary manifestations in the writings of British publicists, Langer, *Diplomacy of Imperialism,* I, chap. III.

[51] As a principle of historical causation it inspired Lord Salisbury's "Dying Nations" speech, May 4, 1898: "You may roughly divide the nations of the world as the living and the dying . . . the weak states are becoming weaker and the strong states are becoming stronger. . . . The living nations will gradually encroach on the territory of the dying, and the seeds and causes of conflict amongst civilized nations will speedily appear." Biological determinism besides being presented as a causal factor of strife could be, and frequently was, used to bolster ideas of racial and cultural affinity. Spring Rice wrote to Senator Lodge during the Spanish-American War urging American annexations in the Pacific: ". . . let us try while we can to secure what we can for God's language," was the way he put it. Joseph Chamberlain, of course, set great store by Anglo-Saxon and Teutonic racial affinities and these ideas found frequent expression in his public utterances. Moreover, it is only in terms of racial affinity that the devotion of the German nation to the Boer cause can be fully comprehended.

daily press preached the doctrine that colonies and trade depended on
the possession of a strong fleet. In England, where Mahan's work scored
the greatest success, it fixed as axiomatic, if it did not inspire, the proposition that Britain's national and imperial existence depended on
absolute mastery of the sea. The early 'nineties witnessed a powerful
upsurge of navalism, with Dilke, Spenser Wilkinson, H. W. Wilson,
Arnold-Forster and a host of anonymous writers in the press, preaching
the new gospel to willing listeners.[52] In 1894 the doctrine of naval supremacy was institutionalized by the formation of the Navy League. The
purpose of the organization according to the chairman of the executive
committee was "to urge upon the Government and the electorate the
paramount importance of an adequate Navy as the best guarantee of
peace." An adequate navy was defined as one sufficient to command the
sea. "Command of the sea, or in other words, the security of the sea
communications of the Empire, is for us the indispensable condition of
national existence in war, and in peace the sole guarantee of commercial
progress and prosperity." [53] This is scarcely more than a summary and
application of Mahan's thesis to the requirements of Britain's position
as a world power.

In Germany a thorough-going deterministic view of the Empire's
future as a great mercantile and naval power was in the front rank of
all arguments for a strong fleet. The phenomenal rise of German industry, the energy of their merchants and shippers made expansion inevitable; Germany's world interests were growing and whether they
willed it or not she was destined to become a world power. Propagation
of a program in terms of "inevitability" is one of the most effective
propagandist devices. With a merchant marine and an export trade
second only to England's, they maintained only a fifth-rate navy. They
were tempting providence in ignoring the need for adequate protection.
"Without sea-power," wrote Tirpitz, "Germany's position in the world
resembled a mollusk without a shell." And driving the point home with
the Emperor he said: "The points of contact and conflict with other
nations naturally increased during such a process of commercial and industrial development, and sea-power is therefore indispensable if Germany is not speedily to decline." Tirpitz' thought on international relations was cast in a mould of biological determinism. Believing that the
nations lived in a state of nature (*untereinander im Naturzustand leben*),

---

[52] On Mahan's influence and the navalism of the 'nineties see Langer, *op. cit.*, II,
chap. XIII, "The New Navalism."

[53] "The Navy League," *Times,* June 1, 1895; for the circumstances of the League's
foundation and its early history see H. Spenser Wilkinson, *Thirty-five Years, 1874–
1909,* pp. 185–97.

he drew from this biological premise the conclusion that security could be found not in alliance systems or in the improvement of machinery for international understanding, but only in stronger national armaments.[54] These were the basic preconceptions from which were derived most of the arguments in support of German naval expansion.

Since 1890 German statesmen had felt keenly the lack of an adequate naval force whenever they essayed an ambitious rôle in world politics. The formation of the famous flying squadron at the time of the Kruger Telegram had been an object lesson in the purpose and function of a navy. Even before this event William II had championed the cause of German sea-power. He was keen to take advantage of the uproar over the Telegram in the spring of 1896. He brought forward at that time a plan to strengthen Germany's position by the purchase abroad of a squadron of cruisers; and he proposed also to appoint Tirpitz, who was recognized as the coming man in naval affairs, to the ministry of marine in place of the weak Admiral Hollmann. The Emperor's drive failed. Hohenlohe found no enthusiasm among the party leaders for the cruiser proposal. Hollmann was left at the ministry of marine and Tirpitz was packed off to the command of the Far Eastern squadron. The Kaiser was bitter. *"Es gibt schon Leute, die es machen können,"* he is reported to have said.[55]

A year later, after the Reichstag had hashed the modest naval estimates for 1897–98, Hollmann was sacked and Tirpitz recalled from the Far East. Returning to Germany in June 1897, he had only to pull together the various parts of his program, which he had been evolving since 1891, convince the Emperor that a high-seas fleet of battleships rather than cruiser squadrons should be the central feature of the plan, formulate the scheme in a long-range program and work up sufficient political pressure in the country to ensure acceptance by the Reichstag.[56]

The parliamentary situation was more favorable than the fiasco of the estimates in the budget commission indicated. It was not so much apathy or hostility toward the naval question that made the deputies reluctant

[54] Tirpitz, *Memoirs*, I, 77, 162; Hallmann, *Der Weg zum deutschen Schlachtflottenbau*, p. 136.

[55] H. Hallmann, *Krügerdepesche und Flottenfrage* (Stuttgart, 1927), pp. 33–45, 76–79; Hohenlohe, *Denkwürdigkeiten*, pp. 151–58; Langer, *op. cit.*, II, 430–32.

[56] The main points of Tirpitz' program were: (1) two squadrons of eight battleships each with necessary auxiliary craft to be stationed in the North Sea; (2) a schedule of construction spread over a period of seven years; (3) separation of the scheme from party politics by committing the Reichstag in advance to the necessary schedule of payments. The technical, strategical and politico-economic directives were formulated in the famous *Dienstschrift* No. IX of June 1894, and the voluminous memorandum (29 folio pages) of January 3, 1896. (H. Hallmann, *Der Weg zum deutschen Schlachtflottenbau*, pp. 123–25, 173–76; Kehr, *Schlachtflottenbau*, pp. 45 ff.)

to vote funds as it was the instability and manifest planlessness of the Hollmann régime. Tirpitz changed the whole order. The clearly defined objectives, the detailed arrangement of means to ends and the simplicity of his plan overcame objection and robbed the opposition of their chief arguments.

As chief of the naval staff under Hollmann, Tirpitz had witnessed the ineffectiveness of the ministry's propaganda, which was limited to those narrow circles that had a technical or political interest in the navy. He was determined to carry his message of German sea-interests as the great national task of the twentieth century direct to the people and to mobilize the public for effective pressure upon the recalcitrant and apathetic Reichstag. To the work of public enlightenment, therefore, he gave special attention. For over a year before the publication of the first naval bill in November 1897, the problem of German sea-power had agitated the political press. The German Colonial Society, the Pan-German League and the chambers of commerce in the shipping towns had manifested a lively interest in the question. And from the moment of Tirpitz' appointment, before any details of his program were revealed, the political commentators were speculating on what the new "von Roon of the navy" would do. Against this background of public interest the official campaign was inaugurated.

Tirpitz personally visited the princes and the federal ministers soliciting their support and co-operation. A publicity department was established in the ministry of marine with Captain von Heeringen in charge. Von Heeringen also made the rounds of the universities enlisting the support of leaders in the academic world. He met with a ready response from the economists Brentano, Schmoller, Wagner, and Schumacher but was less successful with the historians.[57] Von Heeringen's bureau became the central power plant of the national campaign. Besides enlisting leaders of the academic world and supplying them with material for articles and addresses, the bureau entered into close relations with the editors of newspapers friendly to the cause, providing them with an abundance and variety of information. Every branch of the naval service was called on to deliver material and information for publicity purposes. The naval attachés in foreign capitals reported direct to the information bureau on naval developments. Selections from this material were then put into circulation in Germany through the Berliner Neueste Nachrichten and the Neue Politische Correspondenz. The bureau, further, arranged for selected reporters to witness the maneuvers and cultivated direct relations with the chambers of commerce and the chief

[57] Tirpitz, *Memoirs,* I, 142–43.

agency of German heavy industry, the *Zentralverband deutscher Industriellen.*[58] Scientists and technicians were encouraged to co-operate. "Even the children in the schools were summoned to enlighten their parents on the necessity of building up the navy." [59] Such a many-sided campaign, directed and co-ordinated by a central authority and covering every section of the country, marked a new and significant departure in the organization and technique of official publicity.

A retired diplomat, Von Kusserow, mobilized the Colonial Society and its 20,000 members for the navy campaign. Section meetings were organized by the branch societies; 140,000 pamphlets and 2000 copies of Mahan's *Influence of Sea Power Upon History* were distributed.[60] The Pan-German League, which had been for some time in close touch with the naval authorities, was quite as active as the Colonial Society in agitating for the bill.

The guiding spirit of all this agitation and publicity remained the bureau of information in the ministry of marine. Unquestionably the most effective man in that bureau was Ernst von Halle, who, on the recommendation of Schmoller, was engaged in the summer of 1897 as a statistician and economist. Well trained, with a flair for synthesis as well as statistical detail, he concerned himself chiefly with the propaganda for the educated classes, although he sometimes took a hand in the press polemics through contributions to the Norddeutsche. By his statistical and economic publications on Germany's seafaring interests he did more than anyone else to convince the educated classes that the navy was an economic necessity for Germany and a logical expression of the great maritime interests of the Empire.[61]

As a house organ for naval propaganda the ministry began publication of the *Yearbook for Germany's Maritime Interests,* better known as "Nauticus," which was the editorial pseudonym chosen to cloak the identity of the authors. Tirpitz insisted that it be issued as an unofficial work, although its preparation, financing and distribution was entirely in the hands of the information bureau. Tirpitz tells how a group of deputies and friends, celebrating the passage of the first navy bill at his house, "laughingly toasted the great anonymous journalist, 'Herr Nauti-

[58] Kehr, *Schlachtflottenbau*, p. 96 n.

[59] *Vossische Ztg.,* No. 577, Dec. 9, 1897.

[60] Kehr, *op. cit.,* pp. 98–99. Tirpitz realized Mahan's value as an oath-helper and the translation of his book was made an official enterprise. (Tirpitz, *Memoirs,* I, 145.)

[61] In 1899, at the request of the ministry of marine, a professorship of political economy, with special reference to maritime commerce, was created for Von Halle. In addition to his professorship, Von Halle received 2400 M. yearly as an assistant in the ministry of marine. His chief acknowledged contribution to scholarship was his *Volks- und Seewirtschaft* (2 vols., Berlin, 1902). On Von Halle and the other assistants, their subsidies and honors see Kehr, *Schlachtflottenbau*, p. 102.

cus.' " [62] This publication was partly technical, partly popular. Many of the articles were first published in the *Grenzboten* and *Preussische Jahrbücher* and later reprinted in *Nauticus*. Among the regular contributors were the naval officers Boedicker, Hollweg and Wislicenus; civilian specialists were represented by Von Halle and Ernst Francke, the latter the editor of the *Sozialen Praxis* and correspondent of the Hamburgischer Correspondent and Münchner Neueste Nachrichten. Theodor Schiemann of the Kreuzzeitung and Hugo Jacobi, editor of the Krupp owned Berliner Neueste Nachrichten, wrote the political surveys; while other contributors were drawn from the fields of finance, industry and shipping. In its selection of contributors it showed the principal synthesis upon which Tirpitz erected his program: science, business and politics. While Tirpitz says that the sales of *Nauticus* rose from year to year, it never achieved anything like mass circulation. It served, however, as an informational handbook for editors, deputies, officials, libraries and interested parties who received it free of cost.[63]

While no stone was left unturned by the bureau of information in enlisting the support of the intellectual, financial and political élite, the greater burden of work performed was the establishment and maintenance of contacts with the press. At the beginning of the campaign Privy Councillor Koch was sent to South Germany—where Tirpitz anticipated difficulty—to solicit the co-operation of newspaper editors. Co-operation consisted in the main of receiving news items and articles for publication either direct from the ministry or through an intermediary. Koch met with considerable success on his mission. In Berlin and North Germany editors and journalists were personally approached by Von Heeringen and enlisted for the campaign. A surprising number of editors applied to the ministry for material without having been formally solicited.[64] Tirpitz is far too modest about this part of his work when he says: "We received every newspaper impartially, and gave them all positive information without indulging in polemics. They could do with it just what they

---

[62] Tirpitz, *Memoirs*, I, 147.

[63] For further details see Kehr, *Schlachtflottenbau*, pp. 103–5.

[64] *Ibid.*, p. 109. On the evidence in the ministry's archives the following organs entered into direct relations with the information bureau. South Germany: *Münchner Allg. Ztg., Badischer Landesztg., Schwäbischer Merkur, Fränkische Landesztg.,* (Nürnberg). Western Germany: *Kölnische Ztg., Weser-Zeitung* (Bremen). *Hamburgischer Correspondent.* Eastern Germany: *Schlesische Ztg., Breslauer General-Anzeiger, Danziger N. N.* Berlin: *Reichsbote, Norddeutsche, Berliner N. N., Die Post, Tägliche Rundschau, National-Zeitung.* Periodicals and correspondence services: *Grenzboten, Deutsche Wochenblatt, Berliner Politische Tagesdienst, Nationalliberale Korrespondenz, Neue Politische Correspondenz.* Many others in contact with the bureau through intermediaries (usually retired naval officers) gave space to the naval propaganda. On Von Heeringen's contacts with Hugo Jacobi and Justizrat Fischer see Hallmann, *op. cit.*, pp. 271–72, 278.

liked; a certain gratitude for the material we had given them was always evident, and thus we progressed." [65] In the main the campaign was one of enlightenment and enlistment rather than a rousing polemical campaign against the opponents of the bill. Only with Eugen Richter, editor of the Freisinnige Zeitung and leader of the opposition to the navy bill in the Reichstag, did Tirpitz' staff writers engage in direct polemics. For this purpose they made daily use of the Norddeutsche. [66]

When one turns to the files of German newspapers for the autumn and winter of 1897–98, the effectiveness of Tirpitz' measures is everywhere manifest. Every public meeting was chronicled in the Norddeutsche. Local meetings were organized or sponsored by the Colonial Society, the Pan-German League or unofficial groups interested in naval expansion. Programs were stereotyped. Usually there were three speakers: a retired naval officer, a college professor, and some local official, frequently the mayor or the president of the chamber of commerce. Stock arguments and historical parallels cast in a patriotic mould characterized the speeches. After the rhetoric, a resolution would be proposed, unanimously accepted and telegraphed to the chancellor or the minister of marine. The meetings were not orgies of Anglophobia; generally England figured only as an example of sea-power.

Simultaneously with the publication of the bill the ministry of marine issued a memorandum entitled, "The Maritime Interests of the German Empire," in which was forcefully presented the economic arguments for a stronger navy. [67] Almost without exception editors placed this ready-made case in the forefront of the argument.

In the first weeks following the publication of the proposed navy law the press was glutted with articles expounding the doctrines of the minister of marine. [68] As a specimen for quotation we may take the article entitled, "The Naval Program," published on November 28 in the Free Conservative organ, Die Post. The paper represented the industrial wing

[65] Tirpitz, *Memoirs*, I, 145.

[66] Kehr, *Schlachtflottenbau*, pp. 110–11. The Bureau's relations with the *Norddeutsche* were conducted through Geheimrat Metzler of the editorial staff. (Hallmann, *op. cit.*, p. 282.)

[67] The outlines of the bill had been revealed in the *Kölnische Zeitung* toward the end of September; the context of the bill was published in a special edition of the *Reichsanzeiger* late on Saturday evening, November 27, so that Eugen Richter would be unable to attack it in the *Freisinnige Zeitung* until the following Tuesday. Kehr, *op. cit.*, p. 121; Tirpitz, *op. cit.*, I, 148.

[68] Only selected ones are here cited. "Eine Starke Flotte—eine Lebensbedingung für Deutschland," a series beginning in the *Norddeutsche*, No. 389, Nov. 29, 1897, and "Die Bedeutung der Seemacht für die Staatengeschichte," No. 398, Dec. 8; "Zum Entwurf eines Gesetzes, betreffend die Deutsche Flotte," by Count Eckbrecht von Dürkheim, one of the chief navalists and an intimate of Tirpitz, *Kreuzzeitung*, No. 565, Dec. 3 and Nos. 580, 597, Dec. 20, 22; *Die Post*, Nos. 325, 326, 327, 328, 329, 330, Nov. 27, 28, 29, 30, Dec. 1, 2.

of the Conservative party and its columns were always open to Tirpitz'
journalistic auxiliaries. It began with the familiar theme of how their
navy had not kept step with the advance of their maritime interests and
how necessary it was to restore immediately the proper balance. It then
continued:

All other naval powers have materially increased their navies in recent
decades, even states of second rank in America and in Asia have been actively
concerned in creating a fleet to meet modern needs. A strong navy for us is
an absolutely indispensable means for insuring the peace. Such a fleet is needed
not only to defend our coasts and to protect our merchant marine, but also to
increase our weight in relations to our neighbors, with Russia, France and
England. The value of an alliance with Germany for the first two grows with
every ship that we place in service; and upon England's good will—if only
unwillingly maintained—we can only count if she recognizes in our navy a
stubborn fact that must be taken into account. However, not only in European
waters, but also in foreign seas we must occasionally show our battle flag from
more than a single mast. We must at all times be in a position to give our
ships on foreign duty, which represent our interests as do ambassadors and
ministers, all necessary support. Our ships on foreign stations have real significance only when it is known that behind the little cruiser stands a battle
fleet that commands respect. That is all the more necessary as other states
employ modern battleships in foreign service to represent their interests and
not small cruisers as we do. The events of the last month have unfortunately
demonstrated only too clearly what occurs when we neglect our fighting forces
at sea. It has been a lesson which will not be easily forgotten by those who have
an understanding for the duties and the future of the German Empire. It is
a shameful fact that Germans abroad cannot be protected in the degree to
which they have a right under the spirit of the constitution of the Empire.

Representative of the type of inspired article designed to enlist the
support of the patriotic bourgeoisie, it will be noted that it touched on
every point in the official case for the navy. Beginning with the economic
argument, it stressed the point that other nations with a smaller stake
at sea were building modern fleets, that such a fleet was needed to keep
the peace and protect the German coasts, that Germany's alliance value to
France and Russia would be enhanced and that England's good will
would be insured if the German navy were raised to a respectable
strength, that foreign commerce would follow the flag if it were known
that behind the flag was a great navy, and finally, that only through
fighting strength at sea could they protect the lives of German citizens
and prevent outrages such as had recently occurred in China. It was
indicative of Tirpitz' method of indoctrination that the lesson of sea-
power was not stated in one grand splurge of speech or writing but was
rubbed in gradually by thousands of newspaper articles of which this
is a fair example. By inference or statement all reached a common con-

clusion: the Empire would disappear on the morrow if the fleet were not built.

The line-up of the press on Tirpitz' bill foreshadowed the party divisions in the Reichstag. The National Liberal papers were ardent in their support; Conservative party journals, with the exception of the agrarian Deutsche Tageszeitung, were well-disposed; the great liberal democratic organs—Berliner Tageblatt, Vossische Zeitung and Frankfurter Zeitung —avoided direct opposition to naval expansion in principle, while they criticized the program for a battle fleet instead of cruisers and denounced the fiscal feature of the bill as a dangerous surrender of parliamentary control over finance. Eugen Richter's Freisinnige Zeitung and the Social Democratic press were violently hostile. The press of the Center party, which held the balance of power, blew first hot and then cold, presaging the split in the party on the final vote. Party politics played an important part in the passage of the bill. Domestic issues such as a protective tariff for agriculture, which agrarian interests desired and industrial interests opposed, were brought into the negotiations between the government and the party leaders. When they got to the trading stage, party advantage and economic interest counted for more than foreign policy and national defense. When the Catholic deputy, Lieber, delivered two thirds of the Center votes in support of the bill, he assured its passage and established the hegemony of his party in the Reichstag.[69]

British journalists in later years were prone to assert that the German navy was floated on a tide of Anglophobia; that it was conceived in a spirit of hostility to England, and that it was regarded as the indispensable instrument for the future conquest of Britain's position as the premier world power. To what extent does the contemporary publicity support or invalidate this view? It is axiomatic that measures for strengthening the armed forces of a state must be presented on the basis of defensive rather than aggressive needs. The appeal is always to the nationalistic fear stereotypes of the individual. Elementary precepts of propaganda, therefore, precluded positive agitation against England. On the other hand, the good German bourgeois could appreciate the navy as a line of defense against a possible British attack. And he was told again and again that because of commercial greed and envy England might at any moment launch a mercantilist war against Germany.

There is something almost pathological in the manner in which the journalists portrayed Germany as the single honest nation surrounded by envious thieves waiting only a favorable opportunity to rob her. The

[69] On the party alignments and the domestic issues involved see Kehr, *Schlachtflottenbau*, pp. 122–67.

envy, jealousy and greed of other peoples, and notably the English, were emphasized to convince the German citizen that he was in immediate danger of hold-up and robbery. News items and commentaries were slanted to give the impression that every German success—diplomatic, economic, colonial or scientific—filled the people of neighboring lands with envy, heartburn and hatred. The New Year's survey of Die Post warned that "the world is filled with enemies who look with envious eyes upon our power and our newly won prestige." [70]

That England should have figured prominently in this phase of naval propaganda is understandable. The senseless campaign against German commercial competition, which followed the Kruger Telegram in the summer of 1896, had left its residue of apprehension and ill-feeling. It was easy to revive this apprehension and turn it to the account of semi-official naval publicity. Just the right propagandist weapon, a bald threat of a mercantilist war, was at hand: the famous *Germania est delenda* article published by the *Saturday Review* on September 11, 1897. This article is described by Professor Bernadotte Schmitt as "probably the most provocative diatribe in the annals of newspaper effrontery," and Professor W. L. Langer finds that it "established a new record for extravagance of language." [71] The writer concurs in both judgments. Like so many other senseless expressions of national egoism, in which the records of publicity abound, this article passed unnoticed at home, but did incalculable damage when exported. The article throughout was incendiary in tone, but reached its limit in describing Anglo-German commercial and colonial competition. "A million petty disputes built up the greatest cause of war the world has ever seen. If Germany were extinguished tomorrow, the day after tomorrow there is not an Englishman in the world who would not be the richer. Nations have fought for years over a city or a right of succession; must they not fight for two hundred and fifty million pounds of yearly commerce?" Describing the ease with which the British navy could destroy their uncomfortable commercial rival the writer closed with the Catonian appeal: *Germania est delenda.*[72]

Since Frank Harris had assumed the editorship in 1894, the *Saturday Review* had been dedicated to an anti-German crusade. German trade rivalry was a phobia. As early as 1895 the *Review* had said: "We English have always made war upon our rivals in trade and commerce, and our

[70] No. 357, Dec. 31, 1897.

[71] B. E. Schmitt, *England and Germany* (Princeton, 1918), p. 155; Langer, *Diplomacy of Imperialism*, II, 437.

[72] For fuller quotation see Langer, *op. cit.*, II, 437–38; Hoffman, *Great Britain and the German Trade Rivalry,* p. 281.

chief rival in trade and commerce today . . . is Germany. In case of a war with Germany we should stand to win much and lose nothing." [73] This line could not have been too popular, for the *Review* lost to Strachey's *Spectator* its position as the leading Conservative weekly; its circulation dwindled and its financial position was precarious. Certainly on economic and political questions its eccentric policies could hardly have attracted a sound body of supporters.[74] During the summer and autumn of 1896, when panic over German trade rivalry gripped the British editors and publicists, Harris and the *Saturday Review* were in the middle of the stream, but a year later, when the *Review* published its *chef d'œuvre,* the Times and other papers were analyzing the annual trade reports and statistics and somewhat shamefacedly admitting that their alarms of the previous year had been exaggerated.[75]

Whatever may have been the article's significance as an index of British opinion, it certainly achieved the widest currency in Germany. Around it was woven an illusion of universality conveying the impression that all Britain would welcome a war with Germany as a means of eliminating a competitor. Indirect rather than direct evidence points to the information bureau in the ministry of marine as the agency responsible for its introduction to the German press. Published on September 11, the *Saturday Review's* fanfaronade was not reported by the German correspondents in London. Presumably they were accustomed to these outbursts. A full two months elapsed before it began to circulate in Germany. On the eve of the publication of the naval bill it served as a text for a front page article in the Kreuzzeitung ("The German Naval Question," Nov. 13) by Count Eckbrecht von Dürkheim, an active naval propagandist in close touch with Tirpitz and the ministry of marine. In another lead article in Die Post, a journal that took its material direct from Tirpitz' bureau, it was paraded as a warning to those in Germany who were already taking up a position hostile to naval expansion.[76] It achieved even greater pub-

---

[73] Aug. 24, 1895. In a tirade against the products of German industry the *Review* described them as of a character "to give a reasonably civilized being a fit of apoplexy," and cited as examples "the knife blades that curl up when pressed point downward; the cottons that would make good sieves if the size were blown through; the woolens that never came within miles of sheep; and the sherry that never saw a grape." (Jan. 16, 1897.) Other examples of Harris' aberrations appear in the issues of Jan. 25, Sept. 19, Dec. 19, 1896; March 13, May 22, Dec. 11, 1897.

[74] It is doubtful if Harris himself composed these effusions, but that the policy was his is shown by the fact that this line was taken up when he became editor in 1894 and dropped immediately when Harold Hodge took over in 1898. If anything, Hodge's policy (1898–1913) was pro-German. For an amusing description of Harris as editor of the *Saturday Review* see H. G. Wells, *Experiment in Autobiography* (N. Y., 1934), pp. 436–42.

[75] *Times,* Oct. 4 and Dec. 28, 1897; but especially Hoffman, *op. cit.,* pp. 255 ff.

[76] No. 323, Nov. 25. Another diatribe from the English periodicals, unearthed and paraded through the German press at this time, was entitled "The Megalomania of

licity when it was splashed on the front page of the sensational Lokal-Anzeiger in an article entitled "The 'English Friendship' and the Naval Question." It was used to support the conclusion of a navalist writing in the Hamburger Nachrichten on December 25. "That England will seize the first opportunity when circumstances are favorable to wage war against Germany is no idle speculation," the writer concluded.[77] There was scarcely a German newspaper actively engaged in the naval propaganda that at some time during the campaign did not quote or allude to this article. Very soon it appeared in the periodical and book press where it maintained its currency until it was worn smooth and flat by so much passing around. More than any other one screed it helped to establish the thesis that a British attack because of economic jealousy was a possibility against which they must prepare.

British "envy" and "jealousy" worked along with other stock arguments put out by the navy's propaganda bureau. The sneers and petty cavils, which were not difficult to find in the British press, gave color to the thesis. Basically, however, it was wholly irrational and artificial. Envy is the dissatisfaction that one person experiences because another possesses what he cannot. Germany possessed nothing that the English did not have in great abundance—a magnificent colonial empire, a great merchant marine, vast capital, industrial resources, commercial and technical experience. Could the British have been envious of the Germans when they possessed all these things to a degree the Germans could never hope to achieve? The British position was rather analogous to that of an old, rich, and powerful concern witnessing the establishment of an aggressive young rival. At first the British attitude was one of scornful indifference; by the close of the century they were forced to recognize the success of the new competitor, and what was more damaging still to British pride, was the recognition of the necessity for studying German methods. At this time one heard much in England of German technical training, the application of science to industry and the reliability and steadiness of the German workman—all with the view of applying the spur to their own business men and industrialists. There was no demand

England" (*Spectator,* Jan. 16, 1897). Inspired by a provocative article in the *Hamburger Nachrichten,* the *Spectator's* reply purported to show what would result from an Anglo-German war, namely, the seizure of German colonies, destruction of her foreign trade and commerce, and the blockade of her seaports. In such a war Germany would be isolated because other powers "would most of them be not a little pleased to see the most arrogant Power in Europe suffer a few wholesome humiliations."

[77] *Lokal-Anzeiger,* No. 569, Dec. 5; *Hamburger Nachrichten,* No. 302. Eckart Kehr (*Schlachtflottenbau,* pp. 91–92) is in error when he regards this article as a British reaction to the German naval agitation preliminary to the introduction of Tirpitz' bill.

from any responsible quarter that aggressive action be taken to put a competitor out of business.

Nor did the launching of the German naval program create any marked excitement in England. The political aspects of the fight for Tirpitz' bill were reported in routine fashion. The navy law itself was analyzed and commented on at the time of publication and a few ill-natured remarks were forthcoming on the anticipated uses of the fleet when it became a reality.[78] The executive committee of the Navy League issued a routine statement in which it pointed out that all of England's enemies were strengthening their fleets and that greater efforts would be required to maintain British supremacy.[79] That the German navy might some day challenge the English was not even considered. If it gave them trouble it would do so only by a coalition with France and Russia. But outside Navy League circles no great concern was displayed in the British press. In the following March, when Tirpitz' bill became law, public attention was centered upon the Far Eastern crisis and with the exception of the Times, the German navy law was editorially ignored and barely noticed in the news reports. In fact the approval of the bill by the Reichstag corresponded in point of time with a marked détente in the public relations between the two countries. And behind the scenes Chamberlain and Hatzfeldt were exploring the possibility of an Anglo-German alliance.

[78] These came from the *Standard* (Dec. 1), the *Daily Mail* (Dec. 1), and the *Morning Post* (Nov. 30), and were linked more closely with the Kiao-chow seizure than with the navy.

[79] *Morning Post,* Dec. 16.

CHAPTER VII

BRITAIN'S NEED AND GERMANY'S PRICE

Es gibt keine allgemeingültigen Rezepte einer staatlichen Presspolitik, und eine Presspolitik, deren Methoden man öffentlichen darlegen könnte, ist keine Presspolitik mehr.

Walther Heide, *Diplomatie und Presse,* p. 19.

No topic has aroused greater interest among students of diplomatic history than the abortive Anglo-German alliance negotiations at the turn of the century. Each new piece of evidence, from the publication of Eckardstein's memoirs to the recently published third volume of Garvin's biography of Joseph Chamberlain, has been analyzed and glossed by eager scholars in England, Germany, and America. Because of the human propensity to speculate on "what might have been," earlier studies tended greatly to exaggerate the importance of these negotiations. Certainly, Chamberlain's talks with Hatzfeldt in the spring of 1898 were of no more consequence than Salisbury's less spectacular attempts to reach a standstill agreement with the Russians. Both were acting under the compulsion of a press and parliament aroused over Russian poaching in Britain's Far Eastern preserve. Salisbury sought to buy the Russians off; Chamberlain tried to propagate the idea of a common Anglo-German-American front in the Far East.

In so far as Germany was concerned, a distinct improvement in press relations favored and facilitated the colonial secretary's tactics. Since 1896 petty backbiting and recriminations had disturbed Anglo-German relations. Now the authorities took action to remedy this situation. Not the least important of the efforts in this direction was Queen Victoria's personal intervention. Sir Theodore Martin, who had served the Queen as a special emissary on more than one occasion, was authorized to interview the leading London editors and to persuade them, if possible, to adopt a more reasonable attitude toward Germany. Martin was able to report to the Queen on January 13, 1898, that "all the leading Journals will adopt a quite altered tone towards the Emperor of Germany and the German people." Assurances of a conciliatory attitude were given by the editors of the Standard, Daily Telegraph, Morning Post, Daily News, Daily

Chronicle, St. James's Gazette, Pall Mall Gazette, the Globe, and Punch. Concluding his report to Victoria, Sir Theodore wrote: "It is most unfortunate that there should be very generally prevailing in this country a very bitter feeling against the Germans. Everyone whom Sir Theodore has seen has mentioned this, and none more emphatically than the Editor of *The Times* [Mr. G. E. Buckle]. Commercial rivalry has something to do with it; but not very much." [1]

It seems altogether reasonable to attribute to the Queen's intervention the softened judgments of the British press on the Kiao-chow episode and the reserve maintained toward the passage of the German naval law. Hatzfeldt, unaware of the influence brought to bear behind the scenes, commented in his report of January 22 on the sudden abatement of hostile criticism in the English papers.[2] This change provided a more favorable atmosphere for the private and public gestures that Chamberlain began to make a few weeks later toward an understanding with Germany.

At the end of March, Chamberlain, with the knowledge and consent of his cabinet colleagues, engaged the German ambassador in a series of exploratory conversations. These discussions, which the Germans treated as a game of hide-and-seek, have been the subject of much discussion and many judgments. There is no need to extend the record of this debate.[3] However, two points of significance should be noted here. First, the directors of German policy skilfully avoided a commitment that would have soured their relations with St. Petersburg; second, while they opposed Chamberlain's haste to strike a business deal and sign a contract, they kept his hopes green by advancing the more cautious view that a period of propagation and ripening was required. In this connection they repeatedly emphasized the importance of mutual accommodation in small things with a view to improving their public relations and preparing the way for a future general agreement between the two countries.[4]

[1] *Letters of Queen Victoria,* III, 224–25. For the immediate effect of the Queen's action on a particular journal, the *Pall Mall Gazette,* see F. J. Higginbottom, *The Vivid Life,* pp. 197–99.

[2] *G. P.,* XIV, 147.

[3] Except on minor points pertaining to publicity, the writer is in substantial agreement with the narrative and conclusions of W. L. Langer (*Diplomacy of Imperialism,* II, chap. XV) and Gerhard Ritter (*Die Legende von der verschmähten englischen Freundschaft, 1898–1901,* Freiburg, 1929), p. 19. More conventional interpretations are F. Meinecke, *Geschichte des deutsch-englischen Bündnisproblems;* Eugen Fischer, *Holsteins grosses Nein* (Berlin, 1925); G. P. Gooch, *Before the War* (Lond., 1936), I, 198 ff. Garvin's *Life of Chamberlain* (vol. III, 241–77) is particularly important for the memoranda on Chamberlain's conversations with Hatzfeldt. See also Arthur Balfour's amusing letter to his uncle, Lord Salisbury, in Blanche E. C. Dugdale, *Arthur James Balfour* (2 vols., N. Y., 1937), I, 189–91.

[4] *G. P.,* XIV, 212, 222, 236, 247. The Emperor's comment on this point is interesting: "Yes; and above all immediate discovery and exposure of all anti-German art-

While nothing concrete came from the Chamberlain-Hatzfeldt conversations, the colonial secretary was encouraged to present his indictment of splendid isolation to the public. At the same time, by relating this proposed policy change to events in the Far East, his pronouncement took on the character of a public demonstration against Russian activity in that region. At Birmingham on May 13, Chamberlain delivered his famous "long spoon" speech, in which he attacked Russia, deplored the policy of spendid isolation, and advocated an "Anglo-Saxon alliance." Turning to the Far East he reviewed the train of broken promises that had finally landed the Russians in Port Arthur and Talienwan. He dismissed Salisbury's effort to come to an understanding with Russia by citing the proverb, "Who sups with the devil must have a long spoon." Surveying the future of England's trade interests in the Chinese Empire he said: "If the policy of isolation which has hitherto been the policy of this country is to be maintained . . . then the fate of the Chinese Empire may be, and probably will be, hereafter decided without reference to our wishes and in defiance of our interests." The alternative to exclusion was the enforcement of the principle of the open door. And to do this "we must not reject the idea of an alliance with those Powers whose interests are most nearly approximate to our own." [5] Germany was not mentioned in this connection, but an earlier reference to the Crimean War, which had shown that England could not seriously injure Russia unless she was allied to "some strong military power," established the connection in people's minds.

Chamberlain's clear, vigorous, and unconventional language startled the journalists and politicians of two continents. The astonishment in England was the greater since Salisbury only a week before at the Primrose League banquet had spoken slightingly of "the jargon about isolation," and had assured the country that England could hold her own against all comers.[6] British and continental publicists, knowing nothing of the Chamberlain-Hatzfeld talks, were puzzled as to whether Chamberlain's utterances constituted a maneuver or a program. He had denounced isolation, insulted Russia, thrown a kiss toward America and hinted at a continental flirtation. It is not surprising that the editors of the serious London dailies were taken aback. These men were, by and large, conventional in their attitudes toward foreign affairs and diplomacy and were, therefore, more wary than Chamberlain in painting the perils of isolation and the need for allies. To betray their great need, they thought,

---

icles launched in the English press through foreign influence, which betray our stupid press into attacks upon England." (*Ibid.*, XIV, 226.)

5 *Times* report, May 14, 1898.

6 *Times*, May 5, 1898.

would cause the seller to raise his price. As a result the Post, the Standard, and the Daily Telegraph endorsed the speech in a vague and non-committal way, while the Times undertook to correct the impression created abroad that it was a distress signal and that great profits were in sight for the salvagers.[7] Leading Liberal organs, the Westminster Gazette and the Daily News, took a party line and condemned the speech as "indiscreet," "maladroit," and as evidence of "a most plentiful lack of judgment." [8]

Partisan feeling aroused by the Birmingham episode was aired in the Commons' debate on June 10. Chamberlain, attacked by the opposition, restated his views in a much more moderate manner. He weakened his reference to alliance, but boldly asserted that "at all events, I am perfectly ready to say now that I desire better relations with Germany, and I believe . . . that our interests in China are much more nearly allied to the interests of Germany and China than they are to the interests of Russia." The opposition speakers—Harcourt, Asquith, and Dilke—did not deny that an understanding with Germany would strengthen England in the Far East, but they predicted that Germany would be unlikely to offer herself as a relay horse for Chamberlain's policy.

Far from being a cool, rational airing of opinions on foreign affairs, the debate was rather a fierce exchange of blows for party advantage. Chamberlain bore the brunt of the opposition attack as the Liberal leaders played up the contradictory public statements of Chamberlain and Salisbury. Asquith scored a neat rhetorical point when he reminded his hearers that for fifty years Britain had carried unaided the burden of empire. "What have we done, what have the people of Great Britain done or suffered," he asked, "that we are now to go touting for alliances in the highways and byways of Europe?" [9] The same partisan and personal spirit is found in the press reaction to the debate. The Liberal Daily News, for example, praised Asquith for his spirited attack on Chamberlain. "He neither underrates him, as Mr. Gladstone sometimes did, nor overrates him, as Sir William Harcourt always does, but holds up the ingeniously inflated bubble, and then quietly pricks it. The result is a noisy explosion of gas, and the silent fall of a scarcely noticeable pulp." [10] In short, the issues were so confused, the press so imperfectly informed,

---

[7] *Times,* May 16; *Morning Post,* May 14, 23, 26; *Standard,* May 14, 16; *Daily Telegraph,* May 14, 16.
[8] *Daily News,* May 14, 16, 18; *Westminster Gazette,* May 15, 16, 17.
[9] *Parl. Deb.,* 4th ser., vol. 58, 1347. Dilke, Asquith, Curzon, Labouchère, Harcourt, and Chamberlain spoke in the order named. (*Ibid.,* pp. 1317–1438.)
[10] June 11, 1898. Mr. Spender wrote in the *Westminster Gazette:* "The ominous thing is that Mr. Chamberlain desires an alliance with Germany in order to give substance to what, up to the present, has admittedly been 'bluffing.' " (June 11.)

and the partisan feeling so bitter that anything like a discussion of Chamberlain's program on its merits was out of the question.

German press reaction to the debate stirred up by Chamberlain was not conditioned by any knowledge of what had been going on behind the scenes, but rather by the losing diplomatic battle waged by Great Britain against Russian influence at Peking. The silence of the Norddeutsche was eloquent; the Kölnische Zeitung was evasive and reserved. Allowing for variety in shading and emphasis, the comment in Conservative, National Liberal and Democratic journals shows the following pattern. Chamberlain's Birmingham speech was a cry for help and a shocking exposure of Britain's impotence. It would be a mistake for Germany to back England, for she was the losing horse. Where doubts existed as to the outcome of Anglo-Russian rivalry, it was easy for the editors to paint a picture of Germany's comfortable position between the two contestants, both of whom courted German assistance and good will. Special emphasis was given to Chamberlain's reference to an Anglo-Saxon alliance, while his allusion to "a strong military power" on the continent was ignored. A better impression was produced by Chamberlain's frank avowal of a desire for better relations with Germany in the Commons debate of June 10. With few exceptions a cordial endorsement was accorded this outspoken declaration from which the word "alliance" had been dropped.[11]

Further improvement in the public relations between the two countries resulted from the attitude of the German public authorities and the press toward the British campaign for the reconquest of the Sudan. Kitchener's first victory over the dervishes at Atbara inspired William II to send a congratulatory telegram to Queen Victoria. This was released by the British foreign office to the press.[12] The Emperor repeated the telegram act when the River War was brought to a successful conclusion by the annihilation of the Mahdi's forces at Omdurman on September 2. At the foot of the Waterloo column in Hanover he himself announced the English victory to his assembled soldiers and led the cheers for the Queen and their British comrades in arms.[13] Press reception of the news in Germany was quite in the same spirit. "A victory for civilization over barbarism," "a common victory for European culture," and one "which the whole enlightened world welcomes," were some of the generous com-

[11] *Norddeutsche*, Nos. 114, 135, May 17, June 12; *Vossische Ztg.*, Nos. 224, 268, 271, May 14, June 11, 14; *Berliner N. N.*, Nos. 224, 226, May 14, 16; *Kreuzzeitung*, No. 229, May 18; extracts from the party press quoted in the reviews in the *Norddeutsche* and the *Berliner Neueste Nachrichten*.

[12] *Standard*, April 11; *Daily Telegraph*, April 13, 15; *Morning Post*, April 13, 18; *Westminster Gazette*, April 13.

[13] *Letters of Queen Victoria*, III, 274. He also sent a congratulatory telegram to Kitchener.

ments that accompanied the detailed reports of the battle circulated by the Reuter and Wolff agencies. Compliments for the bravery of the British troops and the skilful campaign conducted by Kitchener were strongly to the fore, and although the victory signified a great advance for British imperialism the usual note of envy or carping criticism was entirely absent.[14]

Even Saunders of the Times had to acknowledge "the sympathetic and generous spirit" with which the German press had followed the Sudan campaign, although he attributed the change largely to official dictation. "Journals which hitherto have assumed a very acrimonious tone at the mere suggestion of British interests have suddenly veered round, evidently owing to the magic wand of official inspiration, and now praise what they once abused. In fact, certain official organs have received an intimation from above to pave the way, by means of well-timed hints and suggestions in regard to future politics, for the announcement that political Germany has altered her helm by a few points." [15] Doubtless the influence of the foreign office was brought to bear upon the press through many channels, but that influence did not directly affect more than a fraction of the German newspapers. It was favorable events that produced favorable publicity.

Simultaneously with the German expression of good will toward Britain's success in the Sudan, came the announcement of the signature of the Anglo-German agreement over the Portuguese colonies. The events leading up to this act do not require elaborate restatement. From the first sharpening of the Anglo-Boer crisis in South Africa, British authorities worked feverishly to padlock the only open door to the South African Republic—Delagoa Bay and the railroad from Lourenço Marques to Pretoria. For a time in July 1898 the prize seemed within their grasp when the Portuguese government, to bolster its shaky financial structure, turned to the London government for a loan. At this point Berlin intervened and by making a feint toward co-operation with Paris to block British desires, forced an opening through which they eventually emerged, after two months of hard bargaining, with the agreement of August 30, 1898. As is well known the agreement provided for joint participation in any loan that might be made to Portugal, with the customs revenues of the Portuguese colonies of Mozambique, Angola, and Portuguese Timor earmarked as security. The specification of the territorial lines within

[14] *Lokal-Anzeiger,* No. 415, Sept. 5; *Berliner Tageblatt,* No. 450, Sept. 5; *Münchner N. N.,* No. 411, Sept. 7; *National-Zeitung,* No. 508, Sept. 8; *Freisinnige Zeitung,* Sept. 5; *Frankfurter Zeitung,* Sept. 5; and reports of the *Times, Daily News* and *Daily Mail* correspondents, Sept. 5, 6, 7.
[15] *Times,* Berlin dispatch, Sept. 7.

which the customs revenues should be assigned to the two lending powers was tantamount to a contingent division of spheres of influence. A
secret convention provided for the reversion of the colonies to the signatory powers, along those same lines, in case Portugal should lose or
abandon her sovereign rights. In this event, England would secure southern Mozambique, which included Delagoa Bay, while the Germans would
get Mozambique north of the Zambesi, about three fourths of Angola,
and Portuguese Timor.[16] True, the agreement was conditional upon the
materialization of the Portuguese loan. When the government squeaked
through the crisis without mortgaging the colonial revenue, the convention remained merely *Zukunftsmusik*. One clause in the agreement, however, had immediate application and that fact deserves more emphasis
than most writers have given it. Article II of the secret convention stated
that "from the conclusion of the Conventions of this day's date," the two
parties would "abstain from advancing any claim of whatsoever kind to
the possession, occupation, control, *or exercise of political influence,* in or
over those portions of those Portuguese provinces in which the Customs
revenues have been assigned to Great Britain [or to Germany]." [17] In
its narrowest sense this article meant that the German government abandoned its policy of opposition to British interests in Delagoa Bay. In a
larger sense it was a renunciation, lock, stock and barrel, of the policy of
the Kruger Telegram, an abandonment of Marschall von Bieberstein's
pro-Boer policy, and the removal of the last obstacle to British predominance in South Africa. This was a reversal of policy and a renunciation
that was very much in the thoughts of the German negotiators, and they
therefore felt that they were entitled to heavy compensations. "In giving
England a free hand with regard to Delagoa Bay and its hinterland,"
wrote Bülow to Hatzfeldt, "we take a step which will stir up in the entire
German nation a feeling of painful disappointment, because with the
passage of years the Boers have become the object of a sentimental sympathy which, as in all cases of sympathy, cannot be combated on grounds
of logic. The Emperor's Government, must, therefore, if it is not to suffer
capitis diminutio, be in the position to show that its policy has not merely
been one of renunciations, but that evident advantages have been
gained." [18] From the policy of neutrality toward the Transvaal dispute
the German authorities never wavered even during the days of the Boer

[16] The best accounts of the diplomacy of this episode are Langer, *Diplomacy of
Imperialism,* II, 519–29, note especially the instructive map on p. 525 ; Garvin, *Life of
Chamberlain,* III, chap. LXI ; Gooch, *Before the War,* I, 206–11. The chief sources
are *B. D.,* I, 44–86 ; *G. P.,* XIV, 259–367.
[17] *B. D.,* I, 73.
[18] Bülow to Hatzfeldt, June 22, 1898 ; *G. P.,* XIV, 274. Frequently repeated during
the course of negotiations. *Ibid.,* XIV, 296, 305, 323.

War when they were set upon by the entire German press for their indifference to the fate of the Boer kinsmen. Since British statesmen had never admitted any German rights to a voice in settling the fate of South Africa, they naturally placed no value upon this renunciation, but rather regarded it as a hold-up. Chamberlain was forthright in his opinion: "The only advantage to us is the assurance of Germany's abstention from further interference in Delagoa Bay and the Transvaal—in other words, we pay Blackmail to Germany to induce her not to interfere where she has no right of interference. Well! it is worth while to pay Blackmail sometimes. . . ." [19]

In spite of Chamberlain's resentment at "blackmail," this part of the agreement registered an immediate gain for Britain. As the Portuguese loan never materialized the Germans drew no benefit from it. This makes the secret Anglo-Portuguese declaration of October 14, 1899, in which England renewed the ancient treaties of alliance obligating her to respect the integrity of the Portuguese colonial empire, seem all the more a sharper's trick. However, this step was not taken with the calculated idea of nullifying the German agreement of the preceding year, but to realize the original British intention of closing the open door to the Transvaal at Delagoa Bay. Only at the very outbreak of the Boer War were the British able to secure in return for this declaration an engagement by the Portuguese to close Lourenço Marques to the further importation of arms and munitions destined for the Transvaal.[20] Renewal of the ancient accord with Portugal was the price paid for this highly important object. Had British ministers been pressed on the charge of double dealing at the outbreak of the Boer War, doubtless they would have offered the same defense that a German chancellor offered under similar circumstances at the outbreak of another war—"Necessity knows no law."

From the beginning of the negotiations terminating in the agreement of August 30, 1898, the Germans had insisted upon complete secrecy. But on the very day the accord was signed, a rumor appeared in the press that important engagements marking a new departure in the relations between the two countries had been concluded. The manner in which the rumor was taken up and inflated in the press to force partial disclosures by the authorities, and how these disclosures were made the

[19] Garvin, *Life of Chamberlain*, III, 315.
[20] *B. D.*, I, 93–94. Garvin's labored defense of British action misses fire entirely, because of his misunderstanding of this declaration. (Garvin, *op. cit.*, III, 320 ff.) Instead of binding Portugal to "benevolent neutrality," it bound her not to proclaim neutrality at all in the Boer War. A proclamation of neutrality would have necessitated, under international law, the granting by Portugal of belligerent rights to the Transvaal.

basis of partisan attack and official defense, presents a striking example
of the difficulties inherent in the conduct of secret cabinet diplomacy in
an era of rapid communication, universal literacy, and omnipresent publicity.

The Pall Mall Gazette scooped competing journals with a series of
sensational articles on the new Anglo-German accord. The agreement, it
claimed, was of a comprehensive nature and extended even to "an offensive and defensive alliance in certain eventualities." Celebrating the
end of "splendid isolation," it said: "The achievement of close relations
with Germany is creditable to our statesmanship, and we shall be all the
stronger for it in the critical times that are so clearly imminent. . . ." [21]
The Pall Mall's fantasies produced a crop of glosses, affirmations, and
contradictions almost as remote from the truth as the original Pall Mall
statement. Central to the whole discussion was the question whether a
union of British and German interests to oppose and block Russia in
the Far East had been effected. This line of speculation and exaggeration was particularly embarrassing for the Wilhelmstrasse, where the
possible implications of the accord for Russo-German relations had been
carefully canvassed in advance.[22] It was imperative that these wild rumors be promptly scotched. On September 3, the Kölnische Zeitung
published a Berlin telegram flatly denying that there had been a change
of front in German policy. But that did not mean they had not come to
an agreement on a special question, "for example, a joint loan to Portugal whose needy financial condition may sooner or later require such
action." [23] This communication found a place next morning in the first
left-hand column on the front page of the Norddeutsche, a position that
stamped it as an official pronouncement. Other journalists inquiring at
the foreign office were apparently given the same information, for we
find the Berliner Tageblatt denying that a secret alliance had been concluded and stating that they had "definite assurance" that the accord in
no way touched their relations with Russia.[24]

These official tips were reproduced in practically all the German papers and quickly ended the chatter about a secret alliance. They did not
dispose of the public curiosity as to the real nature of the transaction.
Furnished with the broad hint that it was a colonial deal, the press
sleuths, bent on ferreting out the answer, began to send up trial balloons

---

[21] *Pall Mall Gazette,* Sept. 2, 3, 7.
[22] See Holstein's memorandum in *G. P.,* XIV, 342–44. Holstein had anticipated the
possibility of rumors and exaggerations of a nature disturbing to their relations with
Russia.
[23] *Kölnische Ztg.,* No. 853, Sept. 3.
[24] No. 450, Sept. 5.

labeled Near East, Far East, Zanzibar, Samoa, etc. One by one these were pricked by semi-official denials until only the ones labeled South Africa, Delagoa Bay, and the Portuguese colonies were left in the air. Confirmation came from several sources within the next month. An article by Lucien Wolf (Diplomaticus) in the *Fortnightly Review* gave the main outlines of the agreement, and the Lisbon correspondent of the Berliner Tageblatt secured from Portuguese authorities a fairly accurate summary of the convention.[25] There were other disclosures from time to time, some spurious, some bearing signs of authenticity. However, the exact apportionment of spoils in case the Portuguese empire were mortgaged to England and Germany was not revealed. The public was left in the dark as to the size of the German legacy.

Presumptuous efforts to force a disclosure on this point usually brought a sharp, brusque reprimand. When the Lokal-Anzeiger professed to give the correct details, an official denial was issued through the Wolff Bureau; when the Lokal-Anzeiger persisted in its course, the Reichsanzeiger issued an official statement: "The Berlin Lokal-Anzeiger continues to advertise itself with revelations as to the content of the Anglo-German agreement in spite of the denial published by Wolff's Telegraphic Bureau. We are authorized to state that its assertions rest upon impudent and clumsy invention." [26]

Nevertheless, enough of the agreement became known to raise a cry in colonial and Pan-German circles. The general conclusion arrived at, and this was not denied in official pronouncements, was that England's pre-emption rights over Delagoa Bay had been recognized in return for assurances of compensation in other parts of the Portuguese dominions. That this signified a complete reversal of previous German policy and put the seal upon British predominance in South Africa was clearly understood. The publicity reaction to this fact ran in three main channels. There was first the acceptance of the accord without any great display of enthusiasm but rather with resignation coupled with gloomy hopes that adequate compensation had been secured.[27] In these journals, which were among the most important and widely circulated in the country, were frequent expressions of approval of the agreement as a sign of improved relations with England. While little positive enthusiasm was manifested by this group, there arose a wail of protest and disappoint-

[25] "The Anglo-German Agreement," *Fortnightly Review,* October 1898, pp. 627–34, was quoted widely in the German press; *Berliner Tageblatt,* No. 513, Oct. 9.
[26] Quoted in the *Norddeutsche,* No. 366, Dec. 31, 1898.
[27] *National-Zeitung,* Nos. 501, 526, Sept. 4, 19; *Berliner Tageblatt,* Nos. 450, 452, 500, Sept. 5, 6, Oct. 2; *Schwäbischer Merkur,* No. 207, Sept. 6; *Münchner N. N.,* Nos. 408, 409, 411, Sept. 5, 6, 7; *Kölnische Volksztg.,* Nos. 770, 783, Sept. 5, 9; *Frankfurter Ztg.,* Nos. 243, 244, 247, Sept. 3, 4, 6.

ment in another section of the press, numerically insignificant but extremely vocal. "Abandonment of the Boers!" and "A betrayal of Niederdeutschtum" was the keynote struck by the Pan-Germans, the racialists and the colonialists. Only one really important journal moved in this current—the Lokal-Anzeiger—and its attack was oblique rather than frontal.[28] But the other journals made up for their lack of numbers by the violence and bitterness of their dissent. Here the Leipziger Neueste Nachrichten, the Rheinisch-Westfälische Zeitung and the insignificant Deutsche Zeitung, edited by the super-patriot and racialist, Dr. Friedrich Lange, took the lead. They seized upon the government's renunciation of the policy recorded in Marschall's published dispatch to Hatzfeldt of February 1, 1895: German interests, it was said at that time, require the maintenance of the Transvaal as an independent state, in accord with the treaties of 1884, and the guarantee of the status quo with regard to the railway and port facilities in Delagoa Bay. In official circles, continued the critics, it was now alleged that an adequate price had been secured for the abandonment of this position, but how was the public to know that the compensation was really adequate when the terms of the agreement were secret? Their attitude throughout was similar to that of the opposition speaker in the House of Commons, who said: "I am not acquainted with the intentions of the Government, yet I feel it my duty to state that I mistrust them." For better than two months these stubborn campaigners continued to shout: "Treason to the Boers!" [29]

A prolonged and melancholy howl of dismay was likewise raised in Pan-German and colonial circles. Resolutions of dissent from the government's action were passed first by the local chapters of the Pan-German League and the Colonial Society and subsequently by their respective national executive committees. The latter organization addressed its complaint to Chancellor Hohenlohe and drew from him the assurance that, while political considerations prevented immediate publication, vital German interests were adequately safeguarded.[30] This was the only

[28] *Lokal-Anzeiger,* Nos. 413, 416, 451, Sept. 4, 6, 27. "Das Ende der Woche hat uns noch ein neues Bild gebracht. Germania und Brittania drücken sich liebvoll ans Hertz. Mit dicken Thränen der Rührung in den Augen betrachtet John Bull das schöne Bild. Misstrauische sieht der deutsche Michel zu, und wenn Michel ein Berliner ist, könnte er sich versucht fühlen, der sorglosen Germania zuzurufen: 'Halt man det Portmonnaie fest!'" (Sept. 4.)

[29] The best record of this agitation is to be found in the *Deutsche Zeitung,* whose editors combed the German press for every sign of criticism and dissent. Special articles and citations from other journals in almost every issue from September 3 onward, but particularly important are Nos. 233, 237, 238, 266, Oct. 4, 8, 9, Nov. 11.

[30] *Berliner Tageblatt,* Nos. 511, 513, Oct. 8, 9; *Münchner N. N.,* No. 469, Oct. 11; *National-Zeitung,* No. 580, Oct. 20.

public pronouncement carrying full official responsibility, but an extensive defense campaign was carried on in the semi-official and inspired press.

The government's counter-offensive opened with a series of Berlin telegrams to leading provincial papers defending the foreign office against the charge of selling out the Boers. The similarity of argument and phraseology indicate their common origin. England, it was pointed out, had an option on Delagoa Bay if Portugal at any time wished to dispose of it. If that contingency should arise, Germany would have no legal ground for opposition. Under the agreement just concluded Germany would receive valuable compensation. As for abandoning the Boers, the public was reminded that the situation had changed materially since the Kruger Telegram. When the Boers unwisely refused to make any reforms, the German government had no choice but to secure its interests as best it could. That was the purpose of the present agreement.[31] A political communication appearing in the Süddeutsche Reichskorrespondenz, a provincial correspondence service frequently used by Bülow, upheld the foreign office refusal to publish the details of the accord. Foreign policy, it was said, concerned the achievement of particular immediate and future objectives—not the satisfaction of the curiosity of the newspaper public. If certain indicated eventualities should arise it would then be time to inform public opinion of all that was of importance in the agreement.[32] The foreign office defense of secrecy as against publicity was subsequently elaborated in longer articles in Die Post, the National-Zeitung, and the Schlesische Zeitung.[33]

Typical in sentiment and language was the article entitled, "Zur Weltlage," appearing in Die Post. The report of a general alliance between England and Germany was as absurd, said the writer, as the charge that the abandonment of Delagoa Bay was a diplomatic defeat. Would those who are denouncing the government, have Germany champion every anti-English element on African soil whether genuine German interests are involved or not? "Fortunately German diplomacy does not have to respond to every demonstration in the realm of public opinion as is the case in the purely parliamentary state. In the field of colonial policy it will also follow the course that appears most ad-

---

[31] *Kölnische Ztg.*, No. 847, Sept. 7; *Münchner N. N.*, No. 208, Sept. 7; *Die Post*, No. 244, Sept. 7; *Frankfurter Ztg.*, No. 247, Sept. 7. The *Kölnische's* telegram was conspicuously reprinted in all leading German papers.

[32] Quoted in *Die Post*, No. 248, Sept. 11.

[33] "Zur Weltlage," and "Das deutsch-englische Abkommen und die öffentliche Meinung," *Die Post*, Nos. 248, 269, Sept. 11, Oct. 2; "Deutschland, England und Transvaal," *National-Zeitung*, No. 548, Sept. 10; *Schlesische Ztg.*, No. 235, Oct. 6, 1898.

vantageous in furthering German interests. In the face of repeated demonstrations of sympathy for the Boers we must, nevertheless, give German interests preference over those of the Transvaal." Then follows in this article the explanation that the treaty did not give Delagoa Bay to England; England's option there has existed for more than a decade. If it were eventually used Germany would receive important material compensations. And in conclusion the writer said: "For the pacification of certain colonial enthusiasts, this much can be said with absolute certainty: A second Zanzibar-Helgoland treaty will never be concluded." The pattern of this and similar articles is simple—the realistic view is opposed to the sentimental, the agreement is defended on the ground that they would be compensated for something they could not prevent, the extremists are rebuked and the moderates praised.

Outside the ranks of the semi-official and inspired journals strong support for the government in its publicity dilemma was not forthcoming.[34] Despite the filtering of official views into the press and the endorsement of the agreement by some independent writers, the general tone of the press toward the abandonment of the former German policy in South Africa was mistrustful if not openly hostile. The skeptical attitude and the covert sniping of large circulation papers such as the Berliner Tageblatt, the Lokal-Anzeiger, the Vossische Zeitung, and the Münchner Neueste Nachrichten was of more than ordinary significance.[35] And no one in official position could lightly ignore the section of the press, variously referred to as expansionist, Pan-German, or Bismarckian, which kept up the steady chant:

> Wir weichen züruck von Ort zu Ort,
> Der alte Respekt ist eben fort.

From the beginning it was evident that the spokesmen in the press could not easily be weaned from their sentimental attachment to the Boer cause. Why did not Bülow take the bull by the horns and make an

[34] A notable exception was the Kreuzzeitung, which published two long articles supporting the foreign office. "Realpolitik nicht Gefühlspolitik" was the theme of these articles. The writer deplored "the extraordinary political shortsightedness of those who regarded it as Germany's duty to protect the interests of Boers and Afrikanders in South Africa." "One should not be sentimental in these questions, but that appears to be the case as soon as one begins to discuss the Anglo-German agreement." (Nos. 465, 489, Oct. 5, 19, 1898.)

[35] The Berliner Tageblatt, for example, featured on the front page a dispatch from its London correspondent in which were quoted the following lines from a letter purporting to come from a German friend in South Africa: "Das mit der Abtretung von Delagoabai Deutschland ganz und gar Südafrika an England preisgiebt, daran ist doch kein Zweifel. . . . Südafrika wird künftig von England monopolisirt. Deutschland erleidet in Südafrika bei Englandern, Boeren, und Deutschen eine gewaltige moralische Niederlage." (No. 486, Sept. 24.)

official statement of the government's revised policy toward the South African question instead of operating exclusively through the inspired press? Why did he not say officially to the nation what he confided to the British ambassador—that this agreement "removed from discussion the question of Delagoa Bay, which threatened to embitter relations between the two countries, and to cause an estrangement which it might take thirty or forty years to overcome"?[36] Taking the contemporary official view of the matter some of the reasons are obvious. First, such action would have constituted in effect a repudiation of the Kruger Telegram and an admission of error in the policy that had inspired it; and second, withdrawal from South Africa could not be publicly avowed without indicating the exact extent of the anticipated compensation, and since that was to be found in the colonial possessions of a friendly state diplomatic decorum forbade an official statement. By signing the agreement with England the German government committed itself to neutrality in the Anglo-Boer struggle, but in so doing set itself in opposition to national sentiment. Thus were the seeds of future embarrassment sown. For when the South African War broke out in the autumn of 1899, a swift current of pro-Boer enthusiasm whirled the country away from the course of official policy. During the Boer War, English observers interpreted the German scene in terms of their own experience, professing to see in the rabid Anglophobia of the Teutonic Know-Nothings a clear reflection of the attitudes and opinions of the directors of German policy.

While the agreement over Delagoa Bay and the Portuguese colonies was a source of immediate embarrassment to the German government, and of immediate relief to the British government, the general policy of the latter was facilitated in still another direction. In contemporary publicity the strictly neutral attitude assumed by the German government and press in the Fashoda crisis of the autumn of 1898 was linked directly to the rapprochement with England. Not a word of comfort or encouragement for the French during their hour of humiliation was forthcoming from across the Rhine. Here Germany played the rôle which Englishmen thought she should be happy to play without compensation and with scarcely any thanks; namely, by assuming a rather ominous neutrality to make France conscious of the power that menaced her continental position. Meanwhile the British worked their will against France in colonial matters.

German diplomatic documents reveal the care that was taken to avoid injury to English susceptibilities by any show of sympathy for France.

[36] *B. D.*, I, 108.

They reveal also the skepticism with which Bülow, the foreign office, and the Emperor regarded the French attempts to start a flirtation with Berlin as a signal to the British not to press them too hard.[37] The press followed the lead given by official policy. Throughout the Fashoda crisis the Norddeutsche maintained a severe reserve, reporting developments but never expressing or quoting an opinion. Die Post, which was closely watched as a reflector of official views, never departed from the line that Germany was "absolutely indifferent" toward the quarrel over the Sudan.[38] The Münchner Neueste Nachrichten leaned toward the English side, while the three leading democratic journals—Vossische Zeitung, Berliner Tageblatt, and Frankfurter Zeitung—were impartial in their reporting and noticeably reticent in their judgments.[39] The London correspondent of the Kreuzzeitung championed the English cause and Schiemann in his weekly review of foreign affairs predicted that the French would have to withdraw.[40] Germania, the Center party organ, the National-Zeitung and the popular Lokal-Anzeiger did not deviate from the general line in their treatment of the affair.[41] Almost alone among German papers the super-chauvinistic Deutsche Zeitung embraced the French cause. The editor, Friedrich Lange, prayed for a political miracle that would give the French a victory over the hated British.[42] Making due allowance for traditional German suspicion of France and the influence of the foreign office with certain sections of the press, the complete reserve of German editors is still somewhat puzzling. The abusive and violent tone of the London press toward France must have awakened in German minds painful memories of Kruger Telegram days, when Germany was the object of British wrath. That German publicists refrained from baiting the London editors on this occasion

[37] *G. P.*, XIII, 237–73, XIV, 371–426. When Münster, the German ambassador in Paris, reported that opinion was swinging toward a rapprochement with Germany, the Emperor noted on the margin of the dispatch: "Ein bischen spät! das hätte vor 3 Jahren in der Transvaalzeit gemacht werden müssen." (*Ibid.*, XIV, 393.) Press utterances were no less definite: *Lokal-Anzeiger* (No. 547, Nov. 23): "Wir können kein Bündnis mit dem unruhigen Volke brauchen. . . ." *Kölnische Ztg.* (No. 179, Dec. 15): "Wir brauchen uns mit diesen Zukunftsträumen nicht weiter zu beschäftigen." In the same spirit, *Schwäbischer Merkur*, No. 288, Dec. 9; *Vossische Ztg.*, No. 600, Dec. 23. See further E. M. Carroll, *French Public Opinion and Foreign Affairs*, pp. 175 ff.

[38] No. 285, Oct. 18, 1898.

[39] *Münchner N. N.*, Nos. 459, 472, 475, 484, Oct. 5, 13, 14, 20; *Vossische Ztg.*, Nos. 480, 492, Oct. 14, 20; *Frankfurter Ztg.*, Nos. 294, 295, Oct. 24, 25; *Berliner Tageblatt*, (Arthur Levysohn's weekly political review), Nos. 513, 526, 539, 565, Oct. 9, 16, 23, Nov. 6.

[40] Nos. 487, 501, 525, Oct. 18, 26, Nov. 9.

[41] *Germania*, Nos. 225–255, Oct. 1–Nov. 6; *National-Zeitung*, Nos. 518, 525, 541, 588, Sept. 14, 18, 28, Oct. 25; *Lokal-Anzeiger*, No. 528, Nov. 10.

[42] No. 243, Oct. 15 to No. 263, Nov. 8.

testifies to the growth of a more respectful attitude toward British power.[43]

Kitchener's victory at Omdurman and Salisbury's victory at Fashoda, together with the public display of resolute determination to go to war if necessary, surprised some groups in Germany where it had been the fashion for some time to represent the British Empire as a played-out institution and the British people as soft and flabby to the point where their government would retreat and make concessions rather than stand up and fight for national interests. The change was most striking in Conservative circles, which by tradition were anti-British in their outlook. England, in their eyes, had become *Bündnisfähig*. This reversal is strikingly illustrated in the policy of the Kreuzzeitung, the chief organ of German and Prussian conservatism. Schiemann in his weekly review of foreign affairs for November 9, 1898, presented the case:

For years we have represented an anti-English policy in our columns and energetically rejected every attempt that seemed to lead toward an Anglo-German alliance. But we have always given the reasons that determined our attitude. We said that England was not strong enough, either on land or on sea. To a weak England we were nothing more than a desirable friend whose strength would be used to spare herself sacrifices. Meanwhile conditions have fundamentally changed. In her army and navy England has made extraordinary exertions and has shown in the late Sudan campaign that her men are equal to the demands of a severe campaign. With this England we can talk business, and if we have no cause to seek an alliance we are quite justified in seeking an understanding. . . . In the present world situation an understanding with England is a wise political act; that must be admitted even by those who are not England's friends.

While not so frank in admitting a change of opinion, the dampening of the fires of Anglophobia was just as marked in other Conservative papers—Die Post, the Schlesische Zeitung, and the Reichsbote.

Neither at this juncture nor in the later course of the discussion of an Anglo-German alliance is it evident that Conservative circles, as represented by the press, were irreconcilable in their attitude toward political co-operation with England. Friedrich Meinecke has advanced the thesis that the Anglophobia of the Conservative Junker class in Ger-

---

[43] On the British press campaign see T. W. Riker, "A Survey of British Policy in the Fashoda Crisis," *Pol. Sci. Quar.*, March 1929, pp. 54–78. How the British government mobilized the press is told by Kennedy Jones (*Fleet Street and Downing Street*, pp. 96–97). On the geo-political and diplomatic aspects of the Fashoda crisis, W. L. Langer's chapter (*The Diplomacy of Imperialism*, II, 537–80) is distinguished by the broad grasp of the entire problem in its great complexity. M. B. Giffen, *Fashoda; The Incident and Its Diplomatic Setting* (Chicago, 1930), takes into account only the political aspects.

many, which in its political outlook abhorred England as the leader of
Western Liberalism, was fundamental in the failure of Anglo-German
alliance negotiations.[44] The thesis of a ruling class antagonism to the
English *Weltanschauung* as a primary factor in preventing the conclusion of an alliance cannot be reconciled with the realistic attitude assumed by Conservative journals toward the problem of Anglo-German
relations. The irreconcilables were not the Conservatives, but rather the
neo-Bismarckians, the Pan-German professors, the colonialists and the
lunatic fringe of German political life. Publicity for their ideas was afforded by such journals as the Hamburger Nachrichten, the Leipziger
Neueste Nachrichten, the Rheinisch-Westfälische Zeitung, and the Deutsche Zeitung. The irreconcilables would shun England like the plague;
the Conservatives, on the other hand, would admit closer relations and
agreements on specific questions, if not an out and out alliance. At the
same time they wished to maintain the informal entente with Russia,
not allowing German policy to be steered into a collision with their
powerful Slavic neighbor. In this respect there was a general community
of agreement between the Conservative, Catholic, National Liberal, and
Democratic press.

A test of prevailing attitudes in the German political press is afforded
by the reaction to the two speeches delivered by Joseph Chamberlain
toward the close of 1898. Reviewing the foreign and colonial situation
at a meeting of the Conservative Club of Manchester on November 16,
the colonial secretary presented the government's policy in the Far East
in terms of the open door for British products, and stressed in that connection the common interest of England, Japan, Germany and the United
States in maintaining a free market in China. "Therefore," he said, "it
is that I have advocated and continued to advocate, friendly relations
with those Powers whose interests are most in harmony with ours." He
rejoiced at the progress that had been made with regard to Germany; he
saw no place in the world where Britain's interests seriously conflicted
with Germany's; and he thought that without proposing anything in the
nature of a permanent alliance, they could look forward to closer co-
operation in the future.[45]

It is only in its context of current events—the Fashoda crisis, the
Anglo-Russian tension in the Far East, the South African quarrel—

[44] Meinecke, *Geschichte des deutsch-englischen Bündnisproblems, 1890–1901*, pp.
233–34, 260-61.
[45] *Times*, Nov. 17. Editorial approval was general in the Conservative and Unionist journals. *Times, Pall Mall Gazette, Morning Post, Standard*, and *Daily Telegraph*, Nov. 17 and 18. Mr. Spender countered with an editorial entitled, "Isolation
Still Splendid" (*Westminster Gazette*, Nov. 17).

that Chamberlain's mild expression of commendation for the past and greater hope for the future acquired significant meaning. German press reactions were conditioned by the general picture presented by these events. The Berlin foreign office followed the customary technique of giving publicity to an official view without incurring official responsibility. This took the form of a Berlin telegram to the Kölnische Zeitung, which found a prominent place the following day in the Norddeutsche. The telegram read:

We can only greet Chamberlain's statements with approbation. It is not in Germany's interest to stand on bad relations with England. If during the last decade their relations have frequently been disturbed, it has arisen from the fact that Germany in her necessary colonial development has almost everywhere met with the most determined opposition from Great Britain. . . . Effective co-operation between England and Germany can only be assured on the basis of complete equality of treatment for German interests. It was upon such a basis that the good relations that today exist between Germany and Russia were established. It is only upon such a basis that the plan elaborated by Mr. Chamberlain at Manchester can be realized.[46]

The telegram was dispatched, of course, by Dr. Fischer of the Kölnische Zeitung Berlin bureau; it might well have borne the signature of Bülow or Holstein.

In the important German papers the same note of cautious approval, hedged by reservations and hesitancies, greeted Chamberlain's statements, which were widely circulated in an eleven-hundred word dispatch by Wolff's Bureau. The Berliner Tageblatt alone was unreserved in its commendation. In the other journals the cat's-paw-argument was much in evidence as was also a sharp reservation with regard to the maintenance of cordial relations with Russia. Some thought their present diplomatic position was entirely satisfactory, as they were being courted simultaneously by England, France and Russia. Others were doubtful if Chamberlain's fine theory of co-operation would be applied in concrete instances. A few dismissed it as a trial balloon. The irreconcilables were rendered momentarily speechless. Friedrich Lange, editor of the Deutsche Zeitung, reproduced the Wolff report without comment, although he liberally sprinkled the quoted passages with editorial question marks. This was the German journalist's polite way of saying to his readers, "Here the speaker lies." [47]

[46] *Kölnische Ztg.*, No. 1083, Nov. 18; *Norddeutsche*, No. 271, Nov. 19.
[47] *Deutsche Ztg.*, No. 271, Nov. 18; *Berliner Tageblatt*, No. 584, Nov. 17; *Kreuzzeitung*, No. 547, Nov. 23; *Die Post*, Nos. 315, 317, Nov. 18, 20; *Germania*, No. 264, Nov. 18; *Lokal-Anzeiger*, Nos. 538, 540, 547, Nov. 17, 18, 23; *National-Zeitung*, No. 626, Nov. 17; *Schwäbischer Merkur*, Nos. 272, 288, Nov. 21, Dec. 9; *Kölnische Volksztg.*, No. 1017, Nov. 19; *Münchner N. N.*, Nos. 532, 535, Nov. 18, 19.

Speaking at Wakefield on December 8, Chamberlain undertook to correct the impression that he wished to engage German policy for the defense of Britain's interests against France and Russia. "It was idle," he said, "to talk of an alliance in which the advantage is all on one side." They did not expect Germany to pull their chestnuts out of the fire just as they had no notion of pulling Germany's out for her. But there were many questions that affected their mutual interests, and on these it would be much better to agree than to disagree and oppose one another. Referring to the progress that had already been made, he expressed the confident hope "that in the future the two nations—the greatest naval nation in the world and the greatest military nation—may come more frequently together, and our joint influence may be used on behalf of peace and of unrestricted trade." Either by way of a reminder or to flatter British patriots he added: "Meantime in the present state of the world the friendship of this country is not to be despised." [48]

The British correspondents in Berlin described the reception of Chamberlain's second speech as favorable, satisfactory, or complimentary.[49] An examination of the leading journals confirms these reports, and it is scarcely necessary to reproduce the different wordings employed to express the same general attitude. But why the universal tone of satisfaction and commendation evoked by this pronouncement as contrasted to the first? Scanning the various reports and comments, it is evident that the German publicists divined in Chamberlain's revised remarks a limitation of the entente to questions affecting their mutual interests, leaving Germany her freedom of action in all other spheres. Further, in this speech Chamberlain expressed a desire for better relations with the Czar's government, which weakened the impression hitherto prevailing that his main object was to secure a continental sword to throw into the balance against Russia. English friendship on these terms implied no bar to the cultivation of German relations to Russia. And finally, his remarks were generally interpreted as an acknowledgment of the German claim to equality of treatment wherever Anglo-German interests converged. By and large, it was thought that Chamberlain had met every reservation hitherto made in Berlin to Anglo-German co-operation. The new state of relations was jubilantly defined as a policy of friendly understanding and specific agreement from case to case. *Die Politik von Fall zu Fall* became a slogan in the German press.[50] When Bülow touched

[48] *Times,* Dec. 9; Garvin, *Life of Chamberlain,* III, 323.

[49] *Times,* Dec. 10; *Daily Telegraph,* Dec. 10; *Standard,* Dec. 10; *Daily Mail,* Dec. 10. The *Daily News* correspondent warned that by exhibiting eagerness they flattered the Germans and encouraged them to put up the price. (Nov. 18, Dec. 10.)

[50] *Kölnische Ztg.,* Berlin telegram, No. 1161, Dec. 10; republished in the *Nord-*

on the subject of Anglo-German relations in addressing the Reichstag
(Dec. 12) he merely confirmed what had been said with a thousand
voices in the press—that "there were various questions and many points
on which Germany could move in company with Great Britain, and that
willingly, without prejudice to and with the fullest security of other
valuable relationships." [51]

It is evident that the foreign office and the press had found an idea
system equipped with appropriate word symbols—the free hand, the two
irons, the *Politik von Fall zu Fall*—that allowed for co-operation with
England and friendship with Russia. In the relations between London
and Berlin this denoted a clear gain, particularly in the publicity atmosphere created by the press. Since 1896 the journalists on both sides
of the Channel had written with pens dipped in poison and gall. Intervention of the authorities and the course of diplomatic events restored
sanity and produced a considerable degree of toleration. But even in
those journals where the greatest cordiality was displayed toward the
new course, there was no discernible enthusiasm for an alliance. We
may take as a norm of opinion the statement of the Berliner Tageblatt:
"Germany would like to remove all sources of conflict between herself
and England, but she will not be forced into choosing between Great
Britain and Russia." [52]

In view of this attitude, which prevailed in the foreign office as well
as in the press, the whole problem of the Anglo-German alliance negotiations during 1898 assumes a certain air of unreality. This raises the
question of motives underlying Chamberlain's discussions with Hatzfeldt
and his complimentary public pronouncements. It is significant that his
declaration of regard was made in the spring when Britain was hard
pressed by Russia, and was repeated in the autumn when daggers were
drawn over Fashoda. In the latter instance, which coincided with Chamberlain's Manchester manifesto, British tempers were dangerously shortened. War talk filled the air and armaments preparations were being
pushed at full speed. Many continental observers predicted that Britain would make war on France in the spring. What was more natural
under the circumstances than that Chamberlain should threaten France

---

deutsche (No. 290, Dec. 11) and numerous other papers as the official view; com-
ment of *Münchner N. N.*, No. 570, Dec. 10; *Die Post*, No. 337, Dec. 10; *National-
Zeitung*, No. 664, Dec. 9; *Vossische Ztg.*, No. 576, Dec. 9; *Lokal-Anzeiger*, No. 576,
Dec. 9; *Kreuzzeitung*, No. 576, Dec. 9; *Berliner Tageblatt*, No. 628, Dec. 11;
Schwäbischer Merkur, No. 289, Dec. 10. The *Deutsche Zeitung's* only comment:
"Man sieht, Herr Chamberlain ist mit Deutschland sehr zufrieden. Vielleicht etwas
verdächtig zufrieden?" (No. 290, Dec. 10.)
[51] *Fürst Bülows Reden* (2 vols., Berlin, 1907), I, 38.
[52] No. 599, Nov. 25, 1898.

with an Anglo-German alliance? This dovetailed exactly with Salisbury's tactics in the crisis. The day following Chamberlain's speech at Manchester we find the prime minister writing to Victoria endorsing a proposed visit from William II, and stating that it "would certainly do good." "Matters have much changed during the last twelve months, and he [William II] has shown himself disposed to be friendly to this country. The attitude of France makes it desirable that the world should believe in an understanding between Germany and England." [53] It cannot be doubted that much of the warmth put into the discussion of the Anglo-German rapprochement by British statesmen and editors during the autumn and winter of 1898 resulted from the same calculation that moved Salisbury to recommend a display of family hospitality toward the German Emperor.

This significant time relationship stands out more sharply under the spotlight of contemporary publicity than it does in the diplomatic records of the cabinets. Overlooking the publicity aspects of Chamberlain's campaign has led to a general exaggeration of British alliance overtures to Germany. Certainly Garvin's picture of a stubborn German Michael refusing to be led by "Brummagem Joe" into the Promised Land of an English alliance is an unpardonable flight of fancy.[54] Likewise, the thesis sometimes encountered that an ill-informed and short-sighted journalism, or unfavorable "public opinion," kept English and German statesmen from concluding an alliance belongs in the same category. All the wisdom in matters of foreign affairs was not concentrated in the foreign offices and chancelleries. The logic of the situation in 1898 was as evident to journalists as to statesmen. Furthermore, there were enough men of good will in the editorial rooms of London and Berlin, men who were amenable to official suggestion or argument, to have provided favorable publicity for an alliance had the directors of policy set a determined course in that direction. With the future veiled, the exigencies of the moment seemed to be met by the policy of limited agreements and mutual toleration.

This was accepted in London as well as in Berlin, for British confidence in the formula of splendid isolation was partially restored by the collapse of French opposition in the Sudan and the brusque manner in which French overtures were rejected by the German press. The dangerous doctrine that Britain had become too rich and comfortable

---

[53] *Letters of Queen Victoria,* III, 312.
[54] *Life of Chamberlain,* III, *passim.* More valid judgments are those of W. L. Langer, *Diplomacy of Imperialism,* II, 514–16, 529–31; and Gustav Roloff, "Die englisch-deutschen Bündnisverhandlungen im Jahre 1898," *Berliner Monatshefte,* Oct., 1935.

for determined action was now dispelled. British self-confidence achieved a new high.

It was not the overrated alliance gestures, but the agreement over the Portuguese colonies and Delagoa Bay that restored equilibrium in Anglo-German relations. While the immediate consequences of this agreement were beneficial, it became a source of embarrassment when armed conflict broke out in South Africa. German official publicity registered a partial success in defending the new departure, even though it was well understood that Germany was withdrawing as the champion of the Boer cause. Had the South African question been settled otherwise than by war the wide rift that later developed between German popular sentiment and the realistic policy of the Wilhelmstrasse might have been avoided. No one could foretell the future and Bülow gambled on a peaceful settlement. He may also have hoped to have the expected compensation in hand for publicity purposes before either side resorted to arms. *Realpolitik nicht Gefühlspolitik* was an adequate symbol in 1898, but when the Boer War broke out the following year the Wilhelmstrasse found itself caught in a cleft stick.

In evaluating the force of contemporary publicity it would be twisting the facts to represent it as the decisive influence in Anglo-German relations. It doubtless figured in the calculations of both British and German leaders; it set limits to their mobility in negotiations; it did not determine the direction of national policies, neither did it fix the decisions that were taken in Downing Street or in the Wilhelmstrasse. It might be likened to the weather if it were not for the fact that publicity, within limits, could be and was controlled. At this time the publicity weather was improving. That was the general trend, and that was the desire of those who were in a position to inspire and control it.

CHAPTER VIII

THE BOER WAR: CABINET POLICY VERSUS POPULAR SENTIMENT

But whatever the future may bring, one thing is certain: In the glorious history of England a new leaf has been turned showing the performance of the hangman's office on the latter-day disciples of William Tell.

Theodor Mommsen to Max Müller, *Manchester Guardian*, April 11, 1900.

"Like the petrel that precedes the storm, Cecil Rhodes appeared in Berlin in March, 1899," writes Bülow in his memoirs.[1] At the time, however, Rhodes was regarded as the bearer of an olive branch and not as the harbinger of storms. He came to Berlin in the interest of his grandiose scheme of a Cape to Cairo railroad and telegraph line, for which he wished to secure a right-of-way through German East Africa as well as the financial co-operation of Berlin bankers. Politically his project fitted neatly into the formula of Anglo-German co-operation in specific cases.

Rhodes arrived in Berlin on March 10; he was received by the Emperor and entertained at luncheon and dinner; he departed on the 16th after having come to an agreement with the foreign office on the construction of the telegraph line. His conversations about the projected railway were encouraging but inconclusive. With Rhodes and the Emperor it was a case of love at first sight. These two jerry-builders of empire intoxicated one another with the sweep of their vision and the vastness of their plans.[2]

Regarded by the German public as the real author of Jameson's Raid, Rhodes would have been the object of universal vituperation and abuse had he appeared in Berlin at any time during the preceding three years. All the influence of the German foreign office was now used to restrain the press. The Berlin correspondent of the Daily News reported that "the semi-official apparatus has been set in motion with an ability and works with an exactness which is simply marvellous." The gist of all semi-official and inspired statements was that sentiment should be ex-

---

[1] *Memoirs of Prince von Bülow,* I, 338.
[2] *Ibid.,* I, 338–41. Rhodes' own account in "Vindex" (F. Verschoyle), *Cecil Rhodes, His Political Life and Speeches* (Lond., 1900), pp. 719–22.

cluded and Rhodes' proposals considered entirely on their merits. Fanatical idealism should be suppressed in favor of practical politics.[3] Following the official lead, the important papers of large circulation emphasized that Rhodes' past history had nothing to do with the proposals which he had come to Berlin to lay before the government.[4] But pro-Boers and neo-Bismarckians were undeterred by their minority position. They shrilly denounced any traffic with the instigator of the Jameson Raid and impudently demanded that he leave Berlin forthwith. The Hamburger Nachrichten and the Deutsche Zeitung were the most violent in their attacks. Friedrich Lange, the editor of the latter journal, started the rumor that Rhodes appeared at his audience with William II dressed in a brown shooting jacket and tan trousers! When the agreement over the telegraph line was announced in the semi-official press, Lange reviled it as "Rhodes' Victory" and sadly concluded: *"Wir sind nach Kanossa gegangen."* [5]

A chorus of hosannas and hallelujahs went up from the British press on the occasion of Rhodes' official reception in Germany. Bashford, Maxwell, and Saunders puffed the incident for all it was worth in their dispatches from Berlin, while the editors in London filled their columns with encomiums for William II and the statesman-like attitude assumed by his advisers in the matter of Anglo-German co-operation in developing the Dark Continent. "The German Emperor in granting [this interview] finally effaces in a handsome and magnanimous way the irritating memories of his action on the occasion of the Jameson Raid," wrote the foreign editor of the Times. All the stock phrases were paraded in the press—"new era," "good omen," "family tiffs," "civilization and progress," and "hand in hand with the nations of Anglo-Saxon stock," etc. But all this was in reality only so much window dressing that just failed to conceal the real Conservative-Unionist hope, namely, that Rhodes' meeting with the Emperor marked the final end of Boer reliance upon German support and encouragement against England in South Africa.[6]

The sharpening of the Anglo-Boer crisis during the months preceding

[3] *Daily News,* March 13, 1899; *Norddeutsche,* No. 61, March 12; *National-Zeitung,* Nos. 158, 164, 172, 176, March 8, 10, 14, 15 (articles quoted widely by the German and English papers); *Kölnische Ztg.,* Berlin telegram, No. 202, March 14.
[4] *Lokal-Anzeiger,* Nos. 118, 122, March 10, 13; *Vossische Ztg.,* Nos. 120, 127, 131, March 11, 16, 18; *Berliner Tageblatt,* Nos. 129, 132, 135, 144, March 11, 13, 14, 19; *Kölnische Volksztg.,* No. 246, March 14.
[5] The publicity efforts of this group are fully chronicled in Lange's *Deutsche Zeitung,* Nos. 60, 64, 69, 73, March 11, 16, 22, 26.
[6] The most important editorials and Berlin dispatches are: *Times,* March 11, 13, 16, 17, 21, 27; *Pall Mall Gazette,* March 11; *Daily Telegraph,* March 13, 15, 21; *Standard,* March 13, 15, 16, 22; *Morning Post,* March 15, 16, 22. The Liberal *Daily News* and the *Westminster Gazette* were, in contrast, very casual and matter-of-fact about it all. *Westminster Gazette,* March 16; *Daily News,* March 11, 13, 14, 15, 22.

the outbreak of war reacted upon every mood and tense of the relations between Berlin and London. It bore directly on Rhodes' visit to Germany and it determined also the final outcome of the stubborn diplomatic struggle which the Wilhelmstrasse and Downing Street waged over the Samoan Islands. The British, and particularly Lord Salisbury, were reluctant to apply to Samoa the formula of agreement from case to case in the manner desired by Germany, and from March to November 1899 official circles and the public press were vexed and irritated by the dispute over these far-away islands. Rhodes was warmly welcomed by officials in Berlin because they desired to enlist his support on behalf of the German claim to Samoa.[7]

Anyone ignorant of geography would have assumed from the racket made by the German press during these months that a continent was at stake rather than a small island. As Eckardstein bitterly complains, the politicians of the beer table, who were whipped up by the journals under the influence of the navalists and colonialists, did not know "whether Samoa was the name of a fish, a fowl or a girl," but Samoa was something German and German it must remain.[8] Bülow apparently gave the press free rein. This enabled him and the Emperor to point to the excited state of German 'public opinion' as a condition that the British ought to remedy by making concessions; for such a trifle as Samoa they ought not to imperil the good understanding that had been established in their public relations.[9]

It was the outbreak of war in South Africa and Britain's need of German good will that finally melted British resistance to German pressure; the yelping of the press and the complaints and veiled threats of Bülow and the Emperor were secondary factors in bringing the English ministers to agree to German annexation of Samoa. At a time when the entire continent was pro-Boer and interventionist talk filled the air, Samoa was of slight consequence when measured against German good will and neutrality. Moreover, Chamberlain, pressing for a public advertisement of German benevolence, was particularly anxious that William II should pay a visit to his English relatives. But the date for this event was resolutely postponed in Berlin until the British cabinet agreed to German annexation of Samoa. "The policy of the German Empire since Bismarck has been always one of undisguised blackmail," wrote Chamberlain to Salisbury. "I expected that they would press Samoa at

---

[7] Langer, *Diplomacy of Imperialism*, II, 620–24; Holstein to Hatzfeldt, Feb. 24, 1899, *G. P.*, XIV, 580–81.

[8] Freiherr von Eckardstein, *Lebenserinnerungen und politische Denkwürdigkeiten*, II, 41.

[9] *B. D.*, I, 112, 113, 117–18, 126–27; *G. P.*, XIV, 581–675, *passim*.

the present juncture." [10] But in his opinion a display of German benevolence was worth the price, and in this judgment political circles in England concurred. On November 9, 1899, the German press announced the
glad tidings in large headlines: *"Samoa Bleibt Deutsch!"* And one provincial editor said what many people thought: "All hail and victory,
brave Boers! You have fought for us and have won us Samoa!" [11]

For most Englishmen the South African War began with the Boer
ultimatum of October 9, 1899; technically, the Boers were the aggressors,
and everything that preceded Kruger's rash declaration was blanked out.
Lord Rosebery, the leader of the Liberal Imperialists, said that he
"dated from the ultimatum as Mohammedans from the Hejira." [12] For
continental observers the English campaign to subdue the Boers began
with the Jameson Raid; the outbreak of hostilities was only a change of
weapons. Jameson's filibustering, Chamberlain's diplomacy, and Lord
Roberts' military strategy were varying means toward a single end.
While the crisis was developing in the summer and autumn of 1899, a
publicity pattern was formed in which the German press presented the
origins of the Boer War. Reduced to essentials, this pattern, which was
fathered by sentiment rather than judgment, portrayed Chamberlain and
Milner as the willing tools of the Rand capitalists; the citizenship question and other grievances of the Uitlanders were only pretexts serving to
conceal the real issue, which was British determination to conquer all
South Africa; the war was the work of a small ring of unscrupulous
capitalists made up of Englishmen and German Jews whose object was
the acquisition of the rich gold and diamond mines that lay in the Transvaal. It was a war whose origins were "geological"; a war of the Bourse
against the Boers. When not explained in economic terms, a political
frame of reference was employed. Then we have Great Britain, moved by

[10] Garvin, *Life of Chamberlain,* III, 334–35.

[11] *Times, Daily Mail, Daily News, Morning Post, Standard, Pall Mall Gazette,
Daily Telegraph,* Nov. 9, 10. The entire first page of the *Norddeutsche* (No. 265,
Nov. 19) was given over to quotations from all sections of the press celebrating the
victory. Editors who took the line that Bülow had used British embarrassment in
South Africa to squeeze her out of Samoa were sharply called to order in the
Kölnische Zeitung. Details of the negotiations are to be found in *B. D.,* I, 107–31;
G. P., XIV, 567–675; Chamberlain's part is set forth in Garvin, *op. cit.,* III, 324–43;
Eckardstein, who acted as intermediary between Chamberlain and the German au-
thorities, tells his story in his *Lebenserinnerungen,* II, 1–79; Alfred Vagts, *Deutsch-
land und die Vereinigten Staaten in der Weltpolitik* (2 vols., N. Y., 1935), I, chap. X.

[12] J. A. Spender, *Life, Journalism and Politics,* I, 92. The mobilization of the
British press for the Boer War lies outside the limits of this study. Rhodes and his
lieutenant, Jameson, came to London in the spring of 1899 and conferred with leading
journalists and editors, endeavoring to line up the press for a concerted publicity
blast against Kruger on the franchise question. As Mr. Spender puts it, "The walls
of Jericho were to fall to the blasts of a unanimous Press, for which the tune was
to be set by speeches and despatches in the style of the 'new diplomacy.' . . ." (*Ibid.,*
I, 86–87.)

a lust for power and possessed of overwhelming military force, setting out deliberately to conquer a brave and freedom loving people to whose territory she had not the shadow of a legal claim. Almost every newspaper editor in Germany, without regard to class or party affiliation, stigmatized the war as a continuation of the lawless Jameson Raid.

Judging by press utterances the entire German nation was profoundly moved by deep and genuine sympathy for the plight of the Boer people. A survey of the German press from the Vorwärts on the extreme left to the Kreuzzeitung on the extreme right confirms an observation made by Hermann Oncken in 1904: "There can be no question that for many years we have not had in our Fatherland—so divided by political, social and confessional differences—a movement of sentiment and opinion so universal and deeply felt as to overcome momentarily mutual antipathies." [13] To find anything comparable to this wave of sympathy for a foreign people one would have to return to the early nineteenth century when Philhellenism swept the continent.

While sympathy for the Boer heroes was universal, responsible German journalists did not urge the government to intervene against England on their behalf. On the contrary, they generally denied that enthusiasm for the embattled farmers of South Africa connoted active hostility toward Great Britain. Since the conclusion of the Anglo-German agreement of August 1898, a considerable number of German papers, maintaining connections with the foreign office, notably, the Kölnische Zeitung, the Post, the National-Zeitung, the Hamburgischer Correspondent, the Berliner Neueste Nachrichten, and the Kreuzzeitung, had from time to time warned against identifying German policy with Kruger's recalcitrance. During the summer of 1899 they had recommended a policy of conciliation and reform, a position in complete accord with the action of the Berlin authorities, who gave Kruger similar advice.[14] Through both diplomatic and publicity channels the Boers were given to understand that they could expect no assistance from official Germany.

Committed to neutrality in South Africa and unwilling to countenance any interventionist move by the great powers, the German authorities had nevertheless to take into account the deep sentimental attachment of the nation to the Boer cause. The difficulty encountered by the government throughout the war in conditioning its semi-official publicity policy to these facts, is clearly revealed in Bülow's directives for the press on the eve of hostilities. "With regard to the Transvaal crisis our press should

[13] *Historisch-Politische Aufsätze und Reden* (Berlin, 1914), I, 205. A similar judgment is delivered by Kurt Erler in his brief treatment of German pro-Boerism. *Von der Macht der Presse in Deutschland* (Berlin, 1911), pp. 65–83.

[14] G. P., XV, 367–93.

adopt a cool, quiet, business-like tone. If the avowedly official organs must carefully avoid injury to the feelings of wide circles in Germany by conspicuous partisanship for England or ill-natured attacks upon the Boers, so it is to be desired, on the other hand, that, in the event of war between England and the Transvaal, the German press should not repeat the error of the Spanish-American War by taking at the outset, in an unnecessarily clamorous fashion, the side of the weaker party. Everywhere it must be emphasized that when France, Russia, Italy and Austria do not think of incurring English enmity by mixing in the Transvaal question Germany alone cannot push in and engage herself." [15]

Official counsels of neutrality were effective only in the semi-official and inspired press. The Norddeutsche maintained the strictest reserve, confining its news to the reproduction of Reuter's dispatches, and never commenting on the political origins of the struggle. It never countenanced the absurd rumors and atrocity stories that circulated in the irresponsible press. While betraying no sympathy for the Boer cause, it suppressed all news and opinion that might have been interpreted as approval of British policy and aims. In the Kölnische Zeitung English policy received a fairer hearing than in any other German paper. It emphasized the stubborn refusal of Kruger to make reforms, the disabilities under which all foreigners in the Transvaal labored, and warned against the "rustic cunning" of Kruger and his clique. It also reproduced Alfred Austin's letter to Professor Abel, giving the Imperialist side of the question. From time to time during the war it gave publicity to the British viewpoint and at all times avoided the excesses in false news reporting that distinguished a considerable section of the German press.[16] By its indifference to the fate of the Boers and its occasional presentation of the British case, the Kölnische Zeitung became one of the most unpopular papers in Germany.

During the first months of the war, the Berlin Post, whose importance was derived less from its circulation than from its ownership (Herr von Stumm, the industrialist) and its use as a mouthpiece by the foreign office, propagated the official tenets. Calling for moderation and neutrality, it warned against setting Germany in opposition to Great Britain. The Anglophobes, it pointed out, were playing into the hands of the Franco-Russian Alliance, for a British defeat in South Africa would have serious repercussions in Europe. To deaf ears it preached realism as against sentimentalism in foreign affairs, deploring the political immaturity of the Germans, who, after thirty years of national unification,

[15] Bülow to the foreign office, Sept. 20, 1899; *G. P.*, XV, 395–96. For Hammann's labors with the press and especially his difficulties with the Bismarckian *Hamburger Nachrichten* see Eckardstein, *Lebenserinnerungen,* II, 119–24.
[16] Nos. 800, 802, 819, 157, Oct. 11, 12, 18, 1899, Feb. 26, 1900.

were unable to recognize the difference between interests and sympathies as a sound basis for foreign policy. There was not the slightest inclination in official circles, it declared, to depart from the strict neutrality that had been proclaimed at the beginning of the conflict.[17] Similar in purpose and argument were the pronouncements that appeared from time to time in the Krupp owned Berliner Neueste Nachrichten, whose editor, Hugo Jacobi, was in close touch with the foreign office.[18] Official views also found expression in the National-Zeitung, although they were neutralized to a large extent by bitter editorial condemnation of British methods.[19] Although not to be counted in this circle of semi-official organs, two journals of liberal tendencies, the Frankfurter Zeitung and the Catholic Kölnische Volkszeitung, hearkened to the official plea for objectivity in reporting and commenting on the South African struggle.[20] But in the total output of German journalism during the first months of the war, these were but voices crying in the wilderness. The overwhelming impression produced by the press was one of burning partisanship for the Boers and bitter antipathy for the British.

The rift that developed at the outset between official policy and popular sentiment was widened by the Emperor's visit to his English relations in November. Ostentatiously announced by the London press at the outbreak of the war, it provoked opposition in Germany that ran all the way from dignified expressions of regret to violent meetings and resolutions against such a public betrayal of national sentiment. The objections raised by the Vossische Zeitung may be taken as a fair sample of moderate independent press opinion. First, the visit might be misinterpreted as a gesture of official German approval of British policy toward the Boers. Second, the monarchy ought not to set itself in opposition to the feelings of the German people, who condemn Britain's methods and objectives and sympathize with the Boers. Third, while this does not mean that the

---

[17] Nos. 277, 284, 297, 298, 319, 325, 332, 352, Oct. 8, 15, 28, 29, Nov. 19, 26, Dec. 3, 23. Although there is no direct evidence, the phraseology, the thoughts and the classical allusions in some of these articles all point to Bülow as the author. They were accepted by German editors and British correspondents as inspired by the foreign office.

[18] Nos. 485, 514, 545, Oct. 15, Nov. 1, 19, 1899; Nos. 24, 133, Jan. 16, March 20, 1900.

[19] Nos. 633, 639, 661, 699; Nov. 2, 5, 17, Dec. 3. The article of Dec. 3 was significantly entitled, "Politik und Volksstimmung."

[20] Because of the intolerant Protestantism of the Boers, Catholic organs did not wallow so deeply in Boerenschwärmerei. Kölnische Volkszeitung, Nos. 965, 1006, Oct. 15, 27, and subsequent issues throughout the autumn of 1899. The Frankfurter Zeitung published on the front page (No. 288, Oct. 17) Alfred Austin's letter to Prof. Abel, defending Britain's South African policy. The editor repeatedly warned against any unfriendly gesture toward England. (Nos. 298, 302, Oct. 27, 31.) "Eine Schwächung Englands liegt gar nicht im Interesse Deutschlands, wie es auch nicht passen könnte, wenn die Macht Englands auf Kosten Russland bedeutend erhöht würde."

same Germans were necessarily hostile to Britain, they would like, nevertheless, to avoid the appearance of favoring a cause which they regard as unjust. If the Emperor and his advisers persist, it must be made clear that the visit has no other significance than "a personal courtesy toward his royal grandmother." [21] "It is almost without precedent," wrote the Berliner Neueste Nachrichten, "that an act by a German monarch has met with so little approval by his subjects, as the visit of our ruling pair to the other side of the Channel." [22] Officially no cognizance was taken of these objections, but they were answered by inspired telegrams from Berlin. In these it was pointed out that the visit had been planned before the outbreak of hostilities; that Germany's position was one of strict neutrality; that canceling the visit would have more political significance than carrying it out, and would give the impression that German policy favored the Boers against England; therefore, the engagement, which was strictly a family affair, must be fulfilled.[23]

Forthright criticism and demands for cancellation, couched in the strongest language permissible under the German press laws, came from the Pan-Germans, the Agrarians and the neo-Bismarckians. Their agitation was not confined to the press but found expression in organized protest demonstrations in Hamburg and Munich. At the Hamburg meeting, which was attended by about three thousand persons, a speaker brought down the house by asking: "What has become of the second Telegram?" The speakers demonstrated their enthusiasm for the Boers by abusing the English. "Insolent robbers," "cowardly brigands," and "cursed Anglomania," were some of the compliments paid to the British and their policies. Resolutions were voted expressing sympathy for the Boers and requesting the Emperor to postpone his English visit until such a time as it would not appear as a betrayal of their "Low-German kindred." The Munich demonstration, attended by about twelve hundred people, was somewhat more circumspect in its resolutions, which recorded sympathy for the Boer cause and concluded with the hope that "the Imperial Government will consistently pursue a resolute national policy." It is significant that these demonstrations were unreported by Wolff's Bureau and that even the local papers were reticent as to the details of the proceed-

[21] No. 495, Oct. 21. Also Nos. 484, 494, Oct. 14, 20. Similar moderate protests in *Kreuzzeitung,* Nos. 482, 484, 530, 549, Oct. 13, 14, Nov. 10, 22; *Hannoverscher Kurier,* quoted *Deutsche Ztg.,* No. 263, Nov. 8; *Schwäbischer Merkur,* No. 510, Nov. 1; *Münchner N. N.,* No. 512, Nov. 7; *Frankfurter Ztg.,* No. 302, Oct. 31; *Kölnische Volksztg.,* No. 1007, Oct. 27. "It is by no means only the Pan-Germans who do not wish this visit to take place, but the great majority of the German people," declared the latter journal.
[22] No. 545, Nov. 19.
[23] *Kölnische Ztg.,* Nos. 883, 908, Nov. 10, 18; *Schwäbischer Merkur,* No. 523, Nov. 8; *National-Zeitung,* Nos. 652, 661, Nov. 13, 17; *Berliner N. N.,* No. 514, Nov. 1.

ings and speeches. Only the London Times and the Berliner Neueste Nachrichten, the latter ridiculing the demonstrators, gave anything like full reports.[24]

While full reports were suppressed, the responsible journals did not disguise their disapproval of these attempts to intervene by demonstrations and resolutions in the government's foreign policy. A writer in the Vossische Zeitung sighed for a Bismarck who would make short work of these chatterers; and he affirmed that "the majority of the German nation has nothing in common with the Anglophobia of the Pan-Germans and the Anti-Semites." Other writers in the moderate press attacked the demonstrators for so foolishly serving the interests of the Franco-Russian Alliance, and a blistering semi-official reprimand, entitled *Auswärtige Politik im Volksversammlung,* was delivered through Die Post. The Wolff and Reuter agencies and the British correspondents in Germany gave special prominence to these denunciations of political rowdyism.[25] Yet despite the condemnation of the Munich and Hamburg demonstrations, Friedrich Lange was not far from the truth when he said that if the German people could be polled on the Emperor's visit to England it would scarcely get a vote.[26] When the visit occurred (November 20–28) it was practically boycotted as a news event by the German press. If mentioned at all, it was but to deny that it had any political significance.

Before taking up the sequel to this visit—Chamberlain's astounding speech at Leicester—certain other aspects of German publicity in connection with the Boer War require attention. They are not pleasant to deal with, and yet a complete picture requires it. The most important of these matters is that of false news reporting and the circulation of atrocity stories. These inevitable accompaniments of organized slaughter made their appearance in the German press early in the war and continued almost without abatement until its close. During the first phase of the struggle, from October 1899 to Cronje's surrender at the end of February 1900, the demand for war news in Germany was insatiable. In public

[24] *Berliner N. N.,* No. 503, Oct. 26; *Times,* Berlin dispatch, Oct. 26. Dr. Hasse, leader of the Pan-German League, denied that the meetings were organized by his society. Mildred Wertheimer, *The Pan-German League* (N. Y., 1924), p. 143. In the German press they were generally referred to as Pan-German and Anti-Semitic. The papers that moved in this current were the *Deutsche Tageszeitung,* organ of the Agrarian League, Friedrich Lange's *Deutsche Zeitung,* and the *Hamburger Nachrichten.* The intransigence of the latter journal was attributed by Hammann to Herbert Bismarck's inspiration. (Hammann to Eckardstein, Oct. 28, 1899, *Lebenserinnerungen,* II, 119.)

[25] *Vossische Ztg.,* Nos. 502, 520, 525, Oct. 25, Nov. 4, 8; *Die Post,* No. 297, Oct. 28; *Berliner N. N.,* No. 503, Oct. 26; *Times,* Berlin dispatch quoting *Kölnische Ztg.,* and *Weser-Zeitung,* Oct. 25; *Morning Post,* and *Standard,* Berlin dispatches, Oct. 26, 27.

[26] *Deutsche Ztg.,* No. 268, Nov. 14.

interest, as measured by the space accorded it in the press, the war over-shadowed all other topics.[27]

Fully ninety-five per cent of the South African news appearing in German papers came from London. All direct cable connections were in British hands and at Aden the British installed a military censor to control all communications coming over the Zanzibar-Aden line. In fact, the British communications monopoly and censorship completely isolated South Africa from the rest of the world and no news came through except what the British military authorities chose to pass.[28] However, had the cables been free from military censorship the German public would still have been dependent on British news sources. No German paper had regular staff correspondents reporting by cable from South Africa. Even the Lokal-Anzeiger, a journal enjoying one of the largest circulations in Germany, maintained only a pair of occasional correspondents whose dispatches were mailed and hence delayed in publication from twenty to thirty days. An examination of the leading German papers on this point shows a few reports on the South African War taken over from French sources in Paris, Dutch sources in Amsterdam, and from the Transvaal legation in Brussels. Many of these were originally of British origin. In the main, South African news flowed into the German press from London through three channels: first, Reuter's reports circulated by the Wolff Bureau; second, telegraphic reports from the German correspondents in London based on the news reports of the leading British dailies; third, mail dispatches from occasional correspondents who summarized and abstracted reports appearing in the London press.

The restriction of news at its source, the inadequate service of the German press, and the public interest and excitement encouraged the manufacture of news on a large scale. One of the chief sources of such mendacity, in the early days of the war, was the Kabel-Korrespondenz of London, an agency alleged to have been owned or connected with a leading Hamburg paper. Its operators hashed up English reports, flavored them with Anglophobia and Boer victories, added a Pretoria, Johannesburg, or Capetown date line and sold them to about fifty German newspapers, including such prominent journals as the Vossische Zeitung, Hannoverscher Kurier, and Münchner Neueste Nachrichten. After exposure by the London correspondent of the Frankfurter Zeitung,

---

[27] At this time the most popular feature of Schumann's circus in Berlin was advertised in the press as follows: "Original Transvaal Boers—The Only Ones in All Europe. Showing Their Native Customs and Manners—The Boers on Trek—Fighting Scenes between English and Boers."
[28] The Hamburg stock exchange protested vigorously at the inconveniences to business men. *Die Post*, No. 293, Oct. 24; *Lokal-Anzeiger*, No. 501, Oct. 25.

the agency dated its reports from London, but much that it continued to put into them was sheer speculation.[29] An enterprising individual named Farlow, a former editor of the Kabel-Korrespondenz, supplied the Münchner Neueste Nachrichten and the Magdeburgische Zeitung with telegraphic dispatches purporting to originate with independent agents in South Africa. These reports were usually of such a nature as to tax the credulity of the simplest minds. Brussels was another source of manufactured news, and the Berliner Tageblatt's correspondent was one of the most frequent offenders. His sensational reports on the latest events from the seat of war in South Africa were usually introduced with a hint that they originated in the Transvaal legation (*"aus hiesigen Transvaalkreisen"*) at Brussels. In these communications British forces never lost less than 3500 dead and wounded and seventeen guns.[30] No one stopped to recall, evidently, that Dr. Leyds, the Transvaal diplomatic agent, received no dispatches direct from the war zone and that he was as dependent on the British cables as anyone else. Another ingenious exploiter operating in this field was a certain Herr Schröder in Berlin, who had a convenient peripatetic cousin—London, Cairo, Durban—and who was now a salesman, now a doctor and again an engineer. This cousin was always having fortuitous meetings and interviews with British generals, politicians and high officials. These interviews were sold by Schröder to papers appearing in widely separated localities; and the editors apparently never suspected that they were being duped.[31]

While many of the most respectable German journals were uncritically circulating wild reports from sources known to be unreliable, continual detraction and charges of falsification were hurled at Reuter's Agency and London papers receiving reports direct from South Africa. A frequent cross-heading for these reports of British origin, in the Lokal-Anzeiger and other popular journals, was *"Englische Lügenmeldungen,"* *"Englische Lügen,"* or *"Englische Schwindeleien."* [32] Editors sneered at "English bulletins of victory," and the Lokal-Anzeiger, dealing with some contradictory reports, advised its readers not to take them seriously; it would be easier to assume "that the English are simply lying, as they have

[29] *Frankfurter Ztg.*, No. 340, Dec. 8. Among its fabrications were interviews with the Boer leaders.

[30] Some of his reports were so preposterous that his own editor would insert question marks after his statements. *Berliner Tageblatt,* No. 14, Jan. 9, 1900.

[31] These practices were exposed in an article in the *Frankfurter General-Anzeiger.* The Berlin *Post* (No. 89, Feb. 22, 1900) republished the article, and the editor vouched for the truth of the statements on the basis of his own experience with the agents mentioned.

[32] *Lokal-Anzeiger,* Nos. 518, 550, Nov. 3, 19; *Vossische Ztg.,* No. 35, Jan. 22, 1900; " 'Lüge' und 'englische Kriegsbericht' sind in Zukunft synonym" (*Münchner N. N.,* No. 46, Jan. 28, 1900).

so often been proved to have done before." There was scarcely a German paper that did not slant or angle the news in favor of the Boers by headlines or interpretation. Those papers that excluded reports from all uncontrolled sources and maintained a semblance of objectivity in the presentation of news deserve to be mentioned. They were the Norddeutsche, the Kölnische Zeitung, the Post, the National-Zeitung, the Hamburgischer Correspondent, the Frankfurter Zeitung and, to a considerably lesser degree, the Vossische Zeitung. With the exception of the last two papers mentioned, these journals were semi-official, inspired, or subject to influence by the foreign office.

Along with manufactured and tendentious news reports went atrocity stories and charges of uncivilized methods of warfare. They began with charges from military men on both sides that dum-dum bullets were being used. Then from uncontrolled sources came the accusation that the British were misusing the white flag and violating the immunity of Red Cross field hospitals. By innuendo the Vossische Zeitung charged the British with arming and agitating the Basutos against the Boers, and in less responsible papers it was alleged that the Kaffirs were being armed by the British and encouraged to rape, pillage, and burn.[33] The worst kind of villainy and criminality were attributed to the British soldiers. It was alleged that they killed and robbed the wounded, misused their prisoners, shot doctors attending the wounded in the field, and assaulted all Boer women that fell into their hands. Atrocity mongering was not confined to the fanatical pro-Boer press but was indulged in by such respectable papers as the Lokal-Anzeiger, Berliner Tageblatt, Vossische Zeitung, and Münchner Neueste Nachrichten.[34] The respectable Schwäbischer Merkur published a series of articles by H. Reuchlin, entitled "An Historical Survey of British War Measures," in which the writer concluded that it was quite in the British tradition for the soldiers to rob prisoners, assault women, and dynamite farmhouses.[35] The stories upon which these charges were based were not manufactured by the journals that gave them circulation. They were based usually upon alleged accounts from Boer and German officers in South Africa, from un-

[33] *Vossische Ztg.*, No. 523, Nov. 7. Official British denials never quite extinguished this rumor. See Lord Ampthill's letter, authorized by Chamberlain, to Baron Eckardstein, Oct. 25, 1899. Eckardstein, *Lebenserinnerungen*, II, 75.
[34] *Lokal-Anzeiger*, No. 568, Dec. 4, 1899; *Berliner Tageblatt*, Nos. 13, 19, 40, Jan. 8, 11, 23, 1900 (headline: "English Soldiers as Robbers") ; *Vossische Zeitung*, No. 505, Oct. 27, 1900; *Münchner N. N.*, No. 588, Dec. 3, 1899, No. 49, Jan. 30, 1900 (headlines: "Characteristics of the English Hireling Army," and "English Atrocities").
[35] Nos. 112, 114, March 8, 9, 1900. Even more monstrous charges appeared in another series by Alfred Pfister: Nos. 586, 601, Dec. 15, 23, 1899, Nos. 85, 99, 156, Feb. 21, March 1, April 3, 1900.

balanced Boer sympathizers, or were taken over completely from obscure and uncontrolled news sources.

When such allegations appeared in supposedly serious journals, it is not difficult to imagine the excesses indulged in by the more sensational and mendacious organs. From this source came a steady stream of poisonous slanders, insults and defamations directed at the British army and its commanders. All of this filth was collected and published (December 1900) in a volume entitled *Hunnen in Südafrika,* by a Dr. Vallentin, who claimed to have served as a staff-captain in the Boer army. A shameless book, symptomatic of mental illness, it was reviewed and quoted at length in the gutter press. Another complete record of atrocity mongering is supplied by the files of Friedrich Lange's Deutsche Zeitung. Since enough has already been said about the subject to show its characteristics, there is no need to go raking things up from this sewer.[36]

A more painful subject even than false news and atrocity stories is the handling by the humorous magazines of England's rôle in the Boer War. Many writers have referred to this sorry subject. Honorable Germans both then and later have condemned the excesses and stupidities in the strongest terms, and English writers have excused them as less offensive than similar products of the Parisian press. Exactly what do the files of *Lüstige Blätter, Ulk, Kladderadatsch,* and *Simplicissimus* reveal of the inflamed state of mind that prevailed in certain German circles at this time? In the main it is a record of foul aspersions, odious lampoons, and debased caricatures. A few examples will tell the story. *Kladderadatsch,* less vulgar and common than the others, repeatedly caricatured John Bull as a pickpocket, a Hooligan and a race-track tout. An offensive poem had for a refrain the words: "The Prince of Wales remains at home." Another jingle was directed against the Kaiser's visit to England in November 1899, and Chamberlain's Leicester speech was greeted with the words: "The friendship of bandits is undesirable. You are too gracious, Mr. Chamberlain." Another cartoon shows the Prince of Wales with a brigade of uniformed dogs, inspecting the wounded soldiers returning from South Africa. This gross caricature bore the caption, "The Prince of Wales fulfills his duty as commander of the famous dog brigade on the occasion of the return of his wounded subjects." Upon the Prince's accession to the throne he was portrayed as leaving the gaming table surrounded by low company, male and female. A poem, "Der Bundesgenosse," celebrated the British-Kaffir "alliance." Kitchener, Roberts, Milner, and Chamberlain were the butt of unending ridicule and slan-

---

[36] The following issues are noteworthy: Nos. 274, 282, Nov. 21, Dec. 1, 1899; No. 287, Dec. 8, 1900; Nos. 239, 241, 294, Oct. 11, 13, Dec. 15, 1901.

der.[37] *Simplicissimus* surpassed all its contemporaries in brutality and grossness. At the outbreak of war it published a caricature of an Englishman and a Scotsman standing on the sea-shore looking towards South Africa. One remarks to the other: "For five shillings a day we can hire fellows to fight this war for the honor of our country. No English gentleman would stoop to this dirty work." English military reverses were welcomed with an insulting cartoon entitled, "England's Dream in South Africa," which depicted Queen Victoria as an inebriated old market-woman with a whiskey bottle at her side, trying vainly to pluck an ostrich. A vulgar café scene was captioned with an unprintable insult to the Prince of Wales. Another cartoon showed a giant King Edward crushing women and children in a concentration *Lager* and complaining that the blood squirted up on his crown. Still another issue presented an odious caricature of two British soldiers which bore the legend: "The Boers have killed our pal Bob. Tomorrow morning we will kill five of their children." [38] Every canon of decency, fair play, and good taste was violated weekly by this brawling claque.

False news and atrocity tales in the daily press and grotesque slanders in the so-called humorous periodicals are the more obvious evidences of Anglophobia. But insensate partisanship warped even the ordinary functions of news presentation and comment. Countless German papers republished an article from the Indépendence Belge, professing to reveal the holdings of the Chamberlain family in Kynoch's Ammunition Company, the Birmingham Small Arms Company Ltd., and the Bank of Africa. By the side of this 'revelation' they published a charge made by Labouchère in his weekly *Truth,* that Kynoch's had executed large contracts for the Boer government just before the outbreak of hostilities and that these armaments were now being used to kill Englishmen. The inevitable comment was, "Business before everything else, even one's country." [39] English reverses in the first months of the war led to a general disparagement of the British soldier and the "hireling" army. Unflattering comparisons were made between the British system of recruitment and the German system of universal service, which made every citizen a soldier. The army in South Africa was likened to the French Foreign Legion, composed of "hirelings" and "mercenaries," unrepresentative of the nation and covered only as an organization by the British

---

[37] *Kladderadatsch,* Nov. 12, 19, Dec. 10, 17, 1899; Feb. 3, March 12, Aug. 8, 1901, for specific examples.

[38] *Simplicissimus,* Jahrgang 4, Nos. 31, 32, 42; Jahrgang 6, Nos. 20, 32, 33.

[39] *Vossische Ztg.,* No. 23, Jan. 15, 1900; *Lokal-Anzeiger,* No. 587, Dec. 15, 1899. For the Kynoch debate in the House of Commons see Garvin, *Life of Chamberlain,* III, 614–16.

flag.[40] In all but the semi-official and inspired press Boer victories were joyfully proclaimed, and the prophets in the editorial rooms announced the impending defeat and disintegration of the British Empire. When, after five months, the tide of battle turned with Cronje's surrender at the end of February 1900, the news was received as though it had been a German defeat. "Three thousand Boers captured by forty thousand Englishmen. What a glorious victory!" sneered the Vossische Zeitung.[41]

Enthusiasm and sympathy for the Boer cause was further demonstrated by public contributions of considerable sums of money. Funds to equip medical units, to assist the wounded, to aid prisoners of war, to care for widows and orphans were solicited throughout the country. The General Netherlands Society, with headquarters in Antwerp, and the Pan-German League were most active in this work. The latter organization raised better than half a million marks in the early days of the war. Fifteen thousand marks were contributed to a special fund solicited in twelve days by the readers of the insignificant Deutsche Zeitung. The notes accompanying these gifts breathed hatred of the English as well as pity for the Boers. *"Für die Buren zum Heil, den anderen wünscht möglichst viel Keil,"* wrote one contributor, while another accompanied his gift with a crude tirade against the *"verdammten Mixed Pickles."* [42] No reproach can attach to the humanitarian gestures on behalf of the Boers, but the excess of Anglophobia was a mockery of political common sense.

During the first phase of the war a great responsibility rested upon the British correspondents in Germany and the news editors in London. Should the whole truth be told with chapter and verse cited from the organs of German publicity, or should the popular aspect of "Boeritis" and Anglophobia be subordinated to the government's neutrality and the official efforts to stem the tide through the inspired press apparatus? The position might well be taken that so long as the official world held to its policy of strict neutrality, the excesses of popular feeling were of no consequence, and in the interest of future relations between the two countries should be ignored or minimized. Such, in general, was the course pursued by Bashford of the Daily Telegraph, Maxwell of the

---

[40] Theodor Schiemann in the *Kreuzzeitung*, Nos. 564, 595, Dec. 1, 29; *Schwäbischer Merkur*, No. 465, Oct. 5; *Vossische Ztg.*, No. 593, Dec. 19, 1899.

[41] No. 98, Feb. 28, 1900.

[42] *Deutsche Ztg.*, Nos. 247, 253, 262, 269, Oct. 20, 27, Nov. 7, 15, 1899; No. 213, Sept. 12, 1900. During the year 1901, local and district branches of the Pan-German League listened to 106 lectures on the Boer War. The German Colonial Society, with 30,000 members, hearkening to the official thesis that German colonial aims could best be achieved in co-operation with England, held aloof from organized demonstrations. (Wertheimer, *The Pan-German League*, pp. 84–86, 113.)

Standard, Harrison of Reuter's Agency (chief of the Berlin bureau, June 1899 to December 1904), Morrison of the Daily News, and the correspondents of the Daily Mail and the Morning Post. They did not deny in their reports that hostility to British policy was universal, but they refrained from extensive quotation and specific details. They covered the case by saying, "the majority of independent organs are not favorable to the English cause," and they passed over the wilder manifestations of Anglophobia by explaining that "the hostility of the Bismarckian press was to be expected." The corps of British correspondents looked to the foreign office for authoritative statements of official policy rather than to a frenzied popular press. That individual assurances were forthcoming from this quarter is attested by the number of dispatches that begin with the words, "I have unimpeachable authority for. . . ." or "The following observations emanate from a very trustworthy quarter. . . ." They devised a formula that ran something like this: "I am glad to say that the anti-English outbreaks of some German papers have been viewed by leading personages here with great dissatisfaction." They sympathetically chronicled the inspired articles appearing in the Kölnische Zeitung, Die Post, and Hamburgischer Correspondent in which the Anglophobes were taken to task for their excesses and cautioned to restrain their utterances. Throughout, they maintained that the attitude of the government was absolutely loyal and that the ravings of the Bismarckians and Pan-German chauvinists could and should be disregarded. The Emperor's telegram to his British regiment, his visit to England, and the semi-official preachments against sentimentalism in foreign policy were all interpreted by the correspondents to mean that the German government would join no continental coalition to put stones in Britain's path. All this was cited as gratifying proof that despite the "babble of the non-official press" the Emperor and his ministers would countenance no mischief-making.[43] The Berlin correspondents realized that the foreign office officials were quite out of sympathy with the Anglophobia of the press and that they were using all their resources to combat it, short of a public frontal attack upon nationalist circles where feeling against English policy was most intense.

Alone in the group of Berlin correspondents, George Saunders took an independent line, apparently with the full approval of Chirol and Moberly Bell. Under the impact of "Boeritis" and Anglophobia, which he encountered on all sides, he completely lost his balance, and his dispatches

[43] This summary is based upon the Berlin dispatches (October 15, 1899–February 29, 1900) of the Daily Telegraph, Daily Mail, Daily News, Reuter's Agency, Standard, and Morning Post, the papers and agencies which at that time maintained regular Berlin service.

often degenerated into tirades against everything German. To what extent mass sentiment in Germany was moved by genuine sympathy for the Boers and how much by innate dislike of the English people and their symbols of power is a question to which there is no answer. From the beginning Saunders took the line that pro-Boer sympathy was only an excuse and an occasion for the expression of ancient and chronic Anglophobia. Assurances that official policy remained uninfluenced by the storm in the press he brushed aside as of little consequence in the face of the incontestable ill will of the German populace. When the Kölnische Zeitung made a slip in its plea for a realistic attitude toward the struggle in South Africa and recommended reserve and a free hand in view of possible eventualities, he seized upon it as an official statement (which it probably was) and, giving it a malignant interpretation, he described it as the policy "of a hyena or a vulture of the battlefields waiting for the issue of the fray in order to prey upon the vanquished." (Oct. 20, 1899.) When the Kölnische Zeitung's editor protested this interpretation, Saunders devoted a full column to lecturing the editor and the German foreign office, and then stepped before the Times' audience to take a bow for having performed a deed of great national importance. Saunders never forgot the slip made by the semi-official organ, and on the average of once a week he dragged it into his dispatches. In that one sentence he purported to find the real key and the true meaning of official German policy. Neutrality and friendship were but a cloak for foul designs that would mature in the future against the British Empire. Saunders further reported every excess of pro-Boerism and Anglophobia that appeared in the German press, and himself undertook the task of refuting and denying all rumors and unsubstantiated charges. For completely usurping the editorial function he made an ingenious excuse: "I know it is not primarily my business to reply to these regrettable ebullitions . . . but my excuse and my reason is that I sincerely desire to show how futile this journalistic blank shot is in order to prevent the calamity of its being taken seriously in England." (Oct. 20, 1899.) While most of the British correspondents tended to play down popular hostility and to focus attention on the loyalty of the government, Saunders went to the other extreme.[44]

In official Berlin circles the attitude assumed by Saunders and Chirol caused alarm and apprehension. The Times was read in Great Britain for its foreign dispatches by every person of importance in the journalistic,

[44] Isolated from other material and studied in series, Saunders' dispatches show how a great untruth can be established by reporting selected facts. The most significant dispatches in the early days of the war are, Oct. 2, 13, 17, 18, 19, 20, 23, 26, Nov. 4, 11, 20, 25, Dec. 27.

political, financial, and intellectual world. It mattered little that the other British correspondents were reserved in reporting German popular hostility so long as Saunders and the Times kept the publicity spotlight centered upon the Anglophobes, the Pan-Germans and kindred associations. Bülow desired Saunders' removal from Berlin; he tried to enlist Chamberlain's co-operation by portraying the Times' correspondent as the chief obstacle to a good understanding between the two countries. Writing to the German ambassador in London, he said:

A difficulty, which is not to be underrated, in the way of improving Anglo-German feeling is the Times correspondent, Saunders. Twice or three times a week he gathers bitter criticisms of England and sends them to London, without explaining that the sharpest of them are from opposition [*frondierenden*] and Agrarian papers, that is, from journals which hate their own government more than they do England and wish thereby to create difficulties. The English press, however, comments on every statement as though it came from "an authoritative source" and the Times writes sour leading articles which evoke replies in the same spirit from our side. This can go on indefinitely if Saunders remains. I told you previously that Saunders, by his own admission, is a personal opponent of Chamberlain. It is Chamberlain's affair to remove the cause if the effect upon his policy is unwelcome. The German government can do no more than it has already done. It requires both good nerves and strong determination to maintain German policy free from every anti-English connection, despite the continuous discouragement afforded us by England's policy, press and people.[45]

A week later, when Bülow visited England with the Emperor, he complained to Balfour about Saunders' reporting in the Times, and the British minister, according to Bülow, agreed to use his influence to bring about a change. Reporting his impressions to Holstein and Hohenlohe, the German foreign secretary noted: "In general there is no question that the feeling in Britain is much less anti-German than the feeling in Germany is anti-British. For that reason those Englishmen who, like Chirol and Saunders, know from personal observation the acuteness and depth of Germany's unfortunate dislike of Britain are the most dangerous to us. If the British public clearly realized the anti-British feeling which dominates Germany just now, a great revulsion would occur in its conception of the relations between Britain and Germany." Until his transfer to Paris in 1908, Saunders remained a thorn in the flesh of German officials.[46]

Complaints against Saunders and the Times were not limited to diplomatic conversations. From the beginning of the war the inspired German press called attention to his activity and charged him with misrepre-

[45] Nov. 15, 1899; *G. P.*, XV, 412–13.
[46] Bülow, *Memoirs*, I, 372–73, 391; *G. P.*, XV, 413–20 (mem. Nov. 24, 1899).

sentation, personal bias, and a desire to sow dissension between England and Germany.[47] Several attempts were made to bring influence to bear on the Times during the next six months. Lord Rothschild interceded with the editor, Mr. G. E. Buckle; Sir Thomas Sanderson, permanent under-secretary at the foreign office, remonstrated with Chirol; and Bülow endeavored to influence Chirol and Saunders by appealing to Lascelles, who was on intimate terms with both men.[48] These efforts had no discernible effect on the Times' editorial position or on Saunders' reports from Berlin.

Chirol's attitude toward the whole matter is revealed in the report of a conversation Eckardstein had with him in January 1900. Chirol complained that the attitude of the German press was far more objectionable than that of the French or Russian press; he was bitter over the caricatures of the Queen and the Prince of Wales that had appeared in the *Witzblätter,* and incensed over the slandering of the British army by the circulation of atrocity stories. He intimated to Eckardstein that he preferred to pay the price to win over open enemies like France and Russia rather than rely on a dubious friendship with Germany. Eckardstein, who as first secretary of the embassy had charge of press relations, was disturbed over the insults to the royal family and the British army, and realized that they were alienating influential people in England. He therefore suggested to Holstein that a strong statement be published through Wolff's Bureau denying current atrocity stories that touched the honor of the British soldier. If his advice was followed, the news agency statement attracted little attention in the press.

That the Wilhelmstrasse did what it could to induce moderation in the treatment of news is illustrated in Bülow's directions to the press bureau on the occasion of the British rout at Ladysmith, toward the end of October 1899. "With regard to the British defeat at Ladysmith our press should assume a calm and quiet tone. Public acclaim and too clearly manifested *Schadenfreude* would only direct English resentment against us, when we are not equal to her on the sea; and at the same time it would strengthen the hopes of the French and the Russians that we were ready to allow ourselves to be pushed alone into conflict with England. Without false sentiment for, but also without impolitic agitation against England our press must limit itself to the clarification of the following

[47] "Lügennachrichten der Times," *Die Post,* No. 286, Oct. 17, 1899; *ibid.,* Nos. 287, 296, Oct. 18, 27; *Kreuzzeitung,* No. 497, Oct. 22, a satirical article on Saunders' journalistic methods; *Berliner N. N.,* Nos. 17, 68, Jan. 11, Feb. 10, 1900. The *Daily Telegraph* (Oct. 23, 1899) condemned the *Times'* policy as "ill-judged, dangerous, and unjust to the peoples and the Governments of both countries."
[48] Eckardstein, *Lebenserinnerungen,* II, 184–85; *G. P.,* XV, 496–97, 521.

points of view: (1) the army command has not fulfilled the expectations held of it in England, (2) it must be shown what England will do to make good this serious set-back in Africa, (3) we must wait and see what reaction this English defeat will have on the attitude of France and Russia." [49] The foreign office appeal did not go unheeded in responsible journalistic quarters if we can accept the testimony of the Daily News and Reuter's correspondents in Berlin. The former telegraphed: "The press here does not express the pleasure so widely entertained by the German public at the victory gained by the Boers"; and the latter reported that "The German press comments on the disaster at Ladysmith are almost without exception dignified, soldierly, just, and intelligent." [50]

Although its efforts to influence the press were on occasion attended by some measure of success, the foreign office was unable to reverse the general current of pro-Boer and anti-English sentiment. Outside of counseling moderation and calm, the authorities centered their arguments in the inspired press on the theme of *Realpolitik*. Germany would gain nothing by England's destruction as a world power, it was pointed out; wild outbursts of Anglophobia in the German press played directly into the hands of the French and the Russians, who were working with all their resources for a permanent breach between England and Germany; Germany's colonial and commercial development could best be achieved in co-operation with Great Britain rather than in open opposition to her; Germany's position as a continental and world power should not be prejudiced by sentimental considerations arising out of the South African War; realities and not sentiment should determine German foreign policy. In the main, all but the irreconcilable Bismarckian and Pan-German editors recognized the validity of the official thesis, but pretty consistently refused to surrender their right of judgment on British policy. Official relations with England need not be involved, they repeated again and again; however, we are quite justified in criticizing British policy and British methods and in demonstrating our sympathy for the aggrieved party in this unjustifiable war. "Heaven forbid that for thirty pieces of silver the German nation should sell its conscience and its character!"

In this situation the elements of conflict are clear: A skilled political élite pursuing a cabinet policy based upon the realities of the diplomatic and military system is arrayed against a national sentiment that insists upon a moral judgment, which finds expression through parliament,

[49] Bülow to the foreign office, Oct. 31, 1899; *G. P.*, XV, 414 n.
[50] *Daily News*, Nov. 2; Reuter's report, Nov. 2, 1899, published in innumerable British papers.

political parties and popular journalism. In the organs of the press and
sometimes in the same article the official and the popular thesis found
expression side by side. This gave to German publicity a curious dualism,
representing as it did on the one hand a passionate appeal to uninstructed
sentiment and on the other a calm invocation of political reason. Only in
a bureaucratic subject-state, in contrast to the citizen-state, could such a
contradiction have long endured. Bülow realized that this duality would
be misleading when reported in a parliamentary country like England,
and that is why he rightly feared the activity of Chirol and Saunders and
worked to bring the German journalists and publicists out of their trance
of "Boeritis." But outside the semi-official press, German editors never
learned the A and B of his *Realpolitik.*

In view of the embarrassments that beset the directors of German
foreign policy as a result of the attitude assumed by the press toward
Britain and the Boer War, Chamberlain's amazing speech at Leicester
on November 30, 1899, was just about the greatest disservice to Anglo-
German relations that he could have performed. Bülow puts it mildly
when he calls it a *"gaucherie."* [51] Under the circumstances Chamberlain's
use of the word "alliance" was nothing less than a gross stupidity. What
were the circumstances? For weeks the Berlin foreign office had been
saying through the semi-official press that the Emperor's visit to England
was a strictly family affair, that it had been planned before the outbreak
of the Boer conflict, and that no political commitments of a far-reaching
nature would be discussed or considered. All this was said to make the
visit palatable to an aroused and hostile public. The very fact that the
visit took place was highly significant, for it was tantamount to an official manifesto that Berlin statesmen would hold aloof from any continental combination against England and would join in no collective
action with regard to the South African War that would be embarrassing
to Great Britain. This was fully realized in informed political circles, and
some English editors sought to make great political capital out of the
approaching visit.[52] This was what had been feared in Germany and
every tendency to exploit it in that sense provoked bitter resentment in
the Fatherland.

[51] Bülow, *Memoirs,* I, 385.

[52] The grossest example was the *Daily Mail* (Nov. 17) which published a large
picture of the Emperor with the inscription, "A Friend in Need is a Friend Indeed,"
and accompanied it with an article sometimes referred to as the "boot-licking editorial." It set a new record for political bad taste by asserting that the Emperor
was two thirds English, that he preferred the English system of education to the
German, and that he preferred English sports to German military exercises. Mr.
Spender, who fully grasped the situation, urged his journalistic colleagues not to
make the visit a source of embarrassment to the Emperor by boisterous language
or political exploitation. (*Westminster Gazette,* Nov. 17, 1899.)

The visit began with a humorous incident. When the Emperor, landing at Portsmouth, stepped on English soil for the first time in four years, the band struck up the old tune, "Oh Willie, We Have Missed You!" Appreciating the humor of the situation, the Emperor had the bandmaster presented and cordially shook his hand and thanked him.[53] The same spirit of cordiality and good will prevailed during the visit. The conversations between William II and Von Bülow on the one side and Chamberlain and Balfour on the other were general in nature, and did not go beyond confirmation of their friendly understanding and promises to continue the policy of agreement in specific questions as they should arise in the future.[54]

The sequel to the visit is well known. On the day after the Emperor's departure from England, Chamberlain, in a brief thirty minute speech at Leicester, did what informed and responsible British editors had studiously avoided during the imperial visit. By loosely employing the term "alliance" and "a new Triple Alliance" he provided every disgruntled element in Germany with material for an attack on the government; his words confirmed the apprehension which had been entertained in that country with regard to the English visit.

The pertinent passages of Chamberlain's speech have been frequently reproduced.[55] After denouncing the French press for its gross caricatures of British royalty and calling upon the French "to mend their manners," he spoke warmly, first, of the rapprochement between the United States and Britain, and second, of the extension of their understanding to include Germany:

"The union—the alliance, if you please—the understanding between the two great nations is indeed a guarantee for the peace of the world. But there is something more which I think any far-seeing English statesman must have long desired," he continued, "and that is that we should not remain permanently isolated on the Continent of Europe; and I think that the moment that aspiration was formed it must have appeared evident to everybody that the natural alliance is between ourselves and the great German Empire." Pointing to their community of interest, he went on to say: "It is not with German newspapers that we desire to have an understanding or alliance; it is with the German people . . . [and] if the union between England and America is a powerful factor in the cause of peace, a new Triple Alliance between the Teutonic race and the two great branches of the Anglo-Saxon race will be a

[53] London correspondent, *Schwäbischer Merkur*, No. 557, Nov. 28.

[54] Chamberlain revived the question of an alliance but the discussion was kept on an academic level. For the conversations see Langer, *Diplomacy of Imperialism*, II, 656–59; Bülow, *Memoirs*, I, 354–403, *passim*; Garvin, *Life of Chamberlain*, III, 496–506.

[55] Langer, *op. cit.*, II, 658–59; Garvin, *op. cit.*, III, 506–8. Complete text, *Times*, Dec. 1, 1899.

still more potent influence in the future of the world." In the next sentence he qualified the word "alliance." "I have used the word 'alliance' sometimes in the course of what I have said, but again I desire to make it clear that to me it seems to matter little whether you have an alliance which is committed to paper or whether you have an understanding which exists in the minds of the statesmen of the respective countries."

Chamberlain's utterances exploded like a bombshell in the editorial offices. The bellicose Daily Mail used the "new Triple Alliance" as a club to shake at the French; an alliance between England, Germany, and the United States, with Italy, Austria, and Japan in the background was "something to make these foul-mouthed Parisians shiver." "If they cannot cease their insults," blustered the Daily Mail, "their colonies will be taken from them and given to Italy and Germany . . . and France will be rolled in the 'blood and mud' in which her press daily wallows." (Dec. 1.) Considerable approval of Chamberlain's qualified statements with regard to "alliances" and "understandings" was expressed in the British provincial press, but in the metropolitan journals, where the significance of Chamberlain's *faux pas* was understood, there was much criticism and some abuse.[56] The Pall Mall Gazette said: "The Colonial Secretary has produced much the same effect as the funny gentleman in the old Punch picture, who is represented as entering a drawing room on all fours, under the impression that the function to which he has been invited is a children's party." (Dec. 2.) The Times (Dec. 1) icily regretted that Chamberlain "employed so loosely a term with a precise and defined meaning he did not desire to convey." The Standard and the Daily Telegraph warmly approved Chamberlain's intentions, but they thought that to speak of a formal alliance was a bit premature and might be misinterpreted. (Dec. 1.) The Liberal Daily News (Dec. 1) said: "There is nothing that makes us wish so much to hear Lord Salisbury as a speech on foreign politics from Mr. Chamberlain." Mr. Spender pointed out how ill-timed was the speech: "If, immediately after the German Emperor's visit we make the large claim of an 'alliance,' we put the Emperor in an embarrassing position and lay ourselves open to disclaimers which will check and damage a good cause." (Dec. 1.) Summarizing the first effects of the speech, the Times editor said: "We are only sorry to see that our estimate of its indiscretion has been almost universally confirmed both at home and abroad." (Dec. 4.)

Early reports from Berlin bore out the doleful predictions made in London. The Daily News correspondent noted that by speaking of alliances Chamberlain had made Bülow's task of bringing the German

[56] Provincial papers: *Sheffield Telegraph, Newcastle Daily, Cardiff Mail, Glasgow Daily Record, Newcastle Journal, Birmingham Daily Gazette,* Dec. 1–5, 1899.

public around from its "absurd Anglophobia" all the more difficult. (Dec.
2.) Saunders reported to the Times (Dec. 2) that the German reaction
could be summarized as *"C'est magnifique, mais ce n'est pas la politique."*

In those journals where independent judgments were ordinarily found,
protests were polite but none the less definite. The Frankfurter Zeitung
said that people in Germany would hear nothing of an "alliance" with
England, although they were not opposed to an understanding in specific
questions if it were to Germany's advantage. Levysohn in his weekly review in the Tageblatt and Schiemann in the Kreuzzeitung scored Chamberlain, "the father of the South African War," for exploiting a private
visit in an inconsiderate fashion by thus playing the German Empire off
against France and Russia. For the same reason the Schwäbischer Merkur and the Münchner Neueste Nachrichten, important National Liberal
papers in South Germany, condemned this unhappy fruit of the "non-
political" visit to England. Chamberlain, the Vossische Zeitung explained, feared that the difficulties into which he had plunged his country
would be exploited by England's enemies; hence his desire to give the
impression that for rear-guard purposes Germany was Britain's "natural
ally." "Joseph Chamberlain undoubtedly meant to say something pleasant to us," declared the Lokal-Anzeiger, "when he called us his ally; but
we wouldn't be proud of it even if it were true. . . . We want neither
his written nor his unwritten alliance." Almost alone among the non-
governmental papers, the Socialist Vorwärts welcomed the speech as a
sign that Germany had ceased to be a Russian vassal and was drawing
closer to England and the United States. "The German people," it added,
"is not identical with the Anglophobe Junker and Capitalist press." With
this exception, all the comments bore out the prediction of the London
press that Chamberlain had made a bad blunder.[57]

With the first hot blast from the press, the foreign office officials
rushed in with the diplomatic fire extinguishers. Their object was two-
fold: to counteract the criticism of the government and to protect Chamberlain from the consequences of his friendly, though misguided, gesture
towards Germany. In a prominent front page position the Lokal-
Anzeiger published a statement from "a well-informed source" in which
it was said that Chamberlain had exaggerated somewhat in order to impress his hearers and the English newspaper readers; that the Emperor's
and Count Bülow's conversations with English statesmen had shown a

[57] *Frankfurter Ztg.*, No. 333, Dec. 1; *Berliner Tageblatt*, No. 1148, Dec. 9;
Schwäbischer Merkur, No. 565, Dec. 2; *Münchner N. N.*, Nos. 557, 558, Dec. 2, 3;
Vossische Ztg., No. 565, Dec. 2; *Lokal-Anzeiger*, No. 567, Dec. 3; *Kreuzzeitung*,
No. 571, Dec. 6; *Vorwärts*, No. 282, Dec. 2.

desire on both sides to promote good relations; and that the government
was not contemplating an alliance or anything inconsistent with strictly
German interests. Telegrams from Berlin correspondents of several
prominent papers repeated this formula with only slight variations in
wording.[58] In the Kölnische Zeitung, where the initiated looked for
official reactions, Chamberlain's remarks were received with sympathy
and understanding. In an article republished in the Norddeutsche and
cited by the British correspondents as the official view, it was pointed
out that Chamberlain himself had been careful to explain his use of the
term "alliance." He had not meant a formal treaty of alliance with binding obligations, but a mutually friendly co-operation in questions affecting their common interests. "In this sense Chamberlain's words will
meet with complete understanding and honest assent in Germany, not
only on the part of all professional politicians, but from all those as well
who desire the maintenance of world peace on a permanent and dignified
basis." [59] Two days later the speech was again interpreted for the German
papers in a fair and reasonable article, which concluded with this admonition: "There is no need for us to repulse gruffly such practical evidences of a desire to meet us as were contained in Mr. Chamberlain's
recent speech." [60] However, outside the circle of the inspired and semi-
official press there was little inclination to place other than the worst
interpretation on Chamberlain's words and motives. His statement that
it was not with the German newspapers that he desired an understanding
or an alliance, was not overlooked in Germany; and this sharp thrust did
not incline the editors to soften their criticism or to hearken to the semi-
official voice of reason and understanding.

After Chamberlain's warm and impulsive words at Leicester, Bülow's
Reichstag speech, on December 11, seemed like a jet of cold water.
Students of diplomacy have argued long over whether his failure to reciprocate was a shabby trick and a violation of his word. The charge
rests upon Chamberlain's assertion that in the course of his talks with
Bülow the German foreign secretary had expressed the hope that Chamberlain would, on some occasion, speak of their good understanding as
including also the United States, on condition that he would reciprocate
in the Reichstag.[61] The contemporary evidence as to Bülow's commitment
rests entirely upon Chamberlain's own assertions—a letter to Eckard-

[58] Lokal-Anzeiger, No. 564, Dec. 1; Frankfurter Ztg., No. 334, Dec. 2; Münchner
N. N., No. 558, Dec. 3; Hamburgischer Correspondent quoted by Die Post, No. 332,
Dec. 3. Articles of like tenor appeared in Die Post, No. 332, Dec. 3; Berliner N. N.,
Nos. 565, 584, Dec. 2, 14; and the National-Zeitung, No. 695, Dec. 1.
[59] No. 945, Dec. 2; Norddeutsche, No. 284, Dec. 3.
[60] Kölnische Ztg., No. 951, Dec. 4.
[61] Garvin, Life of Chamberlain, III, 510.

stein of December 1, the day following his Leicester speech, and a communication to Lascelles, the British ambassador in Berlin, on the day following Bülow's speech in the Reichstag. In neither of these communications did Chamberlain say that Bülow had promised to second his speech with a Reichstag declaration.[62] And in Bülow's own record of his talk with Chamberlain there is reference only to a desire that the colonial secretary use his personal and political influence in the interest of greater harmony between Germany and the United States.[63] Certainly the evidence is hardly sufficient to fix upon Bülow the responsibility for having inspired Chamberlain to announce to the world, after the manner of the fashionable intelligence of the day, that "a marriage has been arranged and will shortly take place." [64]

The occasion of Bülow's Reichstag speech was the announcement by the federal government that they proposed shortly to introduce a second navy bill that would double Germany's sea-power. Bülow undertook to establish the necessity of the new measure. His speech was a great trumpet blast calling Germans to the standard on which was inscribed the word *Weltpolitik*. In the course of his remarks he touched upon their relations with the various powers; his reference to England was just as friendly as to France, Russia, the United States, and Japan. But coming so soon after Chamberlain's warm words, Bülow's by contrast gave the impression of a deliberate snub. With England, he announced, they were ready to live in peace and harmony on a basis of complete equality and mutual consideration. And later he assured his hearers that they were not forgetting that their center of gravity was on the continent and that their position there rested upon the Triple Alliance and "our good relations with Russia." [65] Needless to say, Bülow's exposition of their foreign relations met with approval in the German press. With a few words he had completely taken the wind out of the sails of the pro-Boers, the Bismarckians, and the Agrarians, who day in and day out had been attacking the government's pro-British policy. Moreover, the ill will over the Emperor's visit to England and its unhappy sequel evaporated like a mist before the sun, and what counted heavily with Bülow as a person, he became again the object of favorable and complimentary publicity.[66]

---

[62] Eckardstein, *Lebenserinnerungen*, II, 111–13; Garvin, *op. cit.*, III, 512.
[63] *G. P.*, XV, 417.
[64] For the opposite view see Garvin, *op. cit.*, III, 510–13; Willy Becker, *Fürst Bülow und England, 1897–1909* (Greifswald, 1929), pp. 140 ff.
[65] *Fürst Bülows Reden*, II, 88–97.
[66] *National-Zeitung*, No. 717, Dec. 12; *Schwäbischer Merkur*, No. 581, Dec. 12; *Die Post*, No. 342, Dec. 13; *Münchner N. N.*, No. 573, Dec. 13; *Kreuzzeitung*, No. 583, Dec. 13; *Kölnische Volkszeitung*, No. 1170, Dec. 15; *Kölnische Ztg.*, No. 975, Dec. 12.

Bülow's coolness toward England was motivated by other considerations than his love of applause, although this was an important factor. There was the whole-hearted sympathy of the nation for the Boers and its concomitant hostility toward England. Moreover, just at this juncture a serious political crisis was precipitated by the Conservative party over the Prussian canal bill, and Bülow was careful not to widen the breach by antagonizing this group on matters of foreign policy. The National Liberal party, chief supporters of *Weltpolitik* and the naval policy, did not regard with favor an English connection implying German subordination. The Center party, too, had to be coaxed to support the desired naval increase. In fact, if the navy bill were to be brought safely into port, the government could not ignore national feeling on the major question of foreign policy. Finally, in explanation of Bülow's attitude, it must be remembered that in his Reichstag address he was presenting the need for expanding their national defenses, and it is axiomatic that responsible authorities support such a request not by painting a rosy picture of foreign relations, but rather by painting the devil on the wall.

Cool reserve rather than warm complaints marked the reception of Bülow's remarks in the British press; but court and political circles, if we can believe Eckardstein, were deeply resentful at the foreign secretary's failure to return the ball. Bülow himself labored under no misapprehension as to the effect of his words in England and he sought by personal contact to weaken their impression. Eckardstein was instructed to explain to Chamberlain that the exigencies of Reichstag politics had dictated his address. The day was past when Prince Bismarck, secure as the absolute dictator of German foreign policy, could ride roughshod over the feelings of the nation; Hohenlohe and Bülow had to take that important factor into account. British authorities should not be misled by the thoroughly tendentious and incorrect interpretation of Bülow's words so industriously propagated by the French and Russian press. Germany, they could be sure, would have nothing to do with any proposal conceived in hostility to England.[67] A moral or political judgment of the whole episode seems of little consequence as compared to the fundamental problem here revealed, namely, the failure of diplomatic institu-

---

[67] Holstein's instructions to Eckardstein, authorized by Bülow, Dec. 16, 1899. Eckardstein, *op. cit.*, II, 126–27. Replying to Holstein on Dec. 21, Eckardstein wrote: "Everyone who knows Count Bülow's difficult position in the face of German public opinion, can naturally understand his speech. Here in England the great mass of the people has not so far discerned in it any point or coldness toward England, but on the other hand, for some days, I have had to withstand the attacks of politicians, ministers, and the Rothschilds, as well as the royal family. Fortunately I have succeeded in quieting them somewhat—even Chamberlain, who was apparently inclined to see in the speech a jet of cold water directed at him personally."

tions and techniques, inherited from the age of dynastic cabinet politics, to function in a new situation dominated by universal suffrage, mass literacy, electrical communications and the popular press.

In the winter of 1899–1900 all matters of German foreign and domestic politics seemed entirely lacking in order and harmony. The war in South Africa and the Kaiser's visit to England had opened up a gap between government and people; in the field of party politics the Conservatives were in open revolt against the Canal bill; the Agrarian League was increasingly truculent in its demands for tariff reform; the Willing Worker's Bill—called the Prisons Bill by the Socialists—was rejected in the Reichstag on second reading; industry, agriculture and labor seemed hopelessly pitted against one another. How could any common element of national legislation be abstracted from these conflicting groups? The navy bill, which Bülow put in the headlines by his speech of December 11, was the catalytic agent. It satisfied national sentiment; it was a catharsis for Anglophobia; and it furnished the ground for political coalition among the loyal state parties in the Reichstag.

The first navy bill had established the principle of Tirpitz' high-seas fleet; the second bill by doubling the number of battleships provided for the creation of a really formidable weapon of aggression and defense. The agitation that accompanied the passage of the bill conformed in its general outlines to the pattern established by Tirpitz and his lieutenants in 1897–98. However, one important new weapon of public agitation and enlistment had been forged in the meantime—the Navy League. Its creation marked the entrance of the heavy industries, the mercantile interests and the financiers into the ranks of the naval enthusiasts. Organized April 30, 1898, at a meeting to which prominent men had been invited by the Prince of Wied, the forces behind it were revealed by the packing of the central committee with representatives of the Rhenish steel industry and the appointment of Viktor Schweinburg as general secretary. Schweinburg, who served as a journalistic mouthpiece for Dr. Miquel, minister of finance, vice-president of the Prussian state ministry, and an important political cog in the government, was also business manager (since 1897) of the Krupp owned Berliner Neueste Nachrichten. Prominent in the directing committee of the new Navy League were H. A. Bueck, general secretary of the *Zentralverband Deutscher Industrieller,* and Oktavio Freiherr von Zedlitz, leader of the Free Conservative party and a representative and spokesman for the heavy industries. But a naked profit motive masquerading as the representative of national idealism, was more than disinterested patriots could stand. Led by a group of Berlin university professors and Heinrich Rippler, the editor of the Tägliche Rundschau, a savage campaign was begun against the dominance of these forces in the Navy League. Bueck and Zedlitz withdrew almost at once from the central committee, but it took a concentrated and violent campaign to oust the unsavory Schweinburg from the secretaryship. Thus cleansed, the League forged ahead as the protagonist of a great national cause. Behind the scenes it was, of course, dominated by the same interests that founded it—the Ruhr, Rhenish, and Saar steel magnates, the ship building and engineering concerns, and the Bremen, Hamburg, and Lübeck shipping interests.[68] During the year 1900, League membership grew from a quarter of a million to better than a half million; the number of local branches increased from 286 to 1010; and during the first six months of the year, three thousand navy lectures were delivered under League auspices. Members received the official publication, *Die Flotte,* and slightly more than two hundred newspapers subscribed to the League's press service, the *Allgemeine Marine und Handels-Korrespondenz.*[69]

The thesis that the Navy League was "little more than a government department" is quite untenable.[70] It was anchored in the profit motive of German industrial capitalism, and masquerading as an idealistic national organization it sought to generate mass pressure the better to dictate to the state on an essential policy. This is what distinguished it from the British Navy League, rather than that one was "private" and the other "governmental." German authorities welcomed and encouraged the propaganda work of the League, but deeply resented its efforts at various times to dictate construction policies.

Most active in promoting the naval program as a business affair were the two "interest newspapers," the Berliner Neueste Nachrichten, owned by Krupp and Donnersmarck, and their associates, and the Berlin Post, owned by Freiherr von Stumm, "the uncrowned king of the Saar," armor plate manufacturer, and principal owner of the Dillinger Hüttenwerke.[71]

[68] The financial records, showing contributors, have never been published. On the founding of the League and the "Affair Schweinburg," which finally resulted in the legal process Schweinburg-Rippler, see *Berliner N. N.,* No. 202, May 2, 1898; H. A. Bueck, *Deutsches biographisches Jahrbuch,* 1914–16, pp. 187–90; *Der Zentralverband Deutscher Industrieller von 1876 bis 1906* (Berlin, 1902–5), vol. I, *passim; Berliner N. N.,* No. 1, Jan. 2, 1900; *Die Post,* No. 2, Jan. 3, 1900; Kehr, *Schlachtflottenbau,* pp. 168–71, 183–88.

[69] *Times,* Jan. 26, 1901.

[70] A. S. Hurd and H. Castle, *German Sea Power* (N. Y., 1913), p. 213; B. Schmitt, *England and Germany,* p. 210.

[71] Krupp and Stumm owned the principal patents on improved armor plate. (F. Hellwig, *Freiherr von Stumm-Halberg,* pp. 292–93.) On the activity of business interests on behalf of the navy, and the profits derived from naval expansion, see Kehr, *Schlachtflottenbau,* pp. 208–44. Adolf Woermann, who led the Hamburg shippers and chamber of commerce in the agitation for the second navy bill, had been refused a capital loan for his German East Africa Line by the bankers because his

The publicity issuing from these journals from January to June 1900, is the most cynical that can be imagined. After having armed the Boers the munitions concerns were now engaged on British war orders. In their press they followed the foreign office lead in one column, crying down public "Boeritis" and advocating the maintenance of friendly relations with England, while in the next column, in their naval propaganda, they boomed the fleet as an anti-British instrument and a necessary measure for German industrial and commercial expansion!

In the remainder of the press, the campaign was a duplication of that of 1898. The Norddeutsche was monopolized for six months by the navy department; the activity of Tirpitz' publicity bureau is evident on every hand. The variety and volume of articles appearing in one provincial newspaper over a sixty-day period is suggested by the following list from the Schwäbischer Merkur: "The Growth of German Maritime Interests from 1896 to 1898"; "The German Marine and an English Blockade"; "The Navy Bill and the Reichstag"; "South Germany's Maritime Interests"; "The Development of German Shipbuilding"; "Maritime Interests and Blockade"; "The German Navy and the German Laboring Class"; "The Navy of the United States of America." [72] These articles doubtless brought a tang of salt air to the nostrils of the good burghers of Stuttgart. As in the campaign for the first bill, the German professors—Schmoller, Lamprecht, Dietrich Schaefer, Du Moulin-Eckart and others—took an active part. Lamprecht lectured in Berlin on the subject, "A Strong German Fleet, A Necessity in our Historical Development"; and Schmoller spoke before a large meeting on "Germany's Economic Future and the Navy Bill." The peroration of a speech delivered by the fiery Du Moulin-Eckart is enlightening: "The navy is also our sword. We want our place in the sun. We stand now at the crossroads. We must go forward or retreat. The world looks to us. With firm faith in our power and in God, we must work with all our might in the service of German culture and German life, so that the words of the poet will be realized: *'Und es soll an deutschem Wesen, Einmal noch die Welt genesen.'* " [73]

It should be noted in passing that in the publicity on behalf of the navy

---

vessels (Bundesrath and General) were unprotected from British seizure. Kehr, *op. cit.,* p. 241, citing Woermann's letter to the secretary of the Hamburg chamber of commerce, Jan. 10, 1900.

[72] Some of these articles ran through two or three issues. Nos. 47, 50, 60, 65, 67, 69, 79, 83, 87, 91, 93, 96, 102, 103, 107, Jan. 30, 31, Feb. 6, 9, 10, 12, 17, 20, 22, 24, 26, 27, March 2, 3, 6.

[73] *Berliner Tageblatt,* No. 29, Jan. 7, 1900; *Norddeutsche,* No. 12, Jan. 16, 1900; Gustav Schmoller, *Zwanzig Jahre Deutsche Politik* (Munich, 1920), *passim.* The *Norddeutsche* provides a complete record of every aspect of the propaganda for the second navy bill.

bill England was not paraded as the object of German naval expansion. Nor was current hostility to England directly exploited in official propaganda for the benefit of Tirpitz' program. Doubtless, this was an expression of official reluctance to define publicly the foreign political task which naval armaments were designed to perform. Historical fulfillment, industrial advance, twentieth-century mission, requirements of the power-state, all the slogans and the catchwords of *fin-de-siècle* imperialism, rather than specific formulation of fighting tasks, framed and symbolized the appeal for sea-power. This accords with Eckart Kehr's conclusion with regard to the popular ideology crystallizing around the navy laws. "The fleet was not built in response to a concrete foreign political requirement, but in response to the characteristic, vague, undiscerning belief that armaments and war were agencies serving the moral and spiritual progress of mankind." [74]

Nor can one pass lightly over the general thesis of Kehr's book: that the German navy was not constructed in response to the necessities of the foreign situation, but was the resultant of class conflicts within the state. Briefly, he conceived the central feature of German social politics in the last decade of the century to be a three-sided struggle between the representatives of industrial wealth, landed wealth, and the proletariat for hegemony in the state; the navy bill was the compromise measure that enabled the first two groups to co-operate, in the spirit of Miquel's *Sammlungspolitik,* against the anti-state parties of social discontent. The feudal agrarian forces sanctioned the fleet desired by the industrial commercial groups, while the latter, in turn, agreed to the upward revision of agricultural tariffs. The complete overhauling of the Caprivi tariff system in the interests of German agriculture followed immediately upon the passage of the navy bill.[75]

[74] *Schlachtflottenbau,* p. 418. Kehr cites a significant incident showing the reluctance of the authorities to specify the objectives of naval policy. When Vice-Admiral Valois (retired) published a brochure entitled, *Seemacht, Seegeltung, Seeherrschaft* (Berlin, 1899), in which he placed Anglo-German relations as the central feature of the naval question and blockade and starvation as the proper aim of German naval strategy against England, the navy department kept it entirely out of the publicity emanating from the press bureau and thereby reduced its effect to a minimum. Kehr, *op. cit.,* pp. 388–89, based on a notice in the navy department archives.

[75] Kehr, *op. cit.,* pp. 201–5, 259, 262–69, 328, 331, 358. For the legislative interrelationships of the navy bill, the canal bill, the famous Lex Heinze, and the meat imports bill, see Hohenlohe, *Denkwürdigkeiten der Reichskanzlerzeit,* pp. 525–76; Bülow, *Memoirs,* I, 343–49, 360, 599–601. The clash of economic group interests is illustrated by the meat imports bill, desired by the agrarians and opposed by the shippers and importers. Representatives of the Hamburg-America line and the North German Lloyd called upon Hohenlohe and argued as follows: the shipping companies would lose important traffic; the price of meat would be raised to German consumers; popular resentment would further strengthen the Social Democrats;

While accommodation and compromise of economic and class conflicts made possible the passage of the second navy bill, the public agitation produced the atmosphere which was also necessary to its success.
And even though Anglo-German relations did not figure strongly in
official publicity, it cannot be denied that current Anglophobia was a
factor in influencing public attitudes toward the naval program. Hostility
toward England was raised to fever pitch by the seizure and search of
German mail steamers by British naval authorities early in January 1900.
This exercise of a belligerent's right to stop contraband goods probably
accomplished more for the navy bill than all the labors of Tirpitz' information bureau. J. A. Spender's prediction at the time was amply fulfilled: "The *Herzog, General,* and *Bundesrath* will most likely prove to
be the parent ships of a good many future men-of-war." [76]

On December 28, the imperial mail steamer, *Bundesrath,* belonging to
the German East Africa Line, was stopped by British naval authorities
in the neighborhood of Delagoa Bay, and on the suspicion that it carried
contraband of war was taken into Durban and subjected to a prize court
examination. Within the next ten days two other vessels owned by the
same company were seized and searched by the British. The *Herzog* and
the *General* were promptly released, but the *Bundesrath,* which was
completely unloaded even to its coal, was not freed until January 17.
Exasperated by the unaccountable delay, the Wilhelmstrasse bombarded
London with protests couched in language so aggressive that they
aroused the ire of Lord Salisbury and his officials. Ruffled feelings were
by no means smoothed down by the British government's final admission
of error, assurance of greater care on the part of naval authorities in the
future, and the promise of indemnity to the shipping line.

The resentment and the bitterness which these seizures engendered in
Germany is almost indescribable. Writers in the press, unversed in international law, interpreted these incidents as arbitrary and unjustified
demonstrations of British sea-power. False news played no small part
in inflaming minds on both sides of the Channel. When the *Bundesrath*
was taken into Durban, the correspondent of the Central News Agency
(British) reported that it had on board five heavy guns, fifty tons of
ammunition, seven thousand saddles and 180 trained artillerymen, all
destined for the Transvaal. The Hamburg shipping line promptly released the ship's manifest to the press, and when the British search produced no contraband but proved the cargo invoice correct in every

---

the middle class parties and the government would lose voting support. (Hohenlohe,
op. cit., pp. 566–67.)
 [76] *Westminster Gazette,* Jan. 18, 1900.

detail, the German papers resounded with the phrase "lying British press reports." [77] When the clamor in the German press first began, Reuter's Agency released a dispatch saying that friendly conversations were in progress in Berlin in the matter of the seizure, but that no official protest had been lodged. The Wolff Bureau in Berlin immediately replied by announcing that a sharp official protest had been promptly presented and that conversations were taking place in London.[78] The Wilhelmstrasse's tactical move was commended by the German press.

It has been said that in Germany Britain's conduct met with universal indignation and condemnation. When we break this generality down into its components of individual and group publicity, some rather significant differential qualities are revealed. No use was made by the authorities of the Norddeutsche, either to increase or relax the public tension. In its inspired and independent comment the Kölnische Zeitung began by softening its news reports and pouring oil on the waters. However, the long delay and the growing exasperation in official circles provoked a sharply worded Berlin telegram, which, published in special type, was accepted in both the German and British press as a semi-official pronouncement. Relating the facts and reprehending the endless delay encountered in London, the telegram concluded: "If the English government considers it important to avoid undermining completely the relations that have previously been maintained with Germany, she would do well to pay greater attention to German national feeling than she has hitherto seen fit to do." [79] The armor plate press, Die Post and the Berliner Neueste Nachrichten, did not go so far in vilifying the British government as the more popular and sensational journals, but day after day they hammered home the idea that these incidents would not have occurred if Germany had possessed a strong navy, and that lack of a naval arm must be repaired with all possible speed.[80] The popular Lokal-Anzeiger was more concerned with stirring up Anglophobia than with making capital out of the affair for the navy bill. Its language was rude to extremes as it engaged the Times and the Morning Post in bitter polemics. A highly sensational report described how the English officers and sailors treated the cargo of the General; it was alleged that one third

[77] Westminster Gazette, Jan. 3; Die Post, No. 7, Jan. 5; Vossische Ztg., No. 7, Jan. 5; Münchner N. N., No. 29, Jan. 18, 1900.
[78] Reuter's, Jan. 3; Wolff's Bureau, Jan. 4.
[79] No. 40, Jan. 16; also Nos. 5, 14, Jan. 3, 6. The Kölnische Zeitung did not fail to indicate the significance of the incident for German naval requirements.
[80] Berliner N. N., No. 5, Jan. 4 to No. 39, Jan. 24; Die Post, No. 5, Jan. 3 to No. 33, Jan. 20. "Only a strong navy can protect the ideal and material values of the German nation, the brightness of German honor, and the products of German thrift out there on the far seas." (Die Post, No. 29, Jan. 18.)

of the cargo was damaged, a part of it stolen, and the remainder dumped back in the hold without order or sorting. This account was illustrated with photographs of English sailors unloading the ship under the direction of British officers.[81] The Berliner Tageblatt was less sensational in its reporting, but editorial resentment was strongly expressed. Arthur Levysohn, in his weekly review, said that the British had underscored in a historical fashion every argument put forward by William II and his ministers on behalf of the naval program.[82] Beginning with mild protests and scholarly articles on neutral and belligerent rights, the Vossische Zeitung became day by day more aggressive in its reports and comments, although like the Frankfurter Zeitung it was careful to present the affair in such a way as to avoid direct encouragement or approval of the navy law.[83] The Catholic Kölnische Volkszeitung, reflecting the bargaining proclivities of the Center party and its hesitancy toward the navy law, ignored the connection between sea-power and the seizure and search of German mail steamers.[84] It is in the National Liberal papers, the supernationalist journals of rank, that one finds the wildest excesses. They denied that British action had anything to do with belligerent rights, contraband, or any other matter affecting the war in South Africa; it was simply a calculated move on the part of the British government to ruin the German East Africa Line, which had long been a thorn in the side of British shippers. Others said that this was a move to recover by force on the sea the prestige that England had lost on land in fighting the Boers; the British interpretation of sea law was simply a form of "robbery"; they were trying to create a pretext for the seizure of Delagoa Bay. Every effusion of this kind ended with a tearful plea for a navy that would preserve them from such indignities at the hands of the arrogant British.[85]

In another group of papers, denunciation of England was matched by equally bitter attacks upon the German government and its foreign policy. These journals did not form a homogeneous group, but represented malcontent nationalistic factions. Among the more aggressive were the Agrarian Deutsche Tageszeitung, the Bismarckian Hamburger Nachrichten, the Pan-Germanic Leipziger Neueste Nachrichten, the independent Tägliche Rundschau, favorite paper of the German civil servants

[81] Nos. 2, 3, 10, 12, 33, 37, 40, Jan. 3, 7, 12, 20, 23, 25, 1900.
[82] No. 11, Jan. 7; also Nos. 3, 5, 6, 10, 24, 28, 35; Jan. 3, 4, 6, 14, 16, 20.
[83] *Vossische Ztg.*, Nos. 4, 5, 10, 25, 32, 33, Jan. 4, 5, 7, 16, 20; *Frankfurter Ztg.*, Nos. 2, 4, 17, Jan. 3, 5, 18.
[84] Nos. 4, 9, 11, 51, 57, 58, Jan. 2, 4, 5, 18, 20.
[85] *National-Zeitung*, Nos. 1, 4, 11, 21, 41, Jan. 2, 4, 8, 12, 20; *Schwäbischer Merkur*, Nos. 7, 8, 13, 27, 31, Jan. 5, 10, 18, 20; *Münchner N. N.*, Nos. 3, 5, 8, 34, Jan. 3, 4, 5, 10, 21; *Nationalliberale Korrespondenz*, releases Nos. 6, 7, Jan. 5, 6.

and teachers, and such catch-penny organs as the Berlin Kleine Journal and Deutsche Zeitung. The Agrarian editors declared that the argument "If we only had a fleet . . ." was not valid. The government would not use a fleet if it possessed one because it was dominated by the cowardly desires of a ring of international capitalists and industrialists; they suspected a disgraceful secret agreement with England and hoped that the interpellations in the Reichstag on British "sea-robberies" would force its disclosure. This was the wildest of all the outbursts, but in all the papers in this group is to be found a common pattern of complaint against the government's policy of dependence on England and subserviency to the British court and foreign office. The seizure of German ships was the fruit of this policy; and all parties should unite in the Reichstag to bring the issue before the public instead of leaving it to be whispered about by diplomats behind closed doors.[86]

In so far as the public clamor over the *Bundesrath* strengthened the government's naval campaign, it was not unwelcome to the Emperor, Von Bülow, and Tirpitz. But it was definitely embarrassing when directed by the malcontent publicists against the government's foreign policy. William II on his own initiative endeavored to canalize the publicity by releasing to Wolff's Bureau a telegram which he had sent to the King of Württemberg. "I hope that events of the last few days," he said, "will have convinced ever-widening circles that not only Germany's interests, but also Germany's honor, must be protected in distant oceans, and that to this end Germany must be strong and powerful on the seas." [87] After making public this telegram, he wrote to Hohenlohe demanding that Tirpitz bring in immediately the final draft of the proposed navy law. This would satisfy outraged patriotic feelings and furnish a lightning rod against more serious attacks from the public on England and the Queen.[88]

Politicians were so aroused over the *Bundesrath* affair that an accounting in the Reichstag could not be avoided. Three hundred deputies signed the notice of interpellation and all the circumstances pointed to a stormy debate. By appealing to party leaders, Bülow succeeded in postponing the interpellation until the mail steamer had been released and Lord Salisbury had given the desired assurances for the future.[89] The final Reichstag scene, which took place on January 19, was carefully

[86] *Correspondenz des Bundes der Landwirthe,* quoted in the *National-Zeitung,* Nos. 9, 12, Jan. 6, 9; *Deutsche Tagesztg.,* quoted in *Tägliche Rundschau,* No. 4, Jan. 6; *Leipziger N. N.,* quoted in *Tägliche Rundschau,* Nos. 2, 7, Jan. 4, 10; *Tägliche Rundschau,* Nos. 3, 4, 5, Jan. 5, 6, 7 and subsequent issues, particularly the press review.
[87] Wolff's release to German papers, Jan. 9.
[88] Hohenlohe, *Denkwürdigkeiten,* pp. 555–56.
[89] *G. P.,* XV, 461, 463–64.

staged. Every pot-house politician was there swelling with indignation and anxious to delight his constituents by flaying the British government. Apparently by advance agreement with the leaders of the National Liberal, Center, Conservative, and Progressive parties, the interpellation was introduced by deputy Möller of the National Liberal party. His words were sharp but courteous. When he mentioned Kruger and the Boers, his listeners cheered; when he said that notwithstanding what had happened, the British were "an honorable people," a wave of scornful laughter swept the Reichstag. Bülow then replied for the government. His speech and manner were stiff and curt as he gave expression to the public sense of injury and injustice; he let it be known that the government had acted with determination and force and that in consequence they had received full satisfaction. Podbielski, minister of posts, followed Bülow to explain certain technical features affecting the mails. Then, when Liebermann von Sonnenberg, the rabid Anglophobe and Anti-Semite, moved to open general debate, he was voted down by an overwhelming majority and the Liebermanns and Hasses, the Anti-Semites, Agrarians, and Pan-Germans, were left enraged and disappointed as the Reichstag proceeded to other business.

Behind the cleverly arranged scene were serious problems involving personalities, party relationships, and national sentiments. The official report of the Reichstag proceedings reveals nothing of the motives, temper and tactics of the stage managers. In this respect the accounts in the papers by the parliamentary reporters are much closer to reality.[90]

From the beginning of hostilities in South Africa a considerable section of the political and news press had been attacking the government for its benevolent attitude toward Britain as evidenced in the Emperor's visit to Windsor and the statements put out by the foreign office through the semi-official and inspired press. The critics of the administration, pro-Boers, Agrarians, neo-Bismarckians, and Pan-Germans, had seized the national flag and proclaimed themselves the bearers of true German sentiment, as contrasted to the government which was pursuing a foreign policy opposed to national feeling. The seizure of the German mail steamers turned the outcry of malcontent groups into a torrent of Anglophobia, which by implication was a criticism of official policy. For the government this was both an embarrassment and an advantage. It was an embarrassment in so far as it branded official foreign policy as anti-national; it could be made advantageous if turned into channels of naval agitation. It fell to Bülow to resolve the dilemma in the Reichstag. A

[90] Especially *Vossische Ztg.*, No. 32, Jan. 20; *Berliner Tageblatt*, No. 35, Jan. 20; *National-Zeitung*, No. 41, Jan. 20; *Berliner N. N.*, Nos. 31, 32, Jan. 19, 20.

highly developed sensitivity to collective attitudes and an unusual mastery of chiaroscuro in speech fitted him for this delicate operation. The sharp admonitory tone assumed toward Great Britain, and his reference to "the legitimate excitement of German public opinion," identified the government with the nation's grievance and met the requirements of all groups except the extreme nationalists and the Agrarians.[91] In this way Bülow placed the government at the head of the parade and led the demonstrators away from further excesses of Anglophobia. Only by voicing the national resentment with clarity and force was he able to avoid an open debate on the interpellation. Without bringing the navy bill directly into his speech, his words were angled in a manner to indicate that the passage of the navy bill was an immediate national necessity. Aroused patriotic emotions were to work themselves out not in senseless Anglophobic outbursts, but in a politically useful direction on behalf of national armaments. Thus analyzed the navy bill assumes the character not alone of a compromise of domestic class conflicts, but of a national catharsis for highly charged emotional attitudes.

Did Bülow count the ultimate cost in terms of Anglo-German relations? His solution was for the emergency and not for the long run. It illustrates the primacy of domestic over foreign policy. Except for the grumbling of the Times and the Morning Post, there was no general outburst of resentment in the British press. Nor did the navy bill itself strike British publicists as a grave menace to Britain's supremacy on the seas, although it was recognized that if Tirpitz' paper program became a reality, it would affect the naval balance throughout the world. At the moment the British had other irons in the fire and they were skeptical of Germany's ever realizing her naval ambitions. Bülow in his speech before the Reichstag on December 11, 1899, had pointed to the development of world policy and sea-power as the great task of the twentieth century: "In the coming century Germany will be either the hammer or the anvil." This stirring prophecy provoked a tart comment in the Times: "It is hardly probable," wrote the editor (Dec. 12), "that Germany will ever again become the anvil of Europe, but it is still less likely that, even as a 'World-Power,' she will be the hammer of the seas."

[91] *Fürst Bülows Reden,* I, 103–8.

CHAPTER IX

SMASHING FOREIGN WINDOWPANES

You all remember when we left the shore
Of Rule Britannia, we in concert swore
We'd do our best on reaching these localities
To show our undisputed Nationalities,
To show contempt in everything we did!
Tell me, my comrades, how have we succeeded?
            W. S. Gilbert, *La Vivandière.*

At no time during the long struggle in South Africa was interventionist talk entirely absent from the columns of the continental press. True,
for the most part it was idle chatter and wishful thinking. But in Paris,
Vienna, St. Petersburg and Berlin the champions of the Boer cause kept
the subject alive and followed hopefully every move of the diplomats. It
was realized that without Germany the other powers could not act.
Therefore any indication of hardening attitudes toward Britain was sufficient to start the publicity mills. Interventionist hopes had been raised
when Germany bristled up over the *Bundesrath* affair. Another incident
that gave encouragement to Anglophobes and pro-Boers occurred in
January 1900. When a socialist journal in the Rhineland revealed that
Krupp was occupied with munitions orders for England, there was so
much criticism from all sections of the German press that the government advised the manufacturer to refrain from filling orders for either
combatant.[1] Might not the German government be moved still further
by mass pressure? Such must have been the hope of many Boer sympathizers.

At this time events in South Africa took a turn more favorable to the
British. Cronje's forces were surrounded and captured and Kimberley and
Ladysmith were at last relieved. Everything seemed to indicate that if
the continental powers were to organize for mediation they would have
to do so soon. Muraviev, the Russian foreign minister, took the initiative
and made his proposals to Berlin—joint action by France, Russia, and

[1] *Norddeutsche*, No. 10, Jan. 13, 1900; *Berliner Tageblatt*, Nos. 22, 24, 29, Jan. 13,
14, 17; *Vossische Ztg.*, No. 20, Jan. 13; *Die Post*, Nos. 21, 22, Jan. 13, 14. Also
G. P., XV, 452.

Germany to mediate between the combatants and bring the war to an end before the Boer republics were annihilated. Bülow sidestepped the embarrassing proposal by demanding that, as a condition of German co-operation, the three powers guarantee one another's territory. Such a condition involved French recognition of the Treaty of Frankfort, and on this rock Muraviev's 'peace ship' foundered and sank. Subsequent recriminations and tale-bearing by Muraviev, Delcassé, the Kaiser, and Bülow reflect no credit on any of the participants.[2]

While this little game was played out behind closed doors of the foreign offices, the subject of mediation was debated in the press of continental capitals. Here again the utterances and warnings of the inspired German press dovetail exactly with official policy as revealed in the documentary record. When the pro-Boer press took the interventionist bait put out from Paris and St. Petersburg, officially ear-marked articles made their appearance in the Kölnische Zeitung, Die Post, National-Zeitung, and Berliner Neueste Nachrichten. The burden of their refrain was that it would be suicidal to join a Franco-Russian combination for the purpose of diminishing British power. Do not be led by Anglophobia into countenancing the schemes of Germany's enemies, they said, for the real object of the Franco-Russian press campaign is not simply a continental league but the estrangement of England and Germany and the complete isolation of the latter; at the end of the proposed action Germany would be at the mercy of the Franco-Russian Alliance.[3]

Even more positive action than the launching of inspired articles was taken by the authorities against the interventionists. The latter had consistently appealed to Bismarck as authority for a pro-Russian orientation. Bülow caused Bismarck's speeches to be combed for statements on the value of English friendship for Germany and had these launched in the press. To counteract some of the mischief being done in England, he endeavored to establish the thesis that German opinion was less hostile than the French. To prove it the press was scoured for clippings and

---

[2] For complete details and a final judgment see Langer, *Diplomacy of Imperialism,* II, 662 ff.; Willy Becker, *Fürst Bülow und England,* pp. 152–61.

[3] *Kölnische Ztg.,* No. 62, Jan. 23, 1900: "Deutschlands auswärtige Politik," a defense of official policy against Bismarckian, Pan-German, and pro-Boer critics. *Berliner N. N.,* No. 42, Jan. 26: "Los von England," a polemical attack on the *Hamburger Nachrichten* for its advocacy of a continental coalition against England. *Die Post,* No. 22, Jan. 14: "Das deutsche Reich und die gegenwärtige Weltlage," a plea for *Realpolitik* against *Gefühlspolitik* and a slap at the interventionists. *Vossische Ztg.,* No. 60, Feb. 6: "Die Hetzerei gegen England" flatly rejects the coalition policy with which the French and Russian press tempts Germany, and points out the inevitable results of falling into such a trap. Important articles in the same vein: *Die Post,* Nos. 45, 57, 103, 105, Jan. 27, Feb. 3, March 2, 3; *National-Zeitung,* No. 78, Feb. 5; *Schwäbischer Merkur,* Nos. 60, 64, Feb. 6, 8.

these were forwarded to Eckardstein for circulation in the British papers. Eckardstein and Hammann further undertook to check on those London correspondents who were supplying the Lokal-Anzeiger with sensational anti-British articles. In line with his duties as liaison officer between the embassy and the press, Eckardstein used all his influence to secure favorable reactions from the Daily Mail, the Daily Telegraph, the Morning Post and a number of evening journals. All these measures were not without some success, but the Kaiser was overly optimistic when he wrote the Prince of Wales at the end of February: "With superhuman efforts Bülow and I have slowly got the better of our Press, swamped as it was with articles, roubles, and francs from both sides, to create anti-British feelings which our neighbors harbor most themselves!" [4]

As a matter of fact, German observers in London were becoming apprehensive at the signs of growing sensitivity, nervousness and irritability toward the German press attacks. Count Metternich, who was in charge of the embassy during Hatzfeldt's illness in the spring of 1900, expressed his deep concern over this matter in private reports to Hohenlohe and Bülow. He noted that the attitude of indifference to German criticisms was giving way to a general feeling of deep bitterness and hostility toward everything German. What was still more dangerous was the growing conviction in influential circles that improprieties of the German newspapers could have been prevented by official intervention, and that in view of restrictions placed by law upon the German press the authorities were not without responsibility for some of the journalistic attacks. The publication of the bluebook on the *Bundesrath* incident, reproducing the peremptory dispatches originating in Berlin, had touched the Englishman's sense of national honor, while many who had heretofore discounted the hostility of the German press and held to the friendliness of the government were now beginning to wonder if this might not be illusory. Altogether it was a gloomy forecast that Metternich made for the future.[5]

Underlying and mediating the shift in British attitudes, noted apprehensively by Metternich, was the apparatus of news reporting and the network of communications. The campaign carried on by Saunders and Chirol was having its effect. The Berlin correspondent began to report on the odious productions of the German *Witzblätter,* a matter to which

[4] *G. P.,* XV, 560; Lascelles to Salisbury, Feb. 9, 1900, *B. D.,* I, 251; Hammann to Eckardstein, Feb. 2, 1900, Eckardstein, *Lebenserinnerungen,* II, 199. William II repeatedly expressed the opinion that the bad behavior of the German press was the result of Russian and French bribery. (*B. D.,* I, 253; Waldersee, *Denkwürdigkeiten,* II, 444.)

[5] Metternich to Bülow, March 19, 1900; Metternich to Hohenlohe, March 24; *G. P.,* XV, 484–97.

he had heretofore alluded only in general terms. Irritating incidents were exploited in the Times' news columns.[6] While other correspondents and editors were more circumspect, information and testimony on the German public's hostility toward England came home through many channels —tourists on vacation, commercial travelers, readers of German newspapers and periodicals, and by word of mouth from officials and society folk. The Athenaeum Club had on file for its members a collection of lampoons culled from the German humorous magazines. The accepted patterns of vilification were becoming familiar to the English public.

But just as the British were responding to the German stimulus, the fire and fury of the German press began to abate. Official influence had something to do with it, but more effective than that was the military success of Lord Roberts and Kitchener in South Africa. Beginning with the relief of Kimberley on February 15, the British marched steadily forward to the occupation of Pretoria on June 5. With no Boer victories to chronicle, many German editors lost their enthusiasm for South African news. Moreover, from midsummer on, the Boxer rebellion in China, the drama of the besieged legations, and the resultant military action and international diplomatic intrigue crowded the Boer War completely off the front page. "The War in South Africa" gave way to "The War in the Far East." When Kruger's departure from the Transvaal was announced on September 13, it was regarded by German editors as the beginning of the end, and South African news in the large circulation journals dried up to a mere trickle. Even the hot love of Friedrich Lange was chilled as he explained to the readers of the Deutsche Zeitung that, after all, the Boers were just naïve peasants who could not comprehend the moral imperative of fighting to the bitter end for an ideal.[7] Had the war ended with Lord Roberts' brilliant campaign and the proclamation of annexation, had there been no year and a half of bitter guerilla warfare, Anglo-German relations would have been spared much.

Following the summer lull, however, South African news came back into the headlines with President Kruger's arrival in Europe. With the

---

[6] The *Times* reported that when Prince Henry's flagship left Portsmouth harbor, the German sailors cheered the Boers. The Emperor was greatly agitated by this "arrant lie." (*B. D.*, I, 254.) In spite of official denials the rumor persisted in the British press that the Boer army was staffed with Prussian officers and that the German East Africa Line was carrying to Delagoa Bay "hundreds of suspicious looking persons" whose ultimate destination was the Transvaal. (*Berliner N. N.*, No. 64, Feb. 8, 1900.)

[7] No. 214, Sept. 13, 1900. Retrospective articles accepting the reality of the English triumph and the extinction of the republics appeared in the *National-Zeitung*, Nos. 536, 588, Sept. 21, Oct. 21; *Vossische Ztg.*, No. 473, Oct. 9; *Kreuzzeitung*, No. 474, Oct. 10; *Lokal-Anzeiger*, No. 462, Oct. 3; *Berliner Tageblatt*, No. 517, 525, Oct. 11, 15. The *Tageblatt's* articles were sharply critical of Kruger and his advisers.

Boer armies smashed and Pretoria occupied by the British, the sole hope of survival lay in outside mediation. By touring Europe and arousing popular demonstrations Kruger and his advisers hoped to force the hands of continental statesmen. In France, Kruger had a rousing reception. His diplomatic agent, Leyds, then wired the Wilhelmstrasse that the Boer president was coming to Berlin. The Emperor, the chancellor, Von Bülow, and Baron Holstein agreed that the visit would be embarrassing. Before Kruger left Paris Leyds received a broad hint to that effect, but it was disregarded and Kruger and his party started by short stages for Berlin. At Cologne, where "Uncle Kruger" was the center of a spontaneous mass demonstration, he was intercepted by Tschirschky, who in the government's name requested him not to come to Berlin because the Emperor would be unable to receive him.[8]

That serious repercussions would result from this action was foreseen. The boisterous reception accorded the old man in France had been fully publicized by the German press. For days the Pan-German and pro-Boer journals had been calling for a national demonstration of sympathy for the Boer cause. Simultaneously with the announcement that the visit was "postponed," the government gave out its reasons for declining to receive the Transvaal president. These were stated in numerous telegrams sent by Berlin correspondents and agencies to the provincial papers, but in the Lokal-Anzeiger appeared a special article from an "authoritative source" which was set off from other news and editorial matter by special type on the front page. The substance of this official statement was as follows: The popular demonstrations in France for Kruger had not helped the Boers; Kruger's sudden change of plan, and his decision to come immediately to Berlin instead of proceeding to Brussels, was a political surprise and aroused the suspicion that he was acting on advice received in Paris. The matter thus took on an entirely different aspect, for it impinged upon German foreign policy. It seems that people in Paris, continued the statement, are like those who can not or will not help a man in need, but are only too willing to give him recommendations to their friends. "What serious purpose would have been served by entering into a discussion of President Kruger's intentions, and thereby perhaps awakening in him hopes that never could be fulfilled?" [9]

[8] G. P., XV, 549–50. Holstein to Hohenlohe, Dec. 4, 1900; Hohenlohe, Denkwürdigkeiten, pp. 598–600. The Emperor was motivated primarily by considerations of the evil effect of popular demonstrations on the British. But the telegram, which Bülow alleges Queen Victoria sent to William II, asking him not to receive Kruger, does not appear in the Letters of Queen Victoria, the British Documents, or Die Grosse Politik. (Bülow, Memoirs, I, 544.)

[9] No. 565, Dec. 3. Ironically this statement appeared side by side with a poem by Ernst von Wildenbruch, "Deutschlands Wilkommen an Paul Krüger."

"Useless" was the word that summarized Bülow's defense later in the Reichstag. And he might have added, "embarrassing."

That a word spoken, a decision taken, can set the entire press of a country by the ears is one of the impressive phenomena of publicity. A storm of protest swept the country. Of the important news and party journals only the Kölnische Zeitung, the National-Zeitung, and the Vossische Zeitung championed the official course. The Post, which usually functioned as a Wilhelmstrasse amplifier, was significantly silent. The Conservative Kreuzzeitung and the Berliner Neueste Nachrichten agreed that the reception would have been useless, but they took strong exception to the brusqueness with which Kruger was warned off. Outside of these journals criticism ranged all the way from the dignified disagreement of the Berliner Tageblatt and the Frankfurter Zeitung to the mad ravings of the Hamburger Nachrichten, Rheinisch-Westfälische Zeitung and the Berlin Tägliche Rundschau. The "air of Olmütz," "a national mourning," "a blot on the German soul," "a great injury to the German nation," were some of the comments appearing in the Agrarian, Pan-German and Bismarckian papers. Many National Liberal papers in the provincial cities joined the Hannoverscher Kurier in demanding an official statement in the Reichstag that the rebuff to Kruger was not delivered out of consideration for English feelings. The Frankfurter Zeitung wanted to know why the Kaiser could go to England but could not receive Kruger. To the Berliner Tageblatt the government's action was "an affront to the national soul"; and "In view of Kruger's reception in France every German must feel ashamed." "How is it that so great a power as the German Empire has sunk so low that London can dictate who shall and who shall not be received in Berlin?" asked the Rheinish-Westfälische Zeitung. Friedrich Lange said that every letter received in his editorial office had the same refrain: "I am ashamed to be a German." The official Socialist organ, Vorwärts, drew from the affair the Marxian moral of the bankruptcy of the bourgeois state. And on every hand was heard the bitter jest: "The Kaiser fears only God and his Grandmother."

The picture presented by the press was one of agreement between the Socialists, Agrarian Conservatives, the greater part of the National Liberal and Progressive papers, together with the Pan-German and Bismarckian journals. Bülow, who had only succeeded Hohenlohe on October 17, could not have been very happy over this first major decision as chancellor.[10]

[10] Only a few of the critical articles can be cited here: *Hannoverscher Kurier,* quoted in *Kreuzzeitung,* No. 568, Dec. 5; *Rheinisch-Westfälische Ztg.,* quoted by

Public sentiment was arrayed in hostile opposition to a bureaucratic cabinet policy. The clash was concentrated and focused in the Reichstag. On December 10, when the house began to debate the foreign office budget, the attacks made in the press were repeated from the tribune. Bülow's defense was not a complete success. Instead of directing his remarks to the question, "Why was Kruger snubbed?" he cleverly turned the major issue into a minor one, and launched into a long explanation of the government's neutrality policy toward the Boer War. Bülow did not explain how Kruger's reception would have injured German neutrality. Their policy, he declared, was in no way subservient to England; on the other hand, it would be madness to go tilting at English windmills in whatever part of the world they might be whirling.[11]

Debate on this subject was opened again on December 12, when Bülow spoke in reply to the Pan-German deputy, Dr. Hasse. When Kruger was unceremoniously bowed out of Germany, Hasse, the president of the Pan-German League, and Dr. Reismann-Grone, editor of the Rheinisch-Westfälische Zeitung, together with a delegation of League officials, rushed off to The Hague to present Kruger with an address in which the Pan-Germans, in the name of the German people, condemned the foreign policy of the Kaiser's government. Further, the local sections, upon orders from headquarters, had begun to organize public protest demonstrations against the government, while the press that shared Pan-German views pushed abuse and vituperation to the very limits of the press law. Hasse's impassioned attack upon the government's foreign policy in the Reichstag, and his ridiculous diatribe against England, made Bülow's task easy. The chancellor had only to present the issue to the nation as a choice between the foreign policy pursued by the government and the foreign policy recommended by the Pan-German leader. All but the irreconcilables admitted that prudence and sanity excluded the Pan-German policy as an alternative.[12]

In lecturing Hasse on the subject of political behavior (rejecting both "pure moral philosophy" and the "ale-house bench" as acceptable bases of foreign policy), Bülow focused attention on the Pan-German

---

Deutsche Ztg., Nos. 286, 289, Dec. 7, 11; Berliner Tageblatt, No. 619, Dec. 6; Berliner N. N., No. 567, Dec. 4; Deutsche Tagesztg., and the Reichsbote, quoted Vossische Ztg., No. 580, Dec. 12; Frankfurter Ztg., No. 344, Dec. 13; Vorwärts, Nos. 281, 288, Dec. 3, 11; Deutsche Ztg., Nos. 283–97, Dec. 4–20, which provides a complete record of press criticism.

[11] Fürst Bülows Reden, I, 161–68.

[12] Stenographische Berichte des Reichstags, X Legislaturperiode 2 Sess. (Dec. 10, 12, 1900), pp. 413 ff., 470 ff.; Fürst Bülows Reden, I, 161–75; Mildred Wertheimer, The Pan-German League, pp. 144–47; Lothar Werner, Der Alldeutsche Verband, 1890–1918 (Berlin, 1935), p. 145; Bülow, Memoirs, I, 543–49.

League. The advantage gained by diverting the issue to their ridiculous conduct, was pursued by launching a heavy campaign in the inspired press against the Leaguers and their senseless intervention in foreign policy. This campaign reached a climax in a long article in the Kölnische Zeitung directed at *"ein bubenhafte Hetzartikel eines Alldeutschen Blattes."* The writer concluded that "the Pan-Germans make the German nation a laughingstock throughout the world." [13] With this the entire tribe of self-appointed nation savers turned on the Kölnische Zeitung. The Leipziger Neueste Nachrichten published a statement that in the secret account books of the De Beers Mining Company were two entries for "Special Agitation Purposes," listing "Cologne 60,000 pounds" and "Berlin 350,000 pounds." It implied that the Kölnische Zeitung's attitude toward the Boer question was a consequence of bribery. Friedrich Lange said that it was the *"Weltblatt"* on the Rhine which news vendors handed over with a knowing laugh when a customer simply asked for *"Die Charakterlose."* [14] This exchange of calumnies might have gone on for days. On December 17, however, news of the sinking of the naval cadet ship, *Gneisenau,* taking a heavy toll of life, brought a readjustment of news values, and the Kruger snub dropped out of the headlines. It was not without reason that people said of the new chancellor, Bülow: "He has luck."

However, within two months after the Kruger incident the same issues were raised in more acute form by William II's long stay in England on the occasion of the illness and death of Queen Victoria. From January 19 to February 5, 1901, the Emperor was in attendance at the English court, and when he departed from London he was the object of a popular demonstration such as he had never experienced before in England.[15] Historians have cited this demonstration as evidence of the Kaiser's recovery of popularity in England—as the final erasure of pencil marks from a carelessly drafted Telegram. Moreover, it is supposed to have set the stage for the subsequent alliance negotiations. All

[13] No. 975, Dec. 14. Heartily supporting the campaign were the *Vossische Ztg.* (Nos. 574, 582, 585, Dec. 8, 13, 14), *Berliner N. N.* (No. 582, Dec. 13), *Weser-Zeitung,* (quoted *Kölnische Volksztg.,* No. 1134, Dec. 15), and the *Kölnische Volksztg.* (Nos. 1128, 1141, Dec. 13, 17).

[14] The record of the controversy and the charges of bribery on both sides are in the *Deutsche Zeitung,* Nos. 290, 292, 293, 294, 298, Dec. 12, 14, 15, 16, 21, 1900. Bülow illustrates his difficulties with the Pan-Germans by the following tale: Walking one day in the Tiergarten, he met Dr. Hasse and reproached him for creating difficulties for their official policy. Bülow quotes Hasse's reply: "As a representative of the people it is my right and my duty to express the real sentiments of the German people. It is Your Excellency's duty, because you are the Minister, to see that our foreign relations do not suffer as a result." (Bülow, *Memoirs,* I, 549.)

[15] *Times, Daily Mail, Daily Telegraph, Westminster Gazette, Morning Post, Daily News, Pall Mall Gazette,* news reports and editorials, Feb. 5, 6, 1901.

this may well be true, but how did it affect the Emperor's relations with his own people?

Except in the Kölnische Zeitung, the buckets of praise poured over the Kaiser by English editors awakened no response in Germany. On the contrary, the visit and its dénouement intensified suspicion and hostility. The rift between the Emperor and the nation, occasioned by the conflict of sympathies over the Boer War, was widened by the granting of the Order of the Black Eagle to Lord Roberts, by the Emperor's appointment as a field marshal in the British army, and by his long absence from Germany, particularly over his birthday. The bestowal of the Black Eagle upon Roberts was a matter of universal regret. Even the Kölnische Zeitung, when the rumor first appeared, expressed the hope that it was unfounded.[16] More ominous, perhaps, than any other feature of the general press criticism was an article appearing in the Kreuzzeitung, entitled "On the Emperor's Return." It was a manifesto and a lecture from Junkerdom, stressing the duty of a monarch to his subjects. The editor began by expressing sympathy for the Kaiser in his bereavement and acknowledging the obligation that took him to England. But the Emperor must consider national as well as family ties. All true Prussians were proud of the tradition of loyalty to the monarchy, the editor continued; they rejoiced that the king possessed real power, and they wanted to preserve the position of the throne. It would be preserved only if the traditional Prussian loyalty to the crown were not brought into disrepute, if the people were convinced that under their ruler they had nothing to fear, and if the conviction prevailed that the monarch was at one with the sentiment of the nation. It was doubtful if that were so today, and the editor referred to the numerous letters of protest and criticism which he had received from men whose loyalty to the monarchical principle was unquestionable. He then recited the incidents connected with the Emperor's stay in England which had given rise to these apprehensions and doubts. In conclusion, he expressed the fear that a breach was opening between the sovereign and his people and that the unity between ruler and subjects, so essential to a strong monarchy, was rapidly being undermined.[17] This article is summarized at some length to illustrate the extent to which opposition was aroused in the most loyal circles in Germany. There is no reason to review the outpourings

[16] Quoted *Deutsche Ztg.*, No. 39, Feb. 15, 1901. Of the more violent protests that of the *Münchner N. N.* is typical: "Even as a Knight of the Order of the Black Eagle, Roberts is still to us Germans no more than the inglorious commander of a bankrupt army in the most disgraceful and most hateful, predatory war that England has ever fought." (No. 67, Feb. 9, 1901.)

[17] No. 66, Feb. 8, 1901. Coming from the official organ of the Conservative party, the article created a sensation and was quoted in all important German papers.

of the more intransigent critics of the Kaiser and his government. The affair ran its course in the press, following closely the pattern of the Kruger incident, and reaching its climax in the Reichstag debate of March 5. Bülow with his customary facility again papered over the cracks. He reduced the Emperor's actions to the level of those of a private individual, stroked down the pro-Boers by asserting Germany's independence of Great Britain, and quieted the fears entertained in other quarters that he was playing fast and loose with Germany's relations to Russia.[18] Instead of the anticipated washing of linen, the multitude witnessed a washing of hands.

Bülow's curtness toward England and his affability toward Russia foreshadowed the declaration made ten days later on Germany's policy in the Far East. Referring to British concern at Russian encroachments in Manchuria, he announced that that province did not come within the scope of the Anglo-German agreement of October 16, 1900. The diplomacy of the Chinese problem is so complex and confusing, so long-drawn out and so difficult to follow, both in the diplomatic documents and the press, that its importance in bringing about the diplomatic revolution at the turn of the century is easy to overlook.[19] In the words of the Manchester Guardian the Far Eastern crisis began "when first the Germans took a 'coaling station' and soon found that the coaling station had a province attached to it. Then there were the Russians, who went to Port Arthur 'to pass the winter' and have stayed there ever since. Then there were the British, who took Wei-Hai-Wei to encourage the Chinese to resist aggression." (June 16, 1900.) With the Boxer uprising and the international military occupation, in the summer of 1900, a new stage was reached. Russian operations in Manchuria and intrigues in Peking were again the object of British mistrust and alarm, the more so since Britain was involved with the Boers in South Africa. In the German press a general feeling of uneasiness and alarm was manifested at the possibility of more serious complications in their world policy. The accord of October 1900, between London and Berlin, which announced a common policy in dealing with the Chinese puzzle, was greeted in both countries as a measure of relief and insurance. On every hand, reported a London correspondent, one heard the words: "Well, in China we are all right." [20]

---

[18] *Fürst Bülows Reden,* I, 185–94. Outside the semi-official and inspired press, however, Bülow's remarks had a cool reception.
[19] Professor Langer in his *Diplomacy of Imperialism* (vol. II, chaps. XXI and XXII) has fully elucidated the reaction of the Far Eastern question on the diplomatic alignments of the European Powers.
[20] *Berliner Tageblatt,* No. 550, Oct. 29, 1900.

But from the beginning a misunderstanding prevailed as to whether the German government was bound to support Britain in opposing Russian activity in Manchuria. When the first test came with the Russian demands on Peking, in January 1901, it became absolutely clear that in the Yangtze Agreement (as Bülow insisted upon calling it), England had not found a bulwark against Russia in northern China, but had rather accorded to Germany a certain measure of interest in the Yangtze valley. In giving the German interpretation of the accord, Bülow remarked: "As regards the future of Manchuria, really, gentlemen, I can imagine nothing which we regard with more indifference." [21] This improvement on Bismarck's "What is Hecuba to us?" was designed to quiet the clamor in the German press against the government's Far Eastern policy, which it was feared would lead to a breach with Russia. It was also, none the less, a statement of a principle of German policy, namely, that Germany would not co-operate with any power in China against the Czar's government. British policy was based on the belief, or on the hope, that this proposition was untrue. Questions were asked immediately in parliament and the contradictory Whitehall interpretation of the accord was given.[22] Later, in August, the bluebook on China appeared, which again provoked questions in parliament. The bluebook, which one critic called "a record of German unfriendliness," supplied the answer. The influential élite who really determined British foreign policy were completely disillusioned. They had put the bucket into an empty well. The Times' editor, reviewing the Far Eastern transactions in light of the bluebook revelations, drew the conclusion that "in no circumstances whatever, where our interests and those of Russia come into conflict, can we expect the slightest real support from the 'honest brokers' of Berlin." [23] Finding the Germans a broken reed so far as British interests in the Far East were concerned, the London authorities turned to the Japanese and concluded with them the alliance of February 1902.

The several stages through which the misunderstanding over the Yangtze Agreement passed, cannot obscure its importance for Anglo-German relations. It marked unmistakably the point at which British authorities turned away from Berlin. It marked the end of the policy of understanding and parallel action that had been inaugurated with the Portuguese colonies accord in 1898. When, toward the close of the next

[21] *Fürst Bülows Reden,* I, 202–3.
[22] *Times,* parliamentary reports, March 21, 29, 1901; Langer, *op. cit.,* II, 700–2, 722.
[23] *Times,* Aug. 26, 1901.

year (1902), the two governments sought to revive that policy in dealing with Venezuela, the outcry in the press and in parliament was so great
as to threaten the existence of the cabinet.

In view of the breakdown in substantive policy, the alliance negotiations pursued during the spring of 1901 have about them an air of
artificiality. The tension over Manchuria and the interminable war in
South Africa provided the setting. Any chance of success was largely
vitiated by Eckardstein's improper and misleading reports to his superiors
in Berlin. Throughout, the conversations never exceeded the bounds of
the academic, and because of the widely divergent views and the conflict of personalities—Salisbury, Lansdowne, Holstein, Hatzfeldt and
Eckardstein—they never had any great promise of success. They were
brought to a close, in May, by a practical veto imposed by Salisbury.[24]

The impression of unreality which surrounds the Eckardstein-Lans-
downe conversations is considerably heightened when one turns to the
contemporary press. A publicity build-up for the engagement contemplated by the negotiators was wholly lacking. Had one authentic whis-
per about these conversations reached the public there would have been
an explosion without parallel in the German press. It would have required steadier nerves and thicker skin than Bülow possessed to have
withstood the storm. Salisbury's remark on this point shows a genius for
understatement: "A promise of defensive alliance with England would
excite bitter murmurs in every rank of German society. . . ." [25]

The snubbing and misunderstandings on both sides, which ended the
policy of "agreement from case to case," had their counterpart in a bitter
press campaign that shortened tempers and embittered public relations
as no previous campaign had done. The invisible strands of mutual good
will and regard that bound individuals in Berlin and London snapped
under the tension. Chamberlain's alleged slander of the German army in
the War of 1870 brought German Anglophobia to a rousing crescendo.
No hands stretched out by diplomats could bridge the gap that opened
up between the peoples.

This particular occurrence presents so many arresting aspects of the
interrelationships of national chauvinism and mass publicity under modern conditions of rapid communication that it will be treated here at considerable length. It had as a background the German public's partisan-

---

[24] Langer, *Diplomacy of Imperialism,* II, 727–34, 740–42. The negotiations are set
forth in great detail by Willy Becker, *Fürst Bülow und England,* pp. 203–93;
also Johannes Dreyer, *Deutschland und England in ihrer Politik und Presse im
Jahre 1901* (Berlin, 1934), pp. 67 ff.; G. Ritter, *Die Legende von der verschmähten
englischen Freundschaft,* pp. 26–40.
[25] *B. D.,* II, 69; Langer, *op. cit.,* II, 734.

ship for the underdog in the Boer War, the universal condemnation of British military methods, and the widely held belief that the English army was composed of brigands who had perpetrated unmentionable atrocities in South Africa. Any other orientation would have produced no response to Chamberlain's likening of British war methods in South Africa to German methods during the Franco-Prussian War.

Continental as well as English observers predicted in the autumn of 1900 that the war in South Africa would soon be brought to a close. No one could foresee that almost two years of guerilla warfare lay ahead. To conquer the stubborn foe British commanders employed methods that met with almost universal condemnation throughout the civilized world. In Germany, where sympathies were already engaged in the Boer cause, this second phase of the war excited compassion for the victims and fed the fire of Anglophobia. The systematic destruction of Boer farms and the wasting of the country, the removal of the women and children to concentration camps, the use of blockhouses and barbed wire, the expulsion of foreign Red Cross medical units from the field of operations, which deprived the Boers of medical aid—these and other measures provoked the hottest condemnation in the German press. The feeling was fed from many sources. Germans, deported from the Transvaal by British military authorities, returned to the Fatherland and in the meetings of the Pan-German League found a free forum for expressing their hatred of England. A nephew of Christian De Wet toured Germany and spoke before packed houses (4000 in Frankfort) on the inhumanity of British war methods.[26] Another focus of public agitation was the *Deutsche Buren-Centrale* organized, with headquarters in Berlin and Munich, to co-ordinate the raising of funds for the Boers.[27] Whenever Dr. Leyds visited Berlin, the entire publicity resources of the most widely circulated papers were at his disposal.[28] Many of the worst excesses appearing in the foreign press, particularly in French and Irish Home Rule organs, were uncritically reproduced in German papers.[29] In October and November 1900, the Socialist Vorwärts created a sensation with

---

[26] *Frankfurter Ztg.*, No. 36, Feb. 5, 1901.

[27] *Berliner Tageblatt*, No. 542, Oct. 24, 1900. From July 1, 1901, it published jointly with the International League for Assistance to the Boers a fortnightly journal called *Der Burenfreund.*

[28] *Berliner Tageblatt*, No. 52, Jan. 29, 1900, front page interview with photograph.

[29] *Die Post* (No. 521, Nov. 6, 1900), for example, quoted at length an article by Jean Carrère in the *Matin*, in which the writer slandered the British colonial troops: "The men were mostly the collected scum of the towns and seaports. . . . There were robbers of the worst sort amongst them, especially Australians, and still more South Africans." From the Irish *Freeman's Journal* was reproduced the canard that Lord Roberts had given an order to take no Boer prisoners. (*Münchner N. N.*, No. 34, Jan. 21, 1901.)

its "Letters from the Huns"—letters from German soldiers with the Boxer expedition. It balanced this with a similar series in December entitled, *"Das Hunnentum in Südafrika,"* in which British war measures were painted in lurid colors.[30]

Strange as it may seem to a post-War generation accustomed to aerial warfare against civilian populations, it was the system of concentration camps that set the stage for the outburst over Chamberlain's unguarded comparison of British and German methods of warfare. During the winter of 1900–1901 reports began to appear of the burning and dynamiting of farms, and the removal of non-combatants to concentration camps. But the public was totally unprepared for the report released by Miss Hobhouse (June 19, 1901) on conditions in these camps—the disease and malnutrition, lack of clothing and shelter, and above all, the shocking child mortality. Almost simultaneously with this record was published a report to President Steejn by General Smuts on British treatment of civilians.[31] As a rather moderate example of the effect produced by these disclosures we may quote the Vossische Zeitung, which described the conduct of military authorities in South Africa as no better than that of the Turks in Bulgaria and Armenia. How could the British people look on in silence "while its hireling troops perform deeds of savagery among the free Christian people of the Boers, while the farms of men who are fighting for their independence are burnt to the ground, their wives and daughters outraged, and their old men and children driven together and left to die of hunger and disease?"[32] When the concentration camps became a political issue between the government and pro-Boers in England, when Campbell-Bannerman let fall the words "methods of barbarism," when the war office, to counter exaggerated reports, finally published the child mortality figures for the camps, a virulent publicity fed the partisan audience in Germany. In pictures, in articles and in verse the British were anathematized for making war upon helpless women and children.[33]

---

[30] Particularly No. 280, Dec. 1, 1900.
[31] *Vossische Ztg.,* No. 292, June 25, 1901.
[32] No. 298, June 28, 1901.
[33] Some verses by R. V. Gottschall on the concentration camps were quoted in many papers:

> "Ein Mordbefehl, wie ihn Herodes gab,
> Spannt mit dem Tode Weib und Kind zusammen,
> Ein jedes Lager wird ein Massengrab
> Und ringsum leuchten der Verwüstung Flammen;
> Das Haus, der Fleiss der Bürger steht im Brand,
> Schmachvoller Tode trifft mutige Rebellen;
> Es wird zum Heim das Heimatlose Land
> Den wilden Tieren und den Raubgesellen."

It was at this point, in October, when the German nation was aroused by British "methods of barbarism," that Chamberlain, speaking in defense of the government's conduct of the war, sought to justify their methods against the Boers by an unfortunate appeal to examples from other countries at other times. At a political meeting in Edinburgh on October 25, Chamberlain said: "I think that the time has come—is coming—when measures of greater severity may be necessary (Hear, Hear, and cheers), and if that time comes we can find precedents for anything that we may do in the action of those nations who now criticize our 'barbarity' and 'cruelty,' but whose example in Poland, in the Caucasus, in Almeria, in Tongking, in Bosnia, in the Franco-German war, we have never even approached (Cheers)." [34] The Wolff Bureau dispatched from London a four hundred word summary of Chamberlain's speech in which was reproduced a fairly accurate translation of this passage.[35] Very soon, however, the actual words employed by the colonial secretary were forgotten, and in the press and on the platform it was alleged that Chamberlain had said that British war methods in South Africa were far less barbarous than those employed by the Germans in the war of 1870. Having been fed for two years on the rankest and vilest of atrocity stories about the British troops, the Germans put an interpretation on Chamberlain's statement which he had not the remotest intention of conveying.

It may seem surprising that since Chamberlain lumped the wars of France, Spain, Russia, and Germany together for purposes of comparison, no violent reaction was produced except in the latter country. The answer is simple. Excluding 1870, the examples adduced were civil or colonial wars. The Franco-Prussian War, however, was associated in the German mind with the birth of national unity and greatness, and it was celebrated by the upper and middle classes as the most glorious, idealistic, and justifiable of all wars; it was not, therefore, to be compared with bush-fighting or "a war of conquest for the possession of gold and diamond mines."

Articles on "England's Moral Decline," "The Alva of South Africa," etc., in *Schwäbischer Merkur,* Nos. 428, 467, 474, 587, Sept. 13, Oct. 7, 10, Dec. 16; *Vossische Ztg.,* No. 501, Oct. 25; *Lokal-Anzeiger,* No. 511, Oct. 31; *Kreuzzeitung,* Nos. 477, 486, 496, 497, Oct. 11, 17, 22, 23.

It ought to be pointed out that no more condemnatory language was employed in the more responsible German press than in the *Manchester Guardian* and the *Daily News,* and many of the articles appearing in Germany were taken over directly from these journals. The *Manchester Guardian* (Oct. 23, 1901), for example, demanded that the government "clear the English name of the stain of barbarity and the shame of conquering Boers by destroying their children."

[34] *Times,* Oct. 26, 1901.

[35] Published evening papers, Oct. 26, morning papers, Oct. 27.

It was quite accidental that Chamberlain's remark gave rise to a campaign of vituperation extending over two months. Appropriately hostile criticisms were passed upon the colonial secretary's comparison by the Berlin press and the larger provincial papers. No more notice was taken of it in the newspapers for a week.[36] The impulse to a national demonstration came, not from the journalists through the press, but from organized groups of university students and faculty, veterans' associations, and local branches of the Pan-German and Colonial societies. In the beginning the press merely gave publicity to these movements, made their action a matter of national record, and stimulated imitation on the part of other groups. Soon, however, the emotionalized attitudes of the newspaper public made it impossible for all but the hardiest of editors to maintain a strictly reportorial rôle. Henceforth, the journalists took the lead in the national campaign of resentment against the slandering of "Saint Sedan" by a foreign statesman. At this time, too, the agitation left the ground of protest against an individual English statesman and assumed the character of an Anglophobic crusade.

The pattern for the agitation in the societies was set by the students and faculty of German universities. At the University of Greifswald a demonstration meeting was called and resolutions passed condemning Chamberlain for slandering the German army. This action was noticed but not given great prominence in the press.[37] The next meeting of consequence was organized by the students of the University of Berlin. The rector intervened to prevent an official demonstration, so the affair was held outside the university. The meeting was addressed by Herr Baecker, one of the editors of the pro-Boer Deutsche Zeitung, a disabled Boer commander named Banks, who spoke on English atrocities in South Africa, and Professors Gierke, Kahl, and Wagner. At the conclusion of the meeting it was resolved that the "meeting rejects Chamberlain's comparison of our sacred German war of 1870–71 to England's war of conquest in South Africa with all its breaches of the law of nations. We reject it as a brutal insult to our most sacred memories, as a defamation of our heroic dead, and as an insult to our national honor."[38] After the Berlin demonstration of November 6 the meetings became so numerous

[36] *Kreuzzeitung*, No. 504, Oct. 26; *Berliner N. N.*, No. 504, Oct. 26; *National-Zeitung*, Oct. 26; *Berliner Tageblatt*, Oct. 26; *Frankfurter Ztg.*, No. 297, Oct. 26; *Schwäbischer Merkur*, No. 510, Oct. 31; *Lokal-Anzeiger*, No. 504, Oct. 26; *Vossische Ztg.*, No. 504, Oct. 26; *Deutsche Ztg.*, No. 253, Oct. 27. Chirol, who was in Berlin at the time, is of course mistaken in attributing the revival of the agitation to the press. (*Fifty Years in a Changing World*, p. 297.)

[37] *Lokal-Anzeiger*, No. 514, Nov. 1; *Berliner N. N.*, No. 516, Nov. 2; *Münchner N. N.*, No. 510, Nov. 3; *Frankfurter Ztg.*, No. 303, Nov. 1.

[38] Full accounts in the *Lokal-Anzeiger*, No. 523, Nov. 7; *Deutsche Ztg.*, No. 263, Nov. 8; and *Kölnische Ztg.*, No. 873, Nov. 7.

that a complete record is impossible. Demonstrations attended by three thousand people or more were organized by the Pan-German League in Munich, Kassel, Hanover, Stuttgart, Göttingen, and Hamburg. In other cities the demonstrations were organized jointly by the League and the Colonial Society. In Leipzig, Cologne, Bielefeld, Duisburg, Marburg, and other cities, meetings were sponsored by the local veterans' organizations. Student group demonstrations were held at the universities and technical colleges at Breslau, Hanover, Darmstadt, Rostock, Bonn, Munich, Göttingen and Stuttgart. At Giessen, Professor Hermann Oncken was the principal speaker at a meeting of students and faculty, which subscribed to a resolution that Chamberlain's utterance was based upon a lack of knowledge hardly creditable to a minister, and which should have shamed even a half-educated Englishman. In Munich the students and faculties of the university and the technical college united in a meeting which was addressed by Dr. von Stengel and the Pan-German professor, Count du Moulin-Eckart.[39]

The clergy who blessed the banners of war, and the organized veterans who waved them, followed the academicians in notifying the public that their feelings were outraged. The Thuringian Pastors' Society adopted resolutions against Chamberlain's insult to the German nation; other ministerial groups followed its example. A protest manifesto circulated among the Protestant clergy of the Rhineland received 680 signatures. At the outset an effort had been made to stampede the national organization of Soldiers' and Veterans' Societies into the protest movement, but upon the intervention of the military authorities the directing committee in Berlin refused to issue a proclamation in the name of the society and called upon its constituent groups to refrain from agitation.[40] This did not prevent local and state groups from taking independent action. In Württemberg and Anhalt the directing committee, representing 160 affiliated societies with 12,000 members, issued a violent protest. "We positively reject the comparison of our great justifiable war with the robber expedition of the English nation in Africa, which was undertaken for despicable financial gain, and in which the English hireling bands destroy defenseless women and children like robbers and murderers."

[39] The latter declared that the *furor teutonicus* had not gone to sleep, but had raised itself when Chamberlain dared "to compare the deeds of heroes with the handiwork of robbers. . . . A people who fought a war for gold would not know what it was to feel insulted in its *Waffenehre*." (*Münchner N. N.*, No. 542, Nov. 22.) At Jena the students hanged Chamberlain in effigy; at the foot of the gallows sat King Edward drinking from a champagne bottle. Among the spectators, "Goldaktien aus Johannesburg" were distributed which bore the inscription, "Deutscher Michel, das lässt du dir gefallen." (*Kreuzzeitung*, No. 524, Nov. 7.)

[40] Bülow, *Memoirs,* I, 638. On the mores of the *Kriegervereine* see Alfred Vagts, *History of Militarism* (N. Y., 1937), pp. 386–90.

Similar public protests were made by the united soldiers' and veterans' societies in Baden and Saxony. An army chaplain, in a memorial service for those fallen in 1870, declared that "If Chamberlain's words were true then we would have no right to stand in reverence by the graves of our dead."

In the absence of sponsoring groups in the smaller towns, meetings were called by local pastors and teachers. In these districts the agitation continued until mid-December. The resolutions were all cut to the same pattern, although some showed greater ingenuity in vituperation than others. All rejected Chamberlain's comparison as an insult to the German people's army, most of them condemned British barbarism in South Africa, and better than a majority demanded that the "odious comparison" be repudiated in the semi-official press, by the chancellor in the Reichstag, or through some other official channel. The directors of the Hamburg demonstration, more original than the others, added another demand—the deportation of George Saunders, correspondent of the Times. This brings us back to the part played by the press in this witches' Sabbath of chauvinism.[41]

When the demonstration meetings first began, the editors almost without exception justified the agitation on the basis of Chamberlain's alleged insult to the nation. As the more sober minded began to raise doubts as to where it all might lead, they were attacked by the wild men as traitors.[42] Some ignored the agitation in the beginning, but as popular frenzy mounted they were forced into the middle of the current, unless they were willing to forego popularity with their readers. The Kölnische Volkszeitung, the journal with the largest Catholic circulation in Germany, stood aloof until November 18, when it plunged into the stream, launching a wild attack on Chamberlain and feeding its readers with a review of the worst atrocity stories that had appeared in the European press. It linked this campaign with a demand that some concession be made to German national feeling by a statement in the Norddeutsche or a declaration by the chancellor.[43] Some of the editors leaped joyfully into the fight, others no doubt were forced reluctantly into the popular cur-

---

[41] Apart from the regional papers where local demonstrations were chronicled at length, the best record is found in the *Deutsche Zeitung*, which devoted practically its entire space to the propaganda of the movement from November 1 to December 15. The agitation among the soldiers' and veterans' societies is fully recorded in the *Kreuzzeitung*, No. 524, Nov. 7 to No. 552, Nov. 25. A collection of testimonials of indignation from one hundred college professors, deputies and journalists was published in February 1902 under the title, *A German Protest Against English Barbarity in the Boer War*.

[42] The *National-Zeitung* and the *Vossische Zeitung* were so attacked by the *Kreuzzeitung* editors. (*Kreuzzeitung*, No. 529, Nov. 10.)

[43] Nos. 1030, 1034, 1042, Nov. 18, 19, 22.

rent. The London correspondent of the Berliner Tageblatt distinguished himself for vile abuse of Chamberlain, while Arthur Levysohn, the editor, put a stamp of approval upon the public demonstrations.[44] The Vossische Zeitung, which in the beginning took the view that the agitation was exaggerated, warmed up as the public demonstrations progressed. Chamberlain had slandered the German army; his words had not been misinterpreted; and no one could say that German resentment was unjustified. Finally, the editor gave space to a tirade from "one of our London representatives," which equaled anything to be found in the catch-penny chauvinist journals. It was a vitriolic attack on Chamberlain's record in domestic and foreign politics, in which he was denounced as "the son of a shopkeeper" and a "born intriguer who took into politics all the tricks and dodges of the successful manufacturer and shopkeeper, and who still pursues in his dealings with foreign powers methods which secured for him a large fortune as a maker of screws." [45] This bit of blackguardism was only matched by the Deutsche Zeitung's remark that "in the head of the worried screw manufacturer from Birmingham, one screw must have become loose." [46]

Because of his barbed reporting of patriotic hysterics, Saunders came in for a large measure of abuse in the German press. On November 2 he wrote a galling dispatch to the Times describing the indignant reception accorded Chamberlain's speech. He laid the blame for the outburst on the German press, which had fed the people with "infamous lies" about the conduct of British soldiers in South Africa. In the war of 1870, he patronizingly remarked, German soldiers had conducted themselves "almost" as blamelessly as had British soldiers in South Africa. The university demonstrators were described as the "educated and half-educated members of the German universities." Indignantly the Hamburger Nachrichten, which served on all occasions as a practicing medium for communication of the ideas of the departed Prince Bismarck, declared

---

[44] Nos. 563, 586, 592, Nov. 5, 17, 21. The London correspondent wrote on Nov. 5: "But where the English have shown the most execrable brutality, the worst ferocity, has been in preventing foreign countries from sending ambulances to attend the sick and wounded. In this measure the English have reached the culminating point of their infamy, and have placed themselves, so to speak, outside the pale of civilization. These Pharisees, with their mouths always full of the words of liberty and humanity, dare to affect indignation when they are assailed by reproaches by Germans in common with all civilized nations. . . . The German people possess a store of imperishable idealism, while the English people are characterized by a gross and vulgar materialism which, under the cloak of religious hypocrisy, shrinks from nothing. Under such circumstances do not speak to us further of the blood that is supposed to be thicker than water."

[45] Nos. 550, 556, Nov. 23, 27.

[46] No. 262, Nov. 7: "Unser Freund Joë." Further, the writer said: "The Russian minister Ignatiev had the title 'Father of Lies'; he will have to bow modestly in his grave to the greater son in pious England."

that in the Prince's day, Saunders would have been immediately deported. In the Deutsche Zeitung, the Kreuzzeitung, the Hannoverscher Kurier and other journals, Saunders was vehemently denounced. One writer referred to him as "little Chamberlain" who imitates "big Chamberlain" with "his hemming and spitting." [47] In the next seven years Saunders, who incidentally had a German wife and a Prussian officer as a brother-in-law, was to repay these jibes and jeers a hundredfold.

Another feature of the press campaign was the reiterated demand for an official repudiation of Chamberlain's "insult." In some instances, this took the form of abashed excuses for the frantic demonstrators; the agitation, said the apologists, would not have gone so far if the government had spoken out for the nation. "We are simply fulfilling a duty to our own self-respect," wrote the editor of the Schwäbischer Merkur. "If the government is embarrassed by this popular movement it is its own fault, for it had the power to prevent the whole indignation demonstration by a simple declaration in one of its recognized press organs." An apologist in the Berliner Neueste Nachrichten said: "Five lines in the Norddeutsche Allgemeine Zeitung would have been enough to hold back the anti-Chamberlain demonstrations in Germany or to banish them in time." Arthur Levysohn expressed the same opinion in the Berliner Tageblatt. Organs of all political shades joined the Catholic Kölnische Volkszeitung, the Deutsche Zeitung, and the National Liberal Hannoverscher Kurier in urging the government to speak for the nation through the Reichsanzeiger or the Norddeutsche. Many of the demonstrators in their resolutions deplored the passivity of officials in a matter involving national honor. [48]

What do the semi-official and inspired papers reveal of the official attitude toward Chamberlain's *faux pas* and the counter demonstrations? For one thing they show the inability of the official publicity machine to overcome a popular trend, and they reveal also the unwillingness of officials to oppose the aroused nationalists. Some efforts to furnish an official view of the incident are noticeable in the first days of the agita-

---

[47] *Times,* Nov. 2; *Kreuzzeitung,* Nos. 520, 525, Nov. 5, 8, quoting *Hamburger Nachrichten* and *Hannoverscher Kurier; Deutsche Ztg.,* Nos. 260, 262, Nov. 5, 7.

[48] *Schwäbischer Merkur,* No. 534, Nov. 14; *Berliner N. N.,* No. 544, Nov. 15; *Berliner Tageblatt,* No. 597, Nov. 24; *Kölnische Volksztg.,* No. 1034, Nov. 19; *Deutsche Ztg.,* No. 271, Nov. 17; *Hannoverscher Kurier,* quoted by *Kreuzzeitung,* No. 525, Nov. 8; *Münchner N. N.,* No. 526, Nov. 13; *Konservative Korrespondenz,* quoted *Deutsche Ztg.,* No. 265, Nov. 10; *Deutsche Volkswirtschaftliche Korrespondenz,* quoted *Deutsche Ztg.,* No. 262, Nov. 7: "Soll also unser Volk nicht das Vertrauen zur Leitung unserer auswärtigen Politik verlieren, so wird Graf Bülow gut thun, sich in Kürze darüber klar zu werden, was er in Sachen Chamberlain zu thun gedenkt und seinen Entschluss öffentlich kundzugeben."

tion, but they went quite unheeded.[49] Alone of the several papers which generally served to put the government's views before the public, the Kölnische Zeitung opposed the popular mood. Even in doing this it put itself into the position of guard and counselor, rather than a front-line fighter. From time to time it pointed out that Chamberlain was being misquoted in the demonstration meetings, that the French, the Russians, and the Austrians were not reacting, and that the agitation was doing irreparable damage to Anglo-German relations.[50] That even this cautious opposition reacted unfavorably upon its circulation is attested by Von Mühlberg, the under-secretary of state for foreign affairs. Discussing the press campaign with Buchanan, the secretary of the British embassy, Mühlberg said: "The Government . . . were doing all they could to moderate the language of the press, and I would, no doubt, have noticed the difference in tone between those papers which were more or less in touch with the Government, and those that did not seek inspiration from official quarters. It was, however, unfortunately a fact that, while the circulation of the latter class of journals was increasing, that of the former was falling off. This was the case with the 'Koelnische Zeitung,' many of whose regular readers had deserted it for the pro-Boer 'Koelnische Volks-Zeitung'." [51]

After a fortnight, when it seemed that tempers were cooling, fresh fuel was piled on the flames by publication of a letter from Chamberlain's secretary to Mr. Marriner, London correspondent of the Vienna Neue Freie Presse. The gist of the secretary's communication was that Chamberlain felt he had nothing to retract, and that the agitation in Germany was "artificial." Chamberlain, who could always find the right word for the British masses, could always be depended on to find the wrong word for a foreign audience. Every German editor and commentator seized

[49] *Lokal-Anzeiger,* No. 536, Nov. 15, quoted by all papers as semi-official. Here it was stated that popular indignation was justified, but they should not be drawn into general political enmity toward England; the Wilhelmstrasse could not lodge an official protest in London because Chamberlain was not speaking for the government; Russia, Austria, and France were named by Chamberlain, as well as Germany, and they were not protesting; only France and Russia would be benefited by an official collision between London and Berlin. Similar articles in *Berliner N. N.,* No. 528, Nov. 9; Berlin telegram, *Frankfurter Ztg.,* No. 312, Nov. 10.

[50] No. 876, Nov. 8; No. 900, Nov. 17; and No. 908, Nov. 20, calling Reichstag deputy Trimborn to account for grossly misquoting Chamberlain. The deputy admitted the misquotation, saying that he had taken his version from a protest resolution passed at another meeting! In the same number is a long article which was probably written or dictated by Bülow. Compare: "Auch wir sind der Meinung, dass auf einen groben Klotz unter Umständen ein grober Keil gehöre," with "Auf grobe Klötze gehörten grobe Keile," which was Bülow's formula for the Chamberlain incident. (*G. P.,* XVII, 150.)

[51] Buchanan to Lansdowne, Nov. 20, 1901; *B. D.,* I, 262.

on the word "artificial" and made out of it a new provocation. "The agitation is absolutely spontaneous, and the German government has gone to great lengths to suppress it, but it has not succeeded," declared the Kölnische Volkszeitung.[52] It was doubtless the prospect of more violent recriminations that led Bülow and his advisers to publish a semi-official statement in the Norddeutsche on November 22.

Considerable thought and time must have gone into the drafting of this pronouncement. It began with a justification of the popular resentment. It then continued: "We, at least, are unable to see that the demonstrations of offended national feeling in academic circles demand any kind of official or semi-official enlightenment or admonition; unless it is to say that it would be unfair to extend to the English government and to the English people the justifiable indignation excited by the expressions employed outside parliament by a single minister. Meanwhile, any number of serious German papers have emphasized this point of view with sufficient explicitness, and have sincerely deplored that through Mr. Chamberlain's inconsiderate and wounding remark the anti-English feeling engendered in German popular circles by the Boer War should have again been stirred up. . . . We cannot join in the demand which has been made here and there at public meetings that in the interest of the German army, official steps should be taken against unofficial utterances of a foreign minister. The reputation acquired by the German army throughout the entire civilized world by its discipline, its humanity and its bravery stands far too high to be affected by erroneous and inadmissible comparisons." [53] The brief statement, throughout, reveals the triple purpose of its drafters, namely, to satisfy the popular clamor at home for an official response, to make this strong enough to deprive the agitators of an excuse for promoting further disturbances, and to do this without assaulting directly the hotly besieged citadel of official Anglo-German friendship. As it turned out it was a sufficient plaster for wounded patriotic feelings, but its effect in England was deplorable.

With the abatement of popular clamor produced by the Norddeutsche's pronouncement, the more moderate journals began to cry "Halt." In the Kölnische Zeitung, the Berliner Tageblatt, the Frankfurter Zeitung, the Kreuzzeitung, and numerous other responsible papers the official view began to prevail: Further agitation would only serve the cause of Germany's enemies in Paris; England must not be driven into the arms of

---

[52] No. 1042, Nov. 22. Also *Deutsche Ztg.,* No. 274, Nov. 22; *Berliner N. N.,* No. 546, Nov. 21; *Lokal-Anzeiger,* No. 546, Nov. 21; *Deutsche Tagesztg.,* quoted in *Frankfurter Ztg.,* No. 324, Nov. 22. "I have seldom seen the masses so keenly aroused, so vehemently indignant," wrote the *Daily Mail* correspondent (Nov. 22).
[53] No. 274, Nov. 22.

France and Russia; the atrocity stories, which formed the emotional basis of the resentment toward Chamberlain, were in the main sheer fabrications; the reaction produced by the demonstrations in England were having an adverse effect on German trade. These and other arguments were advanced on behalf of sanity and the future security of the national foreign policy. By mid-December the demonstrators and their press claque were silenced.[54]

Press polemics and popular demonstrations against a foreign country, or its representatives, have as their corollary measures of defense in the country attacked. We must now turn to the British press and view the other side. Excluding Saunders of the Times, the English correspondents in Berlin were markedly reserved in reporting the popular agitation loosed by Chamberlain's remarks. They discounted this aspect of the affair while they emphasized the government's lack of sympathy with the senseless and dangerous popular agitation. The English editors commented in the same vein.[55] Saunders, unlike his colleagues, reported the agitation in detail and consciously, or unconsciously, sharpened every unlovely feature. These reports, in turn, formed the basis of bitter editorial comment.[56]

The Norddeutsche pronouncement of November 22 came as a distinct shock to the English correspondents in Berlin, who had been playing up the Wilhelmstrasse's resistance to popular clamor. It was as though a practical jokester had stolen their clothes and left them nude before the public. The feeling of betrayal sharpened dispatches and editorial comment. As an example we may cite a dispatch from the Reuter correspond-

[54] Schiemann in the *Kreuzzeitung*, No. 552, Nov. 25; *Frankfurter Ztg.*, Nos. 324, 328, 334, Nov. 22, 26, Dec. 2; *Berliner N. N.*, No. 550, Nov. 23; *Berliner Tageblatt*, No. 604, Nov. 28, quoting *Süddeutsche Reichskorrespondenz* (directly inspired); *Kölnische Ztg.*, No. 922, Nov. 25; the *Norddeutsche* (No. 279, Nov. 28) began to quote approvingly all these warnings from the other journals. *Kölnische Volksztg.*, attacking the Pan-Germans, "who had established political rowdyism as a formal political system" (No. 1108, Dec. 12, 1901).

[55] Dispatches and editorials in the *Daily Telegraph, Standard, Morning Post, Pall Mall Gazette,* and *Daily Mail,* Nov. 1 to Nov. 22. Reuter's correspondent, Mr. Harrison, was notably reticent and cautious. The correspondent of the pro-Boer *Daily News* took the position that the grievance was legitimate.

[56] A *Times* leader of November 20 contained the words "flimsy pretext," "poisoned wells of German public opinion," "campaign of lies and slander," "stream of calumny," "abominable falsehoods." It concluded that "such a widespread and protracted campaign against a foreign country could hardly have assumed these overwhelming proportions, had it not been regarded at first with official tolerance, if not with indulgence." Popular sentiment may not count in Germany, continued the writer, but it does in England. "These daily manifestations of German hatred are gradually sinking into the heart of the British people, and it would be an unfortunate day for both nations if the belief were to gain ground in England that . . . the passionate enmity of the German people must be regarded as a more powerful and permanent factor in moulding the relations of the two countries than the wise and friendly statesmanship of German rulers."

ent, Mr. Harrison, who only rarely exchanged the rôle of reporter for that of interpreter.

The lesson taught by the whole affair is very obvious. The hysterical talk of professors, veterans, Pan-Germans, and professed Anglophobes, is not due to "Boeritis," but to Anglophobia, which is no prôduct of the Transvaal war, but is the result of accumulated rancour dating from the Vienna Congress. Germans, from the highest officials down to the man in the street, have participated in this outburst against Mr. Chamberlain. . . . The press did not create the feeling. The feeling has been there, accumulating for decades. So forcible an outburst was possible, because the nation was ripe for an anti-English demonstration. Things will resume their normal course, but the public have seen their strength and are fully aware of it. Should the German Government ever desire to make use of it, the nation will respond as one man.[57]

Coming from Reuter's Agency, which rarely went beyond bare factual reporting, the dispatch created something of a sensation.[58]

There was nothing like unanimity, however, in British press judgments. The Daily Mail, which was generally accounted more tribal in its attitudes than other journals, did not spring to Chamberlain's defense. "Is there any real reason why Mr. Chamberlain should not make a frank and plain statement to the world that . . . he had no wish to insult Germany?" asked the editor. The pro-Boer Manchester Guardian and the Daily News could scarcely conceal their pleasure at the colonial secretary's misstep [59]; and Mr. Spender complained that "it is not convenient or dignified that we should have perpetually to make these explanations, nor will the aggrieved parties continue to believe us indefinitely when our apology consists in saying that Mr. Chamberlain has not yet reached the years of discretion." The Liverpool Daily Post, a Liberal Imperialist paper, regretted the misunderstanding, which "is all due to Mr. Chamberlain's recklessness of speech when he seeks to make a telling point upon the platform." [60] The foreign angle of the incident was further obscured by sharp attacks of the Imperialist journals on the Radicals and pro-Boers, who were blamed for creating the impression abroad that the British military authorities were guilty of employing "methods of barbarism" in South Africa.

[57] Published November 25 in all papers subscribing to Reuter's service.
[58] For example, it evoked from the *Daily Telegraph*, the most Germanophile of English papers, a sharp warning to the effect that Britain might be driven to take her friendship and co-operation where they would be gladly welcomed. Many of the editors had sharpened their tone since the official statement in the *Norddeutsche* showed the German government moving to conciliate the demonstrators. *Daily Telegraph*, Nov. 25; *Times*, Nov. 23, 27; *Pall Mall Gazette*, Nov. 22; *Liverpool Daily Post*, Nov. 23; *Birmingham Daily Post*, Nov. 23; *Scotsman*, Nov. 22.
[59] *Manchester Guardian*, Nov. 22; *Daily News*, Nov. 23.
[60] *Daily Mail*, Nov. 22; *Manchester Guardian*, Nov. 22; *Daily News*, Nov. 23; *Westminster Gazette*, Nov. 22; *Liverpool Post*, Nov. 23.

The total campaign, with its farrago of frenzy and fantasy, false motivation and partisan polemics, was dead when Bülow gratuitously revived it by a rude public thrust at Chamberlain. In the Reichstag debate on the foreign office budget (January 8, 1902), the Chamberlain incident was brought up by one of the speakers. In replying to the debater's point, the chancellor completely identified the government with the demonstration of national resentment. He began by advising ministers who sought to justify their policy to leave foreign countries out of the discussion or to adduce their examples with the greatest care. "It is altogether intelligible that a people like the German, who have become so thoroughly identified with their glorious army, should revolt against any appearance of misrepresentation which touches its heroic character and the moral basis of our national struggle for unity. But the German army stands too high, its escutcheon is too bright for them to be affected by warped judgments. Anything of the kind is well answered by the reply which Frederick the Great gave when he was told that somebody had been attacking him and the Prussian army: 'Let the man alone,' said the great King, 'and do not excite yourselves. He is biting on granite.' " [61] When the debate was resumed two days later, Bülow intervened to reprimand the anti-Semitic deputy, Liebermann von Sonnenberg, for calling Chamberlain "the most notorious scoundrel on the face of God's earth," and describing the British army as "a pack of robbers and a gang of thieves." [62] On this occasion, Bülow employed more conciliatory language, but it was his original assault on the platform manners of the colonial secretary that was stenciled indelibly upon the public mind by the press reports. On January 12, Chamberlain, speaking at Birmingham, made his historic reply: "What I have said, I have said. I withdraw nothing, I qualify nothing, I defend nothing. . . . I do not want to give lessons to a foreign minister and I will not accept any at his hands. I am responsible only to my own sovereign and to my own countrymen."

The attacks on Chamberlain in the Reichstag and his defiant rejoinder rallied the British press to his defense. The Daily Telegraph castigated Bülow and hailed Chamberlain's remarks as "sentences of clear steel," "worthy of England." Speaking through the Westminster Gazette, Mr. Spender said: "Count von Bülow declared that it was 'altogether intelligible' that when their 'glorious army' was attacked, the feeling of the German people should rise up in protest. It is in similar fashion 'altogether intelligible' that we in this country should be hurt at the attacks

[61] *Fürst Bülows Reden*, I, 242. Bülow's account of this incident in his *Memoirs* (I, 635–38) is a labored apologetic.
[62] *Ibid.*, I, 245–46.

on an army to which we are equally attached." The Pall Mall Gazette referred to Germany as a country that played "Jackal" to England in the markets of the world, and noting the abatement of criticism in the German press exulted that "the whole pack of 'ill-bred curs,' as Mr. Chamberlain called them, are coming sulkily to heel. . . ." Chamberlain's original remark was indiscreet, said the Daily Mail, "but we are not prepared to accept foreign rebukes, administered with even less tact and discretion, to our public men, or to sit in sackcloth and ashes at a foreign censor's behest." In the Standard's opinion, Chamberlain's retort suited the provocation and was "required by our self-respect." And the Tory Morning Post declared that "Mr. Chamberlain was never so strong in the support of his countrymen as he is at the present moment." The Globe, the Liverpool Courier, the Sheffield Telegraph, the Scotsman, the Birmingham Daily Post, and many other provincial journals echoed the London commentators. Of leading English papers only the Manchester Guardian, the Daily News and the Daily Chronicle would not concede that Bülow's remark was an impertinence and Chamberlain's retort justifiable.[63]

But it was in the Times that the most significant reactions were found. While Saunders emphasized the most painful features of the Reichstag debates, Chirol, or his deputy, denounced Bülow editorially for pandering to the sentiment of the Pan-Germans. He regretted that Bülow had not apologized for "the flood of obscene and unmanly falsehoods with which the German press has persistently sought to befoul the military honour of England." Referring to Liebermann von Sonnenburg's rhodomontade, he said: "Seldom if ever has a friendly nation been so grossly insulted in a foreign Parliament, and never within our memory has the insult met with such mild rebuke. . . ." More important than Chirol's blasts on the editorial page was the stream of letters from emotionally aroused readers demanding a boycott of German goods and denouncing German "arrogance, malevolence, and falsehood." [64] As an informational feature the Times published two articles entitled, "The Literature of Anglophobia," in which the writer reviewed the worst examples of the lampoons and scurrilities that had appeared in the German gutter press.[65]

[63] Daily Telegraph, Jan. 13; Westminster Gazette, Jan. 9; Pall Mall Gazette, Jan. 15; Daily Mail, Jan. 9; Standard, Jan. 13; Morning Post, Jan. 13; Daily News, Jan. 9, 10, 14; Manchester Guardian, Jan. 13; Daily Chronicle, Jan. 13, 1902.
[64] Times, Jan. 9, 11, 15, 16, 21. I assume that the editorials were from Chirol's pen. The foreign editor of the Times not only edited the cable and diplomatic news but also wrote the leading articles in this field. On the duties of the Times' foreign editor see A. Tyrkova-Williams, Cheerful Giver, The Life of Harold Williams (Lond., 1935), pp. 253–337, passim.
[65] Familiarity with the subject and internal evidence, such as the use of the word

He dwelt at length on those touching the royal family and the army, before going on to describe another class of pamphlets, "which reveals the true inwardness of German Anglophobia." At this point he introduced the propaganda publications of the navy campaign, which showed that "the German people have set their heart upon possessing a weapon with which they know that alone they can hope to gratify their hatred of Great Britain." All continental Anglophobia was attributed to the inspiration furnished by the German press, the comic magazines, and the manufacturers of atrocity stories. Behind this campaign, he hinted, was the German government. No other people "had adopted the Boer cause with such passion, not of sympathy . . . but of blind, unreasoning, and unaccountable hatred for the British nation as the German people have done." [66] These two articles contained the most damaging and wounding evidence of the extent to which Anglophobia had been carried in certain quarters in Germany. Henceforth, every contemporary British complaint placed the slandering of the army and the royal family in the foreground.[67] We cannot measure the effect of this publicity on contemporary attitudes and opinions, but considering the politically influential circle which depended upon the Times for foreign news it certainly could not have been inconsiderable.

Contemporaries, of course, could not estimate the significance of this unsavory controversy. In perspective it stands out as the real turning point in public relations, just as the breakdown of co-operation in the Far East marks the turning point in diplomatic relations. By the end of the year 1902, the following pattern of ideas and relationships was pretty firmly established in the historical armory of writers in the British press: (1) German Anglophobia during the Boer War was occasioned less by sympathy for the Boers than by universal hatred and enmity toward England; (2) this feeling had been inspired and nourished by the German government in order to float the German navy; (3) the naval policy represented a national effort to implement German designs on the British Empire; (4) only the refusal of France and Russia to co-operate had thwarted German official efforts to organize intervention against England during the Boer War.[68] This stereotype of German attitudes and policies, contrary to the facts in almost every detail, was moulded and

---

"lucubrations," points to Saunders as the author, although they may have been written by Chirol, who had just returned from Germany.

[66] *Times*, Jan. 13, 14, 1902.

[67] See for example, Alfred Rothschild's letter to Eckardstein of Feb. 20, 1902. Eckardstein, *Lebenserinnerungen*, II, 380–83.

[68] As Saunders put it in one of his dispatches (June 3, 1902), "no European coalition was possible, largely owing to the almost invariable attitude of the Tsar and to the friendly and skillful diplomacy of M. Delcassé."

hardened in the heat of the encounter between Bülow and Chamberlain.

At the bottom of it all was the reporting of false news, the manufacturing of atrocity stories, and the moral indignation aroused by the concentration camps. Then on the basis of a condensed report of Chamberlain's speech, consisting of a four hundred word summary and the quotation of a single sentence, a national protest campaign of unprecedented violence, which the German government was powerless to check, swept the country. Chamberlain's original remark was obscured; and aroused patriots imagined that he had indulged himself in not less than an hour and a half of calumny at the expense of the German nation in arms and its glorious war for national unity. A particularly acute impression was made in Fleet Street and Downing Street by the fact that the German nation alone, of those whose methods of warfare were drawn in for comparison, responded with violent demonstrations of *Englandhass*. From this was drawn the conclusion that of all the continental nations the German was filled with a peculiar and intense hatred of Great Britain, which had behind it more than a natural sympathy for the underdog in the Boer War. In light of this experience might not their notions as to the distribution of England's friends and foes on the continent require a radical revision? In ever widening circles among the élite of diplomacy, politics, journalism and finance this question was answered in the affirmative.[69]

By far the greater share of individual responsibility for the turn taken by Anglo-German relations rests upon Bülow. The chancellor used the semi-official press apparatus to cry down "Boeritis" when it was embarrassing to his policy, but placing as he did a high value on favorable personal publicity, he refused to listen to his advisers who urged him not to pander to the extremists by affronting Chamberlain in the Reichstag. While he disapproved of the demonstrations, speeches, and resolutions of the Anglophobes, he chose to overcome the opposition between popular sentiment and official policy by aligning himself with the demonstrators. Count Metternich, the newly appointed ambassador to England, warned him well in advance of the almost certain consequences of an official rebuke to Chamberlain.[70] Metternich's worst fears were fully

---

[69] Indicative of the shift is the revision between 1900 and 1902 of the British invasion stereotype. In 1900 military critics, who can only function in relation to such a stereotype, were still thinking in terms of a French invasion. Harold Begbie quotes Spenser Wilkinson as follows: "It isn't pleasant to think about, I admit. . . . Ever since the fall of the Empire there has been no discipline in the French Army. If they come we shall know something of the real horrors of war. Plundering will not be the worst of their enormities." (*Pall Mall Gazette*, Aug. 8, 1900.) By 1902, the Germans occupied the rôle traditionally assigned to the French.

[70] *G. P.*, XVII, 198 n. Letter dated Nov. 19, 1901.

realized. In a private letter to Bülow he said: "I wouldn't give two pence for Anglo-German relations." But Bülow was impenitent. The provocation came from Chamberlain, and *"Auf grobe Klötze gehörten grobe Keile. . . .* Now we are quits." Ever the optimist, he hoped that time would bring better things and that the irritation would turn out to be only skin-deep.[71]

Not only does it appear that Bülow disregarded Metternich's advice but he also rejected that of his closest advisers in the foreign office. Holstein, writing a year later to his cousin, was in a position to say, "I told you so."

Richthofen, Hammann (chief of the press bureau) and I tried in vain to dissuade Bülow from his anti-English demonstrations, but he followed the advice of Pan-German Hasse, Moscow-Arnim and such like people. . . . As a matter of fact we did the English a very decisive service during the war when we rejected a Russian proposal for mediation. But since our actions were friendly and our speech unfriendly we found ourselves sitting between two stools (we, that is Bülow). Both sides reproached us, the one because too little was done, the other because too much was said and printed. Bülow held stubbornly to his course and would not take our advice, although we three were in complete accord.[72]

When Bülow jauntily referred to English irritation as a passing mood, he was indulging in wishful thinking. In the course of the following year gloomy reports were sent by Eckardstein and Metternich on the opinions of influential people, the behavior of the press, and the emotionalized attitudes of the man in the street.[73] Writing confidentially to Richthofen a year after the Chamberlain-Bülow incident, the ambassador reported:

As long as I have known England, I have never observed here such bitterness toward another nation as at present exists toward us. It is *not* attributable primarily to commercial rivalry, but it is the expression of sentiment which in consequence of the attitude of the German people during the Boer War now finds its echo here. . . . These observations do not apply . . . to the relations of the English government to us; they describe, however, the popular feeling which also must be reckoned with. The least ill-humor toward us prevails in the higher circles of society, perhaps also in the lower classes of the population, the mass of the workers. But of all those that lie in between, and who work with brain and pen, the great majority are hostile to us.[74]

[71] *G. P.*, XVII, 149–52, Bülow to Metternich, March 13, 1902.
[72] Holstein, *Lebensbekenntnis,* p. 214. Holstein to his cousin, end of November 1902.
[73] Chamberlain, who was bitterly resentful, assured Eckardstein that public hatred of Germany was so deep-rooted that even the strongest ministry would have to reckon with this factor. *G. P.*, XVII, 221–25; Eckardstein to Bülow, Sept. 14, 1902.
[74] *G. P.*, XVII, 234–35; Metternich to Richthofen, Jan. 19, 1903.

An examination of the press only serves to confirm the impressions recorded by the honest Metternich. What the diplomats were whispering to one another behind closed doors, the publicists and journalists were shouting from the housetops. It all dovetails exactly and out of the total picture emerges the indubitable conclusion that when the Anglophobia of the German people broke through to England through the channels of publicity in December 1901, the reaction was no passing irritation but a deep-rooted, ineradicable mistrust of the ultimate aims and objectives of imperial German policy. The reports of Dr. Otto, the sensible correspondent of the Frankfurter Zeitung, of Dr. Gaupp, the scholarly representative of the Münchner Neueste Nachrichten and the Hamburger Fremdenblatt, of Dr. Hans Esser, one of the ablest of the Kölnische Zeitung's foreign staff, of Dr. Otto Brandes, correspondent of the Tageblatt, and of Moritz Sasse, of the Vossische Zeitung, confirm in general and in detail the reports of the diplomatic representatives.[75]

Efforts to undo the mischief were not lacking in Berlin, where, during the summer of 1902, a regular campaign of conciliation was launched in the semi-official and inspired press. Every canard affecting Anglo-German relations was bluntly exposed in the Norddeutsche. Richthofen, in the Prussian Diet, denounced the Anglophobes and the slanderers of the British army. A conciliation committee of university professors was organized to work among the intellectuals, and strong resolutions were voted by the Berlin Merchants' Guild condemning uncontrolled *Englandhass*, which was costing Germany millions of marks in orders and contracts.[76] But the damage could not be so easily undone.

In England bitterness and resentment grew. Every incident seemed to deepen the mistrust and enmity. As a measure of this trend we may cite the visit of the Boer generals to Berlin in October 1902. Although the conquered leaders of the Boer armies were received by the premier and foreign minister of France, without protests in England, there was an immediate flare-up in the London press when it was announced that in Germany they would be received by the Kaiser. The report was inflated

[75] Gaupp to the *Münchner N. N.*, No. 496, Oct. 25, 1902, stating that the British believed that German policy was a menace to the Empire. "Wer in der Lage ist, dem englischen Volk den Puls zu fühlen, weiss, dass Tausende von Engländern aufrichtig an diese Theorie glauben, und dass ihre Zahl täglich wächst. Nicht 'Neid auf den deutschen Handel'—er spielt heute praktisch keine Rolle mehr—sondern Angst von Deutschlands Absichten ist die eigentliche Quelle der wachsenden Feindseligkeit gegen Deutschland." In the same tone, Esser to the *Kölnische Ztg.*, Nos. 879, 903, 1017, Nov. 9, 16, Dec. 28, 1902, and No. 333, April 24, 1903; Moritz Sasse to the *Vossische Ztg.*, Nos. 15, 18, 600, Jan. 10, 11, Dec. 23, 1902; Dr. Otto to the *Frankfurter Ztg.*, Nos. 354, 355, Dec. 22, 23, 1902 and No. 113, April 24, 1903; Otto Brandes to the *Berliner Tageblatt*, No. 20, Jan. 12, 1902.

[76] Reported in the *Times*, May 9, July 22, 29, 1902.

until people began to talk of a new Kruger Telegram. Eckardstein, who was nearing the end of his service as liaison officer at the German embassy, was bombarded with inquiries and warnings from Fleet Street editors. From Moberly Bell he received a hastily scribbled appeal to use his influence to prevent the audience. If the Kaiser received the generals and then came shortly thereafter to England, as was his intention, "there will be absolute disaster," wrote the manager of the Times. "I have never in the whole course of my experience known feeling so strong and—what is to me more serious—more restrained in the firm belief that it *cannot* be true. Nor is this, as generally, among the lower classes only. There was language used today by elderly opulent City men that, at the time of the [Jameson] raid, was only used by the lower classes—and some idea of what people are feeling may be gathered from the fact that some of us are concerting serious measures to prevent disturbance." [77] The communications from the London embassy, the serious warnings in the Post, Times, Standard, and Daily Telegraph, and the *Radau* in the sensational journals awakened the Emperor and his ministers to the seriousness of the situation. When a hitch occurred in fixing the procedure of presentation, William II seized upon this as a pretext, declared the audience question closed and forbade the civil service and the military to participate in the reception of the visitors.[78] To avoid the appearance of truckling to the British press, a semi-official statement was published in the Norddeutsche attributing the Emperor's decision to the Boers' refusal to comply with the customary formalities in securing an audience.[79] When the generals arrived in Berlin (Oct. 17), they received a tumultuous welcome from the populace. Great crowds lined the route from the railway station to the hotel and loud cheers for the South African heroes were mixed with ironic cries of "Lord Bülow" and "Viscount of Richthofen." The Conservative Reichsbote denounced the chancellor for spending an entire evening at the *"Bunte Theater"* to see a sort of *"Tingel-Tangel"* when he could not find fifteen minutes to receive the Boer generals.[80] As on the occasion of President Kruger's visit, the

[77] Letter in facsimile (Oct. 1, 1902), Eckardstein, *Lebenserinnerungen*, II, 416–17.
[78] Emperor's mem., *G. P.*, XVII, 231; and related documents, *ibid.*, XVII, 225–34. Eckardstein's account is a complete misrepresentation. According to Holstein it was he and Richthofen who saved the situation. Holstein, *Lebensbekenntnis*, pp. 214–15.
[79] *Norddeutsche*, No. 237, Oct. 9, 1902 (special type, first page, under "Politischer Tagesbericht"); No. 243, Oct. 16, stating that no official notice would be taken of the public reception; No. 244, Oct. 17, a longer official explanation in reply to the bitter attacks of the Conservative, Pan-German, Bismarckian, and National Liberal organs.
[80] Quoted *Münchner N. N.*, No. 489, Oct. 21; further accounts of the demonstration, *Münchner N. N.*, 484, 485, 486, Oct. 18, 19; *Schwäbischer Merkur*, Nos. 470, 481, 482, 483, Oct. 9, 16, 17; *Berliner Tageblatt*, Nos. 527, 528, Oct. 16, 17; August Stein's account, *Frankfurter Ztg.*, No. 289, Oct. 18; *Kölnische Volksztg.*, No. 927.

German government, reluctant to give offense in London, snubbed the Boers and, in consequence, suffered attacks in the German nationalist press.

The true measure of English popular hostility to Germany only appeared when the cabinets undertook to renew the policy of co-operation in problems involving mutual or parallel interests. When Balfour's government joined Germany in a debt collecting sortie against Venezuela, in the winter of 1902–3, they ran head-on into a stone wall of press opposition. In the newspapers the inception of this venture was linked to the Emperor's visit to England, in November, although in fact the two incidents do not seem to have been related.[81] The first diplomatic moves to secure the desired satisfaction from the Venezuelan government provoked no outcry, but when the co-operating authorities instituted vigorous action—blockade, seizures, and bombardment—the American press took alarm and began to raise the issue of the Monroe Doctrine. With but few exceptions the English journalists turned on their own government, castigating the ministers for embarking upon an ill-considered adventure which was leading them on to a collision with the United States.

Only the Edinburgh Scotsman and the Daily Telegraph, whose foreign editor, Iwan-Müller, was one of Balfour's confidants, actively defended the cabinet. Disregarding party lines, the journalists labeled the affair the "Venezuelan Mess," caviled at the "alliance" with Germany, and decried the stupidity of their diplomats, who were repeating the folly of the Yangtze Agreement. "Whither is Germany Leading Us?", "Six Years of German Policy," "Why Are We Tied to Germany's Tail?", "Great Britain in German Leading Strings," and "Germany's Bad Faith" were some of the headlines in the abusive campaign launched by the Daily Mail.[82] The leaders of the Liberal opposition were in complete accord with the Times in condemning an unholy alliance with Germany, which seriously jeopardized their friendship with the United States.[83] Writers

---

Oct. 18, graphic account of the conduct of the Berlin crowds; *Times,* Sept. 30, Oct. 9, 16, 17, 20.

[81] William II was in England from November 8 to 20. Although he put himself out to be gracious and held a conference at the embassy for leading English journalists, the press maintained its chilly tone. Reports of Dr. Gaupp to the *Münchner N. N.,* Nos. 518, 522, 549, Nov. 7, 10, 26, 1902; *Daily News,* Nov. 21; *Westminster Gazette,* Nov. 10; *Pall Mall Gazette,* Nov. 8, 10; *Daily Telegraph,* Nov. 8; *Times,* Nov. 8. The *Daily Mail* (Nov. 7, 8, 9, 10, 11) took up the cry of Strachey's weekly *Spectator* and harped on the question, "What Does the Emperor Want?" The Emperor's dispatch (Nov. 12, 1902) to Bülow shows a realistic appreciation of prevailing sentiment in England toward Germany. *G. P.,* XVII, 115–17.

[82] Dec. 16, 17, 23, 1902; Feb. 2, 5, 6, 13, 14, 1903.

[83] Speeches by Campbell-Bannerman and Grey, reported in the *Times,* Dec. 16,

and speakers reviewed the history of previous efforts at co-operation with Germany and showed how they had always worked out to the disadvantage of Great Britain. The Yangtze Agreement was cited more frequently than any other incident as proof of German unreliability and double-dealing. "The fact is that no state trusts Germany," declared the Liverpool Post, "and after the Yangtze Agreement it is amazing that the British Government should have been led into the present trouble in German company." How could the foreign office undertake to act "with a Power that gives unexpected interpretations of treaties before the ink is dry?"[84] Solemnly the editors warned the government that Germany was a "fatal partner," and "a deadly rival," who "will embroil us with the United States"; Germany was out to grab territory and protestations to the contrary were "worthless." The Daily News, associating the enterprise with the Emperor's visit to England, denounced it as "a secret conspiracy, hatched in a palace, but now happily destroyed by publicity." The Manchester Guardian denounced the government for plunging thoughtlessly into a frivolous debt collecting mission. J. A. Spender was not averse to friendly co-operation with Germany, "but in no sphere are we less willing to give our conscience into Germany's keeping than in matters affecting our relations with the United States." The Pall Mall Gazette and the Birmingham Post attacked the foreign office on one day and defended the government and the party from Liberal criticisms on the next.[85]

The British are accustomed to look to the national poets for the expression of deepest national emotions in a time of stress and crisis. Swinburne, the poet of freedom, had voiced imperialist sentiment during the Boer War when he referred to the women and children in the deadly concentration camps as "whelps and dams of murderous foes." In the new moment of national peril Rudyard Kipling published in the Times, on December 22, a poem entitled "The Rowers," which the editor endorsed because it expressed "a sentiment which unquestionably prevails far and wide throughout the nation. . . ." In this poem the victorious "Rowers" are returning home from South Africa, when they are told

---

1902, Feb. 7, 1903; letters by Sir Robert Giffen, Sir Charles Beresford, and Gibson Bowles, Dec. 18, 20; editorials, Dec. 20, 1902, Jan. 26, Feb. 4, 17, 1903.

[84] *Liverpool Daily Post,* Dec. 22, 1902, Feb. 14, 1903.

[85] *Daily News,* Dec. 22, 27, 1902; *Manchester Guardian,* Dec. 9, 12, 16, 18, 22, 23, 1902, Jan. 26, 1903; *Westminster Gazette,* Dec. 16, 1902; *Birmingham Daily Post,* Dec. 13, 15, 26, 1902, Jan. 2, 9, Feb. 2, 16, 1903; *Pall Mall Gazette,* Jan. 21, 23, 24, Feb. 14, 1903. Views similar to those cited above were expressed by the *Daily Chronicle, St. James's Gazette, Evening News* (London), *Yorkshire Post,* and *Glasgow Herald.*

that they must change their course to South America. Then "The Rowers" sing:

> Last night ye swore our voyage was done,
>   But seaward still we go;
> And ye tell us now of a secret vow
>   Ye have made with an open foe!
>
> The dead they mocked are scarcely cold,
>   Our wounded are bleeding yet—
> And ye tell us now that our strength is sold
>   To help them press for a debt!
>
> In sight of peace—from the Narrow Seas
>   O'er half the world to run—
> With a cheated crew, to league anew
>   With the Goth and the shameless Hun!

This "frenzied poet of great talent," as Bülow referred to Kipling in the Reichstag, was rebuked by Lord Lansdowne, and sharply called to order by Liberal editors. Spender's genial humor produced the following suggestion: "Our poets and men of letters seem somehow to lose all sense of the value of words when they take to politics, and it would be well if on the approach of international quarrels we could, as Plato proposed for the poets of his Republic, crown them with bay leaves, call them beautiful and gifted persons, and then politely escort them across the frontier until quieter times." (Dec. 22.) Had there been any desire among German editors to renew the feud with their British confrères, no one could say that they had not ample provocation. But with a few unimportant exceptions the German journalists in the Venezuelan affair never abandoned a careful reportorial rôle.[86]

The complete transposition of moods and symbols was the subject of a private letter from Count Metternich to Bülow. "The Venezuela affair shows that the anti-German feeling created here during the Boer War is still stronger than common sense or the self-interest of the English. The delusion which seized our own public opinion during the Boer War has now moved across the Channel. . . . Personally I consider that this sentiment has been caught from Germany. We ourselves are recovering, but here the crisis of the fever and therefore the delirium have only just been reached." [87]

---

[86] Co-operation with England was approved in all but the Socialist, Agrarian, and Bismarckian papers. Bülow had an easy time defending his policy in the Reichstag. (*Fürst Bülows Reden*, I, 397–401.)

[87] Bülow, *Memoirs*, I, 642. On the diplomacy of the Venezuelan affair see *B. D.*, II, 153–74; *G. P.*, XVII, 241–92; A. L. P. Dennis, *Adventures in American Di-*

This incident, which irritated the British people and left the Balfour government making embarrassed excuses to its own parliamentary majority, made the cabinet nervous and timid about co-operation with Germany. It was unfortunate, therefore, that the question of British participation in the Bagdad Railroad should have been raised so soon after the Venezuelan "mess." When the first concession was granted to the Deutsche Bank, in November 1899, it met with the approval of British writers in the press. The Times, for example, said: "There is no Power into whose hands Englishmen would more gladly see the enterprise fall, because there is none which has made such substantial advances in the direction of our own liberal economic policy. . . . It would be gratifying could the co-operation of this country and Germany, already established in more than one quarter of the globe, be extended to a region in which we must always on many grounds have a substantial interest." [88] At that time the British foreign office regarded participation, with adequate guarantees, as desirable. Early in 1903, when the German financiers approached a group of London capitalists, the government indicated its willingness to examine sympathetically the political concessions essential to the co-operation of British capital.[89] The official attitude was explained by Balfour in the House of Commons on April 7, 1903, in response to a question from Gibson Bowles. On April 23, replying to another question from the same source, Balfour announced that after further consideration his government found that they could not give the desired assurances. In the short interval between April 7 and April 23, the ministry had been blown around by a publicity storm of knife-edged intensity. The agitation against British participation began with an article in the April number of the National Review; it was taken up by John St. Loe Strachey in the weekly Spectator and passed then to the Daily Mail and shortly to every daily publicity organ in the country except the Daily Telegraph, the Standard, and the Daily Graphic. The political opposition originated with the strong Russophile group of publicists in London, the economic opposition came from the eastern steamship companies, particularly the P and O Line, and the emotional drive, which inflated the affair to national proportions, was supplied by the deep and abiding public dislike of any form of co-operation with Germany. Balfour's first statement in the Commons favorable to the project led numer-

plomacy (N. Y., 1928), pp. 282–309; Alfred Vagts, Deutschland und die Vereinigten Staaten in der Weltpolitik, II, chap. XV.

[88] Nov. 30, 1899; letter from Lord Newton, Times, Dec. 4; Morning Post, Dec. 13, 1899.

[89] Mem. by Dr. Rosen, March 16, 1903; G. P., XVII, 435. Lansdowne to Sir E. Cassel, Feb. 4, 1903; B. D., II, 179–80.

ous editors to cite and quote the objections raised in the *National Review* and the *Spectator*. Henceforth, reason departed as the railroad was contemptuously referred to as the "Bagdad Bungle," and branded a "Pan-German scheme," "a financial fraud," "a political conspiracy," and a "wild cat project." The danger to British interests in the Near and Far East was painted in lurid colors. On April 18, the Times, heretofore silent, joined the chorus of opposition. The battle was won when it published, on April 22, the text of the convention under which the Turkish government granted the concession to the German consortium. Thinking that the opposition could be silenced by placing all the cards on the table, Arthur Gwinner of the Deutsche Bank sent a copy of the convention to the Times editor. The latter published the document, but accompanied it with an *ex parte* statement and a smashing editorial against British participation. It was the Times' editorial and not the text of the convention that was republished and made the subject of approving comment in all the leading metropolitan and provincial papers. On April 24 Balfour announced the government's retreat and Gibson Bowles, who had led the agitation in parliament, boasted, in an address to the Royal Asiatic Society, that he was there "to drive the last nail into the coffin of the Bagdad Railway." [90]

All the contemporary comment agrees in referring the defeat of the railway project to public hostility to Germany. "Nobody will deny," said the Daily Telegraph, "that the opposition to British co-operation in the construction of this railway springs almost entirely from exaggerated Germanophobia." (April 23.) Lord Esher, who was associated with Cassel and Revelstoke in the financial negotiations, wrote in his diary: "The Government are frightened and run away. . . . But the German Emperor is a Bogey just now in certain quarters; and the English people, led by a foolish half-informed press, are children in foreign politics." [91] Metternich, the German ambassador, and Bernstorff, who had succeeded Eckardstein as counselor of the embassy, attributed the British government's change of front to the same cause.[92] C. E. Dawkins, who represented the Morgan interests, wrote to Gwinner explaining the circum-

---

[90] Report in the *Scotsman*, April 25. The summary of the campaign in the press is based on the following editorial and news reports: *Daily Mail* ("Another German Agreement?"), April 4, 9, 16, 21, 22, 24; *Times*, April 9, 18, 20, 22, 24 (congratulates government for rejecting "insidious and dangerous proposals"); *Pall Mall Gazette*, April 9 (quoting *National Review* and *Spectator*), 22; *Manchester Guardian*, April 9, 15, 23 (reprinting *Times* leader), 24; *Westminster Gazette*, April 22, 25; *Daily News*, April 21, 22, 23; *Scotsman*, April 9, 24; *Birmingham Post*, April 23, 24; *Liverpool Post*, April 21, 23, 24; *Glasgow Herald*, April 20, 23.

[91] *Journals and Letters of Viscount Esher* (Lond., 1934), I, 396–97. According to Esher the Imperial Defense Committee favored the railway on strategical grounds.

[92] *G. P.*, XVII, 438–39, 440, 448–49.

stances. The undertaking had been sacrificed to the "very violent and bitter feeling against Germany exhibited by the majority of our newspapers and shared in by a large number of people." The campaign, he said, had been originally inspired by the Russian embassy in Paris. The clamor, which was then raised in the entire press, occasioned a split in the cabinet; Lansdowne could not carry the ministry. "The anti-German feeling prevailed with the majority; London really having gone into a frenzy on the matter owing to the newspaper campaign which it would have been quite impossible to counteract or influence." [93] Lansdowne shifted part of the responsibility to the business men, pointing out that the outcry caused the financiers to shy off quite as much as the government. "If it had not been for the 'scuttle' of the financiers, I should have been in favor of sticking to our position." In later years he expressed regret that they had yielded to an "insensate outcry." [94]

The Venezuelan episode and the Bagdad Railroad affair showed the strength of popular feeling against Germany. The political élite and the aristocracy, like the proletariat and the financial world, seemed to have had no unalterable hostility to co-operation with Germany. But it must have been crystal clear to the British ministers that any political proposal bearing the label "Made in Germany" could not be entertained unless they were willing to face a hostile press and an aroused, articulate middle class. The policy of political co-operation in special cases was ended. The Venezuelan affair marked the parting of the ways for England and Germany.

To realize how far this road has led we must turn for a moment from the disintegration of Anglo-German relations to the concurrent campaign in England for a complete reorientation of British policy. Since 1896, the idea of rapprochement to France and Russia had been entertained by the government and advocated from time to time in both official and private publicity. But the conditions of success for such a movement were not present until the end of 1901 and the beginning of 1902, when the conviction became firmly established in England that the German people were the avowed enemies of Great Britain and the Empire. The first drive originated in private publicity circles, particularly the half-crown monthlies, which began to preach the "German menace" as the primary cause for reconsidering their Russian policy. That was the burden of the widely advertised article that appeared in Leo Maxse's *National Review* in November 1901. Advance copies of the article were

[93] Dawkins to Gwinner, April 23, 1903; *G. P.*, XVII, 442–43.
[94] *B. D.*, II, 196; Lord Newton, *Lord Lansdowne: A Biography* (Lond., 1929), p. 254. The opposition in the cabinet was apparently led by Chamberlain.

sent to all the British dailies and to continental writers on foreign affairs of established reputation. It made something of a smash hit in the daily press and gave rise to considerable perturbation in the Wilhelmstrasse.[95] However, the group appeared to be 'stymied' for the moment by the conclusion of the Anglo-Japanese Alliance, in February 1902, which of course was an announcement that Great Britain had thrown in her lot with Japan in the Far East and would not capitulate to Russia.[96] The publicity drive was then revised to make France the main object of a rearrangement of British friendships. This went much better. Soon a weekly forum for these ideas was secured in Strachey's *Spectator,* and by mid-summer 1902 the Times, the Daily Mail and the Daily Express were ardently advocating the same reorientation of British policy. By the time the Emperor visited England, in November 1902, the movement had progressed far enough for the *Spectator* and the *Saturday Review* to accuse him of coming over specifically to kill the rapprochement between Britain and France.[97]

From several sources came the matrix of ideas that moulded British attitudes for the next decade. Wilkinson and Arnold White paraded the menace of the German naval program through the columns of the Morning Post, the Daily Express and the Daily Mail.[98] Other writers presented Pan-Germanic fantasies as the genuine objectives of official German policy. W. T. Arnold, former chief leader writer on the Manchester

---

[95] Johannes Dreyer, *Deutschland und England . . . im Jahre 1901,* pp. 47–52. The pseudonym, "A. B. C.," seemed to cover a changing personnel. According to information from "a trustworthy source," Metternich reported that the authors of the article in the November issue were Maxse, Sir Rowland Blennerhasset, and the Russian financial agent, Tatitschew; of the December article, Maxse, a journalist named Baumann, and Evelyn Ashley. (*G. P.,* XVII, 534–36.) Blennerhasset explored this line of policy for the readers of the *Times* in an article entitled, "England, Germany and Russia" (Aug. 31, 1901). J. L. Garvin, under the pseudonym "Calchas," was advocating the same course in the *Fortnightly Review.* Besides writing the chronicle of foreign affairs, Garvin was a prolific contributor of articles, employing three pseudonyms, "Calchas," "Pollex," and "X." Janet Courtney, *The Making of an Editor, W. L. Courtney* (Lond., 1930), pp. 161, 177–78.

[96] *G. P.,* XVII, 554–59.

[97] Dr. Gaupp's report to the *Münchner N. N.,* No. 525, Nov. 12. Even the Anglo-French *Versöhnungspropaganda,* as Theodor Wolff noted, had a point against Germany. "Every unfriendly word uttered in any part of the world about Germany, every American newspaper attack, every article in the *Novoye Vremya* against the Bagdad Railway, every rumor of German expansionist designs is carefully noted in the *Temps,* and the *Matin,* which receive the *Times* news reports and spread them before the French public." (*Berliner Tageblatt,* No. 218, May 1, 1903.)

[98] Wilkinson had been harping on the naval question intermittently since November, 1900 (*Morning Post,* Nov. 15, 1900). Arnold White's activity was the subject of a long report by Dr. Gaupp to the *Münchner N. N.,* No. 506, Oct. 31, 1902. The *Daily Mail* took up the cry in May 1902: "Before Blotting Out England—What Germany Expects to Do Before 1950" (May 31, 1902); "The German Navy; at Whom Is It Aimed?" (Nov. 5, 1902). The German naval menace was agitated sporadically during 1901 in the *Times* and *National Review.* (Dreyer, *op. cit.,* pp. 56–59, 111–13.)

Guardian, published the well-known series of articles in the *Spectator*, entitled "German Ambitions as They Affect Britain and the United States." [99] Saunders, in a dispatch captioned "German Anticipations," raised the perennial bogey of German annexation of Holland, while Wickham Steed discovered the famous Pan-Germanic atlas in which half the states of Europe were "coloured in the same tint as the existing German Empire!" [100] Moreover, Chamberlain in his two great speeches of May 15 and 28, 1903, launching his imperial preference campaign, took his stand on an anti-German platform, and cited Germany's refusal "to recognize Canada as part of our Empire" and her "threatening of South Africa, Australia and New Zealand," as the menace which his program was designed to meet. German economic competition again became an outstanding feature in a nation-wide political campaign.

When these ideas are synthesized they form a summa, or a pattern, that remained dominant in British publicity for a decade. First, attempts at co-operation in the Far East had exposed the unreliability and double-crossing tendencies of German policy; second, the Boer War had shown that the German nation to a man was filled with implacable hatred of Great Britain; third, Pan-Germanic doctrine revealed that German national ambitions could only be achieved by tearing down the British Empire; fourth, Germany was forging the instrument of that policy by constructing a great fleet. The overthrow of England and the establishment of the commercial and naval supremacy of Germany was "the governing idea of her national imagination." It was under the impress of this pattern that the articulate public revolted against the government's policy of co-operation in the Venezuelan affair and in the Bagdad Railway. Under the impact of a great emotional crisis (the Boer War) a transformation was wrought in individual attitudes and stereotypes. Enduring hostility to Germany became the driving power of the rapprochement to France. King Edward's visit to Paris in May 1903, and Loubet's return visit in July, found a united English press championing an Anglo-French understanding. The agreement of April 8, 1904, simply brought official policy into line with altered publicity stereotypes.

[99] Pseud. *Vigilans sed Aequus*. The articles were published in book form early in 1903. See Amy Strachey, *St. Loe Strachey: His Life and His Paper* (Lond., 1930), pp. 236–37.

[100] *Times*, Feb. 15, 21, 1900. Saunders' dispatch led to an interpellation in the Commons and provoked polemics in the German press against the *Times*. (*Norddeutsche*, No. 35, Feb. 11; *Berliner N. N.*, No. 83, Feb. 19; *Die Post*, No. 85, Feb. 20; *Daily Telegraph*, Feb. 20, 1900.)

CHAPTER X

PUBLICITY AND THE DIPLOMATIC REVOLUTION

The one way of making an Anglo-German conflict not inevitable is to act as though it were certain to occur.

J. L. Garvin, *Quarterly Review,* July 1908.

The conclusion of the Anglo-French agreement of April 8, 1904, marked the most important change in the relations of the European cabinets since the scuttling of the Reinsurance Treaty by Bismarck's successors. The continental system to which European statesmen had conditioned their thinking since 1891 was revolutionized. For German policy the consequences were far-reaching. All the effects were not immediately apparent, but it did not require any peculiar astuteness to foresee that German world policy would now be deprived of any British support or encouragement.

Much has been written in condemnation and defense of the Bülow-Holstein policy. Certain it is that they miscalculated the trend of British diplomacy, stubbornly clinging to the false assumption that Britain would never come to terms with France and Russia. Certain it is, too, that they overestimated Britain's dependence on German benevolence. Prior to 1904 Bülow's policy of the "free hand," which was based on the opposition of the Dual Alliance to the British Empire, the natural enmity of the Bear and the Whale, had yielded concrete returns to Germany. While the "free hand" had usually meant a thumb in the balance on England's side, the premises and conclusion of the Wilhelmstrasse theory appeared faultless. "We are and always shall be England's most convenient support," wrote Richthofen in a significant memorandum on the relations of the two states. "Our power absorbs Russian and French fighting forces to such an extent that Russia and France are prevented from adventurous undertakings against England here or there, and, as a result, England's power is maintained in a *status quo.* We, on the other hand, are not asking for any of England's possessions; all we want is to be left in peace and that, when England feeds from the foreign dish of some weak nation, she will let us have our share." [1] Doubtless, all would

[1] Bülow, *Memoirs,* I, 590–91. The dispatch, which is dated Feb. 5, 1901, expresses the attitude of the permanent officials toward the question of an Anglo-German alliance.

have gone well enough if Germany's continental position between the jaws of the Franco-Russian nut-cracker had not necessitated constant courting of Russia. This introduced into German policy a fatal dualism, the consequences of which the Wilhelmstrasse was reluctant to contemplate. Moreover, the German method of demanding their share from the English dish soured the British more and more toward co-operation with Germany; they did not like a policy that required constant bargaining with Berlin. The word "blackmail" became all too common in the English vocabulary of politics and diplomacy. Publicists and statesmen became more strongly inclined to consider a large and substantial 'pay-off' to France and Russia, as against a continuation of the old policy of distributive risks among the powers whose interests in particular circumstances chanced to coincide with those of the British Empire.

Before the authorities in Berlin had fully comprehended the danger, the relationship that had enabled Germany to expand her colonial interests was withdrawn and bestowed upon France. The road was blocked for further colonial acquisitions; efforts at expanding German economic interests overseas would meet with British opposition. This was the first and most obvious consequence of the Anglo-French understanding. Holstein saw it clearly and threw the blame on Bülow. Writing to his cousin on April 10, 1904, he said:

Politically I am not happy. The perverse attitude during the Boer War now bears its fruit in the entente between France and England. Not I alone, but also other members of the political division of the foreign office made every effort three years ago to convince Bülow that he should oppose the immoderate enmity toward England in the Reichstag, and particularly the scandalous caricatures of the comic magazines. But the good Bülow would rather swim with than against the current. Now what a pickle we are in. England and France will hardly attack us, that is not what I fear, but we shall be unable to make any overseas acquisitions. I do not demand such acquisitions but a great mass of people cry out for them and wonder why none fall to us. Indeed, but how shall it be done? Against England and France an overseas policy is impossible. We could have gone along with England and could today have had the position which France has, that is, good friends with both England and Russia. But we missed the opportunity and Delcassé shows that he is the wiser.[2]

Another effect of the new alignment on Germany's position only became evident with the passage of time. Normal friendly relations between Germany and the Entente partners were made practically impossible by the nature of the understanding itself. Depending as it did on sentiment and a sharing of common views of policy, instead of a written alliance, the Entente was an extraordinarily sensitive and delicate tie. As aptly

[2] Holstein, *Lebensbekenntnis,* p. 231.

characterized by one writer, "It partook more of the nature of a jealous engagement than of a trustworthy and tolerant marriage. Each party was particularly mistrustful of any playing by the other with Germany." [3] As a result Anglo-German relations no longer depended simply on the will of Berlin and London and the temper and spirit of their respective publicities, but they were henceforth conditioned by Germany's relations to France. British officials were unable to consider any friendly gesture toward themselves or any dispute between Paris and Berlin strictly on merit. German diplomacy incurred a doubly difficult task, for in calculating the effect of any move the susceptibilities of both the British and French had to be anticipated and taken into account. Anglo-German relations were thus deprived of their independent foundation. Moreover, a deep suspicion met every attempt on the part of official or unofficial parties in Berlin to effect a rapprochement with either of the western neighbors. Every move of this kind was certain to be branded either in London or Paris as a dark plot designed to weaken or disrupt the Entente.

Although ineptitude and aggressiveness were largely to blame for the dilemma which now confronted the Germans in their vital foreign policy, a certain amount of sympathy for them as the objects of a pariah-like attitude cannot be withheld. For eight years Germany was held in diplomatic quarantine, and whenever she sought to expand her interests—in Africa, the Near East, the Orient—she encountered a stone wall of Entente opposition. To this situation must be attributed in part at least, the attitude of defiant aggressiveness which henceforth distinguished German foreign policy. The unaccommodating spirit in Berlin on the naval question in the years to follow, was but a natural reaction under the circumstances. Isolated and blocked along every possible channel of expansion, and her policies the object of the rankest suspicion in every quarter, it is not surprising that rapid expansion of her naval forces should have met with the approval of all parties in Germany except the Social Democrats. Efforts in this direction were quite naturally inter-

---

[3] E. N. Anderson, *The First Moroccan Crisis, 1904–1906* (Chicago, 1930), p. 402. This is by all odds the best account of the diplomacy of this period. The author's own volume (*Germany and the Diplomatic Revolution: A Study in Diplomacy and the Press, 1904–1906,* Philadelphia, 1931) treats of the publicity of these years and forms a counterpart to Prof. Anderson's book. Together they constitute the main sources of this chapter. The excellent article by R. J. Sontag, "German Foreign Policy, 1904–1906" (*Amer. Hist. Rev.,* Jan. 1928), should not be overlooked. Other works that have since appeared and which afford new information or viewpoints are C. W. Porter, *The Career of Théophile Delcassé* (Philadelphia, 1936); A. Combarieu, *Sept ans à l'Elysée avec le Président Loubet* (Paris, 1932); M. Paléologue, *Un grand tournant de la politique mondiale, 1904–1906* (Paris, 1934); Friedrich Rosen, *Aus einem diplomatischen Wanderleben. Auswärtige Amt—Marokko.*

preted abroad as material proof of potentially aggressive designs against the possessions of her neighbors. Germany's neighbors sought to banish this feeling of insecurity by increasing their armaments. Thus did the European cabinets move in a vicious spiral which led in the end to disaster.

Not less important than the revolution in diplomatic alignments was the accompanying revolution in contemporary English stereotypes of Germany and the Germans. We noted in the last chapter the outward signs of changing attitudes of British politicians, diplomats, and publicists toward German foreign policy. Under the emotional impact of the Boer War the average British stereotype of the Teutonic cousin and his country was likewise transformed. The day when the Germans were regarded as a nation of poets and philosophers had long passed—that belonged to the early nineteenth century. During the 'nineties the Germans were seen as a nation pursuing their even way under an efficient paternalistic government, a nation in which the professors with their *Schrifts* and *Blatts* occupied a place in society second only to the military. This nation consumed less alcohol and published more books than either France or England, and led the world in the application of science to technology and industry. Workers were insured by the state and the railways were efficiently operated by the same agency. Industrial wages were lower than in England, but the disciplined, intelligent laboring class maintained a higher standard of physical well-being than the same class in England. German cities had no slums, and the garbage was not hauled off in open carts but in closed dust-proof cars. These folk were just a trifle smug and self-satisfied, a little difficult to entertain, but assiduous, resolute, and disciplined. That the German succeeded in whatever he undertook was a widely held view. But after 1901 this tolerant view is rarely found in the press. With the twentieth century, the popular British press produced a new type of German in a new milieu. He becomes an over-disciplined, goose-stepping individual, suffering the bureaucratic régime like a stupid dolt. Does not the *Hausherr* have to register his newly hired servant at the police station and notify the authorities when he changes his residence? The German ideal of the social-state was a matter of obloquy in contrast to the British ideal of the independent individual. The German was socially inferior, given to pedantic forms of politeness, heel-clicking, and parade-ground smartness. He wore evening dress in daytime! The German woman was always a *Hausfrau* and the German husband ruled his family like a Turkish pasha. Judged by the public prints the German constitution was a feudal document; dueling was the chief occupation in university and army circles; "military murders" were everyday occurrences; German editors passed at least half their time in jail under sentence for *lèse-majesté;* and German foreign relations were conducted with a perfect blend of diplomatic cunning and political immorality. German *Weltpolitik,* when it was not used as a stimulus to panic, was ridiculed and misrepresented. Why should the Germans desire colonies? Those they had brought them no advantage. Only the English were born colonizers and knew how to govern backward peoples. "The Teutonic colonist prefers the freedom of a British régime to the intolerant bureaucracy of his own country's sway," was the proud boast of British imperialists. Germany was no longer the land of the categorical imperative; on the contrary she was wallowing in materialism—her ideal was profits and her cult was brute force. This composite stereotype of the German nation became basic for the selection and reporting of news from Germany. And day by day the popular papers, with their novel standards of news value, authenticated the picture. During the next eight years diplomatic developments were conditioned by these current myths.

The conclusion of the sweeping Anglo-French agreement came as a shock to the Emperor, Bülow, and Holstein. Its full significance was not appreciated, although suspicions as to secret clauses were not lacking. Through Hammann and the press bureau, Bülow furnished the official view for those papers in touch with the Wilhelmstrasse. Putting a good face on a bad matter it was announced that the agreement left Germany's position untouched and was therefore not a cause for irritation or jealousy.[4] Attacked by the Pan-Germans and Bismarckians for leading Germany into isolation, Bülow launched an article in the Kölnische Zeitung placing the responsibility on the German jingoes, who "through their systematic agitation against England and their fanatical enthusiasm for the Boers made the Anglo-French rapprochement possible."[5] In England the Germanophobes regarded the agreement as an instrument to be employed against Germany. According to Bernstorff, who was now in charge of the London embassy's press relations, this was not the interpretation placed on it in Downing Street. On the contrary, foreign office officials had urged H. A. Gwynne, the director of Reuter's Agency, to counteract this interpretation so far as it was within his power to do so. "For our part," wrote Bernstorff, "it is naturally very difficult to influence public opinion since the journalists are already armed with their old prejudices. Frequently at night in their editorial rooms they forget what they have promised me in the afternoon."[6]

[4] Hale, *op. cit.,* pp. 38–40; Anderson, *op. cit.,* pp. 141–43.
[5] No. 408, April 22, 1905, "Die Presse und das Ausland"; O. Hammann, *Bilder aus der letzten Kaiserzeit* (Berlin, 1922), 42–43; Hale, *op. cit.,* pp. 40–41.
[6] Bernstorff to Bülow, April 16, 1904; *G. P.,* XX, 14–21. Hale, *op. cit.,* p. 42.

The first move of German diplomacy was in the direction of repeating the pattern of the Anglo-French rapprochement in the hope of concluding a similar agreement with England. An arbitration treaty between the two governments was negotiated, and a visit by King Edward to Kiel and a return visit of a German naval squadron to Plymouth were arranged. When Lansdowne approached the German officials to secure adherence to the proposed change in the status of Egypt, he was met with a suggestion that this issue be made the center of a general clearing agreement such as England had concluded with France. The Germans got nowhere on this line; Lansdowne stamped their proposal as "a great piece of effrontery"; and the Germans had to be content with a restricted agreement covering their minor interests in Egypt.[7] Nor were they more fortunate in their efforts to improve public relations. All official manifestations of cordiality were received in the English press with suspicion and misgivings; their new friendship with France should not be jeopardized by a too ardent flirt with Germany. On the subject of the arbitration treaty even the Manchester Guardian, though it welcomed the treaty, thought that Anglo-German hostility "springs from forces too manifold and lying too deep to be radically affected by an agreement of this slight description."[8] When the German squadron visited Plymouth, a Daily Mail writer impudently insinuated that it had been sent to spy on British naval preparations.[9] The exchange of naval courtesies had an unforeseen publicity effect. King Edward's visit to Kiel and the return visit of the German squadron to Plymouth focused public attention on the German navy and its steady growth. Although German naval progress had figured since 1901 in occasional articles in the press, and Saunders had reported extensively on it in his dispatches to the Times, it now became for the first time the concentration point for the combined publicity of the British press. German attempts to improve the tone of public relations accomplished the very reverse of what had been intended.

This alarmist campaign over the navy was revived in the autumn by the Dogger Bank incident, which was attributed by the Times to nervousness induced by German warnings to the Russian authorities to be on the lookout for Japanese torpedo boats in the North Sea. At the same time articles appeared in *Vanity Fair* and the *Army and Navy Gazette* advocating a preventive war against Germany; and on December 12 the admiralty announced an important redistribution of naval forces, involving a greater concentration of power in the Channel and North Sea. The

---

[7] Anderson, *op. cit.,* pp. 148–51.
[8] Hale, *op. cit.,* pp. 48–50. Detailed report on the press by Metternich, July 14, 1904; *G. P.,* XXIII, 10–12.
[9] *Daily Mail,* July 11, 1904.

tone of the press, the loose talk in British naval circles, and the significant redistribution of maritime strength caused a war scare in Berlin.[10] German fear of an English surprise attack was not diminished by the statement of Sir Arthur Lee at a public meeting on February 3, 1905, that the North Sea was a danger spot, but that the English navy was ready and could get in the first blow before the other side had time to read the declaration of war in the newspapers. Lee's careless remark produced expressions of indignation in the German press and something akin to panic in the highest circles. Of itself it revived the clamor for increased naval armaments as a safeguard against an English preventive war. Under the impulse of fear, the naval authorities in Berlin were authorized to proceed with new plans for expansion. These were embodied in a supplementary navy law and accepted by the Reichstag in March, 1906.[11]

After the initial failure of German diplomats to establish their relations with England on the same basis that had been accorded the French, they turned to direct action. The ground chosen was Morocco, where the French, without so much as a nod of recognition toward Berlin, had proceeded to fasten their control on the Sultan's dominions by dispatching a 'reform mission' to Fez. Under pressure from Bülow and Holstein, the Kaiser made his spectacular landing at Tangier on March 31, 1905, and Bülow announced in the Reichstag that Germany would defend her rights and interests in Morocco against French encroachment. Thus Europe moved into the Moroccan crisis. While the principals were France and Germany, British sympathy as well as British policy was fully engaged. In forecasting English reaction to the German coup, Bülow and his technical experts blundered like simpletons. Dissatisfaction expressed in some quarters with the insufficient commercial guarantees for the future of British trade in Morocco had encouraged German diplomats to believe that British support of France would be at best perfunctory. They thought that by stressing the open door policy and by refraining from a direct attack on the Entente Cordiale a revival of press polemics could be avoided. Indeed so anxious were the Berlin statesmen to prevent such a war of opinion that a quasi-censorship of news dispatches from German correspondents in London was discussed and approved, although apparently not put into effect.[12]

The legal grounds advanced through the semi-official organs in Berlin

---

[10] "Das erste Deutsch-Englische 'War Scare,' November–Dezember, 1904"; *G. P.*, XIX, 353–80. Hale, *op. cit.*, pp. 56–71. Victor Eulenburg to Bernstorff, Aug. 14, 1904; *Memoirs of Count Bernstorff*, pp. 90–91. Bülow, *Memoirs*, II, 80–81.

[11] For the genesis of the new law and the temper of German naval authorities see A. Tirpitz, *Aufbau der deutschen Weltmacht* (Stuttgart, 1924), pp. 13–30.

[12] Mühlberg to Metternich, April 4, 1905; *G. P.*, XX, 603.

as the basis of German intervention were brushed aside by the commentators in the British press as mere pretexts designed to cover an attack on the Entente Cordiale. To demonstrate the solidarity of the Anglo-French connection, reciprocal fleet visits were announced, King Edward showered attention and favors on M. Delcassé, the French foreign minister, and a British agent was dispatched to Fez to support the French mission then negotiating with the Sultan. English journalists in their zeal for defending their ally were more French than the French themselves. By their ardor in attacking Germany and encouraging France, they raised the suspicion that the British were trying to promote a war between Teuton and Gaul. Metternich and Bernstorff could do nothing to check the Germanophobia of the London press. Their difficulties were described by Bernstorff in a letter to Bülow: "With regard to influencing the press, unfortunately little can be accomplished in such disturbed times. After one has spoken to the journalists, one's ideas can be found in the next leading articles, but such influence lasts only twenty-four hours. Then the stream continues as of old and the single favorable editorial disappears without trace in the torrent. The journalists have just as little desire as the ministers to expose themselves to the attack of the Germanophobe ring." [13] Even Lucien Wolf, foreign editor of the Daily Graphic, who was closer to Bernstorff and the German embassy than any other London journalist, was blown around and forced to take a position antagonistic to Germany's policy.[14]

However, the crusading zeal of the London editors was considerably blunted by Delcassé's resignation on June 6, when from the universal criticism of the French minister by his own press, it was realized that English Hotspurs had contributed not a little to that disaster by their too ardent attacks on Germany. For they had created the suspicion in France that the Anglo-French agreement was being used as an instrument for provoking the neighbor across the Rhine. When Delcassé's successor, Rouvier, accepted the German demand for a conference, the British press, conforming to official policy, accepted the situation and promised the most loyal support to France whatever the course she might decide to steer. The bellicose tone of the London journals toward

[13] April 22, 1905; *G. P.*, XX, 609–15. For details of the press campaign see Hale, *op. cit.*, pp. 105–6.

[14] See Wolf's letter of explanation to Bernstorff, April 5, 1905; *Memoirs of Count Bernstorff*, pp. 80–81. In appointing Bernstorff to succeed Eckardstein, Bülow made much of the former's successful cultivation of the press while stationed in Munich and expected him to repeat his successes in London. Bernstorff could do little in that disturbed period, and he had constantly to contend with Eckardstein's intrigues. Bernstorff gives an account of his four years in London and reproduces some letters from Lucien Wolf, Valentine Chirol, and Sidney Whitman. (*Ibid.*, pp. 67–91.)

Germany, however, was not entirely abandoned. On the announcement that British fleet maneuvers would be held in the Baltic—the first time in many years—the Agrarian Deutsche Tageszeitung and the Conservative clerical Reichsbote made senseless comments which were telegraphed to London by the British correspondents, and made the subject of incendiary and provocative attacks in the Conservative and Unionist press.[15] The violence of the British press recalled the days of the Kruger Telegram and the storm produced by Bülow's reprimand to Chamberlain in the famous *Granitrede*. To the readers of the newspapers war seemed imminent.

The newspaper brawl reached crisis proportions with the publication of a series of revelations by Stéphane Lauzanne in the Matin in early October. Reviewing the incidents leading to Delcassé's resignation in June, the French journalist alleged that the British promised armed support if the French cabinet rejected the German demand for a conference. In Germany these disclosures were taken as proof of the existence of an "assassin's plot" instigated by the British. Britain had endeavored to use Delcassé as a convenient tool to precipitate a conflict between France and Germany. In his directions to the press bureau Bülow stated that the disclosures were not to be treated too skeptically. Moreover, they brought water to the naval wheel, and he wrote Tirpitz that he could make his demands in the supplementary naval bill as high as he wished. He could guarantee their acceptance.[16] That the British had ranged themselves on the side of Germany's hereditary enemy, to the extent of contemplating armed assistance, produced a profound embitterment in German diplomatic and press circles.

Discounting the inaccuracies and exaggerations of the Matin revelations, they revealed to the public the pass to which Anglo-German relations had been brought. They also signified the failure of German efforts to bring about a new alignment of the powers through a rapprochement with Russia and an eventual reconciliation with France. The Anglo-French understanding had impressed Berlin authorities with the danger of a reconciliation between England and Russia. This possibility was no longer scorned as "music of the future." Russia's plight in the war with Japan, during 1904–5, afforded an opportunity for demonstrations of friendship by the Emperor William and his government. An attempt was made in the autumn of 1904 to conclude a definite political alliance with the Russian government. Upon the Kaiser's initiative the idea was

---

[15] Metternich to Bülow, Aug. 14; *G. P.*, XX, 653–54. Hale, *op. cit.*, pp. 176–78.

[16] See Bülow's detailed directions for the press bureau, *G. P.*, XX, 664–69; Tirpitz, *op. cit.*, p. 25; Hale, *op. cit.*, pp. 195–99.

revived in the summer of 1905 at the famous Björkö meeting. At this time Bülow regarded Morocco as powerful bait which might be used to draw France into the Russo-German camp as contemplated in the treaty concluded under such dramatic circumstances by the Kaiser and the Czar. Germany had already demonstrated to the French by vigorous interference with their plans in Morocco that an entente with England could not save them from German trouble making. But the Matin revelations provoked in the entire French press violent demonstrations against any connection with Germany, and gave the final coup to the Kaiser's dream of a continental triplice. The French attitude was the determining factor because Russia's financial need arising out of the war placed her policy in French leading strings. While Lamsdorff and Nelidov were scuttling the Björkö treaty they were diligently clearing the ground for the Anglo-Russian entente.[17]

It is in this larger frame of shifting continental alignments that the first phase of the Moroccan crisis must be considered. In the dénouement, at the Algeciras Conference, no other course was open to Bülow and his advisers but to make of Morocco an end in itself and to enforce as far as they could their cherished principle of international control. In this game all the trumps were held in Paris—the agreement with England, the secret accords with Italy and Spain and the financial necessity of the Russian government. It is not surprising that at Algeciras the Germans found themselves hoisted by their own petard.

As the opening date for the conference approached, a feeling of false optimism developed in Berlin. This was induced in part by the change of government in England, when the Balfour cabinet was succeeded, in December, by a Liberal ministry headed by Campbell-Bannerman with Grey at the foreign office. While the wish may have fathered the thought, Metternich counted on a more understanding attitude on the part of the new ministry and, perhaps, a weakening of British support of France. Moreover, in private circles outside the press, such concern had developed over the bitter newspaper polemics of the summer that a movement for understanding and reconciliation was undertaken. Two public meetings were arranged, which were attended by a considerable number of influential men and women. Metternich thought these meetings had more significance for British feelings and attitudes than the editorials of papers like the Times.[18]

[17] On the Russo-German alliance negotiations see Anderson, *op. cit.*, chaps. X and XV. On the accompanying publicity, Hale, *op. cit.*, pp. 191–202, 207–10.
[18] *G. P.*, XX, 679–84; Anderson, *op. cit.*, pp. 311–18; H. Schöttle, *Die Times in der ersten Marokkokrise* (Berlin, 1930), pp. 112–13. The optimism of Berlin was not

Fundamentally there was no change in foreign policy with the advent of the Liberals to power. To be sure there were vague expressions of a desire to extend the policy of ententes to include Germany. But in platform pronouncements, private conversations, and in the press, a resumption of friendly relations with Germany was made conditional upon the Germans swallowing without protest the French policy in Morocco. Not only did Grey repeat Lansdowne's warning to Metternich that in the event of war arising out of the Anglo-French agreement the pressure of opinion in England would preclude British neutrality, but he went much further and sanctioned the well-known military conversations between the respective general staffs. From the diplomatic preparations made in London, it is evident that Grey and his advisers were as determined as the French to beat the Germans at all costs, and the military conversations indicated a willingness to consider the ultimate consequences of unqualified support of French demands.[19]

The Algeciras Conference was the first international congress to be exploited by the new journalism for the instruction or entertainment of the masses. From the possibility of its failure followed the possibility of war; and the element of conflict was present to a large degree in the diplomatic action itself, which placed it high in the scale of modern news values. More than fifty newspaper correspondents were sent to Algeciras to report this international conflict of wills and personalities. There were twenty French correspondents, six English, four American, three German, and the remainder Italian, Spanish, and Austrian.[20] The physical limitations of Algeciras contributed much to the unsatisfactory relations that developed between the delegates and the journalists. The little Spanish town, scarcely more than a village, had only two hotels. The diplomats occupied one, the journalists the other. During the long delays, which marked the progress of the conference, the journalists were forced to make out of every rumor and minor incident an event of world importance. After the first week the local color of Algeciras, and the three wives brought to the conference by the Moroccan delegate, El Mokri, had been exploited to the limit in countless atmosphere articles.[21] Thereafter, the dearth of news of a sensational kind led to the outright fabrication of interviews, journalistic espionage, and general badgering of the

shared by all the German diplomats. See Monts' letters to Tschirschky, in Monts, *Erinnerungen*, pp. 419–24.

[19] Anderson, *op. cit.*, pp. 322–47; *B. D.*, III, 169–227.

[20] See the list in A. Tardieu, *La conférence d'Algésiras* (Paris, 1907), pp. 503–4. The list is by no means complete.

[21] *Figaro* (Paris), Jan. 31, 1906, cartoon entitled "The Gaieties of Algeciras, or Three Wives for El Mokri."

delegates. The American representative, Mr. White, told the German ambassador in Rome after the conference, that everything could have been arranged a month sooner if it had not been for the "press vermin." [22] Tattenbach, the German delegate, complained of three fabricated interviews in one week.[23] Except for a few favored correspondents the delegates held aloof from the press representatives, which contributed to the general reporting of fantasy and conjecture. Only the French deputation at the conference was prepared to deal with a large group of newspaper correspondents. The way in which M. Billy managed the press relations of the French delegation and oriented the entire correspondents' corps in the interest of his government's policy was described to Holstein by a non-German observer as a "perfectly brilliant technical performance." [24]

Full proof of this statement is furnished by a glance at the reports appearing in the world press from Algeciras. In all but the dispatches of the three German correspondents, the conference publicity was hostile in the fullest measure to the German position. Particularly in the reports circulated by Reuter's Agency and Havas, as well as in the reports of the special correspondents to the Paris and London dailies, Germany's advocacy of the open door and the principle of internationalization was represented as a cloak for sinister designs. Editors and correspondents, writing in the tradition of *fin-de-siècle* imperialism, portrayed France as the defender of European interests and the missionary of civilization, while Germany was branded as a barrier to progress and a protector of barbarism. Politically everything hinged on who was to restore order in Morocco and control the police. German refusal to accept a joint Franco-Spanish mandate was represented as downright petty and unbecoming to a great power. Any show of firmness toward the diplomatic coalition which formed at Algeciras, led immediately to the arraignment of Germany as a willful disturber of the peace eager to provoke hostilities. Not only did the German delegates find themselves isolated around the green table, except for Austrian support, but in world publicity they were isolated by the commanding position held by Reuter, Havas, and the London press in the field of international press communications. Even Wolff's reporting of the conference was inadequate; and most of the German journals followed the conference proceedings

[22] "This rabble dogged the footsteps of the delegates, annoyed them and misrepresented their statements." White made an exception of Cortesi of the Associated Press, and the three German correspondents, Rieger of W. T. B., Baron von Zedlitz of the *Lokal-Anzeiger,* and Dr. Rosenberg of the *Frankfurter Zeitung.* Monts to the foreign office, April 12, 1906; *G. P.,* XXI, 346.
[23] *Figaro* (Paris), Feb. 19, 1906.
[24] Holstein to Radolin, Feb. 10, 1906; *G. P.,* XXI, 152–54.

through the sharply angled Havas and Reuter dispatches transmitted either by their own correspondents, or, as was frequently the case, by the Wolff Bureau itself.

An outstanding publicity feature of the conference was the concerted campaign in the French press against Germany. Led by Tardieu in Le Temps, it was clamorous, bitter, and provocative. In Germany the journalists maintained a studied reserve, leaving all polemics to the semi-official organs. Greater use was made of the Norddeutsche to combat the French press campaign than in any previous diplomatic crisis of similar proportions. But even in the Norddeutsche and the Kölnische Zeitung the Wilhelmstrasse's measures were mainly defensive, taking the form of denials and corrections. The remainder of the press merely amplified the semi-official statements put forth in the Norddeutsche.[25]

The one German attempt to make positive use of the weapon of publicity to influence the negotiations was a lamentable failure. On March 10, when the German delegates broke the tiresome deadlock on the police question by meeting French demands more than half-way, they put the French in a position where they faced acceptance of a favorable compromise, or the shouldering of the onus for breaking up the conference. Among all the delegates the feeling was strong that France should accept the German proposal. A dispatch from Count von Zedlitz to the Lokal-Anzeiger, however, put the colors on too thick, in that it stated that after the German conciliatory move the French delegates were completely isolated in the committee. Tardieu immediately published in Le Temps the dispatch from St. Petersburg to the Russian delegate, instructing him to support unconditionally the French demands. He followed this with a summary of Grey's instructions to Nicolson which were identical in import. The tumult thus created in the press completely nullified Bülow's efforts to bring concerted pressure on the French by a circular dispatch to the various capitals stressing the reasonableness of the German position in the face of French intransigence.[26]

Although the part played by Sir Arthur Nicolson at Algeciras, in

[25] The polemics of the *Norddeutsche* were directed mainly at Tardieu and *Le Temps*. They were revived a year later by an article published in the *Revue des deux mondes* and the appearance of Tardieu's volume, *La conférence d'Algésiras*. Hammann contributed long anonymous critiques, based upon German documents, to the *Kölnische Zeitung* and the *Grenzboten, Kölnische Ztg.*, No. 338, March 30, 1907; "Um Algeciras," "Von einem deutschen Diplomaten," *Grenzboten,* March 21, 1907.

[26] On this incident see Anderson, *op. cit.,* p. 383; Tardieu, *La conférence d'Algésiras,* p. 330; *B. D.,* III, 304; *G. P.,* XXI, 274–75, 312–20; *Norddeutsche* polemics against Tardieu, March 20, 21, 23, 27; Tardieu's articles in *Le Temps,* March 18, 21, 23, 26. Apparently all relevant French diplomatic documents went through Tardieu's hands, although the French ministers disclaimed responsibility for the violent campaign which he carried on in *Le Temps.* Tardieu received the Cassini instructions from the Russian ambassador in Paris.

seconding every French proposal, was no secret, the German press remained quiet toward England. Had there been any desire to pick a quarrel exception might readily have been taken to the steady stream of critical reports that appeared in the Times, the Morning Post, the Pall Mall Gazette, the Daily Telegraph, the Daily Mail, and the Standard. The Manchester Guardian was the only journal of any consequence in England that judged German diplomacy at Algeciras on its merits.[27] The other extreme was represented by Edgar Wallace's reports to the Daily Mail from Algeciras, and the sensational leading articles in which the editor commented on these lucubrations.[28] Aside from the Manchester Guardian and the Westminster Gazette, the important journals agreed in ascribing to German policy two aims: first, to demonstrate to the French how dangerous was their friendship with England and how little protection it afforded; and second, to obtain a naval base and a colonial foothold on the Atlantic coast of Morocco. As Metternich described the prevailing British attitude: "Here the Moroccan question is generally regarded as a test of the Anglo-French entente, and our Moroccan policy as an attempt to smash it up." [29]

In only one article was the German case put fairly in the London press. Lucien Wolf, with Count Bernstorff's approval, published in the Pall Mall Gazette, on March 6, an article entitled, "The German Grievance," in which he presented the official German thesis. It was passed over in dead silence by the daily press, and its only noticeable effect was to stimulate William Tyrrell, Grey's private secretary, to write a long memorandum refuting Wolf point by point.[30] The other side of the picture presented by the British press was, of course, the daily reiteration of the foreign office thesis that French demands arising out of the agreement of April 8, 1904, must be supported by Great Britain without reservations, to the end that their political entente should be preserved unimpaired. With the conclusion of the conference, the general opinion expressed was that its success was attributable solely to the solidarity of France and England in facing together the unjustifiable pretensions of German diplomacy. The Entente Cordiale had received a baptism of fire at Algeciras and had emerged strengthened and fortified in every respect.

[27] "The Kaiser's diplomacy before the Conference may have been roughshod, but, so far as we can see, Germany's action at Algeciras has been straightforward, logical, and on the whole, considerate." (March 10, 1906.)

[28] *Daily Mail*, Feb. 12, 14, 19, 26, 27, March 5, 12, 19, 23, 28, 1906.

[29] *G. P.*, XXI, 51–52.

[30] *B. D.*, III, 347–49. Wolf, who employed the pseudonym, "Diplomaticus," besides being foreign editor of the *Daily Graphic*, was a prolific contributor of articles on foreign affairs to the *Westminster Gazette, Pall Mall Gazette*, the *Times* and numerous periodicals.

Germany's Moroccan action, and its related moves, can only be accounted a lamentable failure. It failed in its initial move to get into the circle of Franco-British friendship; it failed to achieve William II's dream of a continental league; it failed to separate France and England; it failed even to achieve limited German aims in Morocco, for the Act of Algeciras was not a settlement—it only provided a future battleground for the two contestants. Despite the collapse of Bülow's policy in all its larger aspects, the outcome of the Algeciras Conference was presented to the German public as a diplomatic victory. The suspicion of colossal failure was not absent from many minds it is true, but such was Bülow's skill in putting bright colors on an otherwise dark canvas that the official thesis was widely accepted. The chancellor had counted on this. When the conference deadlocked on the critical question of the police and Bülow took the negotiations out of Holstein's hands, he called in Hammann and August Stein for consultation. He put to them this question: Which course would have the least disastrous publicity results, the recall of the German delegation and the break-up of the conference, or surrender to France on the police question depending on press influence to disguise the retreat as a victory? Hammann and Stein were both of the opinion that the latter course was not only preferable but also possible of achievement, so Bülow abandoned the substance of his Moroccan policy and embraced the shadow of international control under a joint Franco-Spanish mandate.[31]

It was not entirely Bülow's skill in manipulating the press and the Reichstag that made this national deception possible. It must be remembered that the mass of documentary material incorporated into many narratives today, was not available to contemporaries for the formation of a broad judgment. When doubts arose, they would be generally resolved in favor of the government. For one must reckon on the majority of editors and publicists taking the patriotic view, which precluded direct attacks on their own statesmen, admissions of national failure, or signs of weakness and fear. The Social Democratic charge that the Moroccan policy was a mistake, and that German isolation was its fruit, contained a larger element of truth than the official thesis, but for patriotic reasons the Socialist interpretation did not find general acceptance in the press.[32]

Officially inspired publicity ignored the failure of the Wilhelmstrasse

---

[31] Rosen, *Aus einem diplomatischen Wanderleben,* I, 257. Tschirschky wrote to Monts on March 28, 1906: "Sie machen sich keinen Begriff von der Abhängigkeit B[ülows] von der Presse. Hammann ist eigentlich der 'leitende.'" (Monts, *Erinnerungen,* p. 441.)

[32] For the Social Democratic view see *Vorwärts,* No. 80, April 5, and Bebel's criticism in the Reichstag. *Norddeutsche,* parliamentary report, April 8, 1906.

to restore the international balance and to avoid isolation; attention was focused on the immediate results of the Algeciras Conference. Here it was pointed out that Bülow's formula for the conference—"neither victors nor vanquished"—had been realized, and that all essential points in the German program had been attained. The principle of internationalization had been legally sanctioned; the principle of the open door, with full protection for German economic interests, had been established; and it had been successfully demonstrated that Germany could not be treated as a *quantité négligeable* in a question of world importance. Such was the substance of interpretative articles appearing in the Norddeutsche and the Kölnische Zeitung. These judgments, appropriately embroidered, were repeated in the press of all groups except the Socialist and Pan-German. In the Reichstag, too, the party spokesmen approved the chancellor's explanations of the past and accepted his optimistic predictions for the future. No peculiar magic or irresistible charm enabled Bülow to blind the nation to the truth; politicians and publicists, as well as diplomats, felt the compulsion to save face.[33]

England was really the victor at Algeciras. But in all the press discussion that marked the close of the conference and the end of the immediate crisis, the German publicists were conciliatory toward her and ignored the part she had played at Algeciras. In official circles, too, resentment was suppressed as Tschirschky, the foreign secretary, went to work to relax the tension between Berlin and London. Grey and Haldane had assured Metternich that only their obligation to support France at Algeciras stood in the way of extending the hand of reconciliation, and once the question of Morocco was out of the way they would come out publicly on behalf of better relations with Germany.[34] The expectations built upon these assurances were not realized. Distrust of German motives had taken deep hold on the British diplomats and foreign office officials. That Germany had bullied France over Morocco because of Anglo-French friendship was as firmly held in official circles as in the press. When Tschirschky expressed a desire to improve their relations his overtures encountered suspicion and reserve. Eyre Crowe wrote on

[33] *Kölnische Ztg.*, No. 335, March 29, 1906; *Norddeutsche*, April 3. Bülow's statement in the Reichstag on April 5 was simply an elaboration of the thesis presented in this article. Not only the thought but in some instances the wording is identical (*Fürst Bülows Reden*, II, 303–6). Supporting the official view: *Die Post*, April 4; *Kreuzzeitung*, March 31; *Münchner Allg. Ztg.*, No. 153, April 3; *Frankfurter Ztg.*, No. 91, April 2; *Lokal-Anzeiger*, April 1; *Vossische Ztg.*, No. 152, March 31, 1906. The *Berliner Tageblatt* was more critical. Theodor Wolff complained that "optimism was a peculiar and chronic ailment of German diplomacy," and Arthur Levysohn summed up the conference results by quoting the old saw, "Be satisfied with a little, for more is not to be had." (*Berliner Tageblatt*, March 30, April 1.)

[34] *B. D.*, III, 209–11, 263–64; *G. P.*, XXI, 45–52, 106–8, 424–31.

the dispatch reporting Tschirschky's gesture: "All this talk about an 'understanding' between the two countries has an air of unreality. . . . Past history has shown us that a friendly Germany has usually been a Germany asking for something, by way of proving our friendship." And Grey concurred, as he noted, "All that is necessary is for the Germans to realize that they have got nothing to complain of." [35]

It was, therefore, with disguised or open disapproval that Grey and the foreign office officials observed the private efforts to stimulate favorable propaganda for Anglo-German reconciliation. The initiative came from the Anglo-German Friendship Committee organized by Lord Avebury in the autumn of 1905.[36] With its co-operation several German delegations were entertained in England after the manner of the exchange visits which had inaugurated the Entente Cordiale. A group of German burgomasters and a labor delegation were entertained in May 1906, and in June a delegation of German editors and publicists visited England. From the friendly reception accorded these groups, Tschirschky, the German foreign secretary, drew the unwarranted conclusion that "the period of estrangement between England and Germany is past." [37] But when the Kölnische Zeitung pointed to the uneasiness created in Paris by the visit of the German journalists as a measure of the visit's success, Saunders flashed a warning in the Times. On the basis of Saunders' dispatch to the Times, Crowe wrote a memorandum in which these words occur: "In the interest of our understanding with France it may become necessary to take some steps to counteract the impression which the sudden and indiscriminate fraternization with the very men who have for years poured out the venom of their hatred of England in their papers . . . cannot but tend to produce in Paris." Grey dismissed the propaganda of reciprocal visits in a significant marginal note. "There is nothing more in what has been said about Germany lately in this country than a gratification of the desire to gush, which is very strong just now. And it is as difficult to restrain gushing as it is to restrain tears, when people desire to cry." [38] Similarly, it was with considerable anxiety and suspicion that the foreign service personnel followed the meeting between Edward VII and William II at Cronberg, in August 1906. Likewise, a visit by Haldane to Berlin, to study the organization of the war office, was at first opposed by the foreign office officials. Their objections, how-

[35] B. D., III, 357–58.
[36] Manchester Guardian, May 2, 1906. Statement of their program and appeal for funds. Lord Avebury was president, R. E. Markel, secretary, and Sir C. Ernest Tritton, treasurer.
[37] Times, May 24, June 26; Manchester Guardian, May 17, 19, 25; Pall Mall Gazette, June 26; Daily Mail, June 27; Frankfurter Ztg., Nos. 167, 170, June 19, 22.
[38] B. D., III, 359–60.

ever, were overruled by a cabinet decision. The reluctance of British diplomats to sanction any conciliatory gesture toward Germany for fear of offending the French became a permanent factor conditioning the relations between Berlin and London. The French were aware of this and exploited it with consummate skill.[39]

The cabinet, or rather those members of the cabinet who were allowed now and then a peep at the mysteries of the foreign office, were not in complete accord with the permanent officials. For the latter, the arrangement of ententes was an exclusive system designed to serve as a bulwark against Germany's aggressive policies of expansion. The Liberal ministers, on the other hand, were profuse in their assurances to Metternich that their understanding with France, and their move to reach an agreement with Russia, did not preclude friendly relations with Germany. At the same time they let it be understood that the entente with France was, and would remain, the pivot of British foreign policy, and that they were bent on establishing their relations with Russia on a similar basis. The difference between the cabinet and the permanent officials was one of emphasis rather than design.[40]

Before the Liberals came to power, Haldane and his friends had assured Metternich of their desire to bring about an entente with Germany similar to their agreement with France, and the German ambassador had written to Bülow that "If the Liberals get into power, they will go to work on this systematically." [41] This prediction was never fulfilled. One year in office, and the experience of the Algeciras Conference, saw the Liberal leaders embracing and strengthening the policy of the preceding Conservative government and adopting gradually, if sometimes reluctantly, the views of the permanent officials. If anything, the suspicion of German policy was greater among the Liberal leaders than it had been among their predecessors. The brusqueness of German policy and the frank acknowledgment of *Machtpolitik* was more repellent to Liberals than to Conservatives, and in the eyes of the former the need for checking it was therefore the greater. It is significant that during the Algeciras Conference we find Grey saying, "An *entente* between Russia, France and ourselves would be absolutely secure. If it is necessary to check

[39] On the Cronberg visit and Haldane's reception in Berlin see *B. D.,* III, 366–84. At the Cronberg meeting, Hardinge, who accompanied the King, told Tschirschky that in London they welcomed the improvement that had taken place in the previous four months, and assured him that "the improvement would be maintained provided that there were no more surprises and no attempt made to injure our relations with France or to thwart our negotiations with Russia." (*Ibid.,* III, 367.)

[40] On the division of power over foreign policy between the cabinet, the foreign secretary, and the permanent officials, see the highly instructive monograph by Margaret Boveri, *Sir Edward Grey und das Foreign Office* (Berlin, 1933), *passim.*

[41] Bülow, *Memoirs,* II, 224.

Germany it could then be done." [42] A Liberal government, however, could not publicly sanction and promote a policy of power politics. That is why the system of ententes was always presented to the public as an expression of the government's desire to promote peace by removing all points of difference between England and France and England and Russia. Thus critics were forestalled and Liberal consciences were untroubled.

By the end of 1906, the revolution in British foreign policy was complete and the course for the next six years clearly defined. The measure of the change that had occurred—the shift from co-operation with Germany and the Triple Alliance to co-operation with the Dual Alliance—is provided by Eyre Crowe's famous memorandum on Anglo-German relations, which stated the basic assumptions of the new departure, and the counter-memorandum by Lord Sanderson, in which he defended the older policy and warned against the perils of the new course. [43]

Crowe's antipathy for Germany amounted to a phobia; that is a matter of record and not of speculation or inference. This is strange in view of the fact that he had a German mother and a German wife. A psychoanalyst would doubtless interpret his political views in terms of a bipolar love hate obsession. But into that matter we need not go. Crowe's astounding memorandum, in its emphasis on the background of historical forces, in its sweeping generalizations, with its detailed elaboration of alternative views to be eliminated by skilful dialectic so as to leave in the end but one logical conclusion, is more characteristic of the *Geheimrat* in the Wilhelmstrasse than the British permanent official in Downing Street. Crowe's memorandum shows a strong German tendency to drug reason with theoretic assertion and to subordinate facts to a predetermined pattern. Sanderson's memorandum, on the other hand, was typically English—factual, barren of theory, dispassionate, standing for fair play. Allowing for the fact that Crowe's memorandum was a slashing indictment of the policy with which Sanderson had been associated for many years, the latter's brief in defense of that policy was remarkably dispassionate and sane.

A considerable part of Crowe's memorandum was taken up with an

---

[42] *B. D.,* III, 267. On an alarmist memorandum by Crowe he wrote: "The Germans do not realize that England has always drifted or deliberately gone into opposition to any Power which establishes a hegemony in Europe." (*Ibid.,* III, 359.) For Metternich's appraisal of Grey's attitude see *G. P.,* XXI, 441–48.

[43] Mr. Eyre Crowe, "Memorandum on the Present State of British Relations with France and Germany," Jan. 1, 1907; Lord Sanderson, "Observations on printed Memorandum on Relations with France and Germany," Feb. 21, 1907. (*B. D.,* III, 397–431.) Crowe was chief clerk in charge of the Western Division, and Sanderson had just retired as permanent under-secretary, a post which he had occupied since 1894.

historical review of Anglo-German relations since the foundation of the German Empire. Crowe presented it as an unrelieved record of Machiavellian duplicity. From this appeal to history he worked up a pattern which led inevitably to the conclusion that, whether by conscious or accidental design, German policy was tending toward world hegemony, which involved striving for maritime ascendency, absorption of her smaller neighbors, and the destruction of the British Empire. Britain stood for the Powers of Light, Germany for the Powers of Darkness. Past experience and clashing ideologies precluded future co-operation between the two governments and made war a likely possibility. With appeals to Mahan on the nature of the Empire and the significance of sea-power, Crowe pointed out that Britain's safety lay in the supremacy of her navy and the maintenance of the balance of power, coupled with vigilant opposition to German intrigues and maneuvers to upset the balance of world political forces.

Sanderson, in his counter-memorandum, not only attacked the historical accuracy of Crowe's narrative of diplomatic incidents, but also took sharp issue with his interpretations and conclusions. The purpose of his notes, he said, was "to show that the history of German policy towards this country is not the unchequered record of black deeds which the [Crowe] Memorandum seems to portray." Typical of the difference in spirit that animated the two documents is the contrast between their analogues for the tendencies and methods of German diplomacy. For Crowe the record of German policy was a record of "political blackmail." Sanderson, on the other hand, describes the Germans as *"les Juifs de la diplomatie,"* whose motto is "nothing for nothing, and very little for sixpence." While he admitted that the Germans were hypersensitive and disagreeable antagonists, they nevertheless were not ungrateful for friendly support. Crowe scored the German press bureau and Bernstorff's activity in trying to influence the London journalists. Sanderson laid a just share of blame on the English press for its scare-mongering and its disturbance of relations between the two countries. "It has sometimes seemed to me," Sanderson wrote, "that to a foreigner reading our press the British Empire must appear in the light of some huge giant sprawling over the globe, with gouty fingers and toes stretching in every direction, which cannot be approached without eliciting a scream." In closing, he uttered a prophetic warning:

It is at all events unwise to meet her [Germany] with an attitude of pure obstruction, such as is advocated by part of our press. A great and growing nation cannot be repressed. It is altogether contrary to reason that Germany should wish to quarrel with us though she may wish to be in a position to face a quarrel with more chances of success, than she can be said now to have. But it would be a misfortune that she should be led to believe that in whatever direction she seeks to expand she will find the British lion in her path.

Unfortunately this valedictory from Lord Salisbury's able associate was consigned by Grey and Hardinge to the archives, whereas Crowe's provocative memorandum had been sent to Campbell-Bannerman, Lord Ripon, Asquith, Morley, and Haldane!

Sanderson belonged to the older generation of officials and diplomats. By 1907 there was only one man in an important post in the foreign service who shared and represented his views. That was Lascelles, the ambassador at Berlin, who because of his known pro-German leanings was regarded with a certain mistrust in the foreign office and, in consequence, was practically without influence.[44]

When we leave the portals of Downing Street and proceed to Fleet Street, seeking the inspiration or reflection of the views that had come to prevail in the British foreign office, it is at once apparent that Crowe's memorandum was attuned to contemporary publicity. It would not be exaggerating in the least to say that it was a composite of the views and opinions which had been advanced by the publicists in the periodicals in 1901, which had received a remarkable "build-up" during the next three years, and which had established itself, under the impact of the Moroccan crisis, as the predominant view in the daily press. There was nothing in Crowe's indictment which had not been advanced again and again in the periodical and newspaper press by Chirol, Saunders, Maxse, Garvin, Dillon, Strachey, Wilson, Blennerhassett, Repington, Wilkinson and others. In fact, the section of the memorandum dealing with England's position as the world's greatest colonial and naval power was only a *précis* of Spenser Wilkinson's *The Great Awakening*.[45]

It would be ridiculous to conclude from the record of intercommunication and stimulation, between British diplomats and the above-mentioned publicists, that there was a plot to direct British foreign policy into anti-German channels. True, William II was inclined to see it that way, and always added a splash of color by attributing adverse publicity in London to the reckless and wholesale distribution of Russian roubles and French

---

[44] Boveri, *Lord Grey und das Foreign Office,* pp. 134–38. In the foreign office more weight was given to the alarmist reports of Tower and Cartwright from Munich than to Lascelles' mild and conciliatory reports from Berlin. Crowe would invariably cover the former with approving minutes, reserving for the latter his comments of disparagement and disapproval. (See for example, *B. D.,* III, 350–55, 433–38.) Particularly noteworthy is Hermann Lutz' study, *Eyre Crowe: Der böse Geist des Foreign Office* (Stuttgart, 1931), pp. 1–49.

[45] Spenser Wilkinson, *Thirty-five Years, 1874–1909,* pp. 62, 187, 221, 316–19. Crowe was Wilkinson's brother-in-law; they were most intimate friends besides, and shared the same political *Weltanschauung.*

francs. In the Kaiser's private demonology Wesselitzsky, the London correspondent of the Novoye Vremya, and Saunders, "a first class scoundrel," occupied high places.[46] Even Metternich, who was not given to inventing conspiracies, seriously considered the possibility of the existence of a secret intrigue against Anglo-German relations, especially on the part of writers in the reviews.[47] We may dismiss the idea that those journalists who worked to effect a revolution in British foreign policy were the blind tools of a foreign power; they had no motive other than that of serving what they regarded to be the national interest.

However, between British officials and British journalists there was much informal collaboration and co-operation. Crowe in the foreign office and Wilkinson as chief leader writer on the Morning Post made a good team. Spring Rice corresponded regularly with Chirol, Strachey, Maxse, and Garvin, supplying them with material for articles on the "German menace." [48] At Algeciras and later at St. Petersburg, Sir Arthur Nicolson worked in the closest relationship with Mackenzie Wallace of the Times.[49] Chirol was absolutely trusted in the foreign office and he doubtless gave as well as received advice and information. Colonel Repington, also of the Times, had good connections in Downing Street. Lord Esher, located in a strategic position in King Edward's official family, was in close touch with Maxse, Repington, Garvin, Kennedy Jones, Northcliffe, and other writers in this circle.[50] This interchange of ideas between directing officials and the Maxse-Chirol group of publicists is an established fact of which too much perhaps should not be made, but which certainly cannot be dismissed as inconsequential.

If Lord Sanderson's memorandum had been circulated among leading London journalists, it would have met with as little approbation as it did in the foreign office. By 1907 Sanderson's views were outmoded in the press. Mr. Spender of the Westminster Gazette, Lucien Wolf of the Daily Graphic, Scott and Montague of the Manchester Guardian, Mas-

---

[46] See for example a characteristic outburst to Alfred Beit. *G. P.,* XX, 690–96.

[47] "The publicists, particularly in the reviews, give information which I can only attribute to diplomatic whispers from a foreign source." Metternich to Bülow, July 9, 1904; Bülow, *Memoirs,* II, 41. Metternich meant the Russian embassy.

[48] In this Spring Rice had the consent of his superiors, subject to the restriction that he himself did not publish or receive pay. (Gwynn, *Letters and Friendships of Cecil Spring Rice,* II, 144.) In 1912, when Spring Rice was detailed to Washington, after four years in Stockholm where he had spent his considerable leisure writing letters about the 'German menace,' one of his friends wrote: "I think it will be a good thing for you, being removed for a time from the German orbit, and I hope you will spend a few years forgetting all about them. I suppose you'll take to making our flesh creep with the Yellow Peril instead." (*Ibid.,* II, 174.)

[49] Harold Nicolson, *Lord Carnock* (Lond., 1930), pp. 171, 224, 311.

[50] *Journals and Letters of Viscount Esher* (Lond., 1934), II, 225, 230, 293–95, 301, 307, 331, 437.

singham and Gardiner of the Daily News brought more understanding to
the Anglo-German problem than any other journalists whose names
come to mind. And yet they belong properly on the middle ground
occupied by Grey himself. Their attitudes sprang largely from their Liberalism, their advocacy of pacific policy so closely associated with the
Liberal ideology, their abhorrence of blatant jingoism involved in Ger-
man-baiting as practiced in the Times and Daily Mail, and in their belief
that the international order should rest on some other basis than military
force.

In one important respect Crowe's memorandum did not reflect current
publicity trends. In his opinion, which was shared by almost the entire
diplomatic personnel, it was Germany's hegemony plans, her political
ambitions, her untrustworthy and aggressive diplomacy that necessitated
counter-measures on Britain's part. Crowe did not place the naval question prominently in the foreground. On the face of it this is surprising
for out of the Moroccan crisis had come an important amendment to
the German naval law (passed on second reading, March 1906). However, it must be recalled that in 1905–6 Fisher introduced the Dreadnought type of battleship. His boast that he had devalued the German
navy at one bold stroke was taken at face value in inner government
councils. The cabinet scaled down expenditures for new construction
during the next three years.[51]

Outside government circles, however, the events of the years 1904–6
had focused public attention on the naval question and established
it as the predominant issue in Anglo-German relations. For the writers
in the press German naval policy became the yardstick by which all
German assurances and protestations of friendship were measured. The
naval question was not simply a problem for the specialists in naval
affairs and politics. Beginning in 1906 it was dramatized for the masses
under the head of "Invasion." Through the press, in plays, and in novels
the fear of a German invasion was planted in thousands of minds. The
father of many sensational invasion stories was the brochure by a young
German general-staff officer, Franz von Edelsheim, published in 1901
under the title "Overseas Operations: A Study." Studying the naval
arm as an adjunct to the army, the author examined the problem of a
surprise landing of six German divisions in England, which would conquer the country even though the main German navy was destroyed by
the British fleet. This booklet became a star witness thereafter in many

<hr/>

[51] For the state of naval opinion in 1906 see *G. P.*, XXIII, 27–53; Austen Chamberlain, *Politics from Inside*, p. 55; Blanche E. C. Dugdale, *Arthur James Balfour*
(2 vols., N. Y., 1937), II, 31–32.

invasion scares.[52] In March 1906, the Daily Mail began publication of the serial by William Le Quex in three parts, "The Invasion of 1910," "The Siege of London," and "The Revenge." The naval chapters were written by H. W. Wilson, a prolific writer on naval affairs and one of the editors of the Daily Mail. "The Invasion of 1910" reproduced the pattern of Edelsheim's technical study—a sudden declaration of war, a naval battle in the North Sea while English forces were weakened by withdrawals for foreign service, and the landing of a German army on the East coast. There were many variations of the topic in subsequent popular literature and the theme was dramatized in the famous invasion play "An Englishman's Home." How seriously these fantasies were taken by the public cannot be determined, but at least they familiarized large numbers of people with the idea of German invasion plans, creating thereby a predisposition to popular response whenever the naval question came before the public and parliament. These same effusions, which were to increase in number during the next four years, must also have contributed powerfully to the acceptance of the thesis that the Germans were striving for European and world hegemony.

Bülow and the Kaiser were at great pains to counteract the agitation in England over the German navy. In public and in private they repeated their well-worn formula that German naval development had no aggressive significance, least of all where England was concerned; it was simply a sensible measure of defense adjusted to their needs as an expanding commercial and colonial power.[53] Far from convincing any British publicist, these assurances merely heightened mistrust. Moreover, it was easy to turn them against Germany by charging that guile and falsity was a peculiar stock-in-trade of German diplomacy.

By the end of 1906 the directors of German policy faced an international situation which four years before they had dismissed as "music of the future." At court, in the Reichstag and in the press dissatisfaction was rife. The words "isolation" and "encirclement" were frequently encountered in the political press. Critics of Bülow's policy became more outspoken during the summer and autumn. Criticism was to be expected from the Pan-Germans and the Socialists, but when the Conservative and

---

[52] It was published as propaganda material during the War under the title, *Germany's Naval Plan of Campaign Against Great Britain and the United States* (Lond., Toronto, N. Y., 1915). "By Freiherr von Edelsheim, in the service of the German General Staff in 1901." See Kehr, *Schlachtflottenbau*, pp. 354–58; Schmitt, *England and Germany*, pp. 210–12; *G. P.*, XVII, 590; H. Lutz, *Eyre Crowe*, pp. 11–26, where the origin of this publication is thoroughly probed.

[53] Bülow's interview with J. L. Bashford, *Nineteenth Century*, December 1904; Reichstag speech, Dec. 5, 1904; interview with Sidney Whitman, *Daily Mail*, Sept. 4, 1906. With William II it became a habit to reassure every Englishman he met.

National Liberal journals began to relate their anxiety over the foreign
situation to Bülow's lack of force and firmness and to criticize his light-
hearted optimism when speaking of their diplomatic position, the chancellor was seriously disturbed.[54] Not only were alarming rumors circulating about the foreign situation but in domestic politics everything
was at sixes and sevens. The Center journalists and politicians were exposing the scandals in the imperial colonial administration. Conservative
journalists complained of a lack of steadiness in the government and
hinted at the "personal régime" as the cause. Harden was beginning his
exposures in the *Zukunft* which were to lead to the shocking Eulenburg
scandals. Everything was shaping up toward the dissolution of the
Reichstag and the famous Hottentot election. "There prevails at present
in Germany a political neurasthenia which is highly deplorable," wrote
Tschirschky to Monts.

In the Reichstag on November 14, Bülow made one of the longest
speeches of his career, lasting fully two hours. It was no jesting, optimistic charmer who spoke this time, but a serious statesman defending his
policy, reassuring his countrymen, and warning Paris, London, and St.
Petersburg of the danger involved in trying to isolate Germany. Bülow
reviewed their relations with each neighbor in turn, and concluded that
Germany was in no immediate danger of isolation; there had been times
when it was much closer than at present. "A nation of sixty millions with
an army such as the German is never isolated, as long as it remains true
to itself, as long as it does not give itself up," he declared. His remarks on
Anglo-German relations constituted one of the most important passages
in his speech. Germany had no desire to force herself in between England and France or England and Russia; good relations between England and Germany were not incompatible with the Entente Cordiale if the
latter pursued peaceful designs. But danger lurked in a policy of exclusive ententes, he warned.

The Entente Cordiale without good relations between the powers and Germany would be a danger to European peace. A policy directed at German encirclement, the creation of a ring of powers around Germany to isolate and
cripple her, that would be a policy dangerous to the peace of Europe. The
creation of such a ring is not possible without exercising a certain pressure.
Pressure produces counter-pressure, and out of pressure and counter-pressure
explosions can finally arise.

[54] How sensitive Bülow was to these criticisms is revealed in a long letter to his
brother (Bülow, *Memoirs*, II, 252–61) in which he deprecated "This continual crying
of stinking fish [which] forges excellent weapons for foreigners to use against us."
See also the correspondence between Tschirschky and Monts (Monts, *Erinnerungen*,
pp. 444–52).

Between Germany and England there was no real cause for misunderstanding, he said. Their naval program was not directed against her, and they had no idea of building a fleet to rival England's; but it was their right and duty to build a fleet commensurate with their overseas interests. He mentioned approvingly the recent visits of German delegations to England, cautioned the journalists to avoid giving injury by engaging in polemics, and prophesied fairer weather for the future. "The needle of the political barometer has happily gone from Rain and Wind to Changing." [55]

Bülow's speech made a strong impression on his immediate hearers, but it did not silence the pessimists and critics in the press. After the first unfavorable press reaction he wrote to Hammann complaining of the unpolitical nature of the Germans and their lack of understanding for foreign affairs. Hammann was requested to launch in the newspapers the idea that his speech had found more understanding in the English, French, Russian, and American press than in the German. "He [Bülow] wants always to be praised in the press," wrote Holstein to his cousin. "That is his misfortune, for the journalists have naturally known it for a long time." [56] It would perhaps be unfair to say that the major objective of Bülow's politics was to be praised by the press, but it was for him the only yardstick by which he measured success and failure. Bülow's oratorical skill could not remove the apprehension in the country; and the press bureau could not turn the barren policy of the preceding years into a success, but there was much truth in one of the chancellor's neat sentences: "In Germany we are all becoming too nervous, both Right and Left, above and below."

[55] *Fürst Bülows Reden,* II, 306–44. The danger of pursuing a policy of exclusive ententes had been the thesis of a semi-official article in the *Deutsche Revue* of September, 1906. Advance proof sheets were sent to the *Times,* which published a summary and a leading article on September 5. The *Times* interpreted the German request for a seat at the Anglo-French table as an attempt to dictate to Great Britain who her friends should be. See also Bertie's memorandum on this article in *B. D.,* III, 385–88.

[56] Holstein, *Lebensbekenntnis,* p. 269; Hammann, *Bilder aus der letzten Kaiserzeit,* pp. 45–46. Bülow's own account is a glowing picture of a great oratorical triumph. (*Memoirs,* II, 289–92.)

CHAPTER XI

INTERVIEWS AND INDISCRETIONS

We publish inelegant extracts from each other's leading articles, we dwell on the indiscretions of our leading public men, and in some subtle way we create an atmosphere in which indiscretions and untoward incidents seem to grow of themselves. This newspaper atmosphere is one of the most difficult things to explain or define, but we all know it and we all yield to it. There comes a moment when the newspapers of the two countries seem to get on each other's nerves, and neither can say or write anything about the other except in a state of acute irritation.

J. A. Spender, Conference on Anglo-German
Understanding, October 30, 1912.

From 1906 to 1909 the diplomatic intercourse between London and Berlin was limited to the settlement of routine business. No projects were initiated, no direct clashes occurred, no important negotiations absorbed the energies and tried the patience of diplomats and officials. The inactivity on this wire was in marked contrast with the great affairs that were settled between London, St. Petersburg, Paris, Madrid, and Tokyo. The Entente wires hummed with activity. Grey's greatest concern was to bring the Russian agreement safely under cover and to consolidate the entente with France. While he was thus occupied his attitude toward the Germans was one of icy reserve. Bülow, on the other hand, lacked the originality, the energy, and the courage requisite for a bold departure in reordering Germany's diplomatic position and in neutralizing the encircling tendencies of the Triple Entente. He was content to hold office, repeat the old slogans and catchwords on all occasions, and like Mr. Micawber wait for the day when something would turn up.[1]

On winning English good will and abating suspicion he lavished the arts of rhetoric and diplomacy, employing the old formulas and the approved techniques. There were Reichstag declarations, newspaper interviews, press maneuvers to counteract Germanophobia, imperial visits

---

[1] Writing to Grey on April 19, 1907, Lascelles complained that Bülow "lets things slide and I am told does absolutely nothing but prepare the brilliant speeches which he makes to the Reichstag." (*B. D.*, VI, 28.) And Tschirschky wrote to Monts on May 25, 1907: "B[ernhard] B[ülow] tut weniger denn je, so dass mir sogar Hammann neulich die Frage stellte, ob ich eigentlich wisse, was B[ülow] den ganzen Tag triebe." (Monts, *Erinnerungen*, p. 451.)

to England, and exchange visits of professional and vocational deputations, much politeness, and many small acts of friendliness and regard. In fact everything was sanctioned and tried that promised to produce favorable press comment, for in so far as Bülow pursued a positive policy toward England it was a publicity policy pure and simple. With the full approval and overzealous co-operation of the Kaiser, Bülow pursued this line until the Daily Telegraph affair brought his house of cards tumbling down and exposed the complete bankruptcy of his policy.

It is the purpose of this chapter to develop the narrative of the major incidents in this three year campaign and to point out their significance. It is not easy to bring the seemingly unrelated events into a pattern of relationship. The efforts of officials to influence the press, the German encirclement fears and alarms, the exchange visits of press delegations, the Kaiser's visit to England, the Tweedmouth letter, and the Daily Telegraph interview present a kaleidoscopic movement of accidents, private intervention and official moves. And yet in all of this there is a detectable design of motive, attitude and action. It is supplied by Bülow's firm faith in the arts of diplomacy and publicity. These he employed to conceal unwelcome realities from the German people, while attempting at the same time to turn foreign suspicion of Germany into good will.

In every conversation between German and English diplomats the press and the state of current publicity became, like the weather in social conversation, a subject of comment and generally of complaint. The German reports, memoranda and marginal comments bristle with strictures on the London press.[2] Although British officials recognized that false news and exaggerated reports circulated by the press worked considerable mischief, they were inclined to take it much more philosophically than the Germans. Grey developed a formula with which he customarily countered Metternich's complaints. "[He] thought it was a great mistake to pay attention to these things. The Press would not lead; it would only follow." [3] He would find the German press equally exasperating if he dwelt on newspaper sensations. Grey and the foreign office officials were reluctant to acknowledge any influence with the journalists; they were unwilling, except on rare occasions, to correct errors and misstatements by issuing *démentis* through Reuter's and other agencies; and they were always extremely cautious about repudiating, on behalf of the govern-

---

[2] "The Emperor seems to have the English press on the brain," wrote Crowe on a dispatch from Lascelles reporting William II's objection to something that had appeared in the *Standard* and the *Illustrated London News*. (*B. D.*, VI, 12–13.)

[3] *Ibid.*, VI, 208. Grey was not consistent. When Metternich would urge upon him the desirability of cabinet members taking the lead, then he would reverse his formula. (*Ibid.*, VI, 90.)

ment, senseless articles or aggravating lampoons.[4] The German tradition of attempting to guide and influence the press in the interest of governmental policy was in sharp contrast to English practices. The Germans could never quite believe that the English were sincere in this matter. The relations of the government to the press constituted a basic misunderstanding between London and Berlin.[5]

The documentary record reveals one instance of an English minister intervening directly to influence the press. Haldane was closer to Metternich than any other cabinet member and was most active in the work of conciliation after the Algeciras Conference. His efforts were directed, in part, toward moderating the tone of a group of British publications. He called on Mr. Buckle, the editor of the Times, and endeavored to bring him around to a more moderate attitude, but without success. He also saw Strachey, the editor of the *Spectator*. Maxse of the *National Review* was "a madman" with whom nothing could be done; and the editor of the weekly *Outlook* swam in the same current. Haldane had more success with the editor of the Tribune and prevailed upon him to take a more conciliatory line. The Westminster Gazette and the Daily News were, of course, already friendly toward Germany. The fanaticism of the others, Haldane thought, was so well known and so completely discounted that they exercised little influence. Metternich dissented from this view, pointing out that the *National Review,* the crudest of the agitators, had become one of the most widely circulated periodicals among the British élite.[6] Altogether, Haldane's efforts achieved very little.

No truce in press attacks, friendship demonstrations, or reassuring words from Bülow could rid German politicians and publicists of the fear of coalitions and encirclement. Black pessimism, which gave rise to attacks on the chancellor, the foreign office and even individual German diplomats, weighed heavily on the country. In 1907 newspaper scares and alarms followed every manifestation of Entente activity. For pur-

[4] Sharp disapproval was elicited, for example, by the naval attaché's apology to Tirpitz for a *Punch* cartoon on the German navy. *Ibid.,* VI, 3. For an instance of Grey's attitude toward issuing official denials through the press see *G. P.,* XXI, 428–29.

[5] With regard to the British view of the German press, Crowe alone among British officials was consistent. Every aspect of publicity unfavorable or derogatory to England he attributed to the official inspiration or encouragement of the German press bureau.

[6] Metternich to Bülow, May 8, 1906; *G. P.,* XXI, 427–31. On another occasion Metternich wrote: "The Englishman, even the educated Englishman, is apt to think that his monthly reviews exert no political influence because they are only read by the few. I am not of that opinion. The impulse that influences the masses proceeds from the few, and even abstract scientific thoughts, if they are deep and stirring and contain a new truth, will form the minds of a new generation." Quoted by Bülow, *Memoirs,* II, 41.

poses of illustration we shall consider two incidents: first, King Edward's Mediterranean cruise and his meetings with the Italian and Spanish sovereigns; and second, the preliminaries of the Hague Conference.

In the German public mind King Edward had become the personal symbol of a campaign to isolate Germany and divest her of international importance. This was the theme of an article appearing in the Neue Freie Presse on the occasion of his meeting with the King of Spain at Cartagena and with the Italian sovereign at Gaeta, early in April 1907. The article was reproduced and commented on in the Kölnische Zeitung. It produced a panic in banking and political circles in Germany. Lascelles described the incident in a dispatch to Grey. "The day before yesterday, Berlin went stark staring raving mad," wrote the British ambassador. "There was a fall of six points in German securities on the Bourse and a general impression that war was about to break out between England and Germany." To check the panic the foreign office published a positive reassurance in the Kölnische Zeitung, which in Lascelles' opinion "calmed people's minds and brought them back to a state approaching sanity." Lascelles attributed the ridiculous fears entertained in Germany to the lack of a responsible and energetic statesman at the head of affairs capable of checking or directing public opinion.[7]

The same nervous suspicion was exhibited in connection with the discussion of the disarmament question and the approaching Hague Conference. Campbell-Bannerman had started the ball rolling in his article on "The Hague Conference and the Limitation of Armaments," published in the *Nation* on March 2, 1907. (The article "disgusted" King Edward.) The subjects of German encirclement and isolation and the limitation of armaments were considered together in a full dress debate on foreign affairs in the Reichstag on April 30. Taking the press comment before and after the debate and reducing it to the simple formula of the "man in the street" we get the following result: "First England isolates us and now seeks to disarm us." Here and there in the press it was bluntly stated that the object of British diplomacy was to isolate Germany at the coming conference and to brand her before the world as the disturber of the peace.[8]

[7] *B. D.,* VI, 28; Lee, *King Edward VII,* II, 538–44; also Cartwright's description of this incident and the general nervousness and tension in Germany, *B. D.,* VI, 29–32.

[8] "England und die Abrüstungs Frage," *Schwäbischer Merkur,* No. 155, April 4; "Keine Nervosität," *ibid.,* No. 183, April 20; "Zur Weltlage," *ibid.,* No. 190, April 25; *Münchner N. N.,* Nos. 205, 216, May 1, 8; *Daily Mail,* Berlin correspondence (April 12, 18) quoting *Die Post, Reichsbote, Rheinisch-Westfälische Ztg., Kölnische Ztg., Berliner Tageblatt, Tägliche Rundschau,* and *Deutsche Tagesztg.; Times* Berlin correspondence, May 1; *Manchester Guardian,* May 3. *B. D.,* VI, 15, 28.

It was incomprehensible to Englishmen that such an interpretation of their foreign policy could be seriously held in Germany. On the other hand, the view entertained in England that German policy aimed at world hegemony and the destruction of the British Empire seemed ridiculous to Germans. Many people, under the circumstances, concluded that the Anglo-German problem was just an unfortunate misunderstanding arising from irrational fears and a lack of accurate and reliable knowledge. Since the press was the recorder and stimulator of these inaccurate and misleading views, many thought that the press itself was fundamentally at fault and that the journalists had become conscious propagandists of misunderstanding. This train of thought led logically to the conclusion that if English editors had more knowledge of Germany, and if the Germans likewise could come to England and see for themselves how unfounded were their suspicions as to British aggressiveness, the misunderstanding which lay at the bottom of Anglo-German tension would be removed. This was the line of thought that prompted the exchange of visits between leading English and German press representatives in 1906 and 1907. As Theodor Barth expressed it, they wanted the journalists to see the other country "through their own eyes and not through their old prejudices." The original suggestion for the visits came from the peace apostle, W. T. Stead, who interested the Anglo-German Friendship Committee and the journalistic organizations in the proposal. Enthusiastic support in organizing the exchange of hospitality was given by the editors of the two leading Liberal journals, J. A. Spender of the Westminster Gazette and A. G. Gardiner of the Daily News.

During the week of June 20–28, 1906, the German journalists were entertained in England. The party of fifty editors and publicists who made the trip included the most prominent journalists in Germany. Excluding the Social Democratic press, whose directors refused to participate in this bourgeois fraternization, every important German newspaper was represented. In the party were: Hermann Ten Brink of Germania, Paul Dehn of the Reichsbote, Friedrich Dernburg of the Berliner Tageblatt, Dr. Grunwald of the Vossische Zeitung, Hugo von Kupffer of the Lokal-Anzeiger, Dr. Rippler of the Tägliche Rundschau, Otto Runge of the Norddeutsche, Dr. Fitger of the Weser-Zeitung, Ernst Posse, editor of the Kölnische Zeitung, Dr. Drill of the Frankfurter Zeitung, together with the editors of the leading papers in Hamburg, Hanover, Karlsruhe, Königsberg, Leipzig, Magdeburg, Munich, and Stuttgart. Some of the participants had distinguished themselves in the past by their Anglophobia, particularly in the Boer War period; and for them this journey may have been a pilgrimage of repentance. Their reception and entertainment in London was beyond reproach. Considerable publicity was given the movements of the delegation in the Liberal journals and in the Daily Telegraph, but the visit made no great stir outside of professional circles. In the various social affairs arranged for the visitors, a number of cabinet ministers participated, notably Lloyd George, Mr. Bryce, Winston Churchill, and Haldane. Grey and the foreign office officials held aloof. The Times, the Morning Post, and the Daily Mail refused to co-operate in any way in the reception and entertainment of the guests. Moberly Bell and Arthur Walter attended, as private persons, a banquet given by Alfred Rothschild in honor of the German visitors.

In the German press the publicity given to the visit was complete to the minutest detail, which was not surprising since the leading editors and journalists made up the party. A number of the participants put their observations and impressions into articles that were published in the daily and periodical press. These reports reveal the good impression made on the German guests by the hospitality and good fellowship which they enjoyed in England.[9]

When a delegation of forty British journalists returned the visit next year (May 27–June 7) they went as the invited guests of the German press, but found themselves the central point of a national good will demonstration. The Times and Daily Mail had agitated against the visit and, together with the Morning Post, *National Review,* and *Spectator,* were, of course, unrepresented.[10] In its news reports from Berlin, the Times ignored the delegation until the German under-secretary, Mühlberg, delivered an important political pronouncement at a banquet for the British visitors. The Times in reporting the speech had to inform its readers that a party of British editors was visiting Germany! With the exceptions just mentioned, the leading Liberal and Conservative-Unionist papers of London and the provinces were represented. Among the outstanding members of the delegation were J. A. Spender of the Westminster Gazette, Gardiner of the Daily News, Sidebotham of the Man-

[9] I have drawn for this account upon a dissertation for the master's degree in the University of Virginia Library by Mr. Francis F. Wayland, entitled, "Anglo-German Press Relations, 1906–1907." Further, W. T. Stead's report in *Review of Reviews,* vol. XXIV (1906); for the list of the German journalists and affiliations, *Daily Telegraph,* June 20, 1906. For the attitude of the British foreign office see B. D., III, 359–62.

[10] *Times,* May 2, 1907, letter from "Journalist" urging that British editors refuse the German invitation. The Berlin correspondent of the *Daily Mail,* F. W. Wile, reported that the English journalists would not be welcome in Germany. (May 21, 22.) When events proved the contrary he played the visit down. *Daily Mail,* May 28, 29, 30, June 1, 1907.

chester Guardian, Pryor of the Tribune, Lucien Wolf of the Daily
Graphic, F. J. Higginbottom of the Pall Mall Gazette, Sidney Low of
the Standard, J. Ellershaw of the Daily Telegraph, W. Wetherell of the
Liverpool Post, J. S. R. Phillips of the Yorkshire Post, and J. Davidson
of the Glasgow Herald. The *Empire Review* was represented by Sir C.
Kinloch Cooke and the *Review of Reviews* by W. T. Stead. Headed by
Prince Hatzfeldt an official reception committee had been organized in
Germany with membership drawn from the highest levels of official,
academic, and business life.

The visit to Berlin took place in an atmosphere of high politics. They
had an informal audience with the Emperor at Potsdam, Bülow entertained them at a garden party, and official Berlin turned out to the
great banquet given in their honor at the Zoological Garden. At least
three officials of highest ministerial rank, among them Tirpitz, Mühlberg, Posadowsky, Dernburg, Bethmann-Hollweg, and Bülow, attended
every function arranged for the visitors. Extending an official welcome
at the banquet, Von Mühlberg assured the guests that German armaments were purely defensive, that their foreign policy was pacific in
spirit, and that they desired cordial relations with England. Mr. Spender,
speaking for his British colleagues, stamped their visit with a political
purpose when he said: "We are here not only to enjoy your hospitality,
but to take counsel together and to see if we cannot help our two countries in their relations with each other." At Dresden, Munich, Frankfort, and Cologne, the British delegation was entertained by local provincial committees; wherever they went in South Germany they noted
the same good will and desire for British friendship. In the Rhineland
they were the object of friendly popular demonstrations.

The publicity that accompanied the visit was astounding. From two to
five columns daily were given to chronicling the speeches and the activities of the group in every leading journal in Berlin and the provinces.
The reports of the British journalists, appearing in the English press,
were taken by the news agencies and the special correspondents and
telegraphed back to Germany to heighten the publicity effect.[11] The impressions of J. A. Spender, A. G. Gardiner, Sidney Low and Mr. Sidebotham were reproduced verbatim in the German press. From the reports of those who participated in the visit one universal impression
emerges, namely, that the German people were sincerely desirous of good
relations with Great Britain. An extremely sour note was injected into

[11] The *Münchner N. N.*, for example, published from one to three columns daily
on the front page. Nos. 246, 254, 255, 257, 263, 264, 266, May 28, June 2, 3, 4, 7, 8, 9.
Likewise the *Kölnische Zeitung, Berliner Tageblatt, Vossische Zeitung, Frankfurter
Zeitung,* and *Norddeutsche.*

all this by the editors of the Times and the Daily Mail, who worked to destroy the impressions of the visit by insinuating that the delegation had only seen the equivalent of Potemkin's Russian villages. Maxse in the *National Review* and Garvin in the *Fortnightly* were depreciatory and cynical toward the whole affair. Garvin asserted that the participants had been induced "to place their political judgment under chloroform," that they had been "compromised" by an "irrelevant hospitality" and had since "constituted themselves the apologists for German policy." [12]

What was accomplished by these visits and exchanges of hospitality? The tangible results were not great and the intangible results are difficult to assess. We can, however, detect here and there signs of the revision of old points of reference from which the journalist wrote his articles on foreign affairs. For example, the Manchester Guardian leaders ceased to present the German nation as a police-ridden people crushed by absolutism and militarism. The Radical editors had seen enough of municipal socialism in German towns and cities to destroy the old illusion that the people were struggling under a reactionary feudal despotism. It is strange to read in the Manchester Guardian a dispatch from Mr. Sidebotham describing Germany's position in Europe and her geographical-military necessities, and cautiously suggesting that "more allowance should be made in England for the fact that the army is regarded as a national institution in a sense that is quite unknown in England." The idea is expanded in a later editorial: "Both countries [England and Germany] in some sort are island Powers, the one in the sea, the other in Europe. Transfer to the German Army all the conservative sentiment that the Englishman feels toward his fleet, and we are in a way to understand how the German can seem army-mad to our eyes and yet boast himself as unaggressive on land as we at sea, and with equal sincerity." [13] Those who participated in the German tour undoubtedly gained in objectivity.

Mr. Spender, according to a dispatch from Metternich, returned from Berlin convinced that only groundless misunderstanding prevented complete reconciliation. What was needed at this point was action by the two governments and he suggested certain questions which might be used as a basis of negotiation—the Bagdad Railway, the Far East, and the

---

[12] *Times,* May 31, 1907; *National Review,* July 1907, p. 683; *Fortnightly Review,* July 1907, pp. 156–57. Sidney Low's article in the *Contemporary Review* (July 1907, pp. 1–16) represents the opposing viewpoint; also J. Mackinnon, *The British Journalists in Germany* (Aberdeen, 1907). F. J. Higginbottom, who represented the *Pall Mall Gazette,* has described the visit in his memoirs, *The Vivid Life* (Lond., 1934), pp. 190–97; and Spender has recounted his impressions in *Life, Journalism and Politics,* I, 201 ff.; also Frederic Whyte, *Life of W. T. Stead,* II, 283–86.

[13] *Manchester Guardian,* June 10, July 4, 1907.

Congo. But the net result of the visit for Spender seems to have been disillusionment. He tells us in his memoirs that from Mühlberg's welcoming speech to the journalists he received the distinct impression that the end of naval competition was in sight. But "when the new Naval Law of April, 1908, appeared . . . I felt that I had been misled, and that no further assurances from the Germans about shipbuilding were worth anything." [14]

In the long run nothing fundamental in Anglo-German relations was altered by the reciprocal visits. Daily journalism depended on events and occurrences which were recorded in the press and subjected to commentary. However much good will the publicists brought to their daily task they could not direct or alter the course of events. Without parliamentary or public support, the *Reklame* for improvement in relations, resulting from direct journalistic action, could not counteract Grey's unenterprising nature or overcome the influence of his advisers. Fleet Street alone could not dominate Downing Street.

While direct journalistic action was incapable of shifting the axis of British policy, it did result in a temporary cessation of gratuitous attacks and recrimination. Edward VII's visit to Wilhelmshöhe in August, the announcement of the Anglo-Russian agreement in September, and William II's visit to England in November, therefore, occurred in a favorable publicity atmosphere. Not too much was made of the meeting of the sovereigns in the press of either country, but Bülow improved the occasion by releasing an interview through J. L. Bashford, which was packed with his customary expressions of official optimism.[15] When the signing of the Anglo-Russian accord was announced, a month before publication, Bülow noted instructions for the press bureau. "It is important," he wrote, "that the agreement be received quietly and objectively if, as I assume, it corresponds to assurances given us by England and Russia, and is not puffed up as an Anglo-Russian alliance or represented unnecessarily as injurious to German interests." [16] The British press made acceptance of this view of the accord easy, for they treated it as an Asiatic agreement without significance for European alignments.[17]

[14] *Life, Journalism and Politics,* I, 205; *G. P.,* XXI, 516.
[15] *Westminster Gazette,* Aug. 16, 1907.
[16] Marginal note, Sept. 1, 1907; *G. P.,* XXV, 40.
[17] While the editors of the *Guardian* and the *Daily News* pulled long faces over the capitulation to Russian autocracy, the agreement had a good press in England. *Daily News,* Sept. 25; *Manchester Guardian,* Sept. 26, 27; *Times,* Sept. 26; *Pall Mall Gazette,* Sept. 25; *Daily Mail,* Sept. 26; *Westminster Gazette,* Sept. 25; *Glasgow Herald,* Sept. 26. Earlier in the summer a number of Socialists and Radicals had published a joint protest in the *Times* (June 11). Among the signers were: Ramsay Macdonald, G. B. Shaw, George Cadbury, John Galsworthy, J. A. Hobson, Fisher Unwin, Justin McCarthy, and R. S. Watson.

In all the leading German papers the agreement was received and commented on in the sense indicated and recommended by Bülow. It was emphasized that Berlin had been consulted by both parties whenever German interests were involved; that although the agreement had its inception in the period of the *Einkreisungspolitik,* it was deprived of any point against Germany by the rapprochement that had since been effected between Berlin and London; and that German economic interests in Persia were fully safeguarded by the adherence of both parties to the principle of the open door.[18]

This era of good feeling continued through the period of William II's state visit to England in November. On this occasion toleration and forbearance in handling certain potentially disturbing incidents enabled officials to avoid embarrassment and to thwart the activity of mischief makers. One such incident occurred in connection with preliminary arrangements for the visit, and in itself illustrates how the intervention of the press can influence directly, without reference to public opinion, the course of foreign affairs. When the journey was first announced, it was reported in the press that Bülow would accompany his sovereign to England. The King and the cabinet wanted William II to come, and were much exercised when a sudden imperial whim threatened to upset all plans; but Grey and Hardinge, the latter permanent chief of the foreign office, did not want Bülow to accompany the Kaiser. For this would advertise the political importance of the affair and might create misgivings in Paris. To prevent this Grey pointed to Bülow's unpopularity in England and the danger of press polemics, and Hardinge wrote Lascelles that the editor of "a very important paper" had already informed him that he proposed to publish an article making clear that Bülow's presence would be unwelcome. On October 10, the Times brought a leading article attacking the chancellor as the originator of all mistrust of German diplomacy, declaring that his foreign policy had collapsed in consequence of England's ententes, while Fisher's surprise Dreadnoughts had postponed the realization of his naval aims. Responsibility for the insults and calumnies of the Boer War period were charged to him, and it was suggested that he wanted to come to England as a penitent for his past misbehavior. Lascelles thought the article, which was probably

[18] *Kölnische Ztg.,* 1005, Sept. 27; *Norddeutsche,* No. 229, Sept. 29; *Süddeutsche Reichskorrespondenz* quoted by *Schwäbischer Merkur,* No. 454, Sept. 28; *Münchner N. N.,* Nos. 416, 453, 462, Sept. 6, 27, Oct. 3 (Berlin telegrams); *Frankfurter Ztg.,* No. 267, Sept. 26; *Kölnische Volksztg.,* No. 837, Sept. 27; *Vossische Ztg.,* No. 454, Sept. 27; *Berliner Tageblatt,* No. 495, Sept. 29 (weekly review of politics). William II was not taken in by all the window dressing; he realized that the agreement by and large was unfavorable to Germany's position in Europe. (*G. P.,* XXV, 45, 47; marginal comments.)

from Chirol's pen, "intentionally mischievous," calculated to provoke polemics in the German press with a view to spoiling the good will effect of the imperial visit.

And so it might have done if prompt counter-measures had not been taken. Writing in the Westminster the same evening, Spender delivered a semi-official repudiation of the venomous attack.

If it were not that the *Times* gives itself something more than a semi-official air in its article this morning on certain aspects of the German Emperor's visit to this country, we might afford to pass its observations in silence as a characteristic outburst from a quarter where anti-Germanism is a kind of obsession. . . . It seems necessary to say as clearly and promptly as possible that the *Times* is not speaking either for the Government or, as we firmly believe, for the public in this matter, but solely for itself and the comparatively few who share its limited and prejudiced point of view.

The prompt repudiation by the Westminster and the general condemnation which the Times' spiteful article provoked in other journals, averted angry replies from the German press. Grey seemed embarrassed and regretful, but at the same time he was greatly relieved when Bülow definitely abandoned the idea of accompanying the Emperor and, instead, sent Schoen, who had just displaced Tschirschky as foreign secretary. Writing to Hammann, the press director, Bülow cited as his reason for refraining from the visit the fact that no English prime minister or foreign secretary had accompanied an English sovereign to Germany in twenty-nine years. While he was not a stickler for form, he said, a certain reciprocity in such matters had to be observed.[19]

No jarring note from the press disturbed the pleasant exchange of amenities during the state visit, which lasted from November 10 to 18. Schoen released an interview to Reuter's Agency full of the usual diplomatic platitudes; a party of English journalists, who had made the trip to Germany in June, was received by the Emperor at the German embassy; and after conclusion of the formal visit the Emperor went to Highcliffe Castle, near Bournemouth, which had been placed at his disposal by an English friend and admirer, Colonel Stuart Wortley.

It was here in the circle of German companions and English friends that the Emperor engaged in those political discussions which provided the material for the famous Daily Telegraph interview which was to

[19] *B. D.*, VI, 81–90; *G. P.*, XXIV, 15–16; Hammann, *Bilder aus der letzten Kaiserzeit*, p. 49; Lee, *King Edward VII*, II, 553–63. Grey's assumption that political capital would be made out of the visit to the injury of their relations to France was unfounded. Bülow impressed it upon Hammann that the visit must be handled by the press with the greatest tact and that Germany desired not only good relations with England but also general peace and quiet.

startle the world a year later. Fully two thirds of that interview was devoted to the explanation of his own actions and his country's attitude toward England during the Boer War. How did the conversations at Highcliffe Castle take this particular historical turn? The Times in its attack on Bülow had given a wholly one-sided account of German policy during those painful years. Moreover, while William was at Highcliffe Castle, the December issue of the *National Review* appeared with an article which claimed to give an authentic account of German attempts to form a coalition against Britain during the South African War.[20] This article, or the Times' leader, may have been the point of departure for the Kaiser's declarations to Stuart Wortley and his circle. One thing is certain, William II was trying to set everyone right on the intervention story and to put German policy in a favorable light before his English hosts. His remarks on these topics were even conveyed directly to the English public through the press. An interview with J. L. Bashford was published in the popular *Strand Magazine,* one of the Emperor's favorite periodicals, in January 1908. It caused no trouble. But another interview, appearing in the Manchester Daily Dispatch, was almost a rehearsal, without the repercussions, of the Daily Telegraph incident.

On December 4 the Manchester paper published what purported to be an interview with the Emperor, in which he warmly repudiated Pan-Germanic aims and ambitions as they affected Germany's neighbors, and ridiculed the idea of a war between England and Germany. Reuter's Agency, on official authority, denied the authenticity of the interview. When the London correspondent of the Dispatch revealed that the manuscript notes had been submitted in advance to the German embassy and there corrected and approved, a second announcement was forthcoming from Reuter's. From this it appears that the enterprising journalist had pieced together his interview from information passed on by a guest at Highcliffe Castle, and that the manuscript was then sent to the embassy where its publication was authorized on condition that the contents be labeled as the views of "many personages in Germany." Fortunately, the English papers, with the exception of the Times and the Daily Mail (Dec. 4, 5, 6), ignored the incident and it was not wired to Germany by the news agencies. Since it contained many of the statements later appearing in the Daily Telegraph it might, however, have been exploited in a mischievous fashion if English editors had desired to play it up.

Equally remarkable was the forbearance of the British press toward the Kaiser's indiscretion in writing his well-known letter to Lord Tweed-

---

[20] "Germany and England; Some Unpublished Pages of German Diplomacy," by "Ignotus."

mouth shortly after his return to Germany. In this letter he strongly protested the attempts then being made to raise a scare in England over the
new German navy law, and the tendency even in official circles to define
British needs in terms of Germany's new program. After Admiral Fisher
launched the first Dreadnought, no battleship construction was undertaken in Germany for over a year. The supplementary law of 1906 indicated that the Germans would follow the English lead, but Tirpitz
really entered the building competition in the new type with the supplementary law of 1908. This bill reduced the life of battleships from
twenty-five to twenty years and provided for regular replacement of the
older types by Dreadnoughts. The replacement program and the schedule
of new ship construction were merged; this combined schedule called
for four Dreadnoughts annually for the years 1908–11, two ships annually from 1912 to 1917, and three ships annually thereafter as a permanent rate.[21] On the day after the Emperor left Windsor and returned to
Highcliffe Castle (November 18), the draft of the proposed supplementary law was published in the Norddeutsche. While William II was
still in England and before the Reichstag began consideration of the
measure, British press comment was guarded.[22] But soon navalists began
to demand that the German challenge in this newest and most formidable
type of vessel be met by providing proportional increases in the British
estimates, which were then being considered by the cabinet. In anticipation of the naval budget for the year 1908–9, Grey, Haldane, and Tweedmouth spoke in political meetings on British armament needs, the Navy
League issued a public manifesto, and in the press the forthcoming estimates were a subject of comment and speculation. It was quite natural
that the German naval law, then before the Reichstag, should have occupied a prominent place in this discussion.[23]

A split in the Liberal cabinet over armaments expenditure encouraged
the agitation. A considerable group of Radicals in the Commons, through
their leaders in the ministry, were demanding material reductions in the
interest of economy and social security legislation. According to reports
coming from cabinet sources, reductions in the 1908 estimates had twice

[21] Tirpitz, Memoirs, I, 265–68; E. L. Woodward, Great Britain and the German
Navy (Oxford, 1935), pp. 153–56; B. D., VI, 68–76, analysis of the law by the British
naval attaché.
[22] W. T. Stead endeavored to repeat his journalistic feat of 1884 in his "Truth
About the Navy" campaign by writing in the Review of Reviews on "Plain Talk
About the Navy." His article attracted some attention in the daily press but did not
start a big scare. Times, Nov. 19, Dec. 31; Pall Mall Gazette, Nov. 20; Daily Mail,
Nov. 25, Dec. 23, 26; Manchester Guardian, Dec. 20, 1907; G. P., XXIV, 25.
[23] See the reports of Metternich, Stumm, and the German naval attaché during
December 1907 and January 1908, G. P., XXIV, 25–32; Tirpitz, Aufbau, pp. 67 ff.

been made at their demand. And still they were not satisfied. The Radical bloc in the Commons was in revolt and five ministers—Lloyd George, Harcourt, and Burns were the leaders—threatened to resign if further reductions were not made. By agreement a Radical amendment from the floor was postponed until the scheduled time for debating the army and navy estimates. Meanwhile, the army appropriation was slightly pared to make a showing of economy. All this occurred during the first week of February.[24]

The strongest argument against the Radical case was the new German navy law; and it was pushed well into the foreground. It was in consequence of the public discussion and agitation over the German program that the Emperor addressed a letter direct to Lord Tweedmouth protesting vehemently against press exploitation of the German bogey for party purposes. "It is absolutely nonsensical and untrue that the German Naval Bill is to provide a Navy meant as a 'Challenge to British Naval Supremacy,'" wrote the Emperor. He then gave an *ex parte* analysis of the new bill, which was designed solely to meet Germany's minimum defense requirements. England ought to arrange her naval program on the same basis and leave Germany out of the discussion. "For it is very galling for the Germans to see their country continually held up as the sole danger and menace to Britain by the whole press of the different contending parties considering that other countries are building too and there are even larger fleets than the German." He then repudiated as a gross calumny the statement made by Lord Esher in a published letter to the Imperial Maritime League, in which the Deputy Governor of Windsor Castle, said that every German from the Emperor down wished the downfall of Sir John Fisher.[25] "Now I am at a loss to tell whether the supervision of the foundations and drains of the Royal Palaces is apt to qualify somebody for the judgment of Naval Affairs in general. As far as regards German affairs naval the phrase is a piece of unmitigated balderdash. . . ."[26] This highly irregular action in addressing directly the minister of a foreign government angered King Edward, to whom his nephew had also written informing him of his letter to Tweedmouth, and it nettled Grey and his advisers. Tweedmouth wrote a personal note in reply; Edward responded in a letter in which he clearly showed his displeasure over this "new departure," and the foreign office prepared a

[24] Details of the cabinet crisis in *Journals and Letters of Viscount Esher*, II, 280–84.

[25] An outgrowth of the Fisher-Beresford quarrel, Esher's letter was addressed to the recently organized Imperial Maritime League refusing to support its proposed investigation of Fisher's administration of the navy. *Daily Telegraph*, Feb. 6, 1908.

[26] The letter is reproduced in *G. P.*, XXIV, 32–35; Tirpitz, *Aufbau*, pp. 58–61.

memorandum defending the English press in its citation of the German naval program as one of the factors which authorities must take into account in determining their naval requirements.[27]

There the matter might have ended but for Tweedmouth's indiscretion in talking everywhere about the letter. Soon it was common gossip in the clubs. The debate on the estimates was scheduled for the first week in March; the cabinet had finally agreed on expenditures, but the rank and file Radicals in the Commons were threatening revolt. On March 6 the Times published a letter from Colonel Repington, its military correspondent, under the sensational heading "Under Which King?" revealing that the Emperor had written direct to Tweedmouth, and charging that "this letter amounts to an attempt to influence in German interests, the Minister responsible for our Navy Estimates." The coup had been concerted in advance between Repington, Buckle, and Chirol and the letter was supported by a leading article describing the Kaiser's communication as an underhand attempt to retard British building and "to make it more easy for German preparations to overtake our own." [28] Serious repercussions were anticipated by Metternich and Bülow, who were taken quite unawares, and preparations were made to publish the correspondence if matters became serious.[29]

Had such a bomb been exploded in 1905 it would have started a dangerous conflagration. As it was, it produced sensational headlines, but no anti-German campaign. On the contrary, the Times was generally denounced for its attempt to raise a scare by the violation of private correspondence. Of fifteen London and provincial papers only two approved the Times' action.[30] It may have been envy that inspired the Daily Mail to rebuke the Times; but whatever the motive it left no one in doubt where it stood. The imputation of a German plot to compromise a British minister in his proper allegiance was dismissed as "neither more nor less than a mare's nest." "The indiscretion, if there is one, lies with the men who told the Times military correspondent about it, and with the Times for making the worst instead of the best of it." The whole episode, it said, was trivial, having about it the "touch of comedy rather than of

[27] G. P., XXIV, 35–47; B. D., VI, 132–36; Lee, King Edward VII, II, 606–9; Esher, Letters and Journals, II, 285–89.

[28] Times, March 6; Charles À Court Repington, Vestigia, pp. 284–86. The provincial papers had advance notice of the letter and the editorial. Everything was done apparently to assure the widest publicity.

[29] Two considerations prevented immediate publication: the Emperor's racy reference to Esher, and Tweedmouth's communication to William II of a copy of the British estimates in advance of their presentation to parliament. There was a double indiscretion; William II was exposed, Tweedmouth was not.

[30] All are quoted in the Westminster Gazette, March 7, 1908.

tragedy." [31] In parliament, the matter was handled with great tact by Asquith, while the opposition suppressed any desire it may have had to make party capital out of the indiscretion. Bitter attacks were, of course, made on the Times by the German journalists, but the complete repudiation of its tactics by the English press and the skillful way in which the matter was disposed of in parliament met with appreciative comment in all the leading papers.[32] In so far as the Times' coup represented an effort to stir up trouble in the press and make bad blood between the two countries it was a complete failure.

It was not, however, without effect upon British naval politics. Repington himself repudiated any design to stir up trouble between England and Germany. "But our object was not to embroil England and Germany but to warn the Kaiser off the grass, and to fire a shot among the Radical geese who were preventing the Cabinet from doing its duty." [33] In a second communication to the Times, published a week after the Tweedmouth exposé, Repington explained the motives underlying the original publication. "I had observed with much anxiety that our Navy Estimates had apparently been twice revised owing to pressure from the left wing of the party in power. I saw plain evidence of a weakening of the Government's purpose at a psychological moment . . . when firmness and tenacity were indispensable for the future security of the State. The German Emperor graciously supplied the tonic indispensable for the health of his Majesty King Edward's Ministers." [34] The Tweedmouth incident placed the Liberal ministry at a disadvantage in resisting Conservative pressure on the naval issue. So it was that Balfour secured for the first time an unqualified pledge from Asquith that the cabinet would institute a program of Dreadnought building during the next three years that would positively assure British superiority over Germany in this class. On March 14 Lord Esher noted in his journal: "The event of the past few days has been the success of A. J. B. in drawing from Asquith a declaration about the Navy, which never would have been obtained but for the Kaiser's letter. . . . So good has come out of evil, if evil it was." [35]

---

[31] *Daily Mail*, March 7, 9, 10.

[32] Particularly the *Frankfurter Ztg., Vossische Ztg., Berliner Tageblatt, Münchner N. N., Schwäbischer Merkur, Kölnische Volksztg., Kreuzzeitung* and *Kölnische Ztg.*, issues of March 9 and 10, 1908. For the brief statements by Asquith, Tweedmouth, Lansdowne, and Rosebery see *Parl. Deb.*, 4th Ser., vol. 185, 1067, 1072–77.

[33] Repington, *Vestigia*, p. 291. Esher's prediction that "Repington will have ruined his chances of keeping in touch with Government Officials after this business," was not borne out by subsequent events. (*Journals and Letters*, II, 293.)

[34] *Times*, March 1, 1908.

[35] *Letters and Journals*, II, 295. *Parl. Deb.*, 4th Ser. vol. 185, 1335–38.

Shortly after the Tweedmouth episode a general shake-up in the cabinet brought McKenna to the admiralty and Lloyd George to the exchequer. In framing the estimates for 1908–9, the Radicals had had their way. The new construction program for the year 1908 provided for only two new vessels of the Dreadnought type. And while the total estimates showed an increase, the amount to be spent on new construction was less than had been spent the previous year. Everyone at all conversant with naval affairs realized that the new German Dreadnought program was a fact that would have to be faced the next year if England were not to be outnumbered in this category in 1911 or 1912. As early as May 5, 1908, McKenna agreed to present to the cabinet an admiralty program specifying four Dreadnoughts in the 1909 estimates, and, if necessary, six. Fisher was jubilant.[36] The Liberal ministers were apprehensive. The vast increase in expenditure that would be required to maintain British supremacy in Dreadnoughts, threatened the program of social security legislation to which the party and its leaders were pledged. While the Radical press inveighed against uneconomic expenditure for armaments, the Conservative-Unionist journals puffed the threat to British naval supremacy, partly out of real concern, but also partly to smother and discredit the socialistic measures of the government. Out of the clash of opposing social and political philosophies emerged a serious problem affecting Britain's relations to Germany. If the Liberal government could reach an agreement with Germany on restriction of shipbuilding, which would obviate the need for a colossal construction program in 1909, Britain's naval margin would remain unaffected, their social security program would be assured, and their Conservative-Unionist opponents would be deprived of a powerful weapon of political agitation and obstruction. Here was a chance to dish the Germans as well as the Conservatives. Thus domestic polity furnishes the key to Anglo-German relations during 1908.

Into the details of the many diplomatic approaches, official and semi-official, that were made to the Germans in this matter we need not go. The importance of the naval question to the British government and public was the theme of numerous dispatches from Metternich. Almost every conversation he had with influential men pivoted on this issue. When Lloyd George visited Germany, ostensibly to study social security systems, he endeavored, unsuccessfully, to get in touch with Bülow for a discussion of the naval problem. Another avenue of approach was sought through conversations between Ballin and Cassel. When King Edward visited William II at Homburg in August, Sir Charles Hardinge,

---

[36] Fisher to Esher, May 5, 1908; Esher, *Journals and Letters,* II, 309–10.

in the easy atmosphere of the billiard room, broached the subject of German naval construction in a conversation with the Emperor. It only brought him a snub and a flat refusal to consider any suggestion from another country as to the proper measure of German armament. During the autumn and winter inconclusive discussions took place between Berlin and London on a possible deal in which political concessions by England would be bartered for a reduction in the German building rate of capital ships. When the Germans suggested a neutrality pledge, this was interpreted in the foreign office as a demand for repudiation of their ententes with France and Russia. The British took even less kindly to this proposal than the Germans had to the suggestion that they guarantee England's naval supremacy by gearing their construction rate down to the exigencies of the English exchequer and the tax sensitivity of the British electorate. No one can blame the British for desiring to equate naval predominance with low expenditure, neither can one blame the Germans for sticking to their naval law in the face of British cultivation of a system of ententes that deprived German diplomacy of all freedom of movement.[37]

During the summer of 1908 two notable demonstrations of Entente policy and friendship created alarm and perturbation in Germany and revived the panic of the previous year over encirclement. Toward the end of May, President Fallières paid a state visit to London and on June 9–10 King Edward met Czar Nicholas at Reval. A lively discussion in the press on turning the Anglo-French Entente into an alliance accompanied the public formalities of the French visit. Followed immediately by the Reval meeting, the impression that great political schemes were on foot was emphasized. A midsummer nightmare seized the German journalists. The barren formality of the Reval reunion, with nothing tangible to report but the usual toasts, left a free field for the workings of the journalistic imagination. Outwardly, the most significant feature of the King's journey was the presence in his suite of Sir John French and Admiral Fisher. To the continental mind this could mean only one thing—military and naval conversations between England and Russia. The Anglo-Russian agreement, which had been publicized as an understanding limited to the Middle East, was now invested with European significance. Entente publicists in England, France, and Russia

---

[37] These discussions were, of course, unknown to the public. For detailed narratives, see Woodward, *Great Britain and the German Navy*, pp. 167–202; S. B. Fay, *Origins of the World War* (2 vols., N. Y., 1928), I, 233–45; Becker, *Fürst Bülow und England*, pp. 327–28; Brandenburg, *Von Bismarck zum Weltkriege*, pp. 248–65; Lee, *King Edward VII*, II, 614–20. The chief documentary sources are *B. D.*, VI, 108–200; *G. P.*, XXIV, 23–163, XXVIII, 3–81; Tirpitz, *Aufbau*, pp. 67 ff.

hailed the event as the concluding step in the formation of a solid bulwark against the aggressive designs of German policy; while it was not an alliance, it could be turned into one if need should arise. In the popular journals, such as the Berliner Tageblatt and the Lokal-Anzeiger, the Baltic festivities dominated the front page and produced alarmist headlines. Numerous interviews with this and that diplomat "who prefers not to reveal his identity," were spread before the public. In every way the press contributed to the state of nervous apprehension that prevailed in the country.[38] The mounting madness reached panic proportions with the publication in the Dortmunder Zeitung of alleged remarks made by the Kaiser at the military review at Döberitz. William II was quoted as having said: "Yes, it now appears as though they wanted to encircle us. We will know how to bear that. The Germans have never fought better then when forced to defend themselves from all sides. Just let them come on. We are ready." [39] From these words it was concluded that war might break out at any moment.

From the beginning of the agitation over the forthcoming Reval meeting the government, through its semi-official press apparatus, had sought to allay public apprehension. The assurances that had been received from London and St. Petersburg had been passed on to the press, but with little positive effect. In the week following Reval, authorized statements representing the official view were circulated by the Wolff Bureau, and Bülow, or one of his subordinates, publicized the official thesis in an interview with the Berlin correspondent of the Neue Freie Presse. There was no cause for nervousness; the alliance of Germany and Austria was a sufficient bulwark against any possible danger; German policy had not been hindered by the various ententes and would not be hindered in the future. "The alleged encirclement of Germany was nothing more than a phrase." [40] To quiet the alarm produced by the Döberitzer slip, Bülow

---

[38] *Berliner Tageblatt*, Nos. 285, 292, 294, 298, June 6, 11, 12, 14; *Münchner N. N.*, Nos. 254, 258, 260, 266, 273, 282, May 31, June 3, 4, 7, 12, 18; *Kölnische Volksztg.*, Nos. 491, 502, 504, 509, 530, June 5, 10, 12, 19. The *Norddeutsche* published optimistic articles designed to dispel the apprehension produced by sensational reports in other papers. (Nos. 136, 138, 143, 144, June 12, 14, 20, 21.) Paul Michaelis, the editor of the *Tageblatt*, summed it up well when he wrote: "Aber es bleibt allerdings das Bedenken übrig, das wir mehr und mehr durch das Netz von Bündnissen, das über Europa und Asien gezogen worden ist, in unserer Bewegungsfreiheit gehemmt werden."

[39] Quoted in *Berliner Tageblatt*, No. 299, June 15, and in practically all German papers.

[40] Quoted *Berliner Tageblatt*, No. 300, June 15. Interview with Dr. Paul Goldman. Goldman did not name Bülow but the expressions as well as the ideas are unmistakably his. Goldman was a source of information for the Wilhelmstrasse on the public relations between Austria and Germany. (*G. P.*, XXV, 473.) Other interviews were released through the Berlin correspondents of *Le Temps, Petit Parisien,* and *Süddeutsche Reichskorrespondenz.*

authorized or actually wrote the article on "International Uneasiness" appearing in the Norddeutsche on June 20. Admitting possible future diplomatic difficulties, the article counseled against pessimistic anxiety and the exaggeration of possible dangers. Germany was accustomed to being pilloried by the press in other countries as the instigator of all evil and the universal disturber of the peace. The statement denied that the Kaiser's speech at Döberitz had been correctly reported; he did not refer to political questions of the day, or use the words "isolate" or "encircle." In conclusion it declared, the German press had a good right to defend itself against the campaigns of foreign suspicion imputing warlike motives, but one must always keep cool. The tension was great enough; there was no need to exaggerate it.[41] Bülow went further in his efforts to quiet alarm and remove anxiety by addressing to the Prussian ministers at the Federal courts a long dispatch reviewing the international situation as it affected Germany and her ally, Austria. Reval, he declared, had changed nothing, but he admitted that under certain circumstances the new system of ententes and understandings might seriously hamper their freedom of action or possibly result in a powerful coalition against Germany and Austria. The necessity for cleaving to their one reliable ally, runs like a red thread through the long disquisition and foreshadows German policy during the Bosnian crisis of the following winter. Firmness and calm, prudence in their relations to other powers, and the maximum of preparedness would maintain the peace and Germany's position in the world.[42]

The sober admissions contained in this document are in sharp contrast to the optimistic assurances fed to the public through the semi-official press. The contrast is explained partly by the chancellor's conviction that public anxiety and official pessimism would encourage and strengthen Germany's foes and thus increase the danger of further pressure. Partly the optimism of official publicity was dictated by the need for maintaining the prestige of the government. To admit the truth, involved a confession of failure and justified the criticism of Bülow's opponents. As for admitting encirclement, he told Saunders, the Times correspondent, that "He was sick of the word and hoped never to hear it again." [43]

[41] Circulated by Reuter and Wolff as a semi-official pronouncement and published in all daily papers. The Kaiser spoke extemporaneously and no shorthand record was kept. In marginal comments he denied having expressed himself as reported in the press. (*G. P., XXV,* 463.) Bülow who was responsible for the *Norddeutsche* statement, which denied use of the word "encircle," accepts the popular version in his memoirs. (*Memoirs,* II, 352.)

[42] Bülow, *Memoirs,* II, 363–66; full text in *G. P., XXV,* 474–79. On the reaction of the Wilhelmstrasse to the Reval interview and the part played by the press see *G. P., XXV,* 441–94.

[43] *B. D., VI,* 155. Making a farewell call at the foreign office, on the occasion of

The general scare produced in Germany by the Reval demonstration made it next to impossible for directors of German policy to discuss the naval question with the British. Any diminution of their shipbuilding program would have appeared as a retreat before the encircling combination which the press had conjured out of the exchange of visits by the Entente authorities during the summer. Under the constant hammering of Metternich, however, Bülow was gradually shifting his ground and was shortly to take up the cudgels against Tirpitz, but he still held, in agreement with the Emperor, that it was sufficient to assure the British from time to time that Germany's naval program signified no hostile intentions toward England. For better than two years every opportunity, public and private, had been used by Bülow and William II to repeat this assurance, although Metternich and the members of his staff in London reported that these disavowals only increased suspicion and mistrust. "No one will ever persuade the English that a German fleet of thirty-eight battleships, twenty armoured cruisers, and thirty-eight small armoured cruisers, with corresponding torpedo and submarine craft—the total of our units in commission for 1920, if the Navy Law is carried out —is a matter of indifference to England. All the technical arguments we adduce to justify this rate of construction only make the English more mistrustful." [44]

During the summer and autumn of 1908, the agitation in England assumed panic proportions. Invasion fantasies, espionage scares, questions and answers in parliament, and continuous agitation of the fleet question in the press produced an atmosphere charged with tension and alarm. Bülow continued to encourage and stimulate counter-propaganda. In his memoirs he refers with great satisfaction to the public remarks made during the summer by McKenna, Grey, Churchill, and Harcourt, deploring chauvinistic excesses. As an example of how he helped this work along, he cites the interview which he gave to his friend Sidney Whitman for publication in the Standard. Whitman handed him the July issue of the Quarterly Review, which contained an article entitled, "The German Peril," and asked him to comment on it. Describing the article as "a chaos of nonsense," Bülow took up and refuted each point made by the writer. The interview attracted little notice in the British press and convinced no one in authority.[45] It made no more impression than a drop of water on a hot stone.

---

his retirement from the Berlin post, Saunders was received by Bülow, who engaged him in a long discussion of the historical background of Anglo-German estrangement. Saunders' position was taken by J. E. Mackenzie.

[44] Quoted Bülow, *Memoirs,* II, 357.

[45] Bülow, *Memoirs,* II, 419; *Standard,* Sept. 14, 1908; *Quarterly Review,* July

If Bülow's interview in the Standard was something of a damp squib, the next flight into publicity by a highly placed German attracted world-wide attention. For within six weeks after the Whitman interview, the Daily Telegraph article burst like a bombshell in the German chancellery. It should be emphasized here that publication of the Kaiser-interview was quite in line with Bülow's policy of regular public pronouncements designed to calm fears and allay criticism in England. Bülow had taken the lead in this activity and had encouraged the Emperor in the same course. Behind this activity lay the belief that by throwing up a favorable publicity screen they could carry the German navy program through the danger zone of an English preventive war.[46] The Daily Telegraph interview, however, revealed the bankruptcy of the publicity policy that Bülow had been sponsoring for more than three years.

The Daily Telegraph interview will always stand as a symbol of blaz-

---

1908, pp. 264–98. The article on "The German Peril" although unsigned was written by Mr. J. L. Garvin. (Communication from Mr. Garvin, Aug. 26, 1938.) Bülow's criticism in the *Standard* interview drew a rejoinder from Garvin. ("The German Peril: A Rejoinder to Prince Bülow," *Quarterly Review*, October 1908, pp. 576–98.) According to Stephen Gwynn, the original article was based on material supplied by Sir Cecil Spring Rice. (*Letters and Friendships*, II, 144.) This raises the question of official responsibility for press polemics against Germany. On many occasions Grey solemnly assured Metternich that government officials neither sanctioned nor participated in the anti-German publicity crusade, that the government could not restrain the press and that it could accept no responsibility for its utterances. And yet we are told by Stephen Gwynn that when Cecil Spring Rice was minister to Sweden (1908–13) "He used all means that lay within his reach to influence the English press; Leo Maxse of the *National Review*, St. Loe Strachey of the *Spectator*, were in constant correspondence with him; he briefed Mr. Garvin in an article for the *Quarterly Review* edited by his friend Mr. George Prothero; he wrote his view on the German menace in a long letter to Mr. Basil Williams of the *Times*. In all these cases he obtained the consent of his official superiors to his furnishing information, provided that he himself did not write, or receive pay." (*Letters and Friendships*, II, 144.) In 1907 he was writing to Mr. J. A. Spender, of the *Westminster Gazette*, on his favorite theme of German mendacity. (Spender, *Life, Journalism and Politics*, I, 215.) Furthermore, what is the explanation of the letter from Sir Charles Hardinge to an English journalist in Berlin, which Tirpitz reproduces without any explanation as to how it came into his hands? On December 14, 1908, Hardinge wrote to the unnamed journalist: "I am obliged to you for your letter of the 13th. I am glad to hear that you propose to write an article on the lines of what I said to you at Cronberg. I think it may do good. I am not at all certain that events of the last fortnight may not tend towards the desired result, i. e. a discussion on a possible restriction of naval construction and the relinquishment of a scheme of which the Emperor is the chief support. . . . The principal point to emphasize is that although we cannot again approach the Emperor or Government on the subject of naval armaments without exposing ourselves to an undesirable rebuff, the door to such a discussion is not closed. . . . The German naval programme is the crux of the whole situation. Until this question is solved, the unrest now prevalent in Europe is bound to continue. I wish you success in your article. Please regard this as strictly confidential." (Tirpitz, *Aufbau*, pp. 99–100.) If Grey was sincere in his unqualified assurances to Metternich, then he could not have known what his subordinates were doing.

[46] Bülow's statement in his *Memoirs* (II, 422) that the Kaiser-interview was a rude departure from official policy, that its effect was "that of a spring frost in the night, nipping in the bud that understanding which the last few months had seemed so fairly to promise between two great peoples," is nothing but moonshine.

ing indiscretion on the part of highly placed personages in their contacts
with the press. Never has the unpredictability of public relations been so
signally exemplified as in the reactions produced by the Daily Telegraph's
scoop of October 28, 1908. Not only did the article provide a major
sensation for the European press, but its repercussions produced a grave
constitutional crisis in Germany and eventually brought about Bülow's
resignation.[47] The effects of the interview were in the main domestic, but
it had its origin in the international situation.

The substance of the interview is so well known that it hardly seems
necessary to quote or paraphrase it at length. From the interview emerges
the single theme that William II was, and had always been, England's
greatest friend and that the British had nothing to fear from German
policy or German armaments. To the Emperor's remarks, which were
given in direct quotation, no serious objections could be made, although
his naïve egocentrism, which was perhaps unobjectionable in a small
circle over coffee and cigarettes, stood out curiously in cold print. The
article contained four bad blunders: (1) His repeated offers of friendship were distorted and misinterpreted by a considerable section of the
English press, which, together with the fact that prevailing sentiment in
Germany was not friendly to England, made it difficult for him to hold
to his pro-British policy. (2) He had, nevertheless, always been England's true friend; during the Boer War he had refused an invitation to
join France and Russia in a coalition to humble England and had immediately notified his English relatives of the proposal. (3) During the
Black Week of 1899 he had worked out, with the co-operation of his
general staff, a plan of campaign for the British army in South Africa
which he had sent to his grandmother; this plan closely approximated the
one carried out by Lord Roberts. (4) The German fleet implied no unfriendly intentions toward England; it was being built with a view to giving Germany a voice in the settlement of future problems in the Pacific.
Judged entirely from the standpoint of Germany's public relations with
England, only one of these indiscretions was downright harmful, namely,
the statement that prevailing sentiment in Germany was hostile to Great
Britain. In the anti-German papers this was exploited as confirmation of
all that they had been preaching for years.

As to the Emperor's assertion that he had foiled a Franco-Russian plot
to humiliate England during the Boer War, there was really nothing

----

[47] The domestic aspects of this incident are the subject of an undistinguished dissertation by H. Teschner, *Die Daily Telegraph—Affäre in der Beurteilung der
öffentlichen Meinung* (Ohlau i. Schl., 1931). More important is Theodor Eschen-
burg, *Das Kaiserreich am Schiedewege. Bassermann, Bülow und der Block* (Berlin, 1929).

new in this. Public discussion of the interventionist episode began in the *National Review* in December 1907, while William II was at High-cliffe Castle. In the article "Ignotus" stated that William II had tried to induce France and Russia to join in a hostile demonstration against Great Britain. The official German version was given by the Emperor in the Manchester Daily Dispatch interview. Further, in language identical with that employed in the Daily Telegraph he had referred to his action in an interview with J. L. Bashford, who quoted his words in an author-ized article appearing in the *Strand Magazine* in January 1908.[48] In July 1908, André Mévil published in Maxse's *National Review* an article on the diplomacy of the Boer War, again alleging German interven-tionist proposals and giving to Delcassé credit for having blocked the German game. This article, inspired by Delcassé, led Schoen, the Ger-man foreign minister to authorize a rejoinder exposing the legends propa-gated by Maxse and Mévil. Prepared by Friedrich Heilbron, Hammann's associate in the press division, the article was published in Richard Fleisher's *Deutsche Revue* in September.[49] Thus the subject had been well aired in the press before the appearance of the Daily Telegraph interview. It was the international situation in November 1908, that made its retelling a public sensation. For over the European chancel-leries hovered the clouds of the Casablanca incident and the Bosnian annexation crisis. To the readers of the interview, who were not aware that the remarks dated from the previous year, it seemed a calculated attempt to sow dissension at a critical moment between England, France and Russia. To a considerable extent, therefore, the sensation created by the interview is attributable to the timing rather than the content.

The plan of campaign, which had been the key to Lord Roberts' vic-tory over the Boers, referred, of course, to the "Aphorisms" which the Emperor had sent to his uncle in England; in no sense did they con-stitute a military plan of campaign. English readers were of course amazed and amused at William II's unblushing conceit, but in Germany it awakened painful memories of Boer War days, when the nation and the monarchy were ranged against one another on this question. People had never suspected that their own Emperor had thus betrayed their heroic Boer kinsmen in South Africa, and committed treason against

[48] In this article the Emperor's words were: "I cannot comprehend the ill-feeling against me in England. I have acted loyally to England. An offer was made to Ger-many simultaneously from two powerful sides to take advantage of the situation and to interfere in British policy, and I refused point-blank. I instantly telegraphed the nature of the offer to my uncle." (*Strand Magazine,* Jan. 1, 1908, p. 22.)

[49] "Deutsche Intrigen gegen England während des Burenkrieges," "von einem Wissenden." It was laid before the Emperor who wrote affirmative marginal notes on it. *G. P.,* XXIV, 170.

German romantic ideals. This more than any other feature of the article was at the bottom of the November Storm in the press and the Reichstag. The Emperor's statement as to the purpose of the German fleet was doubtless an affront to Japan, but merely claiming a right to a voice in the future problems of the Pacific was no more than leaders in other nations had publicly claimed. Moreoover, William II's obsession with the Yellow Peril was a matter of public knowledge and was therefore readily discounted.

However, the fact remains that had the repercussions been anticipated, the interview would never have appeared. That leads to a consideration of the comedy of errors that led to publication of the article. Colonel Stuart Wortley, the Emperor's host at Highcliffe Castle in November 1907, and the Emperor's guest at army maneuvers in 1908, either from memory or notes, arranged the Kaiser's remarks in the form of an interview purporting to come from a diplomat whose identity could not be revealed. In this he had the assistance of Mr. Harold Spender, who arranged for publication in the Daily Telegraph.[50] Stuart Wortley, acting in good faith and with the best intentions, sent the manuscript to the Emperor accompanied by a letter requesting permission to publish the article in the interest of friendlier relations between the two countries. Acting in a strictly constitutional fashion, William forwarded the manuscript and Stuart Wortley's letter to Bülow, at his summer home in Norderney, with instructions to examine it and make such suggestions and changes as seemed advisable. He made a point of requesting Bülow to attend to it personally and not to send it through the foreign office. The chancellor, who later pleaded a heavy burden of work at the time, forwarded the manuscript to the foreign office with instructions that it be carefully examined and re-typed, with corrections and suggested emendations entered in the margins. He did not ask for an opinion on the advisability of publication. Schoen was absent at the time and the acting secretary, Stemrich, gave the manuscript to Klehmet, the eldest member of the political section since Holstein's retirement and a discreet and conscientious worker. Klehmet, following Bülow's instructions, examined the statements for their historical accuracy, toned down the language in several instances, entered the suggested changes on the margins, and wrote a covering dispatch explanatory of the main points where corrections and revisions seemed advisable.[51] The article, together with the accompanying letters, was then returned to Bülow who either

---

[50] It was offered first to the *Westminster Gazette*, but J. A. Spender refused it on the ground that he was too closely associated with Grey and the Liberal cabinet. *Life, Journalism and Politics*, I, 141.

[51] *G. P.*, XXIV, 167–74.

forwarded it to the Emperor or delivered it to him personally on returning to Berlin. Bülow always maintained that he did not read the manuscript because he was heavily burdened with work and because the draft of the interview was "almost illegible" and written on "very bad and thin carbon-copy paper." [52] He also stated then and later in his memoirs that his instructions to the foreign office and to Müller, who represented the foreign office on his staff at Norderney, covered the advisability and opportuneness of publication. Neither statement is true. The interview as delivered at Norderney was typewritten, the first page on the stationery of the Daily Telegraph.[53] Bülow's instructions to the foreign office were, in fact, limited to examination of the historical accuracy of the statements contained in the interview and did not ask for a general report on the political consequences of publication. In the foreign office they thought that Bülow himself would consider that subject.[54] Some German writers have maintained that Bülow read the manuscript but failed to foresee its explosive effect, and that later, when the storm broke in the German press, he threw the blame on the foreign office by alleging that it passed through his hands unread.[55] The evidence on this point is not conclusive, but it is established beyond question that the chancellor, if he did not read the English manuscript, was at least informed of the main points, and the most dangerous ones at that. For the corrected manuscript was accompanied by a personal letter to his cousin Martin Jenisch, who represented the foreign office in the Emperor's entourage, and in that letter, which Bülow dictated to Minister Müller, he incorporated the memorandum drafted by Klehmet explaining the corrections and emendations that seemed advisable. In Klehmet's memorandum all the points in the interview to which public critics later took exception, were touched upon except the Far Eastern orientation of German naval policy.[56] From the technical details connected with the expedition of the interview emerges the following conclusion: The warm assurance of an English staff officer, Stuart Wortley, and of an able English journalist, Harold Spender, that the article would promote better feeling in England toward Germany carried the

---

[52] Bülow, *Denkwürdigkeiten*, II, 338. The English translation here (*Memoirs of Prince von Bülow*, II, p. 375) is faulty.

[53] *G. P.*, XXIV, 180.

[54] *G. P.*, XXIV, 183–85. Mem. by privy councillor Klehmet, Nov. 6, 1908.

[55] Johannes Haller, *Die Ära Bülow* (Berlin, 1922), p. 140; Anon., *Kaiser und Kanzler im Sturmjahr 1908* (Leipzig, 1929), *passim;* Count Westarp, *Konservative Politik*, I, 38–39; Rudolf von Valentini, *Kaiser und Kabinettschef* (Oldenburg, 1931), pp. 100, 106.

[56] Compare Stemrich to Bülow, Oct 5, 1908, *G. P.*, XXIV, 169, with Bülow to Jenisch, Oct. 11, 1908, *ibid.*, pp. 175–76. Bülow also asserted that he instructed Müller to examine the article; Müller flatly denied this. *Ibid.*, XXIV, 198.

weight of authority with the Emperor and his officials. Wortley, Spender, William II, Jenisch, Bülow, and Klehmet had their attention centered upon the impression that would be created in England; they failed entirely to foresee or even consider the effect of publication on German opinion. Had not the Manchester Dispatch interview, the direct quotations in the *Strand Magazine,* and the Tweedmouth letter passed without serious criticism from the well-drilled and loyal German citizenry?

In this connection another very serious blunder was committed. When the telegraphic report of the interview was received by Wolff's Bureau, a few hours after publication in London on October 28, it was referred to Hammann by Dr. Mantler, the director of Wolff's Bureau. Hammann, who was unaware that such an article existed, immediately perceived the danger inherent in the communication. Should the report be suppressed or released? The technical news problem involved was a difficult one. If the report were suppressed, the German papers having London correspondents would publish it anyway and the others would attack Wolff for its inadequate service.[57] On the other hand, publication by Wolff, under the German publicity system, implied that the facts reported were authentic. Hammann suggested that they permit publication by Wolff and then follow up with a semi-official statement to the evening papers that responsibility for the interview's authenticity rested upon the Daily Telegraph.[58] After consultations between Bülow, Hammann and Schoen, Dr. Mantler was authorized to circulate the London account to Wolff's subscribers.[59] The report was then released without any semi-official statement that would cast doubt on the authenticity of the interview. Then by publication of the Wolff report next day (October 29) in the Norddeutsche, the complete authenticity of the interview was established for German editors and publicists. Not even the accuracy of the Telegraph's reporting could now be questioned. It was the Wolff report that loosed the storm in Germany.

Certainly, the press tactics of Bülow and Hammann were most ill-chosen. They could not, however, have foreseen the universality of the revolt against the government and the Emperor's personal régime, and they doubtless counted on the support of those editors who were subject

[57] Within three hours after publication in London, the *Berliner-Zeitung am Mittag* was out with a complete report of the interview.
[58] Mem. by Hammann, Oct. 28, 1908; *G. P.,* XXIV, 177. For Hammann's part in this episode see his diary notes in *Archiv für Politik und Geschichte,* IV, 545 ff.; Hammann, *Um den Kaiser* (Berlin, 1919), pp. 66–72.
[59] Bülow's statement (*Memoirs,* II, 399) that this was done by Hammann without authorization is false. In fact it was Bülow who made the decision to let it go through without any attempt at evasion or side-stepping. See Dr. Mantler's statement in the *Deutsche Allgemeine Ztg.,* No. 241, June 5, 1931; reproduced *Berliner Monatshefte,* July 1931, pp. 701–2.

to official influence, or friendly to Bülow, to neutralize the criticism of opposition journals. That was the way it had always worked out in the past. On the first day of publication in Germany the press bureau chief was able to influence the Kölnische Zeitung, the Münchner Neueste Nachrichten, the National-Zeitung, the Vossische Zeitung, and the Magdeburgische Zeitung in favor of the government and the Kaiser-interview.[60] The remainder of the important journals, without respect to party, commented unfavorably. As the storm gathered force those journals which at first had praised the interview were blown around by the anger and passion of their readers. Only Theodor Schiemann, the foreign political writer on the Kreuzzeitung, who owed everything to the Emperor's patronage, defended the interview in his weekly survey.[61]

The first outburst of criticism was directed against the Kaiser as it was generally assumed that he had acted on his own initiative in an unconstitutional manner, as he had so frequently done before. Under the circumstances Bülow was constrained to publish an official explanation of how the article had come to be published. In this official communiqué, published on Saturday afternoon, October 31, Bülow cleared the Emperor of responsibility, excused himself by declaring that he had not read the draft of the article, and brought the foreign office into the line of fire by attributing to it official delinquency in examining and passing the interview.[62] Instead of subsiding, public agitation increased. "The privy councillors in the foreign office would approve a declaration of war on the Eskimos if it were proposed by the Emperor," remarked one editor. And the Liberal deputy, Dr. Naumann, writing in the Liberale Kor-

---

[60] *Münchner N. N.*, No. 507, Oct. 29; *Kölnische Ztg.*, No. 1139, Oct. 30, and Berlin telegram, No. 1147, Nov. 1; *Vossische Ztg.*, No. 514, Oct. 30; *Magdeburgische Ztg.*, and *National-Zeitung* quoted in *Tägliche Rundschau*, No. 511, Oct. 30.

[61] *Kreuzzeitung*, Nov. 4. The *Kreuzzeitung*, under the direction of the Conservative committee, sharply criticized the interview as another manifestation of absolutism, but later worked to calm the storm. On the policy of the Conservative party and its official press in this crisis see Westarp, *Konservative Politik*, I, 37 ff. Some important documents from the imperial chancellery and from the Conservative party archives are here reproduced for the first time.

[62] *Reichsanzeiger*, Oct. 31; *Norddeutsche*, No. 257, Oct. 31; Bülow, *Memoirs*, II, 395; *G. P.*, XXIV, 182. The communication was drafted in consultation with Schoen, Hammann, and Loebell, chief of the imperial chancellery and Bülow's right hand. The story subsequently spread by Bülow's enemies that he permitted publication of the interview in order to impose the pressure of public criticism upon William II and to limit his personal initiative, receives little support from the documentary record. But why did Bülow, in informing the Emperor of the unfavorable reaction produced by the interview, enclose only clippings from papers which were extremist in their attacks and which belonged in the ranks of the irreconcilable Bismarckians and Pan-Germans? The press clippings laid before William II were from the *Deutsche Tageszeitung*, official organ of the Agrarian League, the *Tägliche Rundschau*, independent with Pan-German leanings, the *Reichsbote*, Evangelical-Conservative, the *Deutsche Zeitung*, fanatically nationalist, and the *Rheinisch-Westfälische Zeitung*, Pan-German. See *G. P.*, XXIV, 179 n.

respondenz, put the rhetorical question: "Of what value to us is the best army in Europe, when no state can negotiate confidentially with us? Of what value is a navy, when it has for a commander-in-chief one who spends his spare time drawing up war plans for the English?" [63]

Although it was made clear that William II had acted constitutionally in the matter of the interview, this did not spare him from criticism for the substance of his remarks as reported in the Daily Telegraph. It was most improper for him to have spoken so openly and recklessly to Englishmen even in private. The bitterest strictures were delivered upon the Emperor's statement that he had drafted military plans for the British during the Boer War. Unfortunately the Wolff report of the interview, which was what most Germans read, was so worded on this point as to convey a totally false impression of the Kaiser's words. In the Daily Telegraph the Emperor said: "And as a matter of curious coincidence, let me add that the plan which I formulated ran very much on the same lines as that which was actually adopted by Lord Roberts and carried by him into successful operation." In the summary supplied to the German press by Wolff, the Emperor was reported as having said: "The plan which I formulated was actually adopted by Lord Roberts and successfully carried through by him." [64] With respect to this revelation, the Rheinisch-Westfälische Zeitung employed language only slightly stronger than that found in other journals.

What weighs most heavily upon the German soul is that the Emperor worked out the plan of campaign with which our brave kinsmen, the Boers, were destroyed. The German Emperor as an unsolicited strategist against a Low-German people, that is a picture which decades cannot erase. England fought then not only against German blood but also against our interests. . . . Was the Emperor also a party to the plans by which thirty thousand Boer farms were destroyed and plundered and the women and children herded into the deadly concentration camps? In spite of semi-official circulation we can not believe the report is authentic. For no German Emperor ever before so conducted himself, and a German Emperor ought not to conduct himself like that.[65]

However bitter the criticism leveled at the form and substance of the Kaiser-interview, the national revolt, which took Bülow and all his advisers by surprise, did not arise from this one incident, but from a store

---

[63] Quoted *Münchner N. N.,* No. 518, Nov. 5, 1908.

[64] "Der von mir aufgestellte Plan wurde wirklich von Lord Roberts angenommen und glücklich von ihm durchgeführt."

[65] Quoted *Tägliche Rundschau,* No. 511, Oct. 30, 1908; less vehement but in the same strain was Heinrich Rippler in *Tägliche Rundschau,* No. 509, Oct. 29; *Deutsche Tagesztg.,* and *Hannoverscher Kurier,* quoted *Tägliche Rundschau,* No. 511, Oct. 30; *Kölnische Volksztg.,* No. 931, Oct. 29; *Frankfurter Ztg.,* No. 301, Oct. 31; *Schwäbischer Merkur,* No. 525, Nov. 10; *Münchner N. N.,* No. 512, 513, 514, Nov. 1, 2, 3.

of resentment and doubt that had been accumulating with every indiscretion committed by William II in the twenty years since his accession. From every press article emerged a profound sense of impending catastrophe if the system were not changed, if guarantees for a steady, consistent, and discreet policy in the future were not secured. After the first three days the foreign political aspects of the episode disappeared from the picture and the issue was defined as a constitutional question involving the chancellor's responsibility for the personal policies pursued by the Emperor. The demand that the Reichstag should secure guarantees for the future and not limit itself merely to interpellation and debate found expression in the organs of all parties except the Conservative. To the publicists smarting under this home-made humiliation, the debates on November 10–11 were a bitter disappointment. The Reichstag acted as a phonograph, playing over the records already made by the press. Each spokesman presented his party's viewpoint; there was no concerted action for constitutional reform; and as a result of Conservative opposition, the original move to unite the bourgeois parties in an address to the Emperor came to nought.[66] Under the heavy pressure of an aroused press and a hostile Reichstag, Bülow excused but did not defend the Emperor; he "deferred to public opinion instead of to absolutism," and let it be understood that his remaining in office would be conditional on the maintenance of greater reserve by the Kaiser. The Emperor's acceptance of this "pledge" was signaled to the public in an official statement published by Bülow in the Norddeutsche on November 18. The Emperor, depressed and anxious, accepted the chancellor's conditions, but confidence in his chief minister was gone. Deprived of the sovereign's confidence, Bülow's influence with the Reichstag leaders waned. The revolt of the Conservatives against the inheritance tax and the breakup of the Bülow *bloc* was the occasion rather than the cause of his resignation.[67]

Many writers, casually mentioning the Daily Telegraph incident, have

[66] Westarp, *op. cit.*, I, 45–48.

[67] Valentini, *Kaiser und Kabinettschef*, pp. 98–108; Westarp, *Konservative Politik*, I, 48–49, 78–97; R. von Sydow, "Fürst Bülow und die Reichsfinanzreform 1908," in *Front Wider Bülow* (Munich, 1931), pp. 119 ff., based on the archives of the imperial chancellery and the treasury department. Eckardstein (*Die Entlassung des Fürsten Bülow*, Berlin, 1931) tells how the breach between Kaiser and chancellor was made; how he worked with Fürstenberg, Röder, and Ballin in the "Bund der Kaisertreuen"; how they got in touch with the publicist Rudolf Martin and got his published account of Bülow's betrayal of the Emperor into William II's hands. The subject was revived in the press in September 1909, and gave rise to an exchange of letters between Bülow and Bethmann-Hollweg, with the Emperor supplying some interesting comments. *G. P.*, XXIV, 199–210. See also Rudolf Martin's article in *Gegenwart*, February 1909; and his book, *Fürst Bülow und Kaiser Wilhelm II*, (Berlin, 1909).

stated or implied that it provoked the British press to renewed agitation and attacks on Germany. Even a cursory glance over the files of British newspapers shows this to be untrue. In both press and diplomatic circles in England, the Emperor's open-hearted declaration produced amazement mixed with suspicion. When, however, it was perceived that his well-meant but ill-starred effort had involved him in a constitutional crisis, a considerable measure of sympathy for his predicament was expressed. Care and discretion marked Grey's handling of the affair. He was satisfied that "The Emperor has made Germany for the time being the laughing stock of the world," and instead of using the interview as an occasion for further embarrassing the German government, he did what he could to smooth over the difficulty.

This was shown in connection with a second Kaiser interview, which at that very time was being hawked around the newspaper offices in London, New York and Paris. In this interview, granted to the American publicist William Bayard Hale, during the Kiel regatta in the summer of 1908, the Emperor had expressed sentiments toward England diametrically opposed to those published in the Daily Telegraph. What passed for a synopsis of the article, which Hale had prepared for the *Century Magazine,* was offered the Daily Mail for publication, but upon inquiry at the foreign office the editors were persuaded to forego publication.[68] In a private letter to Bertie, the British Ambassador in Paris, Grey gave his reasons for not wishing to see it published. Another interview appearing in France or England would be regarded in Germany as a foreign attempt to 'smear' the Emperor and would create a reaction in Germany in his favor. In the interests of general policy he wanted the matter to rest. He closed his letter with these words: "Never since I have been in office has opinion here been so thoroughly wide awake with regard to Germany, and on its guard as it is now. I haven't the faintest tremor of anxiety about that. Never has the Emperor's position been so low in the world. Why not let well alone!"[69]

While the interview did not disturb normal diplomatic relations it did not further the cause which the Emperor had at heart. On the con-

[68] Esher, *Journals and Letters,* II, 362; Lee, *King Edward VII,* II, 622–23. Another article purporting to be a summary of the interview was published in the New York *World.* It was a gross invention and the *World* subsequently issued a retraction. The original Hale article, prepared for the *Century Magazine,* was suppressed at the urgent request of the Wilhelmstrasse, although unlike the *Daily Telegraph* article it had been carefully edited and everything dangerous deleted by the foreign office. For the suppressed article and the details of its suppression see W. H. Hale, "Thus Spoke the Kaiser" and "Adventures of a Document," *Atlantic Monthly,* May–June, 1934, pp. 513–23, 696–705. Also, Hammann, *Um den Kaiser,* pp. 73–74; G. P., XXIII, 276, 319, XXVIII, 20.

[69] Grey to Bertie, Dec. 1, 1908; B. D., VI, 225–26.

trary it greatly embarrassed the English publicists who advocated a conciliatory policy toward the German Empire and who disapproved of the
Germanophobia of the extremists. As Grey said, "All the pro-Germans
here have been shaken and shocked by the impulsive indiscretion of the
Emperor. . . ." Mr. Spender wrote from this angle in the Westminster
Gazette: "It is a sincere regret to most of us that the Emperor's over-
ture should not have been attended with the results that he desired, but
the German people must not misunderstand that incident. We are grate-
ful to the Emperor for his professions of friendship. . . . But our response was difficult, precisely because we foresaw that the form of the
communication must be an embarrassment to the German people, and
that almost any reply to it would add to the difficulty. If we were silent,
we seemed to be churlish to the Emperor; if we thanked the Emperor
for fighting our battle, we were bound to accept the theory that the German people were hostile." (Nov. 6, 1908.) Harold Spender, who had a
hand in the publication of the interview, wrote to the Daily News commenting on the fury of the German people toward their Emperor. William II ought to have foreseen this. "What was probably not foreseen
by him, and it is certainly a most surprising and extraordinary fact, is
that England should contemplate that fury with satisfaction, and should
even applaud the denunciations hurled at one whose worst fault is that
he had dared to proclaim himself the friend of England." (Nov. 3, 1908.)
The Manchester Guardian lectured the London press on the ungracious
attitude with which it received the Emperor's impulsive declaration.[70]

As was to be expected the Conservative-Unionist press of the capital
was extremely critical. The Times, Daily Mail, and Pall Mall Gazette
seized upon the Emperor's statement that he was in a minority in his
friendly feelings toward Great Britain, and exploited it as a confirmation, on the highest authority, of the thesis they had long maintained.
Their efforts were directed mainly toward making capital for their naval
campaign out of the Emperor's blazing indiscretion. "Forewarned is to
be Forearmed," was the title of a strong editorial in the Pall Mall
Gazette (Oct. 30), while the Daily Mail published an open letter to the
Emperor by the apostle of "two keels to one," W. T. Stead. "Your
Majesty's astonishing revelation that nothing but the frail span of your
own life stands between us and the hostility of a majority of your subjects," wrote Stead, "removes the last vestige of doubt in our minds as
to the duty of laying down six Dreadnoughts, and laying them down at

[70] "It is always ungracious to peck at a heart because it is worn on a sleeve, and
in politics it is usually folly. There is not so much friendliness in the world that any
nation should refuse it when offered." (Oct. 31; also Nov. 3 and 6.) The provincial
press in general was inclined to friendlier judgment than the press of London.

once. The more unfriendly the majority of the Germans may be to us, the more incumbent it is upon us to show our fraternal love by leading them not into temptation, but delivering them from evil, by making our Navy so strong that it will not invite their attack." [71] The Times interpreted the interview as an effort to sow dissension among the powers friendly to England. Dismissing every feature of the interview but the one consistent with the Times' editorial policy, it hammered this point day after day. "What the vast majority of Englishmen will have stamped upon their minds is the Emperor's admission that the majority of the German nation are unfriendly to us, and his contention that this hostile nation means to go on indefinitely enlarging their navy." [72] After the first few days the news interest shifted from international implications to the domestic storm that was sweeping Germany. The debates in the Reichstag and the subsequent 'abstainer's pledge' which Bülow secured from William II were viewed generally in the press as a triumph for public opinion over irresponsible autocracy. Instead of hostile and irritating repercussions, the incident ended without positive gains or losses for Anglo-German relations.[73] This was the opinion expressed by Metternich in a private letter to Bülow, but he warned the chancellor that although the assurances given in the Reichstag of German desire for friendship with England had made a favorable impression, no lasting betterment was to be expected as long as the naval question remained an issue between the two governments; the tension would increase rather than diminish.[74]

Since the Algeciras Conference the German authorities had pursued toward England a publicity policy designed to counteract the alarmist campaign over the "German menace," to halt the encirclement tendencies of British policy, and to ward off the danger of a preventive war. The numerous interviews and pronouncements by Bülow on the pacific aims of German policy, the Emperor's journeys and speeches, the official encouragement and inspiration of individual and group efforts, in both England and Germany, to create a more favorable publicity atmosphere must be accounted a part of that program. Outwardly a considerable structure of Anglo-German friendship had been erected by the various committees and organizations which had sponsored the exchange of hospitalities between technical and occupational groups—laborers, pas-

---

[71] *Daily Mail*, Oct. 30, 1908. While the *Daily Mail* exploited the interview in a sensational manner from the news angle, editorially it was mild and considerate.
[72] *Times*, Oct. 29, 30, Nov. 2.
[73] Metternich's report on individual journal's reactions to the Reichstag debate (Nov. 11); G. P., XXIV, 189–90.
[74] G. P., XXIV, 189 n.

tors, journalists, mayors and municipal officials, trade delegations, etc. The reciprocal visits of journalistic delegations was an ambitious effort to influence directly the men who operated the great engines of publicity and propaganda. Behind all this Bülow and the Emperor assured one another that they were building their "long walls to Piraeus." The November Storm showed the futility of this policy. Bülow himself had to recognize the inadequacy of a publicity campaign to solve the crucial problems of foreign relations.

His approval of a private report submitted by the brilliant Walter Rathenau, after a visit to England early in 1909, shows his realization that interviews and Reichstag declarations were not enough. Rathenau, after painting a picture of England's political and economic condition and the current *malaise* that prevailed in the country, showed how every cause for uneasiness was charged to Germany's account.

So that every English discontent is beginning to be crystallized and summed up in this one concept—Germany. What, in the educated classes, has become a reasoned conviction, comes out in the rank and file, in provincials, and in young people, in the form of prejudice, hate, fantastic misconception, to an extent far surpassing our own best journalistic efforts. It would be superficial and futile to hope that small acts of friendliness, visits of deputations, or Press manoeuvres, could dam up dissatisfaction that flows from so deep a source. Only the ensemble of our policy is capable of at least giving England the impression that, on Germany's side, there is no irritation, no fear, no pressing need to expand and take an offensive attitude.[75]

But even before this warning Bülow had been converted to Metternich's thesis, stated with monotonous regularity in the ambassador's dispatches: If you desire a lasting improvement in our relations with England then you must come to an agreement on naval construction, for the naval question is the taproot of all British mistrust, suspicion, and ill will. Very gently and cautiously Bülow began to work on the Emperor. But William II was intransigent and refused to listen to proposals for slowing down construction. Immediately after the Daily Telegraph affair, when the Kaiser was depressed by the national outburst against the personal regime, Bülow began to bombard Tirpitz with memoranda embodying arguments from the diplomatic viewpoint for relaxation of the Anglo-German tension through a naval agreement. Tirpitz twisted and turned, but withstood the pressure. The correspondence ceased without agreement, and when King Edward visited Berlin in February 1909, the smoothly worn assurances on German naval aims were repeated by both

[75] Bülow, *Memoirs,* II, 477–78.

Bülow and his master.[76] Meanwhile in England the stage was set for the great Dreadnought panic of March 1909.

[76] For the documents on the Tirpitz-Bülow debate see, Tirpitz, *Aufbau*, pp. 93–124; *G. P.*, XXVIII, 3–81. For narratives see Bülow, *Memoirs*, II, 355–56, 465–68, 474–90; Becker, *Fürst Bülow und England*, pp. 346–78; Woodward, *Great Britain and the German Navy*, pp. 195–202; Gooch, *Before the War*, I, 268 ff.; Brandenburg, *Von Bismarck zum Weltkriege*, pp. 258–65; Fay, *Origins*, I, 256–59.

CHAPTER XII

NAVAL HYSTERIA AND PARTY POLITICS

It is the discussions which keep alive popular fears and popular interest, upon which alone rest the Navy Estimates. A nation that believes itself secure, all history teaches is doomed. Anxiety, not a sense of security, lies at the root of readiness for war. . . . An invasion Scare is the mill of God which grinds you out a Navy of Dreadnoughts, and keeps the British people war-like in spirit.

Lord Esher to Sir John Fisher, October 1, 1907.

We had never hoped for British approval during the creation of our sea-power.

Admiral Tirpitz, *My Memoirs*, I, 268.

From 1908 to 1912 every feature of Anglo-German relations was subordinate to the question of competitive naval armaments. The aggressiveness of German foreign policy, the impolitic utterances of fanatical patriots and racialists, the excesses of publicity that played about the German naval program had established the thesis in British minds that the realization of German political aims and ambitions was incompatible with the future security of Great Britain and her Empire. The only force that stood between Germany and the accomplishment of her far-reaching designs was Britain's sea-power. This bulwark, therefore, must not for one moment be placed in jeopardy. This is the simple orthodox pattern to which the problem is ordinarily reduced when viewed externally and in historical perspective. Examined somewhat more realistically in its contemporary publicity setting, it loses its simplicity and becomes grotesquely complex. A thousand crosscurrents are revealed; cause and effect become in many instances almost indistinguishable; and the broad lines of what appears to be a clear-cut problem dissolve into party politics, class rivalries, and the personal intrigues and jealousies of warring factions in the naval service personnel. On each level contending groups and parties are accompanied by a partisan chorus in the press. To follow to their end all these threads of political motivation and behavior is an impossible task. Past actuality can never be recovered. At best in approaching the problem one can only isolate and label certain manifestations of publicity, indicate their source, and guess at their influence on the masses and the agents of the state's authority.

Regarded as the sole line of British defense, the navy engaged all those loyalties which in Germany clustered around the army as the chief symbol and agency of the power-state. The identification of the individual's sense of security or insecurity with the strength or weakness of national armaments was the core of the problem regarded from the public relations viewpoint. In the modern state a persistent advertising of the army and navy, sponsored by official or volunteer agencies, is absolutely essential to the continuance of taxpayer support. The techniques of this propaganda in Great Britain, as they affected the navy, had undergone a notable change with the enfranchisement of the urban and rural masses and the spread of popular literacy. Outstanding was the startling increase in the volume of such publicity and, secondary only to this development, the intensification of such propaganda to shock or panic proportions. In 1884–85, almost singlehanded and through an evening newspaper with not above 13,000 circulation, W. T. Stead brought such pressure to bear with his campaign on "The Truth About the Navy" as to force the Gladstone ministry to launch a vastly increased building program. Even the genius of Stead could not have promoted the great Dreadnought panic of 1909 with a small sized megaphone like the Pall Mall Gazette. The measure of difference is the comparatively small group of parliamentarians and influential party men that Stead had to reach in 1884–85 and the mass electorate that had to be reached and moved in 1909.

There was nothing very subtle or abstract in the promotion of publicity on behalf of the navy. Psychologically the chief objective was to arouse fear, banish the sense of security, and induce anxiety. The activity of those who worked at this business was conditioned by a thousand factors. The temper and receptivity to suggestion on the part of the electorate, the extent of foreign armaments to which individual fear and insecurity was always referred, and a multitude of uncontrolled and unmarked variables reduced the process to a rather low level of opportunism. The fitful nature of the process clearly proves this, and it led a contemporary to describe British naval policy in its public aspects as a state of coma accompanied by fits.

Three main features are presented in the English agitation over the "German Menace": First, German economic progress and direct competition; second, German striving for political hegemony on the continent, which conflicted with the English policy of maintaining a balance of power; third, the extensive naval program launched by Tirpitz, which was regarded as a direct threat to British security. After the Liberal victory in the election of 1906, tariff reform receded into the background as an issue of immediate practical politics, but the agitation continued and played a minor rôle in succeeding party battles down to the War. It was not, however, the basic factor in Anglo-German estrangement. In support of this statement can be adduced the unanimous opinion of the German diplomatic representatives in England—Metternich, Bernstorff, Stumm, Kühlmann, and the naval attaché, Von Coerper. Grey was unusually positive in rejecting economic competition as the cause of prevailing mistrust, and his opinion was supported by Spender, Cromer, Roberts, Rosebery, Balfour and many others. But let us quote the contemporary opinion of Count Metternich, who was no ordinary court diplomat, but an indefatigable student of British bluebooks, trade journals, and commercial reports.

The question, what effect the economic evolution of Germany exercises on the political relations between Great Britain and Germany, cannot be judged from this or that newspaper article or from occasional statements by this or that Englishman. What is really authoritative is the attitude which prevails in the great industrial and commercial centers of Great Britain. Naturally there are certain commercial circles that suffer more from foreign competition than others, and which are more inclined to see a danger in foreign rivalry. In the course of time, I have been in touch with many representatives of industry and commerce in England and Scotland; and I have found nowhere, to the same degree as by them, the sincere desire for the continuation of good relations between the two countries in commerce and politics, and nowhere is the fear so strong that they might be interrupted. If the relations between the two countries could be regulated simply on the basis of commercial interests and by the entire body of representatives of those interests, mutual relations would be excellent today. . . . Germany's trade and industry no longer stand in the foreground of British fears. Both would serve rather as a bond between the two nations if the disturbed political atmosphere itself did not throw an unfavorable light upon the mutually beneficial commercial relations.[1]

Anyone seeking to apply the theory of economic determinism to Anglo-German relations from 1906 to 1914, on the level of trade rivalry, must

[1] Metternich to Bülow, Jan. 1, 1909; *G. P.*, XXVIII, 47. Likewise, Von Stumm, the first secretary in the London embassy, was of the opinion that the number affected directly by economic competition was small and that this rivalry was not an important cause of political hostility. "If, notwithstanding, the English continually refer in their political economy to the critical danger from Germany, it is predominantly a talking point in the protective tariff propaganda." (Mem. by Stumm, July 1908; *ibid.*, XXIV, 88–89.) Similarly Bernstorff to Bülow, April 16, 1904, *ibid.*, XX, 14–21; mem. by Von Coerper, March 14, 1907, *ibid.*, XXIII, 48. For Grey's pronouncement see *B. D.*, III, 277; *Twenty-five Years*, I, 325. Moreover, the correspondence of Ballin, Gwinner, Von Schwabach, Rothschild, Fürstenberg, Beit, Cassel and others speaks volumes against the theory that competition in the field of international finance embittered political relations. See particularly Paul von Schwabach, *Aus meinem Akten* (Berlin, 1927), *passim;* B. Huldermann, *Albert Ballin* (Berlin, 1922); H. Fürstenberg, *Carl Fürstenberg, Lebensgeschichte eines deutschen Bankiers, 1870–1914.*

meet and refute point by point the arguments set forth in this dispatch by Metternich.

The second factor in the British myth and legend about Germany in this period was the striving for continental and world hegemony. This was the basic tenet of the British ruling class. It needs no special documentation. As Grey put it, "She [Germany] has reached that dangerous point of strength which makes her itch to dominate." [2] This belief is inseparable from the third feature of the English agitation over the German danger—the ambitious program of naval expansion. It was distrust of German political objectives and fear of the growing military-naval power of Germany that evoked in England emotions ranging from mild individual concern to public panic. Whether the German threat to British security was a myth or a reality makes little difference. People believed in it and it played a major rôle in British political life. In the same dispatch quoted above, Metternich wrote:

The uneasiness over economic rivalry, the political embitterment, engendered by various causes, have retreated before a new factor that has forced them far into the background. This new factor is the fear, and explicitly not the fear of our economic evolution, but the fear of our development in military-naval power. There is scarcely an Englishman of importance who does not see in the German navy, in the dimensions prescribed by the navy law, and in the tempo of construction, a serious danger to his country. . . . That accounts for the fact that the masses move from one extreme to another, from espionage scare to the fear of invasion, and that every political group can exploit the general anxiety for its own purposes, the one for expanding the navy, the other for the introduction of universal military service, the third for taxing the foreigner in the form of protective tariffs to provide the money for armaments, and the fourth for extending the protective network of international agreements and ententes.

To Metternich's testimony we may add the opinion of the German naval attaché, Von Coerper, who wrote in March 1907:

The steadily increasing sea-power of Germany constitutes the greatest hindrance to England's freedom of political action. That is the central point of the unsatisfactory relations of the two nations to one another. All other frequently advanced grounds—competition in industry, commerce and shipping, partisanship during the Boer War, etc.—are of a subordinate nature.[3]

Attractive and simple as is the pattern of trade rivalry supported by the authority of economic determinism, it cannot be validated in this instance against the record of British political life, which from 1906 to 1914 re-

[2] Grey to Bertie, Nov. 12, 1908; *B. D.*, VI, 217.
[3] Mem., March 14, 1907; *G. P.*, XXIII, 48.

veals hegemony and security fears as the dominant formulae of political agitation and enlistment.[4]

Manipulation of the German bogey on an economic level by the tariff reformers, powerful though their voice was in the daily and periodical press, never engaged the emotions and attitudes of the mass electorate. The advocates of economic retaliation through tariffs remained a pressure group striving for hegemony within the state. On the other hand, it was quite simple to sweep the press and arouse the public, irrespective of party affiliations, to the national danger inherent in Germany's bid for sea-power. The maintenance of British predominance at sea was a credo that recognized no party or class lines.

Moving now from a theoretical to a clinical level we have before us the task of describing the publicity phenomena that accompanied the development of public anxiety on the naval question to the point where it reached the proportions of a great national panic in March 1909. Because of the procedure involved in presenting annual estimates for the navy a certain amount of scare-mongering in the political press and parliament was an accepted part of the British technique of naval budget making. The cabinet, or the committee of the cabinet, usually began consideration of general naval needs for the coming fiscal year in November or December. About January first the publicity on naval expenditure began in the heavy political press. Although cabinet consideration of vital policy was supposed to be secret there were many leaks, and the government was subjected to all kinds of pressures and *Putsche* by the

---

[4] For the pro and con arguments on naval rivalry and economic rivalry see Becker, *Fürst Bülow und England,* pp. 306 ff.; Admiral Galster, *England, deutsche Flotte und Weltkrieg* (Kiel, 1925), pp. 65–71; A. Ziebert, *England und der Bau der deutschen Schlachtflotte in der Aera Bülow* (Endingen, 1927), pp. 157–71; J. Haller, *Die Aera Bülow,* pp. 45–46; Hans Herzfeld, "Der deutsche Flottenbau und die englische Politik," *Archiv für Politik und Geschichte,* January 1926, pp. 97–146; W. Hoch, "Der Ursprung des deutsch-englischen Gegensatzes und die Lehren des Weltkrieges," *ibid.,* March–May, 1923; Eckart Kehr, "Englandhass und Weltpolitik," *Zeitschrift für Politik,* XVII (1928), 515 ff.; A. Grabowsky, "Der Primat der Aussenpolitik," *ibid.,* XVII (1928), pp. 527–42. The strongest argument for commercial competition is presented by Hoffman, *Great Britain and the German Trade Rivalry,* pp. 273 ff. It should be noted that Hoffman's work, while it gives an admirable picture of this problem in the 'eighties and 'nineties when the self-complacency of the British was first shattered by German economic advance, is somewhat sketchy on the period from 1906 to 1914, when the security problem pushed the trade bogey into the background. His thesis that in emotional residues left by successive scares over German economic competition is to be found the subjective motive for British entrance into the War can be neither proved nor disproved for there is no way to measure the emotional residues of individual Britons in July 1914. The main weakness in the latter part of Hoffman's book is the identification of protectionist propaganda, which had been repudiated by the electorate in 1906 and 1910, with public opinion.

press and organized groups right up to March 1, when estimates were published. Publication in full or in summary form usually preceded by a few days the date fixed for debate in the House. Henceforth, until final disposition in parliament, the question was treated in the press as of paramount news importance. Inevitably the line of battle was drawn between economists and expansionists and inevitably the needs for the coming year were placed in a framework of comparison with developments and building policies in foreign countries. At this time, everyone who could get a hearing in the press or in parliament indulged in the pleasant pastime of naval arithmetic. That the necessary political techniques for passing the naval budget in England were productive of publicity that reacted unfavorably on international relations is an observable fact needing no supporting testimony beyond a casual consultation of the English newspaper files from January to April in almost any year. Commenting on the alarm and panic that seized the country in 1909, a writer on the Times (March 22) said that "The people would be quite sane in a fortnight—they always went like this in March."

In Germany, by contrast, the naval laws, which bound the Reichstag to appropriate the funds for carrying out the construction program, freed the German admiralty from the necessity of annual publicity campaigns to keep the deputies to their task. True, the naval appropriations were voted annually, but the Reichstag, by accepting the Tirpitz program in the form of law had obligated itself to foot the bill and to refrain from opposing the scheduled appropriations. Furthermore, the annual estimates in Germany were approved by a Reichstag committee in camera; the serious discussion occurred here and the final action of the Reichstag on the committee's report was in the main a formality. As the cost of ships and their equipment advanced with the transition to Dreadnoughts, the Reichstag 'anted up' without serious protest. In consequence, the promotional campaign of Tirpitz' department and his unofficial agencies was one of steady indoctrination, the maintenance of ground already gained, and the preservation and strengthening of attitudes already established. The shock and panic tactics necessitated by the British parliamentary system and the pay as you go plan were not fundamental in Germany, where the schedule of construction was removed by law from the list of annual debatable issues.

Another technical factor figured prominently in the British system and made the question of naval needs a subject of perennial discussion. British building programs were measured with a rubber yardstick—the two power standard. Superior resources in materials, engineering personnel, and shipbuilding yards made it possible to gear construction programs to the plans of potential enemies, and to meet any challenge with a sudden building spurt—depending on a rapid building rate to assure continued superiority. Tirpitz had boldly estimated the naval needs of the German Empire, or rather gave the appearance of having done so, and embodied his arbitrary goal in the form of law (outwardly at least in ship units, but not in total tonnage, for technological improvements prevented this). Instead of meeting the challenge with a similar long-range program, the British authorities continued to vote annual estimates, which, so far as the shipbuilding vote was concerned, required an annual prediction as to what their needs would be two or three years hence (the length of time required to complete capital ships). Technology, budgetary practice, and the parliamentary tradition all operated in such a way as to loosen annually a flood of publicity and debate in which the discussion concerned principally not the British but the German navy. The German bogey became the recognized means of reconciling the English electorate to steadily mounting naval expenditure. British naval estimates were in a sense "Made in Germany." It never failed, moreover, that the discussion went beyond the mere range of the technical and statistical and overflowed into the field of policy, aspirations, and purpose as symbolized by the German naval program. This annual March circus always added something to the measure of popular fear and hostility and rendered more difficult the maintenance of normal public and diplomatic relations.

Since the panic of 1909 was the culmination of preceding scares, it is essential at this point to recapitulate some of the major developments antedating the great Dreadnought, Fear-All Panic. From the date of his appointment as commander of the Mediterranean Station in 1899, Sir John Fisher's influence was felt in the British naval service. In 1902 he was appointed second sea lord at the admiralty, and in October 1904 he was made first sea lord in Lord Selborne's administration. During the next six years he completely revolutionized the naval arm of imperial defense. This is no place to give a detailed account of Fisher's reform career at the admiralty. It must suffice to point out that he rationalized the British navy by the application of the technological advances of the previous fifty years. Assuming his position as the technical chief of the navy he found a barnacle incrusted service; at his retirement in 1910, he turned over to his successor a technically efficient and highly trained fighting force. J. L. Garvin referred to him as "the genius incarnate of technical change." His slogan throughout the reforming years was, "The efficiency of the Navy and its instant readiness for war." [5]

[5] For Fisher's work at the admiralty see *Memories and Records* (2 vols., Lond.,

Fisher's name will always be associated with the launching of the first Dreadnought and the transition from the older style of battleship to the new all big-gun type. In undertaking the Dreadnought Fisher was merely bringing naval construction abreast of the technical and engineering progress of the previous decades. Technologically Fisher was in the right in bringing out the new type; and momentarily Great Britain scored a great advantage over all competitors. Whether it was politically wise to have taken the lead in a type that made rapidly obsolete all the older ships, in which England possessed a three-to-one superiority, is a point which will always be in dispute. Certainly it did not permanently paralyze and discourage the Germans, as Fisher boasted it would.[6] Instead Tirpitz and his staff went doggedly to work evolving a German version of the Dreadnought and widening the Kiel Canal to accommodate the larger vessels, which now became standard for all the world's navies.[7] Only with the transition to the new type did the Germans have an opportunity to start from scratch with the British.

From the day he took over at the admiralty, Germany was for Fisher the enemy against whom Britain's fleet must be remodeled and prepared. The redistribution of the naval forces, too, must be harmonized with the political realities of the changing international situation. For the naval strategists the North Sea became the focus of attention. The process of concentrating British naval strength in or near home waters began in 1904, was carried still further in 1906, and completed in 1912. As early as 1908 Fisher was triumphantly quoting Admiral Mahan's observation "That 86 per. cent. of the British guns are trained on Germany."[8]

Fisher's reforms were not carried through without serious public reper-

---

1919); R. H. Bacon, *The Life of Lord Fisher of Kilverstone* (2 vols., N. Y., 1929), I, 270–304, II, 1–28.

[6] The Dreadnought differed from its predecessors in three respects: higher tonnage, greater speed, and armament composed of ten guns, all of the highest caliber. The British thought that the German navy law of 1900 would not cover the increased cost of the new type and that the shallowness of the Kiel Canal would discourage imitation.

[7] There was no lack of authority, political and technical, behind the criticism of Fisher's masterpiece. See Lord Sydenham of Combe (Sir George Clarke), *My Working Life* (Lond., 1927), p. 209. Clarke served as military correspondent of the *Times* until 1901, when he was succeeded by Repington; later he served as secretary of the Committee of Imperial Defense until he was knifed by Esher and Fisher. The political objections to forcing the pace in new ship design were stated by Mr. Spender in the *Westminster* (July 26, 1907): "The Dreadnought is the pride of our Admiralty, and, we are told, the envy of the German Admiralty, which is going to lay down several of them without delay. . . . Our superiority in speed of construction always enables us to overtake other Powers when the competition has been started, but it is folly for us, with our established supremacy, to take the initiative in starting a new and expensive line of competition."

[8] Bacon, *op. cit.*, II, 78, 79. For the technical details of redistribution see Bacon, *op. cit.*, I, 295–304; Woodward, *Great Britain and the German Navy*, pp. 84–85, 97–98, 377.

cussions. "When a crab has cast its old shell and is growing a new one it is naturally apprehensive of danger." Agitation was inevitable in a country with a parliamentary system and a highly developed political press. Many people doubted the wisdom of Fisher's measures, many vested interests were disturbed and threatened, and there was too much jealousy among ambitious rivals to allow Fisher's prescriptions to pass unchallenged. The opposition to Fisher crystallized in the insubordination of Sir Charles Beresford and the campaign which he worked up in parliament and in Mayfair drawing rooms. The Fisher-Beresford feud split the naval high command into warring factions.[9]

Fisher could not have withstood his enemies and carried through his reforms without recourse to publicity. He had numerous connections with the press and the cultivation of these connections was his constant concern. While he was still commander in the Mediterranean he entered into confidential relations with Arnold White, a prolific writer on naval subjects. White wrote for the *Referee,* using the pseudonym "Vanoc"; he contributed to the Sunday Sun and the reviews, and was a persistent letter writer to the daily press. Fisher's correspondence with White extended over many years. A score or more of the letters reproduced by Bacon in his biography of Fisher, which contain the injunction "Burn this and don't quote," are to Arnold White, although the recipient is designated as "a friend." Fisher did not rely solely on Arnold White, but conducted a veritable campaign of education among the journalists. J. A. Spender has written that he

cultivated the press unblushingly, from the loftiest and most patriotic of motives. . . . We were to be instructed in the true blue-water doctrine, in the greatness and inevitability of the Dreadnought, in the essential necessity for the British Empire of holding all the narrows of the seven seas, and sundry other articles in the ever-expanding creed of the scientific seaman. . . . He gave with both hands to each in turn, and we rewarded him with such an advertisement of himself and his ideas as no seaman ever received from newspapers, and probably none ever will again.[10]

Under his régime every courtesy was extended to press representatives at naval reviews and inspections. He instituted a system of printed 'hand-

[9] The quarrel is reviewed at length in Bacon's *Life of Lord Fisher,* II, chap. XIII. That Beresford was a quarter-deck politician and a man whose abilities were not commensurate with his ambitions, cannot be denied, but he was not quite the insubordinate rogue that Bacon makes him out to be. See further, Spenser Wilkinson, *Thirty-five Years,* pp. 278–81; E. Halévy, *History of the English People in 1905–1915* (Lond., 1934), pp. 392–94; Lee, *King Edward VII,* II, 598–603.

[10] *Life, Journalism and Politics,* II, 67. When the *Daily Express* published advance information on one of Fisher's reform measures, King Edward laconically noted: "Admiralty evidently on good terms with the *Daily Express."* (Lee, *King Edward VII,* II, 329.)

outs' for the reporters which were known in the trade as "X's broadsides." One journalist was quoted as saying that "never in his whole career had he known such an elaborate attempt to influence the newspapers as was made at Whitehall; not even by a politician whose career depends upon it." [11] In view of this and other evidence there is a certain puckishness in Sir John's disclaimer of trafficking with the press. Writing to Arnold White in February 1910, he said: "I can truthfully say I never sought the press, but I recognized it as the one and only engine that could effect the vast revolution from shipbuilding to bread-making—from kettles to turbines—from fossils to Nelsons—as *without the press it could not have been done.* . . . I never gave *déjeuners* to the Press like Beresford and Co. at Claridge's or in my flagship. . . ." [12]

There was one current of publicity favorable to national defense with which Fisher had no sympathy. That was the agitation sponsored by Lord Roberts and the National Service League for compulsory military service. For Fisher the problem of national defense was summed up in the preamble to the Naval Discipline Act, which categorically stated that it was upon the navy "Under the good Providence of God the wealth, safety, and strength of the United Kingdom chiefly depend." The compulsory service campaign implied disagreement with this tenet, and it was regarded by Fisher and his adherents as a reflection on the rôle of the navy and a move to devalue it in public esteem. "German invasion" was the catchword of Lord Roberts and his followers. They envisaged the secret embarkation and the transport of a considerable armed force across the North Sea and a surprise landing upon the shores of Great Britain, without the navy being able to prevent it. The Bolt-from-the-Blue school, as this group was called, was met on the ground of controversy by the Blue-Water school, which put all its faith in the navy and its ability to prevent such an occurrence. Not all the protagonists to be found in either camp were there purely on conviction that the one or the other was right. In the former was to be found many who took no stock in invasion, but who welcomed and supported any campaign calculated to "wake up England." There were in the Blue-Water school, likewise, influential men, like Lord Esher, who shared Fisher's views, who did not believe that a German invasion in force was technically possible, and yet who countenanced the invasion scares and encouraged the promotional activities of the National Service League. These men of the British ruling

---

[11] Cyprian A. G. Bridge to the *Times,* Feb. 19, 1907.

[12] Bacon, *Life of Lord Fisher,* II, 120. Bacon says of Fisher that "He was the first of our Admirals to make an intelligent use of the Press for the benefit of the Navy." "Fisher felt that publicity was essential to success, and having gauged the consequent disadvantages, he boldly faced them." (*Ibid.,* II, 180, 182.)

class were genuinely concerned with the deplorable showing made by British arms in the Boer War; they pessimistically interpreted it as a deterioration of British moral fiber, and proposed as a solution the compulsory cultivation of national character with cordite.[13]

Even against Fisher's will the Bolt-from-the-Blue agitation reacted in the naval sphere, for to a certain extent popular attitudes aroused by the invasion bogey were referred to the navy rather than to the army. But this did not reconcile Fisher, especially when the Committee of Imperial Defense gave a hearing to the Bolt-from-the-Blue school. The subcommittee hearings on invasion were held during the winter of 1907-8. The subject was a lively topic in the newspaper and periodical press and it crossed at many points the unfavorable publicity that was turned in certain quarters upon Fisher's new broom in naval affairs.[14] Fisher ridiculed the whole affair, while his friend and supporter, Lord Esher, tried to convince him that the invasion bogey was useful in advertising national defense. "Invasion may be a bogey. Granted. But it is a most useful one, and without it Sir John Fisher (Captain Fisher as he then was) would never have got 'the truth about the Navy' into the heads of his countrymen." [15]

Technically qualified experts, both English and German, rejected the possibility of invasion by any force of consequence. Repington and Roberts, who were army men, were exceptions. The World War showed that the German navy was not a bridge to invasion, but a threat to British lines of communication. And yet publicity requirements, purely promotional considerations, necessitated the dramatization of the former and the neglect of the latter.[16]

[13] The belief that the country was not equal to the tasks of empire and that mass democracy would not stand the shock of war was widespread among the intellectuals of the type of Chirol, Spring Rice, Maxse, Garvin, and Strachey. Spring Rice's letters accurately reflect this mood.

[14] The hearings of this subcommittee can be followed in the *Letters and Journals of Viscount Esher*, II, 251 ff. The strongest witnesses for the 'invasionists' were Lord Roberts and Colonel Repington, the military correspondent of the *Times*. See his "Memorandum on Invasion" reprinted in Repington, *Vestigia*, pp. 312–40.

[15] Esher, *Journals and Letters*, II, 249, 251–52. On another occasion Esher wrote to Lord Roberts: "What enables the Admiralty to maintain the Fleet is fear of invasion—which every man understands—and not the fear of starvation, which only a few understand. . . ." (*Ibid.*, II, 390–91.)

[16] Aside from the mass of popular rubbish on invasion the technical and semi-technical literature is extensive. For an intelligent summary of the problem see "Invasion from the Nautical Standpoint," by "Master Mariner," *Contemporary Review*, February 1908, pp. 136–44. Captain Dumas, British naval attaché at Berlin, in his general report for 1907, considered the problem of organized invasion and declared it impossible under existing circumstances. (*B. D.*, VI, 122–24.) The same conclusion was reached by Colonel Commander Gädke in a special article in the *Berliner Tageblatt*, No. 600, Nov. 25, 1908. In the conference of political, naval and military heads, held in Berlin on June 3, 1909, the chief of the general staff, Von

As the subcommittee of the Imperial Defense Committee was launching its hearings on the invasion scare, Sir John Fisher, who felt that the navy was on the defensive in this matter, took the opportunity afforded by the Lord Mayor's banquet to denounce the scaremongers. After assuring his hearers that the navy was never more efficient and never in better position to cope with all emergencies, he said:

> Sleep quiet in your beds, and do not be disturbed by these bogeys—invasion and otherwise—which are being periodically resuscitated by all sorts of leagues (Laughter). I do not know what league is working this one. It is quite curious what reputable people lend themselves to these scares. This afternoon I read the effusions of a red-hot and most charmingly interesting magazine editor. He had evidently been victimized by a *Punch* correspondent. . . . And this is what the magazine editor prints in italics in this month's magazine— that an army of 100,000 German soldiers had been practising embarking in the German fleet. The absolute truth is that one solitary regiment was embarked for manoeuvres. . . . To embark 100,000 soldiers you want hundreds and thousands of tons of transport. You might just as well talk of practising embarking St. Paul's Cathedral in a penny steamer (Laughter).[17]

The league to which Fisher referred was, of course, the Imperial Maritime League, organized to agitate against the first sea lord's policy, the "red-hot but charmingly interesting magazine editor" was Leo Maxse, and the story of the 100,000 men appeared in his *National Review*. In reply to Fisher's thrust, Maxse wrote that "The figure may be exaggerated . . . but all the world except the Defense Committee, and apparently the Admiralty, is aware that Germany is directing her great talents to the problem of embarking and disembarking troops. . . . Since he has been ashore, the First Sea Lord has developed an unspeakable contempt for 'scaremongers'; but when he was afloat he was a public-spirited and patriotic promoter of 'scares'; and he would hardly deny that the present British Navy . . . owes its existence exclusively to the efforts of 'scaremongers.' " [18]

Since invasion was the most dramatic and easily exploited aspect of the defense problem, it continued to engage public attention. The writers of cheap serial and penny thriller fiction seized upon the theme for public exploitation. *The Invasion of 1910* was serialized in the Daily Mail and was commended publicly by Lord Esher, Sir Evelyn Wood, and Colonel Lockwood as a stimulus to enlistment in the Territorials. Other effusions of the same type bore the titles—*The Swoop of the Vulture; The Great Raid; How the Germans Took London; The Invaders, A Story of the*

Moltke, said that he would be embarrassed as to what could be done with the army in case of war with England. Tirpitz, *Aufbau der deutschen Weltmacht*, p. 160.
[17] *Times* report, Nov. 11, 1907.
[18] Letter to the *Times*, Nov. 12, 1907.

Coming War, and *While Britain Slept.*[19] Du Maurier's invasion play, "An Englishman's Home," had a great success on the London stage and was commended by all the enthusiasts of the "Wake up England" group.[20] Another play cut to the same pattern was widely produced by amateur companies sponsored by Lord Roberts' National Service League. Undisguised propaganda for compulsory service, it bore the significant title "A Stitch in Time" and featured the invasion of England by a nation called the "Tradelanders."

No less symptomatic of general anxiety was the public concern with German espionage. The old conservative journals as well as the cheap sensational press opened their columns to the invasion and spy alarmists. In parliament numerous questions were asked about the activity of German agents in England. Countless letters appeared in the press reporting German spies swarming over the country, and ridiculous articles were published by reputable editors. Derived entirely from unsubstantiated rumor and gossip, not one of these popular exposures of alien activity resulted in an arrest. In the popular pre-War conception, espionage was mainly concerned with topography—not with technical secrets which is the post-War stereotype—so German spies were always reported as making maps and taking soundings along the Eastern coast. People were apparently unaware that the ordinance department's sectional maps were offered for public sale as were also all admiralty charts. Yet this did not prevent men like Maxse from assuring a Surrey audience that "German officers trooped to England on staff rides, or disguised themselves as waiters, and hairdressers, and our eastern counties are studded with spies." And Frederic Harrison, the Positivist philosopher, could write to the Times that the German army "has been trained for a sudden transmarine descent on our coast; and for this end every road, well, bridge, and smithy in the east of England and Scotland has been docketed in the German War Office." [21] Even the authorities in the foreign office were infected with the popular spy and invasion panic; rumors and hearsay at second and third hand circulated even here.[22] So fantastic became the spy mania and so overburdened with communications were the letter columns of the press, that the Times published a leader recalling the country to its senses. Poking mild-mannered fun at the growing aberration, the Times said:

[19] Charles Lowe reviews the invasion literature and the more common spy stories in the *Contemporary Review,* January 1910, pp. 42–56.
[20] Esher publicly commended it in a *Daily Mail* interview. See also Northcliffe's letter in Esher's, *Journals and Letters,* II, 367, 369–70.
[21] Quoted by Lowe, *op. cit.,* pp. 45, 47.
[22] Notes by Crowe, Charles Hardinge, and Grey on a dispatch from the naval attaché, Captain Dumas, Feb. 3, 1908. (*B. D.,* VI, 117.)

The craze about spies has grown to so marked a degree, and has so frequently found public expression, that a protest becomes necessary, if we are not to be made ridiculous in the eyes of other nations. Every alien servitor with square-set shoulders is watched with solemn misgiving. If an affable foreigner wanders amid the glades of Epping Forest, or takes a photograph of its leafy splendours, he is made the subject of excited letters to the Press. The waiters who flock to the great caravanserais at the East Coast resorts during our brief summer cannot beguile their scanty leisure by a little sea fishing without raising in the fevered imagination of some onlooker the suspicion that they are taking soundings. . . . There is little in the current outcry about espionage in England that is worthy of the serious notice of a great nation.[23]

Nothing that the Times or any other paper could say was able to dispel the public apprehension. "Those who were forever crying 'wolf' for party purposes, and those whose interest it was to wolf the credulous public out of their pence," found the subject too exciting and profitable to forego its exploitation.[24] From time to time the subject was revived in the respectable as well as the yellow press with a series of articles on "Espionage in England."

Another support for the alarmist campaign was the presence in considerable numbers in England of German barbers, clerks, and waiters. Generally figuring in the espionage stories, they were further regarded as a potential military force organized and prepared to co-operate with an invading German army. In his famous invasion speech in the House of Lords, in November 1908, Lord Roberts said: "It is calculated that there are 80,000 Germans in the United Kingdom, almost all of them trained soldiers. They work many of the hotels at some of the chief railway stations, and if a German force once got into this country it would have the advantage of help and reinforcement such as no other army on foreign soil has ever before enjoyed." It was only a step from Lord Roberts' 80,000 Germans ("almost all soldiers") to Colonel Driscoll's statement that there were 350,000 German reservists in England (more than half the number of the German army on a peace-time basis), and that the arms and ammunition necessary to equip this force were cached near Charing Cross. In the face of existing obsessions and predispositions it mattered not at all that there were no more than ten thousand Germans in England who had performed their military service, that the census of 1901 showed fewer than 50,000 Germans all told in Great Britain and fewer than 250,000 foreigners of all nationalities.[25]

Lord Roberts' great prestige with the British people was based on

[23] *Times*, Aug. 21, 1908.
[24] Lowe, *op. cit.*, p. 55.
[25] *Ibid.*, pp. 53 ff.

solid achievement as a military commander. His public campaign for a
national army on the continental model was attended with the widest publicity. When he spoke on his favorite text in the House of Lords on
November 23, 1908, he added the sanction of authority to the spy and
invasion fictions which agitated the public. Dissenting from the conclusions of the Imperial Committee of Defense, he upheld the possibility of
a German invasion of the island in force, pointing, of course, to conscription as the only safe insurance against such a contingency. It was, therefore, on the highest military authority that the German invasion menace
was again paraded through the press. The scare columns of the newspapers presented articles entitled, "The Horror of Invasion," and "A
Disquieting Thought for Christmas," in which occurred expressions such
as "the sound of guns" and "the shrieks of terrified villagers." [26]

Despite invasion and espionage scares and the agitation of conscrip-
tionists, the vast majority of the public still looked to the navy as the
guarantor of national security. As long as the navy was supreme in the
North Sea and the Channel they could "sleep safely in their beds." When
this supremacy was questioned on the highest authority, in the spring of
1909, the mass feeling of insecurity built up by successive spy and invasion scares rose abruptly to panic proportions.

In many respects the Dreadnought panic of March 1909, is one of
the most complex phenomena presented to the student of politics, diplomacy, and publicity. There is sufficient evidence to make out a case for a
well-engineered plot by armaments manufacturers, naval megalomaniacs,
and unscrupulous politicians to shock the public into yielding up vast
sums for military-naval purposes. There is other evidence that could be
emphasized to support a thesis that the navy scare was promoted by a
knavish opposition party bent on dragging the red-herring of national
defense across the path of a government embarking upon a social reform
program inimical to the interests of the possessing classes. It could also
be presented as a normal feature of the democratic process, resulting from
the admirable and honorable action of a cabinet, which, concerned for the
future security of the nation, laid their cards on the table and took the
people into their confidence. If the nation became panic stricken that was
not the fault of the government but a fault of human nature. In fact, all

[26] *Pall Mall Gazette,* Dec. 17, 1908; the *Times* (Nov. 27) demanded a rehearing
of the invasion question by the Defense Committee. The December issues of the
periodicals—*National Review, Nineteenth Century, Fortnightly*—brought articles on
the subject. For Roberts' speech see *Parl. Deb.,* 4th Ser., vol. 196, 1679-96. Metternich commented: "A year ago the old Field Marshal's speech would hardly have
been possible. It would have been regarded as such an exaggeration that it would
have failed to make an impression. Today it is regarded more seriously, at least not
ridiculed, and the exaggeration is not noticed." (*G. P.,* XXVIII, 18.)

three explanations have been applied singly and in combination to find a rational and ordered explanation of this particular chapter of political motivation and behavior.[27] A narrator's task would be greatly simplified if he could choose one thesis and develop it by bringing together only the material relevant to that particular pattern. A closer approximation of reality requires, however, that all the ascertainable evidence be considered.

Certain primary facts should be stated at the outset. First, the crisis did not result from anticipated immediate danger to British naval supremacy; it was entirely anticipatory, based on conjecture as to the situation that would exist in 1912, "the critical year," as all the writers and speakers referred to it. Second, the crisis concerned Britain's future position in only one category of fighting craft, the Dreadnought. Third, the scare was raised entirely on presumptive evidence of German acceleration of her Dreadnought construction program.

In summary, the issue as to relative strength in the new type of ship was as follows: After Fisher launched his Dreadnought no capital ship was begun in German yards for eighteen months. Two vessels of the Dreadnought class were authorized in 1906, but the keels were not laid until August 1907. Three more were authorized in 1907 and their construction undertaken, while in 1908 the new law provided for four ships annually for the next four years. Although not a single Dreadnought was as yet in commission in March 1909, Germany would have, under the program announced, thirteen capital ships—battleships and armored cruisers—in 1912.[28]

The British, in March 1908, had ten ships of the new type already in commission or in various stages of construction. When all were completed in 1910, it was reckoned that their superiority to Germany would be 2:1 (England 10, Germany 5). With the reluctant approval of the admiralty, the cabinet provided for only two new ships in the 1908 estimates.[29] But in that year under the new law, the Germans stepped their construction program up to four capital ships annually. The British had to expand their program in 1909 or prevail upon the Germans to con-

[27] It is presented as a plot of arms manufacturers and black reactionaries by F. W. Hirst, *The Six Panics* (Lond., 1913); G. H. Perris, *The War Traders* (Lond., 1913), chap. XIII; and in great detail by Philip Noel-Baker, *The Private Manufacture of Armaments* (2 vols., N. Y., 1937), I, 449–510. C. E. Playne attempts a psychological explanation in *The Pre-War Mind in Britain* (Lond., 1928), pp. 129 ff.; and E. L. Woodward, *Great Britain and the German Navy*, chaps. X and XI, ignores the political and publicity aspects and presents a bare narrative from the orthodox British navalist viewpoint.

[28] Construction table given by Captain Dumas, *B. D.*, VI, 128; Tirpitz, *Aufbau*, Appendix IV, "The Naval Laws."

[29] Bacon, *Life of Lord Fisher*, II, 86; Woodward, *Great Britain and the German Navy*, pp. 224–25.

tract theirs. Anxious to fulfill its pledge of "peace, retrenchment and reform," the Liberal cabinet sought during 1908 to effect an agreement with the German government that would secure British supremacy without incurring large additional expenditures in 1909. When their overtures were rejected in Berlin, everyone conversant with naval affairs knew that at least four Dreadnoughts would have to be unertaken in 1909 to assure a safe margin in 1911 and 1912. When McKenna, the first lord of the admiralty, presented his department's demand for six capital ships in the 1909 budget, trouble developed immediately in the cabinet. The admiralty board based its case on German acceleration, predicting that Germany might have twenty-one Dreadnoughts in the spring of 1912, and stating as a "practical certainty" that she would have seventeen by that date.[30]

While torrents of gossip were poured out by the press, a serious crisis gripped the cabinet. It was 'pull devil, pull baker,' with the admiralty bureaucrats on one side and the cabinet economists, led by Lloyd George and Winston Churchill, on the other. The latter held that four would give them a safe margin three years hence. McKenna and Fisher held out for six. Five cabinet sessions on the estimates, during January and February, failed to break the deadlock; threats of resignation were put about by both sides. Grey staunchly supported McKenna. Asquith, deeply concerned for the unity of his government, favored the admiralty request for six; and it was he who in the final session brought forward the compromise which all accepted—four ships to be authorized, and four contingent vessels to be laid down if developments in Germany seemed to warrant this action. This was the "curious and characteristic" solution to which Churchill subsequently referred: "The Admiralty had demanded six ships: the economists offered four: and we finally compromised on eight." [31]

While no official record of cabinet proceedings is available, it is evident from fragmentary reports that the admiralty case was grounded upon German acceleration of her Dreadnought program. They dare not hazard British superiority in 1912 by failing to lay down a large batch of ships during 1909. That was also the case presented by McKenna and Asquith

[30] Admiralty memorandum quoted by Bacon, *op. cit.*, II, 88.

[31] Winston Churchill, *The World Crisis* (N. Y., 1923), I, 33. Further light on the cabinet crisis: J. A. Spender and Cyril Asquith, *Life of Lord Oxford and Asquith* (2 vols., Lond., 1932), I, 253–54; Grey, *Twenty-five Years*, I, 193–94; G. M. Trevelyan, *Lord Grey of Fallodon* (Lond., 1937), 242–44; Lee, *Edward VII*, II, 678–82; Esher, *Letters and Journals*, II, 309, 319, 369–70; Austen Chamberlain, *Politics from Inside*, pp. 149–53. Fisher in a ragging note to Churchill (March 4, 1909), suggested that the four contingent Dreadnoughts be named "Winston," "Churchill," "Lloyd," and "George." "How they would fight! Uncircumventable." (Bacon, *op. cit.*, II, 91.)

to parliament to justify the vast increase in the estimates for new construction. Was there actual acceleration? And what was the nature of the evidence upon which the admirals, the cabinet, and ultimately parliament acted?

First of all was the increased capacity of German yards, marine engineering concerns, armaments and gun manufacturers to turn out ships of the large type. Here the talking point was the capital expansion of Krupp's works, news of which reached the British authorities and the public in a highly exaggerated form. It was said that with their new facilities Krupp's, who were the chief contractors for guns and gun mountings, could turn out enough finished material annually to equip eight vessels of the largest type. It was further pointed out that not only was it possible for the Germans to increase their total output, but also to speed up the construction time, and that in this matter, the British admiralty, which counted on two years as average construction time, could no longer assume an advantage of one year in meeting the German program (thirty-six months for construction, and six months for trials and tests being the ordinary timetable in Germany). Although German capacity to produce had been increased, British spokesmen when they discussed "acceleration" did not always distinguish between acceleration as a fact and the ability to accelerate, which was their main defense in later years when the myth of acceleration was completely exploded.[32]

Second in point of consideration was the possibility that the Germans might use their increased engineering facilities to rush the construction of ships by preparing in advance the materials that they were necessarily slow in producing, such as instruments, guns, and gun-mountings. With such material prepared and assembled, a keel could be laid, and the ship completed in, say, eighteen months, instead of the scheduled thirty-six. Now if increased capacity were employed in this fashion, so reasoned British authorities, the Germans would gain a total of four ships over the official schedule by 1912 and would have in the spring of that year not thirteen Dreadnoughts but seventeen. And if the same formula of acceleration were applied to the 1910 program they would have twenty-one. This specter of phantom squadrons of German Dreadnoughts calling the tune in the North Sea over an inferior British fleet in 1912 or 1913 was employed first by the admiralty board and then by the cabinet to justify the vast increase in shipbuilding expenditure.

[32] Woodward (*op. cit.*, pp. 203–7) summarizes the evidence and the more exaggerated conclusions drawn from it; also Fritz Uplegger, *Die englische Flottenpolitik, 1904–1909* (Stuttgart, 1930), pp. 111–23.

From what evidence were these alarming deductions drawn? How substantial were the foundations upon which the admirals, politicians, arms merchants, and journalists erected that great structure of public fear and apprehension? In distant perspective it seems too slight and puny to have caused a national panic. From the published German schedule of expenditures for 1908, the British admiralty authorities learned that the payments authorized for the ships building in that year were considerably larger than the payments to contractors at the same stage in the construction of the first German Dreadnoughts of the 1906 program. This might mean larger and more costly designs (which was actually the case), or it might mean that the construction rate had been stepped up— the latter being the inference drawn by the British. The admiralty further alleged on the basis of information reaching it, that materials had been collected in advance of laying down of these ships, and that there was strong presumption that the same action was being taken in respect to the projected four Dreadnoughts of the 1909 program.[33] This presumption was founded on rumors that began to crop up in the late autumn of 1908 to the effect that contracts for two of the ships of the 1909 program had already been given out and that the firms were proceeding with the collection and preparation of material. This rumor was confirmed by the naval attaché in Berlin, who added that on fairly reliable evidence he was convinced that one of the keels had already been laid down in the Schickau yards in Danzig.[34] In brief, this meant that the orders for the two ships of the 1909 program had been given six months in advance of their authorization by the Reichstag and before the money for the first stage of construction had been voted.[35]

[33] Woodward, *op. cit.*, pp. 209 and Appendix VI. McKenna later admitted under pressure in parliament that they had drawn the wrong inferences, although he upheld the correctness of his facts. *Ibid.*, pp. 250–51; *Parl. Deb.*, 5th Ser., vol. 22, 2457 ff. Typical of the scare reports that came to the admiralty is one from the naval attaché at Constantinople, based upon a conversation with the representative of the Erhardt firm, Krupp's chief German rival in arms manufacture. He wrote: "From information received it seems safe to say that it is, or was, the intention, of the Emperor to secretly prepare all mountings, ship's plates, ammunition, etc., at Krupp's and then to suddenly commence the creation of a number of battleships sufficient to, at least, equal the naval strength of England. The programme had already been settled; it would only mean manufacturing earlier than expected." (Woodward, *op. cit.*, pp. 480–81.)

[34] Woodward, *op. cit.*, Appendix VI, reports of the naval attaché, Oct. 21, Nov. 16, 1908, Jan. 14 and 21, 1909, pp. 490–93. The keel was actually laid on March 1, 1909. F. Uplegger, *Die englische Flottenpolitik, 1904–1909*, p. 117.

[35] Under German budgetary rules and practices, the money for taking new construction in hand for the year became available on April 1, following approval of the Reichstag. Not a single penny could be paid out until the Reichstag had authorized the expenditure. Specifications and tenders usually required some time to circulate, so that actual construction did not customarily begin until late summer or early winter of the year in which the first money installments were made available. Ger-

So far we have considered only the evidence that came to the admiralty officers and the cabinet through official channels, that is, the naval attachés and the secret service. Summarizing the evidence and the deductions: First, the increase in German shipbuilding plant and capital expenditure at Krupp's, which were incidental to the greater demands imposed by Dreadnought construction at a rate of four per year, was exaggerated and misinterpreted. Second, the assumption that larger installments paid out for ships under construction in 1908 signified acceleration of these ships was likewise false; the new ships were simply more costly than their predecessors. Third, the assumption that the ships of the 1909 program had been begun in the autumn of 1908 was only partially true; contracts for two of the four had been conditionally promised. It was mainly upon these mistaken assumptions that the naval experts grounded the building program for which they sought cabinet approval. When the British diplomatic and naval officials began to question their German colleagues on the matter of "acceleration" and their expectations for the critical year of 1912, they received a stock answer: denial of the rumors of German intention to accelerate and assurances that their building program would not be anticipated—they would have only thirteen Dreadnoughts in the autumn of 1912. Since German statements did not conform to admiralty deductions, suspicion was more thoroughly implanted in British minds. Since Grey, McKenna, Fisher and their associates were clearly disinclined to accept the statements of the German authorities, the British suggestion that the naval attaché be allowed to count the ships in German yards, only angered Tirpitz and his associates, for they took it as a reflection upon their word of honor. Under the circumstances, diplomacy was helpless to dispel the thickening fog of suspicion and mistrust.[36]

Supplementing the information derived by the admiralty from its own agents was the alarmist campaign of rumormongering instituted in the press, the London clubs, and in parliament by H. H. Mulliner, managing

---

man battleships were customarily paid for in four installments, the amount of each payment depending on the stage of construction reached. In the case of the two ships mentioned above, Tirpitz, to take advantage of favorable competitive conditions in the autumn of 1908, had promised them to two private German firms, contingent upon Reichstag authorization in March 1909. Payments were to be made on the ordinary schedule and they were to be completed in three years from the date of Reichstag authorization. Under the strict budgetary control exercised by the Reichstag and the financial authorities, it would have been impossible for Tirpitz to accelerate his building program. On German budgetary control and accounting see "Rechnungshof und Rechnungskontrolle," in *Handwörterbuch der Staatswissenschaft* (2nd ed., Jena, 1901).

[36] For the diplomatic exchanges see *B. D.*, VI, 237–58; *G. P.*, XXVIII, 93–142; Tirpitz, *Aufbau*, pp. 111–62. The fruitless diplomatic conversations are narrated at length by Woodward, *op. cit.*, pp. 210–18.

director of the Coventry Ordinance Company. The exaggeration of military preparations made by other countries has always been an accepted technique for merchandising armaments. But the issue has ramifications extending beyond the field of salesmanship. The socio-economic consequences of the industrialization and mechanization of warfare is too large a subject to be explored here. But certainly a many-branched industry that gave employment to thousands of hands and paid dividends to thousands more, and which depended on the national government as its steadiest customer, could not be indifferent to the defense policies of that government. Entire cities and populous districts in Germany and England depended for their economic well-being on the armaments industry and its subsidiary enterprises. A policy of economy at the admiralty or war office could create serious unemployment and stagnation in these branches of industry. The political consequences of such a condition in any constituency could not be disregarded by politicians and party managers. The nexus of armaments, employment, dividends, politics and salesmanship is well illustrated in the famous Mulliner campaign.[37]

Through the process of industrial integration which marked the early years of the twentieth century, the construction and arming of large ships for the British navy was monopolized by two competing groups. The Armstrong, Whitworth, Vickers ring could build and equip a Dreadnought complete, while the other group, Cammell Laird, John Brown, and Fairfield Shipbuilding Company had to purchase the big guns and mountings from the rival ring. To overcome this disadvantage in bidding for the big ships, they organized and financed, in 1904–5, the Coventry Ordinance Works of which Mulliner was the managing director. But from 1906 to 1909, while Fisher was experimenting with new designs and the Liberal cabinet was cutting expenditure on new construction, the parent companies got no orders for big ships and the Coventry Works received no orders for heavy guns and mountings. Their books during this period were kept in red ink. In May 1906, Mulliner addressed an

[37] The larger problem and the attendant evils are the subject of a voluminous literature. Some significant references in the contemporary records are: *G. P.*, XXIII, 5–7; Tirpitz, *Aufbau*, p. 93; Kehr, *Schlachtflottenbau*, pp. 45–47, quoting a letter from the president of the German Navy League to Tirpitz on the stimulus to stagnant industry and business that would be provided by extending the naval building program; also Kehr, "Die soziale und finanzielle Grundlagen der Tirpitzschen Flottenpropaganda," *Die Gesellschaft*, II (1928), pp. 211 ff. Some critical studies of the arms industry are: G. H. Perris, *The War Traders*; H. N. Brailsford, *The War of Steel and Gold* (Lond., 1914); J. T. Walton Newbold, *How Europe Armed for War* (Lond., 1916); and the most extensive and reliable work to date by P. Noel-Baker, *The Private Manufacture of Armaments*, which reviews the major pre-War scandals.

alarmist letter to the war office, which forwarded it to the admiralty. In
this letter he asked: "Are you aware of the enormous expenditure now
going on at Krupp's for the purpose of manufacturing very large naval
guns and mountings quickly?" The letter was ignored at the admiralty,
and further interviews with officials and much harping on his 'information' failed to elicit the desired orders. In 1908 he renewed his drive on
the naval officials with no better results. He then began a regular campaign of agitation against the admiralty in the ranks of the Conservative
opposition where he found ready acceptance of his information. This
secured him a hearing before the Imperial Defense Committee in February 1909, and apparently on the committee's recommendation he was
heard by the cabinet on March 3, in the presence of Admirals Fisher and
Jellicoe.

Now it is doubtless true as E. L. Woodward says, that Mulliner's
evidence "was . . . corroborative, but not in any sense decisive." [38] But
why was this scaremonger, who, as everyone knew and admitted, had a
business axe to grind in addition to a commendable urge to save the
country, called before the cabinet at all? Avaliable evidence provides no
answer. Was he brought in to provide a little scare for Lloyd George,
Churchill and the other Radicals in the cabinet? All the evidence that
the naval officials and the cabinet needed to act on had been supplied in
the matter-of-fact reports of the naval attaché and the intelligence division. But Mulliner could give them the alarmist's picture that might help
to overcome the opposition of the economists in a divided cabinet.[39] We
can say in concluding this subject that Mulliner's information was not
the basis of the admiralty board's big building program; and his influence
on the cabinet is conjectural; but there can be no doubt that it was Mulliner who primed Balfour, Arthur Lee, and other Conservative leaders
with the information upon which they based their ridiculous assertions
as to German ship-building capacity and the construction of squadrons
of secret Dreadnoughts. To this extent he was the father of the popular
panic.

When the cabinet finally united on the program of four authorized and
four contingent Dreadnoughts for the next year, it devolved upon Mc-
Kenna as the department head and Asquith as the party leader to pre-

[38] *Great Britain and the German Navy*, p. 482.
[39] Mulliner's campaign against the admiralty defeated his immediate purpose. The
naval ordinance department refused to place orders with the Coventry Works until
Mulliner was removed as manager. For the details of the Mulliner affair see Woodward, *op. cit.,* pp. 481–84; Perris, *The War Traders*, pp. 109–16; Hirst, *The Six
Panics*, pp. 59 ff.; P. W. Wilson, "Armaments and Patriotism," *Daily News*, May 23,
26, 1913; and in great detail with all the evidence in Noel-Baker, *Private Manufacture of Armaments*, I, 448–510.

sent and support the estimates in the House of Commons. Their chief concern was the reconciliation of their Radical followers to the increased expenditure. There was every possibility that the struggle in the cabinet would now reappear in the larger membership of the Liberal party in the Commons. If the Radicals refused to support the armaments program the government would fall. As Winston Churchill has said, the re-organized government, with Asquith as prime minister and Lloyd George as chancellor of the exchequer, was "a veiled coalition." [40] The Radical-pacifist element was strong in the constituencies and paramount in the powerful National Liberal Federation, the backbone of Liberal party organization in the country. In the Manchester Guardian, the Daily News, and a large number of provincial papers, the Radicals had ardent journalistic support. They were, moreover, closely allied with the National Council of Peace Societies. These people had followed Campbell-Bannerman's lead implicitly, but they did not trust Asquith, Grey, and Haldane, who were "Liberal-Imps." Bent on social reform and ideologically hostile to the expansion of armaments, they scanned every item in the national defense bill with jealous eyes. The government's naval economies in 1907 and 1908 had not satisfied this group of stalwart Liberal pacifists and economists. They moved an amendment to further reduce the estimates in 1907 and in the summer of 1908 they had sent a deputation to the prime minister to present a memorial on the armaments question. This was followed in November by a manifesto from the National Peace Society against increases in the naval budget for the coming year.[41] When a synopsis of the estimates were published on March 12, the leaders of the little navy group in the House, numbering about one hundred and forty, announced that they would present a motion opposing any increase in appropriations. It was with this party of recalcitrants that Asquith and McKenna were most concerned. They had to use strong medicine to convince this group that the cabinet decision to lay down four Dreadnoughts, with the power to add four more in the course of the year, represented a national necessity.

Addressing a large and attentive House, in the early afternoon of March 16, McKenna outlined the government's naval program for the coming year. The estimates provided for an increase of close to three million pounds, most of which was required for new construction. Two Dreadnoughts were to be laid down in July and two more in November. Parliament was requested to authorize the government, if circumstances warranted it, to proceed with the collection of armaments, machinery,

[40] *World Crisis*, I, 28–29.
[41] For details see Woodward, *op. cit.*, pp. 219–20.

and materials for the rapid construction of four more ships to assure their completion early in 1912. McKenna's supporting arguments, addressed to the Radicals to convince them that the requests were not excessive, referred exclusively to developments in Germany. The gist of his remarks may be summarized: first, the admiralty was no longer certain of the rate at which German shipbuilding was proceeding; second, there had been acceleration of the German ships of the 1908 program, which they expected would now be completed in the autumn of 1910 instead of 1911, as under the original schedule; third, steps were being taken of a similar nature to hasten construction of the four ships belonging to the 1909 program; fourth, the productive capacity of German armaments firms, and particularly of Krupp's, the chief furnishers of large guns and mountings, had been so vastly increased as to make possible the equipment of eight battleships per year. Applying the acceleration formula to the German Dreadnought program, McKenna concluded that in the spring of 1912 Germany would have seventeen instead of the scheduled thirteen. It was to meet this eventuality arising out of German acceleration and German capacity to produce, that the government asked for power to add four additional Dreadnoughts to the regular four in their 1909 program. The four contingent ships would give Britain twenty to Germany's seventeen in the spring of 1912.

McKenna had been defending his department against the Radical criticism of having done too much. He was followed by Balfour who voiced the widespread feeling that in the face of grave danger the government was doing too little. With material and information supplied by Arthur Lee, the naval specialist on the Conservative front bench, Balfour proceeded to demonstrate that Britain would lose her supremacy in big ships within the next two years. Germany was building Dreadnoughts in twenty-four instead of thirty-six months, and was laying down eight instead of four ships a year. Germany would have thirteen new capital ships in 1911 to England's twelve, and in the spring of 1912 she would probably have twenty-one Dreadnoughts to England's twenty, with a visible possibility of twenty-five. It was an alarming picture of earthquake and eclipse that the Conservative leader presented to parliament and the nation.

Asquith, who spoke next, instead of concentrating upon Balfour's fictions and alarms, in the customary tradition of parliamentary debate, allowed them to pass in the main unchallenged and, like McKenna, devoted his attention to justifying the cabinet's program to his Radical party followers. This required re-emphasis of the theme of German acceleration and German capacity to produce Dreadnoughts. The spirit and substance of the prime minister's grave warning are contained in the following passage:

I speak quite frankly to the House, because I am obliged to tell them these matters in order to let them understand why we economists have presented these Estimates to the House—there has been such an enormous development in Germany, not only in the provision of shipyards and ships but . . . in the provision for gun mountings and armaments of those great monsters—those "Dreadnoughts" which are now the dominating type of ship—as to be so serious a development from our national point of view, that we could no longer take to ourselves, as we could a year ago with reason, the consoling and comforting reflection that we have the advantage in the speed and the rate at which ships can be constructed. This is a fatal and most serious fact.

From the standpoint of those anxious for national security, Asquith's defense was in every way as alarming as Balfour's attack.

The gravity and deep concern with which the prime minister spoke, contributed more to parliamentary gloom than the politically discounted predictions of Arthur Balfour. When Asquith sat down at 6:15 no one sought to continue the debate. There was dead silence until the speaker rose and the members trooped into the lobby to discuss with varying degrees of agitation and excitement the revelations of the first lord of the admiralty and the gloomy conclusions drawn by the prime minister. All the dark rumors that had been circulating for some weeks in the clubs, the lobby of the House, and in the editorial rooms seemed fully confirmed on the highest authority. Commenting on the session next day, the Daily Telegraph said: "Such words have not been uttered in the British House of Commons within living memory," and the Observer described the proceedings as "the most startling debate ever heard within the walls of Parliament in time of peace." P. W. Wilson, the parliamentary correspondent of the Daily News, likened the scene, as the two front benches compared their calculations of German shipbuilding, to "a council of war." [42]

Asquith's immediate purpose was accomplished—the squelching of the Radical revolt. The motion to reduce the estimates was not made. But in convincing his supporters that their naval position was serious, requiring

---

[42] *Daily Telegraph*, March 17; *Observer*, March 21; *Daily News*, March 17. Other eye-witness accounts: Austen Chamberlain, *Politics from Inside*, pp. 159–60; W. F. Roach, *Mr. Lloyd George and the World War* (Lond., 1920), pp. 28–29. The debate was continued on March 17, 18, and 22 (*Parl. Deb.*, 5th Ser., vol. 2, 930–95, 1075–1146, 1235–1342, 1483–1562). The Conservatives began the debate on a non-partisan level, but fearing that Asquith would dish them by pledging the government to build the four conditional ships and claim their support on this basis, Balfour hurried to give notice of a vote of censure on the cabinet's Dreadnought building policy. This threw the issue into the party arena and rallied the dissatisfied Radicals to the government. (Chamberlain, *op. cit.*, pp. 162–64.)

heroic measures, he spread alarm in parliament and throughout the country. From the point of view of party tactics and publicity a grave error had been made. Austen Chamberlain analyzed the situation for his father:

> If you ask my opinion, the Government are in a very awkward situation about their Navy Estimates. They have produced wide-spread alarm by their speeches and the whole country is excited and anxious about the situation revealed by Tuesday's debate. The fact is that the Government altogether miscalculated the forces at work. They thought they had got to justify their estimates against a Radical attack on the size of their programme and they prepared their speeches from this point of view. But they were quite wrong. All they said in their defence against the Little Navy men only served to strengthen the real attack—the charge that they are not doing enough.[43]

Lord Esher, in the same vein, noted in his journal on March 20: ". . . meanwhile we have been in the throes of a navy scare. Well engineered, it will bring us our 8 Dreadnoughts." [44] Captain Widenmann, the German naval attaché, reported Fisher's regret over all the fuss, since it was really only an internal party question. "Asquith had to have a little 'Scare' in order to make sure of the Radicals in his own party, and no one in the Cabinet had anticipated that the Opposition would so seriously exaggerate the question." Metternich referring a year later to the scare, expressed the opinion that it was Asquith's ill-chosen tactics that had thrown the naval issue into the arena of party politics and mass agitation.[45] Liberal leaders would probably have rejected the imputation of having consciously employed scare tactics. They would have said that they were providing an illuminant—the opposition and the press turned it into a bonfire.

"We talk of nothing here but the Navy," wrote Austen Chamberlain to his father. For a week following the Commons debate, the publicity in the press was of a scare and panic nature, and for a month thereafter the navy was the party issue of the hour. As the organs of the political élite, the aristocracy, and the world of finance, the Times, Morning Post, and Daily Telegraph always claimed the right to dictate the defense policy of Great Britain and the Empire. In this instance they poured forth a mass of news material of the most alarmist character, while in their editorials they hammered away at the government. "It is a moral necessity

[43] *Politics from Inside*, p. 160.

[44] *Journals and Letters*, II, 378. Behind the scenes, Esher was very busy with publicity. On March 20: "Today I have been with Kennedy Jones and this evening 2 hours with Northcliffe on Navy and then Aeroplanes." On March 28: "The naval controversy has raged all this week. . . . One day I asked Jackie [Fisher] and Kennedy Jones to luncheon. They had not met before. Kindred spirits."

[45] Tirpitz, *Aufbau*, pp. 143, 170. Grey, too, anticipated a scare but not a panic. Trevelyan, *Grey of Fallodon*, p. 243.

that the nation itself be aroused," trumpeted the Daily Telegraph (March 18). "Now for the first time in two centuries the trident is half-wrenched from our hand." The Morning Post, as Lord Charles Beresford's megaphone, had been sharply critical of Fisher's Dreadnought policy. It was scarcely in a position to clamor with the others for more ships of this type, so it directed its attack against the admiralty board. Charging general mismanagement, lack of concrete war plans, cruiser shortage, and faulty distribution of forces, Wilkinson and the naval correspondent demanded the sacking of the board and the institution of a new one.[46] The Times in its usual weighty and sober fashion summed up the situation:

> The net result of two days' debate on the subject is that, whereas only forty-eight hours ago the country was willing to believe that we were safe and more than safe with respect to the Navy, that we could in fact "sleep quietly in our beds," we now know on the admission of the Prime Minister and the First Lord of the Admiralty themselves, that unless we bestir ourselves promptly, steadily, and continuously we are or very soon shall be within measurable distance of a very grave situation indeed. . . . By the admission of the Government and the Admiralty they have allowed themselves to be caught napping again. Once bit, twice shy. The German programme may not be unexpectedly and clandestinely accelerated again, but we have admittedly no pledge to that effect.[47]

Some of the slogans, word symbols, and epithets, which flourished in the news, the special articles, and daily editorials reveal the tendencies of Conservative-Unionist publicity. The Birmingham Daily Post accused the government of pursuing a "temporising policy," and called the proposal for four contingent ships a "discreditable piece of chicanery." "The point is not whether Germany seeks war, but whether we are to allow her to take our place as the supreme naval Power of the world. At present she is in a fair way to do so." [48] The Scotsman announced "a crisis in this country's history," which had been produced by the government's "procrastination and want of foresight." Day after day it harped on "our imperilled bulwarks," while it hewed to the party line in supporting the Conservative motion of censure.[49] The Pall Mall Gazette, which had just received the stimulus of a new editor, F. J. Higginbottom, proclaimed "La Patrie Est en Danger" and described McKenna's speech as an "astounding confession of official credulity, fatuous optimism, and hopeless

---

[46] *Morning Post,* March 17, 19, 22 and subsequently throughout March and April. For Beresford's relations to Spenser Wilkinson, see Wilkinson, *Thirty-five Years,* pp. 278–81.

[47] *Times,* March 18, 1909. Among the leading Conservative-Unionist journals the *Glasgow Herald* alone refused to follow the party line. Editorially it ridiculed the alarm and panic and sharply criticized the Conservative vote of censure. (March 19, 22, 23.)

[48] *Birmingham Daily Post,* March 13, 17, 23, April 15.

[49] March 18, 20, 22, 23, 25, 27, 30.

miscalculation." An alarmist editorial headline declared: "The Sands are
Running Out!" And in the editorial the Pall Mall Gazette said: " 'Who is
on my side' exclaimed the Jewish King in the Scriptures, and as we read,
'There looked out unto him two or three eunuchs.' That is about the case
of the Prime Minister on the present occasion." [50] In the scare columns of
the press the issue was described as "life or death, security or annihilation." Not only was the "cause of British freedom imperilled," but "the
safety, honour, and welfare of the Empire" were at stake. "With a shock
of angry surprise," wrote Garvin in the Observer, "Great Britain has
awakened to the fact that a hand is stretched forth to grasp the trident
without which she falls as no kingdom ever fell before." [51]

Evidence that the naval crisis went far beyond mere party agitation
is supplied by the cheap popular press, which fastened upon the issue, not
because it was a good political scrap, but because their readers were interested. The Daily Mail devoted almost its entire news space to the
scare, publishing special articles, interviews, and editorial prophesy of
the most alarmist nature. Avoiding a party line, which was the policy of
the new journalism for the masses, it gave itself to the task of pure scare
exploitation. "Our sea supremacy is in peril," it told its readers. "That
is the moral of yesterday's debate." England must build two Dreadnoughts to Germany's one or "the historic position of our Navy is lost,
and the Nation and the Empire will live under the shadow of continual
danger." Fact was subordinated to fancy as it estimated the capacity of
English yards at twelve Dreadnoughts and that of Germany at "about
fifteen." Under a typical scare headline—"Britain's Danger; What the
Crisis Has Revealed"—the Daily Mail repeated Balfour's fiction of
twenty-one German Dreadnoughts in 1912. The government's proposal
of four capital ships and four contingent vessels was assailed as "in-
vertebrate trifling with the greatest emergency in our recent history."
"There is only one way of safety: Four Dreadnoughts in June and four
in November. Without that the Empire is on the knees of the Gods three
years hence."

From the publication of the estimates until the Conservative motion
for a vote of censure was announced, the Liberal journalists and publicists were greatly embarrassed. Viewing the increase of three millions in
the budget, the Manchester Guardian complained that "These are not
the ideals which returned the present government to power." But following the revelations made by Asquith and McKenna, it concluded that
"The gravity of the issue is common ground to all parties and needs no

[50] March 18, 22.
[51] *Daily Telegraph,* March 23, 24, 31; *Observer,* April 11.

fresh emphasis." "After the statement of the Government . . . it was inevitable that there should be some corresponding increase in our own programme." [52] The Radical Daily News, owned by the Cadburys, edited by A. G. Gardiner, with Nevinson and Brailsford dividing the editorial writing, regarded the estimates as "a bitter disappointment." After the ministerial statement, it fell in line editorially on the ground that "Our supremacy must be maintained at all sacrifice." The editors, while they did not support the government's program, did nothing to embarrass them, but rather turned their attention to crying down the panic propaganda in the Conservative and jingo press.[53] The Daily Chronicle, which boasted the largest circulation of any Liberal morning paper, announced "The Race in Dreadnoughts" in scare headlines and warmly supported the cabinet on the editorial page. "After their full and frank disclosures of the facts," it said, "the Ministers had no longer to reckon with any serious misgivings on the part of their own supporters." In a prominent front-page position, the Chronicle published a communication from John Leyland, editor of *The Navy* and associate editor of *Brassey's Naval Annual,* on the necessity of naval predominance and the consequences for Great Britain if it were lost. In a doleful conclusion Leyland warned his audience that with the loss of sea-power the Dutch, "from being rulers of a great world-state, fell to the rank of a race of herring fishers." [54] The Westminster Gazette and the Liverpool Daily Post and Mercury, organs of Liberal Imperialism, gave unreserved support to McKenna and Asquith.[55]

When the storm broke in England, the German government took steps to correct the misrepresentations so freely put about with regard to the German shipbuilding program. Metternich was authorized to repeat the official assurances as to the number of ships they would have and to explain the circumstances of "acceleration" of two ships of the 1909 program. To reach the British public Tirpitz made similar statements to the Reichstag budget committee. These were communicated to the press and reported in the English journals on March 18. An even fuller semi-official explanation was given in a Berlin telegram to the Kölnische Zeitung.[56] Here it was said again that the premature allocation of the contracts for

---

[52] March 15, 18. The *Guardian* decried the panic. Viewing the figures comparatively it asked, "What ails the country's nerves that they should twitch as they did yesterday?"

[53] March 13, 17, 18, 20, 22, 27, 30. On the editorial relationships in the *Daily News* see H. W. Nevinson, *The Fire of Life* (Lond., 1936), pp. 234–68.

[54] March 17, 18, 22. The editor of the *Chronicle,* Robert Donald, was one of Fisher's chief advocates and inspired spokesmen in the press. On their relations see H. A. Taylor, *Robert Donald* (Lond., 1935), pp. 54–75.

[55] March 17, 18.

[56] No. 299, March 21, 1909.

two vessels of the 1909 program had been effected in advance of the Reichstag vote of funds in order to get lower prices and to prevent the formation of a ring among owners of private yards. "They would not be completed until three years had passed from April 1, 1909, to April 1, 1912. All suspicions that the rate of building has been expedited beyond that provided in the German Naval Law are entirely without any basis in fact."

How were these assurances received in England? Skeptically by Grey and Asquith, who had accepted the British admiralty computations. So far as the public was concerned they only added to the confusion. In naval arithmetic, as the initiated well knew, two and two did not make four, but five or six, or whatever number you chose. The contradictory figures presented a puzzle: Tirpitz said thirteen, McKenna seventeen, and Balfour twenty-one. The Conservative and jingo papers merely ignored Tirpitz' correction when they did not brand it a lie, and continued to shout "twenty-one." The Liberal publicists found this flat contradiction of the government's statistics exceedingly embarrassing. Some followed the example of Mr. Spender, who pointed out that the German assurance was "all to the good, but we have necessarily to take into account Mr. Asquith's qualification that no charge of bad faith will lie against the German Government if different circumstances arise to alter this intention." [57] This was a polite way of saying that "If Tirpitz is a liar, and we strongly suspect that he is, we cannot call him a liar."

Only the Manchester Guardian made the publication of Tirpitz' statement, and the fuller semi-official explanation in the Kölnische Zeitung, the basis for a full reversal of policy. Henceforth, the Guardian criticized the government leaders for their miscalculations and their use of the word "acceleration," and called on Asquith and McKenna to admit that their calculations were based upon misinformation.[58] While the German disclosure as to the award of contracts prior to Reichstag authorization enabled the Liberal ministers to continue to speak of German "acceleration" it should be stated here that this was not the kind of "acceleration" that McKenna, Asquith, and Balfour had frightened the country with on March 16. At that time they intimated, and of course it was stated as a fact in every newspaper, that the Germans were building secret Dreadnoughts and had contrived to add four ships to the number scheduled for construction between 1908 and 1912.

From March 22 on, the Dreadnought issue was an out-and-out party fight. Speaking before the House on March 22, Asquith endeavored to

[57] March 18.
[58] *Manchester Guardian*, March 19, 23, 24, 27, 30, 31, April 19.

abate the public alarm and to throw the responsibility for the scare upon the Conservatives. With the Conservative-Unionist press aflame and the party leadership pressing the vote of censure, Asquith now criticized "the absurd and mischievous legends," and ridiculed "the old women of both sexes, whose slumbers are at present being disturbed by fantastic visions of flotillas of German Dreadnoughts. . . ." [59] The party journalists took their cue from Asquith's speech; Balfour and the wicked Tories were inciting panic for party purposes. "The plain truth is," wrote one London correspondent, "that the Tories are making a flagitious use of the Navy scare for party purposes. . . . If they cannot sail to power on Tariff Reform they mean to try to do so on Dreadnoughts." [60] The same accusation was made in political speeches by Runciman and Trevelyan, Liberal members of parliament.

By making the Dreadnought program a party issue the Conservatives helped the Liberal leadership out of a serious intra-party predicament. When Balfour demanded that Asquith pledge the cabinet to lay down the four contingent vessels as part of the fixed program, he enabled the Radicals to rally to the government and support the program of four fixed and four contingent ships as a measure of economy and pacifism. The party struggle in the press and in the constituencies turned on the issue of four or eight Dreadnoughts as the fixed program. The Liberals would say: "Trust Grey, McKenna, and Asquith. If the four conditional ships are necessary they will be built in good time." Their Conservative opponents would reply: "Not on your life! Asquith and McKenna admitted they had been caught napping by the Germans, who accelerated their program and secretly increased plant available for shipbuilding. Why should we trust them further? We want eight and we won't wait." The agitation continued on these lines for another month.

By no means all of the people who wrote letters to the editor, made speeches, and organized navy demonstrations were actuated by party considerations or genuine anxiety for national security. Some were influenced by ideological considerations and by the prospect of financial gain. Many Tories puffed the navy scare to distract public attention from social reform. For them the issue was socialism versus national security.

[59] *Parl. Deb.*, 5th Ser., vol. 2, 1503–8. For Mr. and Mrs. Asquith, Dreadnoughts had become a social-embarrassment theme. See the amusing incidents recounted by Austen Chamberlain in *Politics from Inside*, pp. 165, 168.

[60] *Liverpool Post and Mercury*, March 22. Also "Party Politics and the Navy," *Westminster Gazette*, March 22; "The Navy Scare," *Daily News*, March 20, 23; "Party-Made Panic," *Daily Chronicle*, March 23. A bye-election was won during this week in Croydon by the Conservatives on the tariff reform and navy issues. "The scare that won a bye-election," was the final judgment of P. W. Wilson on the crisis (*Daily News*, March 30).

Their arguments were cast in the contemporary idiom but the pattern seems eternal. Mr. Samuel Roberts, Conservative, M. P., and a director of Cammell Laird and the Coventry Ordinance Works, said in the course of the naval debate in the House on March 16: "What is social reform, old age pensions, Free Trade, or Fair Trade, compared with our national security? If we are not safe as a nation what is the use of our spending time in talking about social reform?" [61] The editorial writer of the Pall Mall Gazette complained that "Germany has stolen a march upon us while we have been dawdling in a fool's paradise of humanitarian hypotheses"; and the Daily Telegraph, the mouthpiece of the City, attacked the Radicals "who in the name of social reform . . . have worked for social ruin." Rear Admiral Montague in a public statement expressed the hope that the navy scare would awaken people to the fact that national security was more important than "A continued stream of Radical and Socialistic measures that have produced unrest and want of confidence from one end of the land to the other." The same view was expressed by Major General Thomas Fraser: "We cannot afford to give away on social schemes of improvement what is wanted for national insurance. . . ." A letter writer in the Times roundly scolded the chancellor of the exchequer, "who seeks to rob hen roosts to pay for the Socialist eggs he has hatched." [62] These people would have liked to have seen the Conservative party cry changed to read as follows: "Put down the eight. All else can wait!"

It was almost inevitable under the circumstances that the shipbuilding and armaments firms should come forward and show their wares and tell the country how it could be saved by ordering Dreadnoughts. From a board meeting of Vickers Sons and Maxim, came a statement from Colonel Vickers that they could build three Dreadnoughts in three years and after that one each six months. "He had no doubt," the report states, "that important orders would shortly be forthcoming from the British Admiralty." The Marquis of Graham, a director of William Beardmore and Company, stated in an interview published in the Morning Post that no less than eight ships should be put down if the two-power standard were to be maintained. "As a director of Messrs. William Beardmore and Co., [he continued] I may say that we can lay down two Dreadnoughts at once, and in the course of four months we could lay out a third slip to take a third Dreadnought. We have the plant and the means

[61] Parl. Deb., 5th Ser., vol. 2, 972.
[62] Pall Mall Gazette, March 22; Daily Telegraph, March 19; Morning Post, April 26; Times, March 23.

also of turning out the armour, and guns of all calibres, and each ship could be ready within two years of the laying of the keel." Similar statements were forthcoming from the chairmen of Armstrong-Whitworth, the Thames Shipbuilding Company, and others. All displayed a commendable zeal to do business and to save the country.[63]

A special part in the big navy and jingo propaganda was played by the naval defense associations. The Navy League and its rival, the Imperial Maritime League, issued public appeals, collected funds, and organized public meetings in important centers. The Navy League publicity was focused on a single point—the absolute necessity of eight Dreadnoughts for the 1909 program. Thirty-eight meetings were scheduled in a very short time, the largest being the demonstration at the Guildhall, presided over by the Lord Mayor and addressed by Balfour, Lord Brassey, and Sir F. Flannery. The Imperial Maritime League combined general naval propaganda with a more specific purpose—the replacement of Fisher by Beresford at the admiralty. The line taken by this pressure group can be inferred from the resolution moved at one of its organized demonstrations, "against the passing of our naval supremacy, and the dismissal of Lord Charles Beresford from the command of the Channel Fleet." [64] A third league was floated at this time on the tide of public concern over national defense. This was the organization known as The Islanders, founded by Lord Esher. The idea had been maturing for some time, funds had been solicited, and literature prepared. Unlike its rivals it had no party or factional liabilities; and it had but one advertised objective, the propagation of the thesis that "the British Empire floated on the British Navy." Moreover, it concentrated attention upon the German navy by substituting for the two-power standard the newer rallying cry, "Two Keels to One." "This will do more for a big navy," Esher predicted, "than the Government bill and all the Admiralty bounce." By March 1910 there were 10,000 Islanders, "all real workers, not nonsense people." [65]

In the atmosphere of panic and alarm that prevailed in England, wild manifestations of Germanophobia were inevitable. In parliamentary debate it was impossible to separate entirely the size and development of the German fleet from the assumed purposes of its construction. Even though

[63] *Daily Chronicle,* March 24; *Morning Post,* March 20; *Economist,* April 3. For statistics on the boom in the British armaments industry see Noel-Baker, *op. cit.,* I, 505-7.
[64] League activities reported in the *Observer,* March 28; *Morning Post,* March 25; *Times,* April 1; *Birmingham Daily Post,* May 1.
[65] Esher, *Letters and Journals,* II, 372, 378, 452.

participants observed the forms of international courtesy and prefaced their intensive analysis of Germany's naval program and their prescriptions for meeting it with a statement that they did not harbor any unfriendly feeling toward that power, it nevertheless concentrated public attention on the policies of Germany and piled upon her shipbuilding program all the odium for increased expenditure for British armaments. Less responsible members in debate left the ground of the German program and ranged over the field of intentions and objectives that inspired it. Outside the walls of parliament—in the press and on the platform—practically all restraints were removed. When Mr. Runciman rebuked the press for scaremongering by publishing alarming speculations on the German shipbuilding program, the editor of the Birmingham Daily Post established the case for the newspapers in the following words: "The speculation as to the hypothetical policy of other Powers is as justifiable in the press as it is in the House of Commons, and it is indispensable to the argument." [66]

But it was not simply the speculations and comparisons which were reprehensible, but the emotionalized overtones that accompanied the discussion in the press and in public meetings. We need only to sample some of the more extreme statements to establish their spirit and purpose. J. L. Garvin was thrown into a state of prophetic alarm by ministerial disclosures of German acceleration. "We stand in a crisis of national peril such as for two hundred years has never threatened us in peace or war. By an act of moral treachery, which would justify us in armed reprisals now, a foreign Power has doubled its naval programme in secret, and has gained six months' start in a conspiracy against our life. . . . We must fight before 1910—while we have a full margin of power in hand, or build eight Dreadnoughts now. There is no third way." [67] Munro-Ferguson, a Liberal member of parliament, told an audience that "Our hand held out an olive branch, and it has been met with the mailed fist." [68] Admiral Kennedy, a veteran of the Crimean War, in a public address advocated a naval appropriation of fifty million pounds annually, if necessary, to meet the German challenge. Such a sum would be "a mere fleabite" to what would occur "if any of those scoundrels got an entry into this country." [69] Of all the Germanophobic outbursts the

[66] March 29.

[67] *Observer,* March 21. The *Observer* was owned at this time by Northcliffe. Garvin became editor in February 1908. His Sunday article soon became one of the most authoritative features of British political journalism.

[68] *Daily Mail,* March 22.

[69] *Daily Chronicle,* March 20.

greatest publicity was achieved by Frederic Harrison's letter to the Times (March 18). In this hysterical screed he narrated the rise of "Prussia-Germany" by a series of swift military blows against rivals who had first been lulled into a sense of false security. She was now pursuing the same diplomatic-military strategy against England with a view to her utter annihilation and the appropriation of her Empire. The letter was reprinted or dignified by editorial comment in the Times, Daily Mail, Scotsman, Pall Mall Gazette, Liverpool Post and Mercury, the Observer, and in many journals of lesser importance. It was later included in a popular pamphlet issued by the National Service League, and during the World War it was republished in a volume of Harrison's collected warnings entitled, *The German Peril*.

In many of the platform and press effusions lurked a thinly veiled appeal for war, while British superiority at sea was still beyond question. The case for action was bluntly presented by R. P. Houston, M. P., in a speech before the Liverpool Workmen's Conservative Association. If the prime minister and government were worthy of trust "we would not wait until Germany was strong enough to choose her own time to attack us, but we would now, when we are in a position to do so, call upon her to stop building, or, failing her complying with our demand, declare war upon her and destroy her fleet (hear, hear). That is the policy that ought to be adopted." [70] The temper of leading jingoes and navalists is further revealed in the report of the Navy League meeting in Birmingham. The springboard for all the speakers was the German challenge at sea. According to the Birmingham Daily Post's reporter,

Sir Francis Lowe, M. P., said that of course they all had the most friendly feelings towards Germany—(laughter)—and hoped that the good relations which had so long existed would continue. Lieut. Carolyn Bellairs, M. P., said that he had not the slightest doubt that every sane man in this country thought the German Navy was being prepared in order to try conclusions with Great Britain (hear, hear). . . . The glove had been thrown down and they must lay down two battleships for every one she laid down (applause). Mr. Leo Maxse said that the German Emperor derived immense enjoyment from bamboozling British simpletons. . . . Every German battleship had been floated on an ocean of Anglophobia. . . . Our existence was threatened by a gigantic nation in arms, resolved to secure a redistribution of the good things of this world. . . . Germany had obtained all her successes by taking unsuspecting victims completely unawares.[71]

Now the utterances of the Maxses, the Bellairs, and the Harrisons, to

---

[70] *Liverpool Daily Post and Mercury,* April 22.
[71] Report in the *Birmingham Daily Post,* May 1.

whom scaremongering was a trade, should not be identified with the prevailing attitudes in the country, which were deeply marked by anxiety but which were in the main pacific. Statements like those quoted above were of more consequence when exported than when kept for home consumption. They merely stimulated like-minded people in Germany to demand more armaments as insurance against a preventive war. Here are the words of Count Reventlow, one of the most ardent of German navalists: "The whole policy of England, the speeches in your Parliament, and the articles in your press lead me to the conclusion that a strong Navy is our only safety." [72]

On March 29 the debate on the Conservative motion of censure was held in the House of Commons. The feature of that debate was Grey's speech in defense of the government. In the course of his remarks he acknowledged the official assurance of the German government that they had no intention of accelerating their construction program and that they would have only thirteen Dreadnoughts in 1912. This assurance he accepted without question. What then became of the cabinet's case based on acceleration? Admission of error and retraction was avoided by making a distinction between the German assurance as to official intention and the increase in German plant and shipbuilding facilities, which made acceleration possible if the German authorities should at any time decide to change their intention. It was the power to construct that the British had to reckon with. Grey's speech ended on a pessimistic note as he asked his hearers "to recognize that the whole problem of national defence, from the naval point of view, may be entering upon a stage more grave, more serious, requiring greater care, greater effort than anything we have yet known. It is because there is doubt and uncertainty that our Estimates contain the unusual provision of power to anticipate the future." [73] The significance of Grey's speech for the immediate question of the British naval program was well appreciated by Fisher, who wrote the next day in exultant terms to Lord Esher: "Grey rubbed in two great points yesterday: (i) Lack of information as to German acceleration will be acted on as if acceleration were a fact. (ii) The 8 this year won't affect next year." [74] Fisher's expectations were fully realized. At the end of July, McKenna announced in the House that the four contingent ships would be made a part of the regular 1909 program and would not be counted in the program for 1910.

[72] Interview by the Berlin correspondent, *Westminster Gazette,* April 13, 1909.
[73] *Parl. Deb.,* 5th Ser., vol. 3, 70.
[74] Fisher, *Memories and Records,* I, 190.

While the Conservative motion was easily defeated, Grey's speech did not stop the public clamor. The first sign of abatement came about two weeks later, when the mass circulation papers, such as the Daily Mail and Daily Express, dropped the scare and returned to gaudy adulteresses and the latest crime sensations. As a party issue, however, the navy question was not superseded in the political press until the publication of Lloyd George's famous budget on April 29. To finance social reform and the added cost of reconstructing the British navy the chancellor of the exchequer resorted to revolutionary forms of taxation. His fiscal innovations led to two general elections and ended in the Parliament Act of 1911, the most important constitutional change since the Reform Bill of 1832.

Never before had a British program of naval construction been sustained by such a naked appeal to the action of another friendly power. But the bases of that appeal were wholly fallacious, for there was no acceleration of German shipbuilding and no secret Dreadnoughts. Apologists for the British admiralty have maintained that the discovery of the plan to accelerate made hopeless its achievement, and that with the prompt reaction in England the plan was dropped.[75] There is not a shred of evidence to indicate that the promise of two Dreadnoughts to German private firms, conditional on the Reichstag vote of funds for the 1909 program, had any other than a financial and business motive as explained by Tirpitz. Winston Churchill who, together with Lloyd George, led the fight in the cabinet against McKenna and the admiralty, has written: "Looking back on the voluminous papers on this controversy in the light of what actually happened, there can be no doubt whatever that, so far as the facts and figures were concerned, we [Churchill and Lloyd George] were strictly right. The gloomy Admiralty anticipations were in no respect fulfilled in the year 1912. . . . There were no secret German Dreadnoughts, nor had Admiral Tirpitz made any untrue statement in respect of major construction." [76] As a matter of fact the official schedule of German Dreadnought construction was not fulfilled. When the British admiralty sprung its third surprise on Europe in four years (the Dreadnought and the battle-crusier being the first two) and brought out the 13.5 gun, the German ships of the 1910 schedule were delayed eight months while plans were revised to permit the mounting of larger guns. On March 31, 1912, Germany had only nine Dreadnoughts, instead of thirteen, in commission. England had fifteen commissioned and four

[75] Woodward, *Great Britain and the German Navy*, chap. XII.
[76] *World Crisis*, I, 32–33.

more ready for tests and trials. Not until the spring of 1914 did Germany have seventeen capital ships of the Dreadnought type in commission. Under the circumstances it is difficult to resist the judgment of Alan Bourgoyne, editor of the *Navy League Annual,* that the Dreadnought panic was "one of the most portentous pieces of Parliamentary humbug ever practised on the electorate." [77]

Only a brief paragraph is required to describe the German reaction to the British naval scare. The reckless forecasts and predictions about the German building program made by responsible people in England, and the corrosive publicity that accompanied the scare, might well have provoked violent counter-agitation in Germany. There were, to be sure, some bitter rejoinders in the 'kept press' of the arms manufacturers,[78] and some legitimate protests in the leading journals against the use of the German navy program as a platform for electioneering speeches.[79] But in the main the press comment was restrained. This was in line with Bülow's desire to avoid newspaper polemics. He had already warned Tirpitz, on February 19, that it was "absolutely necessary that our press record only the facts and discuss as little as possible the forthcoming English building program." [80] The tempest in England, moreover, co-incided with the final disposition of the Bosnian affair and a major crisis in bloc politics, both subjects ranking high in the German scale of news values. In consequence, less space was accorded the London reports than might otherwise have been the case. More important than the press reaction was the sharpening of Bülow's desire to reduce the tension by reaching some sort of an agreement with the British. The outcome was the famous conference of June 3 in Berlin, attended by the London ambassador and the highest political and military authorities of the Reich. Largely as a result of Tirpitz' political and technical ob-

---

[77] Cited by H. Lutz, *Lord Grey and the World War* (Lond., 1928), p. 165; and *Noel-Baker, op. cit.,* I, 497. The retardation of the German program was reported simultaneously by the Berlin correspondents of the *Daily News* and *Daily Telegraph,* Oct. 28, 1910.

[78] Particularly the *Rheinisch-Westfälische Zeitung* and the *Berliner Neueste Nachrichten.*

[79] "Die Flottenpanik in England," *Münchner N. N.,* No. 151, March 31; "Gerade und Krumme Politik," *Kölnische Ztg.,* No. 335, March 30; *ibid.,* No. 299, March 21; Count Reventlow in *Tägliche Rundschau,* No. 139, March 24; *Magdeburgische Ztg.,* and *Schlesische Ztg.,* quoted *ibid.,* No. 141, March 25; *Vossische Ztg.,* Nos. 130, 138, 161, March 18, 23, April 6; *Berliner Tageblatt,* Nos. 148, 158, 169, March 18, 23, April 6; *Frankfurter Ztg.,* Nos. 78, 83, 89, March 19, 24, 30; *Schwäbischer Merkur,* Nos. 130, 131, 159, March 19, 20, April 16; *Kölnische Volksztg.,* Nos. 236, 247, March 19, 23.

[80] Tirpitz, *Aufbau,* p. 124; *G. P.,* XXVIII, 59. For Goschen's reports on the moderation of the German press see *B. D.,* VI, 246–49; also Findlay's report from Dresden on the Saxon press (*ibid.,* VI, 258–59).

jections, no promising formula of agreement on the naval question was forthcoming from that conference. The political tension and the danger of preventive war did not call for agreement, but for continued building to the end that they might come more quickly through the danger zone.[81] In the prevailing atmosphere of fear and mistrust the remedy prescribed in both England and Germany was more Dreadnoughts, when the great need was not Dreadnoughts but statesmanship.

[81] Protocols of the conference in *G. P.*, XXVIII, 168 ff.; Tirpitz, *Aufbau*, pp. 157 ff.

CHAPTER XIII

AGADIR: PRUDENT AND IMPRUDENT PUBLICITY

If war should ever come between these two countries, which Heaven forbid!
it will not, I think, be due to irresistible natural laws; it will be due to the want
of human wisdom.

A. Bonar Law, in the House of Commons, November 27, 1911.

The Dreadnought panic crystallized the publicity patterns that henceforth governed all journalistic presentation of the British security problem and England's relation to the continental power system. These patterns, which remained relatively stable until disrupted by war, were
three in number. According to the Conservative Imperialist press, the
strongest military power on the continent—so ran the thesis—was
striving also for naval predominance. Fired by ambitions for world trade
and empire, and nursing hostile designs on the independence of her
small neighbors—Holland, Belgium, Switzerland, and the Scandinavian
countries—Germany was embarking on a campaign to establish political
hegemony in Europe. Similar attempts by other powers in the past had
always been a grave danger to the Empire. In the present situation the
British navy was the sole bulwark against the accomplishment of such
a design. Official German protests that her armaments policy cloaked no
war-like aims might be quite true, but they were wholly irrelevant.
Mere superiority in naval and land armaments, if achieved, would place
Germany in a position to enforce a policy destructive of the European
balance of power and grievously detrimental to British interests. To
save Europe from a "brutal Prussian hegemony," they must maintain a
wide margin of naval superiority, vigorously cultivate their political ententes with France and Russia, and avoid giving offense to these friends
by flirting with Germany.

Less rigid and dogmatic was the editorial and news design employed
by the Westminster Gazette, the Daily Chronicle, and the Liverpool
Post and Mercury. In these Liberal Imperialist journals the aggressive
tendencies of German policy were minimized, and the opposition of
England and Germany was attributed to the difference between an island
and continental viewpoint. The Germans were unable to appreciate the
British position with regard to the supreme necessity of maintaining

naval predominance. The British on the other hand, being an island people, did not understand the sensitivity of a continental folk, with land frontiers, to the change in relationships resulting from the British ententes with France and Russia. The British discerned a menace in the German naval program, the Germans saw a potential threat to their security in Britain's understandings with France and Russia. Both illusions could be dispelled by a naval agreement assuring Britain a sufficient margin of safety. In the improved atmosphere, which would result, the cultivation of friendly relations would dispel the illusion that British friendship with France and Russia constituted in any way a threat to Germany's security. While doing everything necessary for their own safety they must always let it be known that they were ready for an agreement on the naval question. And above all they must resist the disastrous fatalism of the doctrine that a failure to arrange the naval question must inevitably lead to war.

In the Radical press, represented particularly by the Manchester Guardian and the Daily News, it was insisted that the issue was not simply one of competitive armaments; the root of the trouble was political. Naval competition was the fruit of the unfortunate policy of exclusive and pointed friendships taken over from the Conservative government. How was it, they asked, that while we have made agreements and arrangements with every power in Europe, not one question had been turned up on which Germany and England could work together? A foreign policy consistent with true Liberalism called for friendships all 'round, and not the exclusive and jealous understandings which were dividing Europe into two heavily armed camps. There is no chance of an agreement on the disastrous armaments question without a prior agreement on policies, which would substitute for the present state of suspicion and hostility one of sympathy and co-operation. If the latter were achieved the tension would disappear and the curbing of expenditure on naval armaments would follow naturally as a measure of common sense.

Now, we may well ask, which of these three patterns more nearly corresponded with the realities of official British policy? The stereotyped view of the European power configuration that prevailed in the Conservative Imperialist journals prevailed also in the foreign office. That Germany aimed at hegemony in Europe was the firm conviction of practically the entire foreign office staff and most of the British ambassadors in key positions—Hardinge, Crowe, Nicolson, Goschen, Bertie, and Cartwright. The security of Britain, and ultimately of her Empire, was linked to the maintenance of the balance of power which could best be secured by unquestionable naval predominance, the cultivation of close understandings with France and Russia, and the preparation of naval and military plans that could meet force with force. Nothing in their view was more pernicious than attempts at political understanding with Germany, which yielded nothing positive and only damaged their credit in Paris and St. Petersburg.

Giving due weight to the threat inherent in the German bid for sea-power, the competition in the economic sphere, the aggressiveness of German policy, and all that that implied for the historic position of Great Britain in European and world affairs, there is still the ring of hollowness in these doctrines as expounded in the Imperialist press. In spite of the tremendous economic advance in Germany since 1871, her resources in capital and raw materials could not match those of the British Empire. Her geographical and political position necessitated the maintenance of a heavy load of land armaments. Further she bore a burden of social services more advanced and more costly than that of any other European country. In spite of much wind and spouting the rôle to which the Pan-German prophets aspired required wealth and resources which Germany did not possess and the lack of which was not to be overcome by her well-disciplined and self-sacrificing population. The expansive force of German policy was strictly conditioned by these fairly obvious factors. All this had been present in Bülow's mind when in response to pressure for still further efforts in the armaments brawl he said: *"Ikarusflüge mache ich nicht mit."* [1]

In British publicity on the German peril all this was overlooked or pushed into the background. Why? Because only by ignoring these realities could the course of British foreign policy be acceptably rationalized. The Anglo-French and Anglo-Russian agreements were made to relieve the dangerous pressure upon certain vulnerable points in the British Empire and its far-flung spheres of economic and political influence. Whether they be called shrewd bargains or capitulations is immaterial, for they were presented in public as the consequences of a welcome rebirth of friendship between nations who were no longer opponents and rivals but good friends. In this reorientation of British policy, and its political linkage with the Franco-Russian Alliance, lurked the implication that the friendship of official Germany was less important than that of France and Russia, a statement which has as its corollary the conclusion that German antagonism and hostility was less dangerous to British interests and more easily borne than that of the Dual

---

[1] Bülow to Hammann, Oct. 2, 1908; Hammann, *Bilder aus der letzten Kaiserzeit,* pp. 60–61.

Alliance. This hypothesis, which admittedly cannot be fully documented, receives support from the timorousness which marked the attitudes of the directors of British foreign policy toward breaches of loyalty by their partners in the Triple Entente. Statesmen in London may have been genuinely pleased with the Franco-German agreement of 1909 over Morocco, but there was the implication of brusqueness in the neglect of the French to consult London during the course of those negotiations. In the Bosnian crisis Grey ranged himself with the Entente in the demand for a conference only to be left in an embarrassing position by the Russian capitulation. Further, to preserve the Entente the British foreign office swallowed Russian chicanery in Persia and even defended the breaches of the 1907 accord in parliament. And when Russia, acting independently of her Entente partners, concluded the Potsdam agreements with Germany, the British diplomats fretted in private, but put a good face on a bad matter in public. All this stood in marked contrast to the painful regard for French and Russian susceptibilities shown by the British whenever they had any dealings with Germany. Reflection upon this point might lead one to conclude that the measure of British resentment toward Germany was directly proportional to the sacrifices, psychological and material, that were necessary to retain the good will of Paris and St. Petersburg; that the tumult over the German menace was a form of over-compensation accompanied by a curious transposition of symbols. Following this line of thought the stereotype of the balance of power, and the British navy standing between an independent Europe and a continent ordered about by militarist Germany, becomes simply a heroic rationalization of Britain's capitulation to France and Russia. Doubtless not one of the three hundred odd men who formulated British policy would have admitted the validity of the above hypothesis, but it explains many features of British public policy that otherwise seem wholly unintelligible.

Had the anxiety over the German danger been thoroughly genuine in the circle of foreign affairs experts, and without any element of compensation or rationalization, some definite action would doubtless have been taken to improve relations by a political agreement with Berlin, or by damping down the highly corrosive publicity emanating from the British agencies of public information and discussion. On the contrary, it was with considerable reluctance that Downing Street officials entered into the negotiations initiated by Bethmann-Hollweg to relax the tension between the two countries. For two years, beginning in 1909, these negotiations were fitfully and fruitlessly pursued—that is, until they were abruptly interrupted by the Agadir crisis. As a basis of agree-

ment Bethmann and Kiderlen proposed a slower tempo in fleet construction and concessions in the Bagdad Railway against a British promise
of neutrality in the event of an armed clash between the Dual and Triple
Alliances. The neutrality formula was wholly unacceptable to Grey and
his professional advisers. As a matter of fact the neutrality question
was answered before it was asked. The prevailing opinion in the ranks
of British diplomats is expressed in a memorandum by Charles Hardinge, drafted in April 1909. An agreement with Germany, he maintained, would be "a trap"; it would "tie England's hands," while Germany consolidated her supremacy on the continent; and in the end
England would be compelled "to take her place amongst the satellites
of the German constellation." In other words, acceptance of a neutrality
formula was equivalent to the abandonment of independence. This view,
expressed so authoritatively by Hardinge, became a fixed dogma in the
influential circles that controlled British policy.[2]

While the naval program and Germany's relations to England were by
no means excluded from discussion in the German press during these
years, they were never the subject of senseless agitation. Protests were
frequently forthcoming in consequence of journalistic exaggerations in
London, but the days of the Boer War were long past when Anglophobia
had been an end in itself. Reflecting the conflict between the Wilhelmstrasse and the navy department, the German editors lined up on the
question of an understanding with England and a curtailment of the
naval program. In general, the liberal journals and those in contact with
the foreign office spoke favorably of an Anglo-German understanding.
Notable in this respect were the Berliner Tageblatt, the Vossische Zeitung, the Frankfurter Zeitung, the Kölnische Zeitung, and the Catholic
journals. More nearly in line with the admiralty viewpoint were the
organs of the Conservative and National Liberal parties and the independent papers with Pan-Germanic leanings. The Social Democratic
press was opposed on ideological grounds to all armaments expenditure.

---

[2] B. D., V, 823–26. The protracted negotiations are conveniently summarized from
the British side in a paper prepared in the foreign office for circulation to the cabinet.
B. D., VI, 631–36, May 24, 1911. Although Kiderlen did not become foreign minister
until 1910, he was Bethmann's technical adviser and guide in opening negotiations
with the British. (E. Jäckh, Kiderlen-Wächter, II, 48–59.) The German record of
the negotiations is in G. P., XXVIII, 199–425. It is perfectly clear that on the part
of the Emperor and the navy department there was neither desire nor inclination to
curtail by agreement their naval program. In England, despite all official and unofficial discussion of the desirability of mutual limitation or reduction, no one in the
admiralty or in any other authoritative position ever undertook to formulate the requirements that would satisfy the British. This curious gap was noted by both
Crowe and Nicolson after the negotiations with Berlin had been going on for nearly
two years. (B. D., VI, 622–23.)

The opinions that found expression in the press, however, were not taken as directives by German statesmen. But they made up a kind of political weather which might condition tactics but which in no wise determined policies.[3]

In England the exigencies of domestic politics kept the Anglo-German problem before the public. The general election in the winter of 1909–10 was precipitated by Lloyd George's budget, but tariff reform and national defense were pushed sharply to the front by the Conservative-Unionists as collateral issues in the campaign. Since for the Englishman the navy was the symbol of his personal security, the defense policy of the government was a favorite topic with Tory campaigners. The Dreadnought scare was still fresh in mind and the Liberals and their Labor allies were always open to suspicion in the matter of appropriations for national defense. It was inevitable, therefore, that in the struggle for ballots politicians should resort to scaremongering. Mr. Balfour set an example for his party henchmen when, speaking at Henley, he said: "Go about at this moment if you will and consult the statesmen and diplomats of the lesser Powers, and I am perfectly confident that you will find among them an absolute unanimity of opinion that a struggle sooner or later between this country and Germany is inevitable. . . ." And he told his audience that he had known Germans of position and character who actually said: "Do you suppose we should ever allow Great Britain to adopt Tariff Reform?"[4] Sir George Armstrong, speaking to a Tory audience at Pembroke, warned his hearers that "the time might come when they would hear the enemy's guns booming in Milford Haven (Oh, Oh! and laughter)."[5] Other speakers and writers enlarged on the danger of invasion and quoted Dreadnought statistics to show that under the Liberal government Great Britain was dropping dangerously behind Germany. To meet this line of attack the Liberal spokesmen on the platform and in the party press were led to make declarations that bordered on the provocative. Speaking at Grimsby, Lloyd George boasted of what the British fleet, which they had kept up to full strength, could do to the German navy in a very few minutes. "There is not a German who does not know that if the German fleet, in a moment of madness, ever attempted to take us, that German fleet

---

[3] Such was Tirpitz' attitude toward the press agitation of the naval critics, Galster, Persius, and Wachenhausen. (Tirpitz, *Aufbau,* p. 152.)

[4] *Daily News,* Jan. 6, 1910. When reproached by Metternich with manipulating the German bogey for electioneering purposes, Balfour, of course, was able to say that he had not stated that this was his opinion, but only the opinion among the diplomats of the minor states. (Metternich to Bethmann-Hollweg, Feb. 10, 1910; *G. P.,* XXVIII, 291–97.)

[5] *Daily News,* Jan. 6, 1910.

would be at the bottom of the German Ocean in a very few hours." [6] Handbills and posters were displayed by both parties, the Liberals showing the inferiority of the German fleet to the English, and the Conservatives representing Britain's margin as dangerously near equality.

German economic competition and the British need for tariff protection was thoroughly publicized in the black bread controversy. A loaf of German black bread symbolized for election audiences and readers of newspapers the relationship between German protectionism and standards of living. Liberal campaign orators would produce a black loaf—the genuine stuff that the German laborer ate—to show their audience that it was vastly inferior to the white loaf eaten by the British worker. The Tory speaker would brandish a loaf to show his audience that it was equally as good as British bread and that the Germans would eat it as a matter of choice. In the press and on the platform a war of words ensued on the edibility and nutritive value of British versus German bread. The Daily News scored a point on the opponents when it unearthed and published from Northcliffe's *Weekly Dispatch* a graphic description of German black bread. "The loaf in appearance is not inviting. Many who see it will go further and say that it is repulsive. The coarse black-brown, dirty colour of the crust is like nothing that we see in England. Cut it and you will notice a peculiar stuffy sour smell. A dozen loaves on a shelf in an ordinary room will make an English visitor who enters say, 'Great Scott! It is close in there! Open the windows!' " [7] Reviewing the Free Trade speeches, special articles, and editorials one receives the impression that the German workers subsisted on sour black bread and horse meat; that in protectionist Germany—also in the United States—workmen were committing suicide in shoals because of hard times and unemployment. In the opposing Tariff Reform publicity German and American workers wallowed in plenty because they enjoyed the blessings of protection. One fact is revealed beyond question by the debate over Tariff Reform in this election, namely, that it was not trade competition that was dominant in British attitudes toward Germany. It was really domestic fiscal policy, free trade *versus* protection, that was at issue. Germany, and also the United States, were both cause and example in the argument. [8]

By far the most important publicity coup in the campaign was the

[6] *Daily News,* Jan. 15, 1910.

[7] *Daily News,* Jan. 5, 1910. In 1903 Northcliffe was conducting a campaign in his papers on the improvement of bread and dramatically sent a correspondent to Germany to bring back samples of the German loaves.

[8] Although the Conservatives gained forty seats in the election, these were won in agricultural and not in industrial areas.

publication by the Daily Mail of the well-known series of alarmist articles on the German danger and England's defenselessness by the Socialist writer, Robert Blatchford. Taken alone and in any other circumstances, this series could be set down as "Wake-up England" articles of the variety which filled the columns of Northcliffe's papers before the War. Published in the midst of the heated campaign over Lloyd George's budget they were doubtless meant to be and were generally interpreted as a clever partisan attack. In the campaign jeremiads of the Liberal press, "Blatchford and Balfour" were symbols of Tory reaction and militarism.

Born in 1851, of mixed English and Italian parentage, Robert Blatchford was apprenticed early in life to a brush maker. Later he served six years in the British army, an experience that enabled him to pose as a military critic. Embracing Socialism, Blatchford began a long career as a radical journalist. In 1891 in collaboration with A. M. Thompson he founded the Socialist journal, the Clarion. In 1894 a series of Blatchford's articles on the social question was reprinted in book form under the title *Merrie England,* and sold twenty thousand copies at a shilling each and a quarter of a million at a penny. Blatchford always boasted that he was first an Englishman and secondly a Socialist; he supported the Boer War and campaigned for conscription. As a matter of fact, he was of that species not uncommon in England known as a jingo Socialist, usually more blatant, more shrill, and shallower than his Tory counterpart. In his later years, like another great popular journalist, W. T. Stead, Blatchford embraced spiritualism. Blatchford commanded a simple graphic style, especially suited to popular journalism and mass propaganda; he had imagination and journalistic flair, but his articles and his memoirs reveal a mind lacking either cargo or ballast, buoyant and impressionable but essentially shallow.[9]

In the autumn of 1909, Blatchford was commissioned by the Daily Mail to report the German army maneuvers. Provided with an interpreter because he spoke no German, Blatchford witnessed the maneuvers and wrote his reports. Returning to England, he was asked by Kennedy Jones, Northcliffe's associate, to write up his impressions of the German menace for the Daily Mail. At first he hesitated, but after reconsidering he agreed to produce a series of ten articles of fifteen hundred words each. For his labor he received ten guineas per thousand words and half the profits from the reprinting and sale in pamphlet form.[10]

[9] Robert Blatchford, *My Eighty Years* (Lond., 1931).
[10] This is the account of the genesis of the articles given by Kennedy Jones (*Fleet*

In the first article, entitled "The Menace," which appeared in the Daily Mail on December 13, Blatchford said: "I write these articles because I believe that Germany is deliberately preparing to destroy the British Empire; and because I know that we are not ready or able to defend ourselves against a sudden and formidable attack." In almost the next sentence he said what every Tory wanted the country to believe about the rising tide of social discontent and the socialistic measures projected by the Liberals to meet the danger. "At the present moment the whole country is in a ferment about the Budget, and the Peers, and the Election. It seems sheer criminal lunacy to waste time and strength in chasing such political bubbles when the existence of the Empire is threatened. . . ." The great menace as he saw it was "the ambition of the Pan-Germans, who are the war party, who are the masters of Germany," to secure world-domination and conquest. It was the Pan-Germanic dream that "was driving Germany into a war of aggression against this country." But more than that "the Pan-Germans menace the honour and the liberty of the British, and the French, and the Danes, and the Dutch. All Europe is to be Teutonised. We are all to be drilled and schooled and uniformed and taxed by Prussian officials, and the Emperor William II is to rule us with a rod of iron."

In the second and third articles, entitled "Evidences of German Hostility" (Dec. 14, 15), he presented the Bismarckian word symbol of "blood and iron" as "the soul of the Pan-German policy." This was supported by a cankered review of the German wars of unification and imperial policy under Bismarck, and buttressed with quotations from the Emperor's speeches, the writings of Treitschke, the provocative statements of German militarists, and the preamble of the German navy law of 1900. He told his readers how he had discovered that there were many soldiers in Germany and how there were also railroads that connected inland parts with the sea ports and that in these sea ports there were "long quays" from which people might go on board ships. From this great discovery he concluded that "Germany has ships, quays, equipment and men ready for an invasion of an enemy's country." That country was

---

Street and Downing Street, pp. 249–53). In his memoirs Blatchford says nothing of his negotiations with Jones, but speaks only of his friend Fenton Macpherson, the foreign editor of the *Daily Mail.* He tells us that his sense of impending national catastrophe impelled him to call Macpherson and offer to do the series without payment. "It was agreed that I should state my case in ten articles of 1,500 words, and Macpherson . . . said he should like the complete thing delivered in three days. . . . I spent the first day on selection and arrangement, wrote 5,000 words on the second day and finished off with 10,000 on the third day." (*My Eighty Years,* pp. 223–24.)

Britain because "Britain alone stands in the way of Germany's realisation of her dream of world-power and domination."

In "Conciliation or Compromise?," the fourth article in the series (Dec. 16), he held up to scorn and ridicule all the efforts of diplomacy and negotiation for limitation of armaments or political understanding as well as all the unofficial efforts at effecting a rapprochement between the peoples. The moves of British diplomacy toward naval limitation he described as "one of the funniest political episodes I can remember." The effect on the Germans he portrayed as follows: " 'Ha,' said the men of blood and iron, 'I smell funk! They are beginning to feel the pinch. Hurry up with those super-Dreadnoughts!' And so it was." The German policy of "blood and iron," which fitted the German theory of war "as a bludgeon fits the hand of a footpad," permitted no compromise. "Arm or surrender; fight for the Empire or lose it. We can choose our alternative; no middle course is open to us."

Having established in the first four articles the reality of the German menace and the threatened eclipse of the British Empire, he turned in the fifth article to the measures necessary to defeat the foul Teutonic plot against an easy-going and pacific nation. Their first need was for "A Man" to take the place of a set of craven politicians who feared to tell the people the truth, who closed their eyes to the danger and refused to take the bold steps required to meet it.[11] The second need was for a conscript army of a half million or a million men, not for home defense but for service on the continent. "The problem of British defence is the defence of France." "The downfall of France is the downfall of the British Empire. The aggrandisement of Germany is the humiliation of Europe." Only by throwing their armed weight in the scales on the weaker side could the balance on the continent be maintained; the defense of the balance of power was the only security against ultimate German domination. The doctrine of the Blue-Water school held against German invasion, but it made no provision against a German conquest of France and the absorption of Belgium, Holland, and Denmark. In other words, "the command of the seas will not enable us to maintain the balance of power. . . . Therefore, the Blue-Water theory is wrong, and Lord Roberts is right."[12]

[11] "Wanted: A Man" (Dec. 17). Blatchford's use of the Old Testament pattern with himself in the rôle of the prophet is so obvious that it scarcely needs to be mentioned. As a people the British had a great heritage but were about to abandon it and forsake the law of life and deny their true destiny; doom threatened them and they needed a Saviour to lead them back to the hard path of duty. It is all there, even the scourging of his own "people" who have become "conceited, self-indulgent, decadent, and greedy," and who "want to keep the Empire without sacrifice or service."
[12] "Armageddon: The Greater Danger," December 18; "The Task," December

In the eighth article of the series Blatchford considered "The Cost." (Dec. 21.) The cost would be great. "But consider the stake. The stake is honour, liberty, and the Empire." The cost of security was as nothing compared to the cost of defeat. "We should have to pay ten times as much as security would have cost us, and after unimaginable suffering we should become 'the conscript appanage' of the men of blood and iron, and should be compelled to serve as German soldiers under German commanders."

In "Soldiering or Slavery" (Dec. 22) he painted a dark future for the British if they did not adopt compulsory service on continental lines. Then he marshaled the other values to be derived from conscription. Starry-eyed he contemplated the mental, moral, and physical advantages of military training for British youth. "I have seen coster boys, mill hands, town-bred hooligans, ignorant, round-shouldered, pallid, unwashed, and morally loose come into a regiment; and in six months they were clean, smart, well-conducted, well-spoken, well-built soldiers. I have seen the transformation effected. I have myself gone through the mill. I am convinced that the Army saved my life."

In the final article (Dec. 23), "A Word for the Homeland," Blatchford reviewed the argument, denied that he was a jingo and an imperialist, and hammered home his theory that in a military sense Britain was no longer an island. She could be attacked on land—in France. Since universal disarmament and a United States of Europe were impossibilities, they had no choice but to maintain the balance of power, which could only be done by universal military service and the preparation for continental war. His closing words were Biblical in their simplicity and appeal: "And the Empire is in danger; and we are unready; and we need a *man*."

In vigor and directness and in the employment of popular stereotype and symbol, Blatchford's articles surpass any other propagandist and promotional piece of the pre-War period in England or Germany. There were no new facts, his program was not original. His few statements of fact were egregiously incorrect, and were, of course, immediately challenged; but this in no wise diminished the working of his articles.[13]

---

20. Blatchford outlined a six point program of salvation: A vote of fifty millions for the navy; a compulsory service bill passed and put into effect immediately; the provision of elementary military training for all schoolboys above the age of ten; establishment of a general staff for the army and navy; increased appropriations for military and naval intelligence; and an appeal to employers to hire British citizens instead of foreigners.

[13] He said for example that the German navy law provided for a fleet of fifty Dreadnoughts and Super-Dreadnoughts. But figures counted for nothing in a statement like the following: "And when I was in Germany a few weeks ago I stood in Essen and looked at the chimney forest of Krupp-town, and reflected that the Ger-

All that Blatchford did was to state shrilly and impolitely, in the language of the common people who made up the million readers of the Daily Mail, what diplomats had been whispering to one another and what had been said a thousand times in the service magazines and in the half-crown monthlies. The German striving for political hegemony, which threatened the general peace and independence of Europe, and the identification of the defense of the Empire with the defense of France were all assumptions that were implicit in the British policy of ententes, in the military conversations initiated with France in 1906, in Haldane's army reforms and the organization of the expeditionary force, and in the co-ordination of French and British naval forces in 1912.

Kennedy Jones says "That the public wanted these writings is shown by the eager way they were accepted and read both in the paper and in the pamphlet. *But they had no permanent effect on the political mind.*" [14] But who can say what their effiect was? To be sure they did not result in the institution of universal military service, but of the millions who read his writings how many were moved to accept the inevitability of war with Germany, the identification of the defense of France with the defense of the British Empire, and the dubious proposition that in a war between the continental alliances the law of self-preservation required British participation?

At the time of publication Blatchford's articles fluttered the dovecots of diplomacy and politics. Lord Esher, writing to his son, enclosed a copy of the Daily Mail "to show you the unscrupulousness of those people," who would "be quite ready to get up a war with Germany in order to cover up their probable defeat on the Budget. I don't think political crime can go much lower than that." "Blatchford—whom they are exploiting—is a socialist and a self-advertising fellow. I suppose the country and the Germans will see through the dodge." The King, according to Esher, "lamented Blatchford's violence." [15] Blatchford's articles were condemned by William II in a conversation with Goschen as "very mischievous and singularly ill-timed." The election speeches and the Daily Mail's publicity evoked a characteristic outburst from the Emperor: "They are all mad in England, and people seem to think that

---

man blood and iron works had recently taken on twenty-eight thousand new hands. . . ." John Leyland quoted Krupp's records of employment to show that not twenty-eight thousand but 2371 workers had been taken on in 1909. Leyland further pointed out that to accommodate 28,000 hands and their families would require the building of a town within the year of something like 100,000 inhabitants. According to a correspondent in the *Westminster Gazette,* the *Daily Mail* editors refused to publish this correction. (*Daily News,* Jan. 5, 1910.)

[14] *Fleet Street and Downing Street,* p. 253. Italics his.
[15] *Journals and Letters,* II, 426, 442.

I am standing here with my battle axe behind my back ready to fall upon them at any moment." [16] The chancellor, Bethmann-Hollweg, too, was angry at the anti-German tone of the election publicity and made no secret of his resentment in conversation with the British ambassador.[17] Grey was not surprised at Bethmann's annoyance and disappointment. He excused the articles and speeches as "not really anti-German but alarmist," and attributed them partly to a genuine anxiety over the German naval challenge and partly to the scare tactics chosen by the opposition for electioneering purposes. "I am not going to be driven out of my course by the Daily Mail and the Peers who are on the stump," he assured Goschen, "but for me or any of us to attempt to moderate their writing and speeches would only lead to the redoubling of their efforts." [18]

Although it exasperated and discouraged Bethmann, the irresponsible publicity of the general election had a cathartic effect. When the new parliament assembled, one of the first items on the agenda was the naval estimates. There was the usual close scanning of German progress and the customary exaggerated forecasts. The Tories went through the motions of condemning the government's proposal of five new Dreadnoughts and five protected cruisers for the year 1910–11 as a betrayal of the two-power standard. The Radicals were regretful, but resigned to the increased program. However, nothing like the panic of the previous year developed. Only in the Northcliffe press, which now included the Times, was the agitation conducted in the old spirit. Here the theme was always the same—the magnitude of German preparations, the insufficiency of British counter-measures.[19]

In the second general election in the year 1910, the question of national defense and Britain's continental policy was not brought so promi-

[16] Goschen to Grey, Jan. 1, 1910; *B. D.,* VI, 434.

[17] *Ibid.,* VI, 319, 435–36.

[18] *Ibid.,* VI, 319.

[19] Notable among the feature articles published in the *Daily Mail* were: A. T. Mahan, "Britain and the German Navy," July 4, 1910, circulated free as a pamphlet and widely discussed in the British and German press; "The Menace in the North Sea," July 15; "The Shrinking Margin of British Safety," July 16; H. W. Wilson, "Is the Navy Ready for War?" on July 8. William Maxwell, who until 1904 had been the *Standard's* Berlin correspondent, was sent to Germany by the *Daily Mail* to write a series of articles on German naval preparations in the North Sea: "The Secret of Borkum," Aug. 29; "Germany and the Netherlands," Aug. 31; "The New Gibraltar" (Helgoland), Sept. 2; "Misconceptions," Sept. 3, sub-headings, "The German Advance, Great Britain Their Objective, Holland's Perilous Position." Also A. T. Mahan, "Britain and the World's Peace," Oct. 31. Typical of the agitation in the cheap periodicals was an advertisement of the *London Magazine,* which featured an article entitled, "German Clerks in Our Midst." It promised "A Wake-up-England article of a different character. What they mean to England's future—these watchful, serious, unostentatious young men you rub elbows with in every crowd." (*Times,* Oct. 20, 1910.)

nently into the foreground of press and platform publicity. Electioneering was concentrated on the House of Lords and Home Rule. With all but the incorrigible fire-eaters a tone of moderation prevailed. Public statements by Asquith, Grey, Metternich, and Bethmann-Hollweg showed that the spirit of accommodation was not lacking and gave rise to hopes that the Anglo-German problem could be solved by agreement. Proof of better feeling is afforded by the spirit in which the British journalists handled the espionage sensation of the year. Toward the end of December 1910, two British officers, Trench and Brandon, were tried and convicted in a German military court for espionage and sentenced to four years' confinement in a fortress. This affair might easily have given rise to bitter press polemics, but the British journals, with few exceptions, took the line that "law is law" and that the officers had had a fair trial.

The momentary improvement in the tone of public relations restored the rhythm of British politics. In the Radical ranks the external relaxation revived the agitation against the mounting naval appropriations. When the estimates for 1911–12 were presented, the reduction-of-armaments group, led by Murray Macdonald and Arthur Ponsonby, again became active. As Mr. Ponsonby caustically remarked, the policy of huge expenditures for armaments was only accepted by Liberalism when Liberals were in office. The Manchester Guardian and the Daily News echoed the dissatisfaction of the Radicals in parliament. It was in reply to the criticisms of his own friends that Grey made his long speech on foreign policy, armaments, and arbitration in the Commons on March 13, 1911. Quite in the spirit of Radicalism Grey deprecated the growing burden of armaments; but it was not England, he maintained, who was forcing the pace. By implication he placed sole responsibility on Germany, whose naval progress was dictated by a legal schedule which could not be changed. The significance of Grey's speech lies in what he omitted rather than what he said. He did not reveal to parliament that in the negotiations of the past two years the German authorities had always expressed their willingness to consider naval limitation if Britain would meet German desires for a political agreement. As a matter of fact, parliament, to say nothing of the nation, never had an opportunity, with all the facts before it, to express a choice between the Entente policy of the foreign office and the cabinet and its alternative, which was a political and naval agreement with Germany.[20]

[20] For Grey's speech see *Parl. Deb.*, 5th Ser., vol. 22, 1977 ff. Grey doubtless felt that publicity for German terms, which were bound to meet with violent objections from Imperialists, Entente enthusiasts, and balance of power advocates, would react unfavorably on the general situation.

Grey's seriousness and moderation, his praise of arbitration and his use of phrases such as "bleeding to death in time of peace," blunted the criticism of the Radicals without in any way affecting the main lines of cabinet policy toward armaments and foreign relations. His speech, furthermore, set a standard for the debate, which was free from the noisy alarmism that had marked similar occasions in previous years. Bethmann-Hollweg replying to Grey, in the Reichstag on March 30, faced a similar political predicament. Inspired by the discussion of Taft's arbitration treaties in the world press, the German Social Democrats had presented a resolution calling on the government to adopt a policy of arms limitation and arbitration. In contrast to Grey's humanitarianism, Bethmann's words seemed stiff and uncompromising, for he ruled out the whole case for disarmament and arbitration as impractical and Utopian as long as "men were men and states were states." In principle the two statesmen were agreed, but in choice of words and tone of address they clashed. However, as Goschen pointed out, although Bethmann's pronouncement was something of a diplomatic blunder when considered as a reply to Grey, it did not signify any disinclination to come to an understanding.[21]

As a matter of fact, it was just at this time that the negotiations for a naval and political agreement, which had been interrupted by the election campaigns in England, were being revived. A new impulse toward agreement came from the formation of a special cabinet committee composed of Asquith, Grey, Lloyd George, Morley, Crewe, and Runciman to assume direction and control of the negotiations. It is evident from chance remarks and hints that the foreign office officials much misliked this assertion of cabinet authority, which they feared lest it disturb the foundations of established policy.[22] But they really had nothing to fear. A leisurely exchange of memoranda, with much attention to tactical advantages on both sides, was begun and continued through the spring and early summer. Then the subject was shelved as the Agadir crisis broke over Europe.

The emergency that threatened to precipitate a general European war had its origins in the conflict and rivalry of Germany and France in Morocco, but it closed in a major crisis involving Berlin and London. Since the Franco-German agreement of 1909, the authorities had sought to implement it with a concrete plan of co-operation. Several ambitious

---

[21] B. D., VI, 616–17. The chancellor's speech is reported in full in the Times, March 31, 1911.
[22] Ibid., VI, 590.

schemes were worked out for economic collaboration in Morocco, but each time a political crisis intervened to postpone final action. One scheme miscarried when the Briand government fell, and M. Pichon was ousted from the Quai d'Orsay. His successor, Cruppi, endeavored to pick up the threads of the negotiations, but met with hostile opposition from the colonial and financial interests behind French policy in Morocco. In a short time he too went out of office and the negotiations were again interrupted. Meanwhile, French military penetration went on apace, until finally in the spring of 1911, under pretext of unrest that endangered European lives at Fez, a military force was dispatched to the Sultan's capital.[23] The Spanish, on the same pretext, followed the French lead, and early in June occupied Larache. While page after page of the Act of Algeciras was thus torn up, Kiderlen was left holding the bag. A salvage operation of major proportions was necessary if Germany were to realize anything from the claims asserted and defended at Algeciras. During the summer of 1911 a myth was propagated in the Entente press to the effect that German intervention was abrupt and brutal and that the manner of her intervention was responsible for the crisis that ensued. To the man in the street it may have been a surprise, but to the political élite familiar with the attenuated symbolism of diplomatic language the storm signals were unmistakable. While the French were marching to Fez, Cambon was warned of the probable consequences; and on April 30 the Norddeutsche published a cautionary notice which was quoted by every leading newspaper in Europe. "Transgressions of the essential provisions of the Algeciras Act," it stated, "would restore complete freedom of action to all powers, and might therefore lead to consequences which cannot at present be disregarded." [24] The initiated knew that Germany would not stand idly by while the French completed their conquest of Morocco.

Three possible lines of action were open to Berlin: first, enforce a return to the strict limitations of the Algeciras Act; second, effect a partition of Morocco between France, Germany, and Spain; third, acquiesce in the *fait accompli* and secure compensation from France for withdrawal of all German claims to a voice in Moroccan affairs. The first possibility was only to be contemplated as a last resort, because the Algeciras Act had already proved to be a broken reed; the second, while doubtless most appealing in Berlin, seemed impossible of achievement because it invited British intervention in consequence of the agreements of 1904; the third, withdrawal and compensation, while less

[23] Freiherr von der Lancken, *Meine dreissig Dienstjahre* (Berlin, 1931), pp. 89–96.
[24] *Norddeutsche,* April 30; *G. P.,* XXIX, 114 n.

attractive than the second, seemed to involve the least danger in accomplishment. It was, therefore, on the basis of colonial concessions in Central Africa (the French Congo) that the Emperor authorized Kiderlen and Bethmann to join issue with the French. At Kissingen on June 20 and 21, Kiderlen broached the subject to Jules Cambon, who proceeded to Paris to acquaint his superiors with German views.[25] Meanwhile, after having lightly broached the subject of compensation, the second step in Kiderlen's planned campaign was taken—the dispatch of the *Panther* to Agadir. This move, described correctly by the mild and moderate De Bunsen, British ambassador at Madrid, as "highhanded and needlessly aggressive," had three interdependent objectives. Kiderlen aimed to impress upon the French the absolute determination of German statesmen to acquire a completely acceptable compensation at all costs, even war; second, to secure in Agadir both a hostage and position of advantage for the period of hard bargaining that was certain to follow; and third, to be in a strategic position if circumstances should open a way for a tripartite division of Morocco. The dispatch of the *Panther* was a symbolical act; at the same time it was a tactical blunder of the first magnitude. It gave rise immediately, in both press and diplomatic circles of the Entente countries, to the complaint that bargaining and agreement with Germany were always barred by her habit of negotiating sword in hand.

Behind a blunt Bismarckian exterior, Kiderlen-Wächter fancied himself a master of indirection. The *Panther* spring was intended to prod the French to come forward with an acceptable proposal and to speed the negotiations, but the circular note to the powers alleged unrest in the neighborhood of Agadir and the threat to German life and property as the excuse for German action.[26] This was an obvious blind and left the public in doubt as to the real German objective. Some observers jumped to the conclusion that the Wilhelmstrasse had surrendered to the pressure of the Mannesmann mining interests and the Pan-Germans and was aiming at the acquisition of a slice of southern Morocco. This conclusion was not unwelcome to Kiderlen as it gave him a stronger bargaining position. The real objective—compensation—was kept in the background. With regard to the press, Kiderlen's policy shows a controlled publicity that revealed too little, and an irresponsible publicity that said too much. Those German newspapers described as "well informed" and those that habitually placed foreign policy above party con-

[25] *G. P.*, XXIX, 101–8, 142–49. Jäckh, *Kiderlen-Wächter*, II, 122–34; Brandenburg, *Von Bismarck zum Weltkriege*, pp. 329–31.

[26] After notification to the powers, the text of the dispatch was given directly to the press. This was an innovation in diplomatic practice.

sideration received the *Panther* coup with reserve. They supported the official fiction of a protective measure as it was elaborated in the Norddeutsche and in the Berlin correspondence of the Kölnische Zeitung.[27] On the other hand, the papers that spoke for the Mannesmann interests, the colonial party, and the Pan-Germans, began a wild clamor, jubilant and expectant, over German acquisition of southern Morocco. The lead in this campaign was taken by the Krupp controlled Berliner Neueste Nachrichten and the affiliated Deutsche Zeitung, by the Rheinisch-Westfälische Zeitung, Die Post, and the independent Tägliche Rundschau. In passing, it might be noted that the ownership and control of Die Post had changed, on April 1, 1910, from the Free Conservative committee to Dr. Theodor Reismann-Grone, a leading Pan-German and publisher of the Rheinisch-Westfälische Zeitung. The chief commentators on foreign policy in the journals mentioned above were: in the Rheinisch-Westfälische Zeitung, Dr. Niessner; in the Post, Dr. Pohl; in the Deutsche Zeitung, Otto Eichler; in the Berliner Neueste Nachrichten, L. Raschdau, a former member of the diplomatic service and a personal enemy of Kiderlen; in the Tägliche Rundschau, the editor Heinrich Rippler and the foreign editor, Oskar Michel.[28] When it leaked out from the French foreign office that Kiderlen and Cambon were negotiating on a basis of compensation for Germany outside of Morocco, these groups and their spokesmen became violent in their opposition to such a settlement. Their unmeasured agitation, with much bandying about of word symbols like "Canossa" and "Olmütz," continued throughout the summer right up to the conclusion and publication of the final agreements.[29]

---

[27] *Norddeutsche,* Nos. 154, 159, 165, July 4, 9, 16; *Kölnische Ztg.,* No. 741, July 3, Berlin telegram: "Es handelt sich bei dem Schritte der deutsche Regierung um Vorsichtsmassregeln, nicht um einen Akt der Besitzergreifung." The following harmonized their policy with the semi-official organs: *Vossische Ztg.,* Nos. 320, 322, 323, 326, 330, July 2, 3, 4, 5, 7; *National-Zeitung,* Nos. 154, 156, July 4, 6; *Berliner Tageblatt,* Nos. 333, 337, 344, 345, July 3, 5, 9, 10; *Frankfurter Ztg.,* Nos. 182, 184, 186, July 3, 5, 7; *Schwäbischer Merkur,* Nos. 304, 305, 307, 310, July 4, 5, 7; *Münchner N. N.,* Nos. 305, 306, 307, 310, 312, 314, July 3, 4, 6, 7, 8; *Kölnische Volksztg.,* Nos. 577, 599, July 7, 14. Many of these journals from July 1–15, like the *Kölnische Zeitung* (No. 749, July 5, "Agadir und sein Hinterland"), published articles enumerating the riches to be found in southern Morocco and the value of the port of Agadir.

[28] P. Gruschinske, *Kiderlen-Wächter und die deutsche Zeitungen in des Jahres 1911* (Emsdetten, 1931), p. 11; Reismann-Grone, *Der Erdenkrieg und die Alldeutschen* (Vienna, 1920), p. 53; *Kölnische Volksztg.,* No. 718, Aug. 22, 1911.

[29] "The Question of Compensation," *Berliner Tageblatt,* No. 862, July 19; "The Compensation," by Count Reventlow, *Deutsche Tagesztg.,* No. 360, July 19; "Compensations," *National-Zeitung,* No. 167, July 19. For the activity of the Pan-German League see L. Werner, *Der Alldeutsche Verband,* pp. 150–51; Heinrich Class' widely distributed pamphlet, *Westmarokko Deutsch!;* and Goschen's report on the Pan-German meeting in Berlin, on August 30 (*B. D.,* VII, 491–92). The Colonial Society likewise campaigned against abandonment of territorial compensation in Morocco. Accounts of their meetings and resolutions in *Berliner N. N.,* Nos. 388, 543, Aug. 1,

In the Entente capitals, Kiderlen's 'conversational opening' at Agadir had a bad press. Assuming a strong condemnatory tone the Northcliffe papers and the Conservative-Unionist press in England probed German action for its motives; these, they alleged, were the desire to bully France, to acquire Agadir as a naval base, and to disrupt the Entente. Germany was essaying a "Kiao-Chau policy in the Atlantic" one writer declared. All entered their customary complaint against "German diplomatic methods." Only one commentator, a special feature writer on the Daily Telegraph, perceived the real German objective, which he described as "the forcible appropriation of one piece of compensation in case another equally satisfactory should not be forthcoming elsewhere." [30]

Liberal editors took a less censorious line in interpreting and commenting on German action. The Daily News, Daily Chronicle, and Manchester Guardian, while they betrayed some uneasiness at the possibility of a German naval base at Agadir, pointed out that it was French evasion or transgression of the Algeciras Act that had paved the way for the *Panther* coup.[31] Because of his close association with Asquith and Grey, special importance was attached to Mr. Spender's views. Writing in the Westminster Gazette, on July 3, he refused to regard German action as a "bolt from the blue." Under the circumstances of French and Spanish action the whole world had been waiting for Germany to move, and it was not surprising that she too had sent a gunboat around to Agadir "to protect her interests." He proposed that all those involved be brought back to the Act of Algeciras; and he noted that Britain was not bound to give France diplomatic support "outside or in conflict with the Algeciras Treaty." This pronouncement, reported in the German press as an indication of official opinion, was obviously responsible in part for the mistaken conception of British policy that developed in Berlin.

Oct. 24; *Schwäbischer Merkur*, Nos. 498, 505, Oct. 25, 30. A defender of the government, writing in the *Grenzboten* (September 1911), asserted that Reismann-Grone's papers were being paid by the Mannesmann brothers for attacking the government. This led to a suit in which Reismann-Grone obtained a judgment of three hundred marks. While a definite financial connection could not be proved, the Reismann-Grone papers were unquestionably the special advocates of the Mannesmann interests. (Reismann-Grone, *op. cit.*, p. 56.)

[30] *Daily Telegraph*, July 4. It is worth noting that the *Times'* editors had cheered the French all the way to Fez, but when the Spanish occupied Larache and Alcazar the *Times* was not pleased. (Editorials and reports April 25, 26, May 2, 13, 25, June 12.) For the reaction to Agadir the following are significant: *Times*, July 3, 4, 6, 7; *Daily Mail*, July 3, 4, 5, 7, 10; *Morning Post*, July 3, 7; *Standard*, July 3, 4, 5, 7; *Birmingham Daily Post*, July 7, 10; *Scotsman*, July 3, 4, 7; *Pall Mall Gazette*, July 3; *Daily Telegraph*, July 5, 7.

[31] *Manchester Guardian*, July 4, 7; *Daily Chronicle*, July 3–15; *Daily News*, July 3–7.

However, on this occasion it was not the Liberal publicists who reflected official opinion. Reference to the *British Documents* shows that the Times and not the Westminster Gazette spoke for Downing Street. In the foreign office the French advance to Fez had been supported and defended from the beginning. Officials could see in it no breach of the Algeciras Act. De Bunsen, who was at that time in London on leave, describes the attitude prevailing in the foreign office as one that "amounted to a declaration that France could do no wrong." It was not France, but Spain and Germany who had torn up the Algeciras agreements.[32]

On July 3, Grey spoke gravely to Metternich of the new situation created by Germany's action. The next day, following a cabinet discussion, he informed the German ambassador that Britain could not be disinterested; that they "must have regard to treaty obligations with France and to British interests"; and that Britain could not recognize any new arrangement in which those interests were not taken into consideration. Almost identical words were employed by Asquith, who made a brief statement in the Commons on July 6.[33] German authorities took these declarations as a simple statement of position. The British maintained later that the Germans had ignored their representations. Rather than push in at this point, Grey and his technical advisers decided to adopt a waiting attitude while the French talked business with Kiderlen.[34]

From the first contact between Kiderlen and Cambon, on July 9, the British officials received detailed reports of the exploratory conversations.[35] These were not reassuring. When Kiderlen pointed to a map of the French Congo and indicated to Jules Cambon the extent of their desires in that region, the British diplomats and officials were taken aback by the size of those demands. Immediately they concluded that German claims were inadmissible and were only proposed in order to wreck the negotiations at the outset; further, they were so far-reaching as to constitute aggression. This was a challenge which France and England must meet with a united front. If they did not line up with France to resist German demands, the French would give in to Germany,

---

[32] De Bunsen's well-founded criticism of the foreign office attitude is set forth in a letter to Noel Buxton, dated December 3, 1911. T. P. Conwell-Evans, *Foreign Policy from a Back Bench* (Lond., 1932), pp. 65–67. For a careful appraisal of British policy based on Volume VII of the *British Documents,* see F. Hartung, "Die englische politik in der Marokkokrise des Jahres 1911," *Berliner Monatshefte,* August 1932, pp. 752–76.

[33] *G. P.,* XXIX, 164–67; *B. D.,* VII, 334, 342.

[34] Grey to Goschen, and Grey to Bertie, July 13; *B. D.,* VII, 360–61.

[35] *Ibid.,* 365–77.

the Entente would smash up, and German hegemony would be fastened upon the continent.[36] Above everything else the British foreign office feared a humiliating colonial partition that would devaluate the Entente in French eyes and cause them to make their own terms with Berlin. That was the reason for Lloyd George's buckling on the shining armor and appearing at the Mansion House as the champion of Britain's national honor. Grey's subsequent explanation in parliament that Lloyd George spoke because they had been left in the dark as to what was transpiring in Berlin—the famous "three weeks of silence"—and because the Germans had left their communication of July 4 unanswered, was merely a parliamentary explanation.

The apprehension of the foreign office and the cabinet was doubtless influenced by what they read in the Times on the morning of July 20, as well as by what they heard directly from the Quai d'Orsay and the British ambassador in Berlin. When Cambon and Kiderlen began negotiations they had agreed that they would make no communications to third parties or to the press. However, as early as July 15 fairly accurate statements appeared in the French press as to German demands for compensation. The leakage in Paris continued as each step was taken in Berlin. On July 20 the London Times, apparently on the basis of articles in the Paris Matin and l'Echo de Paris, published an article giving the details of the German claims for compensation. This was illustrated by a map of Central Africa showing the proposed cession. The text of the article contained one fabrication and one omission. It asserted that Germany was demanding, besides territorial compensation, the reversionary rights which France possessed to the Belgian Congo. The article omitted the important information that the German government, to make the French sacrifice easier to defend in public, would consent to a rectification of the frontiers of Togoland. The tendentious and misleading disclosure was appropriately glossed in the London editorial offices of the leading journals. The bandit parallel—"your money or your life"—was recklessly employed. The Times condemned the demands as "monstrously unfair." No French government, it declared, could accept such terms, and no British government could tolerate such a displacement of power in Central Africa.

On the basis of full information communicated by the French, Grey was in a position to correct the exaggerations of the Times' report; but apparently he was under the influence of the violent press agitation

---

[36] See particularly the minutes by Crowe, Nicolson, and Grey, *B. D.*, VII, 372–79; Nicolson's letter to Goschen, July 18, *ibid.*, VII, 374–75; and Nicolson's minute of July 21, initialed by Grey, *ibid.*, VII, 386.

produced by the Paris revelations when he invited Metternich to call at the foreign office on July 21. He told the German ambassador that he "had been made anxious by the news which appeared yesterday as to the demands which the German Government had made upon France: demands which were in effect, not a rectification of the frontier, but a cession of the French Congo, and which it was obviously impossible for France to concede." He further told Metternich that he was disquieted by the reports of German activity at Agadir; if the negotiations over Central Africa failed, and Morocco should become the direct object of discussion, then the British government must become an active party to the negotiations.[37] Metternich communicated Grey's warning to Berlin and Kiderlen replied with assurances that Germany did not contemplate permanent occupation of Agadir, but sincerely desired a settlement with France on a territorial basis that did not affect British interests. But before this reply could reach London—that is before the system of diplomatic communication had time to function—Grey and Asquith sanctioned the setting off of a rhetorical rocket into the heavily charged atmosphere.

The *British Documents* add little to what is already known of the genesis of Lloyd George's Mansion House declaration. They do, however, illuminate the background of that landmark in political publicity. They reveal, for instance, the discord between the cabinet and the foreign office officials on the question of German action at Agadir and the possibility of Germany acquiring a permanent foothold there. The French officials had from the beginning impressed upon the British ambassador in Paris that such a solution was wholly inadmissible from their standpoint, and the British foreign office accepted the French view; but it is quite evident that the British admiralty, considering the matter in its strictly technical defense aspects, did not regard it as vital and as worth fighting to prevent. Moreover, from the general tenor of the communications within the foreign office it appears that the cabinet would not sanction a commitment of complete solidarity with the French on this point—they did not think the exclusion of Germany from a slice of territory in southern Morocco was worth a war. In other words, British obligations did not cover turning Germany out of Morocco by force just to please the French.[38] Nicolson, Crowe, and Bertie begged that this be not stated uncompromisingly to the French. The issue, they maintained, was broader than Morocco; the general European situation and the balance of power was involved; the foundations of their national

---

[37] Grey to Goschen, July 21, 1911; *B. D.*, VII, 390–91.
[38] Grey to Bertie, July 19 and 20; *B. D.*, VII, 376, 382.

policy would be imperiled if the French were given cause to doubt Britain's loyalty.[39] Apparently the cabinet, on the morning of July 21, reviewed the situation without reaching a decision on the course they would take in the event of a complete break-down of Franco-German negotiations. Grey, therefore, could only underscore, in his interview with Metternich in the afternoon, the original British standpoint, namely, that if France and Germany failed to strike a bargain and Morocco itself became the pivot of discussion they would have to have a voice in the settlement.[40]

Now final decisions affecting the most important questions of foreign policy were reached in the cabinet, but tactical moves, outside of ordinary routine matters, were generally determined by the foreign secretary in agreement with the prime minister. When, therefore, Lloyd George, who was reckoned one of the staunchest of anti-jingoes, proposed to Asquith and Grey, after the cabinet meeting, that he run up the storm signal at the Mansion House that night, they fell in immediately with the proposal.[41] The text of Lloyd George's statement was fixed by agreement between himself, Asquith, and Grey. In fact, Lloyd George was a half hour late at the banquet, and he told Riddell, one of his journalistic confidants, that the delay was caused by the conference at the foreign office.[42] His banker audience thought his tardiness but a part of the bad manners to be expected from a Radical chancellor of the exchequer.

When, in the course of his remarks, Lloyd George reached the well-known nationalistic passage, he read directly from a sheet of paper.

But I am also bound to say this—that I believe it is essential in the highest interests, not merely of this country, but of the world, that Britain should at all hazards maintain her place and her prestige amongst the Great Powers of the world. . . . I would make great sacrifices to preserve peace. I conceive that nothing would justify a disturbance of international good will except questions of the gravest national moment. But if a situation were to be forced upon us in which peace could only be preserved by the surrender of the great and beneficent position Britain has won by the centuries of heroism and achievement, by allowing Britain to be treated, where her interests were vitally affected, as if she were of no account in the Cabinet of Nations, then I say em-

---

[39] B. D., VII, 372–86, passim.

[40] Grey was afraid of drifting and wanted the cabinet to sanction more positive action. See his private note to Asquith on July 19, B. D., VII, 377–78.

[41] Asquith, Churchill, and Grey all agree that the initiative came from Lloyd George. Grey, Twenty-five Years, I, 224–25; Churchill, World Crisis, I, 42–44; H. H. Asquith, Genesis of the War (Lond., 1923), pp. 93–94. A line in a private letter from Nicolson to Cartwright indicates, however, that it was not at all an impromptu proceeding. "The speech of Lloyd George which, I may tell you, was no sudden inspiration but a carefully thought out one, has produced a considerable impression in Berlin and also in Paris. . . ." (B. D., VII, 396.)

[42] Lord Riddell, More Pages from My Diary, 1908–1914, pp. 20–21. Substantiated by the London correspondent of the Birmingham Daily Post, July 31, 1911.

phatically that peace at that price would be a humiliation intolerable for a great country like ours to endure. National honour is no party question.

Such a strong nationalistic note sounded strange from the man who had been branded a "miserable pacifist" during the Boer War. His text gave no indication that he was speaking of the Moroccan dispute. Germany, France, Morocco were not mentioned. Lord Riddell, who was present, and who had been tipped off in advance to the significance of the statement, records that "its importance was not realised by the general company." [43] It was a generalized statement that might have been made by any European statesmen to any patriotic audience. It was a bit of spread-eagleism rather foreign to Lloyd George at that stage of his career, but there was no specific direction, no name and number attached to the message. As a matter of fact, it might well have left commentators running in many directions for its significance, or it might have been overlooked as a generality. But the London press next morning (July 22) sent it speeding on its way to its calculated destination—76 Wilhelmstrasse, Berlin.

Were the leading London editors prepared by the foreign office and the four ministers concerned for the proper reception and interpretation of this official declaration? The memoirs and official records supply no positive answer, but the promptness and harmony of interpretation in the press is strongly indicative of positive direction. Riddell, we know, was given the wink by Winston Churchill, and Arthur Nicolson's cryptic remark to Cartwright, the ambassador in Vienna, may indicate action from this quarter. The strongest evidence of authoritative inspiration is derived from the papers themselves. Particularly is this true of the Liberal organs, which up to this time had been fairly objective in their attitude toward the Franco-German dispute.

Special importance attaches to the treatment of the statement in the Daily Chronicle, whose editor, Robert Donald, was at that time Lloyd George's most intimate journalistic associate.[44] In a flaring headline the Daily Chronicle announced: "Britain Warns Germany—National Honour Is at Stake." Since the passage in question, it declared, was read carefully from manuscript it must be regarded as a statement of the view

[43] *More Pages from My Diary*, p. 21. The London correspondent of the *Manchester Guardian* (July 22) reported that people came away "asking one another almost uneasily what did it all mean?"

[44] On the relations between Donald and Lloyd George see H. A. Taylor, *Robert Donald*, pp. 24–25, 76 ff. The *Daily Chronicle* was Lloyd George's staunchest supporter and he its most frequent inspirer on political policy. A further indication of direction to the press is the fact that the *Chronicle* reproduced only that part of Lloyd George's speech which he read from manuscript. The textual similarity of this passage as reproduced in the *Chronicle, Times* and other journals suggests that it was given as a special hand-out to the representatives of the press.

of the British cabinet. In an editorial entitled, "A Word in Season," it stated that the speech was designed to show that party differences would not hinder England from fulfilling her international obligations; that it would dispel any illusions as to their loyalty to France; and that as a timely warning it was hoped that it would bring the negotiations, which Germany had begun in such an unusual manner, back to safer channels. The Times, in a furious editorial in which German diplomacy was likened to the methods of Dick Turpin, linked the chancellor's fanfaronade with the excessive German demands upon France. Those demands revealed a claim for "absolute European predominance" and Lloyd George's statement was official England's reply to Germany.[45] Mr. Spender, who throughout the long crisis over Agadir avoided all expression of opinion likely to increase the tension, did not comment in Saturday's leader. But a paragraph in the "Notes of the Day" stated that "We heartily agree with these sentiments, though we are bound to add that our agreement does not extend to some of the comments on Mr. George's utterances to be found in our Press this morning. Nothing is to be gained by pretending that the Chancellor of the Exchequer had not in his mind the situation which centers around Morocco." [46] The Daily News, the leading Radical organ in London, did not at first associate Lloyd George's warning with the Moroccan situation. On Monday, however, it blew a blast into the ministerial horn, with an article headed, "The Warning to Germany." "It would be folly," it said, "to mislead German opinion at such a juncture, or to obscure the fact that when Mr. Lloyd George spoke on Friday he spoke for the nation. There is no possibility of national disunion over matters vital to us all." Ignoring the bitter party struggle then in progress over the House of Lords, the Conservative papers of London and the provinces chimed in with the inspired organs and endorsed Lloyd George's statement as a declaration of solidarity with France, an assertion of Britain's legitimate right, and a clear warning to Germany.[47] The ranks closed in the face of a

[45] *Times* (Saturday), July 22. On Monday, July 24, the *Times* published another hard-hitting editorial using Lloyd George's statement as a point of departure. It must not be forgotten that the *Times* was more closely connected with the permanent officials of the foreign office than any other paper.

[46] *Westminster Gazette*, July 22. Reporting Lloyd George's pronouncement, Metternich singled out the three papers, *Chronicle, Times,* and *Westminster Gazette* to illustrate the press reaction. (*G. P.,* XXIX, 206-9.)

[47] The *Morning Post* (July 22, 25) was dignified but positive. The *Standard* reported the speech inconspicuously and without comment on July 22, but on Monday, July 24, it published a leader emphasizing national unity on foreign policy. The *Daily Telegraph* did not comment editorially, but special articles by E. J. Dillon harmonized with the prevailing press attitude (July 27). The general line was followed by the *Daily Mail,* July 22, 24; *Pall Mall Gazette,* July 22; *Scotsman,* July 24; *Birmingham Post,* July 24; *Liverpool Daily Post and Mercury,* July 24.

fancied menace from abroad. Without the institutional aid of a press bureau the government had brought the agencies of opinion and communication into a united front.

From the ranks of the press, the Manchester Guardian was the only deserter. In its service of information and comment it had taken the line that neither their obligations to France nor their strategical position on the Atlantic coast of Morocco was sufficient cause to justify going to extremes. The Guardian's policy was a matter of considerable concern to a government which was under-represented in the country's large caliber daily press. Moreover, the editor and owner of the Guardian, Mr. C. P. Scott, was a power in the Liberal party and a trusted confidant and adviser of the Radical members of the cabinet—Loreburn, Morley, and Lloyd George. From the biography of Mr. Scott, by J. L. Hammond, we get an informative picture of the interreaction between press and politics in a crisis situation.

Alarmed at the Times' exposé on July 20 and the cry of "Robber! Robber!" that went up from the Entente enthusiasts, Mr. Scott went to London on the night train, leaving Montague and Sidebotham in charge in Manchester. Scott breakfasted with Loreburn, who advised him to see Mr. Asquith. Unable to secure an appointment that day, he wrote a letter to the prime minister, not in his capacity as an editor, but as an official of the Liberal party in Manchester. He warned Asquith that a war to prevent Germany acquiring a naval station on the west African coast "would pulverise the party." He returned to Manchester, and that evening (July 20) received an urgent message from Lloyd George asking him as a personal favor not to write anything on the Moroccan situation until he had talked to him. Another note brought an invitation to breakfast with the prime minister. Lloyd George's speech was made that evening while Scott was on the London train. The next morning Scott breakfasted with Asquith and during the day he reviewed the situation with Lloyd George, Churchill, and Grey. The chancellor of the exchequer tried to win him over, saying that "he had found [the Manchester Guardian] much more considered in Germany than any other Liberal paper and if we let the Government down in international controversy it would be inferred that they had no sufficient backing in this country, and give a dangerously false impression of their actual determination, which up to a certain point, was fixed and practically unanimous. . . ." The arguments advanced to convince Scott were those later employed in parliament to justify the Mansion House demonstration: their Moroccan engagements, England's right to be consulted, the danger of a German naval base on the Moroccan coast, and Berlin's failure to respond to Grey's communications. But Scott was not moved from his position that Agadir was not sufficient cause for entering on a course that might lead to war. On July 25 he breakfasted with Grey, and they covered together the same general ground. Scott noted: "All through he [Grey] spoke of the importance of getting Germany to moderate her demands so as not to compel France to reject them, but he never alleged a corresponding need that France should be prepared to make really big concessions in order to pay off Germany as she had already paid off us." [48]

In accord with Lloyd George's request there was no editorial on the speech or the Moroccan situation in the Saturday (July 22) edition of the Guardian. On Monday, however, appeared a leader that was obviously a compromise between Scott's disapproval of Grey's policy and his loyalty to the party. There was no frontal attack on the government or the foreign office, only mildly stated disagreement with their interpretation of British obligations and interests. An oblique warning to the cabinet was contained in the injunction against being more French than the French themselves. Although the Guardian was reserved in comment thereafter until final settlement of the Moroccan dispute, the breach between Scott and Grey on British foreign policy was complete. In November, Scott took the lead in the crusade begun in the press and in the party councils against Grey's entente-balance-of-power policy.

It was enough, however, that Scott did not at the moment attack the government and spoil the demonstration of national solidarity. With the Guardian assuming an attitude of reserve the maneuver was a striking success. The press gave Lloyd George's warning its proper direction; it informed the world that Britain's loyalty to France and the Entente was unshakable. But more than that, it ended the Radical opposition in the cabinet to a broad interpretation of Britain's obligations to France and the system of ententes. When Lloyd George lined up with Asquith, Grey, and the permanent officials, the opposition in the cabinet collapsed.[49] The government was now committed to the foreign office view that the issue was no longer a deal in African real estate, but the foundations of their foreign policy in Europe. At all costs the understanding with France must be preserved. This fundamental consideration determined the British attitude toward the subsequent negotiations between Paris and Berlin. Even when the French became intransigent Grey feared to suggest that a worth-while compensation to Germany in the Congo was reasonable in light of the position they would acquire in

[48] J. L. Hammond, *C. P. Scott,* pp. 153–63.
[49] Churchill, *World Crisis,* I, 42–43.

return in Morocco. In a private letter to Goschen on September 27, he confessed that he dare not press the French about the Congo. In the next sentence he gives the key to British policy: "If I do so we may eventually get the odium in France for an unpopular concession and the whole entente may go." [50]

It was now determined that Britain would be a brilliant second on the dueling ground and not a referee. In consequence, precautionary naval measures were instituted; the military conversations between British and French authorities were resumed, with the full knowledge of the cabinet; the invasion committee of the Committee of Imperial Defense was revived; and every effort was made to implement the Entente against the time when it might become necessary to defend by force the ground which they had taken diplomatically.

Grey, Asquith, Lloyd George, and Churchill have all vigorously defended the Mansion House declaration on the ground that by flashing the red light the Germans were apprised of England's attitude before they had ventured too far on a path leading to war; German intentions, they maintained, were clarified and the Wilhelmstrasse withdrew its unacceptable Congo demands. Peace was preserved. Whether the best means to accomplish that end were employed is debatable. Grey had spoken gravely to Metternich after the cabinet meeting on July 21, and without waiting for a reply from Berlin he sanctioned Lloyd George's statement, which was immediately interpreted by the press as a threat or ultimatum. The resources of diplomacy had by no means been exhausted when the British minister sanctioned a public statement that would have had no point unless it was intended to produce a strong reaction in the press. The French and the Germans were engaged in the preliminaries of bargaining, and if German claims were high Grey was

---

[50] *B. D.*, VII, 545. The thought here is identical with that expressed by Nicolson on July 21, in a private minute for Sir Edward Grey, in which Nicolson portrays the consequences of failure to range themselves unequivocally on France's side. "In any case France would never forgive us for having failed her, and the whole Triple Entente would be broken up. This would mean that we should have a triumphant Germany, and an unfriendly France and Russia and our policy since 1904 of preserving the equilibrium and consequently the peace in Europe would be wrecked. Our naval position in the Mediterranean and elsewhere would be quite altered, necessitating increased naval estimates, while the cessation of our intimate relations with Russia would render our position in Central Asia unstable and insecure. We should even be brought to that position which the Emperor William recently outlined, and be going cap in hand to Berlin to ask what we could do to please him." (*B. D.*, VII, 386.) These statements by Grey and Nicolson reveal the true norms of British policy. It was not really fear of Germany—naval rivalry, commercial rivalry, colonial expansion—that fixed these norms, but rather fear of isolation if the understandings of 1904 and 1907 should go by the boards. This, of course, was not the central feature of publicity in parliament and the press. Opinion and attitude management required the simpler and more direct pattern presented by Anglo-German antagonism.

not so simple minded as to believe that the first asking price was necessarily the final selling price. Moreover, the British had not been rebuffed or insulted; Grey knew every detail of the conversations between Berlin and Paris; and yet the British were the first to take their stand in the market place and shout about "prestige," "humiliations," "vital interests," and exclusion from "the Cabinet of Nations." The unanimity of interpretation and the united front in the press, together with supporting evidence from other sources, points to the conclusion that British officials deliberately chose a publicity technique, with all its unpredictability, and sent the press on a diplomatic mission. Subsequent events showed that, for the time at least, the regular machinery of diplomacy should have been employed.

In Berlin, the significance of Lloyd George's appearance as a foreign office flag-bearer was not grasped immediately. Certainly, it was not related directly to the confidential conversations in progress between Kiderlen and Cambon. The first word put about in the semi-official press and among the Berlin correspondents of the provincial papers was that Lloyd George's pronouncement was not addressed to Germany; it was simply one of those generalities which any statesman might utter on the subject of foreign affairs and national interests.[51] But the interpretation of the speech by the ministerial press in England and the unanimity with which it was related to the current negotiations made the maintenance of this thesis impossible. The direct reports of the London correspondents, particularly those of Dr. Hans Esser to the Kölnische Zeitung, of Bernhard Guttmann to the Frankfurter Zeitung, of Konstantin von Zedlitz to the Lokal-Anzeiger, of C. C. Schardt and Dr. Johannes Schiedel to the Vossische Zeitung, of C. A. Bratter to the Morgenpost, and Dr. Gaupp to the Münchner Neueste Nachrichten and the Hamburger Fremdenblatt, broke down the semi-official interpretation and dispelled the first illusions. Kiderlen dispatched a vehement protest to London, a protest that was directed more against the press interpretation of Lloyd George's remarks than against the pronouncement itself. It was after Metternich had delivered his message at the foreign office that Grey told Churchill that the British fleet might be attacked at any moment without warning.[52]

[51] *Lokal-Anzeiger*, No. 369, July 22; *Frankfurter Ztg.*, Berlin telegram, No. 202, July 23; *Kölnische Ztg.*, Berlin telegram, July 22, No. 819, July 23; *Berliner N. N.*, No. 370, July 23; Berlin reports to the *Times, Daily Mail,* and *Daily News.*
[52] Churchill, *World Crisis,* I, 44–45; *B. D.,* VII, 397–99; *G. P.,* XXIX, 210–14. To McKenna, Grey wrote on July 24: "It is too much to say that relations are strained at the present moment . . . but they might at any moment become strained and we are dealing with people, who recognize no law except that of force between nations, and whose fleet is mobilized at the present moment. . . ." (*B. D.,* VII, 625.)

In the German press the explosion was the greater for having been delayed by the tactics of the press bureau. Misinterpretation was an absolute certainty, for the German editors saw only their side of the case. They knew from official sources and from leaks in Paris that conversations were in progress looking toward a definitive settlement of the Moroccan question by a French pay-off to Germany in the Congo. Then the British chancellor of the exchequer, backed by a united press, appeared on the scene and interposed a provocative veto upon satisfactory compensations in Central Africa, no less than in Morocco. In such moderate papers as the Frankfurter Zeitung, Kölnische Volkszeitung, Berliner Tageblatt, and Vossische Zeitung, there was no violent chauvinistic outburst, but rather intense though restrained resentment that in this irritating manner the British had intervened in the Franco-German negotiations—they had vetoed a port in Morocco, and now had challenged the German right to compensation in the Congo. Britain's policy of blocking every German move toward the realization of a legitimate policy of expansion was a danger to the world.[53] In the National Liberal, Pan-German, and independent chauvinist journals, the leather-lunged national trumpet blowers were in a state bordering on frenzy. On the same old threadbare pretext of her vital interests England intervenes whenever Germany makes a move to secure a place in the sun, they declared. England has undertaken to police the Germans and to keep them out of every corner of the world; she desires nothing so much as to break up the negotiations between France and Germany and to sow dissension between them, because Britain has always drawn her profit from the quarrels of continental neighbors. King Edward is gone, but his policy of hemming Germany in at all costs continues. Lloyd George's saber rattling is not incidental to the present dispute, but demonstrates the whole trend of British policy toward Germany since the turn of the century. In the face of British provocation and threats there is only one answer consistent with our self-respect—a demonstration of our immovable determination to carry through the policy which national necessity forces upon us. No summary statement, such as this,

---

Lloyd George told Riddell that the German government through Metternich had demanded his dismissal from the cabinet, and authorized Riddell to publish the story in his sensational *News of the World*. It appeared as a Paris dispatch on July 30. (Riddell, *Diary*, pp. 21–22.)

[53] *Frankfurter Ztg.*, No. 203, July 24; *Berliner Tageblatt*, No. 373, July 25; *Vossische Ztg.*, No. 365, July 26; *Kölnische Volksztg.*, No. 632, July 25. The Berlin Bureau of the latter paper wrote (No. 634, July 26): "Bei jedem Blick in die englische Presse hat man den unauslöschlichen Eindruck, dass die englischer Politiker—und zwar beider Parteien—nichts so sehr fürchten, als dass Deutschland und Frankreich sich vertragen könnten. . . . Nur eine Freundschaft zwischen den Völkern auf beiden Seiten der Vogesen sähen sie als ein wirkliches Unglück für Alt-England an."

can adequately convey the impression of bitterness and venom produced by these comments.[54]

In an editorial entitled "Imponderabilien," generally cited as inspired, the Kölnische Zeitung took cognizance of the Mansion House speech as interpreted by extremists in London and Paris. "It reminds us of the famous 'Hands Off!' which Gladstone flung at Austria in 1878 when she occupied Bosnia and Herzegovina. We thought the time was past when she [England] could use such language to another country." The German people, it declared, was behind the government's action. This and other imponderables in the situation should not be overlooked by the British and French.[55] The same day an article entitled "What Does England Want?" appeared in the Lokal-Anzeiger. Bearing signs of inspiration and quoted by most of the British correspondents as semi-official, it contained a direct warning that British intervention, as preached by the London press, was quite inadmissible. "Such an attitude, as is displayed by a part of the press, corresponds neither to the concept of loyalty nor the honor of a nation interested in the preservation of world peace," it declared. A more direct statement of official indignation through the Norddeutsche was wisely avoided by the Wilhelmstrasse.

By July 26 the agitation in the press reached war-scare proportions. Certain events reported from London were taken as alarm signals. In modern British politics these have acquired symbolical significance. A special cabinet meeting was announced and Grey reported immediately thereafter to the King, the British ambassador made a hurried trip from Paris to London, the securities market sagged and there was a run on Lloyds for war-risk insurance, a British fleet visit to Norwegian waters was canceled and the London press reported extraordinary naval movements. The German papers advertised these incidents in large headlines and examined their meaning in front page articles. According to the press the diplomatic position was serious if not alarming.[56]

[54] "Lloyd George rasselt mit dem Säbel," and "Die englische Drohung," *Schwäbischer Merkur,* Nos. 337, 344, July 22, 27; "Bange machen gilt nicht!" and "Die englische Einmischung," *Münchner N. N.,* Nos. 346, 349, July 26, 28; "Eine deutliche Ablehnung," *Berliner N. N.,* No. 370, July 24; "Die britische Drohrede," *Die Post,* No. 342, July 24; also *Tägliche Rundschau* editorial, No. 345, July 26.

[55] No. 832, July 27. Goschen quoted from this article in his dispatch of July 27 (*B. D.,* VII, 407–10), in which he also reviewed the comment of the *Frankfurter Ztg.,* the *Münchner N. N., Lokal-Anzeiger, Die Post, Börsen-Courier, Hamburger Nachrichten,* and *Berliner Tageblatt.*

[56] "Die Aufregung um Marokko," *Lokal-Anzeiger,* No. 376, July 26; "Die Interventionen Englands," and "Der Stand der Marokkoverhandlungen," the latter by Theodor Wolff, *Berliner Tageblatt,* Nos. 375, 376, July 26; in the same spirit were *Berliner N. N.,* No. 376, July 26; *Vossische Ztg.,* No. 366, July 26; *Schwäbischer Merkur,* No. 344, July 27; *Frankfurter Ztg.,* No. 206, July 27. Grey instructed Goschen to state to Kiderlen that the English press interpretations of the cancellation of the Norwegian visit were pure invention. (*B. D.,* VII, 622–26; *G. P.,* XXIX, 219.)

The disclosure of German demands in the French press, and the campaign in Paris and London provoked by Lloyd George's speech, had snarled negotiations and produced a first-class public crisis. Neither the Wilhelmstrasse nor the German publicists could fathom British intentions. Were the London statesmen interposing a veto on Franco-German negotiations because English interests in Central Africa were involved? Grey had declared to Metternich that German demands were inadmissible. Would he oppose any settlement that gave satisfaction to Germany? Some of the most important London editors were saying that Britain could not sanction an extensive redistribution of African territory. Did they really want a settlement between France and Germany or were they trying to stir these bitter rivals to war? Clarification was essential if the scare were not to reach panic proportions.

The first move came from the British foreign office. In an authorized statement to Reuter's Agency, which appeared in all the British papers on the morning of July 27 and in the Berlin papers that afternoon, it was declared that nothing had occurred to disturb the *pourparlers* between Berlin and Paris. It was a mistake to assume that Great Britain would participate actively in the negotiations; the cabinet meeting at the foreign office was called to inform the ministers at first hand of the state of affairs. In Morocco the government felt their interests were involved, but a solution outside of Morocco, acceptable to France, would not injure British interests. Finally, it was stated, changes in the disposition of the Home and Atlantic fleets had nothing to do with the current controversy.[57] On the afternoon of the 27th Asquith covered the same ground in a brief statement in the House of Commons. He blessed the Franco-German negotiations, expressing the hope that a solution acceptable to both parties would be reached. "The question of Morocco itself bristles with difficulties," he declared, "but outside Morocco, in other parts of West Africa, we should not think of attempting to interfere with territorial arrangements considered reasonable by those who are more directly interested." Lloyd George's speech he justified on the ground that it was necessary from the first to make it clear that if the negotiations involved Morocco Britain must be consulted because of her interests, her signature on the Algeciras Act, and her obligations to France under the agreement of 1904. He did not know how fully this was at all times understood, and it would have been a grave mistake to allow matters to drift.[58] Balfour arose at the conclusion of Asquith's

[57] *G. P.*, XXIX, 221–22. All leading London and Berlin papers, July 27. The communiqué was probably drafted in the foreign office on July 26 and issued to the press that night.

[58] *G. P.*, XXIX, 223–24; *B. D.*, VII, 406.

statement and performed the established ritual, endorsing the government's stand and declaring that in this matter, which touched British interests and honor abroad, party lines had no meaning. This demonstration of closing the ranks evoked cheers and congratulations from the entire British press.

Published in the German papers on July 28, Asquith's statement confirmed the Reuter announcement of the day before. There was an immediate slackening of the tension and an abatement of rumormongering in the press. Under a streamer headline *"Die Rede des Premierministers Asquith,"* the Berliner Tageblatt devoted the entire front page to the prime minister's statement. Theodor Wolff's accompanying article was appreciative and conciliatory, but he could not conceal a certain bitterness over the general tenor of English policy. The term "British interests," he wrote, was a notoriously elastic concept. It was an English law that "The world is already divided, and England takes pains to see that nothing is traded or changed." [59]

One thing was made very clear to German editors by Asquith's pronouncement, namely, that Morocco as a place for German compensation was quite out of the picture. This was confirmed by an official communiqué, published in Berlin on August 4, which announced that agreement in principle on the object of compensation had been reached by Kiderlen and Jules Cambon. In consequence, the violent attacks upon the government by the Pan-Germans, the colonialists, the Mannesmann brothers and their journalistic allies, were redoubled. The Colonial Society issued a public protest, the Pan-Germans organized a demonstration in Berlin, and the Society of German Industrialists memorialized the government against abandonment of Morocco as an object of compensation. The press gave publicity to these demonstrations, and editorial commentary became every day more bitter and unrestrained. "Agadir must not become Fashoda," was their cry.[60] Among the most extreme attacks was

[59] *Berliner Tageblatt*, No. 379, July 28. Favorable official reaction was recorded in Berlin telegrams to the *Kölnische Zeitung* (Nos. 836 and 838, July 28) and in a statement given to Reuter's Berlin correspondent, Mr. Lester Lawrence. (London papers, July 29.) In general the Reuter communiqué and Asquith's statement were well received, although the prime minister's defense of the Mansion House speech provoked sharp criticism and dissent. *Vossische Ztg.*, Nos. 367, 368, July 27, 28; *Frankfurter Ztg.*, Nos. 207, 210, July 28, 31, quoting *Die Post, Lokal-Anzeiger, Kreuzzeitung,* and the official *Norddeutsche; Kölnische Volksztg.*, No. 640, July 28; *Schwäbischer Merkur,* No. 346, July 28; *Münchner N. N.,* No. 521, July 29; *Tägliche Rundschau,* Nos. 350, 351, quoting the sharper nationalistic comment of the *Reichsbote, Berliner N. N., Deutsche Tagesztg., Rheinisch-Westfälische Ztg.,* and *Schlesische Ztg.*

[60] *Münchner N. N.,* Nos. 361, 362, Aug. 4; *Schwäbischer Merkur,* Nos. 350, 355, 362, July 31, Aug. 2, 7; *Alldeutsche Blätter,* No. 35, Sept. 2; *Kölnische Volksztg.,* No. 72, Aug. 23 (memorial of the *Zentralverband deutscher Industriellen*). Goschen's reports contain a number of references to this agitation, *B. D.,* VII, 445 ff., 491–92.

an article entitled "Crisis and Retreat," published in Die Post, which recalled the days of Olmütz, accused the Emperor of cowardice, and predicted the resignation of Kiderlen and Bethmann. In reply a savage communication was published in the Norddeutsche calling Die Post to order and condemning its "cowardly form of rhetorical questions," its "injury of German interests," and its "dishonorable motives." [61] While the excesses of this publicity were severely condemned in the responsible papers, it is perfectly clear from many columns of report and comment that German resentment at the manner in which the British had intervened was deep and bitter, and that even the opponents of the Moroccan chauvinists thought that the German government had retreated under British pressure.

For the next few weeks the Kiderlen-Cambon negotiations went underground. It was not in this connection that the full measure of German resentment and rancor over "British meddling," which was felt in public circles from the Emperor downward, was manifested. That was evoked by a comparatively trifling incident, a newspaper indiscretion involving the British ambassador in Vienna, Sir Fairfax Cartwright. The editors of the British Documents are of the opinion that the incident was unworthy of the importance accorded it at the time, and that may be true in so far as the diplomatic record is concerned, but it wrecked Cartwright's career and poured poison into the stream of Anglo-German public relations.[62] Briefly, the genesis and circumstances of the indiscretion are as follows: Sir Fairfax Cartwright had gone to Vienna as British ambassador in 1908, after having served as resident minister in Munich and Stuttgart. From the South German capital he had supplied his superiors in London with jaundiced reports on the German press, and on this performance established a reputation as a student of German affairs and a critic of German policy.[63] The proposal to settle him in the Berlin embassy, vacated by Lascelles in 1908, was politely discouraged by the German authorities and he went instead to Vienna. There he worked openly with his French colleague, Crozier, to draw Austria-Hungary away from the Triple Alliance and closer to the Entente. At

---

[61] Die Post, No. 362, Aug. 4; Norddeutsche, No. 183, Aug. 6. See also Goschen's extensive report on this incident in B. D., VII, 438–40. The malcontents found an unexpected ally in Maximilian Harden, who launched a smashing personal attack on the Emperor, Bethmann, and Kiderlen ("the Messiah from Swabia"). "Wilhelm der Friedliche," Die Zukunft, vol. 76, Aug. 5. See also Goschen's report, B. D., VII, 443–45. William II was dangerously incensed by these attacks. (G. P., XXIX, 318–19.)

[62] B. D., VII, 837.

[63] On Cartwright's garbled reporting of the press from Munich see Hermann Lutz, Eyre Crowe, Der Böse Geist des Foreign Office (Stuttgart and Berlin, 1931), pp. 49–58.

the height of the Moroccan crisis, Cartwright was in Marienbad, a fashionable Bohemian resort, whose popularity with international society had been established by the patronage of Edward VII. Present also were the French ambassador to Vienna, Crozier, and Dr. Sigmund Münz, a well-known publicist and writer on foreign affairs, associated with the Vienna Neue Freie Presse.[64] On August 20, Münz had telephoned to his paper the gist of an interview with Crozier on the current diplomatic crisis. It had appeared the next day masked by anonymity and without any trace of its origin. Meeting Sir Fairfax on the promenade, Münz sought his views of the diplomatic situation.[65] On the basis of notes made immediately after his conversation with Cartwright, Münz telephoned again to his paper, reporting the views of the British diplomat, but enjoining the editor to maintain the strictest secrecy as to the source of the remarks. On August 25 the interview appeared in the Neue Freie Presse, under the title "Probabilities and Possibilities in the Question of Peace." But the editor half revealed the source when he added the line, "By an English Diplomat in an Important Position." In the interview, Cartwright began with a disparaging remark apropos of the Moroccan negotiations: "Mountains labor and a ridiculous little mouse is born!" He sharply criticized German policy in raising the issue in the first place and expressed the view that now Berlin had the choice of arousing the dissatisfaction of the Pan-Germans or provoking a conflict with France; should the latter develop, England was on France's side. Germany's policy, he continued, which was challenging and provocative, originated with the clique around the Kaiser and did not have the backing of the German people. There followed severe strictures upon the German government and German diplomatic representatives, who failed in their duty of correctly reporting public opinion in the countries to which they were accredited. He closed with a reference to the unfortunate and embarrassing reaction which German policy was having on Austria's foreign relations.[66]

[64] A good picture of political and social life at this renowned watering place—central Europe's summer capital—is given by Münz in his book, *Eduard VII in Marienbad* (Vienna, 1934). When Lloyd George visited the continent in 1908, Münz had published an interview with the English statesman and endeavored to arrange a meeting between Lloyd George and Bülow, (*Ibid.*, pp. 164–76.)

[65] Cartwright subsequently stated that he refused Münz an interview but that the journalist followed him along the promenade. Münz denied this.

[66] *Neue Freie Presse,* No. 16885, Aug. 25. On the genesis of the interview and its diplomatic consequences, see Münz, "The Cartwright Interview of August 1911," *Contemporary Review,* March 1930, pp. 308–16; B. D., VII, 837–45; G. P., XXIX, 237–44. By far the best account, based upon published material and further inquiries of participants, is by Hermann Lutz, *Deutschfeindliche Kräfte im Foreign Office der Vorkriegszeit* (Berlin, 1932), pp. 21–43. I am indebted to Herr Lutz, the editor of

The editor's indiscretion in adding a by-line, which half revealed the source of the interview (for everyone thought immediately of Cartwright whose Germanophobia was a subject of general gossip in diplomatic and journalistic circles), was deeply regretted by Münz, who wrote immediately in that sense to the ambassador.[67] But the damage had been done. The interview was reported in all the German papers and the Viennese dispatches attributed it to Cartwright. In Berlin, the Vossische Zeitung stirred the fire by publishing an article from the pen of the Austrian historian, Heinrich Friedjung, which reviewed in an unfriendly fashion the ambassador's activities during the previous four years in Munich and Vienna.[68] Over night Cartwright became a devil of intrigue, symbolizing for the man in the street the obstructionist and encircling policy of the British government.

For once William II did not exaggerate when he said to the British military attaché: "What in Heaven's name does your ambassador in Vienna mean by the dreadful statements he has made. . . . My people are furious about . . . it; I cannot tell you how angry they are." [69] At any time the interview would have created a sensation, but coming as it did shortly after Lloyd George's demonstration it enraged the German editors. A torrent of angry denunciation poured from the press. Is Britain through her agents pursuing a policy of intentional provocation? Are the British bent upon goading Germany into war? These were the questions most frequently asked. Out of a simple business question affecting France and Germany the British by their intervention have created an issue that touches German national honor, declared the press critics. The German people will not tolerate a retreat before English threats—such was the general conclusion.[70]

Meanwhile, Cartwright was explaining to his superiors in London, and the diplomats were getting out the usual equivocal denials. Through a series of indiscretions the British ambassador stood charged with a grave breach of diplomatic etiquette. But this scarcely justified the fabri-

---

the German edition of the *British Documents,* for numerous transcripts of contemporary newspaper articles on this subject and the Agadir crisis in general.

[67] The letter, dated August 30, is given in the *Contemporary Review,* March 1930, p. 314.

[68] "Ambassador Cartwright," *Vossische Ztg.,* No. 426, Aug. 28.

[69] *B. D.,* VII, 493.

[70] Most denunciatory was the *Münchner N. N.* (No. 403, Aug. 30), "In King Edward's Tracks." In keeping with its semi-official status, the *Kölnische Zeitung* was more reserved; Nos. 940, 941, 943, 947, Aug. 25, 26, 28, 30. The following are representative reactions: *Berliner Tageblatt,* Nos. 432, 440, 442, Aug. 25, 30, 31; *Berliner N. N.,* Nos. 435, 436, Aug. 27, 28; *Kölnische Volksztg.,* Nos. 730, 740, 765, Aug. 26, 30, Sept. 7; *Tägliche Rundschau,* No. 403, Aug. 29, quoting *Schlesische Ztg.,* and *Der Tag; Kölnische Volksztg.,* No. 748, Sept. 1, quoting *Frankfurter Ztg.,* and *Kreuzzeitung.*

cations and insinuations to which he resorted in his attempt to escape all responsibility. To Grey and Nicolson, Cartwright denied any responsibility for the publication of the interview, stating that he had only a passing word with Münz, who was deaf, and that the greater part of the article was "mere guess-work on his part." He portrayed himself as the victim of a German conspiracy. Tschirschky, the German ambassador in Vienna, aided by the press bureau in Berlin, had organized the affair, so he said, as part of a plot designed to drive him from his post. Cartwright knew that anything reflecting upon Germany would be believed in London, such was the temper in the foreign office. Grey made specific charges out of Cartwright's shaky inferences and in conversations with Metternich over the press agitation taxed the German government with complicity. Instead of probing the origins of the incident by demanding of Cartwright an exact account of what he had said to Münz, Grey threw the blame for the press campaign on the Berlin officials. The attacks upon Cartwright, he assured the Russian ambassador, "had been worked up from German sources." [71]

The first public denial was issued by Cartwright in a telegram to the Berlin Neue Gesellschaftlicher Correspondenz, the second by the London foreign office through an authorized statement by Reuter's Agency. Both merely denied "responsibility" for the interview.[72] Finally, to put an end to the attacks in the German press, a semi-official statement was drafted in Berlin, approved by Grey in informal discussion with Metternich, and published in the Norddeutsche on September 15.[73] The communiqué said: "The Imperial Government, upon inquiry of the British Government, has been informed that the English ambassador in Vienna neither inspired the well-known article in the Neue Freie Presse nor did he make the statements attributed to him by the author. With that the incident is satisfactorily closed for the Imperial Government." After this explicit statement, which went further than the facts warranted, the press subsided. Six weeks later the incident was revived by a question in the House of Commons. Perhaps Grey's suspicions were aroused by this

---

[71] B. D., VII, 493, 839–42; G. P., XXIX, 240–42. Cartwright's insinuations and Grey's assertions are minutely examined and rejected on documentary grounds by Hermann Lutz, Deutschfeindliche Kräfte im Foreign Office der Vorkriegszeit, pp. 35–41. The new materials employed by Herr Lutz include: communications from Dr. Münz, from Count Oberndorff (the then chargé d'affaires in Vienna), from the editor of the Neue Freie Presse, and a letter from Paul von Schwabach to Eyre Crowe (Nov. 1, 1911) denying on the basis of an official inquiry that the German authorities had any prior knowledge of the interview, as charged by Cartwright, or inspired in any way the press campaign against the ambassador.

[72] Kölnische Ztg., Nos. 948, 958, Aug. 28, 31. B. D., VII, 838.

[73] No. 217. Goschen's dispatch reporting its appearance is incorrectly dated. (B. D., VII, 843.)

time. At any rate he asked Cartwright for "the most explicit form of denial that is accurate, in case I want to use it." A week later he had no reply from Cartwright and did not get one until an urgent telegram had reinforced the demand. The declaration Cartwright proposed for delivery in the House merely denied participation in publication, inspiration or previous knowledge of the interview; it did not deny that he had made the statements attributed to him by Münz.

In parliament, Grey linked the Cartwright interview with a false report of a speech by McKenna, which had been taken over from a French source and circulated in Germany by a private press agency. The categorical denial of the McKenna incident covered the 'parliamentary denial' of the Cartwright incident, and the statement was wrapped up in a general rebuke to the press for circulating false news reports. Grey's adroit maneuver conveyed the impression that the Cartwright interview was an invention on the same level with the fabricated statements attributed to McKenna.[74]

By the end of the summer the excesses of journalism had become so galling to statesmen on both sides of the Channel that any mention of the press in diplomatic discussion resulted in bitter reproaches and recriminations. Grey was angry over the McKenna and Cartwright incidents, Kiderlen and Bethmann were exasperated by the English press interpretations of Lloyd George's speech, the Daily Graphic's fictitious accounts of German troop movements, and Repington's disparaging articles in the Times on the German army.[75] The following heated

[74] For Grey's statement see *B. D.*, VII, 656; *Parl. Deb.*, 5th Ser., vol. 30, 1450. The report of McKenna's speech was circulated in Germany by the Press Telegraph agency under a London date line, but it was actually taken from *l'Echo de Paris* and part of the French editorial gloss was reproduced as the words of the British statesman. On Bethmann's initiative the Wolff Bureau and the *Norddeutsche* (No. 230, Sept. 29) corrected the false report the next day. Although Grey made no great effort to penetrate the screen of Cartwright's evasions, he promptly dispatched, with the approval of the cabinet and the King, a stiff formal note to Berlin on the McKenna incident. (*Ibid.*, VII, 648–51.)

[75] Repington's articles, which created a mild sensation, appeared in the *Times* on Oct. 12, 14, 17, 19, 24, 28. The decay of the military spirit in the German army and the inferiority of its equipment and leadership was the burden of Repington's reports. Referring to the lack of spirit, he wrote: "The things which one sees in the look of men in a British or French regiment one seeks in vain in the rather sullen-looking, half-cowed, and machine-made Prussian foot-soldier." One had the feeling that they were driven in their work and "that without the drive of the officers corps they would melt away in the stress of battle." According to the British military attaché, these articles contributed materially to the ill-feeling in Germany toward England. A reply to Repington, entitled "The Times' Criticism of the German Army and Its Political Significance," was published in the *Schlesische Zeitung* under a London date line. It related in detail the alleged scandal that had resulted in Repington's resignation from the British army. Baron Acton, the resident minister at Darmstadt, described it as possessing "astonishing accuracy of detail." (*B. D.*, VII, 645–47, 704; *Schlesische Ztg.*, No. 778, Nov. 4; Repington, *Vestigia*, pp. 303–4.)

exchange took place between Kiderlen and Goschen, when the latter complained that none of the German papers had expressed regret for unjustified attacks on McKenna. Kiderlen: "When, I should like to know, has any English newspaper expressed regrets for its false statements with regard to Germany?" Goschen: "When has any English newspaper published a false report of a speech by a German statesman, and then grossly abused him for what he did not say?" On this performance Goschen was commended by Nicolson and Grey for his "tact and firmness." [76] False news reports, incendiary interviews, and press campaigns that gave heat rather than light did not contribute to the maintenance of peace and harmony.

The ease with which British statesmen overcame opposition in the cabinet and lined up the press in support of a policy of complete solidarity with France, presents a sharp contrast to the domestic difficulties that beset German officials at every stage of the Moroccan negotiations. The Wilhelmstrasse failed completely to convince the press and the political parties of the soundness of their policy and the value of the final settlement. This was not due solely to bureaucratic disregard of public agencies of criticism and support, or to a lack of machinery for keeping in touch with these agencies. According to Bethmann the main objectives of their policy—security for their economic interests in Morocco and compensation in the Congo—had been communicated to the representatives of the Kölnische Zeitung, the Münchner Neueste Nachrichten, the Frankfurter Zeitung, the Deutsche Tageszeitung, the Lokal-Anzeiger, and the Tägliche Rundschau. Moreover, Bethmann and Kiderlen were in a position to influence directly a considerable number of leading journalists. Erzberger was an important link with the Catholic press because of his position in the *Augustinus Verein,* the powerful society of Catholic editors and publishers. They could influence the Kölnische Zeitung through Arthur von Huhn, successor to Justizrat Fischer as chief of the Berlin bureau. Baron von Behr was the link between the foreign office and the Lokal-Anzeiger, whose foreign department was headed by Dr. Troska. August Stein of the Frankfurter Zeitung and Herr Sarvey of the Münchner Neueste Nachrichten afforded direct contact with the two most powerful South German dailies. Schiemann of the Kreuzzeitung was in close touch with the foreign office at all times. The Deutsche Tageszeitung, organ of the Conservative agrarians, was closely connected with Bethmann's secretariat and with the foreign office through the editor, Dr. Oertel, the foreign editor, G. Kreutzberg, and the special feature writer, Count Reventlow. Heinrich

[76] B. D., VII, 655.

Rippler, the independent editor of the Tägliche Rundschau, did not cut himself off from all contact with the government. The imperial chancellery also cultivated relations with the National-Zeitung, the Hannoverscher Kurier, and the Vossische Zeitung.[77] Certainly the machinery for influencing and informing the press was not inadequate.

Likewise, in the case of the political parties, the leaders, excluding the Social Democrats, were informed at the beginning of the government's intentions and objectives. According to Bethmann, when the general aims were thus discreetly disclosed, all but the irreconcilables dropped or ignored the demand for a position in Morocco. What then turned editors and politicians against the government? Two factors are discernible: first, dissatisfaction with the final settlement, and second, Kiderlen's publicity tactics. The first will be considered in its chronological order; the second must be dealt with at this point.

Because successful bargaining required secrecy, Kiderlen insisted at the outset upon complete reserve toward the press on the progress of negotiations. He blamed the leakage in Paris for the snarling of his diplomatic lines and the intervention of the English. With the resumption of negotiations with Cambon, on August 4, he told Goschen that he was "tired of writing *démentis* every morning and I have given strict orders to the Press Bureau to give nothing to the Press and to take no notice of what it says." [78] The secrecy of negotiations, the silence of those really informed, the unconscionable business of the rumormongers, the agitation in the extremist journals—all contributed to produce an atmosphere of nervous tension and alarm. During the first week of September, insecurity and panic seized the business community as French banks began the wholesale withdrawal of their short-term credits from Berlin. Reassuring statements were published in the Norddeutsche, and the anxiety in banking circles was relieved by the direct intervention of Kiderlen and Zimmermann.[79] By the first of November a considerable number of papers were censuring the *Geheimniskrämerei* of the Wilhelmstrasse, which had kept the nation inadequately informed at a time when the highest interests of the country had been at stake. The government's publicity policy, they declared, had induced anxiety and panic at home and misunderstanding and misapprehension abroad.

---

[77] *G. P.*, XXIX, 349; P. Gruschinske, *Kiderlen-Wächter und die deutsche Presse*, pp. 5–7; Jäckh, *Kiderlen-Wächter*, II, 143; information furnished the author by Geheimrat Friedrich Heilbron.

[78] *B. D.*, VII, 432–34.

[79] *Schwäbischer Merkur*, Nos. 414, 416, 422, 440, Sept. 6, 7, 11, 21, quoting the semi-official statements of the *Norddeutsche;* Carl Fürstenberg, *Lebensgeschichte*, pp. 514–15. The relation of the financial crisis to the Moroccan negotiations forms the

With the signature of the Moroccan agreements came the final review and balancing of accounts in the press. On November 3 the Havas Agency published a semi-official résumé of the accords, placing French gains in the foreground and minimizing Germany's compensation. It implied a complete victory for French diplomacy. This version was certain to feed German discontent and heighten the impression that nothing really valuable had been acquired. The Wilhelmstrasse immediately issued a public statement condemning the Havas report for its "omissions and inaccuracies," which were "calculated to create false impressions." A German version of the terms was published the following day, and on November 6 the official texts were reproduced in the Norddeutsche. Before this, however, the Wilhelmstrasse had taken steps to prepare the public and to win support for the settlement by inspired publicity in the Kölnische Zeitung.

It was all in vain, however. Aside from perfunctory approval of the maintenance of peace, the press comment was overwhelmingly hostile. The best argument employed by defenders of the agreement was that as a salvage operation it yielded all that was possible; they must accept the losses incurred in liquidating the mistakes of 1906 and 1909.[80] The liberal democratic trio—the Frankfurter Zeitung, the Vossische Zeitung, and the Berliner Tageblatt—disparaged the colonial gains, which were incommensurate with the risks incurred in their acquisition; they criticized Kiderlen's tactics, and condemned the bureaucratic secrecy of the foreign office; but, at the same time, these journals opposed the extremists and vigorously condemned the abusive ravings of the Rheinisch-Westfälische Zeitung, the Berliner Neueste Nachrichten, the Deutsche Zeitung, the Leipziger Neueste Nachrichten, and Die Post.[81] Almost without exception the National Liberal journals of Berlin and the provinces expressed adverse judgments.[82] Only the Kölnische Zeitung, the Lokal-Anzeiger, and the Norddeutsche, journals closely connected

---

subject of an interesting report by the British consul-general at Frankfort. (*B. D.,* VII, 796–805.)

[80] This was the general line taken by the Conservative and Center press of the Blue-Black bloc. *Kölnische Volksztg.,* Nos. 949, 961, 966, 973, Nov. 6, 10, 11, 14. A public appeal was issued by the Hamburg Bourse, signed by Ballin, Bohlen and others, calling for calmer judgment and warning against giving false impressions abroad. *Frankfurter Ztg.,* No. 313, Nov. 11. A similar appeal for national solidarity was published by Hugo Stinnes in the *Kölnische Ztg.,* No. 1224, Nov. 8.

[81] *Frankfurter Ztg.,* Nos. 300, 308, Oct. 29, Nov. 6; *Vossische Ztg.,* No. 561, Nov. 9; *Berliner Tageblatt,* No. 574, Nov. 10.

[82] *Münchner N. N.,* Nos. 513, 517, 519, Nov. 3, 5, 7; *Schwäbischer Merkur,* Nos. 515, 518, Nov. 4, 6; *Magdeburgische Ztg.,* quoted in *Berliner N. N.,* No. 565, Nov. 5; press review of the *Tägliche Rundschau,* quoting *National-Zeitung* and *Hannoverscher Kurier.* Notable among adverse appraisals was that of Heinrich Rippler, presented in a series of three articles in the *Tägliche Rundschau* ("Marokko-Bilanz," Nos. 523, 524, 525, Nov. 7, 8, 9).

with the government, could find words of praise for the agreement and the work that had gone into its production.[83]

Injected into every comment was bitter criticism of the rôle played by England. Some of the complaints were dignified, some were outrageous diatribes, but all sprang from the same conviction: the diplomatic defeat incurred by the government, which reflected upon the national honor, was in the final analysis a charge upon the English account. Britain was the real victor because she had again made good her claim to sit as a world judge, pronouncing sentence on German policy. England had successfully maintained her old course of holding Germany down and thwarting her legitimate efforts to expand. Although the negotiations had been carried on exclusively with France, that country scarcely figured in the publicity, for it was fully realized that there would have been a different outcome if the British government had not intervened in support of the Entente.

In the Reichstag, where the accords were debated on November 9, 10, and 11, the same spirit prevailed as in the press. But even more so than in the press, the discussion was influenced by party politics. Germany was approaching a general election and party editors and speakers were thinking quite as much of their constituencies as of the Congo. All the middle-class publicity directors and party leaders were setting their sails to catch the strong current of patriotic feeling that was sweeping the country. Circumstances encouraged them to exaggerate and magnify the aspect of the negotiations that bore upon the higher questions of national honor and patriotism; and on this score, Britain and not France was immediately concerned. Bethmann-Hollweg's speech, recommending the agreements to the Reichstag, was uninspired and the tone apologetic. The audience was distinctly hostile and interrupted with whistles, laughter, and ironic cheers. The Berliner Tageblatt summarized the meaning of the speech in one sentence: "We have secured what it was possible to secure without a war, and we refuse to make war for the sake of Morocco." [84] The party spokesmen—Heydebrand for the Conservatives, Bassermann for the National Liberals, Hertling for the Center, and Wiemer for the Progressives, echoed all the criticisms that had been voiced by the political journalists. The Congo compensation was inadequate, German diplomacy inept and confused, the German government

[83] "Das deutsch-französische Abkommen," Kölnische Zeitung, No. 1201, Nov. 4; Lokal-Anzeiger, Nos. 562, 563, Nov. 3, 4; Norddeutsche, Nos. 260, 262, Nov. 4, 7.

[84] No. 574, Nov. 10. The Vossische Zeitung said that to find a precedent for the Reichstag's reception of the chancellor's speech one would have to go back to the speech of Manteuffel, the "November man," following his return from Olmütz. (No. 562, Nov. 9.)

had yielded to intimidation and allowed policy to outweigh honor. The Crown Prince attended the debate and openly applauded the attacks upon England and the gibes hurled at Bethmann. His conduct produced a sensation in the European press.[85] In an evident desire to exclude the British angle from the debate, Bethmann made only a passing reference to Lloyd George's "after dinner speech." Party spokesmen, however, ignored the colonial agreements and concentrated on Anglo-German relations. Heydebrand, the Conservative spokesman, indulged in an outrageous attack on England. Referring to Lloyd George and Cartwright, he said: "We know now where our enemy is. Like a flash of lightning in the dark these incidents revealed to the German people where the enemy was. (Lively agreement.) The German people know now, when it seeks its place in the sun, when it seeks the place to which it is destined, where the state is that believes it can pass final judgment. (Applause.) We Germans are not accustomed to that. If the Imperial Government has not given the answer that was called for, but which remains unknown to us, then the German people will give the answer. (Applause.)" [86] Each speaker paid his respects to Lloyd George and in so doing implied that his own government had failed to defend the nation's honor. The insult was offered in public; why was it not rejected in the same way?

On the second day of debate, the chancellor made a spirited counterattack upon his critics. Laying aside his notes and his air of professorial objectivity he spoke his mind to the chauvinists and the discontented colonialists. He administered a stinging rebuke to Heydebrand, whom he charged with exploiting Anglo-German tension for electioneering purposes. This unexpected strength of defense won for the chancellor considerable ground in the press, which had been as unfriendly as the Reichstag in judging his first speech. But here again domestic politics governed reactions, for the Social Democrats, the Progressives, and the National Liberals would naturally encourage the chancellor in order to widen the gap between him and the leader of the Conservative party. Bethmann's slight success could not obliterate the general feeling that

[85] The Pan-Germans were in ecstasies. Herr Schmock wrote in the *Leipziger Neueste Nachrichten:* "Es zucht ihm [the Crown Prince] in den Händen Beifall zu klatschen! Und wahrhaftig, das zuletzt Erwartete wird zum Ereignis: der Kronprinz applaudiert, er klatscht in die Hände!" (*Berliner Tageblatt,* No. 575, Nov. 10.)

[86] Quoted in all papers, Nov. 9, 10. At a Conservative party rally at Breslau on Oct. 27, Heydebrand had said: "Wenn sogar ein liberales Ministerium, das in England als weniger Kriegslustig gilt, uns die Faust unter die Nase halten konnte und erklärte, über die Welt habe ich allein zu gebieten, so ist das für uns, die wir 1870 hinter uns haben, bitter hart. . . ." (*Münchner N. N.,* No. 513, Nov. 3.)

the press and the Reichstag in the name of the nation had administered a serious rebuke to the bureaucratic government.[87]

The party debates and their reverberations filled the press for days. Meanwhile, the budget committee, charged with examining the accords prior to final action, began its hearings. On November 17 Kiderlen presented a long explanatory statement. It had little to do with the merits of the agreement, but concentrated on the Berlin-London angle, seeking to clear the government of the charge that it had not acted energetically in the face of British interference. To this committee was revealed, for the first time, the sharp official protest that had been made against Lloyd George's Mansion House manifesto and the interpretation put upon it by the British press. The committee report of Kiderlen's remarks filled twelve printed pages, and although the proceedings were customarily secret the government followed the unusual course of releasing through the Wolff Bureau an abstract of more than half the length of the original stenographic report.[88] This publicity measure was clearly designed to counteract criticism of the government in nationalist circles. Kiderlen's report gave almost word for word the communications that passed between himself and Grey during the early summer. This set a new precedent in giving publicity to diplomatic records, a precedent that was not altogether pleasing to the British foreign office.[89] Positive official action was doubtless behind the article in the Lokal-Anzeiger, entitled "What Lloyd George Actually Said." Reproducing the text of Lloyd George's remarks, it sought to dispel the popular legend that an explicit insult had been delivered by the chancellor of the exchequer.[90] From another quarter efforts were made to calm the storm. Twenty leaders of German finance, industry, and commerce issued a public appeal calling on the German people to support the government and to refrain from further injuring national prestige through continuance of the bitter agitation over the Congo treaty.[91] Although these efforts at defense availed little

[87] For details of the Reichstag incident as it affected Bethmann and the Conservative party leaders see Westarp, *Konservative Politik*, I, 154–64.

[88] Released on Nov. 21, published in the German papers on Nov. 22. The Wolff Bureau later issued a statement absolving Kiderlen from responsibility for publication of the secret proceedings. This may have been technically correct, but it is certain that Dr. Mantler would not have taken this step without authorization from some one in authority.

[89] See the comments by Crowe and Grey and the latter's dispatch to Goschen; *B. D.,* VII, 699–700, 715. Grey referred to this procedure as "very unusual" in his speech before the Commons on November 27.

[90] No. 581, Nov. 14. Goschen assumed that it was inspired and reported it to London. *B. D.,* VII, 693.

[91] Circulated by Wolff's Bureau and published in all important papers. (*Norddeutsche*, No. 262, Nov. 11.) This action was taken independently of the government

against the irreconcilables, the more moderate critics recognized that the government had not been lacking in energy in dealing with London.

After Kiderlen had given the German interpretation of the events of July, which was certainly not a version that would be acceptable to London, it was inevitable that Grey should present the British case from the floor of the House of Commons. The date was announced two weeks in advance. Public attention was now focused more sharply than ever on the Anglo-German dispute. In German circles it was felt that they had reached a point where relations with England must either grow worse, or take a turn for the better. In anticipation of Grey's address, the German papers wrote as though he would pronounce whether it was to be peace or war between them. No speech in the pre-War years was given so much advance publicity or reproduced under such flaring headlines as Grey's explanation of British foreign policy on November 27. It was not the fault of the press if the German burghers were not excited to a fever pitch.

When the eagerly awaited speech was in German hands, it was apparent that the public or the editors had anticipated too much, for Grey had not proclaimed the millennium in Anglo-German relations, nor had he urged a declaration of war and a fight to the finish. As a matter of fact the speech, from the German standpoint, changed the situation very little. All the commentators found something to cavil at—he had not renounced Britain's claim to the final word in all colonial questions; he had not explained the grounds on which the British government came to doubt the German declaration of July 1 as to the object of the *Panther's* dispatch to Agadir; he failed to justify the brusque intervention implied in the Mansion House speech; he did not deny Captain Faber's revelations of menacing naval preparations against Germany during the summer; and finally, although his speech was polite in form and unaggressive in tone, it reaffirmed British adherence to the Entente policy that had as a natural corollary hostility and unfriendliness to Germany. In fact, there was scarcely a statement in the speech to which some commentator did not take exception.[92]

---

on the initiative of the banker Helfferich. (Jäckh, *Kidenlen-Wächter*, II, 142.) For the opposing views of journalist and financier on the Moroccan affair see the correspondence that passed between Maximilian Harden and Carl Fürstenberg during the summer. (Fürstenberg, *Lebensgeschichte*, 418 ff.)

[92] Goschen's dispatch (Nov. 29, *B. D.*, VII, 736–41) summarizes and quotes the comments of the *Berliner Tageblatt, Frankfurter Zeitung, Börsen-Courier, Vossische Zeitung, Tägliche Rundschau, Hamburger Nachrichten, Die Post,* and the *Lokal-Anzeiger*. The same criticisms with different shadings were uttered by the Catholic organs, *Germania* (No. 274, Nov. 29) and *Kölnische Volkszeitung* (Nos. 1020, 1023, Nov. 30, Dec. 1), and the South German National Liberal papers, *Münchner Neueste*

erman editors expected of Grey it would be impossible
ut under the circumstances it is doubtful that he could have
e approval of so critical an audience. It is usually a vague stereo-
or an emotional attitude that covers the popular understanding of
complex issue such as the one that divided London and Berlin. In
this instance Theodor Wolff came closer to fixing the terms of German
discontent than any other press commentator when he wrote the following words: "The German people are united on two points that figure
in the debate; the one, that Britain's will shall not pass for law throughout the entire world, and the other, that German policy of the past
months has been a chain of fateful mistakes." [93]

In England, no less than in Germany, when the authorities finally got
around to rendering an account of their recent policy, the government
had to face a certain amount of criticism and discontent. Following the
Mansion House episode, the service of information in the British press
had moved back to domestic issues—the House of Lords and the great
railway strike—and toward the end of September, to the outbreak of the
Turco-Italian War. The protracted Moroccan negotiations were definitely played down in the news until the final agreement was reached,
when the editors expressed general approval of the settlement. The
British public was wholly unprepared for the bitter Reichstag debates,
Kiderlen's disclosures in the budget commission, and the unqualified expressions of resentment and enmity that came from Germany. Sensational revelations of military and naval preparations during the summer
crisis disclosed for the first time how near the country had been to the
brink of war. From the Radical pacifist elements issued the demand that
they have a general stock-taking and consideration of the basic policies
that had so nearly involved the country in armed conflict. The Manchester Guardian, which made itself the spokesman for this group,
phrased the demand as follows: "Now that Morocco is out of the way
and our treaty obligations are exhausted, is this country willing to return to the original conception of the Entente? In plain words, does
the Entente make us friends with France or allies bound to support
her even at the cost of war?" [94]

Nachrichten (Nos. 558, 559, 560, Nov. 28, 29, 30) and *Schwäbischer Merkur* (Nos.
556, 558, 559, 564, Nov. 28, 29, 30, Dec. 2).

[93] *Berliner Tageblatt,* No. 620, Dec. 6. Similarly, the *Vossische Zeitung* declared
that although Grey had stated that England would not stand in Germany's way, if they
put him to the test by acquiring a port in East Africa they would have the threats of
July 4 and 21 in a new edition. (No. 595, Nov. 28.)

[94] Nov. 10. Some of the Conservative journals joined the Radicals in demanding a
general reassessment of policy. Editorials in the *Standard,* Nov. 20, 21, 22.

Grey's speech in the House, on November 27, was not
exposition of British foreign policy for the benefit of the world
it was a defense against serious criticisms of the government in
and in parliament. His address was divided into four parts: in the
part he gave the foreign office version of the events that preceded
Mansion House manifesto and the reasons for British intervention; in
the second part he dealt with the public alarm over the imminence of
war during the summer; in the third part he reviewed the bases of
British foreign policy; and in the fourth he referred briefly to the immediate problem of Anglo-German relations. In narrating the events
that preceded the Mansion House speech, Grey enlarged upon Berlin's
"three weeks of silence," which gave rise to such concern and led to
Lloyd George's proclamation. In the Reichstag and before the budget
commission, Kiderlen and Bethmann had stressed the fact that from
July 1 to July 21 no question, direct or indirect, had been addressed to
them by the British. Grey could not truthfully state that questions had
been asked, but he stressed the failure of the German authorities to provide information. As the cause of British uneasiness he cited the French
press rumors to the effect that the Germans were landing at Agadir
and making treaties with the natives. As cause for greater alarm he
cited the reports that appeared in the press on July 20 as to the exorbi-
tant demands for compensation being advanced by Germany. These, they
feared, would wreck the negotiations between Berlin and Paris. Thus it
appears from Grey's speech that, although he was in the best position
to correct the newspaper exaggerations, he nevertheless made them the
basis of solemn official representations to Berlin, and on top of that
co-operated in the provocative Mansion House gesture.[95] The belated
war-scare, which came after the danger was over, he ridiculed as "a fit
of political alcoholism"; and he ignored all the evidences of military preparations, the disclosure of which in recent weeks had given rise to the
public alarm.[96]

[95] Of course the *British Documents* clearly show that Grey was fully informed
through Bertie at Paris and Cambon in Berlin of every detail of the Franco-German
conversations. They further indicate that Lloyd George was put up to warn the Germans and reassure the French that the Entente still held.

[96] A commotion had been produced in England and Germany by the publication of
a speech by Captain Faber, a Conservative member of parliament, at Andover on November 9. In the course of his remarks, which were designed to show the inadequacy
of the government's military and naval policy, he made inaccurate and exaggerated
statements with regard to British preparations for war against Germany during the
summer. These were taken up in the German press and interpreted as substantial
proof of the thesis of British willingness and preparation for aggression. Articles appeared in the German press examining the disposition of British naval forces, alleging that at the several crisis dates (July 24–27, Aug. 18, Sept. 15–29) the entire
British fleet was concentrated in the Channel and North Sea and that the Far Eastern

Coming to Britain's position in the power alignment of Europe, Grey presented their policy as a continuation of the course inaugurated by the preceding Conservative cabinet. He reaffirmed the government's faith in the ententes with France and Russia. These must remain the bases of British policy, although they did not bar good relations with Germany. The only alternative to the entente system was to return to the old policy of splendid isolation. This was impossible under existing circumstances, for it would "result in other nations of Europe, either by choice or by necessity, being brought into the orbit of a single diplomacy from which we should be excluded." In a short time, under such conditions, he prophesied, they would be building ships against the united navies of Europe. Turning then to the immediate problem of Anglo-German relations, Grey said that their friendships with France and Russia, whose policies were entirely unaggressive, did not preclude good relations with Germany; England had no desire to stand in Germany's way, and he hinted that her colonial aspirations might be satisfied in Central Africa. In concluding, he endorsed Bethmann's slogan of the "clean slate," although he was not noticeably friendly, or optimistic about an immediate improvement in Anglo-German relations.[97]

In the House of Commons Grey drew most of his applause from the Conservative benches; a striking number of his party followers maintained a stony silence. In the debate that followed, the Conservatives completely forswore the rôle of an Opposition. Bonar Law, as party leader, endorsed the government's course and, appealing to national patriotism, called upon his followers to refrain from criticism. Going even further, he proclaimed "that we shall never criticize them even when we think they are wrong, if we believe that there is any danger of our criticism weakening our position among the other great nations of the world." [98] When Bonar Law, toward the end of his address, found those

---

forces were prepared to fall upon the German ships at Tsingtau. Significant for the spirit that prevailed in the press and among the diplomats is the suspicion with which each side regarded the movements of the other; each national group maintained that it had not prepared for aggressive action, but had only taken precautionary measures against attack. Reports of the German naval chief of staff, Von Heeringen, *G. P.*, XXIX, 278–80, 287–89; *ibid.*, XXIX, 261–66; *B. D.*, VII, 716; Tirpitz, *Aufbau*, pp. 249–50; "Seekriegsgefahr von 1911," *Münchner N. N.*, No. 604, Dec. 28; "Britische Freundlichkeiten," *Tägliche Rundschau*, Nov. 29; *Vossische Ztg.*, Dec. 6, No. 609; fullest report on the Faber speech in *Daily Telegraph*, Nov. 20.

[97] *Parl. Deb.*, 5th Ser., vol. 32, 43–65. Asquith too, in his involuted rhetoric, served notice that there would be no change in the direction of policy. "I may add [he said] that we are influenced in our conduct outside the strict letter of Treaty obligations by the desire to maintain . . . the friendships we have formed, and understandings we have entered into, and which, as we believe, have been reciprocal between ourselves and our neighbors." (*Ibid.*, vol. 32, 110.)

[98] *Parl. Deb.*, 5th Ser., vol. 32, 67. Contrast this stand with the bitter and unreasonable censure leveled by German party leaders at their government's foreign policy.

words of conciliation and appreciation for Germany, which Grey had so stiffly avoided, he was heartily cheered from the Liberal benches.[99] Only John Dillon, the Irish Nationalist leader, Ramsay Macdonald, the Labor spokesman, and several Gladstonian Radicals—Noel Buxton, Arthur Ponsonby, Philip Morrell, Josiah Wedgewood—ventured to find fault with Grey's brief for the government. The upper house showed more independence of judgment than the lower. There Lord Courtney launched a scathing attack on Grey; Lord Lansdowne very diplomatically questioned the cabinet's extreme interpretation of the agreement of 1904; and Lord Newton, always sane and moderate, censured the Mansion House declaration as an unnecessarily provocative gesture. Why, he asked, were not the usual channels of diplomacy employed? And to this day the answer is lacking.

In the Conservative press we find a repetition of the performance of the party leaders in parliament. The editors approved the record and championed Grey and the government against "the pro-German Radicals, lineal descendants of the little-Englanders and the pro-Boers." [100] And in the manner of the prime minister and foreign secretary they preached at Germany: She should only be nice and brave and not always be the disturber of tranquillity in the European kindergarten, but take the other nice children as a pattern, who at the moment in Persia, Morocco, and Tripoli were enjoying such harmless, happy games!

Unanimity was lacking in the Liberal press. The Westminster Gazette, Daily Chronicle, and Liverpool Post and Mercury praised Grey's speech, which in their opinion completely vindicated the government's action during the crisis.[101] From the Daily News and the Manchester Guardian came a blast of critical and hostile publicity. Besides the editorials of Sidebotham, Gardiner, and Massingham, there were special feature articles by W. T. Stead, and the letter columns were thrown open to critics of Grey's policy.[102] The chief complaints lodged against Grey and the government were: first, neither Grey nor the prime minister had clarified their relations with France—whether it was an entente

[99] This significant transposition of rôles was noted by several witnesses. London correspondent of the *Scotsman*, Nov. 28; report of the Austrian ambassador, *Oesterreich-Ungarns Aussenpolitik*, III, 602–3; Metternich to Bethmann, *G. P.*, XXIX, 284; Gaupp to the *Münchner N. N.*, No. 557, Nov. 29; C. A. Bratter to the *Morgenpost* (quoted, *Tägliche Rundschau*, No. 558, Nov. 28).

[100] *Birmingham Daily Post*, Nov. 28; *Times*, Nov. 27, 28; *Daily Mail*, Nov. 27, 28; *Pall Mall Gazette*, Nov. 28; *Scotsman*, Nov. 28, 29; *Morning Post*, Nov. 28, 29, Dec. 1; *Daily Telegraph*, Nov. 28, 29; *Standard*, Nov. 28, 29, Dec. 6.

[101] Editorial comment, Nov. 28.

[102] W. T. Stead exploded the myth of "three weeks of silence." Among the critical letter writers were John Dillon, W. Barton, W. P. Byles, De Forest, Napier Malcolm, all members of parliament. (*Daily News, Manchester Guardian*, Nov. 28, 29, 30.)

or an alliance; second, they had not gone far enough in meeting Bethmann on the future of Anglo-German relations; and third, the 1904 agreements had been carried to the point where they divided Europe into two armed camps, precluding independent judgment and disinterested action on the merits of current issues. W. T. Stead was not noted for understatement, but there was probably some truth in his statement that "nine Liberals in ten, in the cabinet and out of it, have been profoundly alarmed by the perils to which the entente policy has exposed us this summer."

While the Conservative and Liberal Imperialist editors were staunch in their defense of the government's policy during the crisis, there was a notable reluctance to continue the acrimonious debate with the German publicists and politicians. Moreover, many of the editors curled the tails of their leading articles with hopeful expressions for the future and warm denials of the German complaint that British policy was directed solely toward thwarting Germany's legitimate ambitions as a great power. When Bethmann, speaking in the Reichstag on December 5, answered Grey in a more aggressive and reproachful tone than he had assumed in his previous utterances, the English editors charged it off to the approaching elections and refused to resume the debate as to who was at fault during the preceding summer.[103] They closed the books, as only editors are privileged to do, by declaring: "We do not care to pursue the matter further!"

In Radical political and journalistic circles the campaign against Grey was intensified. This opposition to the cabinet's foreign policy did not spring up over night, and it was not limited to the Moroccan crisis. Discontent inside and outside of parliament had been accumulating for some time. The general debate simply afforded the critical elements an opportunity to voice their protest against the general policies pursued by the Liberal government since 1906. Four principal issues were raised by the discontented: First, the countenancing of Russian ruthlessness and bad faith in regard to Persia; second, the secrecy with which foreign affairs were conducted and the lack of parliamentary control; third, the steady worsening, under Grey's direction, of their relations with Germany, which during the summer had almost reached the point of open hostilities; and fourth, the turning of a friendly understanding with France into an alliance without the approval or knowledge of parliament.

A very wide range of organizations participated in the campaign to turn the government from its old course and give a new direction to

---

[103] Goschen and Cambon suspected that the speech was written by Kiderlen. When pressed, the foreign secretary did not deny authorship. B. D., VII, 768.

foreign policy. The Anglo-German Friendship Committee, with Lord Avebury as president and Sir Frank Lascelles as chairman, organized meetings in London (presided over by the Lord Mayor), Glasgow, and Edinburgh at which the foreign office policy of exclusive ententes was subjected to serious criticism.[104] The organization of the Liberal Foreign Affairs Group in parliament was a direct result of the Moroccan crisis. During the summer adjournment of parliament, Mr. Noel Buxton paid a visit to Germany and returned alarmed and dismayed at the feeling he had encountered there among official acquaintances. Among his colleagues in the House he collected eighty signatures on a petition to the prime minister calling for government action to remove the impression that Great Britain was pursuing a calculated dog-in-the-manger policy toward Germany. Asquith was not greatly impressed by the memorial; he asked only one question of the committee that presented it: "Are there any Conservatives among the signatures?" In December the petitioners organized the Liberal Foreign Affairs Group under the leadership of Buxton and Arthur Ponsonby. Listed among its specific objectives were the improvement of Anglo-German relations and the counteracting of Germanophobia in the foreign service personnel. At the first meeting, the group recorded its disapproval of any policy "which might seek to oppose the legitimate aspirations of Germany," and urged upon the government "the necessity of taking definite action with a view to reaching an understanding." [105] The National Peace Society, representing twenty-seven organizations, participated in the movement for a reorientation of official policy. "What is wanted," it declared in a public statement, "is a change in the diplomatic view held in both countries." It sent its appeals to all the chambers of commerce and commercial bodies, and three thousand trade union groups, trade councils, and co-operative societies.[106] The Labor party, in conference at Birmingham, adopted a resolution stating "that this Congress believing the anti-German policy pursued in the name of the British Government by Sir Edward Grey to be a cause of increasing armaments, international ill-will, and the betrayal of oppressed nationalities, protests in the strongest terms against it." [107] From this review we see that some of the Liberal party's staunchest allies and supporters in the country and in parliament were thrown into opposition to the foreign policy of

---

[104] The London meeting was held the first week in November, the later meetings in January and February, 1912. (*Manchester Guardian,* Jan. 30; *Times,* Feb. 3.)

[105] T. P. Conwell-Evans, *Foreign Policy From a Back Bench,* pp. 57–59, 81–82; *Manchester Guardian,* Dec. 7; *Daily News,* Dec. 7; *Birmingham Daily Post,* Dec. 10.

[106] *Manchester Guardian,* Dec. 8, 1911.

[107] *Daily News,* Jan. 27, 1912.

the leaders. The "Grey-Must-Go" campaign is generally overlooked by historians and memoir writers because the diverse groups never coalesced for a great positional battle and in the long run their cause was lost; but for the next two years they carried on lively guerilla warfare against Grey and the foreign office.

Grey's opponents found channels of public expression, as well as active allies, in the press of the nation. Some of the ablest journalists in England were his critics—C. P. Scott and H. Sidebotham of the Guardian, A. G. Gardiner and G. H. Perris of the Daily News, H. W. Massingham and H. N. Brailsford of the *Nation*, and F. W. Hirst of the *Economist*. "The Liberal Foreign Secretary," writes J. L. Hammond, "found himself depending almost entirely upon Conservative support, a support often embarrassing and misleading, for among Liberal writers his only steady advocate was Mr. J. A. Spender, the able and experienced editor of the Westminster Gazette. . . ." [108] Efforts were made to restore harmony; but at an arranged meeting between Scott and Grey the two principals could find no common ground. On January 12, acting on Scott's initiative, the Manchester Liberal Federation sent a letter to Grey urging adherence to Liberal principles in the determination of policy, and urging especially a public declaration that the Entente with France involved no presumption of alliance obligations. At the same time Scott published an editorial, from his own pen, appealing to dissatisfied cabinet members to repudiate Grey's entente policy, which consisted in "pandering to Russia and irritating Germany." [109]

We know that some of the cabinet members, notably Loreburn, Harcourt, Burns, and, on occasion, Morley, countenanced the rising of the *Fronde,* if they did not actively encourage it. The turmoil in the press and the revolt in the ranks of the Liberal party were reflected in heated disputes in cabinet meetings.[110] The dissenters, however, were unwilling to break up the government on this issue. A series of resignations, the secession of the Liberal Imperialists, or the secession of the Gladstonian Radicals, would have reduced the party to impotence and returned the Conservatives to power.

[108] J. L. Hammond, *C. P. Scott,* pp. 150–51.
[109] *Ibid.,* pp. 163–65; *Manchester Guardian,* Jan. 13, 1912.
[110] Spender and Asquith, *Life of Lord Oxford and Asquith,* I, 349; *War Memoirs of David Lloyd George* (Boston, 1932–   ), I, 47–48. Metternich, writing to Bethmann on November 24, reviewed the signs of discontent, but predicted that Grey would easily hold his own. "Nevertheless, the dissatisfaction with the direction of England's foreign policy, particularly the dangerous disagreement with Germany into which it has fallen, is sharper than I have seen it for years." (*G. P.,* XXIX, 270.) The cabinet crisis in November arose, according to Lord Esher, over the "imprudent summoning of a packed Defence Committee in August to settle the immediate form of action if war had to be declared against Germany." (*Journals and Letters,* III, 74.)

Grey's position was not seriously threatened. However, to assume that he was impervious to scoldings from the ranks of his own party would be a mistake. It is part of the Grey legend that he was scornful of press criticism and popular agitation touching the business of his department. On this occasion he was resentful of the press attacks and irritated by the intrusion of the pressure groups. Speaking in his constituency, on January 21, he took note of "the severe attacks from certain quarters in the Liberal Press with regard to foreign affairs." He answered his critics by saying that it was not "his foreign policy" but that of the cabinet of which he was a member.[111] The invocation of cabinet solidarity exposed the weakness of his opponents. If the cabinet split, the government would fall.

However, no responsible ministry could ignore the current of conciliation that swept the country in the winter of 1911–12. The Radicals and Laborites represented the extremes in criticism of Grey and the recent trends in foreign policy. Outside these groups was a considerable body of opinion which approved the government's support of the Entente during the summer, but which was not entirely in accord with the outward character of recent foreign policy. In these circles there was a genuine desire to relax the tension and disprove the charge that Britain harbored the idea of bearing down on Germany and keeping her in Coventry. This was reflected in the foreign affairs debate in parliament on November 27. It was even more marked in the conclusion of the debate on December 14. Thirty-two speakers participated in the deliberations, which were entirely free from alarmism and chauvinism. No one can read the report of the debate without being impressed by certain points of common agreement in the utterances of the speakers. One notes, first, the genuine concern expressed over the critical condition that had developed in recent years in their relations with Germany; second, the refusal to accept the thesis propagated so assiduously in a section of the press that war with Germany was inevitable; third, the spirit of self-criticism, which found that perhaps unwittingly their policy had been too heavily weighted against the realization of entirely legitimate German ambitions; and fourth, the hope that the government and the foreign office would take some positive action to relax the tension between the two countries and dispel the atmosphere of bitterness and resentment that prevailed in Germany. Not from any one speech or statement, but from an accumulation of them comes the conclusion that it was the desire of the Com-

[111] G. M. Trevelyan, *Grey of Fallodon*, pp. 217–18; *Manchester Guardian*, Jan. 22, 1912.

mons that the slate be not only cleaned but something new and more agreeable written upon it.[112]

Between the reality of England's position in the Triple Entente and the pressure from the press and parliament to appease Germany there was a fundamental incompatibility. The highest aim of British policy during the crisis had been the maintenance of unity in Entente ranks.[113] The authors and exponents of that policy could hardly renounce it in the hour of victory. Therefore, in consequence of the Radical and Labor revolt and the strong current of conciliation that developed in the country, the cabinet entered upon an equivocal line of action. Behind the scenes and in secrecy the Entente was extended and defined by the Grey-Cambon letters and the redistribution of naval forces looking toward Anglo-French co-operation in a European war. On the other hand, to meet what the custodians of high policy always referred to as "our unfortunate parliamentary exigencies" Grey and Asquith began that series of denials to embarrassing questions, which tended to obscure rather than to clarify Britain's position in the European alignment. At the same time, when the opportunity arose, they sanctioned a dramatic public gesture to conciliate their critics—they sent Haldane to Berlin.

[112] *Parl. Deb.*, 5th Ser., vol. 32, 43–166, 2543–2662. This was further the burden of numerous dispatches from Metternich reporting on English opinion during November, December, and January. (*G. P.*, XXIX, 250–92, XXXI, 72.) The same current was running strongly in the Conservative journals, the *Daily Telegraph, Morning Post, Standard,* and *Scotsman.*

[113] Note the frantic efforts of Grey, Nicolson, Buchanan, and Bertie to buck up the Russians, when at a critical moment St. Petersburg assumed a dubious attitude toward its French ally. (*B. D.*, VII, 464–480.)

CHAPTER XIV

THE TENSION RELAXED?

The Triple Entente has no meaning or reality for us, and we owe no manner of allegiance to it.

Manchester Guardian, January 6, 1914.

The unmistakable signs of revulsion of British opinion following the Agadir crisis did not appease immediately the wrathful German politicians and publicists. Apart from the Social Democratic press, the mood of publicity was resentful and suspicious. To friendship speeches and demonstrations the Germans replied with the slogan originated by William II and his ministers: "We want deeds not words." This was the refrain in every article touching the Anglo-German problem. Given the temper prevailing in the Fatherland, it was child's play for Tirpitz to project and secure acceptance of a supplementary navy law. In military minds the situation had its simple logic; they had received a box on the ears over Morocco—they must bring in an armaments bill to show the world that they would not endure another. Party leaders, too, entertained this view; the Conservatives, National Liberals, and Progressives were pressing for such a bill and the Center, although reserved, would probably vote for it. It was public knowledge that measures for a considerable increase in both arms of the fighting forces were being prepared for submission to the new Reichstag early in 1912.[1]

Metternich and Kühlmann from their observation post in London were deeply impressed with the many signs of British desire to be more accommodating to Germany. They thought British statesmen were on the point of stepping out of their way, and that by agreement Germany might be assured a rich future as a great colonial power. Introduction of a supplementary navy law would give the armaments screw another turn, spoil the atmosphere for a deal, and at the same time increase the danger of an armed clash with the Triple Entente.[2] The chancellor and the foreign secretary accepted the case presented by the London representatives.

[1] Admiral Hopmann, *Das Logbuch eines Seeoffizers* (Berlin, 1923), pp. 379–84; Tirpitz, *Aufbau,* pp. 199 ff.; *B. D.,* VI, 660, VII, 639–41, 750–51; *G. P.,* XXXI, 31–33.
[2] This was the gist of numerous reports from Metternich, but the alternatives are most clearly stated in Kühlmann's dispatch of January 8, 1912. *G. P.,* XXXI, 87.

There then ensued a sharp tussle between Tirpitz and Bethmann, the former insisting that security was to be achieved in further armaments, the latter taking the position that diplomacy and agreement were safer. Kühlmann, in London, was working upon the press with all the influence at his command. It is evident from the tenor of London dispatches appearing in the newspapers, that he had considerable success in mobilizing the German correspondents on the side of the embassy. One of Dr. Gaupp's private reports to the Münchner Neueste Nachrichten found its way through the Berlin bureau of that journal to the imperial navy department.[3]

Bethmann was no match for Tirpitz. He did not have the unqualified support of the Emperor, and the temper of the parties and their publicity spokesmen was not favorable. Almost his only chance of a creditable and satisfactory solution lay in the possibility of a political agreement assuring Germany that England would not be on the side of her enemies in a continental war. With such an agreement the political need for further naval increases would disappear. That had been Bethmann's major aim in foreign policy since 1909, and its realization seemed nearer than ever before when Haldane made his historic visit to Berlin in February 1912.

To enter into a detailed account of this mission and its aftermath is not necessary for the purpose of this book. The considerations that moved the British cabinet to undertake this venture in what the skilled élite of the foreign service disdainfully called "amateur diplomacy" were: first, to satisfy the pro-German sentiment in the cabinet, in the party, and in the press; second, to abate by a public gesture of conciliation and good will the feeling in Germany that British policy was wilfully obstructionist where the desires of that government were concerned; and third, to head off if possible any further considerable increase in the German naval establishment. Given the motives of the two parties, the field of discussion fell naturally into three parts: a formula of neutrality, or a "political understanding," naval expenditure, and colonial matters. All three issues were explored in Haldane's conversations with the Emperor, Bethmann and Tirpitz. Haldane returned to London in a highly optimistic mood with a copy of the German supplementary naval law in his pocket. The negotiations on the neutrality formula were then continued through the German embassy in London. But neither party really had a free hand and they were practically foredoomed to failure. It is abundantly clear that Grey and Asquith backed by the foreign service experts, Nicolson, Crowe, Goschen, and Bertie, had no intention of accepting Bethmann's neu-

[3] On Kühlmann and the press and the Gaupp incident see Tirpitz, *op. cit.,* 191, 296.

trality formula, which would bind England's hands in a continental war. As signs of suspicion and anxiety appeared in Paris and St. Petersburg, the British became more and more reluctant to continue the conversations. Further, the German concessions on the supplementary law were considered inadequate by the technical advisers at the admiralty. Misunderstanding and suspicion soon cropped up. When the British raised objections to the supplementary law and began to shy off from the neutrality formula, the Berlin authorities thought Haldane was being disavowed. The counter proposals made by the British authorities to Bethmann's neutrality formula encouraged the suspicions of Tirpitz and the Kaiser that the British were trying to trade them out of the supplementary law without giving effective guarantees in the vital matter of British policy.

By the end of March negotiations had come to a standstill. The foreign office officials were opposed to any formula that might compromise their relations with France and Russia, while the prime minister began to incline to the view that they were being led on a wild goose chase. On April 10 Asquith wrote to Grey that he was "becoming more and more doubtful as to the wisdom of prolonging these negotiations with Germany about a formula. Nothing, I believe, will meet her purpose which falls short of a promise on our part of neutrality; a promise we cannot give." [4] According to Poincaré, Nicolson told the French chargé that the cabinet "only continued the discussions with Count Metternich to ease their consciences, but nothing would come of it." [5]

The permanent officials and ambassadors were not inclined to favor and assist the step taken by the cabinet and they were genuinely relieved when it failed. Their main concern was to bury the neutrality formula without unduly exciting the feelings of the mourners. Nicolson had been fearful from the beginning that they might be "entrapped" in some engagement that would "offend the French and render them suspicious." For, as he wrote to Goschen, "I have always maintained, and I have impressed as far as I can on those dealing with these matters, that it would be far more disadvantageous to have an unfriendly France and unfriendly Russia than an unfriendly Germany. The latter . . . can give us plenty of annoyance, but it cannot really threaten any of our more important interests, while Russia especially could cause us extreme embarrassment . . . and it would be most unfortunate were we to revert to the state of things which existed before 1904 and 1907." To Bertie, the Haldane mission was an "absurd" and "foolish move," intended "to satisfy the Grey-must-go radicals." And Goschen congratulated Nicolson:

---

[4] B. D., VI, 745.
[5] The Memoirs of Raymond Poincaré, 1912 (N. Y., 1926), p. 107.

"They have tried to bustle us into a hampering formula and I rejoice that they have failed. You have been foremost in this good work." Nicolson's influence in holding the cabinet to the foreign office policy cannot be overemphasized. Grey at the time was preoccupied with the coal strike conferences and Nicolson dealt directly with the cabinet members.[6]

Tirpitz and the German naval enthusiasts were just as pleased at the failure to reach a settlement, for they saved their supplementary law, won a resounding victory over the civilian chancellor, the foreign office, and the hated London ambassador, Paul Metternich. The latter's recall in May was a direct consequence of the failure to reach a political agreement, and it symbolized the triumph of armaments megalomanics over common sense.[7]

Only in the field of colonial matters and the Bagdad railroad did the Haldane mission bear fruit. Conversations on these subjects were begun and final agreements were worked out and awaiting signature when war broke out in 1914.[8]

In England the report of Haldane's journey to Berlin was received with approval and satisfaction by the Liberal editors, and with open expressions of misgivings and hostility by the Times, Daily Mail, and Pall Mall Gazette; the remaining important Conservative-Unionist journals were reserved in their comment. The atmosphere for Haldane's stay in Germany was not greatly improved by Churchill's speech at Glasgow, in which the chief of the admiralty made an uncompromising declaration of Britain's naval determination and ticked off the German navy as a "luxury." His statement was welcomed by the Pall Mall Gazette (Feb. 12) as "a very useful corrective to Lord Haldane's 'all-things-to-all men' demeanour among German statesmen." The same writer warned against a policy of "promiscuous affection." "The general flirt is trusted by nobody. The man who boasts 'a heart like a hotel' becomes the target of universal coolness and suspicion." The navalists and Germanophobes, who like Sir John Fisher were incensed at the sight of a "British Cabinet

---

[6] B. D., VI, 687, 747, 750.

[7] For the intrigues of the German naval attaché and the admiralty against Metternich, see Tirpitz, Aufbau, pp. 197–338, passim.

[8] Detailed narratives of the Haldane mission are to be found in Fay, Origins of the World War, I, 299 ff., and bibliography, p. 300; Bernadotte E. Schmitt, "Lord Haldane's Mission to Berlin," in the Crusades and Other Historical Essays (N. Y., 1928), pp. 245–88; Brandenburg, Von Bismarck zum Weltkriege, pp. 358–71; and in the relevant memoirs of the chief participants, Haldane, Grey, Asquith, Churchill, Tirpitz, and Bethmann. The materials in the British Documents (vol. VI, 666–761) do not change the main outlines, but they afford invaluable details on the working of the foreign office machine and the question of cabinet direction of foreign affairs.

Minister crawling up the back stairs of the German Foreign Office in carpet slippers," were jubilant at Churchill's proclamation of the dogma of British naval supremacy. But Churchill was severely criticized by the Liberal journalists for the substance as well as the inopportuneness of his remarks.[9] Although they did not provoke an outburst in Germany, Churchill provided the German Anglophobes with another slogan— *Luxusflotte*.

Haldane's appearance in Berlin thawed the iciness of the German press toward Great Britain. Innumerable kites were flown in an effort to penetrate the secrecy that surrounded his mission. From press speculation one derives the impression that the British lord chancellor came to Berlin with a bag full of concessions. More important than journalistic vaporings, however, was the change in the spirit of press commentary. The democratic organs—Vossische Zeitung, Berliner Tageblatt, and Frankfurter Zeitung—welcomed this gesture of good will without reservations. Conservative commentators, particularly Schiemann in the Kreuzzeitung, expressed their willingness and desire to bury the hatchet. The National Liberal journals of the provinces—Kölnische Zeitung, Münchner Neueste Nachrichten, and Schwäbischer Merkur—which only a few months before were intractable on the subject of future relations with Britain, turned around and followed the new trend. These journals together with the independent nationalist organs, such as the Tägliche Rundschau, made one significant reservation in discussing Anglo-German agreement, namely, that their defense requirements on land and sea were not to be made the object of any deal. While making this reservation, their tone was as cordial as the Conservative and Democratic press. The semi-official and inspired journals—the Norddeutsche, Lokal-Anzeiger, and Kölnische Zeitung—emphasized Haldane's mission as an *Orientierungsreise*, and welcomed it as a new point of departure and caught up and amplified from both the British and German press every hopeful and friendly comment. Only the Center press failed to respond. The powerful Kölnische Volkszeitung held to the pre-election line—Britain was not to be trusted, this was just another effort to take them in.[10]

[9] Bacon, *Life of Lord Fisher*, II, 144; Churchill, *World Crisis*, I, 100–104; *Manchester Guardian, Daily News*, Feb. 10, 12. Lloyd George's disapproval is recorded in Riddell, *More Pages From My Diary*, p. 37. Austen Chamberlain disapproved of the Cabinet's overtures to Germany. (*Politics from Inside*, p. 412.)

[10] *Berliner Tageblatt*, No. 41, Feb. 10; *Vossische Ztg.*, Nos. 73, 105, Feb. 9, 27; *Frankfurter Ztg.*, No. 40, Feb. 10; *Tägliche Rundschau*, Nos. 67, 69, 77, 78, Feb. 9, 10, 15, 16 (reproducing in its "Press Review" significant comment from the press of all parties); *Münchner N. N.*, Nos. 70, 74, 83, Feb. 9, 11, 16; *Schwäbischer Merkur*, Nos. 70, 72, 77, 83, Feb. 12, 13, 16, 20; *Norddeutsche*, Nos. 34, 35, 37, 39, 40, 41, Feb. 10,

Public optimism was further heightened by Asquith's statement in the House of Commons on February 14 and by Bethmann's equally cordial reply in the Reichstag on February 15. Lord Crewe spoke in the same vein in the House of Lords, and Grey, speaking a few days later at Manchester, found the most cordial words of his entire official career for describing Anglo-German relations. In the Reichstag, Bethmann's statement was greeted with vigorous applause by all parties.[11]

One parliamentary advantage, which must not be overlooked, accrued to Asquith and Grey in consequence of the Haldane mission. They could point to it, and they did so again and again, as concrete evidence of their desire to meet the wishes of their Radical followers. Critics were thus partially disarmed, and as long as it was not revealed that the negotiations had failed of agreement on the fundamental problem, the party leaders could say, as they did say quite correctly, that the negotiations initiated by Haldine were being continued.

One of the curious features of the Haldane mission was its effect upon publicity. The millions of newspaper readers never knew that in its most ambitious aspects it had failed. It was portrayed by both governments in their official and semi-official publicity as a new departure in diplomatic relations and a move toward better understanding. It put a damper on Anglophobia in the German nationalist press; it cooled off heads, although diplomatically it was not productive of great results.

Other forces outside the administrative circle were working to relax the dangerous tension. As an example of unofficial efforts along this line we may refer briefly to the symposium on Anglo-German relations in the periodical *Nord und Süd,* which attracted considerable public attention in the summer of 1912. Dr. Ludwig Stein, a former professor of philosophy at Bern, had just assumed the editorship of Paul Lindau's magazine, *Nord und Süd.* Stein was well known as a leader of the peace movement in Europe, having been associated with Baroness Bertha von Suttner (*Friedensbertha*) and Dr. Alfred Fried in the direction of the Society for International Peace. Taking for his slogan *"Détente entre Entente et Alliance,"* he made his magazine a forum for discussion of the more acute international tensions resulting from the Agadir crisis. He was encouraged to undertake the campaign by Bethmann-Hollweg, who regarded it as a publicity counterpart to his own diplomatic program. Stein went to London and arranged for a symposium of English views

11, 14, 16, 17, 18; *Kölnische Ztg.,* No. 159, Feb. 12 (Berlin telegram); *Kölnische Volksztg.,* Nos. 126, 142, 143, 164, Feb. 11, 16, 23.

[11] *Vossische Ztg.,* Parliamentary correspondent, No. 85, Feb. 16. The official report noted "Lebhafte Zustimmung im ganzen Hause" and "Lebhafte Bewegung und grosser Beifall."

for the June issue. In securing his articles he had the assistance of Haldane, Tyrrell, and Charles Trevelyan. Mr. Balfour wrote the lead article; and among many others who contributed their views were Haldane, Bonar Law, Sir Frank Lascelles, Alfred Rothschild, J. L. Garvin, Noel Buxton, Rufus Isaacs (Viscount Reading), and Ramsay Macdonald. In the July issue Prince Lichnowski had the lead article, answering Mr. Balfour; and he was supported by statements from Arthur von Gwinner, Adolf Wermuth, Dr. von Holleben, Count Posadowsky, Bassermann, Stinnes, Thyssen, Rathenau, Theodor Wolff, and Wilhelm Wundt. A hundred thousand copies of each issue were furnished to English and German agencies and societies, both official and unofficial, for distribution. The articles were not limited to a polite exchange of compliments, but presented a frank discussion of issues that separated the two peoples and their governments. The fact that so many leading men could be brought together in a general presentation of viewpoints is indicative of the new trend in publicity.[12]

As a matter of fact the bellicosity of the Agadir crisis did not reappear in the responsible press of either country until they were actually at war in 1914. More forbearance, consideration and sanity were displayed by the publicists and journalists in the two years before the final crash than at any time since the days of the Kruger Telegram. Many indeed must have shared the impression that J. A. Spender has recorded in his memoirs. "From 1906 till November, 1911, the prospect of war with Germany was always before us, and during the last part of this period we lived in constant dread of it. But from 1911 onwards things had seemed to be gradually on the mend." [13] It is this trend in public relations that has enabled some writers to argue convincingly that by 1914 Anglo-German differences were removed from the causes of conflict in Europe. On the other hand, writers who confine their attention to the documentary record of diplomacy point out that during this same period British statesmen were forging links with the Dual Alliance that would make partic-

---

[12] L. Stein, *Aus dem Leben eines Optimisten* (Berlin, 1930), pp. 194–208. Lichnowski's reply to Balfour, which was submitted to Bethmann and William II for approval, so pleased the latter that when the London embassy became vacant through Marschall's sudden death he went over the heads of his chancellor and foreign secretary and appointed Lichnowski. What particularly pleased William II was Lichnowski's rejection of the English position that they renounce their fleet program as the price of British friendship. Writing in a vein that delighted his sovereign, he said: "Eunuchen haben bekanntlich Zutritt zum Harem, das Mittel ist zwar einfach, aber nicht schmerzlos. Wir wollen weder in einen Harem, noch auch uns entmannen." (*Ibid.*, pp. 172–79.) Lichnowski was not an opponent of German naval policy and *Weltpolitik*, but on the contrary he was wholeheartedly convinced of their political necessity. His writings during the War and subsequently show commendable wisdom after the event, but they do not represent his attitudes in 1912.

[13] *Life, Journalism and Politics*, II, 4–5.

ipation in a war against Germany more than a mere contingency. The latter school is right. While the publicity barometer moved from Stormy to Changing and Fair, the fundamental questions of armaments and political orientation were not resolved in agreements. It was a contradiction that we have noted before of publicity moving on one level and policy moving on another. However, the rancor that discussion of basic issues formerly evoked was gone.

On March 18 Churchill presented to parliament the naval estimates for the year 1912–13. The new first lord of the admiralty was frank and blunt in laying the policy basis for his first naval budget. Brushing aside all subterfuge and disregarding all the "schools" and "standards" he announced that their program, and hence their expenditure, was based on the naval program of one power—that power was Germany. He announced further, that in the years to come they would gear their construction program to the German schedule so that their proportionate strength in the North Sea in Dreadnoughts would be 16:10. For each additional German ship that might be built under the impending supplementary law, Great Britain would build two. And finally, he forecast a further concentration of their fighting forces in home waters through the transfer of the Malta squadron to Gibraltar and the removal of the Gibraltar fleet to the Channel and the home ports. Although the admiralty was in possession of the unpublished German supplementary law, Churchill had to present the estimates as though the German plans were unknown to him. He promised that if the German plans made it necessary his department would bring in supplementary estimates in July. The facts, and the words in which they were expressed, were cold-blooded but not menacing.[14]

In Germany, where the speech was given wide publicity, it produced an unfavorable reaction. On second thought, however, most of the commentators praised the admiralty chief for his frank and open statement of the naval problem. And some of the closer students of the question, like Captain Persius (retired), pointed out that the ratio 16:10 was not far removed from the ratio 3:2 which was known to be the real goal of the German admiralty.[15]

Bethmann had held up publication of the proposed defense bills as long as negotiations were in train with England on his neutrality formula. When this road was blocked, the chancellor finally agreed to publication and the draft proposals appeared in the Norddeutsche on March

[14] For a detailed analysis of the construction program and the new disposition of naval forces see Woodward, *Great Britain and the German Navy*, pp. 366–71.
[15] *Berliner Tageblatt*, No. 145, March 19, 1912; *Kölnische Ztg.*, No. 308, March 19; *Schwäbischer Merkur*, Nos. 133, 134, March 20; *Frankfurter Ztg.*, No. 79, March 20; *Münchner N. N.*, No. 145, March 20.

22. Under the defense bills (*Wehrvorlagen*) the army received the most attention and the most money. The naval increases seemed slight in comparison. Aside from the increases in personnel they called only for the construction of one additional Dreadnought (above the annual two) in 1913, and one in 1916. A third battleship was envisaged but the date of construction was unspecified. The publication of the defense bill and its passage through the Reichstag was quietly handled in the British press. As a matter of fact the general attitude seemed to be that of relief that the naval provisions were not greater. All the more surprising, therefore, was the alarm bell sounded by Churchill in introducing supplementary estimates in the House on July 22. He opened his remarks with these words: "The direct cause of the Supplementary Estimates which I am now submitting to the House is to be found in the new German Navy Law. . . ." It was not new construction under that law that necessitated British countermeasures, but the maintenance of "nearly four-fifths of the entire German Navy . . . in full permanent commission—that is to say, instantly and constantly ready for war." Sketching the history of the German naval laws, which laid down a policy that "marches unswervingly towards its goal across the lifetime of a generation," he emphasized the danger in the North Sea and dwelt upon its magnitude. In Churchill's speech as well as in the supporting statements of his colleagues, we find the familiar theme—the government laid out these huge sums against its will, under the pressure of competition that came from Germany. It was not England but the neighbor across the North Sea that piped the tune for the mad dance of armaments. The naval race was not begun by England, but to maintain their supremacy they were forced to participate. Circumstances beyond their control necessitated the laying of this heavy burden upon the British taxpayer. Such was the general line of argument which had served to keep the rebellious section of the Liberal party in line on foreign policy and security costs since 1909.

In his speech on the supplementary estimates Churchill revealed to the public a new complication in naval defense policy—Britain's position in the Mediterranean. Announcement of the withdrawal of the battle fleet from Malta and the reallocation of the force to Gibraltar and the home waters, turned public attention toward the most recent developments in that area. The Tripolitan War and the Dreadnought construction programs of Italy and Austria-Hungary were new and disturbing elements. Churchill's announcement of a further redistribution of naval forces was equivalent to an admission that the government was unable or unwilling to maintain a 16:10 predominance of Dreadnoughts in the North Sea and to keep at the same time control of the Mediterranean. The solution proposed by the defense authorities was indicated by the first lord when he announced that a squadron of armored cruisers would be maintained at Malta and that this force "in conjunction with the navy of France . . . would, of course, make a combined force superior to all possible combinations."

Behind the admiralty's announcement lay momentous and vital decisions on policy and strategy. In 1912 British statesmen were faced with three alternatives: first, they could pile on ship construction irrespective of cost and maintain their predominance in both the North Sea and the Mediterranean; second, they could conclude a political agreement with Germany (neutrality formula) that would release the British navy from its anchorage in the North Sea and restore the mobility of British sea-power; third, they could conclude an alliance with France and entrust British interests in the Mediterranean to her charge. Opposition in the cabinet and in the party to unlimited naval expenditure excluded the first alternative. The second was considered and rejected at the time of the Haldane mission, because the technical specialists feared the ultimate consequences to the Empire of cutting loose from the Triple Entente and returning to the situation that existed prior to 1904 and 1907; they could better withstand the antagonism of Germany than the antagonism of France and Russia. The third possibility, alliance with France, was favored by the experts in foreign and defense policies, but with the Radicals in the cabinet and an important section of the party strongly opposed to entering into the continental alliance system, even this course could not be openly pursued. Thus it was that Grey and Asquith, with the approval of their colleagues, instituted half measures. They authorized the naval readjustments, which in European practice would normally have followed only as a result of firm political alliance, while they pretended to the nation and even to themselves that their hands were still free as regards supreme decisions of peace and war.[16] The naval dispositions effected in 1912, whereby the French concentrated their forces in the Mediterranean while the British undertook to protect the Atlantic and Channel coasts of France, placed upon Britain, as many writers have pointed out, the obligations of an alliance without providing the check-reins that were standard equipment on the political harness of a formal alliance.

When in mid-September 1912, the Paris press announced that French naval forces would be transferred from the Channel to the Mediterranean, the significance of this move was not lost on German observers who

[16] See Nicolson's memorandum of May 6, 1912, which was apparently the basis of cabinet action. (*Lord Carnock*, pp. 371-73.) This most radical readjustment and its political consequences—the Grey-Cambon notes—are now revealed in detail in *B. D.*, X, pt. 2, chap. XCVI, "The Mediterranean Agreements."

accepted it as proof of the existence of a naval convention between France and England. However, the movement of forces, which was accompanied by a fanfaronade in the Paris Matin and Temps, provoked polemics in the German press against France rather than against England. The Triple Alliance was due to be renewed at this time and the French move was interpreted as an effort to force Italy out of that combination. Publicity took the form of a *Dreibund* crisis rather than an Anglo-German crisis.[17]

In England the press was remarkably reserved in commenting on the realignment of naval forces. Only the Radicals seized on its political implication, and they found it shocking. For a few days F. W. Hirst, H. W. Massingham, A. G. Gardiner, C. P. Scott, and H. Sidebotham delivered severe lectures to the cabinet on this dangerous departure in foreign policy. "And this tremendous revolution in our national policy [declared the Manchester Guardian] has been made without the knowledge of Parliament by a little knot of men working by methods of evasion and equivocation. Ministers in the past have been impeached for much less." [18]

What language the dissenters would have used had they been aware of the notes exchanged by Grey and Cambon on November 22–23 may be left to the imagination. Grey was able to convince the doubters in the cabinet that their freedom of decision was unrestricted, and yet he was unwilling to submit to free discussion and judgment in the press and parliament the new arrangements that went far toward transforming an informal understanding into a binding obligation. In evaluating this important step, it is difficult to add anything to judgments expressed by other writers. Moreover, the main facts are well known.[19] The recently published documents from the British archives covering these transactions

---

[17] "Die Lage im Mittelmeer" and "Flottenverteilung," *Kölnische Ztg.*, Nos. 1038, 1077, Sept. 17, 28; "Die Drohung und ihr Zweck," *Münchner N. N.*, No. 477, Sept. 15; *Deutsche Ztg.*, No. 257, Sept. 18; *Tägliche Rundschau*, No. 446, Sept. 22; *Hamburger Nachrichten* and *Weser-Zeitung*, quoted *Tägliche Rundschau*, No. 438, Sept. 18. Most important of all was the semi-official response, the jet of cold water at the *Temps* and *Matin* delivered in a Berlin telegram to the *Frankfurter Zeitung* (No. 258, Sept. 15). Set up in widely spaced type and *hochpolitisch* in tone, it was quoted by all papers as semi-official. Italy, so ran the communication, would not be intimidated by the disguised threats of the two inspired Parisian papers. "The value of the Italian fleet is more highly regarded by us than by the two journals whose bold flights in political speculation seem to leave out of account entirely the fact that France also has land frontiers."

[18] *Manchester Guardian*, Sept. 12, 14; *Daily News*, Sept. 16, 19; "Sir Edward Grey's Enemies," *Pall Mall Gazette*, Sept. 17; *Times*, Sept. 16. Kühlmann analyzed carefully the *Times* editorial and Mr. Spender's article in the *Westminster* of September 18. (*G. P.*, XXXI, 543–47.)

[19] Fay, *Origins*, I, 320–24; Schmitt, *Coming of the War*, I, 48–53; Lutz, *Lord Grey*, pp. 91–112; Brandenburg, *Von Bismarck zum Weltkriege*, pp. 390–93; Churchill, *World Crisis*, I, 115–16; *Memoirs of Raymond Poincaré, 1912*, pp. 106–15.

add important details and make possible the sharpening of certain conclusions. They throw into strong relief the Mediterranean origin of the naval convention of September 1912, and the exchange of diplomatic notes in November; they show the tremendous leverage exerted by Paris upon the London cabinet and the brusqueness with which the French refused to make the disposition of naval forces, desired by the British, without a guarantee covering their Channel and Atlantic ports; they show how Churchill's explicit statement of non-committal, in the preamble to the naval convention, was transformed by Poincaré and Cambon into the positive assurance contained in the Grey-Cambon letters; they show that the formula of understanding originated with the French and not, as Grey implies in his memoirs, with the British foreign secretary and the cabinet. With regard to personalities involved, the documents show that Nicolson was keen for the fullest possible commitment, that Grey was compliant, and that Asquith was naïve. The latter could not "see any harm in Cambon's formula; indeed it is almost a platitude." And this was the formula which, as historians have pointed out, was almost identical in wording with the political articles of the Franco-Russian Alliance! Finally, these documents show that of the British ministers involved, Churchill had the keenest insight and the best claim to statesmanship. Apart from the first lord of the admiralty, the other members of the cabinet were apparently satisfied with the first paragraph of Grey's letter to Cambon, which seemed to preserve complete freedom of action, and closed their eyes to the fact that in approving this exchange of notes they were giving explicit cabinet sanction to the military and naval arrangements and to the principle of concerted action of which those arrangements were a concrete expression.[20]

In the press the Radicals criticized the withdrawal from the Mediterranean and the concentration of French forces in that area because they feared that it was based on a secret alliance. The new strategic disposition was criticized by the Imperialists as an extremely dangerous expedient involving the abandonment of vital British interests to the uncertain protection of another power. Henceforth, the Conservatives in criticizing the national defense policies of the Liberal cabinet, concentrated on the abandonment of the Mediterranean. The agitation of the Radicals canceled that of the navalists, and through it all the government held to its course of doubtful expediency.[21]

---

[20] *B. D.,* X, pt. 2, 580–619; *Documents diplomatiques français,* 3rd Ser., III, 19, 79, 270–72, 507–8, IV, 318–22, 535–36, 559–60; an interesting conversation between Nicolson and Austen Chamberlain is recorded in the latter's *Politics from Inside,* pp. 484–86.

[21] The navalist agitation on the Mediterranean question found its loudest spokes-

Four issues dominated Anglo-German relations during the last two years of uncertain peace in Europe. There was first, the problem of Britain's attitude toward the politico-economic expansion of Germany outside of Europe; second, the adjustment and harmonization of policy in the general crisis precipitated by the Balkan Wars of 1912–13; third, the problem of Britain's relation to the continental balance and the alignment of military-political forces; and fourth, the pressure of the German naval program upon Britain's security at home and her imperial interests abroad. The first problem moved toward a satisfactory conclusion as British ministers began "to study the map of Africa in a pro-German spirit." During the next two years a new agreement over the Portuguese colonies and a compromise on the Bagdad Railway issue were hammered out in London and Berlin and were awaiting final action when the War broke out. That European pressures could be relieved through this safety valve was a view firmly held by many people. Its most active champion and promoter was the able counselor of the German embassy in London, Richard von Kühlmann. For two years he labored toward a realizable goal only to see his work go for nothing as the prize was almost within his grasp. Sharing Von Kühlmann's views and assisting in their promotion was Dr. Hans Plehn, London representative of the Wolff Bureau. The latter's brochure, *Deutsche Weltpolitik und kein Krieg!*, published anonymously in 1913 and widely commented on in the daily press, gave currency to Kühlmann's thesis.[22] While perhaps not as enthusiastic as Kühlmann and Plehn, the foreign office in Berlin was content to work along this line. The supplementary navy law of 1912 and the failure to draw England into a neutrality agreement had signified a triumph for Tirpitz over the civilian officials. Until their prestige was restored by a notable success in the political field it was useless to touch the naval question. Lichnowski, the new ambassador in London, and Von Jagow, who succeeded Kiderlen as foreign secretary, were agreed that nothing could be gained and much could be lost by further discussion of the armaments issue. "Let sleeping dogs lie," was an expression that appeared frequently in their correspondence.

Much pessimism was dispelled and a hopeful future prospect opened up by the loyal co-operation between London and Berlin during the Bal-

---

man in the *Daily Mail*. Its shrill protests began when Churchill first hinted at the new departure and continued throughout the summer and autumn. Notable articles: May 27, 30, June 11, July 23, Sept. 12. Special appeals were made by Beresford on June 18 and 22.

[22] Bernhard Huldermann, *Albert Ballin* (Lond., 1922), p. 189. Huldermann is in error when he says that Plehn represented the *Kölnische Zeitung*. The other London correspondents, Dr. Gaupp of the *Münchner N. N.*, C. C. Schardt of the *Vossische Zeitung*, and Dr. Guttmann of the *Frankfurter Zeitung* followed the same line.

kan crisis. This was dwelt upon at various times in public pronouncements by Asquith, Grey, Bethmann-Hollweg, and Jagow. Progress toward agreement on colonial expansion, restoration of confidence through co-operation during the Balkan struggle, and the friendly and conciliatory words of the statesmen induced a friendlier tone in the press of both countries. "The Anglo-German Rapprochement," became a favorite theme with the publicists. It was confidently predicted that the two governments were moving from a *détente* toward an *entente*.

In spite of the apparent progress along these lines, the fundamental postulates of British policy toward the continental grouping remained unchanged. For the realists in the foreign office and in the press the primary consideration was to watch over the balance of power and to preserve the triangular bulwark—London, Paris, St. Petersburg. Those of tender conscience who disliked the terminology of power-politics preferred to speak of the loyalty they owed to their friends and the moral obligation they were under to stand by them in time of need. In either case the intention and the result were the same. British policy showed not the slightest indication of a return to the old Salisbury tradition of disengagement toward the two continental groups and the assumption of the rôle of mediator and balance. On the contrary, as has been generally recognized, Britain's engagements to France and Russia became more extensive and precise. Lichnowski during his two years in London never wavered in his opinion that in a war between France and Germany, Britain would intervene on behalf of France. That he was only half-believed in his own foreign office is a measure of the power of self-deception that prevailed in Berlin.[23]

Professor E. Malcolm Carroll, in his volume on French foreign policy, has shown how completely the policy of equilibrium and its maintenance through the alliance system was assimilated in France by all but a few minority groups.[24] Although dissenting groups in England were larger and politically more powerful, the same idea-system gained wide acceptance as it was constantly drummed into the public by the entire Imperialist press. It is not important in this connection to record all of the variations of the theme. The Times stated it succinctly on April 8, 1914, the anniversary of the Entente Cordiale:

It is this [group system] which affords the world its best hopes of peace in the future. The division of the Great Powers into two well-balanced groups

[23] We find Von Jagow, for example, chiding Lichnowski for his stubborn pessimism on this issue. For Lichnowski's predictions and Jagow's skepticism see *G. P.*, XXXVII, 105, 110, XXXIX, 133. See also King George's statement to Prince Henry in December 1912, *B. D.*, X, pt. 2, 658.

[24] *French Public Opinion and Foreign Affairs*, chaps. XII, XIII.

with intimate relations between the members of each, which do not forbid any such member from being on the friendliest terms with one or more members of the other, is a twofold check upon inordinate ambitions or sudden bursts of race hatred. All . . . know that a war of group against group would be a measureless calamity. That knowledge brings with it a sense of responsibility which chastens and restrains the boldest and most reckless. But they know, too, that to secure the support of the other members of their own group and to induce them to share the responsibility and the risks of such a conflict any Power or Powers which may meditate recourse to arms must first satisfy those other members that the quarrel is necessary and just. . . . The balance of power is now the cardinal factor in the policy of the Old World.

Every malady of the European equilibrium, according to the Imperialist press, would yield to this magic formula.

While the attitude of the political authorities in Germany toward the naval question was *noli me tangere,* it could not be excluded entirely from public discussion. In his naval estimates speech in March 1912, Churchill had announced that his department would in the future lay out their Dreadnought construction program on a 16:10 ratio for the North Sea. Appearing before the Reichstag budget committee, on February 6, 1913, Tirpitz stated that this ratio was satisfactory to the German naval authorities, although he translated the ratio into squadrons, making 8 British to 5 German. (Stating the relationship in squadrons, gave Tirpitz an advantage over the British reckoning in battleship units.) Again on February 4, 1914, in the hearings of the budget commission Tirpitz stated that the proposed ratio was still acceptable to Germany. This unexpected trend toward reasonableness made a good impression on Grey, although it only excited suspicion in the minds of the permanent officials and the British ambassador in Berlin.[25] While Churchill's new construction programs for 1913 and 1914 represented a pretty arbitrary and elastic interpretation of 16:10, in that he drew a line at Gibraltar beyond which they must build for their "world requirements," it was certainly a step toward stability in the matter of relative naval strength. If Tirpitz' acceptance was a ruse, it was Churchill who protested in parliament that this standard was "not eternal" and that it could "not be made a binding international instrument." [26]

Figuring more prominently in the publicity of the period than the matter of ratios was Churchill's proposal for a naval holiday. This proposal, involving a complete cessation in new construction for one year, was foreshadowed in Churchill's speech on the estimates in March

[25] *B. D.,* X, pt. 2, 669–88, 734–41.

[26] Naval estimates speech, March 17, 1914, *Parl. Deb.,* 5th Ser., vol. 59, 1926–28. It is significant that the only temporary check placed upon armaments competition was established in the post-War period by an agreement on a 5–5–3 ratio in capital ships.

1912, formulated in greater detail on a similar occasion in the House on March 26, 1913, and again renewed in a public address at Manchester in October of the same year. Like the discussion of the 16:10 ratio it never reached the point of official negotiation between the two governments. All the technical arguments showing the impracticability of the plan were marshaled by the German admiralty and in due time made their appearance in the press.[27] Bethmann-Hollweg, speaking of the proposal in the Reichstag, was complimentary, even flattering, but avoided endorsement of the plan. There was no need to comb the German press for arguments against the proposals; they were all canvassed by the Conservative press in Great Britain, where objections and criticisms were quite as numerous as in Germany. England and Germany, it was pointed out, could not cease new construction for one year if other powers continued to build. Was it likely that the United States would agree to such a measure? Or France? Or Russia? Or Japan? The Pall Mall Gazette, which under Garvin's editorship had assumed a front-line position in navy propaganda, sent a correspondent to interview shipbuilders and navy yard officials. He reported that in these circles Churchill's plan was regarded as Utopian, but if it were accepted it would give them an opportunity to clean up back work and to remove congestion in their yards caused by the railway strike, large foreign orders, and the heavy demands of the government. One authority interviewed said: "Mr. Churchill is, of course, aware of these conditions, and it is, therefore, rather a smart proposal on his part." [28]

Churchill was no doubt sincere in proposing a truce in naval construction, for he was not a man to take his own ideas lightly. The manner and time of their proposal, however, a broadcast to the nation from the public platform, suggests a tactical maneuver to placate the Radical reductionists.[29] During these two years all of Churchill's public pronouncements

[27] Particularly the semi-official Berlin telegram to the *Kölnische Zeitung,* No. 347, March 28, 1913; *Tägliche Rundschau,* No. 144, March 28; *Kölnische Volksztg.,* No. 266, March 28; *Münchner N. N.,* No. 539, Oct. 21; *Schwäbischer Merkur,* No. 138, March 27; *Frankfurter Ztg.,* Nos. 85, 291, March 27, Oct. 20; *Vossische Ztg.,* No. 154, March 27. Only Captain Persius, naval expert on the *Berliner Tageblatt,* fully endorsed the proposal and urged that it be taken up officially. (*Berliner Tageblatt,* Nos. 154, 534, March 27, Oct. 20.) The *Times'* Berlin correspondent reported that Churchill's second proposal was received with "a mixture of indignation, contempt and pity." (Oct. 21, 1913.) To support this statement he selected quotations that suited his purpose from the *Lokal-Anzeiger, Deutsche Tagesztg., Kreuzzeitung, Berliner Zeitung,* and *Vossische Ztg.*

[28] *Pall Mall Gazette,* March 27, 28. For the reaction to the holiday proposal in naval and diplomatic circles see *B. D.,* X, pt. 2, 689–723; *G. P.,* XXXIX, 34–70; Kühlmann, in his dispatch of October 20, 1913 (p. 53), reported at length on British press reaction to Churchill's Manchester speech; Tirpitz, *Aufbau,* pp. 381–403; Churchill, *World Crisis,* I, 111, 190.

[29] See Churchill's personal letter to Grey and the latter's explanation to Goschen, *B. D.,* X, pt. 2, 721–22.

faced two ways. For the benefit of Conservatives and Liberal Imperialists he could boast, as he did in the House, on July 17, 1913, of the "greatest delivery of warships ever recorded in the history of the British Navy"— a destroyer a week for the next nine months, a light cruiser every thirty days, a super-Dreadnought every forty-five days for eighteen months, and a large batch of submarines. On his next public appearance he could address the extreme Radical wing of the party, deploring the continued increase in naval expenditure, and pointing to the holiday proposal as an earnest of the government's willingness to end the mad race if other nations would only see the reasonableness of their proposals. In this way Mr. Churchill and the cabinet were able to satisfy both the Daily Mail and the Daily News.

Another factor that decisively influenced naval calculations on both sides of the North Sea was the feverish expansion of continental military establishments from 1912 to 1914. The Balkan Wars upset the political balance, and statesmen hurried to cover possible future losses with armaments insurance. In Germany the most far-reaching program of reform and expansion since the Caprivi measures in 1893 was promulgated in the army bill of 1913; and to meet the cost the government was driven to the unprecedented financial expedient of a capital levy to cover the non-recurrent charges. The French replied with their three-year service law, and in Russia large additions were made to the army and more and more money was expended for strategic railroads. All the publicity that necessarily accompanied the expansion of military budgets focused attention upon the insecurities of the continental system. To convince people of the necessity of the sacrifices demanded by the military and political authorities, the dangers had to be made real. There was the usual spate of "next-war" books and the jingo spirit was everywhere in evidence. The utterances of the chauvinists in one country inflamed nationalists on the other side of the frontier and lent weight to their demands for further military increases. The propaganda that accompanied the campaign for the three-year service law in France convinced the Germans that they must arm against the reawakened spirit of *revanche*. In the spring of 1914, the reports of the St. Petersburg correspondent of the Kölnische Zeitung, Dr. Ullrich, on Russian military and naval preparations created a panic in the German press. Even Germans of sound judgment and steady nerves were depressed by the military preponderance that the Russians were piling up against them.[30] Mr. Spender has described a meeting

[30] Theodor Wolff in his *Eve of 1914* (N. Y., 1936), pp. 271–95, gives a vivid picture of the *"Renaissance Latine."* It is quite an adequate summary of the reaction of the German press to events in France in 1913, and is based upon the articles Wolff wrote and published contemporaneously in the *Berliner Tageblatt*. Dr. Anton Jux

with Professor Schiemann, arranged by their mutual acquaintance Richard von Kühlmann, at which the German publicist painted a vivid picture of the oppressive fear in the German world over the Russian danger. Was England going to back the Slavs? [31]

It was this general apprehension and a widely prevalent spirit of defeatism in the game of alliances and balances that provide the emotional backdrop for the expansion of German land forces during these last years of uneasy equilibrium. When one reads the Reichstag debates and the political comment in the press one is impressed with the dissatisfaction and the pessimism over the course of German foreign policy. Their diplomacy had failed in the Moroccan crisis and in the Balkans. A Bismarck could have foreseen the consequences and avoided them. "We all lack diplomatic ability," said one Reichstag deputy. This spirit of defeatism gave rise to a line of thought that ran on as follows : If we cannot play the diplomatic game with success we can organize an army better than anyone else, and the more unsuccessful we are in the first the greater the necessity for the second—one hand washes the other.

The point of all this arming—the fear that it expressed and the further apprehension that it induced—is that it signified a reconsideration of Germany's policy and position in the world. Captain Watson, the British naval attaché, noted that he frequently heard Germans say, "Of course you English have a very large navy compared with us, and we must put our strength into our army." The mirage of *Weltpolitik* based on a navy rivaling that of the leading world power faded before the stark realities of Germany's position as a continental state. As General Bernhardi declared in all of his writings in this period, "Germany was a power in the world, but she was far from being a *World Power*." [32] The strategical and political situation compelled her statesmen to acknowledge that their national existence depended on the maintenance of their land forces. Even Tirpitz realized that when extraordinary sacrifices were being demanded of the people on behalf of the army further expansion of the naval building program, beyond the law of 1912, was impossible. The pressure of the great German army bills was exerted upon the continent ; the naval pressure upon England suddenly slackened.

---

in his monograph entitled *Der Kriegsschrecken des Frühjahrs 1914* (Berlin, 1929), has described in detail the war-scare precipitated in Germany by the dispatches of the St. Petersburg correspondent of the *Kölnische Zeitung* and their repercussions in the diplomatic world. For the reaction in British official circles see *B. D.,* X, pt. 2, 754–72. The British were mistaken in assuming that the campaign was inspired by the German press bureau. Dr. Ullrich, who sent the dispatch that touched off the explosion, acted against the wishes of the German embassy in St. Petersburg. For interesting details see Jux, *ibid.,* pp. 46–73, 244–48.

[31] *Life, Journalism and Politics,* II, 6–7.
[32] F. von Bernhardi, *Denkwürdigkeiten,* p. 366; *B. D.,* X, pt. 2, 714.

While the military budgets of the continental states registered the impact of the Balkan Wars on the balance of armed power, the fever of navalism abated in England. Press discussion and parliamentary debate on the estimates in March and July, 1913, were remarkably apathetic, a fact that was noted and deplored by the Times, Pall Mall Gazette, Glasgow Herald and other champions of unlimited naval construction.[33] The relaxation of tension spurred the reductionists to make a concerted attack on the estimates for 1914. To them it seemed appalling that Churchill should publicly forecast an increase in the admiralty demands for the coming year. Chambers of commerce, organizations of business men and taxpayers, Radicals and Laborites joined in the drive for retrenchment. A hundred members of the government's party in the House called on Mr. Asquith in a body to register their protest. Donald, Scott, and Gardiner attacked Churchill in the Chronicle, Manchester Guardian, and Daily News. There was constant agitation in the press of the industrial and commercial North. Everyone knew that, as in all important matters of national defense and foreign policy, the decision would be made in the cabinet and not in parliament. However, the government's deliberations could be influenced by outside agitation. Churchill, backed by the board of admiralty, asked for fifty-two and a half million pounds, an increase over the previous year of two and a half millions. Mr. Churchill has described the fight that ensued in the cabinet. It lasted for five months. Fourteen meetings were devoted to this one question. There were the customary threats of resignation by the first lord and the admiralty board. Asquith employed masterful tactics of delay until the Radicals had talked themselves out and the issue was overrun by the Irish crisis.[34] In the end the naval estimates were accepted with only a few unimportant reductions.

In a singular example of understatement, Mr. Churchill says that "echoes of the [cabinet] controversy had found their way into the newspapers." As a matter of fact, each contending cabinet faction had its journalistic champions and the rule of cabinet secrecy was more honored in the breach than in the observance. The chief contestants welcomed the support that came to them from the press and the public, and they probably had not a little to do with its stimulation. The publicity and pressure forces were lined up along traditional lines: the National Liberal Federation, led by Sir John Brunner, was the most potent party group agitating for retrenchment; then came the National Peace Council and the Free Churches, supported by the big guns in the Liberal press, the Daily

[33] *Times*, March 18, Aug. 6; *Pall Mall Gazette*, March 14, July 18, 21; *Glasgow Herald*, March 14, 15; *Daily Mail*, July 18, 1913.
[34] Churchill, *World Crisis*, I, 181–87.

News, the Manchester Guardian, the Daily Chronicle, Liverpool Post and Mercury, and a considerable number of less important provincial journals. On the other side of the public controversy was the entire Conservative-Unionist party leadership, the Navy League, Lord Esher's Islanders, the Northcliffe press, the Daily Telegraph, Morning Post, Pall Mall Gazette, the Edinburgh Scotsman, and Birmingham Daily Post. A feature of the furious public debate was the journalistic duel between J. L. Garvin and A. G. Gardiner in the Pall Mall Gazette and the Daily News. Garvin denounced the proposals of the reductionists as a policy of "monumental madness and suicide," and he coined the label "Suicide Club," which he applied to the leaders of the economy movement.[35] Gardiner demanded the striking of two Dreadnoughts from the construction program for 1914. Charging gross waste and extravagance in naval building and operating costs, he urged a thorough investigation of admiralty policies and practices.[36]

Even the ministers slipped out from behind the cabinet curtains to join in the public argument. In an interview published in the Daily Chronicle on New Year's Day, 1914, Lloyd George, spokesman for the economists, called for "a bold and independent step in the direction of restricting the growth of armaments." The impelling reasons he cited for such a move were, first, that England's relations with Germany were "infinitely more friendly now than they have been for years" and second, that the continental nations, particularly Germany, were concentrating their energies and resources on their land armaments. If the Germans ever had any idea of challenging British supremacy, the present military situation would put it completely out of their heads, he declared. This pronouncement, called by Asquith, "A heedless interview," irritated his opponents in the cabinet, encouraged the reductionists in their public agitation, and provoked angry attacks in the French and Russian press. Grey was irked at Lloyd George's intrusion into the field of foreign affairs, for abroad his words were interpreted as a betrayal of England's continental friends. He put the cabinet in a false position by seeming to approve the expansion of the German army, and by proposing that while France and Russia were meeting the German challenge on land, England should take advantage of the situation to reduce her naval expenditure. With one voice the balance-of-power advocates and the navalists repudiated the "monstrous proposal." England must not relax the naval pressure upon Germany, for pressure relieved at one point would be applied

[35] Typical headlines in the *Pall Mall Gazette:* "Hands off the Navy—The New Radical Conspiracy——A National Menace." (Jan. 3, 5, 6, 9, 1914.)

[36] *Daily News,* Jan. 17, 21, 22, 23, 1914. The *Guardian* made similar proposals, Dec. 18, 1913; Jan. 6, 20, 23, 1914.

at another, in this case on land against France and Russia. Loyalty to the Triple Entente required them to keep up their end of the military balance between the two alliance groups. The implications were clear. British strategy and policy were linked to France and Russia; the British navy was not solely an expression of independent empire policy, but an important factor in equating the military forces of Triple Alliance and Triple Entente. No cabinet member could have said this publicly—it would have smashed the government—but Asquith hurried off to Paris to stroke down the French, the Times pontificated on Britain's loyalty to her friends, and one after another of Lloyd George's colleagues repudiated his suggestion of a "bold and independent step in the direction of restricting the growth of armaments." [37]

Grey's ill-humor at the Lloyd George interview is understandable. In the larger field of policy it might lead to the conclusion that the British government was taking the improvement in Anglo-German relations seriously, even to the point of considering defense policy independently of Entente ties. This made the French and the Russians suspicious of Britain, just at the moment when the British foreign secretary was most concerned for the stability of those connections. Furthermore, it heightened the pressure from Paris and St. Petersburg for new tokens of reliability and faithfulness. These took the form of naval conversations with Russia and the placing of Entente relations on a more intimate basis by adoption of a conference procedure between Grey and the French and Russian ambassadors when discussing problems common to the Triple Entente.

Closely connected with the general question of power was the development among European statesmen and publicists of a veritable cult devoted to the exaggeration of the strength of Russia—her position as the leader of Slavdom, her potential resources and wealth, the overwhelming size and power of her army, even the soundness of her national finances and the stability of her government. All this, to the Germans, was a nightmare; and it induced the above-mentioned public panic of March 1914. Bu-

---

[37] Churchill, in an interview with the *Daily Mail* correspondent in Paris; Haldane and Grey in public speeches. Grey's Manchester speech of February 3, 1914, has generally been referred to as a "disarmament plea." Quite the contrary. It was a rebuke to Lloyd George and a tactical maneuver to hold the rank and file of the party in line for the increases. They were assured by Grey that the government was truly Liberal in that it deplored armaments expenditures, but the forces that made such great appropriations necessary were beyond their control. For the genesis of the *Daily Chronicle* interview, the row it caused in the cabinet, and the sensation it created in political circles see Riddell, *More Pages from My Diary*, 192–96; G. P., XXXIX, 72–74; B. D., X, pt. 1, 409, pt. 2, 729–30; extracts from Asquith's letters in Spender, *Life of Lord Oxford and Asquith*, II, 76–77; W. Roch, *Mr. Lloyd George and the War* (Lond., 1920), pp. 13–14, 77–79; *Times*, Jan. 2, 5; *Pall Mall Gazette*, Jan. 6, 9, 16; Grey's Manchester address, *Times*, Feb. 4.

chanan's reports to London helped to inflate the Russian balloon and the diplomatic experts were more determined than ever to maintain their connection with this great power, and not to permit the Triple Entente to wither away and atrophy. It was not fear of Germany that inspired British policy, but fear of Russia lest she become an enemy instead of a friend.[38] The Russians moved cleverly, working on Grey through Buchanan and Poincaré. Sazonov and the Czar urged an alliance, failing that a naval convention such as the English had with France. They underscored their dissatisfaction with the insecure basis of their understanding with England. Something had to be done or the Triple Entente would become a *quantité négligeable*. They intimated that England was just a "fair-weather friend," who would not stand by them if war broke out between Germany and Russia. They hinted further that uncertainty about England's support might cause them to join hands with Germany. There was no surer way to excite alarm in Downing Street. And in consequence we find Buchanan drumming away at his superiors on the necessity of meeting Russian wishes and consolidating the understanding by some more precise and definite arrangement, if not an alliance. "Russia [he wrote] is rapidly becoming so powerful that we must retain her friendship at almost any cost. If she acquires the conviction that we are unreliable and useless as a friend, she may one day strike a bargain with Germany and resume her liberty of action in Turkey and Persia. Our position then would be a very parlous one." Nicolson, too, feared "that if we do not try to tighten up the ties with Russia she may become weary of us and throw us overboard." Picturing the damage Russia could do to the Empire in Asia and the Near East, Nicolson said: "This to me is such a nightmare that I would at almost any cost keep Russia's friendship." [39] Under pressure from Poincaré and the French authorities, Grey secured cabinet consent to communicate to Russia, as a mark of special confidence and trust, the secrets of the Grey-Cambon letters and their military and naval agreements with the French. The cabinet also authorized Grey to proceed with negotiations for a naval understanding with Russia.

At this point it is advisable to digress slightly from the main narrative to comment briefly on this particular phase of British relations, for the concern for the Russian connection was a dominant motive in the 1914 crisis. Here is to be found the key to one of the most important aspects of British policy in the July crisis, namely, Grey's failure to put any pressure on Russia to modify her stand or to prevent reckless military action. The

---

[38] *B. D.*, X, pt. 2, 754–820, *passim*. The only representative, diplomatic, journalistic, or technical, who really got behind the false front and reported Russian conditions as they really were was the British naval attaché.

[39] *Ibid.*, X, pt. 2, 784–86.

agreement with Russia in 1907 had been a real revolution in British Empire policy. For it signified a substitution of co-operation and concilia-tion for the old Victorian tradition of blocking and checking the Musco-vites in Turkey, Persia, Afghanistan, and the Far East. Russian chicanery and bad faith, particularly in Persia, was tolerated and excused by Grey on the ground that on the issue most vital to the Empire, the Indian frontier, the Russians had kept their bargain. According to Grey the alternative to the Russian understanding was to abandon it, prepare all their defenses, and submit the issues to the test of war. Grey did not admit another alternative, which was the policy favored by the Curzon group in the Conservative party. Against knuckling under, they favored a sharp demand on Russia for a more loyal observance of the 1907 agree-ment. A good hard jolt might lead the Russians to cease their gangster politics in Persia, to recall their Hartwigs from the Middle East, and to return to reason. Failing this they could embrace the old policy of meeting pressure with pressure and force with force.[40] But Grey, who had fathered the Russian understanding, and took pride in his parentage, could not bring himself to endanger the baby's life. It made little difference how inconsiderate, humiliating, and immoral were Russian actions in Persia; it made little difference that the Russian understanding was unpopular with his own party and with many Conservatives; it made little difference how petty and fussy Sazonov was on matters which the British thought inconsequential; in fact, no matter how unreasonable Russian demands for diplomatic support, Grey was certain at the critical moment to say, as he did in the Liman von Sanders crisis, "we can't turn our back upon Russia." [41] It is inconceivable that a stiff-necked Tory foreign minister, in the last critical years before 1914, would have allowed an incompetent and unstable person like Sazonov to call the signals and carry the ball on every play. The most disquieting impression produced by a reading of Volume X of the *British Documents* is the contrast between the low opinion which all the British officials and diplomats entertained of Sazo-nov, and the way in which they conformed to his wishes and concurred in his dangerous policies.

News of the Anglo-Russian naval conversations soon reached Berlin. No better example of the use of inspired publicity as an adjunct to diplomacy can be found than the German action to thwart the forging of another link in the Triple Entente. De Siebert, an official in the Russian embassy in London, betrayed the preliminaries to the Wilhelmstrasse.

---

[40] See the record of a significant conversation between H. A. Gwynne, editor of the *Morning Post,* and Austen Chamberlain in *Politics from Inside,* pp. 482–83.

[41] *B. D.,* X, pt. 1, 407; see also the very revealing letter by Grey to Dr. Hodgkin, *ibid.,* X, pt. 1, 898–99.

Von Stumm, director of the political section, revealed the secret to Theodor Wolff, intimating that the game might be stopped if the spotlight of publicity were turned on from an unofficial source. The editor of the Tageblatt cast the information in the form of a Paris letter and published it on May 22. Commenting upon the revelation, the editor pointed out that the contemplated naval arrangement could only be aimed at Germany, that it nullified the progress that had been made toward better relations between the two countries, and that it would arm German chauvinists with powerful arguments for further naval building. Wolff's second article (June 2) appealed to the Liberals in England to preserve the gains made toward reconciliation. This elicited questions in the House of Commons and Grey was put in an embarrassing position. His reply was evasive, truthful enough in itself, but it was not an answer to the question. The Daily News and the Westminster Gazette, which had reacted unfavorably to the Tageblatt revelation, were satisfied by the statement, but the editor of the Guardian pointed out its deficiencies. Urging that the matter be further clarified by renewed questioning, the editor said: "For depend upon it, if any agreement has been concluded, there is not a government in Europe which does not know exactly what it is. The secret, in so far as there is one, is a secret from the British Parliament and people, not from any possible enemy." (June 12.) Following Grey's statement another dose of publicity in the Tageblatt was applied, then followed up by instructions to Lichnowski to express the satisfaction of the German authorities at the British foreign minister's denial of the mischievous press rumors! The naval conversations were unfinished business when the diplomats and publicists were overwhelmed by the final catastrophe.[42] The defeat of the British Radicals on the armaments issue, the compliance of Grey and the cabinet in the matter of naval conversations with Russia, the fear of the diplomatic technicians at possible loss of the Russian connection and the consequences to the Empire of isolation, all foreshadow British policy during the July crisis.

Before taking up the events of the summer of 1914, it seems advisable to summarize and review the main features of British and German policy since the turn of the century. During the Boer War the gaps in Empire defense and the critical danger of encroachments by other powers were clearly revealed; pressure had been applied at every vulnerable point by other powers, not excepting even the United States. Clarification of British policy was the result. Henceforth, so far as the technical specialists

[42] Theodor Wolff, *The Eve of 1914*, pp. 379–86; Nicolson, *Lord Carnock*, pp. 406–9; Prince Lichnowski, *Heading for the Abyss* (N. Y., 1928), pp. 364–73; Grey, *Twenty-five Years*, I, 286–95; R. Poincaré, *Memoirs (1913–14)*, 131–32; B. D., X, pt. 2, 774–814; G. P., XXXIX, 593–645.

were concerned, policy was comprehended in one large question—how can we preserve, most effectively and with the least sacrifice, the psychological and material values of our Empire? The creation of the Committee of Imperial Defense and the liquidation of French and Russian hostility by the sacrifices of 1904 and 1907 constituted the answer to that question. England established a connection with the continental group that formed the counterpoise to the German dominated Triple Alliance. As stated repeatedly by the diplomatic and defense experts, it was easier to keep up the navy and incur German enmity than to abandon the Triple Entente and incur the perils and risks to the Empire that would result from isolation. Far from pursuing a balance of power, the British joined, from force of necessity, the stronger and more dangerous group. The reasons and compulsions were clear enough to experts, but in a parliamentary state with a literate electorate and a free press explanations must be given. For reasons of prestige and political expediency the policy had to be propagated in terms other than those employed by technical experts—hence the inflation of the theme of Anglo-German rivalry. So far as naval competition, trade competition, and Pan-German perils were concerned, the contemporary publicity dealt with symbols that were far from referring exactly to objective facts. The professional directors of policy worked in this medium, but they did not delude themselves as to the realities of the situation. They might serve propaganda, but not to themselves. Realization of the facts began to penetrate the public between 1912 and 1914. Pro-Germans, anti-Russians, isolationists, and pacifists tried to reverse British policy and secure a withdrawal from the continental alliance system, but without success. A relaxation of tension between England and Germany ensued, but the actual trend of policy, under control of the political élite, was in fact in the opposite direction, toward more intimate association with the Franco-Russian Alliance and closer integration of the military power of the Triple Entente. By pursuing Empire security through association with the Dual Alliance the British were landed in a war arising from issues wholly remote from British vital interests.

In the case of German policy, in its broad outlines, we find the same mixture of illusion and reality. Under the leadership of William II, Bülow, and Tirpitz, Germany embarked upon the seas of *Weltpolitik,* breaking with the Bismarckian tradition of continental concentration. Friction with England was inevitable, but Bülow thought they could pivot their policy between Britain and Russia. When they did undertake to support England, in the Bismarckian tradition, they did so in a hesitant, uncertain, and half-concealed manner that awakened mistrust instead of breeding confidence. The transfer of British affection to the Franco-Russian group did not immediately affect Germany's continental position because Russia was impotent after the Russo-Japanese War. By 1912 Russia had so far recovered that she appeared to be rapidly approaching military predominance in Eastern Europe and her policy in the Balkans and the Near East became increasingly aggressive. Thereupon the German dream of *Weltpolitik* turned into a nightmare of the *Zweifrontenkrieg*. To those concerned with policy and security, time seemed to be working against the Triple Alliance and in favor of the Triple Entente. Italy's loyalty was more than dubious, Austria was visibly weakening; Germany could not match the man-power of Russia, the wealth of France, and the sea-power of England. If one assumed the inevitability of war between the alliances, as a considerable party in Germany did, then it was logical not to wait for the opponents to complete their preparations, but to take the initiative at a moment favorable to Germany.[43] While the civilian government held to the idea that it was a national duty to preserve the peace, it cannot be denied that the cult of "inevitability" had gained by 1914 numerous and influential adherents.

[43] Bernhardi was the spokesman of this school of thought. Military men must believe in the inevitability of war; otherwise the practice of their profession is a logical absurdity. When the English ambassador asked Bethmann if Bernhardi's books and articles reflected official views, the chancellor answered "No." Bethmann himself combated Bernhardi's views in an anonymous article published in *Die Post*. ("Ist die Zeit für uns oder gegen uns?") Bernhardi, *Denkwürdigkeiten*, pp. 386–87. For a summary of Bernhardi's views see *Germany and the Next War* (Amer. ed., N. Y., 1914), pp. 85–114.

CHAPTER XV

JULY 1914: MOBILIZING OPINION

J. H. Morgan: "But everything has gone to show that Germany had made up her mind to have a war sooner or later."

Lord Morley: "You mean it was 'inevitable.' That has been said of every war since Hannibal."

News of the murder of the Archduke Franz Ferdinand and his wife reached Berlin late Sunday afternoon of June 28. Single news sheets announcing the tragedy were shoved into the hands of holiday trippers as loaded trams from the Grünewald passed Nollendorf and Potsdamerplatz. As the circumstances of the tragedy became known throughout the country the summer holiday spirit disappeared. Except in the London clubs, where telegrams were posted, Englishmen did not learn of the event until they opened their Monday morning newspapers. The world was shocked, and sympathy for the people of the Dual Monarchy and for the old Emperor found expression in almost every European newspaper. Political observers familiar with Austria's South Slav problem and cognizant of the working of Pan-Serbian propaganda were apprehensive of an immediate crisis, but fears were allayed as no special measures were announced in Vienna. After exploiting the "Mystery of the Royal Funeral," the popular English press devoted its space to other sensations: the Home Rule crisis, a "Moonlight Tragedy on the Thames," involving London's gilded youth, a strike at the Woolwich arsenal, and the championship fight between Carpentier and Gunboat Smith. On July 20 the trial of Madame Caillaux for the murder of Gaston Calmette, editor of Le Figaro, opened and for the next few days shared the 'splash page' with sensational accounts of gun-running in Ulster.[1]

A much greater volume of news from Vienna, Budapest, Belgrade and Serajevo appeared in the German press than in the English. The rumors and assertions of Serbian complicity in the murder plot and the vicious press campaign launched in Belgrade against Austria also received wider circulation and gave rise to numerous expressions of anti-Serbian feeling.

[1] For greater detail on the reaction of the British press to the Serajevo murders see Walter Zimmermann, *Die Englische Presse zum Ausbruch des Weltkrieges* (Berlin, 1928), pp. 11–28; J. F. Scott, *Five Weeks: the Surge of Public Opinion on the Eve of the Great War* (N. Y., 1927), pp. 206–15.

popular as well as the serious press carried prominent news stories under arresting headlines: "Grave European Crisis; Danger of War; Europe Is at the Precipice." This alarming estimate of the situation was based on the Austrian ultimatum, the German government's declaration of solidarity with her ally, and the announcement in St. Petersburg that Russia would not stand aside if Serbia were invaded.

In judging Austria's demands upon Serbia, British journalists were far from agreement. There was no party line to write up to and the foreign office had no suggestion for the press except to warn against disturbing the diplomatic atmosphere by indiscreet publicity.[11] Not even the Northcliffe papers—Times, Daily Mail, and Evening News—were in unison. As for the Conservative-Unionist journals, judgments ranged all the way from that of the Morning Post, which, under H. A. Gwynne's direction, saw the Triple Entente already engaged against the Triple Alliance, to the Standard which declared that "Were Great Britain under similar infliction, our attitude would be precisely that taken by Austria-Hungary." [12] In the Liberal press, judgments were quite as discordant. J. A. Spender wrote that acceptance of the demands would mean the subjugation of Serbia, while the Daily News thought that "most of the ten demands made . . . are such as any State has a right to ask of its neighbours." [13] In most of the reports and comments of the British press a grave view of the situation was taken, especially in light of Russia's probable intervention. There was definite hesitation, however, in going beyond events to consider what England's course would be if the Austro-Serbian dispute developed into a general European war. For the moment the press did not go beyond the immediate crisis and did not look to the government for more than mediatory action.

Unanimous approval greeted Sir Edward Grey's announcement in the House of Commons on July 27 that he had proposed mediation through an ambassador's conference composed of representatives of the four disinterested powers—Germany, France, Italy, and Great Britain. Meanwhile the situation had worsened through the Austrian rejection of the Serbian reply and the recall of her minister from Belgrade; and a greater calamity was impending, for on the next day Austria declared war upon Serbia. Grey's statement turned attention to the rôle played by Germany, because it was generally held that if Berlin would "press

[11] H. Wickham Steed, *Through Thirty Years,* I, 409–12.

[12] *Morning Post,* July 25, 27; *Standard,* July 25. The *Standard* (July 27) characterized Serbia as "a half-civilized and wholly waspish and disorderly little state, whose annals are a dreary record of incompetence, violence, and political crime."

[13] *Westminster Gazette,* July 25; *Daily News,* July 25. For detailed reactions of individual papers see Zimmermann, *Die Englische Presse,* pp. 37–59; E. Anrich, *Die Englische Politik im Juli 1914* (Stuttgart, 1934), pp. 154–64.

Zeitung warned that the German public should not foster the illusion that England would remain neutral under all circumstances. If France became involved through her obligations to Russia, Britain would not repeat what had come to be regarded as the mistake of 1870. To support their cautious warnings they pointed to the gravity of Asquith's statement in the House on July 29, to Grey's careful avoidance of anything that might be interpreted as a neutrality commitment, and to Churchill's ominous activity at the admiralty.[16] These admonitions counted for little. Neither in news dispatches nor in interpretative articles were the imponderables of their relations with Britain—the naval balance in Europe, the fixed policy of supporting France, the effect of a German victory on Britain's vital interests—brought up for review or analysis. Of English concern for the neutrality of Belgium the German public remained wholly uninformed. In so far as the journalists concerned themselves with Britain, it was to utter the shallow judgment that the English being a moral people could not possibly join the defenders of murder.

It was with extreme reluctance that authoritative circles in England faced the realities of continental war. When Russia ordered general mobilization and Germany replied with an ultimatum, it was finally admitted that Europe was over the brink and Britain must make a grave decision. At this moment German attention was concentrated on the dreadful outbreak of war on two fronts. Reports from England dried up to a mere trickle. News services were interrupted by impending mobilization, mails were delayed, some cables went dead under suspicious circumstances, and at the telegraph offices official business took precedence over private messages. Telegraph service outside Germany was subject to many hours' delay. After general mobilization was ordered, the censorship was of course clamped on. Under these conditions practically no independent reports from London reached the German press, and the Wolff Bureau furnished only meager summaries of the Westminster Gazette's articles, which seemed to hold out hope of British neutrality.[17] The German public was uninformed of the diplomatic exchanges between Berlin and London. Moreover, with the dislocation of news service and the stoppage of normal activities incidental to mobilization, the Germans missed the crucial stages of the debate in England on intervention.

[16] *Frankfurter Ztg.*, Nos. 206, 207, 208, July 27, 28, 29; *Münchner N. N.*, Nos. 381, 388, 389, July 28, 31, Aug. 1; London telegram to Berlin *Lokal-Anzeiger* (July 28), reproduced in *Kölnische Volksztg.*, No. 676, July 29.

[17] Wolff circulated to the German press a summary of J. A. Spender's article on July 30 in which he deprecated the efforts of the interventionists to force Grey's hand; Britain must remain the concentration point of forces still working for peace. *Berliner Tageblatt*, No. 383, July 31; *Kölnische Volksztg.*, No. 680, July 31; and numerous other German papers.

When the decision finally became known it was an unexpected calamity. The Germans were in the position of a person who hears the preliminaries of a debate when attitudes seem inclined one way, then withdraws from the council room while the real issues are discussed, and then returns as the vote is taken to find that it has fallen in the opposite sense indicated by the preliminary discussion. The announcement in the German press on August 5 that England had declared war on Germany found the public not only unprepared for the announcement but also uninformed as to the considerations that had led to that decision.

How did it come about that in one short week the British government and the greater part of the newspapers moved from neutrality to intervention? In other words, the old question—Why did England enter the war? For purposes of analysis it is assumed that the ultimate decision was made by the influential. The mass electorate had no opportunity to register its views; there were no public opinion polls for the discovery of the obvious. As a matter of fact, all governments in the crisis functioned autocratically, subject of course to influence and pressure from immediate centers of power. Those centers of power in England, those groups in a position to bring direct influence to bear, we may list as follows: the foreign office, the military and naval authorities, the City, the parliamentary groups, and finally, the newspaper press. All of these authorities of opinion, skill, and wealth had spokesmen in the cabinet; and there all views and opinions came to a focus, and there ultimate decisions were made. In both England and Germany final executive action was taken in a small council of leaders, not in the forum of parliament.

With regard to the first group, the foreign office professionals, judgments were formulated early and the line of action which they desired was clearly stated. In the Austrian ultimatum and Germany's declaration of solidarity with her ally, they saw a deliberate challenge to the Dual Alliance. In the crisis Russia would regard Britain's attitude as a test of reliability, and they must be careful not to alienate her by applying pressure directly or through her ally, France. If the Triple Entente were disrupted, which would follow upon England's failure to support Russia, the position of the Empire in the Far East, in Central Asia, the Near East, and in the Mediterranean would be gravely imperiled. If they remained neutral Britain would incur the hatred of the friends they had betrayed and would not earn the good will of their enemies. "I only pray that England will prove true to herself and to her friends," wrote Buchanan to Nicolson, "as if she deserts them in their hour of need she will find herself isolated after the war; and the hours of our Empire will be numbered." Therefore, the government should declare its solidarity with France and Russia. Moreover, in this course lay the best chance of preserving peace by heading the Triple Alliance back from its dangerous course.[18]

This group, whose views are sketched above, did not embrace all the personnel of the foreign office. There were those who thought that a war from which Russia would emerge victorious over the Central powers would not be a distinct advantage for Britain and the Empire. They were definitely opposed to an immediate and unequivocal invocation of Entente solidarity, for such a declaration would encourage Russia and France to greater intransigence and would end the British government's position as mediator between the disputants. As to eventual action in a continental war, their position should be left open to the last moment. This pattern of action is not so fully documented as the preceding, and yet it was the one followed by Grey. At the foreign office Tyrrell was Grey's main support in the policy of "wait and see."

Military and naval exigencies, the pressure of military time-tables, and hair-trigger calculations of technical specialists bore less heavily on the British cabinet than upon any other government during the crisis. True, the Committee of Imperial Defense was in almost continuous session polishing the plans in anticipation of cabinet action; Churchill at the admiralty was usually two steps in advance of cabinet authorization in naval preparations; and Henry Wilson, chief of staff, a political as well as a military strategist, worked feverishly to line up the Conservative-Unionist leadership for intervention, once it became certain that the continental powers were mobilizing.

In the City, bankers and business leaders were appalled at the prospect of a general war, and through Lloyd George and Asquith their fears and protests were heard in the cabinet room. With those responsible for the larger political and security issues involved, these voices carried no great weight and their dire predictions of economic collapse and chaos were dismissed or discounted as the work of panicmongers.[19]

Among the parliamentary groups the greatest uncertainty prevailed. Attention shifted slowly from the bitter dispute over Ulster to the European crisis. War was expected in Ireland but not in Europe. Since general debate was not permitted until after the cabinet had been brought together on a policy of certain intervention, it is impossible to specify in detail the movement of opinion among the party leaders. But the broad

[18] Minutes, dispatches, and private letters by Eyre Crowe, Nicolson and Buchanan, B. D., XI, 81–82, 94, 156–57, 201, 227, 228–29, 259, 277, 345–46.
[19] Spender, *Life of Asquith*, II, 102; *B. D.*, XI, 228; Anrich, *op. cit.*, p. 369; Lloyd George, *War Memoirs*, I, 61, 68–69.

outlines are fairly clear. Pacifism and hostility to Russia determined Labor party opposition to intervention. This opposition was not overcome by Grey's speech of August 3, or by the appeal of the French Socialist leaders to their British comrades, a move inspired by Cambon. However, on August 6, the party caucus refused to sanction Macdonald's speech opposing the vote of war credits.[20] We do not know how the Irish Nationalist party viewed the crisis in its various critical stages, but after Grey's speech, foreshadowing intervention, John Redmond pledged the party to support the government's decision. Perhaps it was just Irish inconsistency that led the Nationalists to deny history and accept a case based on the principle of sanctity of treaties and defense of the rights of small nations!

The leadership of the Conservative-Unionist party moved with events —from indecision at the beginning to united pressure for intervention toward the end. In the first stage of the crisis Bonar Law expressed doubts to Grey that the rank and file of the party would be unanimous in support of war. On July 30 began the formation of a united front between the Liberal Imperialist ministers in the cabinet and the leaders of the opposition. By agreement between Asquith and Bonar Law the Ulster question was shelved in parliament. There was constant and lively intercourse between the leaders during the critical week. Churchill was the chief link between the Liberal Imperialists and the leaders of the opposition—F. E. Smith, Balfour, Lansdowne, Bonar Law, and Austen Chamberlain. Nicolson and Henry Wilson were active in rallying the Conservative leaders to the support of the interventionist group in the cabinet. The upshot of this activity was the conference of Conservative-Unionist leaders at Lansdowne House on Saturday night, August 1, and the dispatch next morning of a letter to Asquith over Bonar Law's signature. In this communication, the significance of which cannot be overemphasized, the Conservative leaders declared that in their opinion "it would be fatal to the honour and security of the United Kingdom to hesitate in supporting France and Russia at the present juncture, and we offer our unhesitating support to the Government in any measures they may consider necessary for that object." [21]

[20] Ramsay Macdonald's speech of Aug. 3, *Parl. Deb.*, 5th Ser., vol. 65, 1829–31; W. P. Maddox, *Foreign Relations in British Labour Politics* (Cambridge, 1934), pp. 54–55, 159, 197. For Cambon's publicity tactics to influence the Labor party leadership see *Memoirs of Raymond Poincaré (1913–1914)*, p. 277.

[21] Newton, *Lord Lansdowne,* p. 440; Blanche E. C. Dugdale, *Arthur James Balfour* (2 vols., N. Y., 1937), II, 77–80; Austen Chamberlain, *Down the Years* (Lond., 1935), pp. 92–106, contemporary memorandum; Churchill, *World Crisis,* I, 228–30; Anrich, *op. cit.,* pp. 369, 443–46, 469. Anrich mistakes George Lloyd, the Conservative leader, for Lloyd George, chancellor of the exchequer, in analyzing Chamberlain's memoran-

It is significant to note that it was not Belgian neutrality that turned the Conservative-Unionists into a war party, but the obligations of the Entente, the question of national honor and of British interests and security. The decision was stamped with political realism; it was not a moral imperative.

In the Liberal party the old division between the Gladstonian Radicals and the Liberal Imperialists reappeared at the first prospect of a European war. To the Radicals, British participation in a continental struggle arising out of a Russian quarrel with Austria over Serbia was unthinkable. The cabinet members opposed to intervention had a firm basis for support in the attitude of the Radical rank and file, which for years had been threatening revolt against the political and military diplomacy of the Liberal Imperialists. The ministers were in no doubt as to the feelings of this group. If their representatives in the cabinet stood firm, they were numerically strong enough to break the government and turn the reins over to the Conservatives or to a coalition. As late as Sunday, August 2, Asquith noted in his daybook: "I suppose a good number of our own party in the House of Commons are for absolute non-interference. It will be a shocking thing if at such a moment we break up." [22] Here was the basis of an anti-war party such as had formed among the Radicals at the outbreak of the Boer War. That opposition to war in 1914 did not crystallize on party lines is largely due to the political skill of Grey and Asquith. A false move on their part, an attempt to force the issue in advance of events, would have produced a crash. Deaf to considerations of high policy and interest, morally averse to war as an instrument of policy, only a higher moral issue would overcome Radical opposition to intervention. That issue was provided by Belgian neutrality, the sanctity of treaties, and the rights of small nations. On Sunday, August 2, after the morning cabinet meeting Cambon was given official assurance that the British navy would protect the French coasts and shipping. With that the die was cast. But at that time the German march through Belgium was still hypothetical. By pushing the Belgian issue into the foreground, in his speech on August 3, Grey brought all but a few stalwarts like Ponsonby, Morrell, and Wedgewood into line with the cabinet's decision. For the Radical Liberals Belgian neutrality was the bridge over which they passed to reunite with those parliamentary groups—Conservatives, Unionists, Liberal Imperialists, and Irish Nationalists—whose decisions had already been made on the

---

dum. His conclusion that Lloyd George went over to the war party on August 1 is therefore erroneous.

[22] Spender, *Life of Asquith*, II, 85.

grounds of national honor, national interests, the preservation of the Entente, the balance of power, or the security of the Empire. It seems reasonable to conclude that in view of attitudes and reactions of the parliamentary groups Britain was almost certain to intervene in the continental struggle, but without the Belgian issue it is not certain that the government would have had the united support of its own party in the House of Commons.

It was in the cabinet that all the stresses and thrusts of party politics, publicity, and international diplomacy came to bear. As the continental governments took one gambler's chance after another, and with each throw of the dice brought war one step closer, the British ministry was reluctantly making up its mind. The cabinet was united in upholding Grey's efforts at mediation. But there agreement ended. What the government should do if peace efforts failed, left the cabinet hopelessly divided. Grey would have had a strong basis of support in the government for a plea to Russia not to make military gestures that would invite German countermeasures, but expert opinion, which held that this might breach the Triple Entente, apparently deterred him from taking action. On the other hand, a warning in Berlin that if the Central powers moved they must reckon with the British fleet would not have been sanctioned by his colleagues. Confronted with the question of neutrality or intervention, the cabinet was divided as follows: For supporting France, the balance of power, and the preservation of the Triple Entente were the Liberal Imperialists Grey, Asquith, Haldane, and Churchill, together with Crewe and McKenna who were almost certain to follow the prime minister. Resolutely opposed to intervention were Morley, Burns, Harcourt, Simon, and Beauchamp. A larger middle group, undecided, strongly pacific, and opposed to intervention except under extreme provocation, numbered among its adherents Lloyd George, Samuel, Pease, Runciman, Hobhouse, Masterman, and McKinnon Wood.[23] Lord Morley was the leader of the peace bloc, which felt that the cabinet "was being rather artfully drawn on step by step to war for the benefit of France and Russia." In the daily cabinet meetings the discussions ranged over every aspect of the problem, but from Asquith's notes it is evident that two questions were outstanding: First, the nature of their obligation to France (honor and interests); second, the anticipated violation of Belgian neutrality (treaty obligation and interests). The interventionists realized that if any issue could unite the government it was Belgian neutrality, and it was brought before the cabinet as early as July 29.

[23] The composition of the groups may not be exact. The participants themselves are not in agreement as to where some of their colleagues stood.

While the cabinet members who had attended the meetings of the Committee of Imperial Defense were pretty certain that the Germans would strike at France through Belgium, it was hypothetical until the Germans made their demands in Brussels, while the issue of assistance to France was forced upon the cabinet at the outset by the French ambassador, the foreign office, the military officials, and the leaders of the Conservative party. In the middle group in the cabinet—those who insisted that the position be kept open and the decision delayed to the last moment— Lloyd George was the most prominent figure. Had he led the peace group as he at first seemed inclined to do, the cabinet must surely have split and the government fallen, but at the last moment, when the time came to present resignations, he swung around, as Morley says, "to the politics of adventure; and found in the German ultimatum to Belgium a sufficiently plausible excuse." Just as he did in the Agadir crisis, Lloyd George deserted the Radicals and joined hands with the Liberal Imperialists. The peace group was left without a leader and the opposition to intervention collapsed. On Sunday morning, August 2, after long and heated debate, the cabinet authorized Grey to tell Cambon that the British fleet would protect the French coast and French shipping in the Channel. On the following day came the news of the German demands on Belgium and the appeal to the signatory powers. With that, consciences were eased, doubts were resolved, and hesitation ceased. In the end only four members resigned—Morley, Burns, Beauchamp, and Simon—and two of these reconsidered and kept their seats in the council (Beauchamp and Simon). No cabinet could have escaped or denied the obligation to protect the French coast and shipping; it was symbolized by the disposition of the French and British naval forces and it was documented in the *"petit papier"* which Grey and Cambon had exchanged in 1912. This was by no means the only consideration that assured, sooner or later, British intervention. All of the other reasons of policy, interest, and honor were likewise valid. Belgium was not the sole, nor even the major cause of British intervention, but it was the crystallizing issue, and determined the immediate form and time of that intervention.[24]

[24] For the cabinet crisis see Spender, *Life of Asquith,* II, 78–102; Asquith, *Memories and Reflections,* II, 7–14, 24–26; Lloyd George, *War Memoirs,* I, 60–71; A. Birrell, *Things Past Redress* (Lond., 1937), pp. 222–35; Lord Beaverbrook, *Politicians and the War* (N. Y., 1928), pp. 1–16; Anrich, *Englische Politik,* pp. 275–77, 334–36, 396–97, 470–78, 489–91; Schmitt, *Coming of the War,* II, 279 ff. For the influences brought to bear on Lloyd George see *Lord Riddell's War Diary* (Lond., 1933), pp. 1–8. But particularly, the much discussed *Memorandum on Resignation* by Lord Morley (*New Republic,* Oct. 10, 1928, pp. 194–200). Some surviving members of the cabinet who were put in an unfavorable light in Morley's *Memorandum,* have sought to discredit it. It is interesting to note that Churchill, who admits the faulty chronology,

In general, the press was slower than the cabinet and parliament in veering around and supporting a war policy. On Monday, July 27, few Englishmen could have been expecting to enter a European war; a week later, on August 3, war was a practical certainty. In this brief time-span the course of events from neutrality to intervention was written across the press.

In the crisis the press played its customary dual rôle: it recorded the grim decisions taken day after day in the European capitals and, in the name of "public opinion," it gave counsel and advice to the leaders. The service of information was preserved remarkably well, better than in Germany, up to the time when military control was imposed in the continental capitals. There was the inevitable crisis accompaniment of manufactured news, rumors, and uncontrolled fantasy. It also reflected the influence of policy on the news page, once a line was decided upon; and there was a considerable stream of reports from the foreign embassies that were consciously designed to cover up or obscure the facts and to mislead the public in the interest of this or that national policy. On the whole the restraints, interventions, and pressures from the authorities were fewer in Britain than in any other country directly involved in the current wave of madness.

We have seen that the preponderance of editorial opinion in the British press was inclined to justify Austrian action and to condemn Serbia; it supported unreservedly attempts to settle the dispute by mediation; and when this avenue was closed by the Austrian declaration of war on Serbia it favored localization of the conflict. Russia's general mobilization, signaled from Berlin on July 31, and Germany's ultimatum in reply quenched all optimism and forced consideration of Britain's rôle in the coming struggle. The national solidarity of the political press, so marked during the Agadir crisis, was notably lacking. In the early stages of the debate only the Northcliffe papers (Times, Daily Mail, Evening News, and Daily Mirror) and the Morning Post, among the leading journals, demanded that the government immediately and unreservedly proclaim its determination to support France and Russia. H. A. Gwynne, editor of the Morning Post, and Geoffrey Dawson, editor of the Times, were in close touch at all times with the Conservative party leadership at Landsdowne House. As early as July 28, Spenser Wilkinson was writing signed articles for the Post on "The European Crisis," in which he declared that if the general crash came and France were involved

regards it as "none the less, as true and living a presentment of the War crisis within the British Cabinet as has ever been, or probably will ever be, given." *Great Contemporaries* (N. Y., 1937), pp. 84–88.

through her alliance with Russia, then the original issues in dispute were of little consequence and it became England's clear duty to join her friends and fight for the preservation of the balance of power. The obligations of the Entente, honor, duty, and the future security of Britain and the Empire were the points advanced in support of the interventionist plea. Steed, the foreign editor of the Times, was in daily conference with Cambon, Nicolson and the foreign office officials, and the Times' appeals and proclamations strongly reflect and parallel the policy which the permanent officials were trying to force upon Grey and the cabinet.[25] Much of the writing in these journals was obviously designed to buck up the cabinet. Steed has described the Northcliffe editorial council on August 1, in which the publisher, who had allowed Steed a free hand in framing the paper's policy in the crisis, said that he had information that the cabinet would decide against intervention. Should they attack the government in time of national crisis? "If the government 'rat' we must pull off our wigs and go bald-headed against the government," Steed replied. "If we attack the government we may either compel them to stand firm, or bring about the formation of a national government that will do its duty before it is too late." [26] A glimpse such as this of an editorial conference and some slight knowledge of the relations between party leaders and party editors shakes the illusion of universality contained in bold editorial page declarations that "Every Englishman [meaning four or five editors and a cabal of politicians] expects the Government to do its duty. . . ."

Resisting the aggressive drive for intervention launched by the Morning Post and the Northcliffe press were the Radical and pacifist papers, the Manchester Guardian, Daily News, and Liverpool Post. Scott brought all his great personal influence to bear upon the Radical members of the cabinet; he spoke his mind to Illingworth, the chief Liberal whip, and he practically turned the Guardian and its staff over to the campaign for neutrality.[27] A. G. Gardiner, the editor of the Daily News, met the arguments of the interventionists with sharply reasoned answers, which

[25] There is also a significant parallelism between Wilkinson's articles in the *Post* and the foreign office minutes of his brother-in-law, Eyre Crowe.

[26] Steed, *Through Thirty Years,* II, 10–11. For the contacts between Gwynne and Dawson and Lansdowne House see Chamberlain, *Down the Years,* pp. 101–2. All the evidence points to the conclusion that if the Radicals had balked at intervention, the Liberal Imperialists would have formed a coalition with the Conservatives.

[27] Hammond, *C. P. Scott,* pp. 177–81. On August 3, Scott wired Lloyd George: "Feeling of intense exasperation among leading liberals here at prospect of Government embarking on war no man who is responsible can lead us again." Robertson Nicoll, editor of the *British Weekly,* and the non-Conformist "pope" of England, was preparing to stir up the dissenters against the cabinet, but he was persuaded by Riddell to stay his protest. (Riddell, *War Diary,* pp. 6–7.)

even today impress the reader as masterpieces of polemical journalism. The Liverpool Post, conscious of the interests of its great industrial and commercial constituency, was violently opposed to intervention up to the moment when debate was cut short by the declaration of war on Germany.

The other principal Liberal papers—Westminster Gazette, Daily Chronicle, and Yorkshire Observer—were pacific in their utterances, condemnatory of the bellicose campaign in the Conservative press, and clearly averse to taking a positive stand for or against neutrality. Mr. Spender in his memoirs has given us the guiding lines of his editorial policy during the crisis: "to fight for peace until the last moment, and to aim at unity in the Government, if war came, were clearly the two imperative duties." "The situation," he continues, "was beyond journalism, and all that the journalist could hope to do was not to do mischief." Spender avoided the groups of journalists and politicians who were agitating for or against intervention, stayed away from the House of Commons, saw Paul Cambon once, and had only two short talks with Grey during the critical twelve days. In the final edition of the Westminster on Saturday, August 1, he published Bethmann-Hollweg's dispatch to Tschirschky of July 30 as evidence that Germany was trying to restrain Austria. The dispatch was sent personally to Spender by the German chancellor.[28] These papers, while hoping for peace, were waiting, like the great middle section of the party, for the government to unite and give a lead. The position is well expressed in the leading article of the Daily Chronicle on Saturday, August 1, entitled "On the Brink." "What shall be the British attitude? We say frankly that at this stage it is best for those who are troubled by no official responsibility not to start dictating to Sir Edward Grey. There are times and this is one, when the crew of the ship had better be prepared to carry out, in any event, the orders of their appointed captain. . . ." While refusing to commit themselves in advance of cabinet action, these editors did give full publicity to the neutrality agitation. However, after Grey's speech on August 3, foreshadowing intervention, they followed implicitly the lead given by the ministry. In the words of Mr. Spender, "Sir Edward Grey speaks for us when he explains the obligation of honour and interest that rest upon the nation at this moment." (Aug. 4.) [29] After following Grey and the cabinet from neutrality to intervention on a strictly national interest, obligation of honor, and balance of power policy, the

---

[28] *Life, Journalism and Politics*, II, 12–17.
[29] Also *Daily Chronicle*, Aug. 4, "England Refuses to Desert France"; *Glasgow Herald*, Aug. 4: "Sir Edward Grey's words describe for us the path of honour, which is also that of duty and of interest."

mingham Daily Post followed the trend in the London press.[35] In the
entire Conservative press only the Daily Graphic, whose foreign editor
was the Russophobe Lucien Wolf, and the Standard, which had lost most
of its circulation and influence, continued to maintain that Austria-
Hungary was in the right, that Russia by mobilizing was the aggressor,
and that "A war to decide whether the predominant interest in the
Balkans should be that of Russia or Austria is not one in which British
sympathies can be engaged on either side." [36] Like the party leadership,
the Conservative press, by August 2, was united on the necessity of
intervention for the preservation of France as a power factor in the
European system, for the maintenance of the Triple Entente, for the security of the Empire which would be threatened by isolation, for the protection of their vital interests involved in the independence of the Low
Countries, for the maintenance of their honor, their obligations and their
interests.

Toward half-past three in the afternoon on August 3, Grey appeared
before a crowded and tense House to make the statement that was to
decide the fate of nations and change the course of history. There is
no need to give a long résumé of his speech. Its main lines had been
fixed in agreement with the cabinet. His restraint, apparent fair-minded-
ness, and cool detachment obscured the fact that he was appearing before the country as well as parliament as an advocate making the strongest possible bid for support. Grey's presentation of the cabinet's brief
paralleled the line of argument developed by the interventionist writers
in the press, in that he approached the crisis from the standpoint of
British interests, British honor, and British obligations. He carefully
avoided the problem of genesis and responsibility—the Archduke's
murder, Pan-Serbian provocation, and Russian mobilization—and
limited his account to the policy and actions of the British government.
The Entente Cordiale was the theme of the first half of his discourse.
With characteristic British disregard of logic Grey began his speech by
assuring the House that the government had not committed the country
to aid France, but before he had gone far he was telling them that the
government *was* under an obligation which they could not escape; in
fact it had already been honored by the written assurance given to
Cambon the day before. The undefended French coasts, the French fleet
in the Mediterranean guarding vital British lines of communication,

---

[35] Zimmermann, *Die Englische Presse*, pp. 183–87. The *Scotsman* was bitterly
critical of the Radical campaign for neutrality and aggressive in its demands for intervention (July 31, Aug. 1). The *Birmingham Daily Post* was more reserved and inclined to look to the cabinet for a lead (Aug. 1, 3).

[36] *Standard*, Aug. 1; Zimmermann, *op. cit.*, pp. 189–93.

established the absolute necessity of the undertaking. He read the document and it was greeted with a fierce cheer from the opposition benches. With this solemn pronouncement all hopes of standing aside disappeared. The party of Bright and Gladstone, of Morley and Campbell-Bannerman was whipped. The leaders had signed the death warrant of the Liberal party.

The second part of the speech was devoted to Belgian neutrality. They had just received an unconfirmed report, said Grey, of a German ultimatum. Here was a vital British interest as well as a legal obligation of the highest order. The support of France was inseparable from the preservation of Belgian independence and he drew a gloomy picture of France defeated and Belgium, Holland, and Denmark falling "under the same dominating influence." If that should come to pass they would be in a position of the gravest peril. Recognizing the argument of the non-interventionists that they stand aside and use their strength at a later stage in the struggle to secure peace and equitable adjustments, he rejected it as a moral and material impossibility. The burden of war would be less than the risks of standing aside. And then fateful words: "For us, with a powerful Fleet, which we believe able to protect our shores, and to protect our interests, if we are engaged in war, we shall suffer but little more than we shall suffer even if we stand aside." In the peroration he expressed confidence that the ministry would be supported "not only by the House of Commons, but by the determination, the resolution, the courage, and the endurance of the whole country."

No historic speech can be separated from the time, place, and atmosphere of its delivery. For Grey it was a great triumph. From the moment he began to speak it was clearly evident from the applause that he had a majority of the House solidly behind him, although there was a large tract of silence below the gangway on the government side. Sharp fierce cheers from the Tory benches greeted Grey's pronouncements. When he gritted out: "We must face it," the enthusiasm of the Unionists knew no bounds. According to one parliamentary correspondent, "The speech made a painful impression on the Liberal party . . . but its logic seemed the logic of events beyond our control." Another correspondent recalled "the faint applause from the Liberals as some fitful gleam of hope seemed to brighten the horizon—and the fierce outbursts of acclamation with which the Unionists hailed every additional portent of the gathering storm." And still another wrote that "To convince doubters of the soundness of the Government's decision only one thing more was needed—a declaration from Mr. Ramsay Macdonald that the Government was doing wrong. This was given at once." Aside from

Russia and concern for the Empire brought British leaders in 1914 to the point where they acted on the assumption that the Triple Entente was more vital than peace. For political realists, those who believed that the state was power and war was a legitimate instrument of policy, this was complete justification for intervention, although it was symbolized and rationalized as national honor and maintenance of the balance of power. However, for a mass democracy which rejected the aristocratic concept of honor, which was deeply distrustful of the foreign policy of the Liberal Imperialists who dominated the ministry, which found Russia, in general, to be more hateful than Germany, which was Little-Englander rather than imperial in its outlook, intervention had to be presented in idealistic terms. The Germans believed that they were fighting for national existence against foes bent upon their annihilation. To an island folk with "twenty-five miles of ships" to prevent invasion and to keep vital communications intact the same doctrine of necessity would not apply with equal force. That is where the Belgian issue was of supreme importance. It gave a legalistic and moral basis for intervention. The Birmingham Daily Post, which was one of the few Conservative papers that at the outset made Belgian invasion the condition of British participation, reviewing Grey's speech, said: "No one can read Sir Edward Grey's candid analysis of the position without realizing at once that it would be almost impossible for Great Britain to remain in a position of detachment, even though no question of Belgian neutrality arose." (Aug. 4.) It was the Belgian issue that silenced the opposition to a war policy among the Radicals and the Laborites and finally united all those groups and classes that possessed effective leadership and adequate organs of expression. And in the trying years that followed, the liberal idealists, to whom war was immoral, waged war in the name of a new morality. They had repudiated a war for self-interest, for honor, even for security, so they invented a war ideology which made the struggle one for the independence and security of small nations, for the vindication of legal rights against military force; it became a fight for civilization against barbarism, a war against the Kaiser and the Junkers and Prussian militarism. But the highest aim of all was set forth by Mr. Garvin in the Pall Mall Gazette on the day war was declared. "We have to do our part in killing a creed of war. Then at last, after a rain of blood, there may be set the greater rainbow in the Heavens before the vision of the souls of men. And after Armageddon war, indeed, may be no more." This, the most idealistic of aims, became the greatest paradox of the age—war to end war!

INDEX

Abel, Professor, 195
Aegidi, Ludwig, 65
Agadir crisis, 380-419, *passim*
Agrarian League, 54, 217
Algeciras Conference, publicity of, 276-78; Act of, 381
Anderson, Sir Percy, 81, 82
Anglo-Congolese dispute, 96-101
Anglo-French Entente, 266-68; German policy toward, 270-71; and naval convention, 430-31
Anglo-German alliance negotiations (1901), 238
Anglo-German commercial rivalry, 132-34, 166-67, 169, 328-31
Anglo-German Friendship Committee, 282, 416
Anglo-German naval rivalry, 308-9, 312, 327-28, 330, 342-43, 364-65, 427-28, 434-35
Anglo-German relations, summaries of, 102, 187-89, 266-69, 432-33; turning point in, 253, 263; effect of Entente Cordiale on, 267-69; and British domestic politics, 371-72; after Agadir, 413; change in British opinion of, 418-19, 426-27
Anglophobia, during Boer War, chaps. VIII and IX, *passim;* and the German government, 246-47; and Agadir crisis, 407-9
Anglo-Russian Entente, reception in Germany, 300-301; on eve of War, 440-42; and naval conversations, 442-43
Armaments competition (1913), 436
Armaments industry in Great Britain, 346-48; and Dreadnought panic, 358-59
Armstrong, Sir George, 371
Arnold, W. T., 30, 264
Arnold-Forster, H. O., 156
Ashmead-Bartlett, Sir Ellis, 95, 127
Ashton, Lord, 23
Asquith, H. H., 171, 385, 388, 416, 419, 425, 431, 439, 457, 458; on naval program (1909), 350-51; and Dreadnought panic, 356-57; and Agadir

crisis, 398; on German neutrality formula, 422
Astor, William Waldorf, 17, 18
Athenaeum Club, 230
Augustinusverein, 57
Austin, Alfred, 27, 90, 99, 105, 142, 195; and Lord Salisbury, 90-92; and "Jameson's Ride," 121-23
Austria-Hungary, and July crisis, 1914, 447; influence on English press, 448
Avebury, Lord, 282, 416

Bagdad Railroad, 261-63, 423, 432
Balance of power, 375-76, 433, 439-40
Balfour, Arthur, 95, 120, 207, 261, 307, 348, 350, 356, 359, 371, 426, 457, 468
Balkan Wars, 433, 436
Ballin, Albert, 308
Barnard, E. G., 17
Bashford, J. L., 18, 26, 35, 115, 129, 132, 204, 300, 303, 315
Bassermann, Ernst, 407, 426
Bathurst, Lady, 24
Beauchamp, Lord, 459, 460
Behr, Baron von, 404
Belgium, neutrality of, 458-60, 467, 470
Bell, Moberly, 20, 135-36, 297; warns German embassy, 257
Bellairs, Lieutenant Carolyn, 361
Beresford, Lord Charles, 335
Berliner Neueste Nachrichten, 53-54
Berliner Tageblatt, 46-47, 443
Bernhard, Georg, 47
Bernhardi, General, 437, 445
Bernstorff, Count, 78, 262, 273; on the English press, 270
Bertie, Lord, 422
Bethmann-Hollweg, 62, 68, 72, 404, 415, 425, 427, 463; and understanding with England, 369-70; and Blatchford articles, 378; on armaments and arbitration, 380; defense of Agadir policy, 407-9; and Tirpitz, 421; and Haldane Mission, 421-22; and naval holiday, 435; and Bernhardi, 445
Birmingham *Daily Post,* 31-32

471